C0-BPI-191

Articles on American Slavery

An eighteen–volume set collecting nearly four hundred of the most important articles on slavery in the United States

Edited with Introductions by
Paul Finkelman

State University of New York,
Binghamton

A Garland Series

Contents of the Series

VOL. 3

Colonial
Southern
Slavery

Edited with an Introduction
by Paul Finkelman

Garland Publishing, Inc.
New York & London
1989

Library of Congress Cataloging-in-Publication Data

Colonial Southern Slavery/ edited with an
introduction by Paul Finkelman.

p. cm.—(Articles on American slavery; vol. 3)

Includes bibliographical references.

ISBN 0–8240–6783–5 (alk. paper)

1. Slavery—Southern States—History—18th century.
2. Afro-Americans—Southern States—History—
18th century. 3. Southern States—History—
Colonial period, ca. 1600–1775.
I. Finkelman, Paul. II. Series.

E446.C7   1989
306.3'62'0975—dc20   89–23558

Printed on acid-free, 250-year-life paper
Manufactured in the United States of America

Design by Julie Threlkeld

General Introduction

Few subjects in American history have been as compelling as slavery. This should not surprise us. Slavery affected millions of Americans, north and south. Afro-Americans, Euro-Americans, and Native Americans were involved in the system. All antebellum Americans were affected, directly or indirectly, by slavery. Slavery especially affected Americans from 1861 until well after Reconstruction. As Lincoln noted in his famous second inaugural address: "The slaves constituted a peculiar and powerful interest. All knew that this interest was somehow the cause of the war."

The goal of this series is to reprint the key articles that have influenced our understanding of slavery. This series includes pioneering articles in the history of slavery, important breakthroughs in research and methodology, and articles that offer major historiographical interpretations. I have attempted to cover all major subtopics of slavery, to offer wide geographic representation and methodological diversity. At the same time, I have resisted the temptation to reprint highly technical articles that will make sense only to specialists in certain fields. For example, I have not included a number of important slavery related articles on economics, law, theology, and literary criticism (to offer just a few examples) because they appeared to be beyond the interest of most generalists.

I have used articles from a wide variety of scholarly journals. I have also used essays and articles in edited volumes, as long as the main focus of those volumes was not slavery, abolition, or black studies. It is my hope that such books are readily available to scholars and students and will show up through card catalogues or on-line catalogue searches. For the same reason I have not reprinted chapters from books about slavery, which are often found in anthologies. With a few exceptions, I have not reprinted articles that later became chapters of books on the same subject. In a few cases I have strayed from this general rule of thumb. I have also generally avoided essay reviews of books, unless the essays go well beyond the common book review or even essay review format. I have also tried to avoid certain famous historiographical controversies that resulted in large numbers of essays being collected and published. With some exceptions, therefore, I have not included the many articles attacking the "Elkins" thesis or Fogel and Engerman's Time on the Cross. Students and scholars interested in these two enormously important scholarly works, and the criticism of them, will find a great deal on both in their card catalogues. Finally, I have also excluded articles from Encyclopedias and dictionaries. These editorial decisions mean that many famous essays and articles will not be found in these volumes. Indeed, a few very important scholars are not represented because all of their work has been in books that are directly on the subject of slavery. Finally, some important articles were left out because we were unable to secure permission from the copyright holders to reprint them in this series.

This project was made easier by the hard work and dedication of Carole Puccino and Leo Balk at Garland Publishing, Inc. A project of this magnitude would not be possible without the help of a number of other scholars, who read lists of proposed articles and discussed the whole problem of slavery with me. I am especially grateful for the help and suggestions of Catherine Clinton, Robert Cottrol, Jill DuPont, Seymour Drescher, Linda Evans, Ronald Formasano, John Hope Franklin, Kermit L. Hall, Robert Hall, Graham Hodges, Michael P. Johnson, Charles Joyner, Alan Kulikoff, Greg Lind, David McBride, Randall Miller, Alfred Moss, James Oakes, Albert J. Raboteau, Judith Schafer, Robert Sikorski, John David Smith, Jean Soderlund, Margaret Washington, William M. Wiecek, Julie Winch, Betty Wood, and Bertram Wyatt-Brown. Two SUNY-Binghamton students, Marci Silverman and Beth Borchers, helped me with much of the bibliographic work on this project. Carol A. Clemente and the inter-library loan staff at SUNY-Binghamton were absolutely wonderful. Without their patience, skills, and resourcefulness, I would have been unable to complete these volumes.

—Paul Finkelman

Contents

Introduction

How and when Afro-American slavery began in the British colonies that became the United States has been the subject of much controversy among scholars. Tied to inquiries about the origin of slavery is the relationship between slavery, racism, and Anglo-American culture in the seventeenth and eighteenth centuries.

Issues such as these raise some of the following questions: When were blacks first enslaved in Virginia? Were the first blacks to arrive in Virginia treated as slaves? How did the settlers in Virginia and Maryland accommodate slavery to English culture and law? Was the enslavement of blacks the result of a predisposition to racism, on the part of the English, or was racism in the English colonies and the United States caused by the fact that most blacks were slaves? What were the relationships between economic development, English imperial policy, and the growth of slavery in the southern colonies? How did changing mortality rates affect slavery? To what extent was slavery an outgrowth of the system of indentured servitude? How did the development of a landless, free white population affect the creation of a slave society? Did the existence of slavery help pave the way for both the American revolution and democracy in the South? These are some of the many questions raised in examining the origins of slavery in Virginia, Maryland, and to a lesser extent the Carolinas. These questions have led to a multitude of interesting, often contradictory, answers.

Historians can agree on only a few basic facts in explaining the origin of slavery in Virginia. In 1619 the first blacks arrived at Jamestown. Their arrival was noted by John Rolfe some five months later, in a report to the London based officials of the Virginia company. Rolfe quite casually wrote: "About the latter end of August, a Dutch Man of War of the burden of 160 tons arrived. . . . He brought not anything but 20 and odd Negroes, which the Governor and Cape Merchant bought for victual (whereof he was in great need as he pretended) at the best and easiest rate they could."[1]

In 1619 there was no slavery in Virginia. The status of these first black Virginians is unknown. Some scholars argue that they were immediately treated as slaves, while other historians assert that they were treated as indentured servants. The paucity of records for this period make any definitive conclusions impossible. We know that some of the early blacks in Virginia were treated as indentured servants, and that in the 1620s a number of blacks were living in Virginia as free people, including some who probably arrived in 1619. Whether some were being treated as slaves that early is still a matter of debate.[2] Before the 1640s there is no written sanction of slavery by any colonial official, although there are hints in some court records that Virginian's were practicing enslavement of Negroes.

Before 1660 the status of most blacks in the colony remained uncertain, and the existence of slavery remained unacknowledged and unsettled. Before 1660 the existing records, which are admittedly few and often cryptic, suggest many blacks were free or indentured servants, but that an increasing percentage of them were being reduced to lifetime slavery. By the early eighteenth century the overwhelming majority of blacks appear to be enslaved.

Not until 1660, forty years after the arrival of that "Dutch Man of War," did the Virginia colonial legislature, the House of Burgesses, explicitly recognize the existence of slaves in the colony. In that year the Burgesses adopted a law that specifically regulated the importation of "negro slaves."[3] In 1662 the Burgesses provided for the punishment of runaway servants by adding extra time to their indentures. The statute had some special provisions to punish whites who ran away with "negroes who are incapable of making satisfaction by addition of a time" to their indentures, because they were already "slaves."[4]

In December, 1662 the Burgesses declared that the children of African women would follow the status of their mother. This law was extraordinarily significant for the development of slavery in America. First, it was a departure from English common law (*partus sequitur patrem*), which provided that a child followed the religion, nationality, and status of the father. Instead, this was the adoption of the old Roman law of *partus sequitur ventrem* (the offspring follows the dam [mother]), which had previously only been applied to the offspring of domesticated animals. This does not mean that the Burgesses were attempting to reduce blacks to the status of animals, but it does show they wanted to reduce blacks to the status of permanent property. Second, this law was a recognition of the fact that "negro women" might have a dramatically different status than white men and women. Third, the statute may have indicated that black women often had the children of their white masters or other white freemen. If slaves were the only potential fathers of the children of black women, then there would have been no need to change the common law rule of *partus sequitur patrem*. Finally, the law was a conscious decision to reduce the children of black women to slavery whenever possible.[5]

After 1662 the Burgesses regularly enacted laws aimed at negro slaves. These laws, with such titles as "An act declaring that baptisem of slaves doth not exampt them from bondage," "An act about the casuall killing of slaves," "An act for preventing Negro Insurrections," and "An act for suppressing outlying Slaves," indicate the direction of Virginia's lawmakers and the society as a whole. By the end of the seventeenth century the institution of slavery had taken root.[6]

Besides the statutes passed by the colonial legislatures, scholars have a variety of early legal cases that bear on the status of blacks. The reports of these cases are often short, incomplete, and inconclusive. They are usually subject to more than one interpretation.[7] Reports of governors, minutes of the governors and their councils, official English colonial documents, some quantitative data, and a few diaries and other personal records add to our knowledge of the origin of slavery. Like the legal cases, they are often ambiguous and incomplete.

Despite the relatively small amount of evidence, in recent years some of the best work in American history has been on colonial slavery. This question has captured the attention of some of the leading scholars in colonial history, Afro-American history, intellectual history, and legal history. Articles in this volume show the range of the debates over the origin of slavery in the New World. From quantitative studies of the early black population to detailed analysis of the statues and court cases creating slavery, these articles probe the origin of America's peculiar institution.

—Paul Finkelman

Notes

1. John Rolfe to Sir Edwin Sandys, January 1619/20, in Susan M. Kingsbury, ed., *The Records of the Virginia Company of London* (4 vols.: Washington, 1933) 3:243. [Some of the spellings, punctuation, and abbreviations have been modernized.]

2. For one historian who asserts they were treated as slaves, see Robert McColley, "Virginia, Slavery In," in Randall Miller and John David Smith, *Dictionary of Afro-American Slavery* (Westport, Conn.: Greenwood Press, 1988) 781.

3. "An Act for the Dutch and all other Strangers for Tradeing to this Place," Act XVI, March, 1659–1660, 1 Hening 540.

4. "Run-aways," Act CII, March, 1661–62, 2 Hening 116.

5. "Negro womens children to serve according to the condition of the mother," Act XII, December 1662, 2 Hening 170.

6. These and other early statutes are conveniently gathered in Paul Finkelman, *The Law of Freedom and Bondage* (New York: Oceana Press, 1986) 14–19. They are also found in William Waller Hening, ed., *The Statutes At Large of Virginia; Being a Collection of all the Laws of Virginia from the First Session the Legislature, in the Year 1619* (13 Vols., Richmond, Va.: Samuel Pleasants, Jr. Printer to the Commonwealth, 1809–23).

7. Many of the early cases are reprinted in Finkelman, *Law of Freedom and Bondage.*

Further Reading

Ames, Susie.   *Studies of the Virginia Eastern Shore* (reprint, New York: Russell and Russell, 1973).

Ballagh.   A *History of Slavery in Virginia* (Baltimore: Johns Hopkins University Press, 1902).

Breen, Timothy and Stephen Innes.   *Myne Owne Ground: Race and Freedom on Virginia's Eastern Shore* (New York: Oxford University Press, 1980).

Boskin, Joseph.   *Into Slavery: Racial Decisions in the Virginia Colony* (Philadelphia: J.B. Lippincott, 1976).

Craven, Frank Wesley.   *The Southern Colonies in the Seventeenth Century* (Baton Rouge: Louisiana State University Press, 1949).

Craven, Frank Wesley.   *White, Red, and Black: The Seventeenth Century Virginian* (Charlottesville: University of Virginia Press, 1971).

Davis, David Brion.   *The Problem of Slavery in Western Civilization* (Ithaca: Cornell University Press, 1964).

Dunn, Richard.   *Sugar and Slaves: The Rise of the Planter Class in the English West Indies, 1624–1713* (Chapel Hill: University of North Carolina Press, 1972).

Frederickson, George.   "Towards a Social Interpretation of the Development of American Racism," in Nathan Huggins, et al., eds., *Key Issues in the Afro-American Experience* (New York: Harcourt Brace Jovanovich, 1970) 240–54.

Jordan, Winthrop.   *White Over Black* (Chapel Hill: University of North Carolina Press, 1968).

Kulikoff, Alan.

Tobacco and Slaves: The Development of Southern Cultures in the Chesapeake, 1680–1800 (Chapel Hill: University of North Carolina Press, 1986).

Klingberg, Frank J.

An Appraisal of the Negro in Colonial South Carolina: A Study of Americanization (Washington, D.C.: Associated Publishers, 1941).

Littlefield, Daniel.

Rice and Slaves: Ethnicity and the Slave Trade in Colonial South Carolina (Baton Rouge: Louisiana State University Press, 1981).

Morgan, Edmund S.

American Slavery, American Freedom (New York: W.W. Norton, 1975).

Nash, Gary.

Red, White, and Black: The Peoples of Early America (New York: Prentice-Hall, 1974).

Wood, Betty.

Slavery in Colonial Georgia, 1730–1775 (Athens: University of Georgia Press, 1984).

Wood, Peter.

Black Majority (New York: W.W. Norton, 1974).

Colonial
Southern
Slavery

The Cases of Fernando and Elizabeth Key:
A Note on the Status of Blacks in
Seventeenth-Century Virginia

Warren M. Billings*

PROFESSOR Alden T. Vaughan's recent note[1] on the blacks who arrived in Virginia between 1619 and 1630 has once again called attention to the origins of chattel slavery and racial prejudice in America. Using the few scraps of evidence which have survived from that decade, Vaughan suggests that the initial period of contact had profound implications for the development of white attitudes toward the blacks. As he admits, however, these bits and pieces of information serve only to tantalize the investigator; they do not, for example, reveal clearly how a black's conversion to Christianity affected his status. A pair of court cases involving two blacks, a man known only as Fernando[2] and Elizabeth Key,[3] sheds some light on the status of Christian blacks and on how that status deteriorated as a result of hardening white attitudes. In addition, they provide a few hints as to how some of the first laws defining slavery in Virginia came to be adopted by the General Assembly.

Of Fernando nothing is known except that he was "a slave for his life time," who sued for his freedom in the Lower Norfolk County Court

* Mr. Billings is a member of the Department of History, Louisiana State University in New Orleans. He wishes to thank his colleague, David R. Johnson, for his suggestions and comments about the preparation of this note.

[1] Alden T. Vaughan, "Blacks in Virginia: A Note on the First Decade," *William and Mary Quarterly*, 3d Ser., XXIX (1972), 469-478.

[2] Lower Norfolk County Order Book, 1666-1675, fol. 17. All citations to the county records are to the microfilm copies at the Virginia State Library, Richmond.

[3] Northumberland County Record Book, 1652-1658, fols. 66, 67, 85; Northumberland County Record Book, 1658-1660, fol. 28; Northumberland County Order Book, 1652-1665, fols. 40, 46, 49. Copies of the records of both cases will appear, along with other documents relating to blacks, in Warren M. Billings, ed., *The Old Dominion in the Seventeenth-Century: A Documentary History of Virginia, 1606-1689*, to be published by the Institute of Early American History and Culture.

during its August 1667 sitting. Claiming that he "was a Christian and had been several yeares in England," Fernando contended that he ought to serve no longer than an English bondsman. As proof of his conversion he offered in evidence several papers, which the clerk noted were written "in Portugell or some other language which the Court could not understand." Declaring that no cause for action existed, the justices dismissed the suit. Fernando appealed the decision to the General Court, but unfortunately no record of the high court's disposition of the case has survived.

The record for Elizabeth Key is fuller. She was the bastard daughter of Thomas Key[4] and an unnamed slave woman.[5] In 1636, when Elizabeth was five or six years old, Key bound her to Humphrey Higginson[6] for a period of nine years. Sometime between 1636 and 1655 she passed into the possession of Colonel John Mottrom I, a Northumberland County justice of the peace, who died in 1655. As a result of Mottrom's death, Elizabeth Key, through her attorney, William Greensted,[7] in January 1655/6 brought suit for her freedom before the Northumberland County Court. Greensted based his arguments upon three grounds: Elizabeth Key's father was a free man, and by common law children inherited their father's condition; she had been baptized, implying that a Christian could not be held for life; and she had been sold to Higginson for a period of nine years, which had long since elapsed. Although the jury found in her favor, one of the overseers of the Mottrom estate, Thomas Speke,[8] appealed the verdict to the General Court, which ruled Elizabeth Key a slave.[9] Greensted had a final avenue of appeal: he petitioned the

[4] Key (d. 1636?) lived at Blunt Point, near modern-day Newport News, Va., and was a burgess for Denbigh in the General Assembly of 1629/30. H. R. McIlwaine, ed., *Journals of the House of Burgesses of Virginia, 1619-1658/59* (Richmond, Va., 1915), xi.

[5] It is significant, perhaps, that the depositions refer to Elizabeth Key's mother as a slave. Since Elizabeth Key was born circa 1630, the reference to her mother's status suggests that some blacks were already being held as slaves by the end of the 1620s.

[6] Higginson was a member of the Council of State. McIlwaine, ed., *Jours., House of Burgesses*, 82. He was also Elizabeth Key's godfather.

[7] Greensted was a Northumberland County planter, whose name appears in a headright sued out by Mottrom in Aug. 1650. Nell Marion Nugent, comp., *Cavaliers and Pioneers: Abstracts of Virginia Land Patents and Grants, 1623-1800* (Richmond, Va., 1934), 198.

[8] Speke (d. 1659) was a justice of the peace and burgess for Northumberland County.

[9] "Selections from Conway Robinson's Notes and Excerpts from the Records of

General Assembly for a hearing,[10] and the Assembly appointed a committee of burgesses to investigate the matter. On the basis of the burgesses' report, concurring with the findings of the Northumberland court, the Assembly remanded the case to the Northumberland justices for retrial. In the interval between the Assembly's order and the county court's reaffirmation of its original verdict, another of the overseers of Mottrom's estate, George Colclough,[11] obtained from Gov. Edward Digges an order for a rehearing before the General Court.[12] Colclough apparently declined to pursue the matter further, for in July 1656 Greensted obtained an order for a nonsuit against Colclough and William Presly,[13] the third overseer of the Mottrom estate. The last known record of Elizabeth Key is the entry into the Northumberland County Order Book of the banns of her marriage to Greensted.

Both the Key suit and Fernando's case are significant because of what they suggest. First, the cases support the idea that a nexus existed between an African's religion and his status as a laborer in Virginia. Conversion to Christianity evidently conferred upon blacks a rank higher than that of slave. If an African retained his native religion, in all likelihood he stayed a slave, but if he converted or were born into slavery and baptized, his conversion or baptism could provide grounds for his release

---

Colonial Virginia," in H. R. McIlwaine, ed., *Minutes of the Council and General Court of Colonial Virginia, 1622-1632, 1670-1676* (Richmond, Va., 1924), 504. The bulk of the General Court records were destroyed in 1865, so the notes which Robinson had made just before the Civil War are the only guide to many of the Court's deliberations. Robinson did not mention Elizabeth Key by name, noting only "a mulatto held to be a slave and appeal taken." It is almost beyond doubt that the unnamed mulatto was Elizabeth Key. Greensted appealed the case to the next regular session of the General Court. That session would have been in March 1655/6 at the same time the General Assembly met. McIlwaine, ed., *Jours., House of Burgesses,* 95.

[10] Until the administration of Governor Thomas, Lord Culpeper, the General Assembly had authority to hear appears from the General Court. Philip Alexander Bruce, *Institutional History of Virginia in the Seventeenth Century: An Inquiry into the Religious, Moral, Educational, Legal, Military, and Political Condition of the People,* I (New York, 1910), 690-696.

[11] Colclough (d. 1622) was a justice of the peace and burgess for Northumberland; he subsequently married Mottrom's widow, Ursula.

[12] Digges (d. Mar. 1674/5) was a member of the Council of State from York County and one of the Interregnum governors of Virginia.

[13] Presly (d. Jan. 1656) was a justice of the peace and burgess for Northumberland County.

from life servitude. This is the inference to draw from William Greensted's successful plea that her baptism entitled Elizabeth Key to freedom. The same inference is also implicit in Fernando's suit. Fernando believed that he had proof of his conversion, which, if accepted by the court, should alter his status to that of an English servant. That he lost the case is immaterial. Fernando's belief that his religion affected his status is the important fact.

These deductions are buttressed by other evidence. The presence of the two cases suggests the strong possibility of the existence of similar ones that were lost in the destruction of great quantities of Virginia's seventeenth-century legal records over the last three hundred years.[14] Certainly the existence of other suits like Fernando's and Elizabeth Key's may be surmised from the fact that in September 1667 the General Assembly enacted a law which declared that the "conferring of baptisme doth not alter the condition of the person as to his bondage or Freedome."[15] It is highly unlikely that the Assembly would have needed to outlaw suits which seldom occurred. Quite to the contrary, as the act's preamble makes clear, long-standing doubt about the effect of baptism upon the black's status had moved the Assembly to action. Furthermore, the proximity in time of the statute's adoption to Fernando's case suggests a desire to rid the courts of such troublesome litigation in the future.

Conversion may also have conferred certain rights upon blacks. One of these, as Vaughan has implied,[16] was the right to be treated as a servant if a black were christianized before coming to Virginia. Another was obviously the right to sue in court. Although the Key and Fernando cases are the only known instances where religion was a matter at issue, they are not the only examples of blacks seeking to obtain their liberty or a change in status through the courts. At least four other cases are

[14] Of the 23 counties which the General Assembly erected between 1634 and 1692, only six have virtually intact records, five have no surviving records, and the remaining twelve have records which range from a few fragments to fairly complete runs for brief intervals. Not only have these local records suffered frightful damage, but the archives of the colony's provincial government for the period before 1680 have been largely destroyed.

[15] William Waller Hening, ed., *The Statutes at Large; Being a Collection of All the Laws of Virginia, from the First Session of the Legislature in the Year 1619,* II (Richmond, Va., 1823), 260.

[16] Vaughan, "Blacks in Virginia," *WMQ,* 3d Ser., XXIX (1972), 478.

known to exist; in each one the litigant bears a Christian name.[17] So do all of the identifiable free blacks and black indentured servants, as well as those who purchased their freedom or had it given them by their masters.[18]

The adoption of the 1667 baptism law signals a deterioration of these rights as a result of a change in white Virginians' attitudes toward converted blacks—a change which began to occur in the 1660s. At the time Elizabeth Key escaped slavery the number of blacks living in Virginia was small in relation to the colony's entire population.[19] Awareness of their presence was slight, and the blacks presented no serious problems for those Englishmen who employed black labor. Consequently the English, who displayed a prejudiced hostility towards all Africans, were more likely to follow their kinder instincts by treating the few immigrant Christian blacks as servants or by occasionally releasing slaves who had converted. A decade later, when Fernando brought his case to trial, the situation had altered. A rising black population probably increased the frequency of similar court actions, and, more important, the planters were beginning to look upon slavery as a viable alternative to indentured servitude.

As long as local justices of the peace recognized baptism as a reason for changing a black's status from slave to servant or as a basis for releas-

---

[17] Charles City County Order Book, 1655-1665, fols. 604-605; H. R. McIlwaine, ed., *Journals of the House of Burgesses, 1659/60-1693* (Richmond, Va., 1914), 34-35; McIlwaine, ed., *Minutes of the Council*, 354; Northampton County Order Book, 1655-1688, fol. 10.

[18] See, for example, Northampton County Order Book, 1664-1674, fols. 53, 220-221; Accomack County Order Book, 1673-1676, fol. 31; Charles City County Order Book, 1677-1679, fol. 216; Middlesex County Order Book, 1680-1694, fol. 371; Middlesex County Order Book, 1673-1680, fol. 126; Surry County Deeds and Wills, 1657-1672, fol. 349. See also the transcript of the York County Order Book, 1657-1662, fol. 45, Va. State Library.

[19] I base this conclusion upon a count of blacks listed in headrights recorded in the archives of Lower Norfolk, Northumberland, and York counties. That count reveals a total of 30 blacks in the headrights registered between 1637 and 1655 and a total of 105 blacks for the period 1656 to 1667. Since the time when I made these computations, Wesley Frank Craven has published the results of his analysis of Virginia's land records. According to his calculations, between 1635 and 1655 a total of 311 blacks were imported into the colony, and from 1656 to 1667 a total of 732 arrived in Virginia. See Craven, *White, Red, and Black: The Seventeenth-Century Virginian* (Charlottesville, Va., 1971), 85-86. These statistics are rather more suggestive than definitive.

ing him outright, and as long as unfavorable lower court decisions in such matters could be appealed, there were neither means to forestall such lawsuits nor assurances that a planter could retain his slaves. No matter how the courts decided these cases, the planter sustained losses of time and money. If he lost, he had to pay costs; if he won, the slave could not make restitution. The only way to protect a planter's investment and prevent further troublesome litigation was to outlaw its basis. Outlawing baptism as a determinant of status removed an avenue of escape for slaves. The General Assembly's action also reveals a hardening of feeling among the English.

This willingness to substitute harsher treatment for more gentle handling is evidenced by the Englishman's increasing intolerance toward the mulatto. Elizabeth Key's fate suggests a customary practice in some courts of freeing from slavery mulattoes who could prove English paternity. Judges who ruled favorably in these cases evidently rested their decision upon the common law dictum that a child inherited his or her father's condition.[20] As the General Court's unfavorable ruling in Elizabeth Key's suit indicates, not all of Virginia's magistrates agreed with that construction. Conceivably justices could interpret common law as inapplicable to mulattoes.

The contradictory interpretation of the law as it concerned a mulatto's status testified to the lack of provision in the English legal system for coping with the emergence of slavery in Virginia. Moreover, conflicting opinions in the Key case attested to the equivocal definition of slavery in Virginia's law. Were mulattoes Christians or heathens, servants or slaves, Africans or Englishmen? As long as uncertainty existed about the condition of the children of slave women and free men, the planter who owned them remained liable to lengthy and costly court action. Baptizing these children only enhanced the probability of a suit. The obvious remedy was a statutory prohibition of claims like those advanced by Elizabeth Key's attorney.

In December 1662, because "some doubts have arisen whether children got by any Englishman upon a negro woman should be slave or free," the General Assembly made a mulatto's freedom or servitude conditional upon the mother's status. As a further discouragement to miscegenous relations, the law also provided that if "any christian shall committ Forni-

---

[20] Henry Swinburne, *A briefe Treatise of Testaments and last willes*, 3d ed. rev. (London, 1635), 75.

cation with a negro man or woman, hee or shee soe offending shall pay double the Fines imposed by the former act."[21]

The act's preamble demonstrates that litigation like the Elizabeth Key case had caused the Assembly to rectify the inconsistencies regarding the legal use of the word *slave*. There was more at issue, however, than a mere desire to give slavery a clearer meaning in Virginia law. The statute was an attempt to formulate a practical method of defining the status of mulattoes, but the law also carried a deeper intent: it sought to keep the races separate. To make good that intention the statute imposed a stiffer than normal fine for interracial fornication and raised the threat of perpetual bondage for the casual offspring of Englishmen and slave women.

Writing a seldom used civil law doctrine, *partus sequitur ventrum*, into the statute indicates the depth of the lawmakers' desire to prevent miscegenation. Its application to mulattoes also shows how the legislators wished to adapt their legal heritage to a new situation.[22] Reared on the tradition of *stare decisis*, they searched the common law for precedents, but found none because common law had not anticipated the existence of mulattoes. So they ransacked their knowledge of the civil law and discovered a useful definition of status, which satisfied the yearning to remain faithful to tradition while resolving a problem for which tradition afforded no remedies.

Winthrop D. Jordan has characterized slavery as the product of "an unthinking decision,"[23] but the evidence presented here leads to a different conclusion. It shows that while white prejudice and hostility had always relegated the blacks to the lowest ranks of colonial society, the English had once allowed some of them a few legal routes to escape their bondage. Their religion and their paternity were of crucial importance for determining which blacks should become servants. Once white Virginians perceived free blacks and miscegenation as serious threats to the public weal and to their own private interests, they moved to circum-

---

[21] Hening, ed., *Statutes at Large*, II, 170.

[22] Swinburne, for example, clearly stated that the dictum was contrary to the "Lawes of the Realme." Swinburne, *Treatise of Testaments*, 76. See also G. R. Elton, ed., *The Tudor Constitution: Documents and Commentary* (Cambridge, 1962), 152-153, and A. K. R. Kirafly, ed., *Potter's Historical Introduction to English Law and Its Institutions* (London, 1958), 631-637.

[23] Winthrop D. Jordan, *White over Black: American Attitudes toward the Negro, 1550-1812* (Chapel Hill, N. C., 1968), Ch. II.

scribe the African bondsmen's approaches to liberty. The laws of 1662 and
1667 were deliberately calculated to undercut the meager rights of black
laborers by denying them access to the courts. These statutes broke with
tradition, thereby freeing Virginia lawmakers from the past's restraining
influences. But the laws also became the precedents for future legislation
that governed an emerging slave system.

What the Fernando and Elizabeth Key cases reveal is significant,
but not conclusive. The evidence they contain affords an answer to the
question of how conversion affected the black man's status, but it is an
incomplete explanation. There is a hint that some black servants *and* slaves
had once enjoyed certain rights, but these rights began to deteriorate in
the 1660s. The evidence further suggests that the drive to give slavery
statutory definition accelerated after 1660, but again the reasons for this
change are unclear. Finally, linking the two cases with the acts of 1662
and 1667 invites the possibility of further study. A detailed comparison
of all the known lawsuits involving blacks with the slave laws might tell
us more about the process by which the English systematically degraded
and enslaved the blacks during the seventeenth century.[24]

[24] At a future date I hope to publish the results of such a comparison.

Negro Property Owners in Seventeenth-Century Virginia

James H. Brewer*

THREE centuries have passed since there appeared on the Eastern Shore, along the banks of the Pungoteague River, perhaps the first community of Negro property owners in historic Virginia. Within a few years other infant black communities were to be found scattered throughout parts of Tidewater Virginia. The story concerning those forgotten African families, partially revealed by Philip Alexander Bruce nearly sixty years ago, cannot be told in its entirety. However, further light is shed on their economic pursuits in the early colonial period by a somewhat fuller exploitation of the county records of Virginia.

It is highly significant that some of the former Negro servants found the environment of seventeenth-century Virginia conducive to the amassing of property in land or chattel in various ways. For example, a few received land grants ranging from 50 to 500 acres, made possible by the head-rights system. Others acquired their property in chattel; while there were some who came into ownership of land or chattel through grants in the wills of their former masters. Through these various means a class of Negro property owners gradually came into existence. How large this class was, it is not possible to say, but the records seem to indicate that their number was relatively small.

The influx of blacks into the colony during the major part of the seventeenth century was still too meager to affect seriously the social and economic life of Virginia. For example, in 1625 there were only 23 Negroes in Virginia, and by the middle of the century only 300 blacks were to be found, while the whites numbered 15,000. Between 1670 and 1680 the Negro population had increased from 2,000 to 3,000. During the last two decades of the century the Negro population grew rapidly, and by 1700 there were approximately 6,000 Negroes in Virginia. It was during this

* Mr. Brewer is Associate Professor of History at Virginia State College. This essay is part of a larger study which the author is preparing on Negro life in seventeenth-century Virginia.

period that Virginia became disturbed by the increase of blacks within her borders. Her fears were manifested by the enactment of two statutes which listed types of property the Negroes might not acquire. The first law, passed in 1670, prohibited them from owning white servants, while the second act denied to them the ownership of firearms or other weapons.[1]

Even though the rapid increase of the Negro population of Virginia was paralleled by certain limitations placed on their rights of ownership, the Negro never lost his right to own and to alienate his property. This is disclosed by a study of the head-rights system.[2] Beginning in 1651, a few Negro families took advantage of the head-rights custom and received acreage along the banks of the Pungoteague River on the Eastern Shore. The first of such grants was made in July, 1651, to Anthony Johnson of Northampton County, who received 250 acres of land for the importation of 5 persons into the colony.[3] At this time Anthony Johnson and his wife, Mary, were perhaps the wealthiest Negroes in Virginia.[4] After Anthony, other free blacks whose last name was Johnson procured property under the head-rights system in the forgotten Pungoteague Community. For example, John Johnson received as head-rights for the transporting of 11 persons a tract of 550 acres of land.[5] Likewise, John Johnson, Senior, was allowed his claim of 50 acres.[6] When Johnson attempted to increase his land holdings, he was summoned in 1653 to appear in court to answer proceedings instituted by his neighbor, another John Johnson, to recover

[1] William W. Hening, compiler, *The Statutes at Large . . . of Virginia* (Richmond, 1819-1823), II, 280, 481.

[2] This was a law designed to stimulate immigration, which stipulated that the government pledged itself to grant 50 acres of land to any person who would pay the passage of a person to Virginia. The person receiving the grant was required to record with the clerk of his respective county court the names of all persons for whose transportation the claim was made. This statute was one of the means by which the Virginia Negro was able to accumulate land of 50 acres or more. For a more detailed discussion of the head-rights system see Thomas J. Wertenbaker, *The Planters of Colonial Virginia* (Princeton, 1922), 34.

[3] Land Patents of Virginia, 1643-1651, Book No. 2, 326, Virginia State Library. Hereafter cited as Land Patents. See also Court Records of Northampton County, 1651-1654, 226; 1655-1658, 10, Virginia State Library. Hereafter cited as CRNC. The names of the five persons imported are Tho. Bembrose, Peter Bughby, Antho. Cripps, Jno. Gesorroro, and Richard Johnson.

[4] See below, p. 578.

[5] Land Patents, 1652-1655, Book No. 3, 101. The names of those imported are Jno. Edwards, William Routh, Thomas Yowell, Fra. Mayland, William Price, John Owens, Dorthy Riley, Richard Hemstead, Law. Barnes, Row. Rith, and Mary Johnson.

[6] CRNC, 1651-1654, 17.

450 acres of land.[7] The next member of the African community to acquire land under the head-rights was a carpenter by trade, Richard Johnson. Richard was perhaps among the 5 servants imported in 1651 by Anthony Johnson. Three years later he was assigned 100 acres adjoining the property of John and Anthony Johnson.[8]

Soon after various Johnsons had achieved a status of moderate economic importance in the historic Pungoteague community, the records disclose that elsewhere in the colony other free Negroes had made progress in land ownership. For example, in December, 1656, Benjamin Doyle was granted a patent for 300 acres of land in Surry County "for the transportation of six persons into the colony."[9] There is also a record of a grant of 50 acres on April 18, 1667, to Emanuel Cambew of James City County.[10] In the adjoining county of York a deed dated October 28, 1668, calling for the transfer of 50 acres of land in New Kent County, was executed by Robert Jones, a white tailor of Queen's Creek, to "John Harris, a negro his heyers, Executrs, admtrs., and assigns forever."[11] On at least one occasion, a Negro leased land on a long-term basis. Philip Morgan and his heirs were "peacefully and quietly [to] enjoy the 200 acres," for 99 years, when the land was to revert to the owner's heirs.[12]

It hardly needs to be said that in sections of Tidewater Virginia there were many free blacks too poor to acquire land. As free persons, however, they inevitably acquired small amounts of personal property in various forms—cattle, household effects, and clothing. Frequently they received such items when they were freed; others, of course, earned them; and, we suspect, others came by them somewhat illegally. Manuscript records dealing with this kind of property are to be found more frequently than those dealing with land. Even the simple sale of cattle, "a black cow and a red calf" to Emanuel Dregis, is recorded.[13] Negroes were also involved in litigation, which not only became a part of the court records but also disclosed their small property holdings. Thus, in 1647 Tony Kongo was compelled

[7] *Ibid.*, 200. John Johnson sought relief from the authorities by testifying that John Johnson, Senior, "Most unrightly detayneth a patent for 450 acres of land." The decision of the court was not revealed.

[8] Land Patents, 1652-1655, Book No. 3, 294; also 101.

[9] *Ibid.*, 1655-1664, Book No. 4, 71f.

[10] *Ibid.*, Book No. 6, 39.

[11] Court Records of York County, 1664-1672, Book No. 4, 327, Virginia State Library. Hereafter cited as CRYC.

[12] Court Records of Accomac County, 1676-1690, 185, Virginia State Library.

[13] CRNC, 1645-1651, 83. See *Virginia Magazine of History*, XI (1904), 281.

by court order to pay a debt of 382 pounds of tobacco due Lewis White. The mulatto Kongo was allowed thirty days to guarantee payment out of "ye next croppe."[14] A judgment for 486 pounds of tobacco against the estate of Edward Jessop, Negro, is recorded in the court records of Northampton County.[15]

The most remarkable record in property holding, however, is that of Anthony Johnson, "the black patriarch" of Pungoteague Community. Within 7 months after acquiring 250 acres in July, 1651, Johnson's holdings were practically wiped out by an unfortunate fire. Johnson then petitioned the court for relief, and the judgment of the court stated, "be it therefore fitt and ordered that . . . (during their natural lives) the sd Mary Johnson & two daughters of Anthony Johnson be disingaged and freed from payment of taxes and leavyes in Northampton County for public use."[16] Ultimately the enterprising "black patriarch" managed to re-establish himself as a moderate property owner. In 1653 Anthony appeared as a claimant in a suit brought against Robert Parker to recover his Negro servant John Casor. Testimony in the trial discloses that Johnson attempted to show that he was intimidated by Parker to free his black servant because of threats by Parker that the servant would enter suit against Johnson to recover his master's cows as damages. The court ordered that the servant be returned to Johnson.[17] The court records also afford additional evidence as to Johnson's business transactions in an effort to replenish his losses through fire. One record shows that Anthony and his son John sold "two heifers collored black and of three years old . . . unto John Williams his heirs executors and assigns forever."[18] In August, 1659, Anthony managed to enlarge his land holdings when his son John "do hereby bargain and make sail of all my right title and interest of this within . . . patent of land to my father Anthony Johnson Negro. . . ."[19] Finally, a chattel mortgage recorded the same year entailed the exchange of more property within the family when John transferred to his father Anthony "two heifers of two year old and four yearling heifers and one calf . . . and also one black cow. . . ."[20]

[14] CRNC, 1645-1651, 83.

[15] CRNC, 1683-1689, 258.

[16] CRNC, 1651-1654, 161.

[17] *Ibid.,* 10. See also John H. Russell, *The Free Negro in Virginia, 1619-1865* (Baltimore, 1913), 33.

[18] CRNC, Deeds, Wills, 1657-1666, 17.

[19] *Ibid.,* 9.

[20] *Ibid.,* 9.

The growth of a class of Negro property owners was also facilitated by the emancipation provisions of liberal and appreciative masters. Thus, former Negro servants as well as emancipated slaves did not always go forth empty-handed from their masters' services. Many were furnished either land or chattel or both to embark upon their new life as freemen. This was true of two blacks, Philip and Nicholas, of York County. Each was bequeathed a cow and allotted a certain plot of land to cultivate for the "balance of their natural lives."[21] John, another Negro of York County, was emancipated by one Thomas Whitehead, and included among the several items he was bequeathed were the possession of a house and the use of as much land as he could cultivate.[22]

Elsewhere in Virginia other Negroes were recipients of property through wills in the seventeenth century. Notable is the will of Richard Vaughan of Northampton County, which left property to each Negro he set free. A portion of Vaughan's will reads:

. . . and for my old Negro woman . . . and the receive twoe Cowes with calfe (or calves by their side) two suits of clothes and bedd and a Rugge, a chest and a pott with foure Barrells of corn and a younge breedinge Sowe; Likewise my Negro girle Temperance . . . to bee possessed of two cowes and to have their increase male and female. . . .[23]

Continuing, Vaughan's will stated, "that ye three Negro girls be possessed of the plantacon of John. Walthome, being to this plantacon some 144 acres of land; and he to build them a Home twenty-five feete in length and twenty feete broad, with one chimmey."[24] Under the terms of the will of John Carter, of Lancaster County, a married slave couple were to be set free and "allowed . . . the use of a convenient house . . . and as much land as they could cultivate. . . ."[25] Robert Griggs showed equal generosity to a mulatto when he bequeathed him a home and a "certain area of ground for life. . . ."[26] Of greater significance are the terms of the

[21] CRYC, Will of Nicholas Martin, 1633-1694, 109.

[22] Ibid., 1657-1662, 211, 217.

[23] CRNC, 1654-1655, 102.

[24] Ibid., Will of Richard Vaughan, 103. For a more detailed analysis of seventeenth-century wills see Philip A. Bruce, Economic History of Virginia in the Seventeenth Century (New York, 1896), II, 123f.

[25] Court Records of Lancaster County, original vol., 1690-1709, 3, Virginia State Library.

[26] Ibid., 1674-1687, 91.

13

will of John Nicholls, filed in 1697, whereby the two mulatto children of one of his female slaves were to be set free and to have possession of several hundred acres of land. In addition to 310 acres left to the mulatto boy and 200 acres left to his mulatto sister, they were to receive a variety of chattel.[27]

The question concerning the economic activities of the Negro inhabitants of Pungoteague and other Virginia communities is not one of major historical significance. Yet their story in many respects parallels that of other ethnic and cultural groups in seventeenth-century Virginia. For example, some Negroes eventually became financially able to pay for the transportation of indentured servants either from Europe or Africa or both, and in this way they acquired 50 acres for each European or African they imported. Others found it more feasible to purchase their property from native Virginians. However, the bulk of the wealth among the Negro population was in chattel property. Finally, the response by the Negro to the need for economic stability resulted in the now-forgotten communities of Negro property owners in seventeenth-century Virginia.

[27] Court Records of Lower Norfolk County, original vol., 1695-1703, 96, Virginia State Library. See Bruce, *Economic History of Virginia in the Seventeenth Century*, II, 125.

14

A CHANGING LABOR FORCE AND RACE RELATIONS
IN VIRGINIA 1660-1710

Seventeenth-century Virginians were an unruly lot. While New Englanders lived in relative peace with one another, Virginians rioted and rebelled; even in periods of apparent calm, they were haunted by the specter of social unrest.[1] These men witnessed a series of disorders between 1660 and 1683, most of which were local in character, some were only threats of violence, but a few involved several counties and one escalated into a colony-wide civil war.

Wealthy planters and political officeholders at the time offered a simple explanation for these events. In each case opportunists had played upon the hopes and fears of the "giddy multitude," an amalgam of indentured servants and slaves, of poor whites and blacks, of landless freemen and debtors.[2] Nathaniel Bacon was the most successful and therefore the most notorious of these agitators, but there were others. A gang of desperate *"Oliverian Soldiers"* supposedly organized the servant uprising of 1663, and high governing officials believed Robert Beverley, Sr., clerk of the House of Burgesses, had sparked the tobacco cutting riots of 1683. No one will ever know whether the mass of discontented workers fully supported, or even understood, the demands of a Bacon or Beverley. The "giddy multitude" may have taken advantage of divisions within the ruling class to express its anger over economic and social conditions beyond its control. Whatever its goals, control of this group preoccupied the Virginia gentry for nearly a quarter century.

During the 1680s Virginia's time of troubles drew to a close, and by the beginning of the eighteenth century the colony had achieved remarkable social stability. The Glorious Revolution in America which disrupted New York and Massachusetts in 1689 passed almost unnoticed in Virginia. To be sure, the tobacco planters were apprehensive about a band of black Maroons that harrassed the settlers of the northern counties, but there was little talk of a general uprising of poor whites, indentured servants and Negro slaves. The "giddy multitude" which a few years earlier had caused Governor William

Professor Breen is in the history department of Northwestern University. He would like to thank the American Council of Learned Societies for its support of research conducted during the academic year 1971-1972. Professors George M. Fredrickson of Northwestern University and R. Hall Williams of Yale University provided many helpful suggestions while the work was in progress.

Berkeley to despair of ever controlling "a People wher six parts of seaven at least are Poore Endebted Discontented and Armed" had ceased to threaten the colony's internal peace.[3]

Many elements contributed to the transformation of Virginia society during the last half of the seventeenth century, but none seems more curious than the disappearance of the "giddy multitude."[4] This group of malcontents requires closer investigation, but unfortunately, the judicial records and tax lists from this period are incomplete, making it difficult to determine the precise identity of these people. The sources are rich enough, however, to provide substantial information about the general character of the "giddy multitude." By examining this material one begins to understand why the great planters regarded the lower classes as such a serious threat to Virginia's internal security. This analysis should also suggest how the changing composition of the colony's labor force between 1660 and 1710 affected Virginia's progress from chronic disorder to stability and more, how it fundamentally altered the relationship between blacks and whites.[5]

A pamphleteer writing about Virginia at mid-century observed the colony's earliest years had been marked by failure and disappointment. But those unhappy days, he argued, were gone forever, and Virginians could anticipate a new era of prosperity.[6] Evidence seemed to support his claims. The colonists had recently reduced the once powerful Powhatan Confederacy to impotence, pushing local Indians to the frontiers of white settlement. Planters rushed to develop the fertile tobacco-producing lands along the rivers north of the James, first the York and then the Rappahannock and Potomac. What Virginia needed—what it had always needed—was a large inexpensive labor force, workers who could perform the tedious tasks necessary to bring tobacco to market.[7]

In the middle of the seventeenth century, the solution to this problem was the importation of white indentured servants. Some historians have claimed that Virginia planters preferred white laborers to Negro slaves, but the argument is not persuasive. Before the mid-1680s, the mainland colonies did not possess a reliable, inexpensive source of blacks.[8] White Englishmen were available, however, in large numbers. Beginning in the 1650s, indentured servants flooded into Virginia at a faster rate than ever before, several thousand arriving annually.[9] Many came voluntarily. They were people who, in Governor Berkeley's words, arrived in America with a "hope of bettering their condition in a Growing Country."[10] Most signed their indentures while still in the mother country, promising to work for a stated number of years in exchange for the costs of transportation, food, clothes and shelter in Virginia. Almost nothing is known about the class of people who found this offer attractive, but many were probably middling sorts.[11]

Other servants found themselves in Virginia even though they had little or no desire to be there. Unscrupulous merchants called "spirits" took advantage of the labor boom, dumping over the years many English laborers onto the colonial market.[12] The "spirits" operated out of England's major port cities, preying upon the poor, young and unsuspecting. Some victims were enticed to the New World with stories of quick riches; others were coerced.[13] One man testified before Parliament in 1660 that he had been sent "against his will to Virginia" by his sister's "cruell contrivance."[14] Once a vessel left England, the "spirited" servants reportedly received just enough food to stay alive. It was even rumored in the mother country that if a storm threatened the ship, the sailors were likely to throw an old person overboard as a suspected witch. That seventeenth-century Englishmen found such stories credible indicates that the servants' voyage to America could often be a terrible ordeal.[15] Since the "spirits" seldom kept records of their dealings, their share of the servant commerce is difficult to estimate. Historians minimize the extent of this illicit trade, but one author describing the colony in 1649 claimed that the "spirits" were the planters' chief source of indentured servants.[16]

Great Virginia planters expressed disappointment with the quality of their servants regardless of the means by which they had been recruited. The owners of large tobacco plantations wanted hard-working, honest and obedient laborers, but the merchants seemed to be delivering "the very scum and off-scouring" of England.[17] The planters, no doubt, were guilty of hyperbole, combining poor and ignorant persons with a few known criminals into a single category of undesirables. Throughout Berkeley's administration, leaders complained about the "importacon of Newgateers" and "Jaylebirds" whom they regarded as a serious threat to the colony's security.[18] The gentry came to see the servants as a dangerous and untrustworthy group requiring constant surveillance. How much these attitudes affected relations between individual masters and servants is impossible to determine, but the planters' representation of the indentured workers as a bunch of "desperate villans" may have been a self-fulfilling description.[19]

Many servants were as disappointed with their masters as their masters were with them. As early as 1649, rumors circulated in England that "all those servants who are sent to *Virginia* are sold as slaves."[20] Tales of harsh treatment were probably the source of such stories. One man who returned to the mother country reported that he had "served as a slave" in Virginia for nine years and had "endured greate hardshipp."[21] But the servants' unhappiness had deeper roots than hard labor and poor food. Many were not psychologically prepared for life in Virginia, and the frustrations they experienced led in time to bitterness and depression.[22] For a majority of servants the colony had represented a new start, an opportunity to achieve wealth and status denied them in England. Propagandists fed these hopes, depicting Virginia as a land of milk and honey. Indeed, one writer observed that servants about to emigrate spoke of the colony as "a place where food shall drop into their mouthes." Many expected free land at the end of their service.[23] The reality never matched the dreams. Virginia at mid-century burst inflated expectations and shocked all but the well-informed. William Bullock, a pamphleteer writing in 1649, understood this problem and warned planters about purchasing servants who "not finding what was promised, their courage abates, & their minds being dejected, their work is according."[24]

The servants' life did not necessarily improve when they reached the end of their contracts.[25] What the new freeman desired most was land, but no one in Virginia seemed willing to furnish it. Successful planters were not eager to establish commercial rivals. Indeed, contemporaries condemned the covetousness of those members of the Virginian gentry who engrossed "great Tracts of land" and deprived others of the means to achieve economic independence. In his account of Bacon's Rebellion, William Sherwood denounced the colony's "Land lopers" who claimed thousands of acres yet "never cultivated any part of itt . . . thereby preventing others seateing, soe that too many rather then to be Tennants, seate upon remote barren Land."[26] Since before 1680 remote lands meant constant danger from the Indians, many ex-servants chose to work for wages or rent land in secure areas rather than to settle on the frontier. It has been estimated that no more than six percent of this group ever became independent planters. Landless laborers more often became overseers on the plantations, supervising servants and slaves whose condition differed little from their own.[27]

Freemen found themselves tied to an economic system over which they had little control. Fluctuations in the price of tobacco could reduce wage earners and small planters to abject poverty. It was not a question of work habits. According to an account in 1667, a man, on the average, could produce 1,200 pounds of tobacco each year, which after taxes left him with approximately 50 shillings. It left so little, in fact, that the colony's secretary marvelled, "I can attribute it to nothing but the great mercy of God . . . that keeps them [the small planters] from mutiny and confusion."[28] In 1672 Governor Berkeley explained to the English Privy Council that single freemen could hardly maintain themselves by their own labor.[29] They fell into debt, unable to purchase necessary imported goods—especially clothing. Whatever hopes they once entertained of becoming properous planters gave way to anger. Their numbers swelled, and their disappointment must have discouraged those persons who were still indentured. Certainly, no one seemed surprised when the king's commissioners, investigating in 1677 the causes of Bacon's Rebellion, discovered a major part of the rebel army had been "Free men that had but lately crept out of the condition of Servants."[30]

Another component of the "giddy multitude" was Virginia's Negroes. Historians know relatively little about this group. Governor Berkeley thought there were some 2,000 blacks in the colony in 1671, but recent scholarship regards that estimate as high. By the early 1680s, the Negro population had probably risen to three or four thousand.[31] A majority of the blacks in this period appear to have come to Virginia from the West Indies. Around the turn of the century, for example, it was reported on the authority of one planter that before 1680 "what negroes were brought to Virginia were imported generally from Barbados."[32] There is no way of ascertaining how long the blacks had lived on Barbados before transferring to the mainland, but it is doubtful Virginia planters would have invested what little capital they possessed in expensive "unseasoned" laborers who could easily die after a single summer in the tobacco fields. If the blacks had stayed a year or two on Barbados, they probably learned to speak some English. Morgan Godwyn, a minister who had visited the island colony in the 1670s, noted that many

Negroes there not only spoke English, but did so "no worse than the natural born subjects of that Kingdom."[33] Their facility with the English language could have played an important part in Virginia's unrest, for it would have enabled blacks to communicate with indentured servants and poor whites.[34]

The status of black men in mid-seventeenth-century Virginia remains obscure; a few were free, some were indentured servants and most were probably slaves. After 1660 the Virginia legislature began to deprive black people of basic civil rights. Although the process of total debasement was not completed until the 1700s, it has generally been assumed that Negroes were a separate and subordinate group within Virginia as early as Governor Berkeley's second administration (1662-1677).[35] The problem with this interpretation is that it relies too heavily upon statute law as opposed to social practice, and dismisses the fact that some whites and blacks cooperated—even conspired together—until the late 1670s.[36]

No one could deny that many whites saw Negroes as property to be exploited, and these men may have been responsible for shaping Virginia legislation. On the lowest levels of colonial society, however, race prejudice may have developed more slowly than it did among the successful planters. Black and white field hands could hardly have overlooked the things they had in common. For the Negroes the original trip from Africa to the West Indies had been a terrible ordeal. Few whites had experienced a psychological shock of this magnitude, but some of them had been forceably abducted and confined in foul quarters until a ship was prepared to sail, and were then transported to the New World under conditions vaguely similar to those endured by Africans.[37] Although little is known about the relative treatment of whites and blacks in Virginia before Bacon's Rebellion, it is doubtful that English servants fared better than Negroes. Evidence from Barbados at this time reveals that planters there regarded white servants as a short-term investment to be exploited ruthlessly and thus, "for the time the servants have the worser lives [than the Negroes], for they are put to very hard labour, ill lodging, and their dyet very sleight."[38] If such conditions prevailed on the mainland, it would help explain why some poor and indentured whites voluntarily joined with black men to challenge the planters' authority. One should understand, of course, that a willingness to cooperate under certain circumstances does not mean white laborers regarded Negroes as their equals. Indeed, such actions only indicate that economic grievances could sometimes outweigh race prejudice.

Between 1660 and 1685, members of the colony's labor force expressed their discontent in a variety of ways, some by isolated, spontaneous acts of violence, others by larger conspiratorial ventures. If an individual became desperate enough, he or she might strike a master.[39] Disaffected servants and slaves also ran away. The problem of fleeing bondsmen became quite serious in Berkeley's Virginia, and numerous colonial statutes tried to curb the practice. People often ran away in groups, fearing perhaps the Indians or the wilderness itself. Servants and slaves, eager for freedom and lured by rumors of a better life somewhere else, slipped away into the forests. Blacks and whites sometimes fled together, conscious that without cooperation their bid for freedom and escape might fail and bring instead immediate physical punishment and probably additional years of drudgery.[40] Whatever the terrors of flight, there were always persons desperate enough to take the chance. Some even plotted escape on shipboard before seeing America.[41] Planters assumed that the desire for freedom was contagious and that unless runaways were quickly suppressed, other men—black and white—would soon imitate them. When a group of fugitive slaves frustrated all attempts to retake them in 1672, the planters' greatest concern was that "other negroes, Indians or servants . . . [might] fly forth and joyne with them."[42]

Insurrection offered another means by which discontented workers expressed unhappiness with conditions in Virginia. While such organized disturbances were relatively infrequent, an occasional uprising reinforced the planters' fears and remained a source of uneasiness years after the violence had been quelled. During the early 1660s, servants upset the peace in several counties. The first disorder occurred in York and appears to have been sparked by complaints among indentured workers of "hard usage" and inadequate diet. Several conspirators, weary of "corne & water," demanded meat at least two or three times a week. The leader, an indentured servant named Isaac Friend, suggested that his followers petition the king for redress. This idea was dropped when someone pointed out that even if Charles II would listen, the group could never get a letter out of Virginia. Friend then decided that 40 servants should band together and "get Armes & he would be the first & have them cry as they went along, 'who would be for Liberty, and free from bondage,' & that there would be enough come to them & they would goe through the Countrey and kill those that made any opposition, & that they would either be free or die for it." Someone apparently revealed the plans before Friend and the others began their freedom march through Virginia. When the commissioners of York questioned the leader about his actions, he admitted making seditious speeches, but protested that he never intended to put the scheme into operation. Despite Friend's assurance, York officials refused to regard the episode as a servants' prank. They ordered Friend's master to keep close watch over him and warned the heads of all families in the county to take note of "like dangerous discourses."[43]

Two years later officials in Gloucester County, a fast growing region north of York, discovered another conspiracy. The causes of this disturbance are difficult to reconstruct since most of the Gloucester records have been lost and the surviving testimony is inconsistent. In his history of Virginia published in 1705, Robert Beverley, Jr. claimed that veterans of Cromwell's army who had been transported to the colony as indentured servants stirred up "the poor People . . . [and] form'd a villanous Plot to destroy their Masters, and afterwards to set up for themselves." Presumably Beverley drew his information from old planters and local tradition, but the available contemporary documents do not mention "*Oliverian* Soldiers."[44] A Gloucester court in 1663 accused nine "Laborers" of conspiring to arm 30 persons to overthrow the government of Virginia. While extant depositions reveal nothing about the political ideas of this group, they do suggest that some participants regarded bondage as their primary grievance. For example, one member reported that the conspirators had secretly pledged to seize weapons, march on the colonial capital and "demand our freedome." If the royal governor denied this request, the rebels planned to leave Virginia.[45]

The reaction to the attempted servant uprising of 1663 appears excessive unless one considers it in the context of the strained relationship between the major tobacco planters and colonial laborers. After the organizers of the plot had been captured and several executed, the servant who had warned the planters received his freedom and £200. The day on which the conspirators were arrested became an annual holiday.[46] Virginia officials notified Charles II of the details of the insurrection in such exaggerated terms that the king immediately ordered the colonists to construct a fortress to protect the governor and his loyal officials.[47] As late as 1670, the memory of the servant plot could still unnerve the gentry of Gloucester, Middlesex and York. Indeed, when it appeared that the mother country had allowed too many criminals and undesirables to emigrate to Virginia, the leading planters of these counties protested and reminded royal officials of "the horror yet remaining amongst us of the barbarous designe of those villaines in September 1663 who attempted at once the subversion of our Religion, Lawes, libertyes, rights and priviledges."[48]

During the 12 years preceding Bacon's Rebellion, fear of the labor force increasingly affected the character of Virginian society. Although no organized violence against the planters or the government occurred in this period, the laborers—black and white—constituted a subversive element. They were essential to the colony's economic well-being, but at the same time, no one trusted them. It was a foolish plantation owner who did not recognize the danger, for in a community in which so many men were unhappy, even seemingly contented workers might be potential conspirators. The tobacco gentry tried to regulate the lives of their bondsmen, and according to colonial statute, any servant who attended an unlawful meeting or travelled about the countryside without a pass risked arrest.[49] But these measures were insufficient to insure domestic tranquillity. Even if the behavior of the slaves and servants could have been closely controlled (a doubtful proposition at best), the poor freemen remained a threat.[50]

The extent of Virginia's social instability was revealed by events in 1676. Indian raids exacerbated long-standing grievances, and when a young planter named Nathaniel Bacon came forward as spokesman for the discontented, he sparked a civil war. Because Bacon's Rebellion was the most momentous event in seventeenth-century Virginia, it has been the object of intense investigation. Historians concerned chiefly with the behavior of the colony's elite have offered several interpretations of what motivated the leaders of this insurrection.[51] Such analysis is of little value in understanding the "giddy multitude," however, since whatever the aims of Bacon and his lieutenants, there is little evidence their goals were the same as those of their followers. Contemporaries, in fact, believed Bacon had aroused popular fears and frustrations to achieve his own private ends. The House of Burgesses concluded in 1677 that this rebellion, like others before it, resulted from "false Rumors, Infused by ill affected persons provoking an itching desire" in the common people.[52] Indeed, the loyal planters around Berkeley despised

Bacon not so much because he was ambitious or even because he had led an unauthorized march against local Indians, but because he had carried his case to the populace. After Bacon had been captured in June 1676, the governor pardoned him; and even though the rebel leader had defied Berkeley's orders several times and slaughtered a village of friendly Occaneechee Indians, Berkeley believed Bacon's submission to be sincere.[53] But Bacon had already stirred forces beyond his control. His followers demanded action. Within two days of receiving his pardon, Bacon "heard what an incredible Number of the meanest of the People were every where Armed to assist him and his cause."[54] He did not disappoint them. Had Bacon somehow confined the dispute to the upper class, he might have been forgiven for his erratic behavior, but once the servants, slaves and poor freemen became involved, he had to be crushed.[55]

Participants on both sides of the conflict believed it had pitted the rich against the poor, the privileged against the oppressed or as Berkeley described it, the "Rabble" against "the better sort people."[56] There is no reason to doubt the validity of this assessment. To many persons, the Rebellion must have seemed the type of class confrontation which Berkeley and his friends had long feared. "The poverty of the Country is such," Bacon declared, "that all the power and sway is got into the hands of the rich, who by extorious advantages, having the common people in their debt, have always curbed and oppressed them in all manner of wayes."[57] Although historians may discover the Virginian gentry was not as selfish as Bacon claimed, the leader's class rhetoric appealed to a large number of colonists.[58]

It would be interesting to identify these people, to know more about their social status, but the rebels have preserved their anonymity. Surviving records have yielded only a few names out of the hundreds who took up arms against the government. Contemporaries, however, insisted Bacon's troops had been recruited from the lowest ranks of Virginia society. They were the rabble, the disaffected, the vulgar, the indigent. In June 1676, loyalist William Sherwood reported "Now tag, rag, and bobtayle carry a high hand."[59] Philip Ludwell, another prominent colonial official, told an English correspondent that Bacon had raised 500 soldiers "whose fortunes & Inclinations being equally desperate, were fit for the purpose there being not 20 in the whole Route, but what were Idle & will not worke, or such whose Debaucherie or Ill Husbandry has brought in Debt beyond hopes or thought of payment."[60] Another account described the rebel army as a body composed of three parts: "freemen, searvants, and slaves."[61]

The lower-class origins of Bacon's troops receives additional verification from a narrative written by an English sea captain, Thomas Grantham. This rough adventurer arrived in Virginia just as the Rebellion was ending. Bacon had already died, and groups of dispirited rebels throughout the colony were debating whether to surrender or carry on the fight. Grantham volunteered to serve as an intermediary between Berkeley and his enemies. The governor accepted the offer, and the captain set off in his thirty-gun ship, the *Concord*, in search of the rebel bands. At a fortified position called West Point, he persuaded Joseph Ingram and "about 250" soldiers to submit to the governor's authority in exchange for a full pardon. Grantham then travelled three miles more to the plantation of Colonel John West, the rebels' "Chiefe Garrison and Magazine." At West's home he encountered approximately 400 "English and Negroes in Armes." In fact, he confronted the very sort of men that Berkeley's followers had often claimed supported Bacon.

The soldiers complained about Ingram's capitulation, and some urged shooting Grantham on the spot. But the captain knew how to talk himself out of difficult situations and brazenly informed "the negroes and Servants, that they were all pardoned and freed from their Slavery." With other such "faire promises" and a liberal supply of brandy, Grantham won most of the discouraged rebels over to the government, but "eighty Negroes and Twenty English . . . would not deliver their Armes." Perhaps these holdouts realized the captain had no power to grant bondsmen freedom; perhaps they believed fighting in a desperate cause better than returning to their masters. Whatever their reasoning, Grantham was one step ahead of the rebels. He tricked them onto a small boat by promising safe passage across the York River, and when the Negroes and servants were aboard, he threatened to blow them out of the water with the guns of the *Concord* unless they immediately surrendered. His account closes with the return of the captured "Negroes & Servants . . . to their Masters."[62]

The presence of so many black rebels at West's plantation provides evidence that many Virginians in Berkeley's time regarded economic status, not race, as the essential social distinction. Even the gentry seems to have viewed the blacks primarily as a component of the "giddy multitude." If the large tobacco planters could have played the white laborers off against the Negroes, they surely would have. The governor's supporters charged Bacon with many failings: atheism, hypocrisy, pride, avarice; but no one attacked the rebel leader for partiality toward black men.[63] One loyalist account of the Rebellion noted that Richard Lawrence, one of Bacon's advisers, had indulged in "the darke imbraces of a Blackamoore, his slave," but in the narrative literature of this period, such racial comments were rare.[64]

If the colonial gentry had been as worried about the danger of black insurrection in 1676 as they were in the eighteenth century, one would have expected some writer to have condemned Bacon's arming the slaves. The silence on this point is especially strange since it had long been illegal in Virginia for Negroes to bear arms.[65] Englishmen such as Captain Grantham appear to have been more conscious of the mixed racial character of Bacon's army than were the local planters.[66] Possibly the colonists had come to view the entire labor force, not just a part of it, as the threat to their safety. The absence of racial slurs does not indicate that Virginia leaders in 1676 felt no prejudice against Negroes. Rather, the planters may have taken for granted the cooperation of slaves, servants and poor freemen.

Bacon's Rebellion has often been described as a turning point in Virginia's history.[67] The settlement of the insurrection did bring about important political changes, especially in the colony's relationship to England; but it did almost nothing to allay the gentry's fear of the "giddy multitude." The social and economic conditions that had originally caused the labor force to participate in the disorder persisted after calm supposedly had been restored. In 1677, a small and relatively insignificant disturbance near Albemarle Sound in Carolina revealed the degree of the planters' uneasiness about maintaining order within their own colony. The disruption, known as Culpeper's Rebellion, grew out of several local grievances, the chief being the collection of a Parliamentary tax. What bothered the Virginians was not the rebels' specific demands, but the character of the rebels themselves. Observers in Carolina reported that Culpeper's force included the worst elements in colonial society. One person warned that if this band of impoverished whites and blacks succeeded in Carolina, it might soon "make Inroads and dayly Incursions" on Virginia.[68]

An even graver danger was the temptation which the Albemarle community presented to the poor laborers and bondsmen in other colonies. As one Carolinian explained, Virginia leaders hoped for a quick suppression of the rebels, "Being exceeding sensible of the dangerous consequences of this Rebellion, as that if they be not suddenly subdued hundreds of idle debtors, theeves, Negros, Indians and English servants will fly unto them." There is no evidence that Virginia workers actually ran to the Albemarle settlements. The fear of a lower-class exodus, however, is more significant than the fact. The colony's elite assumed a coalition of "servants, Slaves & Debtors" would defy established authority if the opportunity arose, and since Virginia's economy had not improved following Bacon's Rebellion, no one knew when a confrontation might occur.[69]

In 1681, five years after Bacon's death, Virginia's leaders were still worried about the possibility of a general servant uprising. At one point they urged the king to allow the foot companies originally sent to Virginia in 1677 to remain so that the Redcoats could "prevent or suppress any Insurrection that may otherwise happen during the necessitous unsettled condition of the Colonie."[70] And Thomas Lord Culpeper, the colony's royal governor (no relation to the leader of the Carolina disorder), regarded the labor force as the chief threat to internal peace. In 1679 the king had instructed Culpeper to "take care that all Planters and Christian Servants be well and fitly provided with Arms." But after living in Virginia only a short time, the governor realized the crown's order was impractical, if not counter-productive. In 1681 Culpeper scribbled in the margin next to this instruction: "Masters have arms. Servants not trusted with them."[71]

The lower classes once again turned to violence in the spring of 1682. The primary cause of this disturbance was chronic economic depression, although the political ambitions of Robert Beverley, Sr., clerk of the House of Burgesses, probably served as a catalyst for unrest. For several years, over-production of tobacco had brought hard times to everyone. In an effort to raise prices, some Virginians advocated the voluntary cessation of planting. Royal officials, however, discouraged these plans in the belief they would reduce customs revenue (a tax based on the volume of trade). When the colony's governor prorogued the Burgesses preventing any legislation on the issue, people in Gloucester took matters into their own hands.[72] Mobs marched from plantation to plantation, cutting tobacco plants as they went.

Each victim immediately became a fervid "cutter," since once his crop had been destroyed, he wanted to insure that his neighbors did not profit by his loss. The panic spread to other counties, and although Deputy Governor Henry Chicheley quickly dispatched cavalry units to apprehend the leading "mutineers" and to frustrate further "Insurrection and outrages," the rioting and "night mischiefs" continued for well over a month.[73]

After 1682 the character of social violence changed in Virginia. Never again would the "giddy multitude"—indentured servants, black slaves and poor freemen—make common cause against the colony's ruling planters. In fact, the plant-cutting riots were the last major disturbance in which white laborers of any sort took part. Over the next two decades, white men came to regard blacks—and blacks alone—as the chief threat to Virginia's tranquillity.

The transformation came slowly; for several years colonial leaders were hardly aware of it. Late in the summer of 1682, Secretary Spencer predicted new disorders simply because it was the season when "All plantations [are] flowing with Syder." He even thought he detected a spirit of unrest that "Bacon's Rebellion left itching behind it." But no rebellion occurred.[74] In 1683, Governor Culpeper reported that all was calm in Virginia. "All hands are at worke," he wrote, "none excepted. And yet there is an evil spiritt at Worke, who governed in our Time of Anarchy." Again, no disorder followed.[75] Two years later, Governor Francis Effingham asked William Blathwayt, secretary of the Lords of Trade, for a special force of 20 men "in Case any disorder should accidenteally happen," but the Governor undermined the urgency of his request by admitting "all things here are in a peaceable and Quiett Condition."[76] The lower-class whites, the common people, seemed interested in planting tobacco, settling frontier lands and raising families, and none showed much inclination toward organized violence. Not even the Glorious Revolution or rumors that hordes of Maryland Catholics planned to descend upon the colony could stir the "giddy multitude."[77] In 1697, the governor's council in Virginia reported: "The country is in peace and happiness."[78] By 1700, the general uprisings of whites, sometimes supported by a few Negroes, were no more than an unpleasant memory. The eighteenth-century Virginia gentry feared the blacks and the policies of certain aggressive royal governors, but no one expressed apprehension about the poor whites, the tenants, the indentured servants or the debtors. The problem is to explain how this change came about.

Many elements contributed to the transformation of Virginia, but none was more important than the rise of tobacco prices after 1684. In Berkeley's time, the tobacco market had generally been poor. Some years were better than others, but prices never regained the level achieved in 1660. During the last two decades of the seventeenth century, economic conditions improved. The demand for Virginia crops expanded, and poor yields and natural disasters occurred often enough to prevent market saturation.[79] These were not boom years as the 1620s had been, but tobacco prices were high enough to raise the lower classes out of the poverty that had been so widespread before the 1680s.[80] Contemporaries appreciated the relationship between economic improvement and social tranquillity. Governor Culpeper informed crown officials in 1683 that "peace and quietness" would continue in Virginia "so long as tobacco bears a price."[81] The next year Spencer observed that the people had calmed down since they had begun working for a full harvest.[82]

While rising prices reduced social tensions, they did not in themselves bring about the disappearance of the "giddy multitude." The character of the labor force also changed during this period. Before Bacon's Rebellion, planters imported thousands of indentured servants; and because the demand for workers exceeded the supply, planters accepted whomever merchants delivered. After 1680, however, commercial developments outside Virginia altered the servant trade. English companies achieved the capacity to ship Negroes directly from Africa to the mainland colonies and, during the last years of the seventeenth century, tobacco planters purchased slaves in increasingly larger numbers. This new source of labor was not only more economic than the indentured servants had been, but it also allowed planters greater selectivity in the choice of servants. William Fitzhugh, for example, one of the colony's major slave holders, refused to take "ordinary servants," warning a trader, "I would have a good one or none."[83]

A second element affecting the quality of indentured servants was England's crackdown on the "spirits." In 1682 Charles II issued a proclamation regulating the recruitment of servants. No indenture would be valid unless signed before a magistrate in the mother country, and no person under 14 years old could be shipped to America without parental consent.[84] The king's humanitarian act may in part have been an attempt to protect - legitimate merchants from fraudulent suits by individuals claiming to have been abducted. In the early 1680s a group calling itself "the Principall Merchants of England traders to the Plantacions" protested that unnecessary prosecutions had so discouraged traders from carrying servants to the New World that some colonies would soon find themselves with "few white men to Governe & direct the Negroes."[85]

Whatever the causes, the number of indentured servants arriving in Virginia dwindled. Those who did immigrate, however, were of a higher social rank than those who flooded the colony at mid-century. Large planters wanted servants with special skills. In 1687 Fitzhugh advised an Englishman how to establish a plantation in Virginia: "the best methods to be pursued therein is, to get a Carpenter & Bricklayer Servants, & send them in here to serve 4 or five years, in which time of their Service they might reasonably build a substantial good house . . . & earn money enough besides in their said time, at spare times from your work . . . as will purchase plank, nails & other materials."[86] Of the seven indentured servants mentioned in Fitzhugh's will, one was a carpenter, one a glazier and another the planter's own cousin.[87] Unlike the planters of Berkeley's time, Fitzhugh's contemporaries seldom complained that their servants were "desperate villans" recruited from the "very scum" of England. Conditions had changed. The indentured workers who emigrated after the mid-1680s escaped the crushing poverty and frustrations that so embittered the previous generation of servants. For these later arrivals Virginia may well have appeared a land of opportunity.

The poor freemen also became less disruptive in this period. Landless and indebted persons, many of them former servants, had once flocked to Bacon's standard. Yet, by the mid-1680s, no one seems to have regarded them as a serious threat to Virginia's internal security. These people benefited greatly from improved economic conditions. Few at the lowest levels of white society experienced the grinding poverty that a decade earlier had driven desperate men to violence. Food was abundant and clothes easier to obtain. Indeed, by the beginning of the eighteenth century, Virginians boasted of eradicating poverty. The planter-historian, Robert Beverley, Jr., noted in 1705 that the colonists "live in so happy a Climate, and have so fertile a Soil, that no body is poor enough to beg, or want Food, though they have abundance of People that are lazy enough to deserve it." Beverley concluded that compared to European nations, Virginia was "the best poor man's Country in the World."[88] Foreign visitors corroborated Beverley's observation. When a French Protestant, Francis Louis Michel, travelled through Virginia in 1702, he reported finding no poor people and wrote: "It is indeed said truthfully that there is no other country, where it is possible with so few means and so easily to make an honest living and be in easy circumstances." As tobacco prices improved, the less prosperous freemen found wealthier neighbors willing to advance credit. And if a person possessed a special skill or trade, he could command a good wage. "I have seen a common journeyman paid annually 30 lbs. sterling, including his board," one man wrote. "But I have heard of master workmen who receive above a guinea daily."[89]

As always, freemen wanted land. In Berkeley's time, hostile Indians along the frontier and "Land lopers" among the gentry frustrated this desire. After the mid-1680s, however, changes in Virginia reduced these obstructions—the colonists simply removed the Indians. A foreign traveller at the turn of the century discovered that Indians "have not come into the colony to inflict damage, because for one thing they are afraid of the English power, but especially because they are unable to flee from the cavalry." As early as 1687, Virginians counselled prospective colonists that Indians "are not greatly to be feared."[90]

Often the colony's most influential planters, such as William Byrd, William Fitzhugh and Ralph Wormeley, claimed the vacated Indian lands. One means to obtain large tracts in the west was to lead the militia in a successful march against the Indians. "The colonels of these troops," a Frenchman explained, "claimed the plantations of the savages & had them surveyed, so that at the present time [1687] there are large tracts of very good land for sale in Virginia."[91] Some of these men held onto the land, building the vast estates that became an integral part of the Virginia aristocracy in the eighteenth century, but much of the acreage was sold. Several Virginians, in fact, became speculators and showed no desire to discourage small farmers from settling the newly secured territory. Fitzhugh, one of the colony's largest landowners, urged an English associate to promote the planter's Virginia lands, for any transfer "will be doubly advantageous to me first by meeting with an opportunity to serve you through your friends, & secondly, by profitably either selling or tenementing my Land, which till so done, is rather a charge than profit."[92] Easy and flexible terms were offered to interested buyers. Ralph Wormeley, for example, was willing to sell "ten thousand acres of ground he owned . . . for one écu an acre."[93]

If landless freemen could not afford acreage in Virginia, they could move to Carolina or Pennsylvania, areas largely inaccessible before 1680. This practice was fairly common. In 1695, Governor Francis Nicholson complained "many families, but especially young men" were leaving Virginia and Maryland for Pennsylvania where land could be purchased at a lower rate.[94] A visitor to Virginia in 1702 "heard many good reports about Pennsylvania and that some people from Virginia moved there."[95] Whichever option the ex-servant chose—buying land in Virginia or moving—he could anticipate becoming an independent planter. Although relatively few advanced to the highest ranks of society, the freeman's horizons were broader in 1700 than they had been in 1670.[96]

After the 1680s the experience of the blacks in Virginia was increasingly different from that of other colonists. Improved tobacco prices raised white laborers out of poverty, making their servitude endurable and their freemanship secure. But the same economic conditions brought large numbers of Negroes into the colony as slaves. No one knows exactly how rapidly the black population grew after 1680. There seems to have been about 4,000 slaves at the time of the tobacco-cutting riots. Estimates of the size of the Negro population in 1700 range as high as 20,000. Even if this figure is excessive, the number of Africans arriving in Virginia expanded substantially in the last two decades of the seventeenth century.[97]

The leading tobacco planters required no encouragement to make the transition from white to black labor. The wealthiest among them had accumulated enough capital to purchase and maintain large gangs of Negroes. For the first time in the century, English trading companies were able to supply blacks on a reasonably regular basis. The colonists bought all the Negroes the slavers could transport and then demanded more.[98] In 1696, a group of Chesapeake planters and merchants petitioned Parliament to lift restrictions on the African trade, since the company holding the monopoly (the Royal African Company) could not meet the escalating demand for blacks in Maryland and Virginia.[99]

The changes in the slave community were more complex than revealed by population statistics alone. In fact, the sheer growth in numbers only partially explains why whites no longer joined with blacks to threaten planter society. An equally important element in understanding race relations in this period was the Negroes' experience before arriving in Virginia. With each passing year an increasing proportion of slaves came directly from Africa.[100] These immigrants had no stopover in Barbados to learn English or to adjust either physically or mentally to an alien culture. They were simply dumped on the wharves of the river plantations in a state of shock, barely alive after the ocean crossing. Conditions on the slave ships were terrible. One vessel from Guinea unloaded 230 blacks, but reported that a hundred more had died at sea.[101] No white servant in this period, no matter how poor, how bitter or badly treated, could identify with these frightened Africans. The terrors they had so recently faced were beyond comprehension. The sale of the blacks emphasized the difference between races. "The negroes are brought annually in large numbers," a visitor to Virginia recounted at the turn of the century. "They can be selected according to pleasure, young and old, men and women. They are entirely naked when they arrive, having only corals of different colors around their necks and arms." These strange, helpless blacks repulsed the writer who noted that even the Indians seemed preferable to these "animal-like people."[102] His reactions, no doubt, were shared by many white Virginians. In 1699, members of the House of Burgesses described the blacks in a manner unknown in Berkeley's time, claiming it unnecessary to expose slaves to Christianity, since "the gross barbarity and rudeness of their manners, the variety and strangeness of their languages and the weakness and shallowness of their minds rendered it in a manner impossible to attain to any progress in their conversion."[103]

Language became a major barrier between white laborers and the thousands of new black immigrants.[104] Before the 1690s, no one recorded any problem in communicating with Negroes. Indeed, it is difficult to comprehend how servants and slaves could have conspired to run away or rebel had they been unable to understand one another. The flood of Africans directly into Virginia not only made it difficult for whites to deal with blacks, but also hindered communications between blacks.[105] The colonists apparently regarded the great variety of African tongues as a protection against black insurrection. Early in the eighteenth century, Governor Alexander Spotswood, convinced of the need for stricter controls over the labor force, warned Virginians that the slaves' "Babel of Languages" offered no real security, since "freedom Wears a Cap which can without a Tongue, Call Together all Those who long to Shake off the fetters of Slavery."[106]

The blacks hated their status. They ran away whenever possible, and on at least one occasion, formed a small band that terrorized the colonists of Rappahannock County.[107] Rumors of Negro plots made the planters uneasy, with good reason. A group of slaves could easily have seized a plantation and murdered the master and his family before troops could have been summoned.[108] But there was little chance that the blacks at this time could have overrun the colony; without the support of poorer whites and indentured servants, they were badly outnumbered. The white cavalry that hunted down the Indians could have done the same to the slaves.[109] The changes in Virginia society after the mid-1680s had set whites against blacks, the armed, organized forces of the planters against the small, isolated groups of slaves. In Berkeley's time the militia had been regarded as a means of protecting the elite from the entire labor force, but early in the eighteenth century, historian Hugh Jones reported that "in each county is a great number of disciplined and armed militia, ready in case of any sudden irruption of Indians or insurrection of Negroes."[110] The labor force was still the major threat to internal security in Virginia, but now the laborers were predominantly black.

Like the Barbadians, the seventeenth-century Virginians exchanged white servants for Negro slaves, and in so doing, exchanged a fear of the "giddy multitude" for a fear of slave rebellion. By 1700, whites had achieved a sense of race solidarity at the expense of blacks. Negroes were set apart as objects of contempt and ridicule. The whites, even the meanest among them, always knew there was a class of men permanently below them. But the story of Virginia's labor force between 1660 and 1710 was more than a dreary narrative of suffering and oppression. For a few decades, it had been possible to overlook racial differences, a time when a common experience of desperate poverty and broken dreams brought some whites and blacks together. Such conditions were present in the American South during the 1890s, and it is not unlikely that they will appear again.

FOOTNOTES

1. See T.H. Breen and Stephen Foster, "The Puritans' Greatest Achievement: A Study of Social Cohesion in Seventeenth-Century Massachusetts." *Journal of American History*, in press (hereafter cited as *JAH*).

2. The House of Burgesses used the term to describe the followers of Nathaniel Bacon (H.R. McIlwaine, ed., *Journals of the House of Burgesses of Virginia 1659/60-1693* [Richmond, 1914], 73). Similar phrases were common in the 1670s. The last example I have found was a proclamation of 1685 referring to "the Giddy headed multitude" (H.R. McIlwaine, ed., *Executive Journals of the Council of Colonial Virginia* [Richmond, 1925], I, 75).

3. William Berkeley to "Mr. Secretary" [Thomas Ludwell], July, 1676, in the Henry Coventry Papers at Longleat, estate of the Marquis of Bath (microfilm, Library of Congress), LXXVII, fol. 145.

4. The disappearance of the "giddy multitude" was only one of several elements affecting Virginia in the last half of the seventeenth century. Equally important were changes in the character of the colony's ruling class. Between 1650 and 1720, the elite was transformed from a body of factious, socially insecure immigrants into a self-confident, unified provincial aristocracy. The behavior of these wealthy planters has been the object of careful examination and much is known about their role in events such as Bacon's Rebellion. The danger for the historian is not in overlooking the gentry, but in crediting it with too large a responsibility in bringing about social change. On the transformation of the Virginia gentry, see Bernard Bailyn, "Politics and Social Structure in Virginia," in James Morton Smith, ed., *Seventeenth-Century America: Essays in Colonial History* (Chapel Hill, 1959), 90-115; John C. Rainbolt, "The Alteration in the Relationship between Leadership and Constituents in Virginia, 1660 to 1720," *William and Mary Quarterly*, 3rd Ser., XXVII (1970), 411-34 (hereafter cited as *Wm. & Mary Qtly.*).

5. Professor Edmund S. Morgan has discussed the character of Virginia's labor force in the late seventeenth century, analyzing how the transition from a predominantly white, indentured labor force to one composed almost entirely of Negro slaves affected the character of colonial Virginia society and how this process later shaped the manner in which the Founding Fathers defined liberty, freedom and equality. Although Morgan was primarily concerned with the development of the institution of slavery, as opposed to changing race relations, his work was extremely valuable in the preparation of this piece. See "Slavery and Freedom: The American Paradox," *JAH*, LIX (1972), 5-29. George M. Fredrickson carries this discussion forward into the nineteenth century and borrowing a term from the sociologist Pierre L. van den Berghe, describes southern society as an *"Herrenvolk* democracy"—democracy for the master race, but tyranny for

subordinate groups. See the *The Black Image in the White Mind: The Debate on Afro-American Character and Destiny, 1817-1914* (New York, 1972, pb. ed.), 58-110.

6. John Hammond, *Leah and Rachel, or, the Two Fruitful Sisters Virginia, and Mary-Land* .... (London, 1656) reprinted in Peter Force, *Tracts and Other Papers* (Washington, 1844), III, 7-9.

7. See Edmund S. Morgan, "The First American Boom: Virginia, 1618 to 1630," *Wm. & Mary Qtly.*, 3rd Ser., XXVIII (1971), 618-30; Wesley Frank Craven, *The Southern Colonies in the Seventeenth Century, 1607-1689* (Baton Rouge, 1949), 214-15.

8. John Spencer Bassett, ed., *The Writings of "Colonel William Byrd"* (New York, 1901), xi; Craven, *Southern Colonies*, 214-15; K.G. Davies, *The Royal African Company* (London, 1957), 38-44.

9. Wesley Frank Craven, *White, Red, and Black: The Seventeenth-Century Virginian* (Charlottesville, 1971), 5, 14-15.

10. Colonial Office Papers, Class I, Vol. 26, no. 77, Public Record Office, London, microfilm, Yale University Library (hereafter cited as CO).

11. See Katheryne Hunlocke to her daughter, August 3, 1648, *Wm. & Mary Qtly.*, 1st Ser., IV (1895), 174. On the social origins of persons coming to the New World at this time, see Craven, *White, Red, and Black*, 5, 7-9; Mildred Campbell, "Social Origins of Some Early Americans," in J.M. Smith, ed., *Seventeenth-Century America*, 63-89.

12. See George Donne's unpublished essay "Virginia Reviewed," British Museum, Harleian Mss. 7021, 11A-12.

13. Abbot Emerson Smith, *Colonists in Bondage, White Servitude and Convict Labor in America, 1607-1776* (New York, 1971, pb. ed.), 67-74.

14. Leo F. Stock, ed., *Proceedings and Debates of the British Parliaments Respecting North America, 1542-1739* (Washington, 1924-37), I, 269.

15. [Lionel Gatford], *Publick Good Without Private Interest* .... (London, 1657), 9-12.

16. Craven, *White, Red, and Black*, 6-7; [Gatford], *Publick Good*, 5; William Bullock, *Virginia Impartially Examined* .... (London, 1649), 14; *Calendar of State Papers Colonial, 1661-1668*, 98 (hereafter cited as *CSP Colonial*).

17. [Gatford], *Publick Good*, 4.

18. CO 1/25, nos. 26, 28; CO 1/27, no. 9. Although the number of convicts coming to Virginia at this time was small, the colonists may have employed words such as "Newgateers" as general terms to describe lower-class immigrants. On the actual criminals, see A.E. Smith, *Colonists in Bondage*, 89-135.

19. CO 1/25, no. 28.

20. Bullock, *Virginia Impartially Examined*, 13-14.

21. Stock, ed., *Proceedings and Debates*, I, 269; CO 1/49, no. 11; Alexander Moray to Sir Robert Moray, June 12, 1665, *Wm. & Mary Qtly.*, 2nd Ser., II (1922), 159-60. See Oscar and Mary F. Handlin, "Origins of the Southern Labor System," *Wm. & Mary Qtly.*, 3rd Ser., VII (1950), 202-05.

22. For a general discussion of psychological adjustment to an unfamiliar environment in the colonial period, see Jack P. Greene, "Search for Identity: An Interpretation of the Meaning of Selected Patterns of Social Response in Eighteenth-Century America," and David F. Musto, "On 'Search for Identity': A Comment," *Journal of Social History*, III (1970), 189-224. The problem of psychological adjustment to New World conditions is a topic that deserves closer attention than it has so far received. On one aspect of this question, see T.H. Breen and Stephen Foster, "Moving to the New World: The Character of Early Massachusetts Immigration," to be published in the *Wm. & Mary Qtly.*

23. Bullock, *Virginia Impartially Examined*, 2-8, 14; Hammond, *Leah and Rachel*, 12-19. One Englishman captured the servants' attitudes in a conversation before departure to the New World: "There was little discourse amongst them, but of the pleasantness of the soyl of that Continent we were designed for . . . the temperature of the Air, the plenty of Fowl and Fish of all sorts; the little labour that is performed or expected having so little trouble in it, that it rather may be accounted a pastime than anything of punishment" (cited in A.E. Smith, *Colonist in Bondage*, 70).

24. Bullock, *Virginia Impartially Examined*, 14.

25. William W. Hening, *The Statutes at Large; Being a Collection of All The Lawes of Virginia* . . . . (Richmond, 1819-23), II, 388; *Wm. & Mary Qtly.*, 1st Ser., XII (1902), 36.

26. William Sherwood, "Virginias Deploured Condition . . . . " [1676], *4 Collections*, Massachusetts Historical Society, IX (1871), 164; [Gatford], *Publick Good*, 9.

27. Thomas J. Wertenbaker, *The Planters of Colonial Virginia* (Princeton, 1922), ch. V; Philip A. Bruce, *Economic History of Virginia in the Seventeenth Century* (New York, 1896), II, 47; Morgan, "Slavery and Freedom," 20.

28. Thomas Ludwell to Lord John Berkeley, CO 1/21.

29. *Virginia Magazine of History and Biography*, XX (1912), 136-37 (hereafter cited as *VMH&B*).

30. John Berry and Francis Maryson, "A True Narrative of the Rise, Progresse, and Cessation of the Late Rebellion in Virginia. . . . ", *VMH&B*, IV (1897), 127. For the fullest and most recent discussion of the planters' fear of the landless and impoverished freemen, see Morgan, "Slavery and Freedom," 20-24.

31. A.E. Smith, *Colonists in Bondage*, 328; Craven, *White, Red, and Black*, 98; CO 1/47, no. 106.

32. Elizabeth Donnan, ed., *Documents Illustrative of the History of the Slave Trade to America* (Washington, 1930-35), IV, 89; Craven, *White, Red, and Black*, 93-94; Bruce, *Economic History*, II, 84-86; Philip D. Curtin, *The Atlantic Slave Trade* (Madison, 1969), 57-58, 118-19.

33. Craven, *White, Red, and Black*, 94-95; Morgan Godwyn, *The Negro's and Indians Advocate* (London, 1680), 101.

34. I have found no evidence in the colonial statutes or private correspondence to indicate that language was a barrier dividing whites and blacks before the 1680s.

35. O. and M. Handlin, "Southern Labor System," 204, 209-13; Carl Degler, "Slavery and the Genesis of Race Prejudice," *Comparative Studies in Society & History*, II (1959-60), 51-57; Winthrop Jordan, *White Over Black: American Attitudes Toward the Negro, 1550-1812* (Chapel Hill, 1968), 71-75; D.B. Davis, *The Problem of Slavery in*

Western Culture (Ithaca, 1966), 245-47; Craven, *White, Red, and Black*, 75-76; Richard R. Beeman, "Labor Forces and Race Relations: A Comparative View of the Colonization of Brazil and Virginia," *Political Science Quarterly*, LXXXV (1971), 632-35.

36. See below, especially the discussion of Bacon's Rebellion.

37. See A.E. Smith, *Colonists in Bondage*, 67-74; Kenneth M. Stampp, *The Peculiar Institution: Slavery in the Ante-Bellum South* (New York, 1956), 21-22.

38. Richard Ligon, *A True and Exact History of the Island of Barbados* (London, 1657), 43-44; Carl and Roberta Bridenbaugh, *No Peace Beyond the Line: The English in the Caribbean, 1624-1690* (New York, 1972), 24-26, 103-08, 168; A.O. Exquemelin, *The Buccaneers of America*, trans., A. Brown (Baltimore, 1969), 64-66; V.T. Harlow, *A History of Barbados* (Oxford, 1926), 302-06.

39. Hening, *Statutes*, I, 538.

40. *Ibid.*, II, 26, 35; B. Fleet, *Virginia Colonial Abstracts, Charles City County Court Orders, 1664-1665* [Vol. XIII], 37; H.R. McIlwaine, ed., *Minutes of the Council and General Court of Colonial Virginia* (Richmond, 1924), 467; Jordan, *White Over Black*, 75.

41. Hening, *Statutes*, II, 273; *VMH&B*, XX (1912), 137; Bruce, *Economic History*, II, 19-29; Susie M. Ames, *Studies of the Virginia Eastern Shore in the Seventeenth Century* (Richmond, 1940), 88-89.

42. Hening, *Statutes*, II, 35, 299.

43. "Records of the York County Court," *Wm. & Mary Qtly.*, 1st Ser., XI (1902), 34-37; "York County in the Seventeenth Century," *Tyler's Magazine of History and Biography*, I (1920), 266.

44. Robert Beverley, *The History and Present State of Virginia* [1705], ed., Louis B. Wright (Chapel Hill, 1947), 69.

45. "The Servants' Plot of 1663," *VMH&B*, XV (1908), 38-41.

46. Beverley, *History of Virginia*, 69.

47. *Ibid.*, 70.

48. CO 1/25, nos. 26, 28.

49. Hening, *Statutes*, II, 187-88, 195; J.C. Ballagh, *White Servitude in the Colony of Virginia: A Study of the System of Indentured Labor in the American Colonies*, Johns Hopkins University Studies, XIII (Baltimore, 1895), 318; Craven, *Southern Colonies*, 215-17.

50. See, "Surry County Court Records, September, 1672," *VMH&B*, VII (1900), 314.

51. For a review of the historiography on Bacon's Rebellion, see Wesley Frank Craven, *The Colonies in Transition, 1660-1713* (New York, 1968), 137-56. Also, Bailyn, "Politics and Social Structure," 105-15; Wilcomb E. Washburn, *The Governor and The Rebel: A History of Bacon's Rebellion in Virginia* (Chapel Hill, 1957).

52. McIlwaine, ed., *Journals of Burgesses*, 73. See also Richard Lee's comments in the Coventry Papers, LXXVII, fol. 161.

53. Washburn, *Governor and Rebel*, 51-52.

54. Coventry Papers, LXXVII, fol. 144.

55. *Ibid.*, 91, 92. For example, in the mid-1670s Giles Bland, the king's collector of customs in Virginia and the son-in-law of a powerful English official, kept his conflicts confined to the colony's ruling class and thus, escaped with fines and censures. When he later joined Bacon's forces, however, Bland was executed (Washburn, *Governor and Rebel*, 92-93).

56. Coventry Papers, LXXVII, fol. 144.

57. CO 5/1371, 241; Coventry Papers, LXXVII, fol. 442.

58. The Burgesses believed Bacon's class rhetoric had wide appeal. They claimed Bacon gathered an army by arousing "the people with Liberty and free estate from Bondage, and that he would make the meanest of them equall with or in better Condition then those that ruled over them" (McIlwaine, ed., *Journals of Burgesses*, 74).

59. William Sherwood to Secretary Joseph Williamson, June 28, 1676, CO 1/37, no. 17; also, no. 1.

60. Philip Ludwell to Secretary Joseph Williamson, June 28, 1676, *VMH&B*, I (1894), 183.

61. "The History of Bacon's and Ingram's Rebellion" [1676] in Charles M. Andrews, ed., *Narratives of the Insurrections, 1675-1690* (New York, 1915), 94.

62. Captain Thomas Grantham's "Account of my Transactions," Coventry Papers, LXXVII, fol. 301; Andrews, ed., *Narratives*, 92-96; Washburn, *Governor and Rebel*, 87-89; Thomas Grantham, *An Historial Account of Some Memorial Actions . . . .* [London, 1716], ed., R.A. Brock (Richmond, 1882). The servants who supported Bacon were punished as runaways (Hening, *Statutes*, II, 395).

63. If Virginia's black population stood at approximately 2500 at the time of Bacon's Rebellion, then the 80 Negroes identified at West's Plantation represented about three percent of the blacks in the colony. Since at least two thirds of the Negro population must have been women and children, the 80 holdouts probably represented about nine percent of the adult black males. One contemporary source mentioned that other Negroes were taken with Ingram, but since the exact number in that group is unknown, they were not included in the estimates. It is possible, however, that considerably more than ten percent of the colony's adult black males were in arms against Berkeley's government (Washburn *Governor and Rebel*, 80, 209; Andrews, ed., *Narrative*, 94).

64. Andrews, ed., *Narratives*, 96.

65. Winthrop D. Jordan, "Modern Tensions and the Origins of American Slavery," *Journal of Southern History*, XXVIII (1962), 27. The Burgesses passed another act against Negroes carrying weapons in 1680 (Hening, *Statutes*, II, 481-82, 492-93).

66. See, Washburn, *Governor and Rebel*, 209.

67. For example, Bailyn, "Politics and Social Structure," 102; Craven, *Southern Colonies*, 394.

68. William L. Saunders, ed., *The Colonial Records of North Carolina* (Raleigh, 1886), I, 261.

69. *Ibid.*, 248, 260-61.

70. Report to the King, October 31, 1681, *VMH&B*, XXV (1917), 371; *CSP Colonial, 1681-1685*, 134-35; also, *ibid.*, 89; Council of Virginia to the Lords of Trade and Plantations, May 5, 1683, CO 1/50, no. 105; McIlwaine, ed., *Executive Journals of the Council*, I, 4.

71. CO 1/47, no. 106.

72. Sir Henry Chicheley to Sir Leoline Jenkins, May 8, 1682, CO 1/48, no. 68; *VMH&B*, XVIII (1910), 249; Blathwayt Papers, XVI, Nicholas Spencer to William Blathwayt, May 29, 1682 (microfilm, Colonial Williamsburg, Inc.).

73. CO 1/48, nos. 69, 74-I, 81, 95, 97; CO 5/1356, 178; Virginia Council Proceedings, May 10, 1682, *VMH&B*, XVIII (1910), 248.

74. CO 1/49, no. 25.

75. CO 1/50, no. 68.

76. Blathwayt Papers, XIV, Governor Effingham to Wm. Blathwayt, May 13, 1685.

77. On the rumors, see McIlwaine, ed., *Executive Journals of Council*, I, 105; Nicholas Spencer to Privy Council, April 29, 1689, *VMH&B*, XXII (1914), 269-70; Blathwayt Papers, XVI, April 27, 1689.

78. *CSP Colonial, 1696-1697*, 461.

79. L.C. Gray, "The Market Surplus Problems of Colonial Tobacco," *Wm. & Mary Qtly.*, 2nd Ser., VII (1927), 233-34; Warren M. Billings, "The Causes of Bacon's Rebellion: Some Suggestions," *VMH&B*, LXXVII (1970), 419-22.

80. Morgan, "The First American Boom"; Wertenbaker, *Planters*, 64.

81. *CSP Colonial, 1681-1685*, 406.

82. CO 1/53, no. 67; Blathwayt Papers, XVI, Spencer to Wm. Blathwayt, April 3, 1684.

83. William Fitzhugh to Captain Partis, July 1, 1680, *VMH&B*, I (1894), 30; Wertenbaker, *Planters of Colonial Virginia*, 127.

84. A.E. Smith, *Colonists in Bondage*, 74-79.

85. Bodleian Library, Oxford, Ms. All Souls 211 (microfilm, Virginia Survey Report, X75).

86. Wertenbaker, *Planters of Colonial Virginia*, 134-35; William Fitzhugh to Nicholas Hayward, January 30, 1687 in Richard Beale Davis, ed., *William Fitzhugh and His Chesapeake World, 1676-1701* (Chapel Hill, 1963), 202. When officials in the mother country suggested forming a settlement of Irish prisoners of war in Virginia, the colonial council rejected the offer because of the "Dangerous Consequence to the Peace and quiett of this their Majesties Dominion, if many Irishmen should be sent into this Colony . . ." (McIlwaine, ed., *Executive Journals of the Council*, I, 139).

87. Davis, ed., *William Fitzhugh*, 15.

88. Beverley, *History of Virginia*, 275.

89. "Report of the Journey of Francis Louis Michel From Berne, Switzerland to Virginia, October 2, 1701–December 1, 1702," *VMH&B*, XXIV (1916), 124, 287.

90. *Ibid.*, 129; Durand of Dauphiné, *Voyage d'un François Exilé Pour le Religion ....* [1687], ed., Gilbert Chinard (New York, 1934), 143; Craven, *White, Red, and Black*, 64-67.

91. Dauphiné, *Voyage*, 109, 179-80; Bassett, ed., *Writings of Colonel Byrd*, xxi-xxii.

92. William Fitzhugh to Nicholas Hayward, April 1, 1689, *VMH&B*, II (1895), 275; Fairfax Harrison, *Landmarks of Old Prince William: A Study of Origins in Northern Virginia* (Richmond, 1924), I, 177-96. On the large number of small farms in Virginia, see Wertenbaker, *Planters of Colonial Virginia*, 52-53; Manning C. Voorhis, "Crown Versus Council in the Virginia Land Policy," *Wm. & Mary Qtly.*, 3rd Ser., III (1946), 499. Also, on the land speculation of wealthy planters in Maryland, Aubrey C. Land, "Economic Base and Social Structure: The Northern Chesapeake in the Eighteenth Century," *Journal of Economic History*, XXV (1965), 648-49.

93. Dauphiné, *Voyage*, 32, 154-55, 157-59.

94. *CSP Colonial, 1693-1696*, 511; Bassett, ed., *Writings of Colonel Byrd*, xi-xiv.

95. "Report of Francis Louis Michel," 135, 289, 290; Wertenbaker, *Planters of Colonial Virginia*, 138-39.

96. See, Land, "Economic Base and Social Structure," 639-54 for an estimate of social mobility in Chesapeake society.

97. "Report of Francis Louis Michel," 25; Rainbolt, "Leadership and Constituents in Virginia," 428; Wetenbaker, *Planters of Colonial Virginia*, 130-33.

98. Davies, *Royal African Company*, 131-35, 143-51; Davis, ed., *William Fitzhugh*, 21, 122, 127-28. The development of the Virginia labor force paralleled that of the West Indian colonies, although the Virginians did not become dependent on Negro slaves until 20 or 30 years after the islands had done so (see C.S.S. Higham, *The Development of the Leeward Islands Under the Restoration, 1660-1685* [Cambridge, England, 1921], 144-65; Harlow, *History of Barbados*, 327; Burns, *History of the British West Indies*, 302).

99. Stock, ed., *Proceedings and Debates*, II, 183.

100. Curtin, *Atlantic Slave Trade*, 144; Donnan, ed., *Documents of the Slave Trade*, I, 250; Davies, *Royal African Company*, 143; Craven, *White, Red, and Black*, 100-01.

101. "Report of Francis Louis Michel," 117.

102. *Ibid.*, 116, 117; Bruce, *Economic History*, II, 108-09.

103. *CSP Colonial*, 1699, 261. This evidence supports the Handlins' argument that race prejudice grew as the Negro population in Virginia expanded and as the lower-class whites improved their economic status relative to the blacks. Neither of these developments, however, seems to have greatly affected race relations much before the 1680s ("Southern Labor System," 210, 214-15).

104. Separate living quarters also divided white and black workers. A French visitor in 1687 noted that the planters built *separate* quarters for "Christian slaves" and "negro slaves" (Dauphiné, *Voyage*, 119-20). William Fitzhugh constructed three units of "quarters" for his Negro slaves (R.B. Davis, ed., *William Fitzhugh*, 15).

105. Hening, *Statutes*, III, 456.

106. Cited in Rainbolt, "Leadership and Constituents in Virginia," 429.

107. McIlwaine, ed., *Executive Journals of the Council*, 86-87; Effingham Papers, II, October 24, 1687 (microfilm, Colonial Williamsburg, Inc.); Hening, *Statutes*, III, 86; Bruce, *Economic History*, II, 116.

108. On Negro plots, real and imagined, see "Records of Westmoreland County," *Wm. & Mary Qtly.*, 1st Ser., X (1902), 178; Effingham Papers, II, October 24, 1687; Wertenbaker, *Planters of Colonial Virginia*, 128-29.

109. Governor Andros' proclamation calling for the stricter enforcement of acts preventing Negro insurrections was read before the militia in each county (McIlwaine, ed., *Executive Journals of the Council*, I, 317-18). On police powers, see Jordan, *White Over Black*, 82; Hening, *Statutes*, III, 86-87; Morgan, "Slavery and Freedom," 26-27.

110. Hugh Jones, *The Present State of Virginia*, ed., Richard L. Morton (Chapel Hill, 1956), 93.

Over a century ago, Tocqueville named slavery as the source of the American prejudice against the Negro. Contrary to the situation in antiquity, he remarked: "Among the moderns the abstract and transient fact of slavery is fatally united with the physical and permanent fact of color." Furthermore, he wrote, though "slavery recedes" in some portions of the United States, "the prejudice to which it has given birth is immovable".[1] More modern observers of the American past have also stressed this causal connection between the institution of slavery and the color prejudice of Americans.[2] Moreover, it is patent to anyone conversant with the nature of American slavery, particularly as it functioned in the nineteenth century, that the impress of bondage upon the character and future of the Negro in the United States has been both deep and enduring.

But if one examines other societies which the Negro entered as a slave, it is apparent that the consequences of slavery have not always been those attributed to the American form. Ten years ago, for example, Frank Tannenbaum demonstrated that in the Spanish and Portuguese colonies in South America, slavery did not leave upon the freed Negro anything like the prejudicial mark which it did in the United States.[3] He and others[4] have shown that once the status of slavery was left behind, the Negro in the lands south of the Rio Grande was accorded a remarkable degree of social equality with the whites. In the light of such differing consequences, the role of slavery in the development of the American prejudice against the Negro needs to be reexamined, with particular attention paid to the historical details of origins.

I

Tannenbaum showed that in the Portuguese and Spanish colonies there were at least three historical forces or traditions which tended to prevent the attri-

[1] *Democracy in America* (New York, 1948), I, 358–60.
[2] Most recently, Oscar and Mary Handlin, "The Origins of the Southern Labor System", *William and Mary Quarterly*, 3rd Series, VII (April, 1950), 199–222.
[3] *Slave and Citizen; The Negro in the Americas* (New York, 1947).
[4] Gilberto Freyre, *Brazil: An Interpretation* (New York, 1945), pp. 96–101; Donald Pierson, *Negroes in Brazil* (Chicago, 1942), pp. 330–6.

bution of inferiority to the Negro aside from the legal one of slavery. One was the continuance of the Roman law of slavery in the Iberian countries, another was the influence of the Roman Catholic Church, and the third was the long history – by Anglo-American standards – of contacts with darker-skinned peoples in the course of the Reconquest and the African explorations of the fifteenth and sixteenth centuries. Roman law, at least in its later forms, viewed slavery as a mere accident, of which anyone could be the victim. As such it tended to forestall the identification of the black man with slavery, thus permitting the Negro to escape from the stigma of his degraded status once he ceased to be a slave. The same end, Tannenbaum showed, was served by the Roman Church's insistence upon the equality of all Christians and by the long familiarity of the Iberians with Negroes and Moors.

In North America, of course, none of these forces was operative – a fact which partly explains the differing type of slavery and status for Negroes in the two places. But this cannot be the whole explanation since it is only negative. We know, in effect, what were the forces which permitted the slave and the Negro in South America to be treated as a human being, but other than the negative fact that these forces did not obtain in the North American colonies, we know little as to why the Negro as slave or freedman, occupied a degraded position compared with that of any white man. A more positive explanation is to be found in an examination of the early history of the Negro in North America.

It has long been recognized that the appearance of legal slavery in the laws of the English colonies was remarkably slow. The first mention does not occur until after 1660 – some forty years after the arrival of the first Negroes. Lest we think that slavery existed in fact before it did in law, two historians have assured us recently that such was not the case. "The status of Negroes was that of servants", Oscar and Mary Handlin have written, "and so they were identified and treated down to the 1660's".[5] This late, or at least, slow development of slavery[6] complicates our problem. For if there was no slavery in the beginning, then we must account for its coming into being some forty years after the introduction of the Negro. There was no such problem in the history of slavery in the Iberian colonies, where the legal institution of slavery came in the ships with the first settlers.

The Handlins' attempt to answer the question as to why slavery was slow in appearing in the statutes is, to me, not convincing. Essentially their explanation is that by the 1660's, for a number of reasons which do not have to be discussed

[5] Handlin, "Origins of Southern Labor", p. 203.
[6] Virtually all historians of the institution agree on this. See U. B. Phillips, *American Negro Slavery* (New York, 1933), pp. 74–77; J. C. Ballagh, *History of Slavery in Virginia* (Baltimore, 1902), pp. 28–35. More recently, however, Susie Ames, *Studies of the Virginia Eastern Shore in the Seventeenth Century* (Richmond, 1940), pp. 101–10 and W. F. Craven, *Southern Colonies in the Seventeenth Century, 1607–1689* (Baton Rouge, 1949), pp. 217–9 have more than suggested that it is possible that slavery existed in Virginia almost from the very beginning of the Negro's history in America.

here, the position of the white servant was improving, while that of the Negroes was sinking to slavery. In this manner, the Handlins contend, Negro and white servants, heretofore treated alike, attained different status. There are at least two major objections to this argument. First of all, their explanation, by depending upon the improving position of white servants as it does, cannot apply to New England, where servants were of minor importance. Yet the New England colonies, like the Southern, developed a system of slavery for the Negro that fixed him in a position of permanent inferiority. The greatest weakness of the Handlins' case is the difficulty in showing that the white servant's position was improving during and immediately after the 1660's.

Without attempting to go into any great detail on the matter, several acts of the Maryland and Virginia legislatures during the 1660's and 1670's can be cited to indicate that an improving status for white servants was at best doubtful. In 1662, Maryland restricted a servant's travel without a pass to two miles beyond his master's house;[7] in 1671 the same colony lengthened the time of servants who arrived without indenture from four to five years.[8] Virginia in 1668 provided that a runaway could be corporally punished and also have additional time exacted from him.[9] If, as these instances suggest, the white servant's status was not improving, then we are left without an explanation for the differing status accorded white and Negro servants after 1660.

Actually, by asking why slavery developed late in the English colonies we are setting ourselves a problem which obscures rather than clarifies the primary question of why slavery in North America seemed to leave a different mark on the Negro than it did in South America. To ask why slavery in the English colonies produced discrimination against Negroes after 1660 is to make the tacit assumption that prior to the establishment of slavery there was none. If, instead, the question is put, "Which appeared first, slavery or discrimination?" then no prejudgment is made. Indeed, it now opens a possibility for answering the question as to why the slavery in the English colonies, unlike that in the Spanish and Portuguese, led to a caste position for Negroes, whether free or slave. In short, the recent work of the Handlins and the fact that slavery first appeared in the statutes of the English colonies forty years after the Negro's arrival, have tended to obscure the real possibility that the Negro was actually *never* treated as an equal of the white man, servant or free.

It is true that when Negroes were first imported into the English colonies there was no law of slavery and therefore whatever status they were to have would be the work of the future. This absence of a status for black men, which, it will be remembered was not true for the Spanish and Portuguese colonies, made it possible for almost any kind of status to be worked out. It was con-

[7] *Maryland Archives*, I, 451.
[8] *Ibid*, II, 335.
[9] W. W. Hening, *Statutes at Large; being a Collection of all the Laws of Virginia...* (Richmond, 1809), II, 266.

ceivable that they would be accorded the same status as white servants, as the Handlins have argued; it was also possible that they would not. It all depended upon the reactions of the people who received the Negroes.

It is the argument of this paper that the status of the Negro in the English colonies was worked out within a framework of discrimination; that from the outset, as far as the available evidence tells us, the Negro was treated as an inferior to the white man, servant or free. If this be true, then it would follow that as slavery evolved as a legal status, it reflected and included as a part of its essence, this same discrimination which white men had practised against the Negro all along and before any statutes decreed it. It was in its evolution, then, that American colonial slavery differed from Iberian, since in the colonies of Spain and Portugal, the legal status of the slave was fixed before the Negro came to the Americas. Moreover, in South America there were at least three major traditional safeguards which tended to protect the free Negro against being treated as an inferior. In summary, the peculiar character of slavery in the English colonies as compared with that in the Iberian, was the result of two circumstances. One, that there was no law of slavery at all in the beginning, and two, that discrimination against the Negro antedated the legal status of slavery. As a result, slavery, when it developed in the English colonies, could not help but be infused with the social attitude which had prevailed from the beginning, namely, that Negroes were inferior.

II

It is indeed true as the Handlins in their article have emphasized that before the seventeenth century the Negro was rarely called a slave. But this fact should not overshadow the historical evidence which points to the institution without employing the name. Because no discriminatory title is placed upon the Negro we must not think that he was being treated like a white servant; for there is too much evidence to the contrary. Although the growth of a fully developed slave law was slow, unsteady and often unarticulated in surviving records, this is what one would expect when an institution is first being worked out.[10] It is not the same, however, as saying that no slavery or discrimination against the Negro existed in the first decades of the Negro's history in America.

As will appear from the evidence which follows, the kinds of discrimination

[10]   Jonn C. Hurd, *Law of Freedom and Bondage in the United States* (Boston, 1858–61), I, 163, points out that the trade "in negroes as merchandise was ... recognized as legitimate by European governments, without any direct sanction from positive legislation, but rested on the general customs among nations, known both in municipal and international private law". Furthermore, he reported that none of the colonies ever found it necessary to pass laws legalizing slavery. He quotes from the Connecticut Code of 1821: "Slavery was never directly established by statute; but has been indirectly sanctioned by various statutes and frequently recognized by courts, so that it may be said to have been established by law." I, 212 n.

visited upon Negroes varied immensely. In the early 1640's it sometimes stopped short of lifetime servitude or inheritable status – the two attributes of true slavery – in other instances it included both. But regardless of the form of discrimination, the important point is that from the 1630's up until slavery clearly appeared in the statutes in the 1660's, the Negroes were being set apart and discriminated against as compared with the treatment accorded Englishmen, whether servants or free.

The colonists of the early seventeenth century were well aware of a distinction between indentured servitude and slavery.[11] This is quite clear from the evidence in the very early years of the century. The most obvious means the English colonists had for learning of a different treatment for Negroes from that for white servants was the slave trade[12] and the slave systems of the Spanish and Portuguese colonies. As early as 1623, a voyager's book published in London indicated that Englishmen knew of the Negro as a slave in the South American colonies of Spain. The book told of the trade in "blacke people" who were "sold unto the Spaniard for him to carry into the West Indies, to remaine as slaves, either in their Mines, or in any other servile uses, they in those countries put them to".[13] In the phrase "remaine as slaves" is the element of unlimited service.

The Englishmen's treatment of another dark-skinned, non-Christian people – the Indians – further supports the argument that a special and inferior status was accorded the Negro virtually from the first arrival. Indian slavery was practised in all of the English settlements almost from the beginning[14] and, though it received its impetus from the perennial wars between the races, the fact that an inferior and onerous service was established for the Indian makes it plausible to suppose that a similar status would be reserved for the equally different and pagan Negro.

The continental English could also draw upon other models of a differen-

[11]   The Handlins, "Origins of Southern Labor", pp. 203–4, have argued that in the early years slavery meant nothing more than a low form of labor and that it had no basis in law. This is true insofar as statute law is concerned, but, as will appear later, in practice quite a different situation obtained.

[12]   The Handlins, "Origins of Southern Labor", pp. 203–4, argue that the continental colonies could not have learned about a different status for Negroes from that of white servants from the slave trade because, they say, "the company of Royal Adventurers referred to their cargo as 'Negers', 'Negro-servants', 'Servants... from Africa', or 'Negro Persons' but rarely as slaves." They overlook, however, abundant references to Negro slaves in the correspondence of the contemporary Royal African Company. Thus in 1663 a warrant for that company refers to "negro slaves" as a part of its monopoly. *Calendar of State Papers, Colonial*, V, 121; see also p. 204. In that same year the Privy Council wrote that the Spanish were "seeking to trade with our island of Barbada for a supply of Negro Slaves...". And then the letter referred to a "supply of Negro Servants", and later still "for every Negro Person a Slave" and then "all such Negro Slaves". K. Donnan, *Documents Illustrative of the History of the Slave Trade*, (Washington, 1930), I, 161–2.

[13]   Quoted in Donnan, *Slave Trade*, I, 125.

[14]   See particularly, Almon Lauber, *Indian Slavery in Colonial Times Within the Present Limits of the United States* (New York, 1913), Chap. IV.

tiated status for Negroes. The earliest English colony to experiment with large numbers of Negroes in its midst was the shortlived settlement of Providence island, situated in the western Caribbean, just off the Mosquito Coast. By 1637, long before Barbados and the other British sugar islands utilized great numbers of Negroes, almost half of the population of this Puritan venture was black. Such a disproportion of races caused great alarm among the directors of the Company in London and repeated efforts were made to restrict the influx of blacks.[15] Partly because of its large numbers of Negroes, Old Providence became well known to the mainland colonies of Virginia and New England.[16] A. P. Newton has said that Old Providence

forms the connecting link between almost every English colonising enterprise in the first half of the seventeenth century from Virginia and Bermuda to New England and Jamaica, and thus it is of much greater importance than its actual accomplishments would justify.[17]

Under such circumstances, it was to be expected that knowledge of the status accorded Negroes by these Englishmen would be transmitted to those on the mainland with whom they had such close and frequent contact.

Though the word "slave" is never applied to the Negroes on Providence, and only rarely the word "Servant", "Negroes", which was the term used, were obviously *sui generis*; they were people apart from the English. The Company, for example, distrusted them. "Association [Tortuga island] was deserted thro' their mutinous conduct", the Company told the Governor of Old Providence in 1637. "Further trade for them prohibited, with exceptions, until Providence be furnished with English."[18] In another communication the Company again alluded to the dangers of "too great a number" of Negroes on the island and promised to send 200 English servants over to be exchanged for as many Negroes.[19] A clearer suggestion of the difference in status between an English servant and a Negro is contained in the Company's letter announcing the forwarding of the 200 servants. As a further precaution against being overwhelmed by Negroes, it was ordered that a "family of fourteen" – which would include servants – was not to have more than six Negroes. "The surplusage may be sold to the poor men who have served their apprenticeship".[20] But the Negroes, apparently, were serving for life.

Other British island colonies in the seventeenth century also provide evidence which is suggestive of this same development of a differing status for Negroes,

---

[15]   A. P. Newton, *The Colonising Activities of the English Puritans* (New Haven, 1914), p. 258.
[16]   *Ibid.*, p. 260.
[17]   A. P. Newton, *The European Nations in the West Indies, 1493–1688* (London, 1933), pp. 173–4.
[18]   *Calendar of State Papers, Colonial*, I, 249.
[19]   *Ibid.*, pp. 277–8.
[20]   *Ibid.*, pp. 278–9.

even though the word "slave" was not always employed. Though apparently the first Negroes were only brought to Bermuda in 1617,[21] as early as 1623 the Assembly passed an "Act to restrayne the insolencies of Negroes". The blacks were accused of stealing and of carrying "secretly cudgels, and other weapons and working tools". Such weapons, it was said, were "very dangerous and not meete to be suffered to be carried by such Vassals...", Already, in other words, Negroes were treated as a class apart. To reinforce this, Negroes were forbidden to "weare any weapon in the daytyme" and they were not to be outside or off their master's land during "any undue hours in the night tyme...".[22]

During the 1630's there were other indications that Negroes were treated as inferiors. As early as 1630 some Negroes' servitude was already slavery in that it was for life and inheritable. One Lew Forde possessed a Negro man, while the Company owned his wife; the couple had two children. Forde desired "to know which of the said children properly belong to himself and which to the Company". The Council gave him the older child and the Company received the other.[23] A letter of Roger Wood in 1634 suggests that Negroes were already serving for life, for he asked to have a Negro, named Sambo, given to him, so that through the Negro "I or myne may *ever* be able" to carry on an old feud with an enemy who owned Sambo's wife.[24]

There is further evidence of discrimination against Negroes in later years. A grand jury in 1652 cited one Henry Gaunt as being "suspected of being unnecessarily conversant with negro women" – he had been giving them presents. The presentment added that "if he hath not left his familiarity with such creatures, it is desired that such abominations be inquired into, least the land mourne for them".[25] The discrimination reached a high point in 1656 when the Governor proclaimed that "any Englishman" who discovered a Negro walking about at night without a pass, was empowered to "kill him then and theire without mercye". The proclamation further ordered that all free Negroes "shall be banished from these Islands, never to return eyther by purchase of any man, or otherwise...".[26] When some Negroes asked the Governor for their freedom in 1669, he denied they had any such claim, saying that they had been "purchased by" their masters "without condition or limitation. It being likewise soe practised in these American plantations and other parts of the world."[27]

[21] J. H. Lefroy, *Memorials of the Discovery and Early Settlement of the Bermudas or Somers Islands, 1515–1685* (London, 1877), I, 127.
[22] *Ibid.*, I, 308–9.
[23] *Ibid.*, I, 505. Cases in 1676 and 1685 indicate that this practice of dividing the children became the standard practice under slavery in a colony where the parcels of slaves were so small that few masters could have a spouse on their plantations for each of his adult Negroes. *Ibid.*, II, 427, 547–8.
[24] *Ibid.*, I, 539. Emphasis added.
[25] *Ibid.*, II, 30.
[26] *Ibid.*, II, 95–6.
[27] *Ibid.*, II, 293. As late as 1662 the perpetual character of slavery for Negroes was being obscured by their serving for ninety-nine years. See *Ibid.*, II, 166, 184.

45

In Barbados Negroes were already slaves when Richard Ligon lived there in 1647–50. "The Iland", he later wrote, "is divided into three sorts of men, viz: Masters, servants, and slaves. The slaves and their posterity, being subject to their masters for ever," in contrast to the servants who are owned "but for five years...".[28] On that island as at Bermuda it was reported that Negroes were not permitted "to touch or handle any weapons".[29]

On Jamaica, as on the other two islands, a clear distinction was made between the status of the Negro and that of the English servant. In 1656 one resident of the island wrote the Protector in England urging the importation of African Negroes because then, he said, "the planters would have to pay for them" and therefore "they would have an interest in preserving their lives, *which was* wanting in the case of bond servants...".[30]

It is apparent, then, that the colonists on the mainland had ample opportunity before 1660 to learn of a different status for black men from that for Englishmen, whether servants or free.

III

From the evidence available it would seem that the Englishmen in Virginia and Maryland learned their lesson well. This is true even though the sources available on the Negro's position in these colonies in the early years are not as abundant as we would like. It seems quite evident that the black man was set apart from the white on the continent just as he was being set apart in the island colonies. For example, in Virginia in 1630, one Hugh Davis was "soundly whipped before an Assembly of Negroes and others for abusing himself to the dishonor of God and the shame of Christians, by defiling his body in lying with a negro".[31] The unChristian-like character of such behavior was emphasized ten years later when Robert Sweet was ordered to do penance in Church for "getting a negro woman with child".[32] An act passed in the Maryland legislature in 1639 indicated that at that early date the word "slave" was being applied to non-Englishmen. The act was an enumeration of the rights of "all Christian inhabitants (slaves excepted)".[33] The slaves referred to could have been only Indians or Negroes,[34] since all white servants were Christians. It is

[28] Richard Ligon, *A True and Exact History of the Island of Barbados* (London, 1657), p. 43.
[29] *Ibid.*, p. 46.
[30] Quoted in Richard B. Morris, *Government and Labor in Early America* (New York, 1946), p. 499. As early as 1633, on the island of Tortuga, the separation of whites, servants or no, from Negroes was in evidence. At a time of anarchy on the island, "The eighty-odd Englishmen in the island had formed a council among themselves for the government of the colony and to keep in subjection the one hundred and fifty negroes, twenty-seven of whom were the company's property". Newton, *Colonising Activities*, p. 214.
[31] Hening, *Statutes*, I, 146.
[32] *Ibid.*, I, 552.
[33] *Maryland Archives*, I, 80.
[34] It is not known whether there were any Negroes in Maryland at that date. J. R. Brackett, *The Negro in Maryland* (Baltimore, 1889), p. 26 found no evidence of Negroes before 1642.

also significant of the differing treatment of the two races that though Maryland and Virginia very early in their history enacted laws fixing limits to the terms for servants who entered without written contracts, Negroes were never included in such protective provisions.[35] The first of such laws were placed upon the books in 1639 in Maryland and 1643 in Virginia; in the Maryland statute, it was explicitly stated: "Slaves excepted".[36]

In yet another way, Negroes and slaves were singled out for special status in the years before 1650. A Virginia law of 1640 provided that "all masters" should try to furnish arms to themselves and "all those of their families which shall be capable of arms" – which would include servants – "(excepting negros)"[37]. Not until 1648 did Maryland get around to such a prohibition, when it was provided that no guns should be given to "any Pagan for killing meate or to any other use", upon pain of a heavy fine.[38] At no time were white servants denied the right to bear arms; indeed, as these statutes inform us, they were enjoined to possess weapons.[39]

One other class of discriminatory acts against Negroes in Virginia and Maryland before 1660 also deserves to be noticed. Three different times before 1660 – in 1643, 1644 and 1658 – the Virginia assembly (and in 1654, the Maryland legislature) included Negro and Indian women among the "tithables". But white servant women were never placed in such a category[40], inasmuch as

---

[35] Handlin, "Origins of Southern Labor", p. 210; Hening, *Statutes*, I, 411, 539. This is not to say that some Negroes were not indentured servants, for there is evidence to show that limited service was enjoyed by some black men. This was true even during the period after the recognition of slavery in the statutes. In October, 1673, for instance, the Council and General Court of Virginia ordered that "Andrew Moore A Servant Negro", who asserted he was to serve only five years, and who had the support of several "oathes", was declared free. Moreover, his erstwhile master was compelled to "pay him Corne and Clothes According to the custome of the country" and 400 pounds of tobacco and cask for the Negro's service since his time expired and to "pay costs". *Minutes of the Council and General Court of Colonial Virginia*, edited by H. R. McIlwaine (Richmond, 1924), p. 354.

[36] Hening, *Statutes*, I, 257; *Maryland Archives*, I, 80.

[37] *William and Mary Quarterly*, Second Series, IV (July, 1924), 147.

[38] *Maryland Archives*, I, 233.

[39] Handlin, "Origins of Southern Labor", p. 209, implies that these early restrictions were later repealed. "Until the 1660's", the Handlins write, "the statutes on the Negroes were not at all unique. Nor did they add up to a decided trend." In substantiation of this point they instance the "fluctuations" in the Negro's right to bear arms. Their cited evidence, however, does not sustain this generalization. Four references to the statutes of Virginia are made; of these four, only two deal with arms bearing. The first one, that referred to in the text above, indicates that Negroes were not to be armed. The other reference is at best an ambiguous statement about who is taxable and which of the taxables are to serve in the militia. It in no wise constitutes either a repeal or even a contradiction of the earlier statute, which, therefore, must be presumed to be controlling. Their evidence for "fluctuations" in the right of Indians to bear arms suffers from the same weakness of sources. The two statutes they cite merely confirm the right of certain Indians to possess guns and deny them to other Indians. No "fluctuation" in rights is involved.

[40] Hening, *Statutes*, I, 242, 292, 455; *Maryland Archives*, I, 342. The statement in Handlin, "Origins of Southern Labor", p. 217 n, that the "first sign of discrimination was in 1668 when white but not Negro women were exempt", is therefore erroneous.

they were not expected to work in the fields. From the beginning, it would seem, Negro women, whether free or bond, were treated by the law differently from white women servants.[41]

It is not until the 1640's that evidence of a status for Negroes akin to slavery, and, therefore, something more than mere discrimination begins to appear in the sources. Two cases of punishment for runaway servants in 1640 throw some light on the working out of a differentiated status for Negroes. The first case concerned three runaways, of whom two were white men and the third a Negro. All three were given thirty lashes, with the white men having the terms owed their masters extended a year, at the completion of which they were to work for the colony for three more years. The other, "being a Negro named John Punch shall serve his said master or his assigns for the time of his natural Life here or elsewhere".[42] Not only was the Negro's punishment the most severe, and for no apparent reason, but he was, in effect, reduced to slavery. It is also clear, however, that up until the issuing of the sentence, he must have had the status of a servant.

The second case, also of 1640, suggests that by that date some Negroes were already slaves. Six white men and a Negro were implicated in a plot to run away. The punishments meted out varied, but Christopher Miller "a dutchman" (a prime agent in the business) "was given the harshest treatment of all: thirty stripes, burning with an "R" on the cheek, a shackle placed on his leg for a year "and longer if said master shall see cause" and seven years of service for the colony upon completion of his time due his master. The only other one of the seven plotters to receive the stripes, the shackle and the "R" was the Negro Emanuel, but, significantly, he did not receive any sentence of work for the colony. Presumably he was already serving his master for a life-time – *i.e.*, he was a slave.[43] About this time in Maryland it does not seem to have been unusual to speak of Negroes as slaves, for in 1642 one "John Skinner mariner" agreed "to deliver unto... Leonard Calvert, fourteen negro-men-slaves and three women-slaves".[44]

From a proceeding before the House of Burgesses in 1666 it appears that as early as 1644 that body was being called upon to determine who was a slave. The Journal of the House for 1666 reports that in 1644 a certain "mulata" bought "as a slave for Ever" was adjudged by the Assembly "no slave and but

---

[41]   In his well-known emigrant pamphlet, *Leah and Rachel* (London, 1656), p. 12, John Hammond casts some interesting light on contemporary opinion regarding women who worked in the fields in Virginia. "The Women are not (as is reported) put into the ground to work, but occupie such domestique imployments and housewifery as in England ... yet some wenches that are nasty, beastly and not fit to be so imployed are put into the ground..."

[42]   *Minutes of the Council*, p. 466.

[43]   *Ibid.*, p. 467.

[44]   Catterall, *Judicial Cases*, I, 57 n. Mrs. Catterall does not think any Negroes came under this agreement, but the language itself testifies to an accepted special status for Negroes at that time.

to serve as other Christian servants do and was freed in September 1665".[45] Though no reason was given for the verdict, from the words "other Christian servants" it is possible that he was a Christian, for it was believed in the early years of the English colonies that baptism rendered a slave free. In any case, the Assembly uttered no prohibition of slavery as such and the owner was sufficiently surprised and aggrieved by the decision to appeal for recompense from the Assembly, even though the Negro's service was twenty-one years, an unheard of term for a "Christian servant".[46]

In early seventeenth century inventories of estates, there are two distinctions which appear in the reckoning of the value of servants and Negroes. Uniformly, the Negroes were more valuable, even as children, than any white servant. Secondly, the naming of a servant is usually followed by the number of years yet remaining to his service; for the Negroes no such notation appears. Thus in an inventory in Virginia in 1643, a 22-year old white servant, with eight years still to serve, was valued at 1,000 pounds of tobacco, while a "negro boy" was rated at 3,000 pounds and a white boy with seven years to serve was listed as worth 700 pounds. An eight-year old Negro girl was calculated to be worth 2,000 pounds. On another inventory in 1655, two good men servants with four years to serve were rated at 1,300 pounds of tobacco, and a woman servant with only two years to go was valued at 800 pounds. Two Negro boys, however, who had no limit set to their terms, were evaluated at 4,100 pounds apiece, and a Negro girl was said to be worth 5,500 pounds.[47]

These great differences in valuation of Negro and white "servants" strongly suggest, as does the failure to indicate term of service for the Negroes, that the latter were slaves at least in regard to life-time service. Beyond a question, there was some service which these blacks were rendering which enhanced their value – a service, moreover, which was not or could not be exacted from the whites. Furthermore, a Maryland deed of 1649 adumbrated slave status not only of life-time term, but of inheritance of status. Three Negroes "and all their issue both male and female" were deeded.[48]

Russell and Ames culled from the Virginia court records of the 1640's and 1650's several instances of Negroes held in a status that can be called true slavery. For example, in 1646 a Negro woman and a Negro boy were sold to

[45] *Journals of the House of Burgesses of Virginia*, edited by H. R. McIlwaine (Richmond, 1914), II, 34.

[46] *Ibid.*, II, 34–5. His plea, however, was turned down, the Assembly not knowing "any Reason why the Publick should be answerable for the inadvertency of the Buyer..."

[47] John H. Russell, *The Free Negro in Virginia, 1619–1865* (Baltimore, 1913), p. 36. Russell concludes from his survey of inventories of estates for this early period that Negroes were valued from 20 to 30 pounds sterling, "while white servants of the longest term... receive a valuation of not more than £15 sterling". *Ibid.*, p. 35. Catterall, *Judicial Cases*, I, 58 n, upon concluding her investigation of inventories of estates, picked 1644 as the date at which "'servant' standing alone, had generally become synonomous with 'white servant' and 'negro' with 'negro slave', ..."

[48] Catterall, *Judicial Cases*, IV, 9.

49

Stephen Charlton to be of use to him and his "heyers etc. for ever". A Negro girl was sold in 1652 "with her Issue and produce... and their services forever". Two years later a Negro girl was sold to one Armsteadinger "and his heyers... forever with all her increase both male and female".[49] For March 12, 1655 the minutes of the Council and General Court of Virginia contain the entry, "Mulatto held to be a slave and appeal taken".[50] Yet this is five years before Negro slavery is even implied in the statutes and fifteen before it is declared. An early case of what appears to be true slavery was found by Miss Ames on the Virginia eastern shore. In 1635 two Negroes were brought to the area; over twenty years later, in 1656, the widow of the master was bequeathing the child of one of the original Negroes and the other Negro and her children.[51] This was much more than mere servitude – the term was longer than twenty years and apparently the status was inheritable.

Wesley Frank Craven, in his study of the seventeenth-century Southern colonies, has concluded that in the treatment of the Negro "the trend from the first was toward a sharp distinction between him and the white servant".[52] In view of the evidence presented here, this seems a reasonable conclusion.

Concurrently with these examples of onerous service or actual slavery of Negroes, there were of course other members of the race who did gain their freedom.[53] But the presence of Negroes rising out of servitude to freedom[54] does not destroy the evidence that others were sinking into slavery; it merely underscores the unsteady evolution of a slave status. The supposition that the practice of slavery long antedated the law is strengthened by the tangential manner in which recognition of Negro slavery first appeared in the Virginia statutes.[55] It occurred in 1660 in a law dealing with punishments for runaway servants, where casual reference was made to those "negroes who are incapable

---

[49]   Russell, *Free Negro in Virginia*, pp. 34–5. He also reports the instance of a Negro by the name of John Casor who was claimed, in 1655, as a "Negro for his life", but he was rescued from such a status by two witnesses testifying that he had an indenture. *Ibid.*, pp. 32–3.

[50]   *Minutes of the Council*, p. 504. Handlin, "Origins of Southern Labor", p. 216, in arguing the late development of a different status for Negroes as compared with whites in Virginia, says: "As late as the 1660's the law had not even a word to describe the children of mixed marriages. But two decades later, the term mulatto is used..." Such a statement is obviously misleading, for though the Handlins presumably mean statute law, the decisions of the General Court were also "law". The *Oxford English Dictionary* cites references for the word "mulatto" for 1595, 1613 and 1657.

[51]   Ames, *Eastern Shore*, p. 105.

[52]   Craven, *Southern Colonies*, p. 219.

[53]   See especially Russell, *Free Negro in Virginia*, pp. 36–9. See also Brackett, *Negro in Maryland*, p. 37.

[54]   An indication that even freedom for the Negro carried certain disabilities is afforded by an instance reported by Ames, *Eastern Shore*, p. 107 from the Northampton County court records of 1654. For contempt of authority and abuse of certain persons, Anthony Longoe, a Negro, was ordered, almost twenty years after his release from service, to receive "thirty lashes now applied, and tomorrow morning thirty lashes more".

[55]   A year earlier, 1659/60, a statute dealing with trade with the Dutch promised remission of a ten shilling tax if "the said Dutch or other forreiners shall import any negro slaves...". This is the first reference in the Virginia statutes to Negroes as slaves. Hening, *Statutes*, I, 540.

of making satisfaction by addition of time",[56] since they were already serving for life.

Soon thereafter, as various legal questions regarding the status of Negroes came to the fore, the institution was further defined by statute law. In 1662 Virginia provided that the status of the offspring of a white man and a Negro would follow that of the mother – an interesting and unexplained departure from the common law and a reversion to Roman law. The same law stated that "any christian" fornicating "with a negro man or woman... shall pay double the fines imposed by the former act". Two years later Maryland prescribed service for Negroes "durante vita" and provided for hereditary status to descend through the father. Any free white woman who married a slave was to serve her husband's master for the duration of the slave's life, and her children would serve the master until they were thirty years of age. Presumably, no penalty was to be exacted of a free white man who married a Negro slave.[57]

As early as 1669 the Virginia law virtually washed its hands of protecting the Negro held as a slave. It allowed punishment of refractory slaves up to and including accidental death, relieving the master, explicitly, of any fear of prosecution, on the assumption that no man would "destroy his owne estate".[58]

In fact by 1680 the law of Virginia had erected a high wall around the Negro. One discerns in the phrase "any negro or other slave" how the word "negro" had taken on the meaning of slave. Moreover, in the act of 1680 one begins to see the lineaments of the later slave codes. No Negro may carry any weapon of any kind, nor leave his master's grounds without a pass, nor shall "any negroe or other slave... presume to lift his hand in opposition against any christian", and if a Negro runs away and resists recapture it "shalbe lawful for such person or persons to kill said negroe or slave...".[59]

Yet it would be a quarter of a century before Negroes would comprise even a fifth of the population of Virginia. Thus long before slavery or black labor

[56] Hening, *Statutes*, II, 26. The equivalent Maryland statute (1663) referred to "Negroes and other Slaves, who are incapeable of makeing Stisfaction [*sic*] by Addition of Tyme..." *Maryland Archives*, I, 489.

[57] Hening, *Statutes*, II, 170: *Maryland Archives*, I, 533–4. Handlin, "Origins of Southern Labor", p. 215 sees the genesis of these prohibitions in concern over status rather than in objection to racial intermarriage. This seems to be true for Maryland. But in speaking of the Virginia circumstances they write: "It was to guard against the complications of status that the laws after 1691 forbade 'spurious' or illegitimate mixed marriages of the slave and the free..." Actually, however, the Virginia statute of 1691 (Hening, *Statutes*, III, 87) clearly aimed at the prevention of "abominable mixture and spurious issue" by forbidding marriage of "English or other white man or woman being free" with "a negro, mulatto or Indian man or woman *bond or free*". (Emphasis added.)

[58] Hening, *Statutes*, II, 270. The working out of the exact legal status of slave property, however, was a slow one. A Virginia law of 1705 (Hening, *Statutes*, III, 333–4), declared "Negro, Mulatto and Indian Slaves... to be real estate", but there were a number of exceptions which suggest the later chattel nature of property in slaves. In South Carolina slaves were decreed to be real estate in 1690 and not until 1740 were they said to be legally chattels. Hurd, *Law of Freedom*, I, 297, 303.

[59] Hening, *Statutes*, II, 481–2.

became an important part of the Southern economy, a special and inferior status had been worked out for the Negroes who came to the English colonies. Unquestionably it was a demand for labor which dragged the Negro to American shores, but the status which he acquired here cannot be explained by reference to that economic motive. Long before black labor was as economically important as unfree white labor, the Negro had been consigned to a special discriminatory status which mirrored the social discrimination Englishmen practised against him.[60]

IV

In the course of the seventeenth century New Englanders, like Southerners, developed a system of slavery which seemed permanently to fasten its stigma upon the Negro race. But because of the small number of Negroes in the northern provinces, the development of a form of slavery, which left a caste in its wake, cannot be attributed to pressure from increasing numbers of blacks, or even from an insistent demand for cheap labor. Rather it seems clearly to be the consequence of the general social discrimination against the Negro. For in the northern region, as in the southern, discrimination against the Negro preceded the evolution of a slave status and by that fact helped to shape the form that institution would assume.

References to the status of the Negroes in New England in this period are scattered, but, as was true of the Southern provinces, those references which are available suggest that from the earliest years a lowly, differential status, if not slavery itself, was reserved and recognized for the Negro – and the Indian, it might be added. The earliest date asserted in the sources for the existence of Negro slavery in Massachusetts is that of 1639. John Josselyn tells of a Negro woman held on Noddles Island in Boston harbor. Her master sought to mate her with another Negro, Josselyn says, but she kicked her prospective lover out of the bed, saying that such behavior was "beyond her slavery...".[61] Though the first legal code of Massachusetts, the Body of Liberties of 1641, prohibited "bond-slavery" for the inhabitants, it clearly permitted enslavement of those

---

[60]   Like Virginia, Maryland developed its slave law and status long before the Negroes had become an important aspect of the labor force. As late as 1712, Negroes made up only slightly more than 20 per cent of the population. Brackett, *Negro in Maryland*, pp. 38–9. If Virginia was slow in bringing her slave practices out into the open air of the statute books, the same could not be said of Carolina. In the Fundamental Constitutions, drawn up in 1669, it is stated in article CX that "Every freeman of Carolina shall have absolute power and authority over his negro slaves, of what opinion or religion so ever".

[61]   Massachusetts Historical Society, *Collections*, Third Series, III, 231. There is no doubt that there were Negroes at this time in Massachusetts, for in 1638 Winthrop reported that Capt. Peirce brought back from Old Providence "some cotton, and tobacco and negroes..." John Winthrop, *History of New England*, James Savage, ed. (Boston, 1853), I, 305.

who are "sold-to us",[62] which would include Negroes brought in by the international slave trade.[63]

Such use of Negroes was neither unknown nor undesirable to the Puritans. Emanuel Downing wrote to John Winthrop in 1645 about the desirability of a war against the Indians so that captives might be taken who, in turn, could be exchanged

for Moores, which wilbe more gayneful pilladge for us then [sic] wee conceive, for I doe not see how wee can thrive untill wee gett into a stock of slaves sufficient to doe all our busines, for our children's children will hardly see this great Continent filled with people, soe that our servants will still desire freedome for themselves, and not stay but for verie great wages. And I suppose you know verie well how we shall maynteyne 20 Moores cheaper than one English servant.[64]

The following year the Commissioners of the United Colonies recommended that in order to spare the colonies the cost of imprisoning contumacious Indians they should be given over to the Englishmen whom they had damaged or "be shipped out and exchanged for Negroes as the cause will justly serve".[65] Negroes were here being equated with Indians who were being bound out as prisoners: this was treatment decidedly a cut lower than that visited upon white servants.[66] That enslavement of Negroes was well known in New England by the middle of the century at the latest is revealed by the preamble to an act of Warwick and Providence colonies in 1652. It was said that it "is a common course practised amongst Englishmen to buy negers, to that end they may have them for service or slaves forever...".[67]

---

[62] Some events of 1645 indicate that those few words were of crucial importance to the Puritans. That year some Negroes were brought to Massachusetts by a Captain Smith and they were ordered by the Gereral Court to be returned to Africa on the ground that their importation constituted "the hainous and crying sinn of man-stealing". But this was man-stealing only because Smith and his men had captured the Negroes in a raid, instead of buying them from traders. *Records of Massachusetts*, III, 48, 58, 84.

[63] Very early in New England history the concept of perpetual servitude – one of the distinguishing marks of slavery – appears in the records. In 1637 Roger Williams, in pleading for the lives of the captured Indians during the Pequot War, alludes to "perpetuall slaverie" as an alternative to their execution. Massachusetts Historical Society, *Collections*, Fourth Series, VI, 214. The will of John Winthrop, written in 1639, deeded to his son Adam "my island" and "also my Indians there and my boat and such household as is there" Robert C. Winthrop, *Life and Letters of John Winthrop* (Boston, 1869), II, 252. Though at least three white men were sentenced to "slavery" in Massachusetts in the early years, in at least two cases this did not, in fact, amount to perpetuity, for they appear to have been released in a short time. The use of the word as a special form of service, however, is most interesting. *Records of Massachusetts*, I, 246, 310, 269.

[64] Massachusetts Historical Society, *Collections*, Fourth Series, VI, 65.

[65] *Records of the Colony of Plymouth* (Boston, 1859), IX, 71.

[66] John Cotton in 1651 clearly distinguished between slavery and servitude. He wrote Cromwell in that year in regard to the Scottish prisoners sent to New England, that "we have been desirous... to make their yoke easy... They have not been sold for slaves to perpetuall servitude, but for 6, or 7 or 8 yeares, as we do our owne". Quoted in George H. Moore, *Notes on the History of Slavery in Massachusetts* (New York, 1866), p. 17 n.

[67] *Records of the Colony of Rhode Island...* (Providence, 1856), I, 243.

By mid-century, Negroes were appearing in the inventories of estates and, significantly, the valuation placed upon them was very close to that found in Virginia inventories of the same period. Their worth is always much more than that of a white servant. Thus in 1650 "a neager Maide" was valued at £ 25; in 1657 the well-known merchant, Robert Keayne left "2 negros and a negro child" estimated to be worth £ 30. "A negro boy servant" was set at £ 20 in an estate of 1661.[68] A further indication of the property character of Negroes was the attachment by the constable of Salem in 1670 of a Negro boy "Seasar" as the "proper goods of the said Powell".[69]

Despite the small numbers of Negroes in New England in this early period, the colonies of that region followed the example of the Southern and insular provinces in denying arms to the blacks in their midst – a discrimination which was never visited upon the English servant. In 1652 Massachusetts provided that Indians and Negroes could train in the militia the same as whites, but this apparently caused friction. The law was countermanded in 1656 by the statement "henceforth no negroes or Indians, altho servants of the English, shalbe armed or permitted to trayne".[70] Although as late as 1680 it was officially reported to London that there were no more than thirty "slaves" in Connecticut, that colony in 1660 excluded Indians and "negar servants" from the militia and "Watch and Ward".[71]

Edward Randolph in 1676 reported that there were a few indentured servants in Massachusetts "and not above two hundred slaves", by which he meant Negroes, for he said "they were brought from Guinea and Madagascar".[72] But it was not until 1698 that the phrase "Negro slave" actually appeared in the Massachusetts statutes.[73] The practice of slavery was preceding the law in Massachusetts precisely as it had in the South. Though an official report to London in 1680 distinguished between Negro slaves and servants in Connecticut,[74] the law of that colony did not bother to define the institution of slavery. Indeed, as late as 1704, the Governor gave it as his opinion that all children born of "negro bond-women are themselves in like condition, i.e., born in servitude", though he admitted that there was no statute which said so. His

---

[68] Quoted in William B. Weeden, *Economic and Social History of New England* (Boston, 1891), p. 149 n. It was officially reported in 1680 by Connecticut colony that three or four "Blacks" were imported each year from the Barbados, and that they usually sold for £22 apiece. This was much more than the going price for servants. *Public Records of the Colony of Connecticut* (Hartford, 1850–90), III, 298.

[69] Quoted in Lorenzo Greene, *The Negro in Colonial New England, 1620–1776* (New York, 1942), p. 172.

[70] *Records of Massachusetts*, III, 268, 397.

[71] *Records of Connecticut*, III, 298, I, 349.

[72] Quoted in Palfrey, *History of New England*, III, 298.

[73] Hurd, *Law of Freedom*, I, 262. Greene, *Negro in New England*, pp. 65–6, says that in 1670 slavery in Massachusetts became legally inheritable, for in that year the word "strangers" was dropped from the Body of Liberties as a description of those who might be enslaved.

[74] *Records of Connecticut*, III, 298.

contention was, however, that such legislation was "needless, because of the constant practice by which they are held as such...".[75]

During the last years of the seventeenth century, laws of Connecticut and Massachusetts continued to speak of Negroes as "servants", but it was very clear that the Negro's status was not being equated with that of the white servant. The General Court of Connecticut observed in 1690 that "many persons of this Colony doe ...purchase negroe servants" and, since these servants run away, precautions have to be taken against such eventualities. It was therefore laid down that all "negroe or negroes shall" be required to have a pass in order to be outside the town bounds. Any inhabitant could stop a Negroe, free or slave, and have him brought before a magistrate if the black man were found to be without such a pass. Moreover, all ferrymen, upon pain of fine, were to deny access to their ferries to all Negroes who could not produce a pass.[76] Massachusetts in 1698 forbade trade with "any Indian, or negro servant or slave, or other known dissolute, lewd, and disorderly person, of whom there is just cause of suspicion".[77]

By the early years of the eighteenth century, the laws of Connecticut and Massachusetts had pretty well defined the Negro's subordinate position in society. Massachusetts acted to restrict the manumission of slaves by providing in 1703 that "molatto or negro slaves" could be freed only if security was given that they would not be chargeable upon the community. Another law set a curfew upon Indians, mulattoes and Negroes for nine o'clock each night. In 1705 Massachusetts became the only New England province to prohibit sexual relations between Negroes and mulattoes and Englishmen or those of "any other Christian nation".[78] Moreover, "any negro or mulatto" presuming to "smite or strike" an English person or any of another Christian nation would be "severely whipped".[79] In 1717 Negroes were barred from holding land in Connecticut.[80]

Thus, like the colonists to the South, the New Englanders enacted into law, in the absence of any prior English law of slavery, their recognition of the Negroes as different and inferior. This was the way of the seventeenth century; only with a later conception of the brotherhood of all men would such legal discrimination begin to recede; but by then, generations of close association between the degraded status of slavery and black color would leave the same prejudice against the Negro in the North that it did in the South.

[75] Quoted in Bernard C. Steiner, *History of Slavery in Connecticut* (Baltimore, 1893), p. 18.
[76] *Records of Connecticut*, IV, 40.
[77] Hurd, *Law of Freedom*, I, 262–3.
[78] *Ibid.*, I, 263, Massachusetts had prohibited marriages between whites and Negroes, mulattoes and Indians in 1692. Lauber, *Indian Slavery*, p. 253.
[79] Hurd, *Law of Freedom*, I, 263. Rhode Island, too, in 1728, provided that before a Negro or mulatto could be manumitted, security had to given that he would not become a public charge. Hurd, *Law of Freedom*, I, 276.
[80] Greene, *Negro in New England*, p. 312.

It would seem, then, that instead of slavery being the root of the discrimination visited upon the Negro in America, slavery was itself molded by the early colonists' discrimination against the outlander. In the absence of any law of slavery or commandments of the Church to the contrary – as was true of Brazil and Spanish-America – the institution of slavery into which the African was placed in the English colonies inevitably mirrored that discrimination and, in so doing, perpetuated it.

Once the English embodied their discrimination against the Negro in slave law, the logic of the law took over. Through the early eighteenth century, judges and legislatures in all the colonies elaborated the law along the discriminatory lines laid down in the amorphous beginnings. In doing so, of course, especially in the South, they had the added incentive of perpetuating and securing a labor system which by then had become indispensable to the economy. The cleavage between the races was in that manner deepened and hardened into the shape which became quite familiar by the nineteenth century. In due time, particularly in the South, the correspondence between the black man and slavery would appear so perfect that it would be difficult to believe that the Negro was fitted for anything other than the degraded status in which he was almost always found. It would also be forgotten that the discrimination had begun long before slavery had come upon the scene.

CARL N. DEGLER
Vassar College

Origins of the Southern Labor System

Oscar and Mary F. Handlin*

IN the bitter years before the Civil War, and after, men often turned to history for an explanation of the disastrous difference that divided the nation against itself. It seemed as if some fundamental fault must account for the tragedy that was impending or that had been realized; and it was tempting then to ascribe the troubles of the times to an original separateness between the sections that fought each other in 1861.

The last quarter century has banished from serious historical thinking the ancestral cavaliers and roundheads with whom the rebels and Yankees had peopled their past. But there is still an inclination to accept as present from the start a marked divergence in the character of the labor force, free whites in the North, Negro slaves in the South. Most commonly, the sources of that divergence are discovered in geography. In the temperate North, it is held, English ways were transposed intact. But the soil and climate of the South favored the production of staples, most efficiently raised under a regime of plantation slavery.

In this case, however, it is hardly proper to load nature with responsibility for human institutions. Tropical crops and climate persisted in the South after 1865 when its labor system changed, and they were there before it appeared.[1] Negro slavery was not spontaneously produced by heat, humidity, and tobacco. An examination of the condition and status of seventeenth-century labor will show that slavery was not there from the start, that it was not simply imitated from elsewhere, and that it was not a response to any unique qualities in the Negro himself. It emerged rather from the adjustment to American conditions of traditional European institutions.

By the latter half of the eighteenth century, slavery was a clearly defined status. It was

---

* Mr. Handlin is Associate Professor of History at Harvard University. He and Mrs. Handlin have previously collaborated in several significant studies of the relation of government to business in early American history and of the immigrant's role in American culture.

[1] See, in general, Lewis Cecil Gray, *History of Agriculture in the Southern United States to 1860* (New York, 1941), I, 302 ff.

that condition of a natural person, in which, by the operation of law, the application of his physical and mental powers depends . . . upon the will of another . . . and in which he is incapable . . . of . . . holding property [or any other rights] . . . except as the agent or instrument of another. In slavery, . . . the state, in ignoring the personality of the slave, . . . commits the control of his conduct . . . to the master, together with the power of transferring his authority to another.[2]

Thinking of slavery in that sense, the Englishmen of 1772 could boast with Lord Mansfield that their country had never tolerated the institution; simply to touch the soil of England made men free.[3] But the distinction between slave and free that had become important by the eighteenth century was not a significant distinction at the opening of the seventeenth century. In the earlier period, the antithesis of "free" was not "slave" but unfree; and, within the condition of unfreedom, law and practice recognized several gradations.

The status that involved the most complete lack of freedom was villeinage, a servile condition transmitted from father to son. The villein was limited in the right to hold property or make contracts; he could be bought and sold with the land he worked or without, and had "to do all that that the Lord will him command"; while the lord could "rob, beat, and chastise his Villain at his will."[4] It was true that the condition had almost ceased to exist in England itself. But it persisted in Scotland well into the eighteenth century. In law the conception remained important enough to induce Coke in 1658/9 to give it a lengthy section; and the analogy with villeinage served frequently to define the terms of other forms of servitude.[5]

[2] Summarized in John Codman Hurd, *Law of Freedom and Bondage in the United States* (Boston, 1858), I, 42, 43.

[3] William Blackstone, *Commentaries* . . ., edited by St. George Tucker (Philadelphia, 1803), I, 126, 423. For Somerset's Case, see Hurd, *Law of Freedom and Bondage*, I, 189 ff.; also *ibid.*, I, 185 ff.

[4] [Thomas Blount], *Les Termes de la Ley; or, Certain Difficult and Obscure Words and Terms of the Common Laws and Statutes . . . Explained* (London, 1685), 648-652; Hurd, *Law of Freedom and Bondage*, I, 136.

[5] Edward Coke, *First Part of the Institutes of the Laws of England; or, a Commentary upon Littleton . . .*, edited by Charles Butler (Philadelphia, 1853), Bk. II, Ch. 11, Sections 172-212; James Paterson, *Commentaries on the Liberty of the Subject and the . . . Security of the Person* (London, 1877), I, 492; Jacob D. Wheeler, *Practical Treatise on the Law of Slavery . . .* (New York, 1837), 256, 257; Tucker's Appendix to Blackstone, *Commentaries*, I, 43n; Gray, *History of Agriculture*, I, 343 ff.

For, law and practice in the seventeenth century comprehended other forms of involuntary bondage. The essential attributes of villeinage were fastened on many men not through heredity and ancient custom, as in the case of the villein, but through poverty, crime, or mischance. A debtor, in cases "where there is not sufficient distresse of goods" could be "sold at an outcry." Conviction for vagrancy and vagabondage, even the mere absence of a fixed occupation, exposed the free-born Englishman, at home or in the colonies, to the danger that he might be bound over to the highest bidder, his labor sold for a term. Miscreants who could not pay their fines for a wide range of offenses were punished by servitude on "publick works" or on the estates of individuals under conditions not far different from those of villeinage. Such sentences, in the case of the graver felonies, sometimes were for life.[6]

The sale by the head of a household of members of his family entailed a similar kind of involuntary servitude. A husband could thus dispose of his wife, and a father of his children. Indeed, reluctance to part with idle youngsters could bring on the intercession of the public authorities. So, in 1646, Virginia county commissioners were authorized to send to work in the public flaxhouse two youngsters from each county, kept at home by the "fond indulgence or perverse obstinacy" of their parents. Orphans, bastards, and the offspring of servants were similarly subject to disposal at the will of officials.[7]

Moreover servitude as an estate was not confined to those who fell into it against their wills. It also held many men who entered it by agreement or formal indenture, most commonly for a fixed span of years under conditions contracted for in advance, but occasionally for life, and frequently without definite statement of terms under the assumption that the custom of the country was definite enough.[8]

Early modification in the laws regulating servitude did not, in England or the colonies, alter essentially the nature of the condition.[9] Whether vol-

[6] See *Maryland Archives* (Baltimore, 1883 ff.), I, 69 (1638/9), 152 ff. (1642), 187 (1642), 192 (1642); William Waller Hening, *Statutes at Large Being a Collection of all the Laws of Virginia* . . . (New York, 1823 ff.), I, 117; Gray, *History of Agriculture*, I, 343; John H. Lefroy, *Memorials of the Discovery and Early Settlement of the Bermudas or Somers Islands, 1518-1685* (London, 1877), I, 127.

[7] See Hening, *Statutes*, I, 336; also Paterson, *Commentaries*, I, 495; Gray, *History of Agriculture*, I, 343; Susie M. Ames, *Studies of the Virginia Eastern Shore in the Seventeenth Century* (Richmond, 1940), 78 ff.; *infra*, 212.

[8] Paterson, *Commentaries*, I, 494; *infra*, 209.

[9] See Gray, *History of Agriculture*, I, 343 ff.

untary or involuntary, the status did not involve substantially more freedom in law than villeinage. It was not heritable; but servants could be
bartered for a profit, sold to the highest bidder for the unpaid debts of their
masters, and otherwise transferred like movable goods or chattels. Their
capacity to hold property was narrowly limited as was their right to make
contracts.[10] Furthermore, the master had extensive powers of discipline,
enforced by physical chastisement or by extension of the term of service.
Offenses against the state also brought on punishments different from
those meted out to free men; with no property to be fined, the servants
were whipped.[11] In every civic, social, and legal attribute, these victims of
the turbulent displacements of the sixteenth and seventeenth centuries
were set apart. Despised by every other order, without apparent means of
rising to a more favored place, these men, and their children, and their
children's children seemed mired in a hard, degraded life.[12] That they
formed a numerous element in society was nothing to lighten their lot.

The condition of the first Negroes in the continental English colonies
must be viewed within the perspective of these conceptions and realities of
servitude. As Europeans penetrated the dark continent in search of gold
and ivory, they developed incidentally the international trade in Blacks.
The Dutch in particular found this an attractive means of breaking into
the business of the Spanish colonies, estopped by the policy of their own
government from adding freely to their supply of African labor. In the
course of this exchange through the West Indies, especially through Cura-
cao, occasional small lots were left along the coast between Virginia and
Massachusetts.[13]

Through the first three-quarters of the seventeenth century, the Negroes,
even in the South, were not numerous; nor were they particularly concentrated in any district.[14] They came into a society in which a large part of
the population was to some degree unfree; indeed in Virginia under the

[10] *Maryland Archives*, I, 69 (1638/9); Hening, *Statutes*, I, 245, 253, 274, 439, 445;
Ames, *Eastern Shore*, 77; *infra*, 214.
[11] See, for instance, Hening, *Statutes*, I, 167, 189, 192.
[12] Philip Alexander Bruce, *Institutional History of Virginia* . . . (New York,
1910), II, 614.
[13] See Elizabeth Donnan, ed., *Documents Illustrative of the History of the Slave
Trade to America* (Washington, 1930 ff.), I, 83 ff., 105, 106, 151; Gray, *History of
Agriculture*, I, 352.
[14] Philip Alexander Bruce, *Social Life of Virginia in the Seventeenth Century*
(Richmond, 1907), 14; James M. Wright, *Free Negro in Maryland 1634-1860* (New
York, 1921), 13.

60

Company almost everyone, even tenants and laborers, bore some sort of servile obligation.[15] The Negroes' lack of freedom was not unusual. These newcomers, like so many others, were accepted, bought and held, as kinds of servants.[16] They were certainly not well off. But their ill-fortune was of a sort they shared with men from England, Scotland, and Ireland, and with the unlucky aborigenes held in captivity. Like the others, some Negroes became free, that is, terminated their period of service. Some became artisans; a few became landowners and the masters of other men.[17] The status of Negroes was that of servants; and so they were identified and treated down to the 1660's.[18]

The word, "slave" was, of course, used occasionally. It had no meaning in English law, but there was a significant colloquial usage. This was a general term of derogation. It served to express contempt; "O what a rogue

[15] See Gray, *History of Agriculture,* I, 314 ff.

[16] This fact was first established by the work of James Curtis Ballagh, *History of Slavery in Virginia* (Baltimore, 1902), 9 ff., 28 ff. and John Henderson Russell, *Free Negro in Virginia 1619-1865* (Baltimore, 1913), 23 ff. Their conclusions were accepted by Ulrich B. Phillips, *American Negro Slavery* (New York, 1918), 75; although they ran counter to the position of Philip Alexander Bruce, *Economic History of Virginia in the Seventeenth Century* (New York, 1907), II, 52 ff. They were not seriously disputed until the appearance of Ames, *Eastern Shore,* 100 ff. Miss Ames's argument, accepted by Wesley Frank Craven, *Southern Colonies in the Seventeenth Century 1607-1689* (Baton Rouge, 1949), 402, rests on scattered references to "slaves" in the records. But these are never identified as Negroes; the reference is always to "slaves," to "Negroes or slaves," to "Negroes and slaves," or to "Negroes and other slaves," just as there are many more frequent references to "Negroes and servants" (for the meaning of "slave" in these references, see *infra,* 204. Miss Ames also argues that the free Negroes referred to by Russell may have been manumitted. But unless she could prove—and she cannot—that Englishmen in Virginia had a previous conception of slavery as a legal status within which the Negro fell, it is much more logical to assume with Russell that these were servants who had completed their terms. For the same reasons we cannot accept the unsupported assumptions of Wright, *Free Negro in Maryland,* 21-23.

[17] Marcus W. Jernegan, "Slavery and the Beginnings of Industrialism in the American Colonies," *American Historical Review,* XXV (1920), 227, 228; Ames, *Eastern Shore,* 106, 107.

[18] In such a work as [Nathaniel Butler], *Historye of the Bermudaes or Summer Islands,* edited by J. Henry Lefroy (London, 1882), for instance, the term "slave" is never applied to Negroes (see pp. 84, 99, 144, 146, 211, 219, 242). For disciplinary and revenue laws in Virginia that did not discriminate Negroes from other servants, see Hening, *Statutes,* I, 174, 198, 200, 243, 306 (1631-1645). For wills (1655-1664) in which "Lands goods & chattels cattle monys negroes English servts horses sheep household stuff" were all bequeathed together, see *Lancaster County Records,* Book 2, pp. 46, 61, 121, 283 (cited from Beverley Fleet, ed., *Virginia Colonial Abstracts* [Richmond, 1938 ff.]).

and peasant slave am I," says Hamlet (Act II, Scene 2). It also described the low-born as contrasted with the gentry; of two hundred warriors, a sixteenth-century report said, eight were gentlemen, the rest slaves.[19] The implication of degradation was also transferred to the low kinds of labor; "In this hal," wrote More (1551), "all vyle seruice, all slauerie . . . is done by bondemen."[20]

It was in this sense that Negro servants were sometimes called slaves.[21] But the same appellation was, in England, given to other non-English servants,—to a Russian, for instance.[22] In Europe and in the American colonies, the term was, at various times and places, applied indiscriminately to Indians, mulattoes, and mestizos, as well as to Negroes.[23] For that matter, it applied also to white Englishmen. It thus commonly described the servitude of children; so, the poor planters complained, "Our children, the parents dieinge" are held as "slaues or drudges" for the discharge of their parents' debts.[24] Penal servitude too was often referred to as slavery; and the phrase, "slavish servant" turns up from time to time. Slavery had no meaning in law; at most it was a popular description of a low form of service.[25]

Yet in not much more than a half century after 1660 this term of derogation was transformed into a fixed legal position. In a society characterized by many degrees of unfreedom, the Negro fell into a status novel to English law, into an unknown condition toward which the colonists unsteadily moved, slavery in its eighteenth- and nineteenth-century form. The

[19] *State Papers Henry VIII, Ireland,* II, 448; also III, 594 (under Sklaw); see also Shakespeare's *Coriolanus,* Act IV, Scene 5.

[20] Thomas More, *Utopia* (Oxford, 1895), 161, 221, 222.

[21] See Russell, *Free Negro,* 19.

[22] Paterson, *Commentaries,* I, 492.

[23] See Bruce, *Institutional History,* I, 673; Ames, *Eastern Shore,* 72 ff.; E. B. O'Callaghan, ed., *Documents Relative to the Colonial History of the State of New York* (Albany, 1856 ff.), III, 678.

[24] Butler, *Historye of the Bermudaes,* 295, 296. See also Lorenzo Johnston Greene, *Negro in Colonial New England 1620-1776* (New York, 1942), 19, *n.* 25; Arthur W. Calhoun, *Social History of the American Family* (Cleveland, 1917), I, 82; and also the evidence cited by Richard B. Morris, *Government and Labor in Early America* (New York, 1946), 339, 340.

[25] See Abbot Emerson Smith, *Colonists in Bondage* (Chapel Hill, 1947), 158, 186; *Maryland Archives,* I, 41; Gray, *History of Agriculture,* I, 359; Butler, *Historye of the Bermudaes,* 295; Morris, *Government and Labor,* 346. Some of the earliest Negroes in Bermuda and Virginia seem thus to have been held as public servants, perhaps by analogy with penal servitude (Ballagh, *Slavery in Virginia,* 29).

available accounts do not explain this development because they assume that this form of slavery was known from the start.

Can it be said, for instance, that the seventeenth-century Englishman might have discovered elsewhere an established institution, the archetype of slavery as it was ultimately defined, which seemed more advantageous than the defined English customs for use in the New World? The internationally recognized "slave trade" has been cited as such an institution.[26] But when one notes that the Company of Royal Adventurers referred to their cargo as "Negers," "Negro-Servants," "Servants . . . from Africa," or "Negro Person," but rarely as slaves, it is not so clear that it had in view some unique or different status.[27] And when one remembers that the transportation of Irish servants was also known as the "slave-trade," then it is clear that those who sold and those who bought the Negro, if they troubled to consider legal status at all, still thought of him simply as a low servant.[28]

Again, it has been assumed that Biblical and Roman law offered adequate precedent. But it did not seem so in the perspective of the contemporaries of the first planters who saw in both the Biblical and Roman institutions simply the equivalents of their own familiar forms of servitude. King James's translators rendered the word, "bond-servant"; "slave" does not appear in their version.[29] And to Coke the Roman *servus* was no more than the villein ("and this is hee which the civilians call servus").[30]

Nor did the practice of contemporary Europeans fall outside the English conceptions of servitude. Since early in the fifteenth century, the Portuguese had held Moors, white and black, in "slavery," at home, on the Atlantic islands, and in Brazil. Such servitude also existed in Spain and in Spanish America where Negroes were eagerly imported to supply the perennial shortage of labor in the Caribbean sugar islands and the Peruvian mines. But what was the status of such slaves? They had certain

---

[26] See, for example, Craven, *Southern Colonies*, 219.

[27] Donnan, *Documents*, I, 128-131, 156, 158, 163, 164. For continued use of the term, "Negro Servants" by the Royal African Company, see *ibid.*, I, 195.

[28] John P. Prendergast, *Cromwellian Settlement of Ireland* (London, 1865), 53n, 238; Patrick Francis Moran, *Historical Sketch of the Persecutions Suffered by the Catholics of Ireland under the Rule of Cromwell and the Puritans* (Dublin, 1907), 343-346, 356, 363.

[29] See, for example, Genesis, XIV, 14, XXX, 43; Leviticus, XXV, 39-46; Exodus, XXI, 1-9, 16. See also the discussion by Roger Williams (1637), *Massachusetts Historical Society Collections*, Fourth Series, VI (1863), 212.

[30] Coke, *First Institute upon Littleton*, 116a, §172.

property rights, were capable of contracting marriages, and were assured of the integrity of their families. Once baptised it was almost a matter of course that they would become free; the right to manumission was practically a "contractual arrangement." And once free, they readily intermarried with their former masters. These were no chattels, devoid of personality. These were human beings whom chance had rendered unfree, a situation completely comprehensible within the degrees of unfreedom familiar to the English colonist. Indeed when Bodin wishes to illustrate the condition of such "slaves," he refers to servants and apprentices in England and Scotland.[31]

Finally, there is no basis for the assertion that such a colony as South Carolina simply adopted slavery from the French or British West Indies.[32] To begin with, the labor system of those places was not yet fully evolved.[33] Travelers from the mainland may have noted the advantages of Negro labor there; but they hardly thought of chattel slavery.[34] The Barbadian gentlemen who proposed to come to South Carolina in 1663 thought of bringing "Negros and other servants." They spoke of "slaves" as did other Englishmen, as a low form of servant; the "weaker" servants to whom the Concessions referred included "woemen children slaves."[35] Clearly American slavery was no direct imitation from Biblical or Roman or Spanish or Portuguese or West Indian models. Whatever connections existed were established in the eighteenth and nineteenth centuries when those who justified the emerging institution cast about for possible precedents wherever they might be found.

If chattel slavery was not present from the start, nor adopted from elsewhere, it was also not a response to any inherent qualities that fitted the Negro for plantation labor. There has been a good deal of speculation as

[31] I. [Jean] Bodin, *Six Bookes of a Commonweale,* translated by Richard Knolles (London, 1606), 33. For the Portuguese and Spanish situations, see Jose Antonio Saco, *Historia de la esclavitud desde los tiempos mas remotos hasta nuestros dias* (2d ed., Habana, 1937), III, 266-277; Donnan, *Documents,* I, 15, 16, 29 ff.; Frank Tannenbaum, *Slave and Citizen the Negro in the Americas* (New York, 1947), 43 ff., 55; Gray, *History of Agriculture,* I, 110, 304-306; Marcus W. Jernegan, *Laboring and Dependent Classes in Colonial America, 1607-1783* (Chicago, 1931), 25.

[32] See, for example, Edward McCrady, *History of South Carolina under the Proprietary Government 1670-1719* (New York, 1897), 357; Gray, *History of Agriculture,* I, 322.

[33] See *infra, n.105.*

[34] *Massachusetts Historical Society Collections,* Fourth Series, VI, 536 ff.

[35] *Collections of the South Carolina Historical Society,* V (1897), 11, 32, 42, 43.

to the relative efficiency of free and slave, of Negro, white, and Indian, labor. Of necessity, estimates of which costs were higher, which risks—through mortality, escape, and rebellion—greater, are inconclusive.[36] What is conclusive is the fact that Virginia and Maryland planters did not think Negro labor more desirable. A preference for white servants persisted even on the islands.[37] But when the Barbadians could not get those, repeated representations in London made known their desire for Negroes.[38] No such demands came from the continental colonies.[39] On the contrary the calls are for skilled white labor with the preference for those most like the first settlers and ranging down from Scots and Welsh to Irish, French, and Italians.[40] Least desired were the unskilled, utterly strange Negroes.[41]

It is quite clear in fact that as late as 1669 those who thought of large-scale agriculture assumed it would be manned not by Negroes but by white peasants under a condition of villeinage. John Locke's constitutions for South Carolina envisaged an hereditary group of servile "leetmen"; and Lord Shaftsbury's signory on Locke Island in 1674 actually attempted to put that scheme into practice.[42] If the holders of large estates in the Chesa-

[36] For material relevant to these questions, see Lucien Peytraud, *L'Esclavage aux antilles françaises avant 1789* (Paris, 1897), 20 ff.; Gray, *History of Agriculture*, I, 362-370; Bruce, *Social Life*, 16; Ulrich B. Phillips, *Life and Labor in the Old South* (Boston, 1929), 23; Ralph B. Flanders, *Plantation Slavery in Georgia* (Chapel Hill, 1933), 9, 10; Ballagh, *Slavery in Virginia*, 51; Wright, *Free Negro in Maryland*, 21; E. Franklin Frazier, *Negro in the United States* (New York, 1949), 29 ff.; Donnan, *Documents*, I, 174.

[37] See C. S. S. Higham, *Development of the Leeward Islands under the Restoration 1660-1688* (Cambridge, 1921), 143, 165.

[38] Donnan, *Documents*, I, 91, 92, 115-118.

[39] Craven, *Southern Colonies*, 25. There is no evidence to support T. J. Wertenbaker's statement that the demand for Negro slaves remained active in Virginia after 1620 and that if England had early entered the slave trade, Virginia and Maryland "would have been from the first inundated with black workers." See *Planters of Colonial Virginia* (Princeton, 1922), 31, 125; *First Americans 1607-1690* (New York, 1929), 23.

[40] William Berkeley, *A Discourse & View of Virginia* (London, 1663), 4, 5, 7, 8; *Virginia Historical Register*, I, 63; Phillips, *Life and Labor*, 44; T. J. Wertenbaker, *Patrician and Plebeian in Virginia* (Charlottesville, Va., 1910), 137 ff.

[41] Ballagh, *Slavery in Virginia*, 14; McCrady, *South Carolina*, 383; Alexander S. Salley, Jr., ed., *Narratives of Early Carolina 1650-1708* (New York, 1910), 60.

[42] Locke also anticipated a lower form of labor to be performed by Negro slaves. But while the leetmen would be held only by the lords of manors, any freeman would have power to hold slaves. See John Locke, *First Set of the Fundamental Constitutions of South Carolina*, articles 22-26, 101 (a draft is in *Collections of the South Carolina Historical Society*, V, 93 ff.); also Gray, *History of Agriculture*, I, 323-325.

peake colonies expressed no wish for a Negro labor supply, they could hardly have planned to use black hands as a means of displacing white, whether as a concerted plot by restoration courtiers to set up a new social order in America,[43] or as a program for lowering costs.[44]

Yet the Negroes did cease to be servants and became slaves, ceased to be men in whom masters held a proprietary interest and became chattels, objects that were the property of their owners. In that transformation originated the southern labor system.

Although the colonists assumed at the start that all servants would "fare alike in the colony," the social realities of their situation early gave rise to differences of treatment.[45] It is not necessary to resort to racialist assumptions to account for such measures; these were simply the reactions of immigrants lost to the stability and security of home and isolated in an immense wilderness in which threats from the unknown were all about them. Like the millions who would follow, these immigrants longed in the strangeness for the company of familiar men and singled out to be welcomed those who were most like themselves. So the measures regulating settlement spoke specifically in this period of differential treatment for various groups. From time to time, regulations applied only to "those of our own nation," or to the French, the Dutch, the Italians, the Swiss, the Palatines, the Welsh, the Irish, or to combinations of the diverse nationalities drawn to these shores.[46]

In the same way the colonists became aware of the differences between themselves and the African immigrants. The rudeness of the Negroes' manners, the strangeness of their languages, the difficulty of communicating to them English notions of morality and proper behavior occasioned sporadic laws to regulate their conduct.[47] So, Bermuda's law to restrain the insolencies of Negroes "who are servents" (that is, their inclina-

[43] William E. Dodd, "The Emergence of the First Social Order in the United States," *American Historical Review*, XL (1935), 226, 227.

[44] See Wertenbaker, *Planters*, 86 ff.; Wertenbaker, *Patrician*, 144 ff.; Wertenbaker, *First Americans*, 42 ff. In addition it might well be questioned whether large producers in a period of falling prices would have driven out the small producer who operated with little reference to conditions of prices and costs. See *Maryland Archives*, II, 45, 48 (1666); Gray, *History of Agriculture*, I, 231, 232, 276.

[45] Hening, *Statutes*, I, 117.

[46] See *Maryland Archives*, I, 328, 331, 332 (1651), III, 99 (1641), 222 (1648); Gray, *History of Agriculture*, I, 87, 88; Higham, *Leeward Islands*, 169 ff.

[47] See Bruce, *Social Life*, 139, 152; Bruce, *Institutional History*, I, 9.

tion to run off with the pigs of others) was the same in kind as the legislation that the Irish should "straggle not night or dai, as is too common with them."[48] Until the 1660's the statutes on the Negroes were not at all unique. Nor did they add up to a decided trend.[49]

But in the decade after 1660 far more significant differentiations with regard to term of service, relationship to Christianity, and disposal of children, cut the Negro apart from all other servants and gave a new depth to his bondage.

In the early part of the century duration of service was of only slight importance. Certainly in England where labor was more plentiful than the demand, expiration of a term had little meaning; the servant was free only to enter upon another term, while the master had always the choice of taking on the old or a new servitor. That situation obtained even in America as long as starvation was a real possibility. In 1621, it was noted, "vittles being scarce in the country noe man will tacke servants."[50] As late as 1643 Lord Baltimore thought it better if possible to hire labor than to risk the burden of supporting servants through a long period.[51] Under such conditions the number of years specified in the indenture was not important, and if a servant had no indenture the question was certainly not likely to rise.[52]

That accounts for the early references to unlimited service. Thus Sandys's plan for Virginia in 1618 spoke of tenants-at-half assigned to the treasurer's office, to "belong to said office for ever." Again, those at Berkeley's Hundred were perpetual "after the manner of estates in England."[53] Since perpetual in seventeenth-century law meant that which had "not

[48] Lefroy, *Memorials*, I, 308; Smith, *Colonists in Bondage*, 172. For the dangers of reading Negro law in isolation, see the exaggerated interpretation of the act of 1623, Craven, *Southern Colonies*, 218.

[49] That there was no trend is evident from the fluctuations in naming Negroes slaves or servants and in their right to bear arms. See Hening, *Statutes*, I, 226, 258, 292, 540; Bruce, *Institutional History*, II, 5 ff., 199 ff. For similar fluctuations with regard to Indians, see Hening, *Statutes*, I, 391, 518.

[50] Charles M. Andrews, *Colonial Period of American History* (New Haven, 1934 ff.), I, 137.

[51] *Maryland Archives*, III, 141. See also the later comment on the Barbados by Berkeley, *Discourse*, 12; and the complaint of Thomas Cornwallis that the cost of maintaining many servants was "never defrayed by their labor," *Maryland Archives*, I, 463.

[52] That the practice of simply renewing expired terms was common was shown by its abuse by unscrupulous masters. See *infra*, n. 71, n. 78.

[53] Gray, *History of Agriculture*, I, 316, 318 ff.

any set time expressly allotted for [its] . . . continuance," such provisions were not surprising.[54] Nor was it surprising to find instances in the court records of Negroes who seemed to serve forever.[55] These were quite compatible with the possibility of ultimate freedom. Thus a colored man bought in 1644 "as a Slave for Ever," nevertheless was held "to serve as other Christians servants do" and freed after a term.[56]

The question of length of service became critical when the mounting value of labor eased the fear that servants would be a drain on "vittles" and raised the expectation of profit from their toil. Those eager to multiply the number of available hands by stimulating immigration had not only to overcome the reluctance of a prospective newcomer faced with the trials of a sea journey; they had also to counteract the widespread reports in England and Scotland that servants were harshly treated and bound in perpetual slavery.[57]

To encourage immigration therefore, the colonies embarked upon a line of legislation designed to improve servants' conditions and to enlarge the prospect of a meaningful release, a release that was not the start of a new period of servitude, but of life as a freeman and landowner.[58] Thus Virginia, in 1642, discharged "publick tenants from their servitudes, who, like one sort of villians anciently in England" were attached to the lands of the governor; and later laws provided that no person was to "be adjudged to serve the collonie hereafter."[59] Most significant were the statutes which reassured prospective newcomers by setting limits to the terms of servants without indentures, in 1638/9 in Maryland, in 1642/3 in Virginia.[60] These acts seem to have applied only to voluntary immigrants "of our own nation."[61] The Irish and other aliens, less desirable, at first re-

---

[54] We have discussed the whole question in "Origins of the American Business Corporation," *Journal of Economic History*, V (1945), 21 ff. See also Smith, *Colonists in Bondage*, 108.

[55] Russell, *Free Negro*, 34.

[56] Helen Tunnicliff Catterall, *Judicial Cases Concerning American Slavery and the Negro* (Washington, 1926 ff.), I, 58.

[57] *Collections of the South Carolina Historical Society*, V, 152; Wertenbaker, *Planters*, 60; Higham, *Leeward Islands*, 169; Jeffrey R. Brackett, *Negro in Maryland* (Baltimore, 1889), 23.

[58] *Maryland Archives*, I, 52, 97 (1640).

[59] Hening, *Statutes*, I, 259, 459; Gray, *History of Agriculture*, I, 316, 346.

[60] *Maryland Archives*, I, 37, 80, 352 (1654); Hening, *Statutes*, I, 257.

[61] *Maryland Archives*, I, 80, 402-409 (1661), 453 (1662); Hening, *Statutes*, I, 411. The Maryland act specifically excluded "slaves."

ceived longer terms.[62] But the realization that such discrimination re-tarded "the peopling of the country" led to an extension of the identical privilege to all Christians.[63]

But the Negro never profited from these enactments. Farthest re-moved from the English, least desired, he communicated with no friends who might be deterred from following. Since his coming was involun-tary, nothing that happened to him would increase or decrease his num-bers. To raise the status of Europeans by shortening their terms would ul-timately increase the available hands by inducing their compatriots to emigrate; to reduce the Negro's term would produce an immediate loss and no ultimate gain. By midcentury the servitude of Negroes seems gen-erally lengthier than that of whites; and thereafter the consciousness dawns that the Blacks will toil for the whole of their lives, not through any par-ticular concern with their status but simply by contrast with those whose years of labor are limited by statute. The legal position of the Negro is, however, still uncertain; it takes legislative action to settle that.[64]

The Maryland House, complaining of that ambiguity, provoked the decisive measure; "All Negroes and other slaues," it was enacted, "shall serve Durante Vita."[65] Virginia reached the same end more tortuously. An act of 1661 had assumed, in imposing penalities on runaways, that *some* Negroes served for life.[66] The law of 1670 went further; "all servants not being christians" brought in by sea were declared slaves for life.[67]

But slavery for life was still tenuous as long as the slave could extricate himself by baptism. The fact that Negroes were heathens had formerly justified their bondage, since infidels were "perpetual" enemies of Chris-

---

[62] See Virginia acts of 1654/5 and 1657/8, Hening, *Statutes,* I, 411, 441, 471.

[63] *Ibid.,* I, 538, II, 113, 169, 297. The provision limiting the effectiveness of the act to Christians is not surprising in view of contemporary attitudes. See the act of the same year excluding Quakers, *ibid.,* I, 532. For later adjustments of term, see *Maryland Archives,* II, 147 (1666), 335 (1671).

[64] For an example of such uncertainty, see the case of "Degoe the negro servant" (Virginia, 1665), *Lancaster County Record Book,* Book 2, p. 337; also Craven, *South-ern Colonies,* 219. It is instructive to note how that question was evaded by ninety-nine year terms in Bermuda as late as 1662. See Lefroy, *Memorials,* II, 166, 184.

[65] *Maryland Archives,* I, 526 ff., 533; Wright, *Free Negro in Maryland,* 21; Brackett, *Negro in Maryland,* 28.

[66] Hening, *Statutes,* II, 26, 116; Catterall, *Judicial Cases,* I, 59.

[67] Hening, *Statutes,* II, 283; it was reenacted more stringently in 1682, *ibid.,* II, 491. See also McCrady, *South Carolina,* 358.

tians.[68] It had followed that conversion was a way to freedom. Governor Archdale thus released the Spanish Indians captured to be sold as slaves to Jamaica when he learned they were Christians.[69] As labor rose in value this presumption dissipated the zeal of masters for proselytizing. So that they be "freed from this doubt" a series of laws between 1667 and 1671 laid down the rule that conversion alone did not lead to a release from servitude.[70] Thereafter manumission, which other servants could demand by right at the end of their terms, in the case of Negroes lay entirely within the discretion of the master.[71]

A difference in the status of the offspring of Negro and white servants followed inevitably from the differentiation in the length of their terms. The problem of disposing of the issue of servants was at first general. Bastardy, prevalent to begin with and more frequent as the century advanced, deprived the master of his women's work and subjected him to the risk of their death. Furthermore the parish was burdened with the support of the child. The usual procedure was to punish the offenders with fines or whippings and to compel the servant to serve beyond his time for the benefit of the parish and to recompense the injured master.[72]

The general rule ceased to apply once the Negro was bound for life, for there was no means of extending his servitude. The most the outraged master could get was the child, a minimal measure of justice, somewhat

---

[68] See Saco, *Historia de la esclavitud*, III, 158 ff.; Hurd, *Law of Freedom and Bondage*, I, 160; Donnan, *Documents*, I, 3, 4.

[69] John Archdale, *A New Description of the Province of Carolina* (1707), in Salley, *Narratives*, 300. For English law on the question, see Gray, *History of Agriculture*, I, 359.

[70] Catterall, *Judicial Cases*, I, 57; Hening, *Statutes*, II, 260; Locke, *Constitutions*, Article 101; *Maryland Archives*, I, 526, II, 265, 272; Ballagh, *Slavery in Virginia*, 46-48; Russell, *Free Negro*, 21; Wright, *Free Negro in Maryland*, 22; Hurd, *Law of Freedom and Bondage*, I, 210; Brackett, *Negro in Maryland*, 29.

[71] For the feudal derivation of manumission, see Coke, *First Institute upon Littleton*, I, 137b, §204. For the application to servants see Bodin, *Six Bookes*, 33; Hening, *Statutes*, II, 115 (1661/2). The requirement for manumission of servants in Virginia, to some extent, seems to have become a means of protection against labor-starved masters who coerced their servants into new contracts just before the old expired. See Hening, *Statutes*, II, 388 (1676/7).

[72] *Maryland Archives*, I, 373 (1658), 428, 441 (1662); Hening, *Statutes*, I, 438, II, 114 (1661/2), 168 (1662), 298 (1672), III, 139; Bruce, *Institutional History*, I, 45-50, 85, 86; Calhoun, *American Family*, I, 314. Women were always punished more severely than men, not being eligible for benefit of clergy. See Blackstone, *Commentaries*, I, 445n.

tempered by the trouble of rearing the infant to an age of usefulness.[73] The truly vexing problem was to decide on the proper course when one parent was free, for it was not certain whether the English law that the issue followed the state of the father would apply. Maryland, which adopted that rule in 1664, found that unscrupulous masters instigated intercourse between their Negro males and white females which not only gave them the offspring, but, to boot, the service of the woman for the life of her husband. The solution in Virginia which followed the precedent of the bastardy laws and had the issue follow the mother seemed preferable and ultimately was adopted in Maryland and elsewhere.[74]

By the last quarter of the seventeenth century, one could distinguish clearly between the Negro slave who served for life and the servant for a period. But there was not yet a demarcation in personal terms: the servant was not yet a free man, nor the slave a chattel. As late as 1686, the words slave and servant could still be conflated to an extent that indicated men conceived of them as extensions of the same condition. A Frenchman in Virginia in that year noted, "There are degrees among the slaves brought here, for a Christian over 21 years of age cannot be held a slave more than five years, but the negroes and other infidels remain slaves all their lives."[75]

It was the persistence of such conceptions that raised the fear that "noe free borne Christians will ever be induced to come over servants" without overwhelming assurance that there would be nothing slavish in their lot. After all Pennsylvania and New York now gave the European newcomer a choice of destination.[76] In Virginia and Maryland there was a persistent

[73] Ballagh, *Slavery in Virginia*, 38 ff.; Greene, *Negro in New England*, 290 ff.
[74] See Coke, *First Institute upon Littleton*, I, 123a, §187; *Maryland Archives*, I, 526-533; Wright, *Free Negro in Maryland*, 21, 22, 27; Wheeler, *Practical Treatise*, 3, 21; Russell, *Free Negro*, 19, 21; Greene, *Negro in New England*, 182 ff.
[75] [Durand], *A Frenchman in Virginia Being the Memoirs of a Huguenot Refugee in 1686*, edited by Fairfax Harrison, (Richmond, 1923), 95 ff. For laws conflating servant and slave, see Brackett, *Negro in Maryland*, 104. This contradicts the assumption of Catterall, *Judicial Cases*, I, 57, that the status of Negroes was completely fixed by 1667.
[76] The agitation against transportation of felons was also evidence of the desire to supply that assurance. See *Maryland Archives*, I, 464; Hening, *Statutes*, II, 509 ff., 515 (1670); Ballagh, *Slavery in Virginia*, 10; Phillips, *Life and Labor*, 25. The attractiveness of rival colonies may account for the low proportion of servants who took up land in Maryland. See Abbot Emerson Smith, "The Indentured Servant and Land Speculation in Seventeenth Century Maryland," *American Historical Review*, XL (1935), 467 ff.; Gray, *History of Agriculture*, I, 88, 348.

71

effort to make immigration more attractive by further ameliorating the lot of European servants. The custom of the country undoubtedly moved more rapidly than the letter of the law. "Weake and Ignorant" juries on which former servants sat often decided cases against masters.[77] But even the letter of the law showed a noticeable decline in the use of the death penalty and in the power of masters over men. By 1705 in some colonies, white servants were no longer transferable; they could not be whipped without a court order; and they were protected against the avaricious unreasonable masters who attempted to force them into new contracts "some small tyme before the expiration of their tyme of service."[78]

Meanwhile the condition of the Negro deteriorated. In these very years, a startling growth in numbers complicated the problem. The Royal African Company was, to some extent, responsible, though its operations in the mainland colonies formed only a very minor part of its business. But the opening of Africa to free trade in 1698 inundated Virginia, Maryland, and South Carolina with new slaves.[79] Under the pressure of policing these newcomers the regulation of Negroes actually grew harsher.

The early laws against runaways, against drunkenness, against carrying arms or trading without permission had applied penalties as heavy as death to all servants, Negroes and whites.[80] But these regulations grew steadily less stringent in the case of white servants. On the other hand fear of the growing number of slaves, uneasy suspicion of plots and conspiracies, led to more stringent control of Negroes and a broad view of the master's power of discipline. Furthermore the emerging difference in treatment was calculated to create a real division of interest between Negroes on the one hand and whites on the other. Servants who ran away in the company of slaves, for instance, were doubly punished, for the loss of their own time and for the time of the slaves, a provision that discouraged such joint ventures. Similarly Negroes, even when freed, retained some disciplinary

[77] See the complaint of Thomas Cornwallis, *Maryland Archives,* I, 463 ff.

[78] See Hening, *Statutes,* II, 117, 156, 157, 164 (1661/2), 388 (1676/7), 464 (1680); Maryland Archives, II, 30 (1666), 351 (1674); Smith, *Colonists in Bondage,* 110, 228, 233; Bruce, *Economic History,* II, 11 ff.

[79] See Donnan, *Documents,* I, 86, 87; Gray, *History of Agriculture,* I, 352-355; Bruce, *Economic History,* II, 85; Salley, *Narratives,* 204; Higham, *Leeward Islands,* 162 ff.; Craven, *Southern Colonies,* 401; Russell, *Free Negro,* 29; Hening, *Statutes,* II, 511 ff.

[80] See Hening, *Statutes,* I, 401, 440; *Maryland Archives,* I, 107 ff. (1641), 124 (1642), 193 (1642), 500 (1663); McCrady, *South Carolina,* 359.

links with their less fortunate fellows. The wardens continued to supervise their children, they were not capable of holding white servants, and serious restrictions limited the number of manumissions.[81]

The growth of the Negro population also heightened the old concern over sexual immorality and the conditions of marriage. The law had always recognized the interest of the lord in the marriage of his villein or neife and had frowned on the mixed marriage of free and unfree. Similarly it was inclined to hold that the marriage of any servant was a loss to the master, an "Enormious offense" productive of much detriment "against the law of God," and therefore dependent on the consent of the master.[82] Mixed marriages of free men and servants were particularly frowned upon as complicating status and therefore limited by law.[83]

There was no departure from these principles in the early cases of Negro-white relationships.[84] Even the complicated laws of Maryland in 1664 and the manner of their enactment revealed no change in attitude. The marriage of Blacks and whites was possible; what was important was the status of the partners and of their issue.[85] It was to guard against the complications of status that the laws after 1691 forbade "spurious" or illegitimate mixed marriages of the slave and the free and punished violations with heavy penalties.[86] Yet it was also significant that by then the prohibition was couched in terms, not simply of slave and free man, but of

[81] *Maryland Archives,* I, 249 (1649), 348 (1654), 451 (1662), 489 (1663), II, 146 (1666), 224 (1669), 298 (1671), 523 (1676); Hening, *Statutes,* II, 116, 118 (1661/2), 185, 195 (1663), 239 (1666), 266 (1668), 270, 273 (1669), 277, 280 (1670), 299 (1672), 481 (1680), 492 (1682), III, 86 ff., 102 (1691), 179 (1699), 210 (1701), 269, 276, 278 (1705); Thomas Cooper and David J. McCord, eds., *Statutes at Large of South Carolina* (Columbia, 1836 ff.), VII, 343 ff.; Brackett, *Negro in Maryland,* 91 ff.; Phillips, *Life and Labor,* 29; Russell, *Free Negro,* 10, 21, 51, 138 ff.; Bruce, *Social Life,* 138; Bruce, *Economic History,* II, 120 ff.; Ames, *Eastern Shore,* 99; also Addison E. Verrill, *Bermuda Islands* (New Haven, 1902), 148 ff.
[82] See Hening, *Statutes,* I, 252, 433, 438; *Maryland Archives,* I, 73, 97 (1638/9), 428, 442 ff. (1662), II, 396 (1674). For English law, see Coke, *First Institute upon Littleton,* 135b, 136a, §202; *ibid.,* 139b, 140a, §209.
[83] Hening, *Statutes,* II, 114 (1661/2); Jernegan, *Laboring and Dependent Classes,* 55, 180.
[84] Hening, *Statutes,* I, 146, 552.
[85] See *supra,* 213; Wright, *Free Negro in Maryland,* 28-31.
[86] Hening, *Statutes,* III, 86-87, 453 (1705); Brackett, *Negro in Maryland,* 32 ff., 195 ff.; Russell, *Free Negro,* 124; Craven, *Southern Colonies,* 402. For the use of "spurious" in the sense of illegitimate see the quotations, Calhoun, *American Family,* I, 42.

Negro and white. Here was evidence as in the policing regulations of an emerging demarkation.

The first settlers in Virginia had been concerned with the difficulty of preserving the solidarity of the group under the disruptive effects of migration. They had been enjoined to "keepe to themselves" not to "marry nor give in marriage to the heathen, that are uncircumcised."[87] But such resolutions were difficult to maintain and had gradually relaxed until the colonists included among "themselves" such groups as the Irish, once the objects of very general contempt. A common lot drew them together; and it was the absence of a common lot that drew these apart from the Negro. At the opening of the eighteenth century, the Black was not only set off by economic and legal status; he was "abominable," another order of man.

Yet the ban on intermarriage did not rest on any principle of white racial purity, for many men contemplated with equanimity the prospect of amalgamation with the Indians.[88] That did not happen, for the mass of Redmen were free to recede into the interior while those who remained sank into slavery as abject as that of the Blacks and intermarried with those whose fate they shared.[89]

Color then emerged as the token of the slave status; the trace of color became the trace of slavery. It had not always been so; as late as the 1660's the law had not even a word to describe the children of mixed marriages. But two decades later, the term mulatto is used, and it serves, not as in Brazil, to whiten the Black, but to affiliate through the color tie the off-spring of a spurious union with his inherited slavery.[90] (The compiler of the Virginia laws then takes the liberty of altering the texts to bring earlier legislation into line with his own new notions.[91]) Ultimately the complete

---

[87] *Ibid.*, I, 323.

[88] Almon W. Lauber, *Indian Slavery in Colonial Times* (New York, 1913), 252.

[89] See Hening, *Statutes*, I, 167, 192 (1631/2), 396, 415 (1655/6), 455, 456, 476 (1657/8), II, 340, 346 (1676); *Maryland Archives*, I, 250 (1649); Catterall, *Judicial Cases*, I, 69, 70; Lauber, *Indian Slavery*, 105-117, 205, 287; Brackett, *Negro in Maryland*, 13; Craven, *Southern Colonies*, 367 ff.; Ballagh, *Slavery in Virginia*, 34, 47-49; McCrady, *South Carolina*, 189, 478; Greene, *Negro in New England*, 198 ff.; Peytraud, *L'Esclavage*, 29; Gray, *History of Agriculture*, I, 361.

[90] By 1705, a mulatto was a person with a Negro great grandparent. See Hening, *Statutes*, III, 252; also Ballagh, *Slavery in Virginia*, 44; Tannenbaum, *Slave and Citizen*, 8.

[91] See Hening, *Statutes*, II, iii, 170. For other alterations to insert "slave" where it had not originally been, see *ibid.*, II, 283, 490.

judicial doctrine begins to show forth, a slave cannot be a white man, and every man of color was descendent of a slave.[92]

The rising wall dividing the legal status of the slave from that of the servant was buttressed by other developments which derogated the qualities of the Negro as a human being to establish his inferiority and thus completed his separation from the white. The destruction of the black man's personality involved, for example, a peculiar style of designation. In the seventeenth century many immigrants in addition to the Africans—Swedes, Armenians, Jews—had brought no family names to America. By the eighteenth all but the Negroes had acquired them. In the seventeenth century, Indians and Negroes bore names that were either an approximation of their original ones or similar to those of their masters,—Diana, Jane, Frank, Juno, Anne, Maria, Jenny. In the eighteenth century slaves seem increasingly to receive classical or biblical appelations, by analogy with Roman and Hebrew bondsmen.[93] Deprivation by statute and usage of other civic rights, to vote, to testify, to bring suit, even if free, completed the process. And after 1700 appear the full slave codes, formal recognition that the Negroes are not governed by the laws of other men.[94]

The identical steps that made the slave less a man made him more a chattel. All servants had once been reckoned property of a sort; a runaway was guilty of "Stealth of ones self."[95] Negroes were then no different from others.[96] But every law that improved the condition of the white servant chipped away at the property element in his status. The growing emphasis upon the consent of the servant, upon the limits of his term, upon the ob-

[92] Catterall, *Judicial Cases*, II, 269, 358; Wheeler, *Practical Treatise*, 5, 12.

[93] *Lancaster County Record Book*, Book 2, p. 285; Catterall, *Judicial Cases*, II, 7, 8; Greene, *Negro in New England*, 201; Calhoun, *American Family*, I, 190; Bruce, *Institutional History*, I, 673.

[94] No earlier laws covered the same ground. See *Maryland Archives*, II, 523 ff. (1676); Hening, *Statutes*, III, 298, 447-453 (1705); *Statutes of South Carolina*, VII, 343 ff.; Craven, *Southern Colonies*, 217; Morris, *Government and Labor*, 501; Russell, *Free Negro*, 117-119, 125 ff.

[95] *Maryland Archives*, I, 72; Morris, *Government and Labor*, 432; Smith, *Colonists in Bondage*, 234.

[96] Thus the inclusion of the Negroes among the Virginia tithables was at first a recognition of their status as personalities rather than as property. The tax was not intended to be discriminatory, but to apply to all those who worked in the fields, white and black. The first sign of discrimination was in 1668 when white but not Negro women were exempt. See Hening, *Statutes*, I, 144, 241, 292, 356, 361, 454, II, 84, 170, 267, 296; Russell, *Free Negro*, 21; Bruce, *Institutional History*, II, 458, 546 ff. For other difficulties in treating Negroes as chattels see Hening, *Statutes*, II, 288.

ligations to him, and upon the conditional nature of his dependence, steadily converted the relationship from an ownership to a contractual basis. None of these considerations applied to the Negro; on the contrary considerations of consent and conditions disappeared from his life. What was left was his status as property,—in most cases a chattel though for special purposes real estate.[97]

To this development there was a striking parallel in the northern colonies. For none of the elements that conspired to create the slave were peculiar to the productive system of the South. The contact of dissimilar peoples in an economy in which labor was short and opportunity long was common to all American settlements. In New England and New York too there had early been an intense desire for cheap unfree hands, for "bond slaverie, villinage or Captivitie," whether it be white, Negro, or Indian.[98] As in the South, the growth in the number of Negroes had been slow until the end of the seventeenth century.[99] The Negroes were servants who, like other bondsmen, became free and owners of land. But there too, police regulations, the rules of marriage, and the development of status as property turned them into chattel slaves.[100]

A difference would emerge in the course of the eighteenth century, not so much in the cities or in the Narragansett region where there were substantial concentrations of Blacks, but in the rural districts where handfuls of Negroes were scattered under the easy oversight of town and church. There the slave would be treated as an individual, would become an equal, and acquire the rights of a human being. Men whose minds would be ever more preoccupied with conceptions of natural rights and personal dignity would find it difficult to except the Negro from their general rule.[101]

[97] See *Maryland Archives*, II, 164 (1669); Hurd, *Law of Freedom and Bondage*, I, 179; Hening, *Statutes*, III, 333 (1705); Gray, *History of Agriculture*, I, 359; Brackett, *Negro in Maryland*, 28.

[98] *Massachusetts Historical Society Collections*, Fourth Series, VI, 64 ff.; Greene, *Negro in New England*, 63, 65, 125.

[99] *Ibid.*, 73 ff., 319.

[100] For an abstract of legislation, see Hurd, *Law of Freedom and Bondage*, I, 254-293. See also Greene, *Negro in New England*, 126-139, 169, 170, 178, 184, 208 ff.; George Elliott Howard, *History of Matrimonial Institutions* (Chicago, 1904), II, 225, 226; Calhoun, *American Family*, I, 65, 210; J. H. Franklin, *From Slavery to Freedom* (New York, 1947), 89-98; Ellis L. Raesly, *Portrait of New Netherland* (New York, 1945), 104, 161, 162.

[101] Greene, *Negro in New England*, 86, 103 ff., 140; Calhoun, *American Family*, I, 82.

But by the time the same preoccupations would fire imaginations in the South, the society in which the slave lived would so have changed that he would derive no advantage from the eighteenth-century speculations on the nature of human rights. Slavery had emerged in a society in which the unit of active agriculture was small and growing smaller; even the few large estates were operated by sub-division among tenants.[102] After 1690, however, South Carolinians (and still later Georgians) turned from naval stores and the fur trade to the cultivation of rice, cotton, and indigo. In the production of these staples, which required substantial capital equipment, there was an advantage to large-scale operations. By then it was obvious which was the cheapest, most available, most exploitable labor supply. The immense profits from the tropical crops steadily sucked slaves in ever growing numbers into the plantation. With this extensive use, novel on the mainland, the price of slaves everywhere rose sharply, to the advantage of those who already held them. The prospect that the slaveowner would profit not only by the Negroes' labor, but also by the rise in their unit value and by their probable increase through breeding, accounted for the spread of the plantation to the older tobacco regions where large-scale production was not, as in the rice areas, necessarily an asset.[103]

The new social and economic context impressed indelibly on the Negro the peculiar quality of chattel with which he had been left, as other servants escaped the general degradation that had originally been the common portion of all. Not only did the concentration of slaves in large numbers call for more rigid discipline, not only did the organization of the plantation with its separate quarters, hierarchy of overseers, and absentee owners widen the gulf between black and white, but the involvement of the whole southern economy in plantation production created an effective interest against any change in status.[104]

Therein, the southern mainland colonies also differed from those in the West Indies where the same effective interest in keeping the black man debased was created without the prior definition of his status. The actual condition of the Negro differed from island to island, reflecting variations in the productive system, in the labor supply, and in economic trends. But

[102] See Ames, *Eastern Shore*, 16, 17, 30 ff., 37 ff.; McCrady, *South Carolina*, 189; Werkenbaker, *Planters*, 45, 52 ff.; Phillips, *Life and Labor*, 34; Craven, *Southern Colonies*, 210 ff.

[103] Flanders, *Plantation Slavery*, 20; Gray, *History of Agriculture*, I, 120, 278, 349.

[104] [Durand], *Frenchman in Virginia*, 112 ff.; Phillips, *Life and Labor*, 47; Salley, *Narratives*, 207, 208.

with surprising uniformity, the printed statutes and legislative compila-
tions show no concern with the problems of defining the nature of his
servitude. The relevant laws deal entirely with policing, as in the case of
servants.[105] A similar unconcern seems to have been characteristic of the
French, for the most important aspects of the royal *Code noir* issued from
Paris in 1685 were entirely disregarded.[106]

The failure to define status may have been due, in the islands which
changed hands, ·to contact with the Spaniards and to the confusion at-
tendent upon changes of sovereignty. More likely it grew out of the manner in which the Negroes were introduced. Places like the Barbados and
St. Christopher's were at the start quite similar to Virginia and Maryland,
societies of small farmers, with a labor force of indentured servants and
engagées. The Negroes and the sugar plantation appeared there somewhat earlier than on the continent because the Dutch, English, and French
African companies, anxious to use the islands as entrepots from which their
cargoes would be re-exported to Latin America, advanced the credit not
only for purchase of the Blacks, but also for sugar-making equipment. But
the limited land of the islands meant that the plantation owner and the
yeoman competed for the same acres, and in the unequal competition the
farmer was ultimately displaced.[107]

The planter had no inveterate preference for the Negro, often expressed
a desire for white labor. But the limits to the available land also prevented
him from holding out the only inducements that would attract servants
with a choice,—the prospect of landed freedom. From time to time desul-
tory laws dealt with the term of service, but these showed no progression

[105] See *Montserrat Code of Laws from 1668 to 1788* (London, 1790), 8, 16, 38;
Acts of Assembly Passed in the Island of Nevis from 1664, to 1739 (London, 1740), 9, 10, 11, 17, 25, 28, 31, 37, 46, 75; *Acts of Assembly Passed in the Island
of Barbadoes from 1648 to 1718* (London, 1721), 22, 101, 106, 137 ff.; *Acts, of Assembly Passed in the Island of Jamaica from the Year 1681 to the Year 1768, Inclusive* (Saint Jagoe de la Vesga, 1769), I, 1, 57; [Leslie], *New History of Jamaica* (2d
ed., London, 1740), 204 ff., 217 ff. There seem to have been two minor exceptions.
The question of slave status was implicitly touched on in the laws governing inheritance and the sale of property for debt (*Acts of Barbadoes*, 63, 147) and in early orders
affecting term of service. See *Calendar of State Papers, Colonial*, I, 202; [William
Duke], *Some Memoirs of the First Settlement of the Island of Barbados . . .* (Barbados,
1741), 19.
[106] Peytraud, *L'Esclavage*, 143 ff., 158 ff., 208 ff.
[107] See Peytraud, *L'Esclavage*, 13-17; Gray, *Southern Agriculture*, I, 303-309;
Donnan, *Documents*, I, 92, 100, 108-111, 166, 197, 249 ff.; Vincent T. Harlow, *History
of Barbados 1625-1685* (Oxford, 1926), 42.

and had no consequences. The manumitted were free only to emigrate, if they could, or to hang about, hundreds of them "who have been out of their time for many years . . . [with] never a bit of fresh meat bestowed on them nor a dram of rum."[108] The process of extending the rights of servants, which on the mainland was the means of defining the status of the slave, never took place on the islands.

The term, slave, in the West Indies was at the start as vague as in Virginia and Maryland; and when toward mid-century it narrowed down to the plantation Negroes as sugar took hold through the stimulus of the Africa traders, it does not seem to have comprehended more than the presumption of indefinite service.[109] To Europeans, any service on the islands continued to be slavery. For whatever distinctions might be drawn among various groups of them, the slavish servants remained slavish servants. All labor was depressed, Negro and white, "domineered over and used like dogs." That undoubtedly affected emigration from the islands, the decline of white population, the relationships of Blacks and whites, the ultimate connotation of the term slave, the similarities in practice to villeinage, the savage treatment by masters and equally savage revolts against them, the impact of eighteenth-century humanitarianism, and the direction of emancipation.[110]

The distinctive qualities of the southern labor system were then not the simple products of the plantation. They were rather the complex outcome of a process by which the American environment broke down the traditional European conceptions of servitude. In that process the weight of the plantation had pinned down on the Negro the clearly-defined status of a chattel, a status left him as other elements in the population achieved their liberation. When, therefore, Southerners in the eighteenth century came to think of the nature of the rights of man they found it inconceivable

[108] Smith, *Colonists in Bondage,* 294.

[109] See Richard Ligon, *True & Exact History of the Island of Barbados . . .* (London, 1657), 43-47; [Charles C. de Rochefort], *History of the Caribby-Islands . . .*, translated by John Davies (London, 1666), 200 ff.

[110] Smith, *Colonists in Bondage,* 294. For examples of servant legislation, see *Acts of Barbadoes,* 22 ff., 80 ff., 145 ff., 150, 168, 204 ff. (1661-1703). See also Peytraud, *L'Esclavage,* 38, 135 ff.; Donnan, *Documents,* I, 97; Morris, *Government and Labor,* 503; Leslie, *New History of Jamaica,* 89, 148 ff.; Morgan Godwyn, *Negro's and Indian's Advocate* (London, 1680), 12 ff.; Frank W. Pitman, "Slavery on British West India Plantations in the Eigtheenth Century," *Journal of Negro History,* XI (1926), 610 ff., 617; William L. Mathieson, *British Slavery and Its Abolition, 1823-1838* (London, 1926), 44, 50 ff.

that Negroes should participate in those rights. It was more in accord with the whole social setting to argue that the slaves could not share those rights because they were not fully men, or at least different kinds of men. In fact, to the extent that Southerners ceased to think in terms of the seventeenth-century degrees of freedom, to the extent that they thought of liberty as whole, natural, and inalienable, they were forced to conclude that the slave was wholly unfree, wholly lacking in personality, wholly a chattel.

Only a few, like St. George Tucker and Thomas Jefferson, perceived that here were the roots of a horrible tragedy that would some day destroy them all.[111]

[111] See the eloquent discussion in Tucker's appendix to Blackstone, *Commentaries*, I, 35 ff.

The Origin and Nature of African Slavery in Seventeenth Century Maryland

WHITTINGTON B. JOHNSON

THE 1664 ACT IN MARYLAND WHICH ESTABLISHED DE JURE PRACTICES OF PER-petual slavery is one of the most frequently quoted slave laws, yet the context in which it is interpreted belies the true significance of the act and the reason why lawmakers in the colony passed it. Moreover, the nature of slavery in seventeenth-century Maryland differed discernibly from that of the ante-bellum period, yet too often in the past scholars have lumped practices of the colonial period with those of later periods without giving due recognition to their differences.

The legal development of slavery in Maryland has been ably chronicled by a number of scholars, the most recent being Winthrop Jordan who couched the development in an historical context and Jonathan Alpert who viewed it from a different but refreshing perspective, the legal, or lawyer's perspective.[1] This study will seek to answer some questions which were not raised in those studies, namely: Why was the 1664 Act passed? What took precedence, African indentures or the "durante vita" mandate of the 1664 Act? How restrictive were the slave laws in seventeenth-century Maryland? And what was the nature of miscegenation laws?

De facto slavery preceded laws legalizing the practice in the mainland colonies,[2] and Maryland was no exception. Andrew White, a Jesuit missionary who was among the original Maryland settlers, brought a mulatto named Matthias with him and later imported another mulatto, Francisco. Two more original settlers, the Wintour brothers Edward and Frederick, brought an African named John Price with them.[3] These servants may have been slaves, for in 1638 reference was made to slaves in an act of the legislature:

> Be it enacted by the lord proprietor of this province of and with advice and approbation of the freemen of the same that all persons being Christians (slaves excepted) of the age of eighteen years or above brought into this province at the charge and adventure of some other person shall serve such person . . . for the full term of four years . . . [4]

Two conclusions can be drawn from the language of this act, one being that slaves in the text refer to Africans, and perhaps, non-European persons, and the other being that no limit was attached to the length of time slaves could serve. Further evidence to support the contention that slaves were in Maryland at the time is gleaned from a contract in 1642 between John Skinner

Mr. Johnson is associate professor of history at the University of Miami (Fla.).

236

82

and Leonard Calvert, in which the former agreed to deliver to Calvert seventeen slaves, fourteen men and three women.[5] Evidently this transaction was never consummated, for the first notice of an African slave being sold in Maryland was not recorded until 1644.[6]

Reliance upon African slaves, as the chief source of labor, was not a part of the original plans for developing the colony's work force, as is evidenced by Lord Baltimore's instructions of 1635:

> In taking of servants he may do well to furnish himself with as many as he can, in useful and necessary arts: a carpenter, of all other the most necessary; a millwright, a ship-wright, boat-wright, wheel-wright, sawyer, smith, cutler, leather-dresser, miner, fisherman, and gardener. These will be of most use; but any lusty young able man that is willing to labour and take pains although he have no other particular trade will be beneficial enough to his master.[7]

These "lusty young men" were expected to populate manors and fit into an economic system closely approximating that of fifteenth century Europe, but the plan went awry. With so much land available, a disconcerting number of European servants refused to remain on these manors, escaping into the hinterlands and carving out homesteads of their own. Moreover, Marylanders shifted their commercial economic endeavors from growing wheat, corn and "other provisions" to growing tobacco. This shift in emphasis resulted in increasingly larger acreages of land being devoted to tobacco growing which in turn created an increase in demand for more laborers and longer terms of servitude. African laborers, thus became very desirable because Africans could be required to serve longer terms, female slaves could be employed in the fields, runaways were less successful among African slaves and payment of freedom dues could be avoided.[8]

Although the low fertility rate of female African slaves[9] and the slowness of the British merchant to enter the slave trade[10] kept the slave population relatively small for much of the century, African servants were visible in the colony and it was common practice for them to serve for life, as a perusal of inventories of probated estates reveals. The money value of Africans consistently exceeded that of European servants who had limited periods to serve,[11] and that at a time when Europeans brought high prices because of a shortage of their kind.

The highest value placed on any European servant was that of 2,600 pounds of tobacco which was placed on John Hayes by John Scotches in 1659, another European servant on the plantation being assessed at 1,600 pounds of tobacco.[12] A number of inventories valued European servants at 2,000 pounds of tobacco.[13] The inventory of Richard Smith's estate in February, 1662 listed "three men servants at 2,000 a piece," while that same year and month the inventory of William Palmer's estate listed "a Negro woman" at 3,000 pounds, and a 1662 inventory of an estate in Charles County placed the value of "a Negro man and his wife" at 5,500 pounds of tobacco.[14]

A second and better indicator that there were African servants who served for life prior to 1664 is obtained from inventories which listed the duration of time which servants had to serve. In 1658 an inventory of the estate of Cornelius Abraham listed two servants, one with "one crop to make" and the other with "two crops."[15] An inventory of the estate of Robert Taylor in April, 1661 listed three servants, two of whom had four years to serve, while the other had only three years.[16] The inventory of William Stowe in June, 1661 listed twelve servants with terms ranging from three months to 10 years; however, his two African servants, Philip and Margarett, did not have any time designation beside their names.[17] The inventory of the estate of John _____ in January, 1663 listed a manor servant "with four years [at] 2,000, two boys for about 3 years [at] 2,000 . . . 2 man negroes [at] 3,400, and a negro woman for which [is] now born a small negro girl, [at] 2,500."[18] The inventory below was taken after the 1664 Act, but it is consistent with earlier practices of listing servants. African servants have a higher value than European and the latter have duration of service designated, but the African servants do not.

Estate of Sarah Jordan   July 5, 1665

1 man servant having 1 year to serve	1000 (pounds of
1 youth 3 years to serve	1500 tobacco)
1 boy 9 years to serve	1800
1 maid 2 years to serve	900
1 maid 1 year to serve	500
1 Negro woman with a Negro child	4000

Source: Maryland Provincial Testamentary Proceedings, Volume I (1657–1666), p. 147 (in the fourth run of pages), Maryland Hall of Records.

The fact that "Negro servants" in the above inventories served for life obviated the need to designate the duration of their service.

The proof of life service for African servants prior to 1664 is evidenced in an act of 1663 entitled "An Act Concerning English Servants That Runaway in the Company of Negroes and Other Slaves." Not only does the term slave appear in the title of an act for the first time in Maryland but the text of the act clearly indicates that Africans served for life. The statement "divers English servants who runaway in company with Negroes and other slaves, . . . who are incapable of making satisfactory by addition of time"[19] can have no other meaning than that they served for life.

Since African slaves served for life, and evidently had been doing so for several decades without prompting legislation legalizing the practice, I doubt that it was that practice which prompted the 1664 Act; certainly nothing in the debates pertaining to the language of the act suggests that a compelling need to legalize slavery was uppermost in the minds of the lawmakers. Rather, judging from the amount of debate time consumed and the large space devoted to them in the act, the vexing problems of miscegenation and the children born of such unions were the primary reasons for the 1664 Act.[20] Understandably, since the lawmakers addressed the practice of service for life first, historians have stressed this and have ignored the key issues.

According to the act, Africans living in the colony and those imported subsequent to the act were to serve "Durante Vita." The thorny question, however, was the one posed by "divers freeborne English women" who:

To the disgrace of our nation do intermarry with Negro slaves by which also divers suits may arise touching the issue of such woman and a great damage doth befall the masters of such Negroes...

After heated debate the lawmakers agreed to enact legislation which they thought would be severe enough to deter such marriages in the future:

... whereof for deterring such freeborne women from such shameful matches be it further enacted that whatsoever free born woman shall intermarry with any slave from and after the last day of this present assembly shall serve the masters of such slave during the life of her husband and that all the issue of such freeborne woman shall be slaves as their fathers were...[21]

There remained the question of children born prior to the act's passage, which the lawmakers addressed by declaring that they "shall serve the masters of their parents till they be thirty years of age and no longer."[22]

The significance of the 1664 Act, therefore, is not the "durante vita" term, which certainly did not break any new ground in the practice of slavery in Maryland, but the inheritability aspect of slavery which the act introduced, for evidently prior to 1664 children of slaves did not inherit "durante vita" status. If this were so, the law would not have made the distinction in length of service given to pre-1664 Act children vis-a-vis post-1664 Act children.

I doubt if Maryland was the only colony that permitted interracial marriages between free females and slaves, but it was the first, and only colony, which tried to discourage the practice by decreeing slavery inheritable making children follow the status of their father. Moreover, the 1664 Act was less concerned about legalizing a practice—African slavery—that was almost as old as the colony itself than it was with discouraging a practice which was fairly new: the marriage of free English females to African slaves. It should be stressed that in 1664 it was the economic ramifications of miscegenation which worried leaders in the colony.[23]

Even while African slaves were being required to serve for life, a number of Africans were able to secure their freedom after serving only a short term. In 1653, John Babtiste, an African servant, petitioned the Provincial Court for his freedom, claiming that Simon Overzee, who brought him to the colony and subsequently sold him, could not sell him for life since his time of service was restricted by an oral agreement to a set number of years. Babtiste presented credible witnesses who corroborated his testimony and the Court ruled in his favor, ordering him to serve an additional two years after which he was to be freed.[24]

An interesting case reached the Provincial Court in 1676 when Thomas Hagleton petitioned that body for his freedom. Hagleton was an African who formerly lived in London, England, where he was baptized "into Christian faith" and later moved to Durham, England where he became a servant of William Jordan, a tobacco planter, who taught him the tobacco trade and had him converted to Catholicism.[25] After Jordan's death, Hagleton became a servant of one Margery Dutchesses "who consigned the petitioner to Thomas Kemp to serve the term of four years." Sometime in the early 1670s Kemp brought Hagleton to Maryland and indentured him to Major Thomas Truman under whom Hagleton was to serve the remainder of his term. But evidently Truman refused to abide by the agreement, keeping his African servant an additional twelve months before he appealed to the Provincial Court for relief. Hagleton, like Babtiste before him provided credible witnesses to corroborate his story[26] and the Court ruled in his favor.[27] Hagleton, who was assigned fifty acres which he transferred to a Samuel Goosey of Calvert County,[28] subsequently petitioned the Court to gain compensation for the twelve months due him from Truman for unilaterally extending his service, but his failure to follow through on his suit resulted in the 1683 session of the Court ordering that the case "be struck from . . . the dockett."[29]

In 1678, William Upton, another African, petitioned the Court for his release from servitude alleging that his contract with John Price called for a limited term of service, not durante vita. The Court ruled for Upton, ordering that he be given clothing and some corn.[30] And fifteen years later, in 1693, the Court heard the case of Ralph Trunckett who claimed that Gilbert Turberfield was keeping him illegally. Trunckett was born in Madagascar and was brought to England where he was converted to Christianity and "brought up in the Anglican Church." Trunckett claimed that he came to Maryland as a "self indentured servant of Captain Edward Prince" and not as a slave. After the death of Prince, Trunckett and the property of the Captain were inherited by Thomas Prince; his widow married Gilbert Turberfield, who assumed ownership of all her property. Trunckett followed the approach used earlier by Babtiste and Hagleton, with the same results.[31]

However, three other African servants who presented freedom petitions to the Court after the 1664 Act was passed were not successful in gaining their freedom. In its 1679–80 session the Court heard a petition from Charles Cabe but rejected it because he did not support his testimony with sufficient corroborative evidence.[32] In 1693, the Court heard the appeal of Joyce Gidding, a New England-born black, who claimed that her master, Thomas Brooks, did not acquire her service for life. Once again the Court ruled against the petitioner because of insufficient corroborative testimony.[33] A year later, the Court heard testimony of Tom Blanco, but found the evidence presented so untruthful that the sheriff was ordered to jail him and to give him a sound whipping.[34]

The findings in these petition cases show that "durante vita" legislation regarding African servants did not take precedence over the indentures and oral contracts which these servants made. To be sure, Africans did not receive, automatically, the protective umbrella of English common law, but whenever they could show that their servitude was based upon a contractual agreement, whites were obligated to abide by the indenture. The precedent established by these freedom petition cases resulted in a gap developing between the letter of the 1664 Act and its practice.

While the Provincial Court was busy throughout the period ruling on freedom petitions, the legislature was relatively inactive in the field of slave legislation throughout the 1670s and 1680s.[35] But all this changed during the 1690s, when the number of legislative enactments relating to slavery increased. The text of these acts reflects that the assembly had begun to develop a feel for legislating on slavery. Perhaps the most restrictive of the laws was the 1695 act requiring slaves to carry passes signed by either their master, or an overseer, whenever they left the plantation, even if traveling from one to another of their master's plantations. A slave caught off the plantation without a pass was to be punished, but not to the extent of maiming or killing.[36] While this act mirrors the subordinate position of the slave, it is quite apparent that masters did not have life-and-death powers over their African slaves.

Moreover, these masters could not treat their slaves cruelly. Failure to provide slaves with clothing, food and lodging could result in manumission,[37] and brutalizing them could result in criminal prosecution by the colonial government. Accordingly, in December, 1658, Simon Overzee was indicted for fatally beating his "African servant," Anthony. Testimony revealed that Anthony had been stubborn, obstreperous and a frequent runaway. This last charge weighed heavily in Overzee's favor, for running away was one of those infractions that colonists loathed with a passion. As a consequence, Overzee was acquitted after several lengthy court sessions.[38] The fact remains, however, that he was forced to stand trial for killing a slave. Thirty-four years later, a female slave was manumitted because her master cut off her ear,[39] which shows that pressure, albeit sporadic, was exerted on slaveowners to be humane to their slaves.

The manumission of the female slave stemmed from a 1692 act prohibiting masters, mistresses, dames, or overseers from dismembering or cauterizing slaves, the follow through of royal instructions of 1691 which directed governors that "you shall endeavor to get a law passed ... for the restraining of any inhumane severity which ill masters or overseers may use towards their Christian servants and their slaves."[40] Justices of the county courts were authorized to manumit "dismembered and cauterized" slaves. This act also stated that if masters denied "sufficient meat, drink, and clothing or shall unreasonably burden their servants or slaves beyond their strength with labor or deny them necessary sleep"[41] upon proof being presented to the justice of the county court, first and second offenders were fined; third offenders, though, were to lose the service of that slave or servant, he being declared free.[42] Moreover, the 1692 act released servants and slaves from chores on Sundays and holidays.[43]

Concomitant with the emergence of laws legalizing and regulating slavery, antimiscegenation laws and tariffs on slave immigrants were also enacted. During the seventeenth century slaves were permitted to marry other Africans, but racially exogamous marriages were discouraged. While the antimiscegenation laws of 1664 and 1681, were limited to African slaves and Europeans, later laws extended the ban to include free Africans and Europeans.[44]

These antimiscegnation laws were Maryland's first legal manifestation of English disdain for Africans:

And for as much as diverse free born English or white women sometimes by the instigation, procurement or connivance of their masters, mistresses or dames and always to the satisfaction of their lascivious and lustful desires, and to the disgrace not only of the English but also other Christian nations do intermarry with negroes and slaves . . .[45]

In succinct terms, the language of the law stated that European women who married Africans were a disgrace to whites everywhere. Although many Maryland slaveowners probably shared this negativism toward Africans,[46] it did not inhibit them from mating their male slaves with European female servants (slaves could not marry without their masters' permission). This course of action was probably forced upon slaveowners because there were so few African females in the colony with whom they could mate their slaves.[47] Since children of a union involving a slave followed the status of their father, the potential monetary gain from a male slave-European female union partially compensated for the revulsion which such unions probably occasioned among slaveowners.

Judging from the number of antimiscegenation laws passed during the last quarter of the seventeenth century, there must have been an increase in the number of interracial marriages, causing consternation among the provincial leadership. These laws were harsh, punishing affected masters, dames, ministers and magistrates, but not slaves and their white mates. The 1681 act quoted above awarded freedom to female European servants who married African slaves, in addition to fining their masters, but this did not stop the practice.[48] There were no laws prohibiting the marriage of free Africans to female slaves, but free Africans who married whites were forced into perpetual servitude, marking the first time that free Africans were enslaved for committing certain acts.[49] In view of the harshness of the punishment meted out to those involved in interracial marriages, racism had replaced economic consideration as the primary reason for enacting antimiscegenation laws.

The last quarter of the seventeenth century also witnessed a significant increase in Maryland's slave population, the majority of which resulted from the slave trade, but there were no legislative attempts to curb this traffic. The chart below shows that the estimated African population in Maryland increased from twenty, or 3.4 percent of the total population in 1640, to 3,227 or 10.9 percent in 1700, which means that during this period the rate of increase of the African population was three times that of the white. Such a pattern reflects the transition of Maryland's economy away from the fairly small, subsistence-style family farms toward the later specialized tobacco plantations worked by slave labor.

Subsequently, the colony attempted to exploit this increase in slave importation by enacting a ten shilling revenue tariff in 1695, payable by the seller within three months after the slave entered the colony.[50] In 1696 and again in 1699, the duty was increased to twenty shillings, payable at the port upon entry of the slave.[51] This marked the end of slave legislation for the seventeenth century.

By the end of the seventeenth century the legal system embracing slavery in Maryland (evolving from earlier de facto practices) consisted of a few laws which legalized slavery by making it inheritable, declared that conversion to

ESTIMATED POPULATION OF MARYLAND 1640-1700

- -	1640	1650	1660	1670	1680	1690	1700
White and African	583	4504	8426	13226	17904	24024	29604
African	20	300	758	1190	1611	2162	3227

Source: *United States Bureau of the Census Historical Statistics of the United States: Colonial Times to 1957* (Washington D.C., 1960), p. 756.

Christianity did not lead to automatic manumission,[52] and restricted the movement of slaves. Tangential laws banned racially exogamous marriages and placed a revenue raising impost on slave immigrants. This was the extent of the slave legal system.

Under the system, slaves were chattels real, the same status held by European servants. According to English law, chattels real were attached to the land, and could not be separated from it; this was not the case with chattels personal.[53] Further, English law accorded the master a right only to his servant's services.[54] The American experience modified English law somewhat by permitting the slave to be detached from the land, but safeguards surrounding the slave's person were retained.

From the standpoint of laws in the books, the slave system practiced in Maryland during the seventeenth century lacked much of the comprehensiveness associated with the "peculiar institution" of the antebellum period. For instance, there were no laws denying slaves the right to testify in court against whites. In freedom petitions, defendants were always white, yet Africans were permitted to state their cases and present witnesses in their behalf. There were no laws defining the legal status of African slaves; depending on the situation, they might be persons, property or both. If we are to be guided by the freedom petitions, once again, slaves were persons, by virtue of the fact that they could be legal partners in a contract and sue in court to redress grievances.

There were some distinct differences, however, between African slaves and European servants, notwithstanding the fact that the term slave and servant were used interchangeably in the vernacular. By 1700, in Maryland the slave was an African who served "durante vita," with the children inheriting the status of their father. European servants, on the other hand, served short terms and their status was not inheritable.

Perhaps this study has demonstrated a need to reexamine the early slave laws in the other colonies to determine if giving de jure status to perpetual servitude was the intent behind the enactment of these laws. Or were they passed to resolve perplexing problems which were created by the presence of African slaves among them? At least the 1664 Act can now be seen in a different and more meaningful perspective as it related to a contemporary seventeenth century problem. It would be interesting, also, to ascertain whether slaves in other colonies were able to gain freedom through the courts (freedom petitions). The irony here is that freedom petitions very well could have established a precedent for Afro-Americans, for historically they have had to petition the court to secure rights as first class citizens. Could freedom petitions be viewed as the first chapter in this long struggle?

Indeed, African slavery in seventeenth century Maryland marks a fruitful beginning point from which to examine the practice of slavery and racial attitudes in other colonies, and during other periods.

REFERENCES

1. Winthrop Jordan, "Modern Tension and the Origins of American Slavery," *Journal of Southern History*, 28 (February, 1962): 18–30; Winthrop Jordan, *White Over Black: American Attitudes Toward the Negro, 1559–1812* (Chapel Hill, North Carolina, 1968), 71–82; Jonathan L. Alpert, "The Origin of Slavery in the United States—The Maryland Precedent," *The American Journal of Legal History*, 14 (1970): 189–221. Alpert contends that, "Although other factors were significant, the heart of early slavery was contractual" (p. 220).
2. In some instances the first slave laws passed in colonies were those designed to abolish slavery. Georgia and Rhode Island abolished slavery, as did New Jersey, although less categorically and New York and Massachusetts stipulated what types of slavery could be introduced. William M. Wiecik, "The Statutory Law of Slavery and Race in the Thirteen Mainland Colonies of British America," *William and Mary Quarterly*, 34 (April, 1977): 260.
3. Ross M. Kimmel, "The Negro Before the Law in Seventeenth Century Maryland," (M.A. Thesis, University of Maryland, 1971), p. 25.
4. *Archives of Maryland*, 70 vols. (Baltimore, 1883–1964), I: 41. Since the act did not identify the racial origin of these slaves, conceivably Indians as well as Africans could have been included under the term. Matthew P. Andrews, *History of Maryland Province and State* (New York, 1929), 21; Jonathan L. Alpert, "The Origin of Slavery in the United States," p. 191.
5. *Archives of Maryland*, IV, 189.
6. Helen Catterall, *Judicial Cases Concerning American Slavery and the Negro*, 5 vols., (Washington, D.C., 1936), IV: 8.
7. Clayton C. Hall (ed.), *Narratives of Early Maryland 1633–1684* (New York, 1910), pp. 98–99; Eugene I. McCormac, *White Servitude in Maryland, 1634–1820* (Baltimore, 1904).
8. Lewis C. Gray, *History of Agriculture in the Southern States to 1860*, 2 vols. (New York, 1941), I; 39–40, 350, 364, 370–71.
9. Russell R. Menard, "The Maryland Slave Population 1658 to 1730: A Demographic Profile of Blacks in Four Counties," *William and Mary Quarterly*, 32 (January, 1975): 33, 39. There were other long run economic advantages which offset the demographic factor of almost a zero (natural) population growth.
10. Gray, *History of Southern Agriculture*, I: 352–53.
11. Carl Degler, "Slavery and the Genesis of American Race Prejudice," *Comparative Studies in Society and History*, 2, (1959): 59; Jordan, "Modern Tensions," p. 25.
12. Maryland Provincial Testamentary Proceedings, Vols. I (1657–1666), 64 (1659), Maryland Hall of Records.
13. Provincial Testamentary Proceedings, I: 22, 32, 80 (in the third run of numbered pages).
14. Provincial Testamentary Proceedings, I: 136, 66, 85 (in the third run of numbered pages).
15. Provincial Testamentary Proceedings, I: 43 (1658).
16. Provincial Testamentary Proceedings, I: 48 (in the second run of numbered pages).
17. Provincial Testamentary Proceedings, I: 24 (in the second run of numbered pages).
18. Provincial Testamentary Proceedings, I: 141 (in the third run of numbered pages). The first name is illegible.
19. *Archives of Maryland*, 66: 291.
20. *Archives of Maryland*, 1: 526–27; Carter G. Woodson, "The Beginnings of the Miscegenation of Whites and Blacks," *Journal of Negro History*, III (October, 1918): 339.
21. *Archives of Maryland*, I: 533.
22. *Ibid.*
23. Oscar and Mary F. Handlin, "Origins of the Southern Labor System," *William and Mary Quarterly*, 7 (1950): 215–16.
24. *Archives of Maryland*, 40: 499.
25. Maryland Provincial Deeds, Liber W. R. C. #1 (1676–1699), 88 Maryland Hall of Records.
26. *Archives of Maryland; Proceedings of the Provincial Court*, 1675–1677, 66: 291.

27. *Archives of Maryland*, 67: 46.
28. Maryland Provincial Patents, Liber 15, pt. 2, 391 Maryland Hall of Records.
29. Maryland Provincial Chancery Court Record, Liber C.D. 1668-1671, pp. 196, 199, 307, Maryland Hall of Records; Maryland Provincial Court Judgments, Liber W.C. (1679-1684) pt. 2, 700, 828, Maryland Hall of Records.
30. *Archives of Maryland*, 69: 122.
31. Provincial Court Judgments D.S.C. (1692-1693), pp. 162-64, Maryland Hall of Records; Kimmel, "The Negro and the Law in the Seventeenth Century Maryland," 59 ff.
32. *Archives of Maryland*, 65: 19.
33. Provincial Court Judgments D.S.C. (1592-1693), 361-362, Maryland Hall of Records.
34. Kent County Court Proceedings, Liber I (1676-1698), pt. 2, Maryland Hall of Records.
35. For the next decade, or two, most of the legislation surrounding slavery enacted by the assembly focused upon miscegenation. See *Archives of Maryland*, 38: 48-49; also Jeffrey Brackett, *The Negro in Maryland* (Baltimore, 1889), p. 104.
36. *Archives in Maryland*, 38: 51-52.
37. *Archives in Maryland*, 12: 203-208, 552, 544-549.
38. *Archives in Maryland*, 41: 190.
39. *Archives in Maryland*, 12: 425-426.
40. Leonard W. Labaree, *Royal Instructions to British Colonial Governors*, 1670-1776, 2 vols. (New York, 1935), II: 507.
41. *Archives of Maryland*, 13: 425-426.
42. *Ibid.*
43. *Archives of Maryland*, 38: 48-49.
44. *Archives of Maryland*, 102: 304-05; 12: 552; 13: 544-49.
45. *Archives of Maryland*, 102: 203-05.
46. Jordan, *White Over Black*, p. 7; Degler, "Slavery and Race Prejudice," p. 62.
47. Adult male slaves outnumbered their female counterparts by about one and one-half to one, this disparity being most pronounced late in the seventeenth century. Russell, "The Maryland Slave Population, 1658 to 1730," p. 39.
48. *Archives of Maryland*, 7: 203-05; This suggests that masters were exploiting the situation. Handlin, "Origins of the Southern Labor System," p. 213.
49. Alpert, "The Origins of Slavery in the United States," p. 211.
50. *Archives of Maryland*, 38: 51-52.
51. *Ibid.*, p. 81.; 22: 497.
52. *Archives of Maryland*, 54: 279.
53. William Blackstone, *Commentaries on the Laws of England*, 4 vols. (London, 1765-1769), Bk. II, 386. According to English law of the period, chattels were divided into two types, real and personal. Chattel real was so designated because it was annexed to real estate (which had both permanence and immobility) and had one quality, immobility. Servants, villeins and slaves were classed in this category because the lord could not dispossess them of their holdings. Chattels personal had neither immobility nor permanence: animals, household goods, jewelry, money, garments and the like were classed in this category. Accordingly, English law made a distinction between servant and animal.
54. Eugene Sirmans, "The Legal Status of the Slave in South Carolina, 1670-1740," *Journal of Southern History*, 28 (1962): 464.

American Chiaroscuro:
The Status and Definition of Mulattoes
in the British Colonies

Winthrop D. Jordan*

THE word *mulatto* is not frequently used in the United States. Americans generally reserve it for biological contexts, because for social purposes a mulatto is termed a *Negro*. Americans lump together both socially and legally all persons with perceptible admixture of Negro ancestry, thus making social definition without reference to genetic logic; white blood becomes socially advantageous only in overwhelming proportion. The dynamic underlying the peculiar bifurcation of American society into only two color groups can perhaps be better understood if some attempt is made to describe its origin, for the content of social definitions may remain long after the impulses to their formation have gone.

After only one generation of European experience in America, colonists faced the problem of dealing with racially mixed offspring, a problem handled rather differently by the several nations involved. It is well known that the Latin countries, especially Portugal and Spain, rapidly developed a social hierarchy structured according to degrees of intermixture of Negro and European blood, complete with a complicated system of terminology to facilitate definition.[1] The English in Maryland, Virginia, and the Carolinas, on the other hand, seem to have created no such system of ranking. To explain this difference merely by comparing the different cultural backgrounds involved is to risk extending generalizations far beyond possible factual support. Study is still needed of the specific factors affecting each nation's colonies, for there is evidence with some nations that the same cultural heritage was spent in different ways by the colonial heirs,

---

* Mr. Jordan is a Fellow at the Institute of Early American History and Culture at Williamsburg, Virginia. An abbreviated version of this article was delivered at the annual meeting of the Southern Historical Association, Chattanooga, Nov. 11, 1961.

[1] See, for example, Irene Diggs, "Color in Colonial Spanish America," *Journal of Negro History*, XXXVIII (1953), 403-427.

depending on varying conditions encountered in the New World. The English, for example, encountered the problem of race mixture in very different contexts in their several colonies; they answered it in one fashion in their West Indian islands and in quite another in their colonies on the continent.

As far as the continental colonies were concerned, the presence of mulattoes received legislative recognition by the latter part of the seventeenth century. The word itself, borrowed from the Spanish, was in English usage from the beginning of the century and was probably first employed in Virginia in 1666. From about that time, laws dealing with Negro slaves began to add "and mulattoes." In all English continental colonies mulattoes were lumped with Negroes in the slave codes and in statutes governing the conduct of free Negroes:[2] the law was clear that

[2] These statements are based on an examination of what I believe to be nearly all the colonial and state statutes concerning Negroes and slaves through 1807. For the use of *mulatto* see the *Oxford English Dictionary* and the private petition to the Virginia Assembly in "The Randolph Manuscript," *Virginia Magazine of History and Biography,* XVII (1909), 232. The word was first used in a statute in 1678: William Hand Browne and others, eds., *Archives of Maryland* (Baltimore, 1883——), VII, 76. Maryland actually created a legally separate class of persons known as "Mulattoes born of white women," and in doing so developed a severe case of legislative stuttering. The difficulty originated in 1664 when the Assembly declared that children were to follow the condition of the father (rather than the mother as in other colonies). It took 35 years to straighten out this matter, but meanwhile some provision had to be made for mulatto children of white mothers, for no one really wanted them to be slaves. The Assembly provided that they should serve until age 31. This group was sometimes treated legally as white and sometimes as Negro, a procedure which seems to have been followed only about through the 1730's. (Virginia in 1691 enacted similar provisions for this class, but apparently abandoned them five years later.) The underlying intention was that mulatto children of white mothers should be free in status, though punished for their illegitimate origin. This was not discrimination between mulattoes and Negroes but between mulattoes of two different kinds of mothers, white and black. The legal confusion and inconsistencies on this matter may be followed in Browne and others, eds., *Archives of Md.,* I, 526-527, 533-534; VII, 176, 177, 203-205; XIII, 290, 292, 304, 306-307, 308, 323, 380, 394, 529, 546-549; XIX, 428; XXII, 551-552; XXVI, 254-261; XXX, 289-290; XXXIII, 111-112; XXXVI, 275-276; XXXVIII, 39; William Kilty, ed., *The Laws of Maryland* (Annapolis, 1799-1800), II, chap. 67, sec. 14. None of the standard secondary sources on the Negro in Maryland offer a satisfactory account of this matter. For Virginia, see William Waller Hening, ed., *The Statutes at Large: Being a Collection of All the Laws of Virginia . . .* (New York, Philadelphia, Richmond, 1819-23), II, 170; III, 87, 137-140, 252. A Virginia militia act of 1777 declared that free mulattoes might serve as "drummers, fifers, or pioneers" (Hening, ed., *Statutes of Va.,* V, 268), but this failure to refer to "negroes and mulattoes" was so unusual that one must suspect inadvertent omission. See also a clear case of such omission in Massachusetts: George H. Moore, *Notes on the History of Slavery in Massachusetts* (New York, 1866), 228-237.

mulattoes and Negroes were not to be distinguished for different treatment —a phenomenon occasionally noted by foreign travelers.[3]

If mulattoes were to be considered Negroes, logic required some definition of mulattoes, some demarcation between them and white men. Law is sometimes less than logical, however, and throughout the colonial period only Virginia and North Carolina grappled with the question raised by continuing intermixture. In 1705 the Virginia legislature defined a mulatto as "the child, grand child, or great grand child of a negro," or, revealingly, merely "the child of an Indian." North Carolina wavered on the matter, but generally pushed the taint of Negro ancestry from one-eighth to one-sixteenth.[4] There is no reason to suppose that these two colonies were atypical, and in all probability something like these rules operated in the other continental colonies. What the matter came down to, of course, was visibility. Anyone whose appearance discernibly connected him with the Negro was held to be such. The line was thus drawn with regard to practicalities rather than logic. Daily practice supplied logic enough.

Another indication of the refusal of the English continental colonies to separate the "mixed breed" from the African was the absence of terminology which could be used to define a hierarchy of status. The colonists did, it is true, seize upon a separate word to describe those of mixed blood. They were forced to do so if they were to deal with the problem at all, even if they merely wished, as they did, to lump "mulattoes" with Negroes. If, however, an infusion of white blood had been regarded as elevating status, then presumably the more white blood the higher the social rank. Had such ranking existed, descriptive terminology would have been required with which to handle shades of distinction. Yet no such vocabulary developed in the American colonies. Only one word besides *mulatto* was used to describe those of mixed ancestry. The term *mustee (mestee, mustize,*

[3] Duc de La Rochefoucault Liancourt, *Travels through the United States of North America . . .* (London, 1799), I, 568; Kenneth and Anna M. Roberts, trans., *Moreau de St. Méry's American Journey, 1793-1798* (Garden City, N. Y., 1947), 301-302.

[4] Hening, ed., *Statutes of Va.,* III, 252; Walter L. Clark, ed., *The State Records of North Carolina* (Goldsboro, N. C., 1886-1910), XXIII, 106, 160, 262, 345, 526, 559, 700, 882; XXIV, 61; XXV, 283, 445; William L. Saunders, ed., *The Colonial Records of North Carolina* (Raleigh, 1886-90), VII, 605, 608, 645. In 1785-87 Virginia altered the definition to one-quarter Negro, but there was no general trend in this direction during the 19th century; see Hening, ed., *Statutes of Va.,* XII, 184; Samuel Shepard, ed., *The Statutes at Large of Virginia, from October Session 1792, to December Session 1806, Inclusive,* New Ser., being a continuation of Hening (Richmond, 1835-36), I, 123.

mestizo, mustizoe) was used to describe a mixture which was in part Indian, usually Indian-Negro but occasionally Indian-white. The term was in common use only in the Carolinas, Georgia, and to some extent New York, that is, in those colonies where such crosses occurred with some frequency. Its use revealed the colonists' refusal to identify Indians and Negroes as the same sort of people, a refusal underlined by their belief that the two groups possessed a natural antipathy for each other.[5] Yet while the colonists thus distinguished persons of some Indian ancestry by a separate word, they lumped these *mustees* with mulattoes and Negroes in their slave codes.

Although legislative enactments provide a valuable index of community sentiment, they do not always accurately reflect social practice. An extensive search in the appropriate sources—diaries, letters, travel accounts, newspapers, and so on—fails to reveal any pronounced tendency to distinguish mulattoes from Negroes, any feeling that their status was higher and demanded different treatment. The sources give no indication, for instance, that mulattoes were preferred as house servants or concubines. There may well have been a relatively high proportion of mulattoes among manumitted slaves, but this was probably due to the not unnatural desire of some masters to liberate their own offspring. Yet all this is largely negative evidence, and the proposition that mulattoes were not accorded higher status than Negroes is as susceptible of proof as any negative. Perhaps the usual procedure of awaiting disproof through positive evidence may be allowed.

A single exception to these generalizations stands out sharply from the mass of colonial legislation. In 1765 the colony of Georgia not only undertook to encourage immigration of free colored persons (itself a unique

[5] See, for example, Hugh Jones, *The Present State of Virginia from Whence Is Inferred a Short View of Maryland and North Carolina,* ed. Richard L. Morton (Chapel Hill, 1956), 50; John Brickell, *The Natural History of North-Carolina . . .* (Dublin, 1737), 263, 273; Anne Grant, *Memoirs of an American Lady; With Sketches of Manners and Scenes in America as They Existed Previous to the Revolution,* ed. James G. Wilson (New York, 1901), I, 134; [George Milligen-Johnston], *A Short Description of the Province of South-Carolina* (London, 1770), in Chapman J. Milling, ed., *Colonial South Carolina; Two Contemporary Descriptions by Governor James Glen and Doctor George Milligen-Johnston,* South Caroliniana, Sesquicentennial Series, No. 1 (Columbia, 1951), 136; Parish Transcripts, Box III, bundle: Minutes of Council in Assembly (1755), 3, New-York Historical Society, New York City. See also Kenneth W. Porter, "Relations between Negroes and Indians within the Present Limits of the United States," *Jour. of Negro Hist.,* XVII (1932), 298-306, 322-327.

step) but actually provided that free mulatto and mustee immigrants might be naturalized as white men by the legislature, complete with "all the Rights, Priviledges, Powers and Immunities whatsoever which any person born of British parents" could have, except the right to vote and sit in the Commons House of Assembly.[6] Thus a begrudging kind of citizenship was extended to free mulattoes. That Georgia should so distinguish herself from her northern neighbors was a measure of the colony's weak and exposed condition. A small population with an increasingly high proportion of slaves and perpetual danger from powerful Indian tribes made Georgians eager for men who might be counted as white and thus strengthen the colony. The legislature went to great lengths in its search —perhaps too far, for it never actually naturalized anyone under the aegis of the 1765 law.

Only rarely in the colonial period did the subject of mulattoes receive any attention from American writers. Mulattoes were so fixed in station that their position apparently did not merit attention. The subject did come up once in the *South-Carolina Gazette,* yet even then it was casually raised in connection with an entirely different topic. An anonymous contributor in 1735 offered the public some strictures on Carolina's *nouveau riche,* the "half Gentry," and attacked especially their imitative and snobbish behavior. For illustration he turned to the character of the mulatto.

It is observed concerning the Generation of *Molattoes,* that they are seldom well beloved either by the Whites or the Blacks. Their Approach towards Whiteness, makes them look back with some kind of Scorn upon the Colour they seem to have left, while the Negroes, who do not think them better than themselves, return their Contempt with Interest: And the Whites, who respect them no Whit the more for the nearer Affinity in Colour, are apt to regard their Behaviour as too bold and assuming, and bordering upon Impudence. As they are next to Negroes, and but just above them, they are terribly afraid of being thought Negroes, and therefore avoid as much as possible their Company or Commerce: and Whitefolks are as little fond of the Company of *Molattoes.*[7]

---

[6] Allen D. Candler, comp., *The Colonial Records of the State of Georgia* (Atlanta, 1904-16), XVIII, 659. The wording of the act is ambiguous, and though free Negroes might have fallen under its provisions, the legislature was apparently thinking only of mulattoes and mustees.

[7] *South-Carolina Gazette* (Charleston), Mar. 22, 1735.

The writer's point, of course, was not that mulattoes were in fact superior to Negroes, but that they alone thought they were. Apparently mulattoes thought white blood to be a source of elevation, a proposition which whites (and Negroes as well) were quick to deny. White blood secured one's status only if undiluted.

A somewhat different aspect of this problem came up in 1784 when it was forced on the attention of a Savannah merchant, Joseph Clay. As executor of a will Clay became responsible for the welfare of two young mulattoes, very possibly the children of his deceased friend. Because the young people were both free, Clay's letter to a gentleman in Ireland offers valuable evidence of what a combination of personal freedom and some white ancestry afforded in the way of social position in Georgia. "These young Folks are very unfortunately situated in this Country," Clay wrote, "their descent places them in the most disadvantageous situation, as Free persons the Laws protects them—but they gain no rank in Life White Persons do not commonly associate with them on a footing of equality— so many of their own Colour (say the mixt breed) being Slaves, they too naturally fall in with them, and even the Negro Slaves claim a right to their acquaintance and Society." For Clay the situation was one of unrelieved gloom, even of horror: "thus a little reflection will present to you what their future Prospects here must be—neglected by the most respectable Class of Society, [they] are forced to intermix with the lowest, and in what that must end—we woud wish to draw a Veil—all the Care that can be taken of them cant prevent it, it arrises from our peculiar situation in regard to these people." Clay went on to recommend as "the most eligible plan" that the children be sent to Europe if his correspondent would accept them as wards. "The Boy might be Bound to some business . . . and the Girl might make a very good Wife to some honest Tradesman." It was essential that they cross the Atlantic: "this alone can save them . . . I think they might both be made usefull Members of Society no such distinctions interfere with their happiness on your side the Water."[8] Clay added finally that several of his friends endorsed his proposal. Apparently America offered little opportunity for blacks to become whites through intermixture. American society, wedded as it was to

---

[8] Joseph Clay to John Wright, Savannah, Feb. 17, 1784, in *Letters of Joseph Clay, Merchant of Savannah, 1776-1793* . . . (Georgia Historical Society, *Collections,* VIII [1913]), 203-204. Further testimony that mulattoes considered themselves superior to Negroes may be found in William Logan to Lord Granville, London, Aug. 13, 1761, Logan Papers, XI, 60, Historical Society of Pennsylvania, Philadelphia.

Negro slavery, drew a rigid line which did not exist in Europe: this was indeed "our peculiar situation in regard to these people."

The existence of a rigid barrier between whites and those of Negro blood necessarily required a means by which the barrier could on occasion be passed. Some accommodation had to be made for those persons with so little Negro blood that they appeared to be white, for one simply could not go around calling apparently white persons Negroes. Once the stain was washed out visibly it was useless as a means of identification. Thus there developed the silent mechanism of "passing." Such a device would have been unnecessary if those of mixed ancestry and appearance had been regarded as midway between white and black. It was the existence of a broad chasm which necessitated the sudden leap which passing represented.

Fortunately it is possible to catch a glimpse of this process as it operated in the colonial period by following the extraordinary career of a family named Gibson in South Carolina. In 1731 a member of the Commons House of Assembly announced in the chamber that several free colored men with their white wives had immigrated from Virginia with the intention of settling on the Santee River. Free Negroes were undesirable enough, but white wives made the case exceptionally disturbing. "The house apprehending [this prospect] to be of ill Consequence to this Province," appointed a committee to inquire into the matter. Governor Robert Johnson had already sent for what seemed to be the several families involved, and the committee asked him to report his findings to the house.

"The people lately come into the Settlements having been sent for," Johnson duly reported, "I have had them before me in Council and upon Examination find that they are not Negroes nor Slaves but Free people, That the Father of them here is named Gideon Gibson and his Father was also free, I have been informed by a person who has lived in Virginia that this Gibson has lived there Several Years in good Repute and by his papers that he has produced before me that his transactions there have been very regular, That he has for several years paid Taxes for two tracts of Land and had seven Negroes of his own, That he is a Carpenter by Trade and is come hither for the support of his Family." This evident respectability so impressed the governor that he allowed the Gibson family to remain in the colony. "The account he has given of himself," Johnson declared, "is so Satisfactory that he is no Vagabond that I have in Con-

sideration of his Wifes being a white woman and several White women
Capable of working and being Serviceable in the Country permitted him
to Settle in this Country upon entering into Recognizance for his good
behaviour which I have taken accordingly."[9]

The meaning of Johnson's statement that "they are not Negroes nor
Slaves but Free people" is not entirely clear. Certainly Gideon Gibson
himself was colored; it seems likely that he was mulatto rather than
Negro, but it is impossible to tell surely. At any rate Gideon Gibson
prospered very nicely: by 1736 either he or a son of the same name owned
450 acres of Carolina land. He continued to own Negroes, and in 1757
he was described as owning property in two widely separated counties. By
1765 the status of Gideon Gibson (by this time definitely the son of the
original carpenter) was such that he was appointed administrator of an
estate.[10] His sister married a wealthy planter, and there is no evidence to
indicate that Gibson himself was regarded by his neighbors as anything
but white.[11] In 1768 he was leading a band of South Carolina Regulators
on the field of battle. The commander dispatched to arrest Gibson was a
planter and colonel in the militia, George Gabriel Powell, who ignomini-
ously resigned his commission when his men sided with the Regulators.
This latter worthy, apparently a kind master to his own Negroes, sought
vindication by attacking Gibson's ancestry.[12] The exact nature of the attack is unclear, but the matter came up on the floor of the Commons, of
which Powell was a member. The prominent merchant-patriot of Charles

[9] Parish Transcripts, Box II, bundle: S. C., Minutes of House of Burgesses
(1730-35), 9.

[10] *South-Carolina Gazette*, Aug. 29, 1743, supplement; Nov. 26, Dec. 10, 1750;
Mar. 3, 1757, supplement; "Abstracts of Records of the Proceedings in the Court of
Ordinary, 1764-1771," *South Carolina Historical and Genealogical Magazine*, XXII
(1921), 97, 127; see also XXIII (1922), 35; [Prince Frederick Parish], *The Register
Book for the Parish Prince Frederick, Winyaw* (Baltimore, 1916), 15, 20, 32, 34.

[11] For this point I am indebted to Dr. Richard M. Brown, of Rutgers University,
who is currently publishing a study of the South Carolina Regulators. He also provided information and references on the younger Gideon Gibson's regulating activities and kindly pointed out to me a useful local history: Alexander Gregg, *History
of the Old Cheraws* [2d ed.] (Columbia, 1905). See this source, 72n, for the marriage of Gibson's sister.

[12] For the Regulators' battle, see Gregg, *Old Cheraws*, 73-74, 139-156; Charles
Woodmason, *The Carolina Backcountry on the Eve of the Revolution; The Journal
and Other Writings of Charles Woodmason, Anglican Itinerant*, ed. Richard J.
Hooker (Chapel Hill, 1953), 176-177. For biographical information on Powell and
his kindness to his slaves, A. S. Salley, ed., "Diary of William Dillwyn during a
Visit to Charles Town in 1772," *S. C. Hist. and Genea. Mag.*, XXXVI (1935), 35,
and n.

Town, Henry Laurens, recorded the conflict in a letter written some years later. Laurens was writing from England of his own conviction that slavery ought to be brought to an end, a conviction that inevitably raised the question of color.

Reasoning from the colour carries no conviction. By perseverance the black may be blanched and the "stamp of Providence" effectually effaced. Gideon Gibson escaped the penalties of the negro law by producing upon comparison more red and white in his face than could be discovered in the faces of half the descendants of the French refugees in our House of Assembly, including your old acquaintance the Speaker. I challenged them all to the trial. The children of this same Gideon, having passed through another stage of whitewash were of fairer complexion than their prosecutor George Gabriel [Powell].—But to confine them to their original clothing will be best. They may and ought to continue a separate people, may be subjected by special laws, kept harmless, made useful and freed from the tyranny and arbitrary power of individuals; but as I have already said, this difficulty cannot be removed by arguments on this side of the water.[13]

Laurens showed both sides of the coin. He defended an individual's white status on the basis of appearance and at the same time expressed the conviction that colored persons "may and ought to continue a separate people." Once an Ethiopian always an Ethiopian, unless he could indeed change his skin.

Gideon Gibson's successful hurdling of the barrier was no doubt an unusual case; it is of course impossible to tell how unusual. Passing was difficult but not impossible, and it stood as a veiled, unrecognized monument to the American ideal of a society open to all comers. One Virginia planter advertised in the newspaper for his runaway mulatto slave who he stated might try to pass for free or as a "white man." An English traveler reported calling upon a Virginia lawyer who was "said to be" and who looked like a mulatto.[14] But the problem of evidence is insurmountable. The success of the passing mechanism depended upon its operating in silence. Passing was a conspiracy of silence not only for the individual

[13] Henry Laurens to William Drayton, Feb. 15, 1783, in David Duncan Wallace, *The Life of Henry Laurens; With a Sketch of the Life of Lieutenant-Colonel John Laurens* (New York and London, 1915), 454. The speaker was Peter Manigault.

[14] Rind, *Virginia Gazette* (Williamsburg), Apr. 23, 1772; J[ohn] F. D. Smyth, *A Tour in the United States of America: Containing an Account of the Present Situation of that Country* ... (London, 1784), I, 123.

but for a biracial society which had drawn a rigid color line based on visibility. Unless a white man was a white man, the gates were open to endless slander and confusion.

That the existence of such a line in the continental colonies was not predominantly the effect of the English cultural heritage is suggested by even a glance at the English colonies in the Caribbean. The social accommodation of racial intermixture in the islands followed a different pattern from that on the continent. It was regarded as improper, for example, to work mulattoes in the fields—a fundamental distinction. Apparently they were preferred as tradesmen, house servants, and especially as concubines.[15] John Luffman wrote that mulatto slaves "fetch a lower price than blacks, unless they are tradesmen, because the purchasers cannot employ them in the drudgeries to which negroes are put too; the colored men, are therefore mostly brought up to trades or employed as house slaves, and the women of this description are generally prostitutes."[16] Though the English in the Caribbean thought of their society in terms of white, colored, and black, they employed a complicated battery of names to distinguish persons of various racial mixtures. This terminology was borrowed from the neighboring Spanish, but words are not acquired unless they fulfill a need. While the English settlers on the continent borrowed one Spanish word to describe all mixtures of black and white, the islanders borrowed at least four—*mulatto, sambo, quadroon,* and *mestize*—to describe differing degrees.[17] And some West Indians were

---

[15] [Thomas Tryon], *Friendly Advice to the Gentlemen-Planters of the East and West Indies* ([London], 1684), 140-141; John Singleton, *A General Description of the West-Indian Islands, as far as Relates to the British, Dutch, and Danish Governments* . . . (Barbados, 1767), 152-153; [Janet Schaw], *Journal of a Lady of Quality; Being the Narrative of a Journey to the West Indies, North Carolina, and Portugal, in the Years 1774 to 1776,* ed. Evangeline Walker Andrews, in collaboration with Charles M. Andrews, 3d ed. (New Haven, 1939), 112; [Edward Long], *The History of Jamaica* . . . (London, 1774), II, 328-330, 332-335; William Beckford, *A Descriptive Account of the Island of Jamaica* (London, 1790), II, 322; Bryan Edwards, *The History, Civil and Commercial, of the British Colonies in the West Indies,* 3d ed. (London, 1801), II, 18-31. The only place in the United States ever to develop an established institution of mulatto concubinage was New Orleans, where the influence of the Spanish and of French refugees from the West Indies was strong.

[16] John Luffman, *A Brief Account of the Island of Antigua, together with the Customs and Manners of its Inhabitants, as Well White as Black* (London, 1789), 115.

[17] *Mulatto* meant one-half white; *sambo,* one-fourth white; *quadroon,* three-fourths white; and *mestize* (which did not imply Indian mixture as it did on the continent), seven-eighths white. Long, *Jamaica,* II, 260-261; Edwards, *History,* II, 18; J[ohn] G. Stedman, *Narrative of a Five Years' Expedition, against the Revolted*

prepared to act upon the logic which these terms implied. The respected Jamaican historian, Bryan Edwards, actually proposed extension of civil privileges to mulattoes in proportion to their admixture of white blood.[18] Such a proposition was unheard of on the continent.

The difference between the two regions on this matter may well have been connected with another pronounced divergence in social practice. The attitude toward interracial sex was far more genial in the islands than in the continental colonies. In the latter, miscegenation very rarely met with anything but disapproval in principle, no matter how avid the practice. Sexual intimacy between any white person and any Negro (that "unnatural and inordinate copulation") was utterly condemned. Protests against the practice were frequent.[19] A traveler in New York reported that the citizens of Albany possessed a particular "moral delicacy" on one point: "they were from infancy in habits of familiarity with these humble friends [the Negroes], yet being early taught that nature had placed between them a barrier, which it was in a high degree criminal and disgraceful to pass, they considered a mixture of such distinct races with abhorrence, as a violation of her laws."[20] About 1700 the Chester County Court in Pennsylvania ordered a Negro "never more to meddle with any white woman more uppon paine of his life." Public feeling on this matter was strong enough to force its way over the hurdles of the legislative process into the statute books of many colonies. Maryland and Virginia forbade cohabitation of whites and Negroes well before the end of the seventeenth century. Similar prohibitions were adopted by Massachusetts, North and South Carolina, and Pennsylvania during the next quarter-century and by Georgia when Negroes were admitted to that colony in 1750. Thus two Northern and all Southern colonies legally prohibited

---

Negroes of Surinam, in Guiana (London, 1796), II, plate opposite p. 98; *Jamaica, a Poem, in Three Parts* (London, 1777), 22-23.

[18] Edwards, *History*, II, 24n.

[19] For a few examples: James Fontaine, *Memoirs of a Huguenot Family*, trans. and ed. Ann Maury (New York, 1872), 350; Eugene P. Chase, trans. and ed., *Our Revolutionary Forefathers; The Letters of François, Marquis de Barbé-Marbois during His Residence in the United States as Secretary of the French Legation, 1779-1785* (New York, 1929), 74; *South-Carolina Gazette*, Mar. 18, 1732; Mar. 28, 1743; May 22, 1749; Elhanan Winchester, *The Reigning Abominations, Especially the Slave Trade, Considered as Causes of Lamentation* (London, 1788), 22n; Klaus G. Loewald, Beverly Starika, and Paul S. Taylor, trans. and eds., "Johann Martin Bolzius Answers a Questionnaire on Carolina and Georgia," *William and Mary Quarterly*, 3d Ser., XIV (1957), 235.

[20] Grant, *Memoirs*, I, 85.

miscegenation.[21] Feeling against intercourse with Negroes was strengthened by the fact that such activity was generally illicit; Americans had
brought from England certain standards of marital fidelity which miscegenation flagrantly violated.

The contrast offered by the West Indies is striking. Protests against
interracial sex relations were infrequent. Colored mistresses were kept
openly. "The Planters are in general rich," a young traveler wrote, "but a
set of dissipating, abandoned, and cruel people. Few even of the married
ones, but keep a Mulatto or Black Girl in the house or at lodgings for
certain purposes."[22] Edward Long of Jamaica put the matter this way:
"He who should presume to shew any displeasure against such a thing
as simple fornication, would for his pains be accounted a simple block-
head; since not one in twenty can be persuaded, that there is either sin;
or shame in cohabiting with his slave."[23] Perhaps most significant of all,
no island legislature prohibited extramarital miscegenation and only one
declared against intermarriage.[24] The reason, of course, was that white

[21] Hening, ed., *Statutes of Va.*, II, 170; III, 86-87, 452-454; Browne and others, eds.,
Archives of Md., I, 533-534; VII, 204-205; XIII, 546-549; XXII, 552; XXVI, 259-260;
XXX, 289-290; XXXIII, 112; XXXVI, 275-276; Edward R. Turner, *The Negro in
Pennsylvania, Slavery—Servitude—Freedom, 1639-1861* (Washington, 1911), 30n;
The Acts and Resolves, Public and Private, of the Province of the Massachusetts Bay
(Boston, 1869-1922), I, 578-579; *Acts and Laws of the Commonwealth of Massachu-
setts* (Boston, 1890-98), IV, 10; Clark, ed., *State Recs. of N. C.*, XXIII, 65, 106, 160,
195; Thomas Cooper and David J. McCord, eds., *Statutes at Large of South Carolina*
(Columbia, 1836-41), III, 20; James T. Mitchell and others, eds., *Statutes at Large
of Pennsylvania from 1682 to 1809* (Harrisburg, 1896-1915), IV, 62-63; also X,
67-73, and the *Pennsylvania Packet* (Philadelphia), Mar. 4, 1779; Candler, comp.,
Col. Recs. of Ga., I, 59-60. Delaware, not considered a Southern colony or state by
contemporaries, passed no outright prohibition until 1807 (repealed the next year)
but provided for heavier fines in interracial bastardy cases than in such cases where
only whites were involved; *Laws of the State of Delaware* (New Castle and Wilmington, 1797-1816), I, 105-109; IV, 112-113, 221.
[22] Samuel Thornely, ed., *The Journal of Nicholas Cresswell, 1774-1777* (New
York, 1924), 39.
[23] Long, *Jamaica*, II, 328.
[24] The exception was Montserrat; the law was probably disallowed: Colonial
Office Papers, Ser. 391, LXIX, 51 (Feb. 16, 1762), Public Record Office, London, for
which reference I am indebted to Frank W. Pitman, *The Development of the British
West Indies, 1700-1763* (New Haven, 1917), 27, where the citation is given as C.O.
391/70, p. 51 (Feb. 16, 1762). This statement on the absence of anti-miscegenation
laws is based on a reading of the statutes of the various islands which, from the nature of the sources, is probably less complete than for the continental colonies. For
obvious reasons only those islands settled primarily by Englishmen have been included: those captured from the French had a different cultural heritage. An act
applying to all the Leeward Islands declared that no "Free Person" should be mar-

men so commonly slept with Negro women that to legislate against the practice would have been merely ludicrous. Concubinage was such an integral part of island life that one might just as well attempt to abolish the sugar cane.

Mulattoes in the West Indies, then, were products of accepted practice, something they assuredly were not in the continental colonies. In the one area they were the fruits of a desire which society tolerated and almost institutionalized; in the other they represented an illicit passion which public morality unhesitatingly condemned. On the continent, unlike the West Indies, mulattoes represented a practice about which men could only feel guilty. To reject and despise the productions of one's own guilt was only natural.

If such difference in feeling about miscegenation has any connection with the American attitude toward mulattoes, it only raises the question of what caused that difference. Since the English settlers in both the West Indies and the continental colonies brought with them the same cultural baggage, something in their colonial experiences must have caused the divergence in their attitudes toward miscegenation. Except perhaps for climatic disimilarity, a factor of very doubtful importance, the most fundamental difference lay in the relative numbers of whites and Negroes in the two areas. On the continent the percentage of Negroes in the total population reached its peak in the period 1730-65 and has been declining since. It ranged from about 3 per cent in New England, 8 to 15 per cent in the middle colonies, 30 to 40 in Maryland and Virginia, 25 in North Carolina, 40 in Georgia, to a high of some 60 per cent in South Carolina. The proportion of Negroes in the islands was far higher: 75 per cent in Barbados, 80 in the Leeward Islands, and over 90 in Jamaica.[25]

---

ried to "any Slave," but this provision was in a section regulating the conduct of free Negroes and almost certainly applied only to them; *Acts of Assembly, Passed in the Charibbee Leeward Islands. From 1690, to 1730* (London, 1734), 138-139. Bermuda in 1663 acted against miscegenation, but this fact merely gives additional confirmation to the pattern outlined above, since the island at the time had fairly close contact with Virginia and never became like the Caribbean islands in economic structure, proportion of Negroes, or social atmosphere. See J. H. Lefroy, comp., *Memorials of the Discovery and Early Settlement of the Bermudas or Somers Islands, 1515-1685* (London, 1877-79), II, 190.

[25] Population statistics for the colonial period are at best merely rough estimates in most cases. I have compiled tables showing the proportion of Negroes in the total population for the principal colonies settled by Englishmen, with figures drawn largely from the following sources: U. S., Bureau of the Census, *A Century of Popu-*

These figures strongly suggest a close connection between a high proportion of Negroes and open acceptance of miscegenation. South Carolina, for example, where Negroes formed a majority of the population, was alone among the continental colonies in tolerating even slightly conspicuous interracial liaisons.[26] Thoroughly disparate proportions of Negroes, moreover, made it inevitable that the West Indies and the continental colonies would develop dissimilar societies. The West Indian planters were lost not so much in the Caribbean as in a sea of blacks. They found it impossible to re-create English culture as they had known it. They were corrupted by living in a police state, though not themselves the objects of its discipline. The business of the islands was business, the production of agricultural staples; the islands were not where one really lived, but where one made one's money. By contrast, the American colonists maintained their hold on the English background, modifying it not so much to accommodate slavery as to winning the new land. They were numerous enough to create a new culture with a validity of its own, complete with the adjustments necessary to absorb non-English Europeans. Unlike the West Indians, they felt no need to be constantly running back to England to reassure themselves that they belonged to civilization. Because they were conscious of the solid worth of their own society, forged with their own hands, they vehemently rejected any trespass upon it by a people so alien as the Negroes. The islanders could hardly resent trespass on something which they did not have. By sheer weight of numbers their society was black and slave.

---

lation Growth, from the First Census of the United States to the Twelfth, 1790-1900 (Washington, 1909); Evarts B. Greene and Virginia D. Harrington, American Population before the Federal Census of 1790 (New York, 1932); Calendar of State Papers, Colonial Series, America and West Indies, 37 vols. (London, 1860——); Alan Burns, History of the British West Indies (London, 1954), 401, 454, 461, 465, 499, 500, 510, 511, 514, 515; Vincent T. Harlow, A History of Barbados, 1625-1685 (Oxford, 1926), 338; C. S. S. Higham, The Development of the Leeward Islands under the Restoration, 1660-1688; A Study of the Foundations of the Old Colonial System (Cambridge, Eng., 1921), 145, 148; Pitman, West Indies, 48, 370, 374, 378; Edwards, History, II, 2. My figures are in substantial agreement with those which may be calculated from a table recently compiled by Stella H. Sutherland in U. S., Bureau of the Census, Historical Statistics of the United States, Colonial Times to 1957 (Washington, 1960), 756, except in the case of North Carolina where her figures yield a proportion nearly 10 per cent higher than mine.

[26] For a New Englander's comment on miscegenation in South Carolina see Mark Anthony DeWolfe Howe, ed., "Journal of Josiah Quincy, Junior, 1773," Massachusetts Historical Society, Proceedings, XLIX (Boston, 1916), 463.

This fundamental difference was perhaps reinforced by another demographic factor. In the seventeenth century the ratio of men to women had been high in America and higher still in the West Indies, where the ratio was about three to two, or, as the sex ratio is usually expressed, 150 (males per 100 females). In the following century it dropped drastically. New England's sex ratio went below 100 as a result of emigration which was as usual predominantly male. Elsewhere on the continent the bounding birth rate nearly erased the differential: in 1750, except on the edge of the frontier, it was probably no more than 110 and in most places less. Perhaps not so well known is the fact that the same process occurred in most of the English islands. Emigration sapped their male strength until Barbados had a sex ratio in the 80's and the various Leeward Islands were balanced in the neighborhood of 100. A significant exception was Jamaica, where in mid-eighteenth century a plentiful supply of land maintained a sex ratio of nearly two to one.[27]

Male numerical predomination was surely not without effect on interracial sexual relations. Particularly where the white population was outnumbered by the black, white women formed a small group. Their scarcity rendered them valuable. The natural reaction on the part of white men was to place them protectively upon a pedestal and then run off to gratify passions elsewhere. For their part white women, though they might propagate children, inevitably held themselves aloof from the world of lust and passion, a world associated with infidelity and Negro slaves. Under no circumstances would they have attempted, nor would they have been allowed, to clamber down from their pedestal to seek pleasures of their own across the racial line. In fact the sexual union of white women with Negro men was uncommon in all colonies. When it did occur (and it did more often than is generally supposed) it was in just those areas to which the demographic factors point—America north of South Carolina, especially in New England, where white women even married Negroes. Such a combination, legitimized or not, was apparently unknown in the West Indies.[28]

[27] Tables of the sex ratios in the various colonies have been calculated from the sources given in the previous note and, in addition, Pitman, *West Indies,* 371-382; Long, *Jamaica,* I, 376.

[28] I have found no cases of white women sleeping with colored men in the West Indies. For this combination on the continent, see extracts from the Court of General Sessions of the Peace [Suffolk County, Mass.], Apr. 4, 1704, Oct. 2, 1705, Apr. 6, 1708, July 4, 1710, Apr. 6, 1714, in Parish Transcripts, Box XVI; James

If a high sex ratio contributed to the acceptability of miscegenation, it may well have enhanced the acceptability of mulatto offspring. For example, there is the striking fact that Jamaica, the only colony where the sex ratio continued high, was the only colony to give legislative countenance to the rise of mulattoes. In 1733 the legislature provided that "no Person who is not above Three Degrees removed in a lineal Descent from the Negro Ancestor exclusive, shall be allowed to vote or poll in Elections; and no one shall be deemed a Mulatto after the Third Generation, as aforesaid, but that they shall have all the Privileges and Immunities of His Majesty's white Subjects of this Island, provided they are brought up in the Christian Religion."[29] In this same period Barbados was barring any person "whose original Extract shall be proved to have been from a Negro" from voting and from testifying against whites.[30] Beginning in the 1730's the Jamaican legislature passed numerous private acts giving

---

Bowdoin to George Scott, Boston, Oct. 14, 1763, in Bowdoin-Temple Papers, XXVIII, 56, Mass. Hist. Soc., Boston, in which Bowdoin wrote that "My Man Caesar has been engaged in an amour with some of the white ladies of the Town. . . ." so he was sending him to Grenada in exchange for produce or another Negro boy; W. H. Morse, "Lemuel Haynes," *Jour. of Negro Hist.*, IV (1919), 22; [Daniel Horsmanden], *A Journal of the Proceedings in the Detection of the Conspiracy Formed by Some White People, in Conjunction with Negro and other Slaves, for Burning the City of New-York in America, and Murdering the Inhabitants* (New York, 1744), 2, 4; *Boston News-Letter*, June 25, 1741; Arthur W. Calhoun, *A Social History of the American Family from Colonial Times to the Present* (Cleveland, 1917-19), I, 211; Helen T. Catterall, ed., *Judicial Cases Concerning American Slavery and the Negro* (Washington, 1926), I, 89-91; II, 12; IV, 28, 32; *Maryland Gazette* (Annapolis), Aug. 19, 1746; James H. Johnston, Race Relations in Virginia and Miscegenation in the South, 1776-1860 (unpubl. Ph.D. diss., University of Chicago, 1937), 199-202; John H. Franklin, *The Free Negro in North Carolina, 1790-1860* (Chapel Hill, 1943), 37, 39; Saunders, *Col. Recs. of N. C.*, II, 704; "Johann Martin Bolzius," 235. For this combination in actual marriage, see Lorenzo J. Greene, *The Negro in Colonial New England, 1620-1776* (New York, 1942), 201-202; Morse, "Lemuel Haynes," 26; Grant, *Memoirs*, I, 86; Calhoun, *Family*, I, 211; Catterall, ed., *Judicial Cases*, II, 11; La Rochefoucault Liancourt, *Travels*, I, 602; *Maryland Gazette*, July 31, 1794; and the case of Gideon Gibson discussed above. A causal connection between the sex ratio and miscegenation has been suggested by Herbert Moller, "Sex Composition and Correlated Culture Patterns of Colonial America," *William and Mary Quarterly*, 3d Ser., II (1945), 131-137, but some of his conclusions must be treated with caution.

[29] *Acts of Assembly, Passed in the Island of Jamaica; from 1681, to 1737, inclusive* (London, 1738), 260-261; see also Long, *Jamaica*, II, 261, 321. This same definition of a mulatto was retained in 1780; *Acts of Assembly, Passed in the Island of Jamaica; from 1770, to 1783, inclusive* (Kingston, 1786), 174.

[30] *Acts of Assembly, Passed in the Island of Barbadoes, from 1648, to 1718* (London, 1721), 112, 153, 171, 213, 226, 267; Richard Hall, comp., *Acts, Passed in the Island of Barbados. From 1643, to 1762, inclusive* (London, 1764), 256.

the colored offspring (and sometimes the colored mistress) of such and such a planter the rights and privileges of white persons, especially the right to inherit the planter's estate. There was objection to this blanching of mulattoes, however, for in 1761 the Assembly restricted the amount of property a planter might leave to his mulatto children, saying that "such bequests tend greatly to destroy the distinction requisite, and absolutely necessary to be kept up in this island, between white persons and negroes, their issue and offspring. . . ." The law failed to destroy the acceptability of the practice, however, for the private acts continued.[31] It was in Jamaica, too, that Bryan Edwards called for extension of civil privileges to mulattoes. And Edward Long, in his history of the island, wrote that those beyond the third generation were "called English, and consider themselves as free from all taint of the Negroe race."[32] Thus Jamaica, with the highest proportion of Negroes and highest sex ratio of all the English colonies, was unique in its practice of publicly transforming Negroes into white men.

The American continental colonist refused to make this extension of privilege. He remained firm in his rejection of the mulatto, in his categorization of mixed-bloods as belonging to the lower caste. It was an unconscious decision dictated perhaps in large part by the weight of Negroes on his society, heavy enough to be a burden, yet not so heavy as to make him abandon all hope of maintaining his own identity, physically and culturally. Interracial propagation was a constant reproach that he was failing to be true to himself. Sexual intimacy strikingly symbolized a

[31] *Acts of Assembly, Passed in the Island of Jamaica, from the Year 1681 to the Year 1769 inclusive.* 2 vols. in 1, with an *Appendix: Containing Laws Respecting Slaves* (Kingston, 1787), I, Table of Acts, 18, 20-25, 30-31; II, Table of Acts, 3, 7-11, 14-15; II, 36-39; *Acts of Assembly, Passed in the Island of Jamaica; from 1770, to to 1783, inclusive,* Table of Acts, 8, 11, 13, 16, 18, 20, 22, 24, 26, 28, 30-31; *Acts of Assembly, Passed in the Island of Jamaica, from the Year 1784 to the Year 1788 inclusive* (Kingston, 1789), Table of Acts, vi-viii, xi, xv-xvi; *The Laws of Jamaica: Comprehending all the Acts in Force, Passed between the Thirty-Second Year of the Reign of King Charles the Second, and the Thirty-Third Year of the Reign of King George the Third* (St. Jago de la Vega, 1792), I, Table of Acts, no pagination: *The Laws of Jamaica, Passed in the Thirty-Third Year of the Reign of King George the Third* (St. Jago de la Vega, 1793), Table of Acts, no pagination; *The Laws of Jamaica, Passed in the Thirty-Fourth Year of the Reign of King George the Third* (St. Jago de la Vega, 1794), Table of Acts, no pagination. See also Long, *Jamaica,* II, 320-323; Edwards, *History,* II, 22-23.

[32] Long, *Jamaica,* II, 332. This general picture of Jamaica is borne out by a work on a somewhat later period; Philip D. Curtin, *Two Jamaicas: The Role of Ideas in a Tropical Colony, 1830-1865* (Cambridge, Mass., 1955), chaps. 1-3.

union he wished to avoid. If he could not restrain his sexual nature, he could at least reject its fruits and thus solace himself that he had done no harm. Perhaps he sensed as well that continued racial intermixture would eventually undermine the logic of the racial slavery upon which his society was based. For the separation of slaves from free men depended on a clear demarcation of the races, and the presence of mulattoes blurred this essential distinction. Accordingly he made every effort to nullify the effects of racial intermixture: by classifying the mulatto as a Negro he was in effect denying that intermixture had occurred at all.

Modern Tensions and the Origins
of American Slavery

By WINTHROP D. JORDAN

THANKS TO JOHN SMITH WE KNOW THAT NEGROES FIRST CAME TO the British continental colonies in 1619.[1] What we do not know is exactly when Negroes were first enslaved there. This question has been debated by historians for the past seventy years, the critical point being whether Negroes were enslaved almost from their first importation or whether they were at first simply servants and only later reduced to the status of slaves. The long duration and vigor of the controversy suggest that more than a simple question of dating has been involved. In fact certain current tensions in American society have complicated the historical problem and greatly heightened its significance. Dating the origins of slavery has taken on a striking modern relevance.

During the nineteenth century historians assumed almost universally that the first Negroes came to Virginia as slaves. So close was their acquaintance with the problem of racial slavery that it did not occur to them that Negroes could ever have been anything but slaves. Philip A. Bruce, the first man to probe with some thoroughness into the early years of American slavery, adopted this view in 1896, although he emphasized that the original difference in treatment between white servants and Negroes was merely that Negroes served for life. Just six years later, however, came a challenge from a younger, professionally trained historian, James C. Ballagh. His *A History of Slavery in Virginia* appeared in the *Johns Hopkins University Studies in Historical and Political Science*, an aptly named series which was to usher in the new era of scholarly detachment in the writing of institutional history. Ballagh offered a new and different interpretation; he took the position that the first Negroes served merely as servants and that enslavement did not begin until around 1660, when statutes bearing on slavery were passed for the first time.[2]

---

[1] "About the last of August came in a dutch man of warre that sold us twenty Negars." Smith was quoting John Rolfe's account. Edward Arber and A. G. Bradley (eds.), *Travels and Works of Captain John Smith . . .* (2 vols., Edinburgh, 1910), II, 541.

[2] Philip A. Bruce, *Economic History of Virginia in the Seventeenth Century* (2

112

There has since been agreement on dating the statutory establishment of slavery, and differences of opinion have centered on when enslavement began in actual practice. Fortunately there has also been general agreement on slavery's distinguishing characteristics: service for life and inheritance of like obligation by any offspring. Writing on the free Negro in Virginia for the Johns Hopkins series, John H. Russell in 1913 tackled the central question and showed that some Negroes were indeed servants but concluded that "between 1640 and 1660 slavery was fast becoming an established fact. In this twenty years the colored population was divided, part being servants and part being slaves, and some who were servants defended themselves with increasing difficulty from the encroachments of slavery."[3] Ulrich B. Phillips, though little interested in the matter, in 1918 accepted Russell's conclusion of early servitude and transition toward slavery after 1640. Helen T. Catterall took much the same position in 1926. On the other hand, in 1921 James M. Wright, discussing the free Negro in Maryland, implied that Negroes were slaves almost from the beginning, and in 1940 Susie M. Ames reviewed several cases in Virginia which seemed to indicate that genuine slavery had existed well before Ballagh's date of 1660.[4]

All this was a very small academic gale, well insulated from the outside world. Yet despite disagreement on dating enslavement, the earlier writers—Bruce, Ballagh, and Russell—shared a common assumption which, though at the time seemingly irrelevant to the main question, has since proved of considerable importance. They assumed that prejudice against the Negro was natural and almost innate in the white man. It would be surprising if they had felt otherwise in this period of segregation statutes, overseas imperialism, immigration restriction, and full-throated Anglo-Saxonism. By the 1920's, however, with the easing of these tensions, the

---

vols., New York, 1896), II, 57-130; James C. Ballagh, A *History of Slavery in Virginia* (Baltimore, 1902), 28-35.

[3] John H. Russell, *The Free Negro in Virginia, 1619-1865* (Baltimore, 1913), 29.

[4] *Ibid.*, 23-39; Ulrich B. Phillips, *American Negro Slavery* (New York, 1918), 75-77, and *Life and Labor in the Old South* (Boston, 1929), 170; Helen T. Catterall (ed.), *Judicial Cases Concerning American Slavery and the Negro* (5 vols., Washington, 1926-1937), I, 54-55, 57-63; James M. Wright, *The Free Negro in Maryland, 1634-1860* (New York, 1921), 21-23; Susie M. Ames, *Studies of the Virginia Eastern Shore in the Seventeenth Century* (Richmond, 1940), 100-106. See also T. R. Davis, "Negro Servitude in the United States," *Journal of Negro History*, VIII (July 1923), 247-83, and Edgar T. Thompson, "The Natural History of Agricultural Labor in the South" in David K. Jackson (ed.), *American Studies in Honor of William Kenneth Boyd* (Durham, N. C., 1940), 127-46.

assumption of natural prejudice was dropped unnoticed. Yet only one historian explicitly contradicted that assumption: Ulrich Phillips of Georgia, impressed with the geniality of both slavery and twentieth-century race relations, found no natural prejudice in the white man and expressed his "conviction that Southern racial asperities are mainly superficial, and that the two great elements are fundamentally in accord."[5]

Only when tensions over race relations intensified once more did the older assumption of natural prejudice crop up again. After World War II American Negroes found themselves beneficiaries of New Deal politics and reforms, wartime need for manpower, world-wide repulsion at racist excesses in Nazi Germany, and growingly successful colored anticolonialism. With new militancy Negroes mounted an attack on the citadel of separate but equal, and soon it became clear that America was in for a period of self-conscious reappraisal of its racial arrangements. Writing in this period of heightened tension (1949) a practiced and careful scholar, Wesley F. Craven, raised the old question of the Negro's original status, suggesting that Negroes had been enslaved at an early date. Craven also cautiously resuscitated the idea that white men may have had natural distaste for the Negro, an idea which fitted neatly with the suggestion of early enslavement. Original antipathy would mean rapid debasement.[6]

In the next year (1950) came a sophisticated counterstatement, which contradicted both Craven's dating and implicitly any suggestion of early prejudice. Oscar and Mary F. Handlin in "Origins of the Southern Labor System" offered a case for late enslavement, with servitude as the status of Negroes before about 1660. Originally the status of both Negroes and white servants was far short of freedom, the Handlins maintained, but Negroes failed to benefit from increased freedom for servants in mid-century and became less free rather than more.[7] Embedded in this description of diverging status were broader implications: Late and gradual enslavement undercut the possibility of natural, deep-seated antipathy toward Negroes. On the contrary, if whites and Negroes could share the same status of half freedom for forty years in the seventeenth century, why could they not share full freedom in the twentieth?

[5] Phillips, *American Negro Slavery*, viii.
[6] Wesley F. Craven, *The Southern Colonies in the Seventeenth Century, 1607-1689* (Baton Rouge, 1949), 217-19, 402-403.
[7] *William and Mary Quarterly*, s. 3, VII (April 1950), 199-222.

The same implications were rendered more explicit by Kenneth M. Stampp in a major reassessment of Southern slavery published two years after the Supreme Court's 1954 school decision. Reading physiology with the eye of faith, Stampp frankly stated his assumption "that innately Negroes *are*, after all, only white men with black skins, nothing more, nothing less."[8] Closely following the Handlins' article on the origins of slavery itself, he almost directly denied any pattern of early and inherent racial antipathy: ". . . Negro and white servants of the seventeenth century seemed to be remarkably unconcerned about their visible physical differences." As for "the trend toward special treatment" of the Negro, "physical and cultural differences provided handy excuses to justify it."[9] Distaste for the Negro, then, was in the beginning scarcely more than an appurtenance of slavery.

These views squared nicely with the hopes of those even more directly concerned with the problem of contemporary race relations, sociologists and social psychologists. Liberal on the race question almost to a man, they tended to see slavery as the initial cause of the Negro's current degradation. The modern Negro was the unhappy victim of long association with base status. Sociologists, though uninterested in tired questions of historical evidence, could not easily assume a natural prejudice in the white man as the cause of slavery. Natural or innate prejudice would not only violate their basic assumptions concerning the dominance of culture but would undermine the power of their new Baconian science. For if prejudice was natural there would be little one could do to wipe it out. Prejudice must have followed enslavement, not vice versa, else any liberal program of action would be badly compromised. One prominent social scientist suggested in a UNESCO pamphlet that racial prejudice in the United States commenced with the cotton gin![10]

Just how closely the question of dating had become tied to the

---

[8] Kenneth M. Stampp, *The Peculiar Institution: Slavery in the Ante–Bellum South* (New York, 1956), vii-viii, 3-33.

[9] *Ibid.*, 21-22.

[10] Arnold Rose, "The Roots of Prejudice" in UNESCO, *The Race Question in Modern Science* (New York, 1956), 224. For examples of the more general view see Frederick G. Detweiler, "The Rise of Modern Race Antagonisms," *American Journal of Sociology*, XXXVII (March 1932), 743; M. F. Ashley Montagu, *Man's Most Dangerous Myth: The Fallacy of Race* (New York, 1945), 10-11, 19-20; Gunnar Myrdal, *An American Dilemma: The Negro Problem and Modern Democracy* (New York, 1944), 83-89, 97; Paul Kecskemeti, "The Psychological Theory of Prejudice: Does it Underrate the Role of Social History?" *Commentary*, XVIII (October 1954), 364-66.

practical matter of action against racial prejudice was made apparent by the suggestions of still another historian. Carl N. Degler grappled with the dating problem in an article frankly entitled "Slavery and the Genesis of American Race Prejudice."[11] The article appeared in 1959, a time when Southern resistance to school desegregation seemed more adamant than ever and the North's hands none too clean, a period of discouragement for those hoping to end racial discrimination. Prejudice against the Negro now appeared firm and deep-seated, less easily eradicated than had been supposed in, say, 1954. It was Degler's view that enslavement began early, as a result of white settlers' prejudice or antipathy toward the first Negroes. Thus not only were the sociologists contradicted but the dating problem was now overtly and consciously tied to the broader question of whether slavery caused prejudice or prejudice caused slavery. A new self-consciousness over the American racial dilemma had snatched an arid historical controversy from the hands of an unsuspecting earlier generation and had tossed it into the arena of current debate.

Ironically there might have been no historical controversy at all if every historian dealing with the subject had exercised greater care with facts and greater restraint in interpretation. Too often the debate entered the realm of inference and assumption. For the crucial early years after 1619 there is simply not enough evidence to indicate with any certainty whether Negroes were treated like white servants or not. No historian has found anything resembling proof one way or the other. The first Negroes were sold to the English settlers, yet so were other Englishmen. It can be said, however, that Negroes were set apart from white men by the word *Negroes*, and a distinct name is not attached to a group unless it is seen as different. The earliest Virginia census reports plainly distinguished Negroes from white men, sometimes giving Negroes no personal name; and in 1629 every commander of the several plantations was ordered to "take a generall muster of all the inhabitants men woemen and Children as well *Englishe* as Negroes."[12] Difference, however, might or might not involve inferiority.

[11] *Comparative Studies in Society and History,* II (October 1959), 49-66. See also Degler, *Out of Our Past: The Forces that Shaped Modern America* (New York, 1959), 26-39.

[12] H. R. McIlwaine (ed.), *Minutes of the Council and General Court of Colonial Virginia, 1622-1632, 1670-1676* (Richmond, 1924), 196. See the lists and musters of 1624 and 1625 in John C. Hotten (ed.), *The Original Lists of Persons of Quality . . .* (New York, 1880), 169-265.

The first evidence as to the actual status of Negroes does not appear until about 1640. Then it becomes clear that *some* Negroes were serving for life and some children inheriting the same obligation. Here it is necessary to suggest with some candor that the Handlins' statement to the contrary rests on unsatisfactory documentation.[13] That some Negroes were held as slaves after about 1640 is no indication, however, that American slavery popped into the world fully developed at that time. Many historians, most cogently the Handlins, have shown slavery to have been a gradual development, a process not completed until the eighteenth century. The complete deprivation of civil and personal rights, the legal conversion of the Negro into a chattel, in short slavery as Americans came to know it, was not accomplished overnight. Yet these developments practically and logically depended on the practice of hereditary lifetime service, and it is certainly possible to find in the 1640's and 1650's traces of slavery's most essential feature.[14]

The first definite trace appears in 1640 when the Virginia General Court pronounced sentence on three servants who had been retaken after running away to Maryland. Two of them, a Dutchman and a Scot, were ordered to serve their masters for one additional year and then the colony for three more, but "the third being a negro named John Punch shall serve his said master or his assigns for the time of his natural life here or else where." No

---

[13] "The status of Negroes was that of servants; and so they were identified and treated down to the 1660's." ("Origins," 203.) The footnote to this statement reads, "For disciplinary and revenue laws in Virginia that did not discriminate Negroes from other servants, see Hening, *Statutes*, I, 174, 198, 200, 243, 306 (1631-1645)." But pp. 200 and 243 of William Waller Hening (ed.), *The Statutes at Large; Being a Collection of All the Laws of Virginia . . .* (2nd ed. of vols. 1-4, New York, 1823), I, in fact contain nothing about either servants or Negroes, while a tax provision on p. 242 specifically discriminates against Negro women. The revenue act on p. 306 lists the number of pounds of tobacco levied on land, cattle, sheep, horses, etc., and on tithable persons, and provides for collection of lists of the above so that the colony can compute its tax program; nothing else is said of servants and tithables. To say, as the Handlins did in the same note, that Negroes, English servants, and horses, etc., were listed all together in some early Virginia wills, with the implication that Negroes and English servants were regarded as alike in status, is hardly correct unless one is to assume that the horses were sharing this status as well. (For complete bibliographical information on Hening [ed.], *Statutes*, see E. G. Swem, *Virginia Historical Index* [2 vols., Roanoke, Va., 1934-1936], I, xv-xvi.)

[14] Latin-American Negroes did not lose all civil and personal rights, did not become mere chattels, yet we speak of "slavery" in Latin America without hesitation. See Frank Tannenbaum, *Slave and Citizen: The Negro in the Americas* (New York, 1947), and Gilberto Freyre, *The Masters and the Slaves: A Study in the Development of Brazilian Civilization* (New York, 1946).

white servant in America, so far as is known, ever received a like sentence.[15] Later the same month a Negro was again singled out from a group of recaptured runaways; six of the seven were assigned additional time while the Negro was given none, presumably because he was already serving for life.[16] After 1640, too, county court records began to mention Negroes, in part because there were more of them than previously—about two per cent of the Virginia population in 1649.[17] Sales for life, often including any future progeny, were recorded in unmistakable language. In 1646 Francis Pott sold a Negro woman and boy to Stephen Charlton "to the use of him . . . forever." Similarly, six years later William Whittington sold to John Pott "one Negro girle named Jowan; aged about Ten yeares and with her Issue and produce duringe her (or either of them) for their Life tyme. And their Successors forever"; and a Maryland man in 1649 deeded two Negro men and a woman "and all their issue both male and Female." The executors of a York County estate in 1647 disposed of eight Negroes—four men, two women, and two children—to Captain John Chisman "to have hold occupy posesse and inioy and every one of the afforementioned Negroes forever[.]"[18] The will of Rowland Burnham of "Rapahanocke," made in 1657, dispensed his considerable number of Negroes and white servants in language which clearly differentiated between the two by specifying that the whites were to serve for their "full terme of tyme" and the Negroes "for ever."[19] Nor did anything in the will indicate that this distinction was exceptional or novel.

In addition to these clear indications that some Negroes were owned for life, there were cases of Negroes held for terms far

[15] "Decisions of the General Court," *Virginia Magazine of History and Biography*, V (January 1898), 236. Abbot Emerson Smith in the standard work on servitude in America, *Colonists in Bondage: White Servitude and Convict Labor in America, 1607-1776* (Chapel Hill, 1947), 171, says that "there was never any such thing as perpetual slavery for any white man in any English colony." There were instances in the seventeenth century of white men sold into "slavery," but this was when the meaning of the term was still indefinite and often equated with servitude.

[16] "Decisions of the General Court," 236-37.

[17] *A Perfect Description of Virginia* . . . (London, 1649), reprinted in Peter Force (ed.), *Tracts* . . . (4 vols., Washington, 1836-1846), II.

[18] These four cases may be found in Northampton County Deeds, Wills &c. (Virginia State Library, Richmond), No. 4 (1651-1654), 28 (misnumbered 29), 124; *Archives of Maryland* (69 vols., Baltimore, 1883-1961), XLI, 261-62; York County Records (Virginia State Library), No. 2 (transcribed Wills & Deeds, 1645-1649), 256-57.

[19] Lancaster County Loose Papers (Virginia State Library), Box of Wills, 1650-1719, Folder 1656-1659.

longer than the normal five or seven years.[20] On the other hand, some Negroes served only the term usual for white servants, and others were completely free.[21] One Negro freeman, Anthony Johnson, himself owned a Negro.[22] Obviously the enslavement of some Negroes did not mean the immediate enslavement of all.

Further evidence of Negroes serving for life lies in the prices paid for them. In many instances the valuations placed on Negroes (in estate inventories and bills of sale) were far higher than for white servants, even those servants with full terms yet to serve. Since there was ordinarily no preference for Negroes as such, higher prices must have meant that Negroes were more highly valued because of their greater length of service. Negro women may have been especially prized, moreover, because their progeny could also be held perpetually. In 1645, for example, two Negro women and a boy were sold for 5,500 pounds of tobacco. Two years earlier William Burdett's inventory listed eight servants (with the time each had still to serve) at valuations ranging from 400 to 1,100 pounds, while a "very anntient" Negro was valued at 3,000 and an eight-year-old Negro girl at 2,000 pounds, with no time-remaining indicated for either. In the late 1650's an inventory of Thomas Ludlow's large estate evaluated a white servant with six years to serve at less than an elderly Negro man and only one half of a Negro woman.[23] The labor owned by James Stone in 1648 was evaluated as follows:

	lb tobo
Thomas Groves, 4 yeares to serve	1300
Francis Bomley for 6 yeares	1500
John Thackstone for 3 yeares	1300
Susan Davis for 3 yeares	1000
Emaniell a Negro man	2000
Roger Stone 3 yeares	1300
Mingo a Negro man	2000[24]

[20] For examples running for as long as thirty-five years, see *William and Mary Quarterly*, s. 1, XX (October 1911), 148; Russell, *Free Negro in Virginia*, 26-27; Ames, *Eastern Shore*, 105. Compare the cases of a Negro and an Irish servant in *Calendar of Virginia State Papers* . . . (11 vols., Richmond, 1875-1893), I, 9-10, and *Maryland Archives*, XLI, 476-78; XLIX, 123-24.

[21] Russell, *Free Negro in Virginia*, 24-41. See especially the cases in *Virginia Magazine of History and Biography*, V (July 1897), 40; York County Deeds, Wills, Orders, etc. (Virginia State Library), No. 1 (1633-1657, 1691-1694), 338-39.

[22] John H. Russell, "Colored Freemen As Slave Owners in Virginia," *Journal of Negro History*, I (July 1916), 234-37.

[23] York County Records, No. 2, 63; Northampton County Orders, Deeds, Wills, &c., No. 2 (1640-1645), 224; York County Deeds, Orders, Wills, &c. (1657-1662), 108-109.

[24] York County Records, No. 2, 390.

Besides setting a higher value on the two Negroes, Stone's inventory, like Burdett's, failed to indicate the number of years they had still to serve. It would seem safe to assume that the time remaining was omitted in this and similar documents simply because the Negroes were regarded as serving for an unlimited time.

The situation in Maryland was apparently the same. In 1643 Governor Leonard Calvert agreed with John Skinner, "mariner," to exchange certain estates for seventeen sound Negro "slaves," fourteen men and three women between sixteen and twenty-six years old. The total value of these was placed at 24,000 pounds of tobacco, which would work out to 1,000 pounds for the women and 1,500 for the men, prices considerably higher than those paid for white servants at the time.[25]

Wherever Negro women were involved, however, higher valuations may have reflected the fact that they could be used for field work while white women generally were not. This discrimination between Negro and white women, of course, fell short of actual enslavement. It meant merely that Negroes were set apart in a way clearly not to their advantage. Yet this is not the only evidence that Negroes were subjected to degrading distinctions not directly related to slavery. In several ways Negroes were singled out for special treatment which suggested a generalized debasing of Negroes as a group. Significantly, the first indications of debasement appeared at about the same time as the first indications of actual enslavement.

The distinction concerning field work is a case in point. It first appeared on the written record in 1643, when Virginia pointedly recognized it in her taxation policy. Previously tithable persons had been defined (1629) as "all those that worke in the ground of what qualitie or condition soever." Now the law stated that all adult men and *Negro* women were to be tithable, and this distinction was made twice again before 1660. Maryland followed a similar course, beginning in 1654.[26] John Hammond, in a 1656 tract defending the tobacco colonies, wrote that servant women were not put to work in the fields but in domestic employments, "yet som wenches that are nasty, and beastly and not fit to be so imployed are put into the ground."[27] Since all Negro women were

[25] Apparently Calvert's deal with Skinner was never consummated. *Maryland Archives*, IV, vii, 189, 320-21. For prices of white servants see *ibid.*, IV, 31, 47-48, 74, 78-79, 81, 83, 92, 98, 108-109, 184, 200, 319.

[26] Hening (ed.), *Statutes*, I, 144, 242, 292, 454. The Handlins erroneously placed the "first sign of discrimination" in this matter at 1668 ("Origins," 217n). For Maryland, see *Maryland Archives*, I, 342; II, 136, 399, 538-39; XIII, 538-39.

[27] John Hammond, *Leah and Rachel, or, the Two Fruitfull Sisters Virginia, and*

taxed as working in the fields, it would seem logical to conclude that Virginians found them "nasty" and "beastly." The essentially racial nature of this discrimination was bared by a 1668 law at the time slavery was crystallizing on the statute books:

Whereas some doubts, have arisen whether negro women set free were still to be accompted tithable according to a former act, *It is declared by this grand assembly* that negro women, though permitted to enjoy their ffreedome yet ought not in all respects to be admitted to a full fruition of the exemptions and impunities of the English, and are still lyable to payment of taxes.[28]

Virginia law set Negroes apart in a second way by denying them the important right and obligation to bear arms. Few restraints could indicate more clearly the denial to Negroes of membership in the white community. This action, in a sense the first foreshadowing of the slave codes, came in 1640, at just the time when other indications first appear that Negroes were subject to special treatment.[29]

Finally, an even more compelling sense of the separateness of Negroes was revealed in early distress concerning sexual union

---

Mary-land: Their Present Condition, Impartially Stated and Related . . . (London, 1656), reprinted in Force (ed.), *Tracts*, II.

[28] Hening (ed.), *Statutes*, II, 267. The distinction between white and colored women was neatly described at the turn of the century by Robert Beverley, *The History and Present State of Virginia*, Louis B. Wright, ed. (Chapel Hill, 1947), 271-72.

[29] Hening (ed.), *Statutes*, I, 226, and for the same act in more detail see *William and Mary Quarterly*, s. 2, IV (July 1924), 147. The Handlins discounted this law: "Until the 1660's the statutes on the Negroes were not at all unique. Nor did they add up to a decided trend." ("Origins," 209.) The note added to this statement reads, "That there was no trend is evident from the fluctuations in naming Negroes slaves or servants and in their right to bear arms. See Hening, *Statutes*, I, 226, 258, 292, 540; Bruce, *Institutional History*, II, 5 ff., 199 ff. For similar fluctuations with regard to Indians, see Hening, *Statutes*, I, 391, 518." But since the terms "servants" and "slaves" did not have precise meaning, as the Handlins themselves asserted, fluctuations in naming Negroes one or the other can not be taken to mean that their status itself was fluctuating. Of the pages cited in Hening, p. 258 is an act encouraging Dutch traders and contains nothing about Negroes, servants, slaves, or arms. Page 292 is an act providing that fifteen tithable persons should support one soldier; Negroes were among those tithable, but nothing was said of allowing them to arm. Page 540 refers to "any negro slaves" and "said negro," but mentions nothing about servants or arms. In the pages dealing with Indians, p. 391 provides that no one is to employ Indian servants with guns, and p. 518 that Indians (not "Indian servants") are to be allowed to use their own guns; the two provisions are not contradictory. Philip A. Bruce, *Institutional History of Virginia in the Seventeenth Century* (2 vols., New York, 1910), II, 5 ff., indicates that Negroes were barred from arming in 1639 and offers no suggestion that there was any later fluctuation in this practice.

between the races. In 1630 a Virginia court pronounced a now famous sentence: "Hugh Davis to be soundly whipped, before an assembly of Negroes and others for abusing himself to the dishonor of God and shame of Christians, by defiling his body in lying with a negro."[30] While there were other instances of punishment for interracial union in the ensuing years, fornication rather than miscegenation may well have been the primary offense, though in 1651 a Maryland man sued someone who he claimed had said "that he had a black bastard in Virginia."[31] There may have been nothing racial about the 1640 case by which Robert Sweet was compelled "to do penance in church according to laws of England, for getting a negroe woman with child and the woman whipt."[32] About 1650 a white man and a Negro woman were required to stand clad in white sheets before a congregation in Lower Norfolk County for having had relations, but this punishment was sometimes used in ordinary cases of fornication between two whites.[33]

It is certain, however, that in the early 1660's when slavery was gaining statutory recognition, the colonial assemblies legislated with feeling against miscegenation. Nor was this merely a matter of avoiding confusion of status, as was suggested by the Handlins. In 1662 Virginia declared that "if any christian shall commit ffornication with a negro man or woman, hee or shee soe offending" should pay double the usual fine. Two years later Maryland prohibited interracial marriages:

forasmuch as divers freeborne English women forgettfull of their free Condicōn and to the disgrace of our Nation doe intermarry with Negro Slaves by which alsoe divers suites may arise touching the Issue of such woemen and a great damage doth befall the Masters of such Negros for prevention whereof for deterring such freeborne women from such shamefull Matches . . . ,

strong language indeed if the problem had only been confusion of status. A Maryland act of 1681 described marriages of white women with Negroes as, among other things, "always to the Satisfaccōn of theire Lascivious & Lustfull desires, & to the disgrace not only of the English butt allso of many other Christian Nations." When Virginia finally prohibited all interracial liaisons in 1691, the

---

[30] Hening (ed.), *Statutes*, I, 146. "Christianity" appears instead of "Christians" in McIlwaine (ed.), *Minutes of the Council*, 479.
[31] *Maryland Archives*, X, 114-15.
[32] Hening (ed.), *Statutes*, I, 552; McIlwaine, *Minutes of the Council*, 477.
[33] Bruce, *Economic History of Virginia*, II, 110.

assembly vigorously denounced miscegenation and its fruits as "that abominable mixture and spurious issue."[34]

One is confronted, then, with the fact that the first evidences of enslavement and of other forms of debasement appeared at about the same time. Such coincidence comports poorly with both views on the causation of prejudice and slavery. If slavery caused prejudice, then invidious distinctions concerning working in the fields, bearing arms, and sexual union should have appeared only after slavery's firm establishment. If prejudice caused slavery, then one would expect to find such lesser discriminations preceding the greater discrimination of outright enslavement.

Perhaps a third explanation of the relationship between slavery and prejudice may be offered, one that might fit the pattern of events as revealed by existing evidence. Both current views share a common starting point: They predicate two factors, prejudice and slavery, and demand a distinct order of causality. No matter how qualified by recognition that the effect may in turn react upon the cause, each approach inevitably tends to deny the validity of its opposite. But what if one were to regard both slavery and prejudice as species of a general debasement of the Negro? Both may have been equally cause and effect, constantly reacting upon each other, dynamically joining hands to hustle the Negro down the road to complete degradation. Mutual causation is, of course, a highly useful concept for describing social situations in the mod-

---

[34] Hening (ed.), *Statutes*, II, 170; III, 86-87; *Maryland Archives*, I, 533-34; VII, 204. Opinion on this matter apparently was not unanimous, for a petition of several citizens to the Council in 1699 asked repeal of the intermarriage prohibition. H. R. McIlwaine (ed.), *Legislative Journals of the Council of Colonial Virginia* (3 vols., Richmond, 1918-1919), I, 262. The Handlins wrote ("Origins," 215), "Mixed marriages of free men and servants were particularly frowned upon as complicating status and therefore limited by law." Their citation for this, Hening (ed.), *Statutes*, II, 114 (1661/62), and Marcus W. Jernegan, *Laboring and Dependent Classes in Colonial America, 1607-1783* (Chicago, 1931), 55, 180, gives little backing to the statement. In Virginia secret marriage or bastardy between whites of different status got the same punishment as such between whites of the same status. A white servant might marry any white if his master consented. See Hening (ed.), *Statutes*, I, 252-53, 438-39; II, 114-15, 167; III, 71-75, 137-40. See also James C. Ballagh, *White Servitude in the Colony of Virginia* (Baltimore, 1895), 50. For Maryland, see *Maryland Archives*, I, 73, 373-74, 441-42; II, 396-97; XIII, 501-502. The Handlins also suggested that in the 1691 Virginia law, "spurious" meant simply "illegitimate," and they cited Arthur W. Calhoun, *A Social History of the American Family from Colonial Times to the Present* (3 vols., Cleveland, O., 1917-1919), I, 42, which turns out to be one quotation from John Milton. However, "spurious" was used in colonial laws with reference only to unions between white and black, and never in bastardy laws involving whites only. Mulattoes were often labeled "spurious" offspring.

ern world.[35] Indeed it has been widely applied in only slightly altered fashion to the current racial situation: Racial prejudice and the Negro's lowly position are widely accepted as constantly reinforcing each other.

This way of looking at the facts might well fit better with what we know of slavery itself. Slavery was an organized pattern of human relationships. No matter what the law might say, it was of different character than cattle ownership. No matter how degrading, slavery involved human beings. No one seriously pretended otherwise. Slavery was not an isolated economic or institutional phenomenon; it was the practical facet of a general debasement without which slavery could have no rationality. (Prejudice, too, was a form of debasement, a kind of slavery in the mind.) Certainly the urgent need for labor in a virgin country guided the direction which debasement took, molded it, in fact, into an institutional framework. That economic practicalities shaped the external form of debasement should not tempt one to forget, however, that slavery was at bottom a social arrangement, a way of society's ordering its members in its own mind.

[35] For example, George C. Homans, *The Human Group* (New York, 1950).

A "PROLIFICK" PEOPLE: BLACK POPULATION GROWTH IN THE CHESAPEAKE COLONIES, 1700-1790

*Allan Kulikoff**
University of Illinois
Chicago Circle

"The Negroes are not only encreased by fresh supplies from Africa and the West Indies," wrote Hugh Jones, a Virginia clergyman, in 1724, "but also are very prolifick among themselves." Thirty-five years later, Andrew Burnaby, an English visitor to Virginia, insisted that "the number of Negroes in the southern colonies is upon the whole nearly equal, if not superior, to that of white men; and they propagate and increase even faster."[1] When Jones wrote his book in 1724, Virginia's black population had just begun to reproduce itself but heavy immigration from Africa continued; by the time Burnaby came to Virginia, the black population of the Chesapeake colonies grew rapidly almost entirely from natural increase.

The population history of Africans and Afro-Americans in the Chesapeake colonies during the century preceding the Revolution can be roughly divided into four periods: 1660-1680, 1680-1710, 1710-1740, and 1740-1780. Each period can be distinguished by its own pattern of immigration and by a differing rate of natural increase or decline. During the first two periods, from 1660 to 1710, black population increased only from foreign immigration; it grew from both immigration and by natural increase during the third period, but it expanded largely from natural increase in the last period. These changes can be documented from two kinds of sources. First, the number of black immigrants can be compared with the total black population. The higher the proportion of immigrants in the total black population, the lower was the rate of natural increase. Secondly, the number of children per woman found in probate inventories permits an approximation to the degree of natural growth. The higher the ratio of children to women, the greater the rate of natural increase.[2]

---

* The author would like to thank Stanley Engerman and Norman S. Fiering for their comments, and the Institute of Early American History and Culture for financial support.

1. Hugh Jones, *The Present State of Virginia* (1724), ed. by Richard L. Morton (Chapel Hill, 1956), p. 75; Andrew Burnaby, *Travels Through the Middle Settlements in North America. In the Years 1759 and 1760. . . .* (London, 1775; Cornell University Press reprint, 1968) p. 111.
2. The only previous analysis of these problems is found in Russell R. Menard's pathbreaking article, "The Maryland Slave Population, 1658 to 1730: A Demographic Profile of Blacks in Four Counties," *William and Mary Quarterly*, 3rd. Ser., 32 (1975): 29-54 (hereafter *WMQ*). This article supports most of Menard's points concerning the early period and extends his arguments up to the Revolution.

125

I

In 1660, no more than 1700 blacks lived in Maryland and Virginia. By 1680, their numbers had increased to about 4600. Most of this increase came from immigration from the West Indies. The West Indian immigration was somewhat different from the African of later years. In the first place, these forced immigrants travelled shorter distances than those coming from Africa and had been seasoned in the New World before coming to the Chesapeake. Therefore, probably fewer of them died enroute or in their first year in the region than those who came from Africa. Secondly, the proportion of female immigrants was greater from the West Indies than from Africa. The sex ratio, men per hundred women, for black adults in Southern Maryland between 1658 and 1670 was only 130, a good deal lower than it was at the height of the African slave trade to that colony.[3]

By 1680, ships had begun arriving from Africa. At least two came in 1679 with a total of 550 slaves and between 1683 and 1687 five more vessels appeared with a total of about 900 Africans.[4] About three-quarters of all blacks who came to Virginia between 1710 and 1718 had been brought from Africa.[5] We know that at least 13,000 Africans came to Maryland and Virginia between 1710 and 1718. Around 1000 black slaves came to Virginia each year in the early 1700s. After a sharp decline in this average to below one hundred in the years from 1710 to 1714, the number increased to nearly 1200 yearly, in the next decade. The 2.4 percent annual increase in the black population of

---

3.   Wesley Frank Craven, *White, Red and Black: The Seventeenth Century Virginian* (Charlottesville, 1971), pp. 84, 93-95, 97, 99; Menard, "Maryland Slave Population," p. 32.

4.   Elizabeth Donnan, *Documents Illustrative of the Slave Trade to America* (Washington, 1930-1935), 4:53-55; "A List of Ships Sent to Gambia by the Royal African Company Since Nov. 1783," T 70/61, 170 Public Record office (PRO); T 70/61, 30; "Case of the Society of Bristol," CO 5/1308, 54, 14-45, PRO. The number of landed Africans is known for only two ships; only the order to sail for Africa is recorded for the others.

5.   Donnan, *Documents*, 4: 17-18, 173-87 corrected with original Naval Officer Returns. My figure for the proportion of Africans in the trade (73 percent) differs from that in Herbert Klein, "Slaves and Shipping in Eighteenth Century Virginia," *Journal of Interdisciplinary History*, 5 (1975): 384 because I counted all the ships with Bristol, Liverpool and London registries carrying over 40 slaves as coming from Africa even when its origin was listed as the West Indies. This procedure can be checked for 1718 when lists of ships from Africa and lists of all slave ships survive. In that year four ships with more than 40 slaves and Bristol, London, or Liverpool registeries were found on the complete list and entered as coming from the West Indies; three of them, (with 83 percent of the slaves) came from Africa but stopped first in the islands. If this correction is applied to 1710-1718, then I misclassified 225 slaves, and the proportion coming from Africa would be reduced to 68 percent.

Virginia—equivalent to doubling of the population every 29 years—was mainly due to the annual increase in black immigration to that colony (see figure 1 and table 1).[6]

Table 1
Growth of Virginia's Native Black Population[a]

Period	Population Increase (to Nearest 50)	Natural Population Increase (to Nearest 25)	Annual Rate of Natural Increase (Percent)[b]	Natural Increase As a Percentage of Total Increase[b]
1700-1710	2,950	- 3,250	-2.0	0
1710-1720	7,250	1,125	0.6	16
1720-1730	10,000	725	0.3	7
1730-1740	23,400	11,600	2.8	50
1740-1750	41,500	32,100	5.0[c]	77
1750-1760	33,450	28,650	2.4	86
1760-1770	47,050	42,100	2.7	89

[a] For sources and computational methods, see appendices 1, 2, and 3.
[b] These rates are based upon the average of the two estimates of the number of surviving immigrants presented in appendix 3.
[c] This figure is clearly too high.

Almost all black immigrants to Virginia after 1720 came from Africa; Africans accounted for 93 percent of all slave immigrants between 1727 and 1740.[7] The numbers of immigrant blacks increased at a rate of 2.9 percent a year and averaged about 1400 each year between 1722 and 1744.[8] By the early 1740s, about 1750 blacks were brought to Virginia each year. Nevertheless, this dramatic increase in the numbers of immigrants was less than the overall increase in black population. In the 1720s and 1730s, black population grew at a rate of about 4.2 percent a year. The shifts in the rate of growth of the black population and in black immigration suggest the beginnings of a natural increase among Virginia's blacks.

Immigration dramatically declined from the mid-1740s to the Revolution, falling at a rate of 4.1 percent a year; by the 1770s, less than 500 blacks came to Virginia in a typical year, a number below that of seventy years earlier.[9] In the 1740s and 1750s, when perhaps 800

6. For the growth of black population see appendix 1. The discussion of the sources and their biases for figure 1 is in appendix 2.
7. Donnan, *Documents*, 4: 188-206, corrected with original Naval Officer records.
8. Figure based upon a logarithmic regression on imports, 1722-1744.
9. Figure based upon a logarithmic regression on imports, 1744-1770.

slaves were imported each year, black population continued to increase by about 4.3 percent each year. As the rate of black immigration continued to decline in the 1760s, the growth rate of the black population also decreased. Black population in Virginia grew at a rate of only 2.7 percent a year between 1760 and 1790. Since the absolute number of slave immigrants declined, while black population rose, the rate of natural population growth must have increased. For example, black population probably increased naturally from 1760 to 1790 at a rate close to 2.7 percent a year. Not only had immigration declined, and ended during the Revolution, but some black Virginians had been taken to Kentucky and North Carolina.[10]

A comparison of the numbers of surviving black immigrants and the total black population will permit estimation of the approximate rate of natural increase (see table 1).[11] In the 1700s, there was a substantial natural decline in the black population that may have been 2 percent a year. The 1710s and 1720s were years of transition. During those decades, there may have been some natural increase, but minimal adjustments in the total population figures eliminate any growth.[12] After 1730, the black population of Virginia grew rapidly from natural increase; from 1730 to 1770, the numbers of blacks increased naturally at about 2.5 percent a year. As the numbers of immigrants declined after 1740, natives accounted for an ever higher proportion of the total growth of black population. Half of the blacks added to Virginia's population in the 1730s were immigrants, but that proportion declined to a quarter in the 1740s, and to a tenth by the 1750s.

II

Patterns of black population growth were similar in Maryland, but the immigration data we have are far sketchier. About 300 slaves a year came to Maryland between 1698 and 1708. In the early 1720s, perhaps as many as 500 to 1000 Africans were forced to come to Maryland during years of peak immigration. Immigration was very high between

---

10.   There were 13,000 blacks in Kentucky in 1790, and most must have come from Virginia. See U.S. Bureau of the Census, *Historical Statistics of the United States Colonial Times to 1970* (2 volumes, Washington, 1976), 28.

11.   The estimates are only as good as three different pieces of information: the numbers of immigrants, the death rates of immigrants, and the level of black population. Since any of the three could be biased (as appendix 3 makes clear), the growth rates presented in table 1 and in the text might be biased in either direction.

12.   I have reduced the 1710 figure from *Historical Statistics* (see appendix 1). If I had used their number, I would have found natural decline in the 1710s and natural growth in the 1700s.

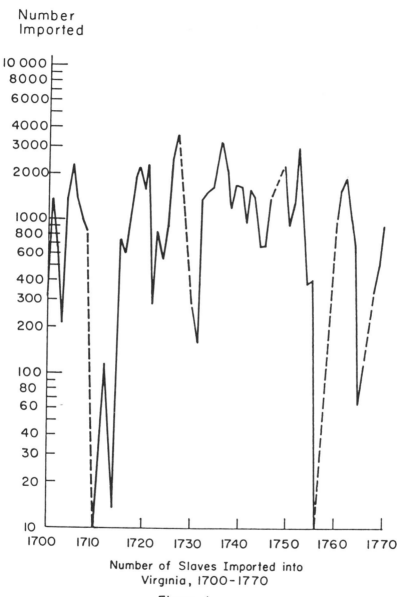

Number of Slaves Imported into
Virginia, 1700-1770

Figure I.

1733 and 1738, low throughout the 1740s, moderate in the 1750s, and high for the last time in the early 1760s. Roughly 550 slaves a year entered Maryland from 1733 to 1738 (and 450 a year during the entire decade). About 200 came in the 1750s, 350 in the 1760s, and 200 in the 1770s. Maryland's tobacco frontier was much smaller than Virginia's and fewer new Negroes were needed in that province. From 1700 to the 1730s the level of black immigration increased at a rate of about 1.9 percent a year; from 1730 to the 1770s, its level declined at a rate of about 2.6 percent a year.[13]

III

As long as most of the adult slaves in the Chesapeake colonies were African immigrants, black population grew mainly by the enslaving of more Africans. The purchase of large numbers of Africans was often a self-defeating process for planters who wished to develop a self-sustaining slave labor force. In the first place, twice as many men as women were imported. This meant that a high rate of female fertility would be required to achieve any natural increase, while female mortality would have to be low in early and childbearing years. Unfortunately, high mortality and low fertility were endemic problems among African immigrants.

When Africans came to the Americas, they left one disease environment and entered another. Since they lacked immunity to the local diseases, many died soon after arrival. Between 1710 and 1718, 5.4 percent of African immigrants to Virginia died before they could be sold.[14] Many others died before the end of their first year in the region, especially from respiratory diseases during the winter and spring following their enslavement.[15] The experience of 32 Africans bought by John Mercer of New Marlborough in Stafford County, Virginia, between 1733 and 1742 suggests the extent of immigrant black mortal-

---

13. For sources and methods of computation, see Allan Kulikoff, "Tobacco and Slaves: Population, Economy and Society in Eighteenth-Century Prince George's County, Maryland," (Ph.D. diss., Brandeis, 1976), 72-75.

14. Philip D. Curtin, "Epidemiology and the Slave Trade," *Political Science Quarterly* 83 (1968): 190-216; Donnan, *Documents*, 4: 175-181. A somewhat smaller proportion (4.8 percent) of those coming from the West Indies died. There were some differences according to port of entry: 4.4 percent died in York; 9.6 percent in Rappahannock; and 5.4 percent in both Upper and Lower James. The difference, if it was not due to lower reporting rates at other ports (unlikely), could be related to slower sales on the Rappahannock.

15. Allan Kulikoff, "The Origins of Afro-American Society in Tidewater Maryland and Virginia, 1700-1790," *WMQ*, 3rd. Ser., 35 (1978), forthcoming. See C. G. Chamberlayne, ed., *The Vestry Book and Register of St. Peter's Parish, New Kent and James City Counties, Virginia* (Richmond, 1937) for an example.

ity in Virginia. Eight of the 32 died by the end of their first year, and at least another seven died before they had lived ten years in Virginia. If both the pre-sale mortality and the deaths at New Marlborough were typical, then less than half of the Africans who were forced to come to the Chesapeake lived even ten years. The life chances of Mercer's African slaves improved the longer they lived on his plantation. An African, age 20, who came to Mercer's farm in the 1730s could expect to live only to age 36. If he survived a year, he would probably live to be 41, and if he lived ten years, he would be age 47 before he died (see table 2).

Table 2

Life Expectation for Thirty-Two Africans Bought by John Mercer of Stafford County, Virginia Between 1733 and 1742

Time Since Arrival	Number Alive	Number of Survivors Per 1000	Preferred Life Expectation (In Years)
At Arrival	32	1000	15.5
One Year	24	750	19.5
Two Years	23	719	19.3
Five Years	22	688	17.2
Ten Years	17	531	16.7

Source: John Mercer Ledger B, Buck's County Historical Society, p. 12, (Film copy at Colonial Williamsburg Research Library). For details of the construction of this table, see appendix 3.

No other similar record of a Chesapeake plantation has yet been found. Does the mortality it records seem reasonable? Mortality was higher during the first three years after arrival in the West Indies: 31 percent at New Marlborough, 36 percent at Worthy Park in Jamaica, and 43 percent on the Codrington plantation in Barbados. However, life expectation of those surviving seasoning seems to be higher in Jamaica; a slave who survived three years at Worthy Park in the 1730s might live another 30 years. Mortality on Mercer's plantation fits the traditional belief that one-third of all black immigrants died during their first three years in the New World. Nevertheless, since it would be expected that Chesapeake mortality was less than that of the islands, the Mercer data might overestimate the extent of black mortality. The apparently high mortality at New Marlborough does demand that the earlier rise of a naturally increasing black population in the Chesapeake than in the West Indies be more fully explained.[16]

16. Michael Craton, *Sinews of Empire: A Short History of British Slavery* (New

Both early death and the sex composition of the immigrant population reduced the African birth rate. Slavers brought over predominantly adult male cargoes. Thomas Cable, a merchant on Virginia's
Eastern Shore, suggested in 1725 that if he "could choose a Cargoe of
Negroes as you propose 200—I would have 100 men able young
Slaves, 60 women, 30 Boys & 10 Girls from 10 to 14 years of age.
Such a Cargoe I could sell to a great Advantage."[17] Slave ships that
reached Virginia closely followed this pattern. They typically contained two men for every woman, and less than a sixth of the migrants were children. Three-quarters of the children were over ten
years of age and another fifth were eight or nine. Two-thirds of the
older children were boys but the younger children were more evenly
divided by sex (see table 3).[18]

IV

African women in the Chesapeake bore few children. Their health
and social condition greatly militated against conception. Many of
these women were so severely undernourished after the middle passage that they could not conceive a child or complete a pregnancy.
The high rate of mortality during the first year suggests considerable
morbidity that may have continued to inhibit conception, and otherwise healthy women may have refused to bring children into slavery
as a protest against their enslavement.[19] Even after they became
healthy enough to bear children, many women remained childless.
Edmund Jenings apparently purchased around twenty African women
and placed them on his quarters in King William County, Virginia, in
the years before he died in 1712. Over two-thirds of the 22 women on

---

York, 1974), pp. 194-195, 365; J. Harry Bennett, Jr., *Bondsmen and Bishops: Slavery
and Apprenticeship on the Codrington Plantations in Barbados* (Berkeley, 1968. University of California Publications in History, volume 62), pp. 54, 60-61, 95.

17.   Thomas Cable to John Walpole, July 16, 1725, Cable Letterbook, 1722-1757,
Maryland Historical Society (hereafter MdHS). I am indebted to John Hemphill for
pointing out this source.

18.   Table 3. There were 597 ages of slaves judged in York and Lancaster courts
(1710-1749 and 1710-1740) where both age and sex were given: 75 percent were between
10 and 14 (with those age 15 excluded); 19 percent were 8-9; 6 percent were 0-7 and
only one percent were 0-4.

19.   Menard, "Maryland Slave Population," 41-42. Regular menstruation requires
"a minimum weight for height, apparently representing a critical fat storage." Rose E.
Frisch, "Demographic Implications of the Biological Determinants of Female Fecun-
dity," *Social Biology*, 22 (1975): 17-22, quote at p. 17. Frisch's ideas are applied to
Jamaica's slave population by Richard S. Dunn, "A Tale of Two Plantations: Slave
Life at Mesopotamia and Mt. Airy in Virginia, 1799 to 1828," *WMQ*, 3rd Ser., 34
(1977): 61-63.

Table 3
Age and Sex Composition of a Typical African Slaver to Virginia

| Group | Composition in Percentages | | | Sex Ratios |
	Males	Females	Total	
Adults[a]	58	27	85	213
Age 10-14[b]	7	4	11	200
Under 10[b]	2	2	4	150
Totals	67	33	100	203

[a] The sex ratio of five ships (with 959 slaves) that entered Maryland and Virginia, 1717-1721, was 213 for adults and 213 for children. Fifteen percent of the Africans were children. When two other ships, one in 1702 and the other in 1727, are added, the adult sex ratio declines to 180 and the child sex ratio decreases to 196 while the proportion of children increases to 17 percent (1152 slaves). The 1702 ship was the subject of long litigation; Robert Carter complained about the atypical composition of the 1727 ship.

[b] The sexual composition of the children represents work with the sources cited above and two series of the ages of immigrant children judged in York and Lancaster counties, Virginia (1710-1749 and 1710-1740 respectively). From 1680 to the Revolution, every black immigrant under 16 had to have his age judged in the local county court or his master would have to pay a poll tax on him. William Waller Hening, *The Statutes at Large: Being a Collection of all the Laws of Virginia* (Richmond, 1819), 2: 479-480; 3: 258-259; 6: 40-41. Apparently more boys than girls died in seasoning, for the sex ratios found in ages judged are only 130 for ages 10-14. The sex ratios given in the table follow the ships' sex ratio for older children but assume that the ages judged were more accurate for younger children. The breakdown between children 0-9 and 10-14 was calculated from the ages judged.

Source: Donnan, *Documents*, 4: 70-72, 100; T 70/1225, 2, 6-7, PRO; "Sale of the Charfield Slaves Begun July 23, 1717 Belonging to Samuel Jacobs and Company, Bristol," Stephen Loyd-John Tayloe Account Book, Virginia Historical Society (VHS); Robert Carter to John Pemberton, July 26, 1727, added to June 28 letter, Carter Letterbooks, VHS; Elizabeth Suttell, "The British Slave Trade to Virginia, 1698-1728," (M.A. Thesis, William and Mary, 1965), pp. 58-59.

his quarters had no children early in 1713 and another fifth had but one child. Some of the women may have been new Negroes purchased in 1712 but others were likely bought as early as 1705 and 1707. Nine of the fifteen childless women lived on quarters where men outnumbered women.[20]

Some African women may not have immediately found husbands. Since far more men than women immigrated, one might expect women to be almost immediately forced into sexual unions. Yet this was not the case on the many quarters of Robert "King" Carter when he died in 1733. Carter owned some native women but bought numer-

---

20. "Inventories of Negroes, etc. on the Estate of Edmund Jenings, 1712-1713," Francis Porteus Corbin Papers, Duke University. The years mentioned were peak years for imports (see Appendix 2).

ous Africans in the years before he died. The adult sex ratio on his plantations in 1733 was 142. About a fifth (36/173) of all the women over 15 were unmarried; four were young native women, but the other 32 were apparently over 20. These women were probably Africans. They tended to live with other unrelated women. Carter encouraged marriage among his slaves and allowed husbands and wives to live together. But even after they married, Carter's African slaves did not begin to have children immediately. In all, 41 percent of the women over 15 on Carter's plantations had no children.[21] The Jenings and Carter data suggest that African women rarely conceived a child until at least their third year in Virginia. The first year they were both unhealthy and unmarried; the second year they may have married but did not conceive. It is entirely possible that the average African immigrant woman did not bear her first child until her fourth, fifth, or sixth year in the region.

In sum, immigrant slave populations in Maryland and Virginia could not reproduce themselves. We can rather crudely present a probable fertility pattern for the sixty women on Cable's "preferred slave ship" from the data just presented. If these women were like other immigrant women, they were mostly in their early twenties when they arrived.[22] By the time they conceived, they were roughly 25 and had at most fifteen fertile years left. If mortality were half that reported at New Marlborough, ten of the 60 women would have died before they had any children. If the other 50 bore children regularly until about age 37, they would have had about 4.4 children each. There would have thus been 3.7 children born for each of the 60 women. If 30 percent of the children died before age 20, and the sex ratio of the adult population was 180, then only .9 native adults would have replaced each African adult in the next generation. But suppose the deaths followed the Mercer table and that the surviving women bore children less regularly. In this case, 19 women would die childless and the remaining 41 women would have about four children each. Each of the 60 women would have borne about 2.7 children and

---

21. Inventory of Robert Carter, 1733, in Carter Papers, Virginia Historical Society (hereafter VHS); Carter bought 80 slaves for his own use in 1727. Robert Carter to William Dawkins, May 13, 1727, Carter Letterbooks, VHS; Carter to Dawkins, June 3, 1727, Carter Letterbooks, Alderman Library, University of Virginia. For number of children per family, see table 4.

22. White immigrant women arrived in the Chesapeake in their early 20s and scholars have assumed that African women did as well. Russell R. Menard, "Immigrants and Their Increase: The Process of Population Growth in Early Colonial Maryland," in Aubrey Land, et al., eds., Law, Society and Politics in Early Maryland (Baltimore, 1977); Menard, "Maryland Slave Population," pp. 45-46.

if 40 percent of the children died before age 20, and the sex ratio of the African population was 200, then two Africans would have been replaced by only one native adult.[23]

This exercise suggests that the African population of the Chesapeake colonies declined at a rate between 0.4 to 2.6 percent per year.[24] Yet the black population did begin to grow naturally sometime around 1730. The key to understanding this change is the increase in the proportion of native black women in the female population of Maryland and Virginia. Native women, both white and black, married younger and had more children than their immigrant mothers. If immigration of African women increased at a slower rate than the numbers of maturing native women, then the proportion of native women in the population would increase, and the number of children per woman (Africans plus Afro-Americans) would also grow. The differences in the fertility of immigrant and native black women can be illustrated by a comparison of the slaves on plantations owned by Edmund Jenings in 1712, King Carter in 1733, and Charles Carroll and Thomas Addison in 1773-1774. Jenings's farm contained mostly Afri-

---

23. I made the following assumptions:

Variable	High Fertility	Low Fertility
Months from Arrival to First Conception	36	36
Birth Intervals (months)	25 in year 3-10	30 in year 3-10
	30 in year 10-15	40 in year 10-15
Death Rate	2.7 percent die before being sold; later mortality half the Mercer Table	5.4 percent die before being sold; later mortality follows Mercer Table
Adult Sex Ratio	180	200
Percent Children Die Before 20	30	40
Births/All Women	3.7	2.7
Survivors at Age 20/Women	2.6	1.6
Survivors at Age 20/Adults	.9	.5

These estimates are deliberately biased against the hypothesis that immigrants could not replace themselves. The birth intervals are especially short for an unhealthy population and even the low fertility estimate might generate too many births. Birth intervals of native women are discussed below. About 40 percent of slave children died in the nineteenth century. See Jack E. Eblen, "New Estimates of the Vital Rates of the United States Black Population During the Nineteenth Century," *Demography*, 11 (1974): 307-308. Data presented below suggests that death rates in the eighteenth century were at least as high.

24. Growth rates were computed from the ratio of survivors at age 20 to adults, assuming that a slave generation lasted 26 years. See notes to table 7 below for justification of that figure.

135

can women: Carter's included both Africans and natives; and Carroll's and Addison's female slaves were almost all natives. There were only .7 children aged 0 to 15 for each woman on Jenings's quarters, but 1.6 on Carter's and 2.3 on Carroll's and Addison's.[25]

The size of families of married women suggests more precisely the dimensions of the difference in fertility between immigrant and native women. Only seven of the 22 women on Jenings's farms had any children: four women had one child, two had four children, and one had five children. While a fifth of the families on Carter's quarters were childless, 41 years later only a twentieth had no children on the other two. And there were proportionately two-and-a-half times as many families with four or more children on the Carroll and Addison plantations than on those owned by Carter. The average household on Carter's farms included two children, but there were three children per family on the Maryland plantations (see table 4).[26]

Table 4

Number of Children in Households on Robert Carter's Plantation in 1733 and Charles Carroll's and Thomas Addison's in 1773-1774[a]

Plantation[b]	Percentage of Households by Number of Children					Mean Size	Median Size
	0	1	2-3	4-5	6+		
Carter	22	18	46	13	1	2.0	2
Carroll & Addison	6	21	39	25	10	2.9	3

[a] There were 140 households on Carter's quarters and 72 on Carroll and Addison's. I have counted as a household every instance where a marriage could be proved: husband-wife-children households, mother-children households, and father-children households. Children who had left the household were not counted, but the sale and transfer practices on the three plantations were roughly similar. Since the age of mothers on Carter's plantations is not known, I could not control for age-structure differences.

[b] Carter had quarters in Lancaster, Northumberland, Richmond, Westmoreland, Caroline, King George, Stafford, Spotsylvania and Prince William Counties. The Addison farms were in southern Prince George's County and the Carroll quarters were located in Anne Arundel County, both in Maryland.

Source: Robert Carter Inventory, Carter Papers, VHS; Charles Carroll Account Book, MdHS; Prince George's Inventories (hereafter PG) GS2, 334-36, Maryland Hall of Records (hereafter MHR).

25. Jenings Inventory; Carter Inventory; Charles Carroll Account Book, MdHS; Prince George's Md., Inventories, GS2, pp. 334-336, MHR. Only children who could be placed with a particular mother or father were counted. If one excludes two old women found on the Jenings plantation, the ratio increases to .8. (with the two old women included, there were 24 females).

26. Some of the differences could have been caused by differences in the age struc-

As the proportion of native adults in the black population increased, the ratio of men to women declined, and this, added to an increase in the proportion of native women among blacks, led to a higher overall birth rate. More boys than girls are born in most populations, but adult sex ratios are close to 100 because more boys than girls die. The effect of an increase in the proportion of native adults on the adult sex ratio is clear: if the entire black population were African, the sex ratio would be about 200; when a third of the adults were Afro-Americans, the sex ratio would drop to 156; and by the time Africans constituted only a third of the adult population, the sex ratio would decline to 125.[27] The black adult sex ratio was also affected by African death rates in the Chesapeake colonies. African men apparently died more rapidly than African women, and this differential mortality also helped lower the sex ratio.[28]

The rate of natural increase of the black population in the Chesapeake colonies depended on the black birth rate, the adult death rate, infant and childhood mortality, and the sex ratio. All of these variables were affected by the composition of the black population. The reasons for natural population increase or decline in any period can best be discovered by a detailed analysis of the available fertility and mortality data. Very little is known about the period before 1680, but a substantial understanding of black population growth after 1680 is possible.

V

The period between 1680 and 1710 was characterized by heavy immigration, low female fertility, and a high death rate. From one-half to two-thirds of all black adults of childbearing age in Virginia in 1708 were immigrants, and the proportion may have been higher in earlier years.[29] Sex ratios in Surry County, Virginia, and on Maryland's

---

ture of the populations. Since female ages were not given on the Carter quarters, no direct comparison can be made. However, the marriage rates on the two plantations were very similar: 83 percent of all women over 15 were married on the Carroll farms; 79 percent on the Carter plantations. This similarity suggests, at a minimum, that there was not a greater proportion of women 15-19 (and therefore probably unmarried or married without children) on the Carter plantation.

27. See George W. Barclay, *Techniques of Population Analysis* (New York, 1958), pp. 64-65, 70-72 for a discussion of sex ratios in closed populations.

28. Menard, "Maryland Slave Population," pp. 32-33 argues that the fact that more old women than old men appeared in inventories suggests that men died more quickly than women.

29. The proportions of immigrants reported here and in subsequent paragraphs are based upon total black immigration adjusted for deaths and numbers of children. For computational procedure, see appendix 4.

Western Shore, reported in figure 2, suggest that the proportion of immigrants among blacks increased from 1680 to 1710.[30] In Surry County, the adult sex ratio increased from 144 between 1679 and 1689 to over 200 from 1690 to 1704. The black adult sex ratio rose in Maryland from roughly 120 in the late 1670's to 174 in the 1710's. Immigrant women gave birth to very few children, and the few native women could not offset their low fertility. The Jenings plantations may have been typical of farms dominated by African adults: there were only .7 children under 16 for each woman on his quarters in King William County in 1713, and only .3 children for each adult. In Maryland, heavy immigration in the late 1690s and early 1700s led to an increasing rate of natural decline of the black population. In the 1690s, there were about 1.3 children per woman and .5 children for each adult, but in the 1700s, the number of children per woman declined to 1.0 and the number of children per woman decreased to .4.[31]

Black immigration nearly stopped in the early 1700s, and picked up only late in the decade. As a result, the proportion of Africans in the adult population of Virginia declined to somewhere between 50 and 58 percent. As the magnitude of immigration decreased, sex ratios became much lower: 126 in York County and 118 in Lancaster County in the 1710s. The black birth rate probably increased as a result, but immigrants were still needed to maintain the population. In the 1710s, there were 1.4 children for each woman and .6 children for each adult in York County. Maryland's population behaved somewhat differently. Adult sex ratios rose from about 150 to 170, indicating that substantial numbers of Africans had been forced to come to southern Maryland. Nevertheless, the number of children per woman rose to

---

30. The data on slave sex ratios presented in figure 2 come from the following sources: Menard, "Maryland Slave Population," pp. 32, 43, (Southern Maryland); St. Mary's City Commission (St. Mary's County); Kulikoff, "Tobacco and Slaves," p. 77 (Prince George's for ages 15-29); York County Orders, Wills, 1710-1770; Robert Wheeler, "Mobility of Labor in Surry County, Virginia, 1674-1703," paper delivered at the Stony Brook Conference, 1975, p. 6.

31. Jenings Inventory; Menard, "Maryland Slave Population," p. 32. I have adjusted Menard's ratios of children to women and children to adults to account for the immigration of children. Each of the statistics from that article (Maryland before 1730) and from York County is based upon ratios of children 0-15 to women or adults; exact ages were rarely given. In each of these cases, I have assumed that there were equal numbers of boys and girls in the native black population, and have called any excess boys immigrants. This may overestimate male immigration of children (sex ratios tend to be over 100 at birth), but underestimate the immigration of girls. These children to women ratios are somewhat difficult to interpret for they represent only a part of a woman's childbearing and include children who died before age 20. However, child/woman ratios greatly below 2 suggest a naturally declining population; ratios near or above 2 suggest natural increase.

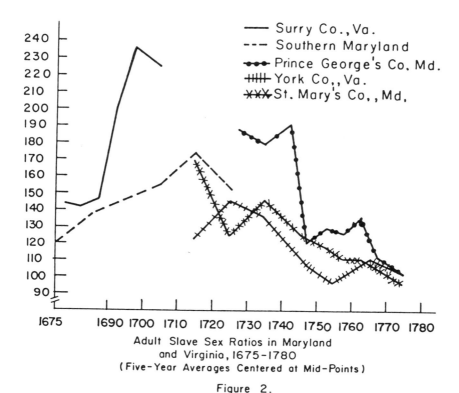

Adult Slave Sex Ratios in Maryland
and Virginia, 1675-1780
(Five-Year Averages Centered at Mid-Points)

Figure 2.

1.5 and the number of children per adult increased to .5. These patterns suggest that large numbers of African men, but fewer African women came to the colony and that many native women reached the peak of their childbearing years during the decade. Maryland's black population still experienced a natural decline but at a slower rate than in the 1690s and 1700s.[32]

A naturally growing black population appeared in both Chesapeake colonies in the 1720s and 1730s despite a surge of immigration and an increasing sex ratio. Between 52 and 69 percent of the black adults of Virginia were immigrants in 1728 and the proportion declined to between 42 and 51 percent by 1740. Sex ratios rose in Prince George's County, Maryland and York County, Virginia, but declined in St. Mary's County, Maryland, and Lancaster County, Virginia (see figure

---

32. York County, Orders, Wills, etc., for the 1710s; figure 2; Menard, "Maryland Slave Population," p. 32; Lancaster Wills, 1710-1725. All Virginia probate materials are in Virginia State Library (hereafter VSL).

2). There were nearly two children for each woman in both Maryland and Virginia. In York County, the number of children per woman increased from 1.6 in the 1620s to 2.0 in the 1730s and the number of children per adult rose from .7 to .8. In southern Maryland in the 1720s, there were 1.9 children per woman and .8 children per adult. During these two decades, the proportion of native women in the black population became high enough to overcome the low fertility of African immigrant women. These native women married in their late teens and had numerous children. Data from a group of thirteen black women born in Prince George's County in the 1710s and 1720s suggest an age of conception for their first child of 17.6 years. A woman in her 20s or 30s during these years would give birth to roughly five children if she lived to age 44, and each adult in the population would be replaced by about one adult in the next generation.[33]

The rate of black natural increase grew dramatically in the years after 1740. African immigration decreased sharply. As a result, only 27 to 34 percent of all black adults were immigrants in 1750, and that proportion continued to decline. Black adult sex ratios declined in all parts of Tidewater Maryland and Virginia. In the 1750s, only Prince George's sex ratio was over 130, and by the 1770s, sex ratios in Prince George's, York, and St. Mary's counties were all below 105. Each woman in the population had to give birth to only two surviving children to insure that every adult was replaced by another adult in the next generation. Black women bore enough children in the pre-Revolutionary years, however, to provide a high rate of natural increase (see figure 3).

VI

Afro-Americans married and began having children in their late teens. The mean ages at the conception of the first child of those slave women born between 1720 and 1759 ranged from 17.5 to 18.5 years and no trend is discernible (see table 5). About 12 percent of these women conceived their first child before age 16 and 70 percent of the women began their childbearing before age 20. Only 3 percent of them had their first pregnancy after age 24.

The impact of early marriage can be seen in an analysis of Charles Carroll's and Thomas Addison's plantations in 1773 and 1774 (also included in table 5). Only 29 percent of the girls age 15 to 19 were

---

33.   Figures 2 and 3; table 5; York Wills, Orders. The meaning of the age at conception and fertility data will be explained below.

Table 5
Age at First Conception of Slave Women
born 1710-1759, Southern Maryland

Decade of Birth of Mother	Mean Age of Women		Total Number of Women
	At Conception of Eldest Child Living With Her	At Estimated Conception of First Child[a]	
1710s	18.4	17.8	5
1720s	18.1	17.5	8
1730s	18.8	18.1	17
1740s	19.3	18.5	71
1750s	17.9	17.6	79

[a] Allowing for the estimated impact of infant mortality.
Source: Prince George's Inventories, libers PD1, DD1, DD2, GS1, GS2, ST1, ST2, MHR; PG 1776 Census in Gaius M. Brumbaugh, *Maryland Records: Colonial, Revolutionary, County and Church* (Baltimore, 1915), 1: 1-89; Carroll Account Book, MdHS (Carroll's slaves in Anne Arundel County). For a detailed description of the biases of this data and computational procedures, see appendix 4.

married or had children, but 90 percent of those 20 to 24 had children. Every woman over 24 on these quarters had given birth. The experience of the women on Carroll's and Addison's farms suggests that marriage and childbearing was not an uncommon experience for women 18 and 19 years of age; four of the seven women (57 percent) 18 and 19 were married and had children. The singulate mean age at birth of their first child for these women was 19.1 (or an estimated 18.4 at conception of the first child), a figure not much higher than those reported in table 5 for the 1740s and 1750s for a larger group of plantations.[34]

These women not only began to have children at a young age, but they bore children at short intervals. Afro-American women lived in monogamous households, and lacked inhibitions against having closely spaced children. Like white women, they experienced a birth nearly once every other year. Birth intervals for 29 Prince George's

34. See table 5 for sources. The singulate mean age is based upon proportions of slave women with children, rather than on the specific ages at which they had their first known child. The statistic reports the mean number of years lived without children by those who have a child by age 40. See J. Hajnal, "Age at Marriage and Proportion Marrying," *Population Studies*, 7 (1953): 111-36 and the application of Hajnal's statistic to slave age at first birth by James Trussell and Richard Steckel, "The Estimation of the Mean Age of Female Slaves at the Time of Menarche and Their First Birth," *Journal of Interdisciplinary History*, 1978. For the proportions marrying here, see appendix 4.

slave women in the 1770s under age 35 ranged from 25 to 27 months; and the mean birth interval for three women on Robert Lloyd's plantation on the Eastern Shore of Maryland in the 1740s was 27 months. Twenty-three women on Francis Jerdone's plantations in York, Spotsylvania, and Albemarle counties in the 1760s and 1770s bore a child about every 29 months. A slave woman who married in her late teens, and lived to 45, would probably have had eight or nine children; women who died in the 20s or 30s, of course, would have fewer children.[35]

These birth intervals accurately reflect the fertility of eighteenth-century slave women. Afro-American women who married from 1740 to 1800 bore about six children and those who completed their childbearing years gave birth to eight children. Slave women throughout the Chesapeake region bore similar numbers of children. Carroll and Jerdone had farms in Tidewater; Jerdone, Jefferson, and Bolling each had a plantation in Piedmont. Fertility might have been increasing slightly from 1740 to the Revolution, but may then have declined during the early nineteenth century (see table 6). Both the Carroll plantation (in Anne Arundel County, Maryland) and Mt. Airy (in Virginia's Northern Neck) were located in the tidewater region of the Chesapeake colonies, but completed families were about one-quarter larger on Carroll's farms before the Revolution than at Mt. Airy in the 1810s and 1820s.[36] Since women at Mt. Airy gave birth to their first child at a mean age of 19.3, this difference might indicate the beginnings of family limitation among Afro-Americans in Tidewater.

---

35. Brumbaugh, *Maryland Records*, 1: 1-88 (Prince George's Census, 1776); Robert Lloyd Farm Book, MdHS; Francis Jerdone Slave Book, VSL. The range for Prince George's women on the census was based upon years between births. The census gives ages of all slaves alive in half the county in 1776. The upward bias in the statistics created by infant and childhood mortality could not be directly measured. A relatively unbiased figure was calculated by excluding women over 35 and choosing only women with three or more children whose eldest child was not over 12 years. The range for Prince George's women was determined by including and excluding women age 30 to 34 from the calculation. The downward bias created by these decisions ought to cancel the upward bias produced by mortality. The method of linking women with children is explained in appendix 5. Birth intervals from the other two sources are based upon exact births. Infants who died in their first few weeks of life apparently were not listed on the Jerdone register; very long birth intervals were therefore excluded. If the interval was greater than 60 months, it was not included; and if interval b was only half the size of interval a, it too was eliminated (e.g. intervals between births 1-2 = 56 months; between 2-3 = 19 months; interval 1-2 not counted). Finally, intervals over 40 months when only two births were recorded were not used. If *all* intervals are included, the mean rises to 32 months. The estimate of the number of children born, given these intervals, is based upon a twenty-year childbearing period.

36. Dunn, "Tale of Two Plantations," p. 58.

Table 6
Family Size on Five Plantations, 1739-1828

Plantation	Years of Birth of First Child	Mean Completed Family Size[a]	Mean Size All Families[b]	Number of Women
Carroll, Md.	1739-1759	7.9	c	11
Jerdone, Va.	1754-1775	8.0	5.8	19
Bolling, Va.	1750-1795	8.3	6.0	25
Jefferson, Va.	1765-1800	7.7	c	c
Mt. Airy, Va.	1809-1828	6.4	c	c

[a] Completed family size is defined as follows: 1) on Carroll plantation, it includes the families of all women 40-60, except for two women who had only one child; 2) on the Jerdone and Bolling plantations, it includes all women with at least seven children and all women who lived through at least 15 childbearing years. There were 10 completed families on Jerdone's plantations's and 14 on Bolling's.

[b] Average number of births per family. No death registers survive for either the Bolling or Jerdone plantations. Women whose families were considered incomplete either died, were sold, or lived through their childbearing years with fewer than 7 children. The Jerdone record included both a register and a family list. The family list apparently did not list children born in the 1750s who died before the list was made in 1770. Five families in this category are excluded.

[c] Data not available.

Source: Carroll Account Book: Jerdone Family Slave Book, VSL: William Bolling Register, VHS: Edwin Morris Betts, *Thomas Jefferson's Farm Book* (Philadelphia, 1953): 1-178 (data provided by Mary Beth Norton: she describes completed family size as "all births between 1765 and 1800"); Dunn, "Tale of Two Plantations," p. 58.

VII

Plantation records hide variations in the black birth rate caused by immigration and changing age structures. Figure 3 shows the numbers of children 0-4 for every woman 15-44 listed by age in Prince George's inventories between 1725 and 1779.[37] This statistic shows the direction and intensity of changes in the overall black birth rate. When African immigration to southern Maryland declined after 1740, the numbers of children 0-4 for each woman increased from .6 in the 1740s to nearly 1.0 in the 1750s. After imports of slaves into the

---

37. PG Census, 1776: PG Inventories, 1725-1780. Data comes from exact ages on the census and from probate inventories which frequently list ages. While only 9 percent of all slaves listed had ages given in the 1730s, this rises to 27 percent in the 1740s and 45 percent in the 1750s and 1760s. Most of those with exact ages were probably natives, but the ages of Africans were estimated with those of natives on a number of large plantations. When the inventory ages can be checked with census data, they appear unbiased. See Menard, "Maryland Slave Population," pp. 32-33: Kulikoff, "Tobacco and Slaves," pp. 81, 455-58.

county increased in the early 1760s, child-woman ratios reached a trough of about .7. When immigration declined in the 1770s, the child-woman ratio again increased to about 1.0. If women alive during the periods of high immigration bore children at the rate implied by the child-woman ratios, then each woman gave birth to about 4.2 children; if they followed the fertility schedule implied by child-woman ratios found in periods of low immigration, then they would have had about six children.[38]

The presence of large numbers of African-born women explains most of the variations in child-woman ratios, but age structure also played a role. About 42 percent of the women between 15 and 44 were in their teens or 40s between 1740 and 1744, when the birth rate was low, but only a quarter were in these two age groups between 1755 and 1759, when the birth rate reached a peak. The adult female age structure was less clearly correlated with the child-woman ratios in the 1760s and 1770s. During these decades, the proportion of women 15-19 and 40-44 ranged narrowly between 30 and 37 percent. The variations in child-woman ratios during periods of low immigration suggest that long and short swings in fertility may have been common among black women in the Chesapeake, with alternating periods of low and high crude birth rates.[39]

Child-woman ratios cannot measure fertility directly because they are "based upon survivors of previous births."[40] If one knows the death rate for children 0-4, then one can compute a total fertility rate from child-woman ratios. Records kept by Robert Lloyd and Robert Carter (of Nomini) suggest that a third of all slave children died between birth and age 5.[41] If one-third of all children 0-4 died before the inventory was taken, then women who survived their childbearing

---

38. This number assumes that the ratio of children 0-4 to women 15-44 can be multiplied by 6 to derive a cohort total fertility rate for the women during their entire childbearing period (on the assumption they have children at the same rate throughout that time). It will be biased downward, however, due to the failure to include all deaths below age 5.

39. For the underlying data see Kulikoff, "Tobacco and Slaves," pp. 455-58. The proportions of women 15-19 and 40-44 are as follows: 57 percent in the 1730s; 42 percent in the 1740s; 36 percent between 1750 and 1754; 25 percent from 1755 to 1759; 37 percent between 1760 and 1764; 30 percent between 1765 and 1769; 35 percent from 1770 to 1774; and 35 percent in 1776. For swings in fertility, see Barclay, *Techniques of Population Analysis*, pp. 204-6 and P.M.G. Harris, "The Social Origins of American Leaders: The Demographic Foundations," *Perspectives in American History*, 3 (1969): 159-346, but especially pp. 311-33.

40. Barclay, *Techniques of Population Analysis*, pp. 24-25.

41. Lloyd Farm Book; Robert Carter Deed of Manumission, 1791-1796, Carter Papers, Duke University. For details, see appendix 6.

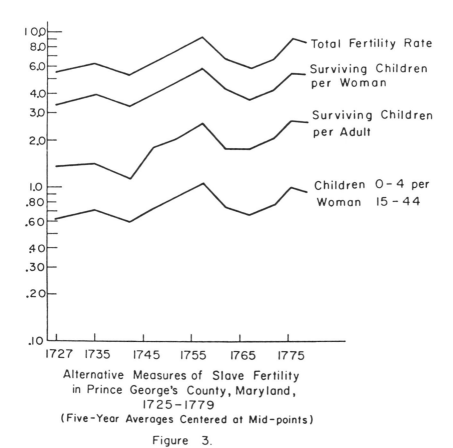

Alternative Measures of Slave Fertility
in Prince George's County, Maryland,
1725-1779
(Five-Year Averages Centered at Mid-points)

Figure 3.

years typically gave birth to between six and nine children. Slave women who followed the fertility schedules of different years produced varying numbers of children: 6 based on the early 1740s, 7 for the late 1740s, 8 for the 1750s, 6 for the 1760s, and 8 for the 1770s.

There was a very slow growth in the total fertility rate between 1730 and 1779, but this growth was achieved by the 1750s. The total fertility rate for the entire period probably approximated seven children. That figure, however, includes years when the lower fertility of African women depressed the total fertility rate. From 1750 to 1779, the mean total fertility rate during times of low immigration was 7.8.[42]

42. This figure excludes 1765-1769, the lowest cohort in the period. The mean is 7.5 when all cohorts are included. The 1776 and 1778-1779 data are counted as one case. See appendix 6.

This figure corresponds closely to the completed family size found on the Carroll, Jerdone, Bolling, and Jefferson plantations (see table 6).

Some of the slave children born in Prince George's died before they reached adulthood but enough survived to insure natural growth. The number of adult children per woman hovered around 3.5 in the early 1740s, then rose to about five by the 1770s. When African immigration increased in the 1760s, the number declined to about four, still above the level of the 1740s. As long as sex ratios remained high, the number of children per adult was less than half the number of children per woman. There were only 1.4 children per adult in the 1730s, and that number did not substantially increase until the 1750s. By the mid-1760s, the sex ratio of black adults reached near 100, and the numbers of children for every adult was nearly half the number of children for each woman.[43]

A comparison of the rates of natural increase computed from Virginia population and immigration data with those drawn from Prince George's adjusted surviving child-woman ratios suggests the probable range of black natural population increase in the Chesapeake colonies.[44] The numbers of blacks would have declined at a high rate in the 1700s without immigration. While the black population may have barely replaced itself in the 1710s and 1720s, substantial natural population growth began in the 1730s, and the rate of growth probably increased in the 1740s and 1750s as the proportion of native women in the population rose. During the 1730s and 1740s, black population grew at about a rate of 2 percent each year. From 1750 to 1779, the growth rate may have been as high as 3 percent a year, but it was probably closer to 2.5 percent (see table 7).[45]

VIII

This essay has attempted to document the changing rates of growth of the black population in the Chesapeake colonies and to suggest why the population grew. The composition of the black population was critical. Afro-Americans married younger, bore more children,

---

43. Figure 2 (PG sex ratios) and appendix 6.

44. The Virginia figures ought to be higher than the Maryland statistics because the Virginia data include children alive at the end of the decade who died before age 20, while the Maryland figures estimate growth rates of the adult population. Nevertheless, the Maryland figures overestimate the growth of the adult population because they are based upon a total fertility measure that assumes that all women reach age 44. Therefore, both figures—despite their biases—roughly measure similar things.

45. The mean rate for Maryland and Virginia during this period is 2.78 (each decade in table 7 counting as one observation).

Table 7
Rates of Natural Increase of the Black Population
of Maryland and Virginia

Decade	Virginia (Based on Total Population and Immigration)	Maryland (Based on Adjusted Ratios of Surviving Children to Adults)[a]
1700s	-2.0	
1710s	0.6	
1720s	0.3	
1730s	2.8	1.3
1740s	5.0[b]	1.6
1750s	2.4	3.3
1760s	2.7	2.2
1770s		3.3

[a] To compute the Maryland rates, the adjusted surviving children to women ratio was divided by two. Then, a growth rate was computed in which the length of a generation was assumed to be 26 years. A female generation is "approximately equal to the average age of mothers giving birth to live daughters." *Multilingual Demographic Dictionary* (English Section) in United Nations Department of Economic and Social Affairs *Population Studies*, No. 29 (New York, 1958), p. 44. The length of the female generation was approximated using the ages of 18 mothers of children under 1 found on the Carroll and Addison plantations in 1773 and 1774. Carroll Account Book; PG Inventories, GS2, pp. 342-346.

[b] Figure is clearly too high.

Source: Virginia, see table 1; Maryland, see figure 3.

and probably lived longer than their African parents and grandparents. Much remains to be learned about the black population. Future research might focus on three areas. First, we need to distinguish the demographic behavior of immigrants and natives in a more systematic way. Age-specific marital fertility rates for natives and immigrants may have been quite similar, with Africans having had fewer children merely because they began their childbearing later than natives. Or fertility rates may have been different. Secondly, we ought to learn if there were substantial regional differences within the Chesapeake. Older, settled tidewater areas differed in many ways from newer piedmont sections in the eighteenth century, and perhaps the demographic behavior of slaves was also different in the two areas. And finally, the essay demands that more comparative work be done. It has long been thought that West Indian slaves failed to reproduce themselves in the eighteenth century. But if the key to understanding black population growth in the Chesapeake colonies is the proportion of native women, then scholars will have to separate the demographic behavior of Africans and natives on the islands. It is surely possible that natives in the West Indies had many children, but that so many slaves were imported every year that natural growth of the entire population could never begin.[46]

Blacks were surely a prolific people in the mid-eighteenth century, but what difference did this fact make in the everyday lives of slaves and their masters? In the first place, sustained natural growth allowed blacks to develop a cohesive family life. Black women bore many children, and masters tended either to keep parents and children together or transfer them (by sale, will or gift) within their own neighborhood. Some large plantations contained large kinship networks by the 1770s, and most slaves knew numerous kin who lived nearby. Secondly, masters had a more reliable labor force. Africans not only died in great numbers, they often refused to work or worked badly. Afro-Americans adjusted to the slave system and took pride in passing skills (both in agriculture and in the crafts) on to their children. And finally, the development of a native labor force reduced local demands for African imports and thereby accelerated the development of a slave community.[47]

---

46.   See Dunn, "Tale of Two Plantations," for an argument that native fertility in Jamaica was very low and Jack E. Eblen, "On the Natural Increase of Slave Populations: The Example of the Cuban Black Population, 1775-1900," in Stanley L. Engerman and Eugene D. Genovese, eds., *Race and Slavery in the Western Hemisphere: Quantitative Studies* (Princeton, 1975): 211-48 for an argument that the native population of Cuba increased naturally.

47.   For extended discussions of these issues, see Kulikoff, "Tobacco and Slaves," ch. 7; Kulikoff, "Origins of Afro-American Society," and Allan Kulikoff, "The Beginnings of the Afro-American Family in Maryland," in Land, *et al.*, eds., *Law, Society and Politics*.

Appendices

1. Black Population Growth

Black population estimates for the colonial period are based upon a few censuses, tithable figures, and the governors' estimates of the total slave population. The ratios scholars use to transform this data into total black population figures are subject to great error, but these are the only surviving data from which a population series can be computed. Black population in Maryland and Virginia was estimated from the series printed in *Historical Statistics*.[1] Several adjustments were made in this data. The 1710 figure for Virginia was apparently too high. In 1708 there were 12,000 black tithables (blacks over 15) in Virginia. When this number was divided by .645 (to account for children and old people), a growth rate computed for the total population from 1700 to 1708, and that rate applied to the period 1700-1710, the number of blacks was reduced from the 23,118 in *Historical Statistics* to 19,350.[2] The growth of Virginia's black population in the 1720s shown in *Historical Statistics* was too low, given the large immigration of Africans, shown in figure 1, and the possible natural increase in that decade. Therefore, I assumed that the black population of Virginia grew at the same rate as that of Maryland during the 1720s, and increased the 1730 Virginia figure from the 30,000 in *Historical Statistics* to 36,600. The 1750 (and 1755) figures for Virginia were independently calculated. Tithable figures, separated by race, survive for most Virginia counties in 1750 and for the entire province in 1755. I estimated the number of black tithables in 1750 by multiplying the 1749 or 1750 tithable figures for whites and blacks (mostly found in county order books at the VSL) by the proportion of black tithes among all tithes in 1755. I then multiplied the number of tithes by two (a number somewhat lower than that suggested by the 1755 Maryland census) to estimate the total number of blacks. This increased the 1750 figure from the 101,452 in *Historical Statistics* to 107,100.[3] The 1755 figure for Maryland was taken directly from the census of that

---

1. *Historical Statistics of the United States: Colonial Times to 1970* (Washington, 1976), 1168, 29, 36.
2. Evarts B. Greene and Virginia D. Harrington, *American Population Before the Federal Census of 1790* (New York, 1932): 139; Russell R. Menard, "The Maryland Slave Population, 1658 to 1730: A Demographic Profile of Blacks in Four Counties," *WMQ*, 3rd Ser., 32 (1975): 32. The proportion of taxables used here is an average of the 1690s and the 1700s. I eliminated unknowns from Menard's table and assumed that all children 0-15 and one-half of the old people were not taxable.
3. The 1750 lists are found in Robert E. Brown and B. Katherine Brown, *Virginia, 1705-1786: Democracy or Aristocracy?* (East Lansing, Mich., 1964): table between pp. 73-74; the 1755 Maryland census is in *Gentleman's Magazine* 34 (1764): 261 and reprinted in part in *Historical Statistics*, p. 1169.

year; and I estimated the Virginia number by dividing the number of Virginia tithables by the proportion of tithable slaves among all slaves in Maryland that year. The 1755 Virginia figure was thus raised to 127,650.[4] The Maryland slave population for 1780 was estimated from the 1782 census, and the growth rate of slaves from 1770 to 1782. By this estimate there were 83,000 blacks in Maryland, about 3,600 more than shown in *Historical Statistics*.[5]

How well do these figures reflect the growth of the black population? There are substantial differences in decennial growth rates for the black population; 1.7 to 6.0 percent for Virginia and 1.9 to 6.0 percent for both colonies. (See table A1). While part of the difference might be explained by varying levels of immigration, another part

Table A1

Average Annual Rates of Growth of the Black Population of the Chesapeake Colonies
1700-1790

Start of Decade	Virginia		Virginia and Maryland	
	Averaged Over Decade	Averages Over Two Decades	Averaged Over Decade	Averages Over Two Decades
1700	1.7	2.4	3.4	3.5
1710	3.2	3.2	3.7	3.5
1720	3.3	4.2	3.2	3.9
1730	5.1	5.5	4.6	5.3
1740	6.0	4.3	6.0	4.2
1750	2.8	2.8	2.3	2.6
1760	2.9	2.3	2.9	2.4
1770	1.6	2.5	1.9	2.6
1780	3.5		3.4	
Mean	3.3	3.4	3.5	3.5
Standard Deviation	1.35	1.08	1.15	.92
Coefficient of Variation[a]	.40	.32	.33	.26

[a] Standard deviation divided by mean.

4. The 1755 list is in Greene and Harrington, *American Population*, pp. 150-51.
5. The 1782 census is reported in Allan Kulikoff, "Tobacco and Slaves: Population, Economy and Society in Eighteenth-Century Prince George's County," (Ph.D. dissertation, Brandeis University, 1976): 428-29.

might be due to errors in the numbers themselves. Growth rates averaged over two decades show less fluctuations and may be more useful in describing long-term population growth. Rates of population growth for the two colonies together show less variation than that for Virginia considered alone.

2. Numbers of Slaves Imported

The standard source for statistics about forced black immigration to Virginia is Elizabeth Donnan's collection of documents. She, in turn, collected her data from naval office records.[6] How accurate are these statistics and can they be used to indicate either the trend or level of slave imports? If all the quarters of any year for all the ports in Virginia (South Potomac, Rappahannock, York, Upper James, Lower James, Accomack) survive, then the total number of slaves recorded by Donnan ought to be nearly complete. Some slaves were probably smuggled each year. However, since the cost of duties was passed on to the buyer, there was no particular reason for eighteenth-century slavers to smuggle significant numbers of African or West Indian blacks into Virginia. And there were so many good ports in Virginia that few black immigrants travelled overland from Maryland or North Carolina. In fact, numerous Africans who came to Virginia must have been immediately sold to men who took them to adjoining colonies. These two biases—underrecording due to smuggling and overrecording due to out-of-province sales—may have cancelled each other.

In general, Donnan accurately collected the data from the naval office records, but spot-checks show that she missed some slave ships. I have added several ships that entered South Potomac with slaves. Donnan did not find any of the slaves who came to York in 1727: she lists 734 imported slaves for 1727 for the entire province, but 3,551 actually came to Virginia that year.

Missing data present much greater problems. From 1700 to 1708 and 1719 to 1726 only imports from Africa are known. West Indian imports during these years were estimated from the proportion of the trade from the Indies in adjoining years. Quarters and years are often missing from the surviving records. I assumed that the numbers of immigrants were nearly complete if the spring and summer quarters (March 25 to September 25) from the major slave ports were present. Around 91 percent of all slaves came during these months. I also

---

6. Elizabeth Donnan, *Documents Illustrative of the History of the Slave Trade to America* (Washington, 1935), 4: 173-234; the 1768-1770 data is from P.R.O. Customs 16/1 reprinted in *Historical Statistics*, p. 1172.

accepted without change one year with somewhat less data. York and Upper James were the major ports. Between 1710 and 1740, York received almost all the African slaves: 72 percent between 1710 and 1718; 78 percent between 1718 and 1727; 81 percent between 1727 and 1733; and 58 percent between 1735 and 1740. Most of the rest went to Rappahannock. Between 1740 and 1755, substantial numbers of Africans came to both York and Upper James; then, Upper James became the dominant port (50 percent of Africans in 1750-1754, 62 percent in 1760-1764) while York faded into insignificance (42 percent in 1750-1754 and 4 percent in 1760-1764). Where data did not meet these standards, I estimated imports by assuming that there was a linear trend between the two nearest years with complete data. These procedures probably missed some slaves, but the trend should not be affected by the omissions. (See table A2).

3. African Life Expectation

Table 2, and part of table 1, were computed from data found on two sides of page 12 of John Mercer's Ledger B. The debit side lists

Table A2
Corrections Applied to Immigration Data

Years	Problem	Correction
1700-1708	Only African imports known	African imports divided by .73, proportion of Africans in trade, 1710-1718
1709	No data	Trend line, 1708-1710
1710-1718	Year of Entry known only for Upper and Lower James	Applied proportion entering James River to all ports
1719-1726	Only African imports known	African imports divided by .86, mean of proportion of Africans in 1718 (.79) and 1727-1740 (.93)
1728-1729	No data	Trend line, 1727-1730
1734	April-June missing for York; Rappahannock missing	Used recorded data
1747-1748		Trend lines, 1746-1749,
1753, 1757		1752-1754, 1756-1758
1759, 1767	No data	1758-1760, 1766-1768

purchases of slaves and columns on the credit side show births and deaths. I counted as Africans all those slaves on whom Mercer paid a duty or those bought "in company." No immigrants were listed by name after 1742, and deaths were recorded only from 1733 to 1749. The year of death is known for 17 of 32 slaves in the table; approximate time of death had to be estimated for the rest.

The number of survivors per thousand of table 1 is relatively accurate, but it must be remembered that it is based upon only 32 observations and the possibility that these slaves were not typical is great. I assumed that all those slaves not found in the death column were alive in 1749. Mercer bought five slaves in 1742 who apparently lived to 1749; I assumed that all five survived ten years and included them among the 17 live slaves. There were no known epidemics from 1749 to 1752 that would have led to deaths among these five immigrants. These procedures may have introduced a slight bias toward longevity, but that bias goes against my hypothesis of high mortality.

Since the dates of death of fifteen slaves are not known, the number of years to live can be computed only with the aid of the Maryland white male immigrant life table presented in a recent article.[7] Life expectation was computed as follows. First, the person-years of those whose death dates are known was calculated. Each person who died within one year was assumed to have lived one-half year; the others to have lived from year of purchase to year of death.[8] All the others lived from at least the date of purchase to 1749. I computed three different estimates of how long the survivors lived after 1749; a) high mortality—all the survivors died in 1750; b) preferred estimate—all the survivors arrived at age 22, lived from arrival to 1749, and then lived the number of years found in the preferred estimate of the Maryland immigrant life table; and c) low mortality—all the survivors arrived at age 22, lived from arrival to 1759, and then lived the number of years found in the preferred estimate. (See table A3).

While none of these estimates is necessarily reliable, the preferred estimate probably best approximates the experiences of African immigrants. The high mortality estimate is no doubt too high, for it assumes that none of these immigrants lived over sixteen years. The other two are based upon the life table for Maryland whites. There must have been some racial differences in mortality (and certainly in

---

7. Lorena S. Walsh and Russell R. Menard, "Death in the Chesapeake: Two Life Tables for Men in Early Colonial Maryland," *MdHM*, 69 (1974): 214.

8. In several instances only the year of death is known, so I have used only the year of death in all cases. One African who died one year and three months after arrival is included with the group who died within a year.

Table A3

Three Estimates of Time Imported Africans Lived in Virginia,
1733-1742

Time Since Arrival	Estimated Years to Live		
	High Mortality	Preferred	Low Mortality
At Arrival	8.1	15.5	18.3
One Year	9.5	19.5	23.3
Two Years	9.0	19.3	23.3
Five Years	6.3	17.2	21.3
Ten Years	5.1	16.7	22.1

immunity to malaria), yet the disease environments in Maryland and on Mercer's plantation may have been very similar for much of the Maryland table is based upon men who lived just across the Potomac River from Mercer. If the Maryland table can be used, then it would seem reasonable to assume that the black and the white life expectations after seasoning were comparable. The preferred estimate corresponds relatively closely to the life expectation of Maryland's white male immigrants after seasoning. They lived about 17.2 years at arrival (assuming a 25 percent seasoning rate like that of Mercer's Africans) and 17.4 years at age 30. This would suggest that more Africans died in their first years in the region than whites, but that black and white life expectation came closer together after a few years.[9] The low mortality estimate not only provides a life expectation that exceeds the white preferred estimate, but shows a decline in life expectation of only one year between the first and tenth year after arrival. Unfortunately, there is no way at present to test these assertions.

4. Black Growth Rates and Proportions of Immigrants Among Black Adults

The population, immigration, and mortality data examined above can be used to estimate both the natural increase of the black population and the proportion of immigrants among black adults. Decennial natural increase was computed by subtracting the number of surviv-

---

9. Walsh and Menard, "Death in the Chesapeake," p. 215 shows the effect of various seasoning rates on white mortality; I have computed the 25 percent death rate in the same way as their lower estimates of seasoning. Of course, this comparison may not be completely reliable because the calculation of the life expectation for these blacks utilizes data from the Maryland immigrant table.

ing immigrants among those who came during the previous ten years from the end-year population. Then an annual growth rate was calculated using the beginning year population and the end-year population minus the surviving immigrants. I calculated two estimates of the mortality of these immigrants. For the high estimate, I assumed that 20 percent died during their first year and that deaths then followed the Mercer table. The lower figure was used for the first year because many slaves imported during the terminal-year would still be alive on 31 December but would die the following winter and spring. The full mortality was allowed for those immigrants who entered previous to the terminal year (allowing also for the 5.4 percent who died before being sold). A linear trend was used to calculate survival between year 5 and year 10. (See table A4). The low mortality estimate was calculated by halving the number of deaths in the high estimate. Each of the estimates of survivors was then subtracted from the terminal year population, and growth rates computed. The amount of natural increase (total population growth-surviving immigrants) and the growth rate of the native born population was then computed for each estimate and presented in table 1. (See table A5). The use of these mortality estimates, rather than the high mortality estimate shown in the Mercer life table presents a lowered computed level of natural increase.

The proportion of immigrants in the black adult population of childbearing age was calculated from a similar series of statistics. Several additional pieces of data were needed: the numbers of black

Table A4

Ratios Used to Calculate Numbers of Surviving Immigrants

Years Since Importation	Ratios for Total Population	Ratios for Adult Population
1 or less	.800	.720
2	.665	.599
3-5	.634	.571
6	.599	.599
7	.566	.566
8	.534	.534
9	.505	.505
10	.477	.477
11-20		.407

Table A5

Number of Surviving Immigrants and Rates of Natural Increase
in Virginia,
1700-1770[a]

Period	Number of Surviving Immigrants (to nearest 50)		Rate of Natural Population Increase (percent per year)	
	High	Low	High	Low
1701-1710	5,250	7,150	-1.3	-2.7
1711-1720	5,450	6,800	0.9	0.2
1721-1730	7,950	10,600	0.7	-0.2
1731-1740	10,250	13,350	3.1	2.5
1741-1750	8,100	10,700	5.1	4.9
1751-1760	4,000	5,600	2.5	2.3
1761-1770	4,150	5,750	2.7	2.6

[a] High and Low refer to high and low mortality estimates. For slave imports, the high mortality estimate yields the smaller number of surviving immigrants and the higher rate of natural increase.

adults, the numbers of children among surviving immigrants, and the proportion of immigrants who survived twenty years. The number of black tithables is known for 1708, 1750, and 1755; the numbers in 1720, 1728, and 1740 were estimated on the basis of the total population in *Historical Statistics* multiplied by the proportion of adults in the black population of Maryland at about that time.[10] Two estimates of mortality were calculated. The high mortality estimate, based upon the Mercer life table, began with the survival ratios computed for the entire population. Then the ratios for the first five years were multiplied by .9 to account for children among surviving immigrants. To compute the low mortality estimate, I halved the number of deaths in the high estimate. To estimate the number of immigrants arriving for the second decade after immigration, the ten-year survival rate calculated in the high mortality estimate was multiplied by the survival rate between ages 30 and 35 and then this number was multiplied by the number of immigrants who entered Virginia between ten and twenty years before the end date. These two estimates of the number of immigrants who survived for twenty years were then divided by the terminal-year adult population to estimate the range of the proportion of adults in the black population. (See table A6).

10. Greene and Harrington, *American Population*, p. 139; Brown and Brown, *Virginia*, table between pp. 73 and 74. The proportions of adults in the total population are found in Menard, "Maryland Slave Population," pp. 32, 43. In each case, I assumed that taxables = all - children and that the proportion taxable = taxable/all. Unknowns

Table A6
Proportion of Immigrant Adults in Total Black Population[a]

Year	Adult Population	Immigration of the Past Ten Years		Immigrants of 11-20 Years Past	Proportion Africans in Population	
		High	Low		High	Low
1708	12,000	5,400	7,300	700	51	67
1720	17,950	5,200	6,650	3,700	50	58
1728	21,150	9,150	12,650	1,850	52	69
1740	36,000	9,600	13,050	5,400	42	51
1750	53,550	7,550	10,450	6,700	27	34
1755	60,000	7,350	10,650	6,150	23	28

[a] High and Low refer to high and low mortality estimates.

5. Age at First Conception of Slave Women

Masters rarely recorded the births of their slave children and never indicated when slave women on their plantation married. The data in table 5 were collected from probate inventories, one large plantation record, and a census that listed every slave in one-half of Prince George's County, Maryland, by age but not by name. The Carroll plantation record, and a number of inventories linked women to children still living with them. Only the Carroll list indicated kin ties between women and children who had left their home. If only one woman, and several children, appeared in an inventory or on the census with their ages given, the woman was called the children's mother. All women under 35 at the time of census or inventory and women between 35 and 40 listed with five or more children, were included. The Carroll record was treated the same as the other data. Age at conception of first surviving child was computed from this data by subtracting the age of the oldest child plus nine months from the mother's age.

These mean ages contain a significant upward bias. First and second children who died before the inventory or census was taken would not be listed on the record. This, of course, would become more likely as the woman and her children grew older. The standards of inclusion mentioned in the previous paragraph reduce but do not eliminate this bias, but the standards probably do eliminate the possibility that eldest children were sold or transferred before the inven-

---

were excluded, and the 1720-1729 ratio was used for 1728 and 1740, while the 1710-1719 ratio was used for 1720.

tory was written. The estimate of the age at first conception began
with the surviving child statistic and then attempted to measure the
impact of infant mortality. Data presented in appendix 6 suggests that
roughly a fourth of all slave infants died during their first year of life.
Therefore, a 25 percent infant mortality rate and a 15 month interval
between conceptions (24 month birth interval) was applied to the
data. It was assumed that females under 25 would have a 25 percent
probability of having their first child die; those between 25 and 29
would have a 25 percent probability of death for both the first two
children; and those over 30, a 25 percent probability of death for all of
the first three children. The mean age at conception of first surviving
child was then adjusted by subtracting the number of months upward
bias, allowing for a 25 percent infant mortality rate and a 15 month interval between conceptions (e.g., .25 × number of females × 1.25
years for those under 25; .25 × number of females × 2.5 years, for
those 25-29; .25 × number of females × 3.75, for those 30+). Then,
the sum of these calculations was subtracted from the product of the
mean age at conception of first surviving child and the number of
cases. The result was divided by the number of cases to derive the
revised estimated mean age.

These adjustments contain both upward and downward biases. To
provide a lower bound for the age of mother at birth, the mortality of
the early children of women over 25 was overestimated. The probability that a quarter of them lost their first two or three children in infancy will be small. By providing an upper bound for the effect of infant mortality, it also provides a lower bound for the age at first birth.
On the other hand, I assumed that no child died above age one, but
before the inventory was taken. The birth interval was deliberately
kept low. If I had used a 27-month birth interval, the number of years
in the calculation would increase .25 years for each child who died.
The revised figures are a mean of .6 years (7.2 months) lower than the
statistics directly computed from the data (standard deviation = .187;
SD/$\overline{X}$ = .312). The largest difference is found for the females born in
the 1740s. Many women in this group were between 27 and 36 years
of age in 1776 and found on that year's census. The small difference
between the two figures in the 1750s cohort stems from the source:
women born in the 1750s were between 17 and 26 in 1776. In all, the
new statistic reduced the universal mean (counting each cohort
equally) from 18.5 to 17.9, and the standard deviation of the cohorts
was reduced from .561 to .406 or from 6.7 to 4.9 months.

There are still some downward biases in the measure. The deaths of
young, unmarried women, and the presence of more young than older

women in a growing population produce downward biases in the ages at first conception. A singulate mean age, based upon proportions of slave women with a child, tends to eliminate this bias.[11] The singulate mean age of slave women at the birth of their first child on the plantations of Charles Carroll and Thomas Addison in 1773-1774 was 19.1. Two married women, ages 19 and 20, were present on Carroll's list but had no children. These women were counted with the group that had children because slave women on these plantations rarely lived with husbands until they gave birth to their first child. It seems probable that both women had given birth to a child who died. Since there was a clear difference in the proportions unmarried in the 15-19 and 20-24 age groups, they were broken into smaller age groups. (See table A7).

6. Measures of Slave Fertility

Slave fertility can be computed from two kinds of records. Several plantation registers survive. (See table 6). These documents do not include ages of mothers or data on infant deaths. Nor are sales or bequests of slave women mentioned. One knows a woman is alive only because she continues to bear children. Some children died as infants and are not found on the birth registers, because children's births were not immediately recorded. Completed families are defined as those of women who lived at least fifteen years between their first and last known children or who bore at least seven children. This procedure estimates completed family size fairly well. The downward bias

Table A7

Proportion of Women Without Children on the Carroll & Addison Quarters

Age Group	Number of Women	Percentage Without Children
15-17	10	90.0
18-19	7	42.9
20-21	10	20.0
22-24	16	6.3
25-39	34	0.0

11.　See J. Hajnal, "Age at Marriage and Proportions Marrying," *Population Studies*, 7 (1953): 111-36 and James Trussell and Richard Steckel, "The Estimation of the Mean Age of Female Slaves at the Time of Menarche and Their First Birth," *Journal of Interdisciplinary History*, 1978.

of missing births may be cancelled by the upward bias of excluding the families of some slave women who ended their childbearing years early, but survived beyond age 44. In computing the size of all families, women who died before age 44 and those who continued to have children on another plantation are included.

Table 6 also includes data from the Charles Carroll inventory. All ages are recorded on this document, and completed families are defined as families of women between age 40 and age 60 listed on the inventory. One can link adult children with their mothers, and Carroll rarely sold any of his slaves. All surviving children of these women are known. However, one does not know the complete childbearing histories of women under 40, nor can one determine the numbers of children who died before the inventory was completed.

Probate inventories can be used to suggest changes in fertility. I used Prince George's County, Maryland, probate inventories from 1725 to 1779 and a 1776 census for half the county to construct a series of different measures of the fertility of slave women. Though these sources contain an abundant data on ages of women and children, one cannot usually link mothers with their children. The number of children 0-4 for each woman 15-44 was the base for all the other measures in figure 3. One could determine the total number of children born to women who followed the fertility schedules of each of the cohorts found on this graph by multiplying each child-woman ratios by six, but that number would exclude many children who were born but who died before the inventory was taken. A total fertility rate can be computed from these child-women ratios only if mortality between 0 and 5 is known. Such a statistic would assume that the child-woman ratio equalled the average of the age-specific rates of these women.

I estimated that 32.7 percent of all children died between age 0 and 5, and divided the child-woman ratios by .673 (1 - .327) and then multiplied that number by 6 to compute the estimated total fertility rate. To calculate the number of surviving children age 20 per woman, one needs to know the proportion of children ever born who died before age 20. The result assumes that all women completed their childbearing years. Here, I used the average of male and female survivorship of West level 8 of the Princeton life tables (.618), the tables that seem to most closely approximate the measured early childhood mortality.[12]

_____

12. Ansley J. Coale and Paul Demeny, *Regional Model Life Tables and Stable Populations* (Princeton, 1968): 9.

Infant and childhood mortality was calculated from two sources. The Robert Lloyd farm book lists the births of 41 children born in the 1740s and 1750s. According to the farm book, three of the 41 children were sold, 7 to 9 died in infancy, and 3 to 5 died as children. This would indicate an infant mortality rate of about 20 percent. The register suggests a possibility of four unrecorded births (birth intervals of 4+ years surrounded by 2 to 2.5 year intervals). Three of the recorded infant deaths are within the first month, so at least some births were immediately entered. About half of all infant deaths occurred in the first month in seventeenth-century England.[13] If one assumes that half the births were recorded immediately, and half at one month, then one ought to add three infant births and deaths to the 41 entries: therefore, 11/44 or 25 percent died in infancy. The childhood data are too limited to use.

The manumission record of Robert Carter of Nomini Hall provides the second source of data on mortality between 0 and 5. Carter listed all slave children to be manumitted in both 1791 and 1796. A comparison of these two lists provides a measure of five-year survival for these children. (See table A8). About one-third of the children age less than one in 1791 died by 1796. Others were born in 1791 but died before the list was taken. The mortality by 1796 of those who were

Table A8
Deaths of Children Under Eleven on Robert Carter's Quarters, Between 1791 and 1796

Age in 1791	Number of Children	Number of Deaths 1791-96
Less Than 1	21	7
1	17	2
2	25	5
3	24	4
4	25	2
5	20	2
6	11	2
7	11	0
8	12	1
9	14	2
10	11	1

13. E.A. Wrigley, "Mortality in Preindustrial England: The Example of Colyton, Devon Over Three Centuries," *Daedalus*, 97 (1968): 568.

less than 1 in 1791 therefore provides a minimal estimate of mortality between 0 and 5. A minimum estimate of infant mortality can be computed by subtracting the death rate of children ages 1 to 4 in 1791, between 1791 and 1796 from the estimate of mortality of children less than 1 in 1791. Here, I averaged the mortality of children between ages 1 and 6, 2 and 7, 3 and 8 from 1791 to 1796, divided that number by 5 (calendar years between 1791 and 1796) and multiplied that number by 4 (years between 1 and 5) to get an estimate of mortality between 1 and 5. The average mortality of children 1-4 was 129/1000. Finally that number was subtracted from the estimate of mortality between 0 and 5 (333/1000). Infant mortality on the Carter plantations approximated 204/1000. The average infant mortality on the Lloyd and Carter plantations was 227/1000. About 12.9 percent of the surviving children died between age 1 and age 5. Therefore, the death rate of children 0-4 used in figure 3 was .327 and the survival rate was .673.

Two ratios based on the number of surviving children are found in figure 3. The first multiplies the total fertility rate by .618 (see above), and measures the number of surviving children per woman. One might add together the number of male and female adults, but some men could not marry because sex ratios remained above 100 for most of the century. I assumed that all men who could marry did marry and have children. The rate of nonmarriage was calculated from the sex ratios. This number was subtracted from 1 to compute the marriage rate, and the marriage rate was multiplied by the number of surviving children per woman to generate the adjusted ratio. (E.g., if the sex ratio was 180, 80/280 of the adults were unmarried (28.6%) and 71.4 percent were married. Sex ratios from Prince George's between ages 15 and 29 were used in making this estimate).[14] This measures the number of surviving children per adult.

Adjusted survival ratios were used to calculate the growth rates for Maryland found in table 7. Rates for five-year cohorts within decades were averaged to compute the overall decade growth rate.

---

14. Kulikoff. "Tobacco and Slaves." p. 77.

The Origins of Afro-American Society in Tidewater Maryland and Virginia,

1700 to 1790

Allan Kulikoff

ALTHOUGH the eighteenth-century Chesapeake planter looked upon newly enslaved Africans as strange and barbaric folk, he knew that American-born slaves could be taught English customs. Hugh Jones, a Virginia cleric, commented in 1724 that "the languages of the new Negroes are various harsh jargons," but added that slaves born in Virginia "talk good English, and affect our language, habits, and customs."[1] How readily slaves in Maryland, Virginia, and other British colonies accepted English ways is currently a subject of controversy. Some scholars hold that the preponderance of whites in the population was so large, and the repressive power of whites over blacks so great, that slaves in the Chesapeake colonies were forced to accept Anglo-American beliefs, values, and skills. Other writers maintain that slave migrants and their descendents created indigenous social institutions within the framework of white rule.[2] This essay

Mr. Kulikoff is a member of the Department of History and Research Associate, Office of Social and Demographic History, at the University of Illinois, Chicago Circle, where he is working on a book about Chesapeake society in the 18th century. An earlier version of this paper was presented at the colloquia at Tufts University, the Institute of Early American History and Culture, and the Univ. of Virginia, and before the Richmond Area American History Seminar. The author would like to thank all the participants at these forums and especially Edward Ayres, Fred V. Cartensen, John Demos, Stanley L. Engerman, David H. Fischer, Herbert G. Gutman, Sarah Hughes, Russell R. Menard, Michael Mullin, and Thad W. Tate for their criticisms. The author also wishes to thank Menard, Ayres, Douglas Deal, Kevin Kelly, and the St. Mary's City Commission for permission to use their data. This essay was completed while the author was a Fellow at the Institute of Early American History and Culture and initial research was supported by the National Science Foundation (GS-35781) and Brandeis University through its Rose and Irving Crown fellowship program.

[1] Hugh Jones, *The Present State of Virginia* . . . , ed. Richard L. Morton (Chapel Hill, N.C., 1956 [orig. publ. London, 1724]), 75-76. For other contemporary comparisons of African and native slaves see William Stevens Perry, *Papers Relating to the Church in Virginia, 1650-1776*, I (Geneva, N.Y., 1870), 264-265, 280, 293, 297.

[2] Gerald W. Mullin, *Flight and Rebellion: Slave Resistance in Eighteenth-*

supports the second position by describing how slaves living in Maryland and Virginia during the eighteenth century developed their own community life.

The proponents of the idea that Afro-Americans developed a distinctive social structure and culture are divided over the extent of the survival of African forms and structures in the Americas. Sidney W. Mintz and Richard Price have recently published a provocative analysis of the process of slave acculturation in the New World. Blacks who were brought to the Americas, they argue, did not have a common culture. Their religious beliefs, kinship systems, and forms of social organization differed substantially. Nevertheless, Mintz and Price add, West Africans did share some values and experiences. For example, each West African group developed different kinship practices, but throughout the region each person located his place in society by his position in his kin group and lineage. When Africans arrived in the New World, their cultural differences were initially of greater significance than the values they shared. They were not "*communities* of people at first, and they could only become communities by processes of cultural change. What they shared at the outset was their enslavement; all—or nearly all—else had to be *created by them*." The features of the society they formed, Mintz and Price assert, depended upon the demands of the white masters, the characteristics of the economy, the demography of slave and white populations, and the extent of ethnic divisions among blacks. As they interacted daily among themselves, slaves learned to cope with ordinary problems of working, eating, marrying, and childrearing under the conditions of slavery. The social institutions they developed were neither imposed by Europeans nor directly taken from African communities, but were a unique combination of elements borrowed from the European enslavers and from various African societies that held common values. "Once effective slave institutions became operative among a miscellaneous aggregate of slaves, that aggregate . . . would begin to become a community. Thereupon, the more divisive or disruptive aspects of life could begin to work themselves out against the existing structure of behavioral patterns," and slaves could place their new, Afro-American structures in a settled social context.[3]

Century Virginia (New York, 1972), chaps. 2-3, argues that native slaves in Virginia assimilated white norms. Herbert G. Gutman, *The Black Family in Slavery and Freedom, 1750-1925* (New York, 1976), chap. 8 and Allan Kulikoff, "The Beginnings of the Afro-American Family in Maryland," in Aubrey C. Land, *et al.*, eds., *Law, Society, and Politics in Early Maryland* (Baltimore, 1977), 171-196, hereafter cited as Kulikoff, "Beginnings of the Afro-American Family," maintains that slaves in the region developed their own society and culture.

[3] Sidney W. Mintz and Richard Price, *An Anthropological Approach to the Afro-American Past: A Caribbean Perspective*, ISHI Occasional Papers in Social Change, No. 2 (Philadelphia, 1976), 1-21. Quotations are found on pp. 9 and 21. I am indebted to Mr. Mintz for permitting me to read versions of this essay before its

Mintz and Price describe a process of cultural change that may have been common in slave societies, but they do not adequately explain how specific social institutions and values emerged in particular areas and they pass over lightly the specific ways in which the economic and demographic structures of a region limited the kind of culture and society that slaves were able to develop. Nor do Mintz and Price suggest how the length of the process of slave acculturation might vary in places with differing economic and demographic structures.

The size of working units, the density of black population, the pattern of African immigration and the proportion of whites in the population greatly influenced the development of slave societies and cultures. Some crops required large plantations; others could be grown on small farms. Since large plantation areas needed more slaves than did small farm regions, they attracted greater numbers of slave immigrants and, consequently, major plantation regions often had greater concentrations of slaves and a larger proportion of immigrants in their slave population than areas dominated by small farms. Slaves who lived on a large plantation in a region where a substantial majority of the people were black and the density of the slave population was great probably had more opportunities to worship their gods, begin stable families, and develop their own communities than did slaves who lived on a small quarter in a preponderantly white country. A slave who lived with many Africans in a place where constant, heavy immigration of blacks kept the proportion of Africans high was more likely to adapt African customs than the slave who lived where migration was sporadic, the proportion of immigrants among adult blacks low, and the numbers of whites great.[4]

The slave economy and black population patterns found in the Chesapeake colonies can be adequately analyzed from existing sources, but the specific content of the culture and society slaves formed is far more difficult to

publication. "Society," as used here, concerns social institutions and structures such as family, government, work groups, or churches; "culture" includes values and beliefs that motivate and justify behavior in a society. A belief that witches ought to suffer death is part of a group's culture, but the act of killing a witch takes place in the society's governmental or religious structures.

[4] These comments are based upon my reading of Mintz and Price, *Anthropological Approach* and upon the following works: Richard S. Dunn, *Sugar and Slaves: The Rise of the Planter Class in the English West Indies, 1624-1715* (Chapel Hill, N.C., 1972); Orlando Patterson, *The Sociology of Slavery: An Analysis of the Origins, Development and Structure of Slave Society in Jamaica* (London, 1967); Peter H Wood, *Black Majority: Negroes in Colonial South Carolina from 1670 through the Stono Rebellion* (New York, 1974); Mullin, *Flight and Rebellion;* and Russell R. Menard, "The Maryland Slave Population, 1658 to 1730: A Demographic Profile of Blacks in Four Counties," *William and Mary Quarterly,* 3d Ser., XXXII (1975), 29-54.

determine. While probate inventories and wills, plantation accounts and vital registers, and British naval office records allow a detailed reconstruction of crop production, slave imports, the distribution of slaves on plantations, and the density, as well as the ethnic and demographic composition, of the black population, the exact connection between these variables and slave institutions, beliefs, and values cannot be precisely defined. However, occasional descriptions of slaves' reactions to their conditions, slave beliefs, and slave behavior can be found in planters' letters, plantation records, local court order books, and newspaper ads for runaways. These kinds of information are used here to suggest plausible connections between demographic structures and slave society, but the data are often fragmentary and much more must be found before firm statements can be made.

Data from tidewater Maryland and Virginia suggest that African and Afro-American slaves developed a settled community life very slowly. Three stages of community development can be discerned. From roughly 1650 to 1690, blacks assimilated the norms of white society, but the growth of the number of blacks also triggered white repression. The period from about 1690 to 1740 was an era of heavy black immigration, small plantation sizes, and social conflicts among blacks. The infusion of Africans often disrupted newly formed slave communities. Finally, from 1740 to 1790, immigration declined and then stopped, plantation sizes increased, the proportion of blacks in the population grew, and divisions among slaves disappeared; consequently, native blacks in the tidewater formed settled communities.

Between 1650 and 1690 two demographic patterns shaped black life. Tobacco was the region's cash crop, and most planters were men of moderate means who could afford few slaves. Therefore, blacks constituted a very small percentage of the Chesapeake population—only about 3 percent (or 1,700) of the people in 1650 and 15 percent in 1690 (or 11,500). Most slaves lived on small plantations of fewer than eleven blacks. Moreover, almost all slaves were immigrants, and most came to the Chesapeake from the West Indies. Some had recently arrived in the islands from Africa; others had lived there a long time or had been born there.[5]

These characteristics led blacks toward assimilation in the Chesapeake colonies. Natives of the islands and long-time residents knew English and were experienced in slavery; new African slaves soon learned English in order to communicate with masters and most other blacks. Blacks and whites

[5] Wesley Frank Craven, *Red, White and Black: The Seventeenth-Century Virginian* (Charlottesville, 1971), 84, 93-95, 97; U.S. Bureau of the Census, *Historical Statistics of the United States, Colonial Times to 1970* (Washington, D.C., 1976), 1168, hereafter cited as *Historical Statistics;* Menard, "Md. Slave Population," *WMQ*, 3d Ser., XXXII (1975), 34-35.

worked together in the fields, and blacks learned to imitate the white servants by occasionally challenging the master's authority. Seventeenth-century Englishmen perceived Africans as an alien, evil, libidinous, and heathen people, but even they saw that their slaves did not fit this description, and whites treated many blacks as they did white servants. Some black residents became and remained free.[6]

After 1660 the lot of blacks deteriorated; stringent racial laws were passed in Virginia each year between 1667 and 1672, and in 1680, 1682, and 1686.[7] The timing of these laws was due in part to the growth and changing composition of the black population. The number of blacks in the Chesapeake colonies doubled in every decade but one from 1650 to 1690, while white population grew more slowly. African slaves began to be imported directly from Africa for the first time around 1680; from 1679 to 1686, seven ships with about 1,450 slaves arrived in Virginia from Africa.[8] These blacks seemed to Englishmen to be the strange, libidinous, heathenish, and disobedient people they believed typical of Africans.

Africans continued to pour into the Chesapeake: from 1700 to 1740, roughly 43,000 blacks entered Virginia, about 39,000 of whom were Africans. The proportion of Africans among all slave immigrants rose from about 73 percent between 1710 and 1718 to 93 percent between 1727 and 1740.[9] Over half, and perhaps three-quarters, of the immigrant slaves went to a few lower tidewater counties, while some of the rest worked in the upper tidewater.[10]

---

[6] Edmund S. Morgan, *American Slavery—American Freedom: The Ordeal of Colonial Virginia* (New York, 1975), 154-156, 310-315; Winthrop D. Jordan, *White over Black: American Attitudes toward the Negro, 1550-1812* (Chapel Hill, N. C., 1968), chap. 1; Ross M. Kimmel, "Free Blacks in Seventeenth-Century Maryland," *Maryland Historical Magazine*, LXXI (1976), 19-25; Warren M. Billings, "The Case of Fernando and Elizabeth Key: A Note on the Status of Blacks in Seventeenth-Century Virginia," *WMQ*, 3d Ser., XXX (1973), 468-474; James H. Brewer, "Negro Property Holders in Seventeenth-Century Virginia," *ibid.*, XII (1955), 575-580.

[7] Jordan, *White over Black*, 71-82. A useful compilation of Virginia's laws on slaves and servants can be found in Betty W. W. Coyle, "The Treatment of Slaves and Servants in Colonial Virginia" (M.A. thesis, College of William and Mary, 1974), 100-108.

[8] *Historical Statistics*, 756; Allan Kulikoff, "A 'Prolifick' People: Black Population Growth in the Chesapeake Colonies," *Southern Studies*, XVI (1977), 391-428.

[9] Elizabeth Donnan, ed., *Documents Illustrative of the Slave Trade to America* (Washington, D.C., 1931-1935), IV, 172-174, corrected with original Naval Officer Returns; Kulikoff, " 'Prolifick' Prople," *So. Studies*, XVI (1977), 391-428.

[10] This assertion is based upon an analysis of slave ages judged in the York and Lancaster counties Court Order Books, 1710-1740, found in the Virginia State Library, Richmond. From 1680 to the Revolution the name and age of every black immigrant under 16 had to be registered with the local court. William Waller Hening, ed., *The Statutes at Large, Being a Collection of All the Laws of Virginia*

The proportion of recent immigrants among black slave adults fluctuated with trade cycles: about one-half in 1709, one-third in 1720, one-half in 1728, and one-third in 1740 had left Africa or the West Indies within ten years.[11] This immigration affected every facet of black life in tidewater, for every few years native blacks and earlier comers had to absorb many recently imported Africans into their ranks.

The demographic composition of slave cargoes suggests that Africans had a difficult time establishing a regular family life after their arrival in the Chesapeake. The slave ships usually carried two men for every woman. Children composed less than one-fifth of imported slaves, and there was a similar surplus of boys over girls. Very young children were infrequent in these cargoes; perhaps three-quarters of them were aged ten to fourteen, and nearly all the rest were eight or nine.[12]

Nonetheless, newly enslaved Africans possessed a few building blocks for a new social order under slavery. Many shared a similar ethnic identity. Data from Port York for two periods of heavy immigration show that about half the African migrants were Ibos from Nigeria, while another one-fifth came from Angola.[13] From 1718 to 1726, 60 percent came from Biafra; between 1728 and 1739, 85 percent migrated from Biafra or Angola.[14] (See Table I.)

(Richmond, 1819-1823), II, 479-480, III, 258-259, VI, 40-41. I estimated the number of immigrants coming to tidewater by (1) multiplying the numbers of ages judged by four to estimate the number of adult immigrants; and (2) multiplied the resulting York total by 10 (York, Gloucester, James City, New Kent, Charles City, Elizabeth City, Warwick, Surry, Isle of Wright, and Accomac-Northampton equalled York's total) and the Lancaster figures by seven (Northumberland, Richmond, Middlesex, King and Queen, King William, and Westmoreland equalled Lancaster's totals). This procedure yielded the following tidewater shares of total Virginia black immigration: 41 to 75% in the 1720s (mean 56%), 41 to 95% in the 1730s (mean 59%), and 19 to 58% in the 1740s (mean 36%).

[11] Kulikoff, " 'Prolifick' People," *So. Studies*, XVI (1977), 391-428.

[12] *Ibid.,*

[13] Most Africans from Biafra were Ibos. Philip D. Curtin, *The Atlantic Slave Trade: A Census* (Madison, Wis., 1969), 157-158, 161, 188, 245; Roger Anstey, *The Atlantic Slave Trade and British Abolition, 1760-1810* (Atlantic Highlands, N. J., 1975), 70-72. Other groups, especially Ibibio, Efkin, and "Mokos," also came from the region. Angola encompassed a larger area and no single group dominated the trade. *Ibid.,* 60.

[14] Curtin, *Atlantic Slave Trade,* 157-158, and Herbert S. Klein, "Slaves and Shipping in Eighteenth-Century Virginia," *Journal of Interdisciplinary History,* V (1975), 388-389, argue from this data that the distribution of Africans migrating to Virginia was relatively random. But both included all Africans who entered all Virginia ports for most of the 18th century. The York totals given in Table I include most of the slaves whose origins were recorded. For example, the 5,818 slaves reported for York, 1728-1739, constitute 46% of all those listed in Donnan, ed., *Documents of Slave Trade,* IV, 40, for the 1727-1769 period and 61% when the vague "Guinea" origin is eliminated.

TABLE I

GEOGRAPHIC ORIGINS OF AFRICANS ENTERING PORT YORK, VIRGINIA,
1718 TO 1739

| Port of Origin | Percentage of Slaves Entering York | |
	1718-1726	1728-1739
Bight of Biafra	60	44
Angola	5	41
Gold Coast	13	5
Senegambia	4	10
Madagascar	9	
Windward Coast	7	
Sierra Leone	1	
Total	99	100
Number Known	8400	5818
Total Number	8613	8786
Percent Unknown	3	34

Source: Elizabeth Donnan, ed., *Documents Illustrative of the Slave Trade to America* (Washington, D.C., 1931-1935), IV, 183-185, 188-204. The categories are taken from Philip D. Curtin, *The Atlantic Slave Trade: A Census* (Madison, Wis., 1969), 128-130.

Most immigrants spoke similar languages, lived under the same climate, cultivated similar crops, and shared comparable kinship systems.[15] When they arrived in the Chesapeake, they may have been able to combine common threads in their societies and cultures into new Afro-American structures with some ease.

Before Africans could reconstruct their lives, they had to survive the middle passage, the demoralizing experience of being sold, and the stresses of their first year in the Chesapeake. The terrible hardships of the middle passage are well known. Africans were often packed naked into crowded and unsanitary ships, coffled together much of the time, and fed a starchy diet. Perhaps one in five died en route. Although they sometimes managed to develop friendships with shipmates that mitigated their misery, these fragile connections were usually destroyed after the ships made port.[16] The survivors

[15] C. K. Meek, *Law and Authority in a Nigerian Tribe: A Study in Indirect Rule* (London, 1937), chap. 1; Ikenna Nzimiro, *Studies in Ibo Political Systems: Chieftancy and Politics in Four Niger States* (Berkeley and Los Angeles, 1972), 25-29; "The Early Travels of Olaudah Equiano" (1789), in Philip D. Curtin, *et al.*, eds., *Africa Remembered: Narratives by West Africans from the Era of the Slave Trade* (Madison, Wis., 1967), 69-88; Jan Vansina, *Kingdoms of the Savanna* (Madison, Wis., 1966), chap. 1 and 191-197.

[16] Daniel P. Mannix and Malcolm Cowley, *Black Cargoes: A History of the Atlantic Slave Trade, 1518-1865* (New York, 1962), chap. 5; Mintz and Price,

arrived tired, weak, and sick from their long voyage. Records from the period 1710 to 1718 indicate that about one-twentieth of them died before they could be sold.[17] The sales took place aboard ship, and the slaves were bought one by one, in pairs, or in larger groups over several afternoons. The buyers were strange white men and women, fully clothed and healthy and speaking an alien tongue, who peered and poked all over the Africans' bodies. After the sale, some shipmates left with different masters, while others were returned to their chains to be sold another day.[18]

Many slaves had to endure the indignity of slave sales many times before they were finally purchased. Early in the century, some slave ships sold Africans in Barbados and then came to Yorktown; in the 1720s and 1730s, slavers went first to Yorktown and then upriver to West Point or to ports on the Rappahannock River.[19] Once they arrived in Virginia, slaves were shown to customers for an average of two to five days before being bought.[20] How often an African was placed on sale depended upon the individual's age, sex, and health, and the state of the market for slaves. Planters purchased healthy men first; women and children were second and third choices; unhealthy slaves were sold last. Women and children were sometimes bought by

---

Anthropological Approach, 22-23. Curtin, *Atlantic Slave Trade*, 277, shows that Nantes traders between 1715 and 1741 lost about 19% of their slaves in transit (mean of five-year cohorts).

[17] Donnan, ed., *Documents of Slave Trade*, IV, 175-181.

[18] Robert Carter Diary, 1722-1727, Sept. 18, 20, 21, 27, 29, 1727, Alderman Library, University of Virginia, Charlottesville; Mullin, *Flight and Rebellion*, 14; Gregory A. Stiverson and Patrick H. Butler III, eds., "Virginia in 1732: The Travel Journal of William Hugh Grove," *Virginia Magazine of History and Biography*, LXXXV (1977), 31-32.

[19] Between 1710 and 1718, 41% of all Africans stopped first in the Islands; 15% from 1732 to 1739 were displayed there first. Donnan, ed., *Documents of Slave Trade*, IV, 175-204, compared with *ibid.*, II, 299-300, 427-432; see also *Virginia Gazette* (Parks), Apr. 21, 1738, and Aug. 10, 1739. Donnan, ed., *Documents of Slave Trade*, IV, 175-206, shows that from 1710 to 1733 from 72 to 81% of African immigrants entered York and 17 to 20% came to Rappahannock (grouped years 1710-1718, 1718-1727, 1727-1733); 1735-1740, 58% York, 18% Rappahannock, 12% Upper James. For West Point, see *ibid.*, 101 (Greyhound, 1723) and *Va. Gaz.*, June 1, 1739. For Yorktown, see *ibid.*, Apr. 8, 1737, and June 8, 1739. For Yorktown and West Point see *ibid.*, Aug. 19, 1739. For Rappahannock (from York), see Augustus Moore to Isaac Hobhouse, May 3, 1723, in Walter E. Minchinton, ed., "The Virginia Letters of Isaac Hobhouse, Merchant of Bristol," *VMHB*, LXVI (1958), 294.

[20] Data are from two ships consigned to Robert Carter: the *John and Betty*, the third ship at Rappahannock in 1727 (2.2 days), and the *Rose*, the last ship at Rappahannock in 1727 (5.3 days). Both ships had high proportions of women and children. Robert Carter Diary, July 17–Aug. 3 and Sept. 18–Oct. 5, 1727; Carter to John Pemberton, July 26, 1727 (added to June 28 letter), and Carter to George Eskridge, Sept. 21, 1727, Robert Carter Letterbooks, 1727-1728, Virginia Historical Society, Richmond. There were three slaves on the *Rose* unaccounted for.

middlemen who took them from the ship and sold them in the interior of the province.[21]

Despite the degradation of the slave sale, Africans made a small beginning toward a new community life as they traveled several days to the masters' plantations. Although they had left most of their shipmates behind, they usually walked in groups and could use the trip to renew old friendships or make new ones. Only about one-third of the Africans in five samples drawn from the years 1689 to 1721 were purchased singly; about one-fourth left in pairs and the rest in larger groups. (See Table II.) Furthermore, slaves destined for different masters may have traveled together whenever a planter who lived more than a day's trip from the sale site asked a neighbor going to the sale to buy a slave for him.[22]

Once they entered the plantation world, African immigrants had to begin to cope with their status. The absolute distinction between slavery and

[21] "Sale of the Charfield Slaves Begun July 23, 1717 Belonging to Samuel Jacobs and Company, Bristol," Stephen Loyd-John Tayloe Account Book, Va. Hist. Soc.; John Baylor Account Book, 1719-1721, Baylor Papers, Alderman Lib., Univ. Va., 139, 162-164; Robert Carter to Messrs. Francis Chamberlayne and Francis Sitwell, July 26, 1720, and Sept. 27, 1727, in Louis B. Wright, ed., *Letters of Robert Carter, 1720-1727: The Commercial Interests of a Virginia Gentleman* (San Marino, Calif., 1940), 41-43, 52-53 (the date is misprinted on the second letter). The 1717 *Charfield* sale record is listed in order of purchase but the day of sale is not indicated (compare Tayloe to Jacobs, July, 1719, Loyd-Tayloe Account Book, where Tayloe relates that John Baylor sold the last slaves to Mr. Robinson with the purchase of two slaves by William Robinson recorded as the next-to-last entry in the sale record). Baylor sold the following slaves, page by page: (1) 17 men, 6 women, 4 boys, 1 girl; (2) 19 men, 9 women, 7 boys, 8 girls; (3) 16 men, 8 women, 5 boys, 1 girl; (4) 7 men, 8 women, 7 boys, 1 girl; (5) 12 men, 4 women, 5 boys, 1 girl. Page 5 included 2 old men, 3 sick women, and a "bursten boy."

[22] Even Robert Carter had slaves delivered to him on occasion. Carter to [?] [May 21, 1728], Carter Letterbooks, Va. Hist. Soc. I estimated distance of purchasers from the *Charfield*, which was berthed at Urbanna on the Rappahannock (John Tayloe to Samuel Jacobs and Co., July 1727, Loyd-Tayloe Account Book), from data in Clayton Torrence, comp., *Virginia Wills and Administrations, 1632-1800* . . . (Richmond [1931]). Only purchasers who lived on the Middle Peninsula or the Northern Neck were included. A buyer was identified with a county if a man with the same name was listed in Torrence or if there were substantial numbers of decedents with his family name in only one county. This procedure is subject to errors of commission and omission. After identifying the purchasers, I assumed that masters lived in the middle of the county, measured mileage from Urbanna on a modern road map, and then multiplied the mileage by 1.25 because colonial roads were rarely direct. I identified the destinations of 75/128 slaves sold at this sale to planters (those probably resold were excluded), and the mean distance traveled was 37 miles, a trip of about two days. For travel times see Allan Kulikoff, "Tobacco and Slaves: Population, Economy, and Society in Eighteenth-Century Prince George's County, Maryland" (Ph.D. diss., Brandeis University, 1976), 338.

TABLE II

THE DISTRIBUTION OF AFRICANS AMONG PURCHASERS IN VIRGINIA, 1689 TO 1721[a]

			Percentage of Slaves Bought			
Number Purchased	Royal African Company 1689-1713[b]	Africa Galley 1702	Charfield, 1717[c] All	Weighted	John Baylor's Sales 1719-21	Prince Eugene 1719 Women & Children
1	38	11	25	30	41	52
2	25	49	27	32	31	17
3	14	11	4	5	4	5
4	9	8	3	3	10	14
5 and over	14	21	42	30	14	12
Total	100	100	101	100	100	100
Number Sold	217	53	150	124	83	58

Notes and Sources: [a] Charles Killinger, "The Royal African Company Slave Trade to Virginia, 1689-1713" (M.A. thesis, College of William and Mary, 1969), 137-148; Donnan, ed., Documents of Slave Trade, IV, 71-72; "Sale of the Charfield Slaves," Loyd-Tayloe Account Book, Virginia Historical Society, Richmond; John Baylor Account Book, 1719-1721, Alderman Library, University of Virginia, Charlottesville.

[b] These statistics are not based upon actual sales but on bills and bonds of planters to the Royal African Company. Killinger used the amount of the bond to determine the number of slaves purchased, a generally accurate method. I included only the numbers of slaves bought in contiguous years. (His data included all purchases of each planter over the entire period.)

[c] The "all" includes all sales; the weighted excludes 26 slaves probably destined to be resold: 7 men, 1 woman, and 2 boys to Christopher Robinson, an Urbanna merchant who died in 1727 with 2 women, 1 man, 4 old women, and 2 children; 7 men and 4 women to John Baylor for Beverly and Lyde (Baylor and Lyde were slavetraders). I also determined that 29 slaves sold in groups greater than 5 probably stayed with their purchasers. Then, using this data, I distributed the unknowns in large sales (over 5) in the same manner as the knowns. The Robinson inventory can be found in Middlesex Wills, 1713-1734, 317-320.

freedom found in the Chesapeake colonies did not exist in West African societies. African communities and kin groups possessed a wide range of rights-in-persons. A captive in war might end up as anything from a chattel, who could be sold, to the wife of one of the victorious tribesmen; he might become a soldier, domestic servant, or agricultural laborer. At first, such outsiders would be strangers, but eventually they or their children could move from marginality to partial or full membership in a kin group or community.[23]

When they reached their new homes, Africans were immediately put to work making tobacco. Most were broken in on the most routine tasks of production. Nearly two-thirds of them arrived between June and August, when the tobacco plants had already been moved from seed beds and were growing rapidly. The new slaves' first task was weeding between the rows of plants with hands, axes, or hoes. These jobs were similar to those that Ibos and other Africans had used in growing other crops in their native lands. After a month or two of such labor, slaves could be instructed in the more difficult task of harvesting.[24] Some Africans refused to accept this new work discipline, either not understanding or pretending not to understand their masters. Edward Kimber, a visitor to the Eastern Shore in 1747, wrote that "a new Negro" (a newly enslaved African) "must be broke. . . . You would be surpriz'd at their Perseverance; let an hundred Men shew him how to hoe, or drive a Wheelbarrow, he'll still take the one by the Bottom, and the Other by the Wheel."[25]

Under these conditions, Africans were often struck with loneliness and illness. For example, Ayuba (Job) Suleiman was brought to Maryland's Eastern Shore in 1730. He was "put . . . to work making tobacco" but "every day showed more and more uneasiness under this exercise, and at last grew sick, being no way able to bear it; so that his master was obliged to find easier work for him, and therefore put him to tend the cattle." A new slave might become so ill that he could not work. Thomas Swan, a planter in Prince George's County, Maryland, bought two Africans in the summer of 1728; in November of that year he asked the county court to refund one poll tax because "one of them has been sick ever since he bought him and has done him little or no Service."[26]

One in four new Negroes died during their first year in the Chesapeake; in some years—1711, 1727, 1737, 1743—mortality seems to have been especially high. In 1727 Robert Carter lost at least seventy hands—perhaps a quarter of all his slaves born abroad and more than half his new Negroes.

[23] Igor Kopytoff and Suzanne Miers, "African 'Slavery' as an Institution of Marginality," in Miers and Kopytoff, eds., *Slavery in Africa: Historical and Anthropological Perspectives* (Madison, Wis., 1977), 3-81.

[24] Donnan, ed., *Documents of Slave Trade*, IV, 188-243; Klein, "Slaves and Shipping," *Jour. Interdis. Hist.*, V (1975), 396-397. For the tobacco-growing cycle see Kulikoff, "Tobacco and Slaves," 354 and sources cited there.

[25] "Eighteenth-Century Maryland as Portrayed in the 'Itinerant Observations of Edward Kimber,'" *Md. Hist. Mag.*, LI (1956), 327-328.

[26] Thomas Bluett, "The Capture and Travels of Ayuba Suleiman Ibrahims," in Curtin *et al.*, eds., *Africa Remembered*, 41; Prince George's Court Record, Liber O, fol. 335, Maryland Hall of Records, Annapolis.

Because Africans possessed some native immunities against malaria, most survived the malarial attacks of their first summer in the region, but respiratory illnesses struck them hard the following winter and spring. Planters considered late spring "the best time of buying them by reason they will be well season'd before the winter."[27] Blacks living in New Kent County, Virginia, between 1714 and 1739 died infrequently in the summer, but deaths rose somewhat in the fall, increased from December to February, and peaked in March and April. The county undoubtedly included many Africans. Whites in the same parish died more frequently in autumn, and less often in spring, than their slaves.[28]

Despite disease and death, new Negroes soon began to develop friendships with other slaves, and to challenge the authority of their masters by attempting to make a new life for themselves off their quarters. They were able to oppose their masters because so many of their fellow workers were also recent immigrants who shared their new experiences under slavery. In the mid-1700s, late-1710s, mid-1720s, and mid-1730s, when unusually large numbers of blacks entered Virginia, these Africans, united by their common experiences and able to communicate through the heavily African pidgin they probably created, ran off to the woods together, formed temporary settlements in the wilderness, and several times conspired to overthrow their white masters.[29]

[27] Robert Carter to William Dawkins, May 13, 1727, Carter Letterbooks, Va. Hist. Soc.; Carter to Dawkins, June 3, 1727, Carter Letterbooks, Univ. Va.; Conquest Wyatt to Richard Wyatt, June 1, 1737, and July 20, 1743, earl of Romney's Deposit, Loan 15, British Library; Robert Bristow to Thomas Booth, Oct. 30, 1710, and Sept. 15, 1711, Robert Bristow Letterbooks, Va. St. Lib.; Elizabeth Suttell, "The British Slave Trade to Virginia, 1698-1728" (M.A. thesis, College of William and Mary, 1965), 58-59; Robert Carter Inventory, 1733, Va. Hist. Soc. Carter owned 733 slaves when he died in 1732. Assume he owned 700 slaves in 1727, that the sex ratio of his native slaves was 100, and that he bought two men or boys (10 to 14) for every woman or girl. Then, he would have owned 222 immigrants. Assume further that the death rate of native workers was equal to West level 5, in Ansley J. Coale and Paul Demeny, *Regional Model Life Tables and Stable Populations* (Princeton, N.J., 1966), 34-35, 130-131. This would yield 10 to 15 deaths among the 248 working natives depending on the growth rate chosen. The remaining 55-60 deaths would yield a death rate of 250 to 270 per 1,000 for all immigrant slaves. If Carter bought 80 slaves in 1726, as he did in 1727, and the death rate of seasoned Africans followed West level 5, then 61 to 68% of the new Negroes would have died.

[28] See the death register printed in C. G. Chamberlayne, ed., *The Vestry Book and Register of St. Peter's Parish, New Kent and James City Counties, Virginia, 1684-1786* (Richmond, 1937). The presence of Africans is suggested by high black adult sex ratios in the register: the adult sex ratio was 151 men per 100 women (and 157 excluding mulattoes), the black child sex ratio was 100, and the white adult sex ratio was 115.

[29] Kulikoff, " 'Prolifick' People," *So. Studies*, XVI (1977), 391-428.

First, Africans had to find or create a common language because there were few speakers of any single African tongue in any neighborhood. Some new slaves may have devised nonoral means of communication soon after arrival, but the large concentration of Ibos and Angolans among the Africans suggests that many spoke similar languages and that others could have become bilingual. Others probably spoke some West African pidgin that they had learned in Africa in order to communicate with Europeans. A new creole language may have emerged in the Chesapeake region combining the vocabulary of several African languages common among the immigrants, African linguistic structures, and the few English words needed for communication with the master.[30]

Almost as soon as Africans landed, they attempted to run away together. Seven of Robert Carter's new Negroes did so on July 17, 1727. They took a canoe and may have crossed the Rappahannock River. Carter sent men "sev[era]l ways" for them, and on July 15 they were returned to him. Enough new Negroes ran away to convince the Virginia assembly to pass laws in 1705 and 1722 detailing procedures to follow when Africans who did not speak English and could not name their master were recaptured.[31]

A few Africans formed communities in the wilderness in the 1720s, when black immigration was high and the frontier close to tidewater. In 1725 the Maryland assembly asserted that "sundry" slaves "have of late Years runaway into the Back-Woods, some of which have there perished, and others ... have been entertained and encouraged to live and inhabit with the Shewan-Indians." Other slaves, who heard of their success, were "daily making Attempts to go the same Way." Any slave who ran beyond the Monocacy River, at the edge of white settlement, was to have an ear cut off and his chin branded with an "R." The assembly, recognizing that Africans habitually ran away, withheld this punishment for new Negroes during their first year in the colony.[32]

---

[30] "Capture of Ayuba Suleiman," Curtin et al., eds., Africa Remembered, 42-43; "Travels of Olaudah Equiano," ibid., 88-89; Gov. Spotswood of Virginia feared slaves could rebel without speaking a common language: "freedom Wears a Cap which Can Without a Tongue, Call Together all Those who Long to Shake the Fetters of Slavery," he wrote in the 1710s. Quoted in Menard, "Md. Slave Population," WMQ, 3d Ser., XXXII (1975), 35. The problem of language was first discussed by Mullin, Flight and Rebellion, 44-47; for pidgins, see Wood, Black-Majority, chap. 6 and J. L. Dillard, Black English: Its History and Usage in the United States (New York, 1972), 73-93.

[31] Carter Diary, July 17, 24, 1727; Hening, ed., Statutes at Large, III, 456, IV, 168-175; Randolph W. Church, ed., The Laws of Virginia, Being a Supplement to Hening's The Statutes at Large, 1700-1750, comp. Waverly K. Winfree (Richmond, 1971), 212-222; Mullin, Flight and Rebellion, 40-45.

[32] William Hande Browne et al., eds., Archives of Maryland ... (Baltimore, 1883-   ), XXXVI, 583-586, XXXV, 505-506, XXXVII, 211, XXV, 394-395. Prince George's Court Rec., L, 515.

At least two outlying runaway communities were established during the 1720s. Fifteen slaves began a settlement in 1729 on the frontier near present-day Lexington, Virgina. They ran from "a new Plantation on the head of the James River," taking tools, arms, clothing, and food with them. When captured, "they had already begun to clear the ground." Another small community evidently developed on the Maryland frontier in 1728 and 1729. Early in 1729, Harry, one of the runaways, returned to southern Prince George's County to report on the place to his former shipmates. He told them that "there were many Negroes among the Indians at Monocosy" and tried to entice them to join the group by claiming that Indians were soon going to attack the whites.[33]

As soon as Africans arrived in the Cheaspeake colonies in large numbers, government officials began to complain about their clandestine meetings. In 1687 the Virginia Council asserted that masters allowed their blacks to go "on broad on Saturdays and Sundays ... to meet in great Numbers in makeing and holding of Funneralls for Dead Negroes." Governor Francis Nicholson of Maryland wrote in 1698 that groups of six or seven slaves traveled thirty or forty miles on weekends to the sparsely inhabited falls of the Potomac.[34]

Whites suppressed clandestine meetings primarily because they feared slave rebellions. Africans pushed to suicidal actions might revolt against the slave system. Revolts were rare in the Chesapeake colonies, where whites heavily outnumbered slaves, but Africans apparently participated in conspiracies in Surry, James City, and Isle of Wight counties in Virginia in 1710, and in Prince George's County, Maryland, in 1739 and 1740. The 1739-1740 conspiracy, which is the best documented, was organized by slaves who lived in St. Paul's Parish, an area of large plantations, where numerous slaveholders had recently bought Africans. The Negroes spent eight months in 1739 planning to seize their freedom by killing their masters and other white families in the neighborhood. Their leader, Jack Ransom, was probably a native, but most of the conspirators were Africans, for it is reported that the planning was done by slaves in "their country language." The revolt was postponed several times, and finally the white authorities got wind of it. Stephen Boardley, an Annapolis lawyer, reported that whites believed that two hundred slaves planned to kill all the white men, marry the white women, and then unite both shores of Maryland under their control. Ransom

---

[33] Mullin, *Flight and Rebellion*, 43-44; quotation is in Michael Mullin, ed., *American Negro Slavery* (New York, 1976), 83; Prince George's Court Rec., O, 414-415.

[34] H. R. McIlwaine, ed., *Executive Journals, Council of Virginia*, I (Richmond, 1925), 86-87; *Md. Arch.*, XXIII, 498-499, also cited in Menard, "Md. Slave Population," *WMQ*, 3d Ser., XXXII (1975), 37-38; Hening, ed., *Statutes at Large*, IV, 128-129.

was tried and executed; four other slaves were acquitted; and the furor died down.[35]

Every attempt of Africans to establish an independent social life off the plantation failed because whites, who held the means of terror, insisted that their slaves remain at home. Running to the woods, founding outlying communities, or meeting in large groups challenged work discipline and cost the planter profits. Nevertheless, substantial numbers of Africans probably participated in activities away from the plantation. Slaves from many different African communities proved that they could unite and live together. Others, though unable to join them, must have heard of their exploits and discovered that a new social life might be possible. Sooner or later, however, Africans had to turn to their plantation to develop communities.

But as late as the 1730s, plantations were not very conducive places in which to create a settled social life. A major determinant was the small size of the slave populations of the plantation quarters. On quarters of fewer than ten slaves, completed families of husbands, wives, and children were uncommon and the slaves, who lived in outbuildings, did not control enough space of their own to run their own lives apart from the master. Table III shows how small the tidewater plantations were. Only 28 percent of the slaves on Maryland's lower Western Shore before 1711 lived on plantations of over twenty slaves, and some of these lived in quarters distant from the main plantation. The rest lived on smaller farms. Quarters were similarly small in York and Lancaster counties in the 1710s. From 1710 to 1740, plantation sizes in Prince George's and Lancaster counties increased, while those in York and St. Mary's stayed the same. If these four counties were typical of tidewater in the 1730s, then 46 percent of the slaves lived on quarters of ten or fewer and only 25 percent resided on units of over twenty (but usually under thirty).[36]

African social structures centered on the family, but slaves in the Chesapeake had difficulty maintaining family life. Men who lived on small quarters often had to find wives elsewhere, a task made more difficult by the high ratio of men to women in much of tidewater. As long as adult sex ratios remained high, men had to postpone marriage, while women might be forced

[35] Herbert Aptheker, *American Negro Slave Revolts* (New York, 1943), 169-170 and sources cited there (Aptheker calls one conspiracy two); Stephen Boardley Letter Books, 1738-1740, 55-58, Maryland Historical Society, Baltimore; *Md. Arch.*, XXVIII, 188-190, 230-232, XL, 425, 428, 457, 523; Prince George's Court Rec., X, 573-576; Chancery Records, VIII, 38-39, Md. Hall Recs. (shipment of 320 Africans in 1734 to Benedict near the site of the rebellion). I checked all of Aptheker's sources in *Slave Revolts*, chap. 8, and the 1710 conspiracy seemed to be the only one in Virginia that included Africans.
[36] The figures are means of the entries of Table III, with each county equaling one observation. Only 9% of Carter's slaves lived on units of over 30 in 1733. See n. 56.

TABLE III

PLANTATION SIZES IN TIDEWATER MARYLAND AND VIRGINIA, 1658 TO 1740

	Proportion of Slaves Living on Units of				
Place and Time	1-5 Slaves	6-10 Slaves	11-20 Slaves	21+ Slaves	Number of Slaves
Maryland Lower Western Shore[a]					
1658-1710	29	22	21	28	1618
1721-1730[c]	17	19	20	44	974
Prince George's, Maryland					
1731-1740	17	26	34	24	842
St. Mary's, Maryland					
1721-1730	26	21	25	28	484
1731-1740	32	22	35	11	524
York County, Virginia					
1711-1720	28	20	22	30	618
1721-1730	29	21	34	16	459
1731-1740	25	30	27	18	446
Lancaster County, Virginia[b]					
1711-1725	29	22	31	17	248
1726-1735[c]	14	18	24	45	322
1736-1745[c]	14	17	18	52	499
"King" Carter's Plantations					
1733	2	14	40	45	733

Note and Sources: Menard, "Maryland Slave Population," *William and Mary Quarterly*, 3d Ser., XXXI (1975), 32, 43; Kulikoff, "Tobacco and Slaves: Population, Economy, and Society in Eighteenth-Century Prince George's County, Maryland" (Ph.D. diss., Brandeis University, 1976), 185; St. Mary's City Commission data from St. Mary's Inventories; York County Orders, Wills, etc., collected by Edward Ayres; Lancaster County Wills (or Deeds, Wills) for years listed; Robert Carter Inventory, Va. Hist. Soc. Inventories tend to over represent the wealthier slave owners and to combine a master's slaves from several quarters in one place; therefore the proportions of slaves who lived on larger units is overestimated. Since the bias remains constant, the changes between periods are usually accurate.

[a] St. Mary's, Charles, Calvert, and Prince George's, 1658-1710; Prince George's and Charles, 1721-1730.

[b] Odd years chosen because the number of cases (slaves) in first period otherwise too low.

[c] Unusually large number of planters with major slave holdings (21+) died. Part of the change shown in the table is due to this fact.

to marry early. Along the lower Western Shore of Maryland, the sex ratio was about 150 in the 1690s and 1700s, but by the 1710s it was under 150 in York County and under 120 in Lancaster County, remaining at those levels until 1740. Even on large plantations men could not count on living in family units, for sex ratios there were higher than on small quarters. During the 1730s the adult sex ratio in Prince George's was 187, but on nine large plantations in that county, each having ten or more adult slaves, it stood at 249. A similar pattern has been found in both York and Lancaster counties at times between 1710 and 1740.[37]

Since most slaves lived on small plantations, the development of settled black community life required visiting between quarters. Sometimes slaves met on larger plantations, getting "drunke on the Lords Day beating their Negro Drums by which they call considerable Numbers of Negroes together." On one Sunday in 1735, Edward Pearson's Negroes with some of his "Neighbours Negroes was Beating a Drum and Danceing but by my Consent" in Prince George's.[38] Slaves probably did not regularly visit friends on nearby plantations, however. Visiting networks could develop only where blacks were densely settled and constituted a large part of the population. The population in tidewater was never over half slave except in a few counties between the James and York rivers before 1740. Only 16 percent of the people in the Chesapeake colonies were black in 1690, but this proportion grew to 25 percent in 1710 and 28 percent in 1740.[39]

The large plantations in tidewater housed masters, overseers, native blacks, new Negroes, and less recent immigrants, while smaller units, with only a few natives or immigrants, tended to be more homogeneous. The concentration of men on large plantations suggests that most African adults were bought by the gentry—a pattern documented by the composition of John Mercer's and Robert Carter's plantations. Mercer bought sixty-nine slaves between 1731 and 1746. These purchases included six seasoned Africans or natives in 1731 and 1732, twenty-five new Negroes from 1733 to 1739, and twenty new Negroes and fifteen seasoned slaves in the 1740s. By 1740 Mercer owned a mixed group of new Negroes, seasoned immigrants, and native

[37] Kulikoff, " 'Prolifick' People," So. Studies, XVI (1977), 391-428; Kulikoff, "Tobacco and Slaves," 77; York County Wills and Orders, XIV-XVIII, Va. St. Lib.; Lancaster County Wills, X-XIII, Va. St. Lib. York adult sex ratios were, in 1711-1720, 126 and 145 on large plantations (numbering five) with 10 or more adult slaves, and the sex ratio on Robert Carter's plantations in 1733 (Carter Inventory, Va. Hist. Soc.) was 153, while the sex ratio in Lancaster inventories, 1726-1735, was 113. Lancaster and York counties inventories in the 1720s and 1730s show large plantation sex ratios about the same or even lower than all plantations, but the number of observations is too small to be certain.

[38] Menard, "Md. Slave Population," WMQ, 3d Ser., XXXII (1975), 37; Prince George's Court Rec., V, 618, 630.

[39] Historical Statistics, 1168; Menard, "Economy and Society," 412; Menard, "Md. Slave Population," WMQ, 3d Ser., XXXII (1975), 35. The statement about the James-York region is based upon later data found in Evarts B. Greene and Virginia D. Harrington, American Population before the Federal Census of 1790 (New York, 1932), 150-151.

children and adults. The composition of Carter's quarters in 1733 shows the culmination of this process. Over half of Carter's 734 slaves lived on plantations where one-fifth to one-half were recent immigrants, and another third resided on quarters composed predominantly of natives or older immigrants. Only one-seventh of his slaves lived on quarters dominated by new Negroes. About one-half (6/13) of the quarters of over twenty slaves, and natives formed a majority of the rest. Most of the farms (11/18) with eleven to twenty slaves included Africans and natives, but five others were peopled by natives. Nine of the eleven quarters where new Negroes formed a majority were small units of fewer than ten slaves.[40]

Most new Negroes learned to be slaves on such diversified plantations. Nearly two-thirds (64 percent) of Carter's recent immigrant slaves lived on plantations with numerous native adults and children, and white overseers resided at almost every quarter. Africans had to learn some English in order to communicate with masters, overseers, and native slaves, and they were put into the fields with other slaves who had already learned that they had to work to avoid punishment and that resistance had to be indirect. Africans saw that a few slaves were given responsibility—and power—over other slaves or were taught new skills. Slaves born in Africa apparently were well acculturated on Robert Carter's quarters. While the great majority of his adult slaves were agricultural laborers, some Africans (who had probably been in the country for a number of years) joined their native friends as foremen who worked under white overseers. Perhaps nineteen of the thirty-three foremen on these plantations were born in Africa. Four other men—possibly Africans—became sloopers (boatmen) on Carter's main plantation.[41]

Nevertheless, Africans and native slaves quarrelled on occasion because of the great differences between their respective experiences. Natives had not been herded into ships and sold into bondage. They were probably healthier than immigrants. Many of them were baptized Christians, and some became believers. To immigrants, by contrast, Christianity was an alien creed, and they sometimes tried to maintain their own Islamic or African religions in opposition to it. Ben, for example, was brought from Africa to Charles County, Maryland, about 1730. According to his grandson, Charles Ball, Ben

[40] John Mercer's Ledger B, Buck's County Historical Society, 12 (film copy at Colonial Williamsburg Research Dept.); Carter Inventory, Va. Hist. Soc. I identified as immigrants all men, women, and children 10-14 who did not live in a family and all husband-wife households. Of course, some immigrants had children, and some of the adults living in sex-segregated households were teenagers not yet married, but this method gives a plausible estimate.

[41] Carter Inventory, Va. Hist. Soc. There were resident overseers on all but two quarters with 9 slaves (of 734). Two overseers supervised two quarters; 63 slaves lived on these four farms.

"always expressed great contempt for his fellow slaves, they being . . . a mean and vulgar race, quite beneath his rank, and the dignity of his former station." Ben never attended a Christian service but held that Christianity was "altogether false, and indeed no religion at all."[42]

The most significant difference between recent immigrants and native blacks can be seen in their family life. A native-born slave on Robert Carter's plantations in 1733 usually lived in a family composed of husband, wife, and children, whereas new Negroes were placed in sex-segregated barracks, and seasoned immigrants often lived in conjugal units without children. Though polygamy was common in some African societies, only one of Carter's slaves managed to keep two wives.[43] Conditions at Carter's plantations were optimal; elsewhere, high sex ratios severely limited the marriage opportunities of African men. At first, older slaves could become "uncles" to younger Africans, and Africans of the same age could act as brothers, but African men had to find wives in order to begin a Chesapeake genealogy.[44] They had to compete with natives for the available women; native women may well have preferred native men, who were healthy, spoke English, and knew how to act in a white world, to unhealthy or unseasoned Africans. Furthermore, newly enslaved African women often waited two or three years before taking a husband, thereby reducing the supply of prospective wives even further. The reluctance of Afro-American women to marry Africans may have been one of the grievances of the Prince George's conspirators in 1739-1740.[45]

Several incidents on Edmund Jenings's plantations in King William County, Virginia, in 1712-1713, suggest that Africans competed among themselves for wives, sometimes with tragic results. George, who lived at Beaverdam Quarter, complained in November 1712 that "his country men had poysened him for his wife," and he died the following February from the poison. Roger, of Silsdon Quarter, apparently wanted more than one wife. In December 1712 or January 1713, he "hanged himselfe in ye old 40 foot Tob. house not any reason he being hindred from keeping other negroes men wifes

[42] Kulikoff, " 'Prolifick' People," So. Studies, XVI (1977), 391-428; Charles Ball, Fifty Years in Chains, ed. Philip Foner (New York, 1970 [orig. publ. 1837]), 21-22; "Capture of Ayuba Suleiman," Curtin et al., eds., Africa Remembered, 42.
[43] Carter Inventory, Va. Hist. Soc. One can identify those who had been in the country a number of years by the ages of their children. Husband-wife households were rare on Charles Carroll of Carrollton's holdings (386 slaves) in 1773-1774; almost all households included children. Husband-wife households are therefore probably immigrant households. For Carroll see Kulikoff, "Beginnings of Afro-American Family," 178-183. Children 10-14 on Carter's plantations are usually listed with parents; where they are not, I assumed that they were immigrants.
[44] Mintz and Price, Afro-American Anthropology, 34-35.
[45] Kulikoff, " 'Prolifick' People," So. Studies, XVI (1977), 391-428; Stephen Boardley thought the conspirators planned to kill black women as well as white men. Boardley Letter Books, 55-58.

besides his owne." The overseer "had his head cutt off and stuck on a pole to be a terror to the others."[46]

Slaves in the Chesapeake colonies failed to establish a settled community life in the times of heavy immigrations in the 1710s, 1720s, and 1730s. Conflicts among Africans and between African and native slaves could never be fully resolved as long as substantial numbers of Africans were forced into slavery in the two colonies. On the other hand, the rate of immigration, the proportion of Africans in the slave population, and the percentage of blacks in the population were never great enough to permit successful communities based mostly upon African institutions and values to develop either on the plantation or away from it.

The demographic conditions that prevented blacks from developing a cohesive social life before 1740 changed during the quarter century before the Revolution, as the immigration of Africans to tidewater Maryland and Virginia declined sharply. Only 17 percent of Virginia's adult black population in 1750 and 15 percent in 1755 had arrived within the previous ten years, and these newcomers went in relatively greater numbers to newer piedmont counties than had their predecessors.[47] The proportion of adult blacks in 1755 who had entered Virginia since 1750 ranged from 4 percent in Lancaster County and 8 percent in York County in tidewater Virginia to 15 percent in Caroline County and 21 percent in Fairfax County, both near the fall line.[48] After 1755, almost all of Virginia's black immigrants went to piedmont counties.[49]

[46] "Inventories of the Negroes etc. on the Estate of Edmund Jenings Esqr, 1712-13," Francis Porteus Corbin Papers, Duke University, Durham, N.C. (film at Colonial Williamsburg).

[47] Kulikoff, " 'Prolifick' People," *So. Studies*, XVI (1977), 391-428; Donnan, ed., *Documents of Slave Trade*, IV, 204-224, shows that in the 1740s, York remained the major slave port, but Upper James (where most new settlement occurred) became the second port: 22% entered Upper James, 53% York, and 11% Rappahannock.

[48] Ages of slaves judged found in Lancaster Orders, IX-X, York Judgments and Orders, 1746-1752 and 1752-1754, Fairfax Orders, 1749-1754 and 1754-1756, all are in Va. St. Lib.; and T. E. Campbell, *Colonial Caroline: A History of Caroline County, Virginia* (Richmond, 1954), 331. I used the Fairfax index to orders located at the Fairfax County Municipal Building, courtesy of Donald Sweig of that county's bicentennial commission. The method of calculating the proportion of immigrants is described in n. 10 above.

[49] The redistribution of African immigrants to piedmont after 1750 can be seen in two ways. First, Upper James became the dominant slave port (50% of slaves in 1750-1754, 62% in 1760-1764), while York fades into insignificance (42%, 1750-54 and 4% 1760-1764). Until the early 1770s, almost all ships on the Upper James went to Bermuda Hundred, a small settlement at the convergence of the Appomatox and James rivers, near present-day Petersburg, and close to the expanding Southside. Donnan, ed., *Documents of Slave Trade*, IV, 219-231; *Va. Gaz.* (Hunter), Sept. 12,

As the number of African immigrants in tidewater declined, the internal division among blacks diminished. These immigrants were under greater pressure than their predecessors to acquire the language, values, and beliefs of the dominant native majority. Like new Negroes before them, they sometimes ran away but with less success. On arrival, they found themselves isolated and alone. Olaudah Equiano, for example, was brought to Virginia in 1757 at age twelve. "I was now exceedingly miserable," he wrote, "and thought myself worse off than any . . . of my companions; for they could talk to each other, but I had no person to speak to that I could understand. In this state I was constantly grieving and pining, and wishing for death." But once slaves like Equiano learned English, they became part of the Afro-American community. Bob, twenty-nine, and Turkey Tom, thirty-eight, were new Negroes who lived on the home plantation of Charles Carroll of Carrollton in 1773. Since Bob and Tom were apparently the only two recent immigrant slaves on any of Carroll's many plantations, they both could participate fully in plantation life. Bob was a smith, a position usually reserved for natives; he married the daughter of a carpenter, and lived with her and their two children. Tom, a laborer, also found a place in the plantation's kinship networks: his wife was at least a third-generation Marylander.[50] Very few Africans probably ever became artisans, but most lived on plantations where they could find wives among the native majority.

The size of quarters increased after 1740 throughout tidewater, providing greater opportunities for slaves to develop a social life of their own. The proportion who lived on units of over twenty slaves doubled in St. Mary's County, increased by half in York County, and grew, though more slowly, in Prince George's. In the 1780s one-third to two-thirds of the slaves in nine tidewater counties lived on farms of more than twenty slaves, and only a sixth to a tenth lived on units of fewer than six. If these counties were typical, 43 percent of tidewater's blacks lived on farms of over twenty slaves, and another 25 percent lived on medium-sized units of eleven to twenty. (See

---

1751, July 10, 30, 1752, Aug. 12, 1752; *ibid.* (Royle), Nov. 4, 1763; *ibid.* (Purdie and Dixon), June 27, Aug. 1, and Sept. 5, 1766, Aug. 11, 1768, May 18, 1769—all are ads for slave ships about to enter the Upper James and bound for Bermuda Hundred. Secondly, ages judged disappear from tidewater court records: from 1755 to 1770, there were 6 ages judged in York (1755-1758 missing), 3 in Lancaster, 15 in Caroline, 41 in Fairfax, and 46 in Prince Edward (1754-1758 and 1765-1769) on the Southside frontier. York Judgments and Orders, 1759-1763, 1763-1765, 1765-1768, and 1768-1770; Lancaster Orders 10-14; Fairfax Orders (from index cited in n. 48) 1754-1756, and Minutes 1756-1763; Campbell, *Caroline County*, 331.

[50] John Blassingame, *The Slave Community: Plantation Life in the Antebellum South* (New York, 1972), 16; "A List of Negroes on Doohoregan Manor taken in Familys with their Ages Decr. 1, 1773," Charles Carroll (of Carrollton) Account Book, Md. Hist. Soc.

Table IV.)[51] The number of very large quarters also grew. Before 1740 few quarters housed over thirty slaves, but by the 1770s and 1780s the wealthiest gentlemen ran home plantations with over one hundred slaves and quarters with thirty to fifty.[52]

Because plantation sizes increased, more Afro-Americans lived on quarters away from the master's house and his direct supervision. On small plantations the quarter could be located in an outbuilding or in a single dwelling. On large plantations "a Negro Quarter, is a Number of Huts or Hovels, built some Distance from the Mansion-House; where the Negroes reside with their Wives and Families, and cultivate at vacant Times the little Spots allow'd them." Slave houses and the yards surrounding them were centers of domestic activity. The houses were furnished with straw bedding, barrels for seats, pots, pans, and usually a grindstone or handmill for beating corn into meal. Agricultural tools and livestock were scattered outside the house, and the quarter was surrounded by plots of corn and tobacco cultivated by the slaves.[53]

[51] Figures are means with the proportion in each county equaling one observation.

[52] The change in the size of the largest plantations cannot be traced through inventories because they often do not properly divide a decedent's slaves among his quarters. Quarter-by-quarter lists of the slaves of Robert Carter in 1733 (Carter Inventory, Va. Hist. Soc.), Charles Carroll (of Carrollton) in 1773 ("Negroes on Doohoregan Manor"), and the manumission record of Robert Carter of Nomini in 1791 (Louis Morton, *Robert Carter of Nomini Hall: A Virginia Tobacco Planter of the Eighteenth Century* [Williamsburg, 1941], Table 9 in the appendix, 284) suggest, however, the dimensions of the change:

Number of Slaves	Percent Living on Quarters of Various Sizes on		
	R. Carter 1733	C. Carroll 1773	R. Carter 1791
1-10	16	2	5
11-20	40	18	9
21-30	35	37	33
31-40	9	10	14
41-50	0	0	17
101+	0	34	22
Total Number of Slaves	733	386	509

[53] "Eighteenth-Century Maryland," *Md. Hist. Mag.*, LI (1956), 327. A plat of a quarter, surrounded by fields, can be found in Moore V. Meek, Ejectment Papers, Box 30. A quarter located in a kitchen is described in Provincial Court Judgments, EI #4, 110-112, Md. Hall Recs. The furnishing and implements at quarters are listed in Prince George's Inventories, TB#1, 93-94 (1726), 32-38, 64-68 (1727); PD#1, 6-10, 26-28 (1729), 247-248 (1734), 426 (1738); DD#1, 56-58; 82-83 (1741), 363

185

TABLE IV
SIZES OF PLANTATIONS IN MARYLAND AND VIRGINIA, 1741 TO 1790[a]

| County and Year | Proportion of Slaves Living on Units of | | | | Number of Cases |
	1-5 Slaves	6-10 Slaves	11-20 Slaves	21+ Slaves	
Prince George's					
1741-1750	14	18	22	48	1,090
1751-1760	11	17	28	44	1,126
1761-1770	13	22	31	35	1,144
1771-1779	10	17	18	55	1,099
1790	11	13	23	52	11,176
St. Mary's					
1741-1750	39	24	27	11	580
1751-1760	21	27	30	23	892
1761-1770[b]	15	20	28	37	1,453
1771-1777	16	26	31	26	831
1790	16	21	25	37	6,985
Anne Arundel[c]					
1783	12	17	29	41	5,855
York[d]					
1741-1750	19	24	36	22	689
1751-1760[b]	12	13	26	49	803
1761-1770	7	17	40	37	663
1771-1780	12	17	33	39	788
1785	16	20	30	33	2,190
James City					
1783	12	22	28	38	2,039
Warwick					
1783	18	26	24	33	897
Charles City					
1784	11	16	26	47	2,808
Middlesex					
1783	10	12	15	63	2,277
Lancaster					
1783	9	20	28	42	3,024

Sources: [a] Kulikoff, "Tobacco and Slaves," 185; St. Mary's Inventories collected by the St. Mary's City Commission; Anne Arundel County Tax Lists, Maryland Historical Society, Baltimore; Bureau of the Census, *Heads of Families at the First Census of the United States Taken in the Year 1790: Maryland* (Washington, D.C. 1907), 92-98, 104-109; York County Wills and Inventories, 19-22, Virginia State Library, Richmond; personal property tax lists for York, 1785, James City, 1783, Warwick, 1783, Charles City, 1783—all at Va. St. Lib.; Nancy Lous Oberseider, "A Socio-Demographic Study of the Family as a Social Unit in Tidewater Virginia, 1660-1776" (Ph.D. diss., University of Maryland, 1975), 202-203 for Middlesex; Bureau of the Census, *Heads of Families at the First Census of the United States Taken in the Year 1790: Records of the State Enumerations: 1782 to 1785, Virginia* (Washington, D.C., 1908), 55-56, for Lancaster.

Notes: The data in the 1780s and 1790 is not comparable with the earlier data for it covers

186

TABLE IV (continued)

all planters listed in tax records and censuses and not a biased inventory sample. The inventory will be biased upward, for more wealthy than poor planters had inventories taken. Nor are the data for Prince George's and St. Mary's in 1790 and Lancaster in 1783 comparable to the other lists from the 1780s, for data from these three counties include all a planter's holdings taken together while the other data are divided into precincts and a planter's holdings in each precinct is separately enumerated.

ᵇ Greater than usual number of planters died.

ᶜ Not entire county. Excludes Annapolis, but includes 12 hundreds of the remaining 18 or 65% of the slaves excluding those in Annapolis. Hundreds from all parts of the county were chosen.

ᵈ In these inventories, but not in any others, I separated the quarters of one planter into separate observations and excluded from the table all slaves on plantations in piedmont. In general, the numbers on large plantations are still far too large.

Afro-Americans made the quarters into little communities, usually organized around families. Because African immigration largely ceased, the adult sex ratio decreased throughout tidewater until it reached about one hundred by the time of the Revolution.[54] Almost all men and women could marry, and by the 1770s many slaves had native grandparents and great-grandparents. Smaller quarters contained a family or two, and larger quarters were populated by extended families in which most residents were kinfolk. Domestic activities such as eating, playing in the yard, or tending the garden were organized by families, and each family member had a part in them. The quarter was the center of family activity every evening and on Sundays and holidays, for except during the harvest, slaves had these times to themselves. Nonresident fathers visited their wives and children, runaways stayed with friends or kinfolk. In the evenings native men sometimes traveled to other quarters where they passed the night talking, singing, smoking, and drinking. On occasional Sundays they held celebrations at which they danced to the banjo and sang bitter songs about their treatment by the master.[55]

(1744); DD#2, 128-129, 219, 322 (1752); GS#1, 245-246 (1758); and GS#2, 257-258 (1772), 357-359 (1775)—all in Md. Hall Recs.

[54] For details, see Kulikoff, " 'Prolifick' People," *So. Studies*, XVI (1977).

[55] Kulikoff, "Beginnings of Afro-American Family," 180-183; *The Journal of Nicholas Cresswell, 1774-1777* (New York, 1924), 18-19; *Md. Arch.*, XLIV, 647-648; Ferdinand M. Bayard, *Travels of a Frenchman in Maryland and Virginia . . . in 1791 . . .*, ed. Ben C. McCary (Williamsburg, 1950), 96; Thomas Bacon, *Four Sermons Preached at the Parish Church of St. Peter, in Talbot County, . . .* (Bath, 1783 [orig. publ. London, 1753]), 56-58; Carville Earle, *The Evolution of a Tidewater Settlement: All Hallow's Parish, Maryland, 1650-1783* (University of Chicago, Geography Research Paper No. 170, 1975), 160-161.

The economy of the quarters was partially controlled by the slaves, since distance from the master allowed them a certain autonomy in small matters. Slaves occasionally slaughtered stock without permission, ate some of the meat, and traded the surplus. Chickens, sheep, and swine were traded to fellow slaves, as well as to peddlars, merchants, and other whites. The danger and excitement of stealing the master's livestock were shared by all the quarter's families. This illegal activity was apparently widespread. A Prince George's planter complained in 1770 that "in the Neighbourhood where I live, it is almost impossible to raise a stock of Sheep or Hogs, the Negroes are constantly killing them to sell to some white people who are little better than themselves."[56]

After 1740, the density of the black population and the proportion of slaves in the population of tidewater both increased, and as a result, the area's slave society gradually spread out to embrace many neighboring plantations in a single network. Ironically, masters provided slaves with several tools they could use to extend these cross-quarter networks. As masters sold and transferred their slaves, more and more kinfolk lived on neighboring quarters, and naturally they retained ties of affection after they were separated. Whites built numerous roads and paths to connect their farms and villages, and their slaves used these byways to visit friends or run away and evade recapture. By the 1770s and 1780s, Afro-Americans numerically dominated many neighborhoods and created many cross-plantation social networks.

The density of black population and the proportion of slaves in the population increased in both Chesapeake colonies. The number of slaves per square mile increased by more than one-third between 1755 and the early 1780s in three tidewater areas. Slaves composed 26 percent of the population of the lower Western Shore of Maryland in 1710, 38 percent in 1755, and 46 percent in 1782. A similar change occurred on the Eastern Shore, and by 1775, the results were visible in tidewater Virginia. In that year, nearly every county between the Rappahannock and the James rivers as far west as the heads of navigation was more than one-half black; over half of Virginia's slaves lived in these counties. Between 40 and 50 percent of the people were black in 1775 in the Northern Neck and in piedmont counties adjacent to tidewater.[57]

Quarters were connected by extensive networks of roads and paths,

[56] Mullin, *Flight and Rebellion*, 60-62; *Md. Arch.*, XXIV, 732-733, XXVII, 155-158, L, 436; *Maryland Gazette* (Annapolis), Oct. 12, 1758, Oct. 18, 1770, Mar 13, 1777; *Va. Gaz.* (Rind), Mar. 17, 1768; Dunlop's *Md. Gaz.* (Baltimore), Nov. 4, 1772; Prince George's Court Rec., EE#2, 99, 543 (1778).

[57] "Number of Inhabitants in Maryland," *Gentleman's Magazine; and Historical Chronical*, XXIV (1764), 261; Greene and Harrington, *American Population*, 154-155; Kulikoff, "Tobacco and Slaves," 202-203, 323, 428-432; Bureau of the Census, *Heads of Families at the First Census of the United States . . . Records of the State Enumerations: 1782-1785, Virginia* (Washington, D.C., 1908), 9-10; Lester J. Cappon *et al.*, eds., *Atlas of Early American History: The Revolutionary Era, 1760-*

which grew remarkably complex during the eighteenth century. For example, Prince George's County had about 50 miles of public roads in 1700, but 295 in 1739, and 478 in 1762. In 1762 there was one mile of public road for every square mile of taxed land in the county. This elaboration of roads made it easier for slaves to visit nearby plantations. Whites could not patrol all these roads, let alone private paths not maintained by the county, without a general mobilization of the white population.[58]

Two Maryland examples from the 1770s and 1780s illustrate the demographic characteristics of places where Afro-American slaves were able to develop cross-plantation social networks. The area around Upper Marlborough, Prince George's county seat, was over six-tenths black and had over twenty-five slaves per square mile in 1783. The region, which covered about 130 square miles, extended to the Patuxent River and included an adjacent area across the river in Anne Arundel County. Perhaps half the blacks in this region lived on quarters of over twenty slaves and another fourth on farms of eleven to twenty. The road network here was the most developed in the county. Elk Ridge was located near Baltimore town. In 1783 its population was about half black, with fourteen slaves per square mile. About six-tenths of the Elk Ridge slaves lived on farms of over twenty blacks, and another one-fifth on units between eleven and twenty. One neighborhood in this area was very heavily black. In 1774, 330 of Charles Carroll's slaves lived at Doohregan Manor on the main plantation and at nine other quarters spread over the 10,000-acre tract. Many social activities could occur in the village of 130 slaves on the main plantation, and a somewhat smaller number among the 143 who lived on farms of 21 to 40 slaves. The rest of Carroll's slaves resided on small quarters of under twenty-one people. Visiting among slaves on Carroll's various quarters must have been common, however, because slaves on one quarter were frequently related by blood and marriage to those on another.[59]

1790 (Princeton, N.J., 1976), 24, 67, 100, 102. The number of slaves per square mile on Maryland's lower Western Shore (Prince George's, Charles, Calvert, and St. Mary's counties) was 12 in 1755 and 18 in 1782; in York, Charles City, James City, and New Kent, 15 in 1755 and 18 in 1790; in Lancaster, Middlesex, Richmond, and Essex counties, 14 in 1755 and 21 in 1790. I multiplied 1755 Virginia tithables by two and divided by square miles. Blacks accounted for roughly 57% of the population in both 1755 and 1790 in York, Charles City, James City, and New Kent and 51% in 1755 and 59% in 1790 of the population in Lancaster, Middlesex, Richmond, and Essex. I multiplied white tithables by two for 1755 and determined the rough proportion of blacks in adult population.

[58] Kulikoff, "Tobacco and Slaves," 327-339; Earle, Tidewater Settlement System, 154-157.

[59] Kulikoff, "Tobacco and Slaves," 205, 532-536; Anne Arundel Summary of

These ideal conditions could not be found everywhere in tidewater. From just north of the Patuxent to just south of the James, plantations were large, black population density was high, few whites were present, and road networks were well developed. Slaves in these areas could create a rudimentary cross-plantation society. By contrast, in other regions on the Eastern Shore and upper Western Shore of Maryland, blacks were a minority, and small planters tilled the soil with their sons and perhaps several slaves. Here whites controlled the environment, and slaves had fewer opportunities to pursue their own activities.[60]

Even within areas of high black populations and large plantations, the opportunities of slaves for social life outside their own plantations varied from place to place. In twenty-eight taxing districts of Anne Arundel and Prince George's counties in 1783, the black population ranged from 27 to 66 percent. Large plantations tended to be located where the population was predominantly Afro-American, but the relationship was not exact: in Anne Arundel in 1783, 18 to 58 percent of the blacks in eight "hundreds" whose population was over half black lived on quarters of over twenty slaves.[61] Neighborhoods close to each other could have very different racial compositions. Taxing districts along the Potomac River in Prince George's, about fifteen miles from Upper Marlborough, were only four-tenths black, and around Oxon Creek, where most of the householders were white tenants, only 30 percent of the people were slaves. Only one-third of the slaves along the Potomac lived on farms with over twenty of their fellows. In Virginia, both James City and York counties were over 60 percent black in the 1780s. Most of the large plantations in these counties were located in upper Yorkhampton Parish, where over half the blacks lived on quarters of over twenty slaves. Only one-third to one-fourth of the slaves lived on big quarters in the remainder of these counties.[62]

Even on large plantations, social life was often insecure. Some slaves were sold or forced to accompany their masters to the piedmont, far away from family and friends: about 20 percent of all slaves in southern Maryland left

1783 Tax Lists, Executive Papers, Md. Hall Recs.; Lyons Creek and Elk Ridge Hundred 1783 Tax List, Md. Hist. Soc.; "Negroes on Doohregan Manor," Carroll Account Book, Md. Hist. Soc. The distribution of slaves on plantations for the region around Upper Marlborough is based upon Lyons Creek Hundred in Anne Arundel and on work in Prince George's inventories. Individual 1783 tax lists do not survive for Prince George's.

[60] These generalizations are based upon study of tax lists cited in Table IV and summaries of 1783 tax lists, Executive Papers for all Maryland Counties, Md. Hall Rec.

[61] The Pearson Product Moment Correlation between percent black and percent living on farms of more than 20 slaves for 12 hundreds (27-61% black) was .744.

[62] Kulikoff, "Tobacco and Slaves," 205; James City Personal Property Tax List, 1783, and York County Personal Property Tax List, 1785, Va. St. Lib. I am indebted to Edward Ayres for helping me with the geography of James City and York.

the region between 1755 and 1782. Even when a slave remained the property of the same white family, he might not live on the same farm for more than a few years. For example, after the Revolution large planters in Elizabeth City County, Virginia, tended to hire out their slaves to tenants and small landowners. A slave might live on a different plantation every year, suffering separation from spouse, children, and friends.[63]

Nevertheless, one-half to three-quarters of the Afro-Americans who lived in tidewater in the 1780s enjoyed some sort of social life not controlled by their masters. Perhaps 43 percent lived on large quarters, and another 4 percent were men who lived in the neighborhoods with many large quarters and could visit nearby farms. Another 25 percent lived on farms of eleven to twenty blacks and could participate in the family and community activities of their quarters. The remaining one-fourth of the slaves were women and children who lived on small plantations. They usually did not travel from quarter to quarter but waited for husbands and fathers to visit them.

The Afro-Americans made good use of these opportunities to create their own society. In the years before the Revolution, they developed a sense of community with other slaves both on their own plantations and in the neighborhood. This social solidarity was shown in several ways. In the first place, Afro-Americans often concealed slaves from the neighborhood on their quarters. Since masters searched the neighborhood for runaways and placed notices on local public buildings before advertising in a newspaper, many runaways were not so advertised. The increasing appearance of such advertisements in the *Maryland Gazette* during the thirty years before the Revolution suggests that slaves were becoming more successful in evading easy recapture. The number of runaways in southern Maryland rose in each five-year period between 1745 and 1779, except the years 1765 and 1769, and the increase was especially great during the Revolution, when some escaped slaves were able to reach British troops.[64]

Most runaways required help from other blacks. Only a small minority were helped by whites, and about three-quarters (22/29) of those so helped in southern Maryland were artisans, mulattoes, or women. Women infrequently ran away, and there were few slave mulattoes and artisans.[65] The majority of runaways traveled from plantation to plantation through a quarter underground. Some joined family members or friends on nearby or

---

[63] Kulikoff, "Tobacco and Slaves," 84-88; Sarah Shaver Hughes, "Slaves for Hire: The Annual Allocation of Black Labor in Elizabeth City County, Virginia, 1782 to 1810," *WMQ*, 3d Ser., XXXV (1978), 260-286.

[64] See Table V; *Md. Gaz.*, Mar. 9, 1758 (notices put up for runaway); Benjamin Quarles, *The Negro in the American Revolution* (Chapel Hill, N.C., 1961), chap. 2.

[65] Mullin, *Flight and Rebellion*, 112-116; *Md. Gaz.*, Apr. 9, 1772, Jan. 29, 1767, Feb. 14, 1771.

TABLE V

MOTIVES OF RUNAWAY SLAVES IN SOUTHERN MARYLAND,
1745 TO 1779[a]

Motive	Percentage of Runaways by Years			Totals	
	1745-1759	1760s	1770s	Percent	Number
To Visit	60	30	58	54	63
To Pass as Free; to Work	20	45	21	25	29
To Escape Maryland	20	25	21	21	25
Number	25	20	72	100	117
Number of Unknowns	35	33	59		127
Total Number of Runaways	60	53	131		244
Percent Unknown	58	62	45	52	

Notes and Sources: [a] All runaway ads published in the *Maryland Gazette* (Annapolis), 1745-1779, the *Maryland Journal* (Baltimore), 1773-1779, and Dunlop's *Maryland Gazette* (Baltimore), 1775-1779, from Prince George's, Charles, Calvert, Frederick (south of Monocacy River), and Anne Arundel counties and any slave born or traveling to those areas. Each slave runaway equals a single observation, but when a slave ran away twice in a five-year period, he was counted only once. Every motive in each ad is counted. If the ad states, for example, that a slave will both visit and try to pass as free, then it is counted in both places. The "to pass as free" column includes all slaves whose masters believed they would attempt to pass for free in Maryland or search for work in the province. The "to escape Maryland" column includes all those headed for Virginia or Pennsylvania and all those attempting to join either Revolutionary or British armies.

even distant plantations; others attempted to pass as free in small port towns, find employment, or leave the region. About one-half of southern Maryland runaways (see Table V) and nearly one-third (29 percent) of Virginia's advertised runaways before 1775 stayed with friends or kinfolk. They hid on quarters or in surrounding woods for a few days or weeks, and then returned voluntarily or were recaptured. Many of the other slaves, who wanted to pass as free, also had to use the plantation underground to reach their destinations, and at least half of them stayed within visiting distance of their family and friends. Only one runaway in four in southern Maryland and one in three in Virginia before 1775 left his home province and tried to begin a new life as a free person.[66]

The slave community, of course, had its share of conflicts, and on

[66] Table V; Mullin, *Flight and Rebellion*, 108, 129. Since the number of unknowns is so large, it is difficult to be more precise. If one eliminates "acculturated" slaves (by Mullin's difinition), then the Maryland and Virginia data become very similar.

occasion a slave assaulted or stole from another slave. Nevertheless, several accounts of these incidents suggest that the rest of the slave community united against the transgressors. Slaves usually refused to testify in court against their fellows, especially when blacks stole goods from whites, but when a member of the black community was hurt, slaves testified against the guilty person to protect themselves or their property. In May 1763 Jack poisoned Clear with a mixture of rum and henbane; she became ill and died the following February. Six slaves who belonged to Clear's master informed him of the act and testified against Jack in Prince George's court. They were joined by three slaves who lived on nearby plantations. The jury found Jack guilty, and he was sentenced to hang. Similarly, when Tom broke into Weems's quarter in Anne Arundel County and took goods belonging to Weems's slaves, six men and women owned by James and David Weems testified against him. He was found guilty and was hanged.[67]

Afro-American slaves had developed strong community institutions on their quarters and in their families and kin groups by the 1760s and 1770s, but the values and beliefs held by members of this community are difficult to determine. Since blacks in the Chesapeake region did not achieve a settled social life until after heavy African immigration stopped and since whites continued to live in even the most densely black areas, one would expect slave culture in the region to reflect white values and beliefs. Even native-born slaves had little choice either about their work or about the people who lived with them in their quarters. Nevertheless, they had a measure of self-determination in their family life, in their religion, and in the ways they celebrated or mourned. The skimpy surviving evidence suggests that when they could choose, tidewater Afro-Americans simultaneously borrowed from whites and drew on the values and beliefs their ancestors brought from West Africa to form a culture not only significantly different from that of Anglo-Americans but also different from the culture of any West African group or any other group of North American slaves.

The way Afro-Americans organized their family life indicates most clearly how they used both African and Euro-American forms to create a new institution compatible with their life under slavery. By the time of the Revolution, most slaves lived in families, and slave households were similar to those of their white masters. About as many Afro-Americans as whites lived in two-parent and extended households. Whites all lived in monogamous families, and only scattered examples of the African custom of polygamy can be found among blacks. Slavery forced the kinfolk of extended families to live very close to one another on large plantations where they

[67] Prince George's Court Rec., XXVI, 343, 357; Anne Arundel Judgments, IB#6, 347-348, 355; Md. Gaz., Dec. 14, 1774.

played and worked together. By contrast, whites only occasionally visited their extended kinfolk and worked their fields only with their children, not with adult brothers and sisters. This closeness fostered a sense of kin solidarity among Afro-Americans. They named their children after both sides of the family (but interestingly enough, daughters were not often named for their mothers). And they sometimes refused to marry within the plantation even when sex ratios were equal: many of the available potential partners were first cousins, and blacks refused to marry first cousins. This may have represented a transformation of African marriage taboos that differed from tribe to tribe but tended to be stricter than those of Chesapeake whites, who frequently married first cousins.[68]

Native slaves occasionally accepted the outward signs of Christian belief. Their children were baptized and sometimes received religious instruction. All three Anglican clergymen of Prince George's County reported in 1724 that they baptized slave children and adults and preached to those who would listen. In 1731 one Prince George's minister baptized blacks "where perfect in their Catechism" and "visit[ed] them in their sickness and married them when called upon." Similar work continued in both Maryland and Virginia in the generation before the Revolution.[69]

Afro-Americans may have superimposed Christianity upon the beliefs, values, and ceremonies learned from African forebears and from each other. Thomas Bacon, a Maryland cleric and publisher of a compendium of the colony's laws, preached to blacks on Maryland's Eastern Shore in the 1740s at services they directed, "at their *funerals* (several of which I have attended) — and to such small congregations as their *marriages* have brought together." Bacon felt that the slaves he saw were "living in as profound Ignorance of what Christianity really is, (except as to a few outward Ordinances) as if they had remained in the midst of those barbarous Heathen Countries from whence their parents had been first imported."[70]

Native slaves retained folk beliefs that may have come from Africa.

[68] Kulikoff, "Tobacco and Slaves," chap. 10, and "Beginnings of Afro-American Family," 175-185; Gutman, *Black Family*, 88-90, chaps. 3-5. Gutman, along with Ira Berlin and Mary Beth Norton, have found extensive kin naming on the plantations of Charles Carroll and Thomas Jefferson during the 18th century. I am indebted to Mr. Gutman for sharing this unpublished data with me.

[69] William Stevens Perry, *Historical Collections Relating to the American Colonial Church*, IV (Davenport, Iowa, 1878), 201, 206, 304, 306-307; Bacon, *Four Sermons Preached*, 4; Thad W. Tate, *The Negro in Eighteenth-Century Williamsburg* (Charlottesville, Va., 1972), 65-75. Prince George's responses in the 1720s and 1730s seem typical of those from other parishes on Maryland's lower Western Shore, but those returns are scattered in Perry, *Historical Collections*, IV.

[70] Thomas Bacon, *Four Sermons upon the Great and Indispensible Duty of All Christian Masters and Mistresses to Bring Up Their Negro Slaves in the Knowledge and Fear of God* (London, 1749), v, vii. Eugene D. Genovese, *Roll, Jordan, Roll:*

Some African medicine men, magicians, and witches migrated and passed on their skills to other slaves. Medicine men and magicians were spiritual leaders in many African communities, including those of the Ibos, and they continued to practice among Afro-Americans who still believed in their powers. William Grimes was born in King George County, Virginia, in 1784; his narrative of his life as a runaway suggests that he was terrified of a woman he thought was a witch, that he feared sleeping in the bed of a dead man, and that he consulted fortune tellers.[71]

Slave music and dance displayed a distinctly African character. In 1774 Nicholas Cresswell, a British visitor, described slave celebrations in Charles County, Maryland. On Sundays, he wrote, the blacks "generally meet together and amuse themselves with Dancing to the Banjo. This musical instrument . . . is made of a Gourd something in imitation of a Guitar, with only four strings." "Their poetry," Cresswell reported, "is like the music— Rude and uncultivated. Their Dancing is most violent exercise, but so irregular and grotesque. I am not able to describe it." The banjo was probably of African origin, and Cresswell's reaction to the dancing suggests that it contained African rhythms unknown in European dance. If the form was African, it was placed in an American context: the slave songs Cresswell heard "generally relate the usage they have received from their Masters and Mistresses in a very satirical stile and manner."[72]

Although these little pieces of data do not add up to a complete description of slave culture in the Chesapeake on the eve of the Revolution, some tentative conclusions can nonetheless be drawn. In several areas, where slaves could choose how to behave, they did not follow white norms but combined African memories with fragments of white culture. The result, however, does not seem to have been heavily African, at least on the surface, and blacks in Maryland and Virginia preserved far less African content in their culture than did slaves in the British West Indies.

African and Afro-American slaves developed their own social institutions in the generations preceding the Revolution, and probably formed their own indigenous culture as well. A period of great disruption among blacks early in the century was followed in the pre-Revolutionary years by a time of settled communities. Newly enslaved Africans came to the Chesapeake colonies in large enough numbers to cause conflicts between native slaves and new

---

The World the Slaves Made (New York, 1975), Book 2, Pt. 1, describes how slaves transformed Protestant religion in the antebellum period and how it differed from white religion.

[71] Charles H. Nichols, Jr., "The Case of William Grimes, the Runaway Slave," *WMQ*, 3d Ser., VIII (1951), 556-558. Grimes was in Georgia when he encountered the witch, but his training in Virginia obviously influenced his belief.

[72] *Journal of Cresswell*, 18-19. Blassingame, *Slave Community*, 27-32.

Negroes, but the migration was too small to allow Africans to develop syncretistic African communities successfully. Africans were forced by their masters to say on the quarter, where natives also lived and where unit sizes were small and sex ratios high. As a result, slaves could not transform individual friendships into community institutions. It was only when native adults began to predominate that the earlier conflicts among blacks were contained, and families and quarter communities began to emerge throughout tidewater. At the same time as immigration of Africans declined, the proportion of natives among blacks grew, the sex ratio declined, and the number of slaves per unit increased. These demographic changes made the development of communal institutions easier.

As slaves responded to the demographic and economic environment of the Chesapeake colonies, they developed indigenous institutions. This essay confirms the overall argument made by Mintz and Price, but further suggests the crucial importance of slave immigration, the density of slave population, the size of units, and the adult sex ratio in the development of slave communities in the Chesapeake colonies. Because demographic and economic conditions in the Chesapeake were not favorable to black cultural autonomy until nearly the middle of the eighteenth century, the development of distinctive social institutions among the slaves of the region was a long process, much slower than Mintz and Price suggest for the West Indies. Detailed study of slave demography and the economics of slavery in various colonies might well show why Afro-American communities and cultures developed at different rates and possessed different characteristics in the Chesapeake, South Carolina, and the West Indies.

Much work remains to be done on slave society in the colonial Chesapeake and in other mainland colonies. Three areas especially require research. First, we need to know a great deal about the internal life of the slave quarters. The impact of Christianity on African and Afro-American beliefs and on slave family and community life needs much further exploration. Only with more details on slave culture in the Chesapeake colonies and elsewhere in the colonial South can the relationships between slave demography and slave culture suggested in this article be adequately tested.

Secondly, we should explore in detail the interaction between whites and Africans and whites and native slaves. Knowledge of which whites Africans saw every day and of the values and beliefs the whites followed will tell us how much Africans borrowed from whites and what ideas and structures may have come from African communities. Slaves obviously could form communities and extended families only if permitted by the masters, for whites could greatly disrupt slave life through the sale of slaves, the organization of work, and the punishment of their chattels. An investigation of the mundane attitudes of masters toward their slaves both in the fields and in the quarters would therefore be very useful.

Finally, this essay deals with only a portion of older settled tidewater areas. In the 1730s and 1740s proportionately more black immigrants went to the piedmont than to tidewater, and after 1755 nearly every African found his new home in a piedmont county. How much of the history of tidewater was repeated in the piedmont? If the population of the piedmont was heavily African, perhaps the characteristics of slave society in tidewater in the 1720s and 1730s were replicated in the piedmont in the 1750s and 1760s. But if enough black migrants from tidewater entered the piedmont, the story of the 1750s and 1760s may have been much the same in the two regions. Of course, it is possible that the relationships between slave demography and slave society documented here did not exist in the piedmont. If that is proven, then the basic patterns described here might be called into question.

To find the answers to these questions will be difficult, for whites in the Chesapeake showed little interest in the internal lives of their slaves. However, much remains to be collected from family papers, probate records, court order books, vestry books, parish registers, and even mercantile records. The search for answers may be difficult but it is certainly worth undertaking when the problems of race and culture that began in the colonial era are still with us.

197

The Maryland Slave Population, 1658 to 1730: A Demographic Profile of Blacks in Four Counties

Russell R. Menard*

ALTHOUGH historians have written extensively on the origins of slavery, the attitudes of Europeans toward Africans, and the status of blacks in the New World, they have paid scant attention to a wide variety of questions concerning the lives of early Afro-Americans.[1] The surviving evidence limits what can be learned about blacks in Maryland and Virginia in the seventeenth century, but it is possible to move beyond the issues that have preoccupied recent scholarship. This essay utilizes probate inventories to explore the changing character of the slave population in four Maryland counties. While the interpretations advanced are tentative, it is hoped that the data will suggest new questions and provide a useful demographic context for future research.

Slaves were personal property and were listed and appraised along with other possessions in the inventory taken shortly after a slaveowner's death. In the absence of census materials and detailed registers of vital

* Mr. Menard is a Fellow of the Institute of Early American History and Culture and a member of the Department of History, College of William and Mary. Earlier versions of this paper were presented at the St. Mary's City Commission Archaeology Seminar in August 1973 and the Indiana University Economic History Workshop in November 1973. He would like to thank participants in both seminars for their perceptive comments. He also wishes to thank Lois Green Carr, Alan Day, P. M. G. Harris, Allan Kulikoff, Aubrey Land, and Gerald and Martha Mullin for helpful criticism. The National Science Foundation provided funds for the research.

[1] The most recent essays include Alden T. Vaughan, "Blacks in Virginia: A Note on the First Decade," *William and Mary Quarterly,* 3d Ser., XXIX (1972). 469-478, and Warren M. Billings, "The Cases of Fernando and Elizabeth Key: A Note on the Status of Blacks in Seventeenth-Century Virginia," *ibid.,* XXX (1973). 467-474. Vaughan's notes provide a guide to the earlier literature. Wesley Frank Craven, *White, Red, and Black: The Seventeenth-Century Virginian* (Charlottesville, Va., 1971), suggests that the concerns are beginning to shift and expand. Gerald W. Mullin's study, *Flight and Rebellion: Slave Resistance in Eighteenth-Century Virginia* (New York, 1972), demonstrates that seemingly intractable sources can yield a wealth of insight into slavery in the Chesapeake colonies.

events, probate inventories provide an indispensable guide to the demography of slavery. They are perhaps the single most informative source for the history of slavery in the Chesapeake colonies, and they have scarcely been tapped. Inventories yield sensitive price information, data on the distribution of labor and the growth of slavery, evidence on the occupational structure of the slave population, insights into white attitudes toward blacks, a guide to the possibilities for family life among slaves, and a useful index to the incidence of miscegenation. They also furnish data for a sex and age profile of the slave population.

This study is based on the 1,618 slaves listed in inventories taken in Calvert, Charles, Prince George's, and St. Mary's counties, Maryland, between 1658 and 1710,[2] and 1,569 inventoried slaves in Charles and Prince George's for the period 1711-1730. The four counties are situated on Maryland's lower Western Shore and are contiguous. Planters in the region were among the first in Maryland to invest heavily in slavery; in the early eighteenth century more than one-half of the colony's slaves lived in the four counties.[3]

The slave population in the region grew at an extraordinary rate between 1658 and 1710. At most, 100 slaves lived in the four counties at the beginning of the period, perhaps 3 percent of the total population; by 1710, over 3,500 slaves lived there, composing 24 percent of the region's population.[4] Rapid growth began in the middle 1670s, with a sharp ac-

---

[2] Using funds provided by the National Science Foundation, the staff of the St. Mary's City Commission gathered the data for all four counties for the period 1658 to 1705 as part of a larger study of wealth in inventories in which I have been engaged with Lois Green Carr and P. M. G. Harris. For the years 1706 to 1710, the data on slaves are drawn only from Charles and Prince George's. The inventories are in the following volumes, all at the Maryland Hall of Records, Annapolis: Testamentary Proceedings, I-IV, XVI; Inventories and Accounts, I-XXV; Charles County Court and Land Records, Q#1; Charles County Inventories, 1673-1717; Prince George's County Inventories, BB#1, 1696/7-1720. Lois Green Carr generously supplied the data for Prince George's from 1706 to 1710.

[3] Two thousand two hundred seventy-eight of the 4,475 slaves listed in the 1704 census lived in the 4 counties. William Hand Browne *et al.*, eds., *Archives of Maryland . . .* (Baltimore, 1883-), XXV, 256, hereafter cited as *Md. Arch.* Despite the column heading "Slaves young and old," the census lists only taxable slaves, men and women age 16 and over, in at least 5 of Maryland's 11 counties and perhaps in 10. Cf., for examples, the Baltimore County tax list for 1704 or the number of taxables in Prince George's with the census returns. Charles is the only county for which it is reasonably certain that an effort was made to include all slaves. Baltimore County List of Taxables (1699-1705), MS 74, Maryland Historical Society, Baltimore; Prince George's County Court Records, B, 340; Charles County Court and Land Records, B#2, 57, Hall of Records.

[4] The estimate of 100 slaves at the beginning of the period is a projection from

celeration in the 1690s. From 1695 to 1708 at least 4,022 slaves arrived in the province, an average of nearly 300 a year.[5] The adult slaves in Maryland before 1710 were almost all immigrants, a fact of major importance for demographic analysis. Prior to the mid-1690s most slaves came to the province from the West Indies, although there was substantial immigration to the Chesapeake colonies directly from Africa in the middle to late 1670s and again in the mid-1680s. After 1695 most of the new arrivals were African-born, without prior experience in the New World.[6]

Because sex and age were important determinants of value, appraisers usually distinguished male slaves from female slaves and sometimes recorded their ages in years. In most cases when sex is not specifically mentioned, it can be inferred from the slave's name. Appraisers often recorded specific ages, but without sufficient frequency or precision to permit a detailed year-by-year analysis. In many inventories appraisers used only broad categories, distinguishing working adults from children and old slaves. Even in those inventories in which specific ages appear, the disproportionate number ending in 0 (20, 30, 40, etc.) suggests frequent guessing. Moreover, appraisers often recorded the ages of some of the slaves in an estate and then lumped the rest—especially the very young and the old—into residual categories. Because of the lack of precision and consistency, I have placed slaves in only three age groupings: 0 to 15 years, 16 to approximately 50, and old slaves. From the appraiser's description and the value assigned each slave, all but 10 percent of the slaves can be placed in one or another of these categories. Classification requires some educated guesswork. In particular, the divi-

---

the number of blacks found in estate inventories. The figure for 1710 is from the census in *Md. Arch.*, XXV, 258-259.

[5] Margaret Shove Morriss, *Colonial Trade of Maryland, 1689-1715*, The Johns Hopkins University Studies in Historical and Political Science, XXXII (Baltimore, 1914), 77-80; C.O. 5/749/pt. II, Public Records Office Transcripts, Library of Congress; *Md. Arch.*, XXV, 257; Cecil County Judgments, E, 1708-1716, 1-9, Hall of Records. A comparison of the entries in the several lists suggests that they do not include all the slaves brought to Maryland during this period. I have discussed the growth of slavery in "From Servants to Slaves: The Transformation of the Chesapeake Labor System" (paper presented at the annual meeting of the Southern Historical Association, November 1972).

[6] The sources of Chesapeake slaves and the organization of the trade need investigation. Useful comments can be found in Craven, *White, Red, and Black*, 74-109; Philip D. Curtin, *The Atlantic Slave Trade: A Census* (Madison, Wis., 1969), 72-75, 127-162; Morriss, *Colonial Trade of Maryland*, 79-80; and K. G. Davies, *The Royal African Company* (London, 1957). Elizabeth Donnan, *Documents Illustrative of the History of the Slave Trade to America*, 4 vols. (Washington, D. C., 1930-1935), is an invaluable collection.

TABLE I

PROFILE OF SLAVES IN CALVERT, CHARLES, PRINCE GEORGE'S,
AND ST. MARY'S COUNTIES, MARYLAND, 1658 TO 1710

	1658-1670	1671-1680	1681-1690	1691-1700	1701-1710	1658-1710
Males 0-15	3	13	21	52	88	177
Females 0-15	5	6	11	42	62	126
Sex ratio	.60	2.167	1.909	1.238	1.419	1.405
Sex unknown 0-15	6	16	25	49	34	130
Total 0-15	14	35	57	143	184	433
Males 16-50	17	48	74	145	241	525
Females 16-50	13	40	54	100	156	363
Sex ratio	1.308	1.200	1.370	1.450	1.545	1.446
Old males	1	2	7	12	19	41
Old females	6	10	15	18	26	75
Sex ratio	.167	.200	.467	.667	.731	.547
Old sex unknown	0	0	0	4	3	7
Total old	7	12	22	34	48	123
Slaves, age, sex unknown	3	22	31	63	55	174
total slaves	54	157	238	485	684	1618
ratio 0-15/16-50	.467	.398	.445	.584	.463	.488
ratio 0-15/females 16-50	1.077	.875	1.056	1.430	1.179	1.193
ratio females 0-15[a]/ females 16-50	.615	.350	.435	.665	.506	.526

[a] Assuming that ½ of the children not identified by sex were females.

sion between working adults and old slaves is imprecise; I may have incorrectly counted as "old" several slaves who were still in their forties. Despite this imprecision at the edges, the results provide a useful profile of the slave population in southern Maryland during the seventeenth century (see Table I).[7]

[7] Throughout this essay I assume that the sex and age profile of the slaves owned by inventoried decedents did not differ in any important respect from that of the slave population as a whole. Unfortunately, the available evidence does not provide an opportunity to test this assumption for the 17th century. However, I did test it against the 1755 census. The sex ratio among adult slaves appearing in Charles County inventories taken in 1755 was 1.22; in the census it was 1.27. The ratio of children to adults in inventories was 1.00; in the census it was 1.10. Charles County Inventories, 4, 1753-1766; *Gentleman's Magazine, and Historical Chronicle,* XXXIV (1764), 261. Allan Kulikoff has compared the sex and age distributions

One striking characteristic was the preponderance of males. Among adults of working age, men outnumbered women by roughly one and one-half to one, with the greatest imbalance occurring at the end of the period when substantial numbers of slaves began to arrive in the Chesapeake colonies directly from Africa. The relative shortage of women reflects the character of the immigrant population. In a tabulation of Virginia headright entries, Wesley Frank Craven found a sex ratio (expressed as the number of men per woman) among black immigrants of 2.464 in the seventeenth century.[8] While Craven was unable to ascertain the sex of a significant proportion of the slaves and therefore suggests caution in the use of this figure, the disparity between the sex ratio calculated from headrights and that found in inventories implies a shorter expectation of life for black men than for women, a hypothesis supported by the fact that among old slaves women outnumbered men by nearly two to one, despite the surplus of males in the other age groups.[9]

The skewed sex ratio apparently reflects the preferences of planters as well as the structure of the immigrant population. The sex ratio among black adults of working age on plantations with ten or more slaves was 1.646, higher than in the slave population as a whole.[10] Even the wealthiest slaveowners—who presumably had some options—did not always provide a wife for each working man on their plantations. This fact supports Craven's suggestion that historians have been too quick to assume that seventeenth-century planters immediately recognized the advantages of a self-perpetuating labor force.[11]

The sex ratio among blacks was similar to that in the white population. Among white immigrants to the Chesapeake colonies in the second half of the seventeenth century, the ratio ranged from 2.5 to 3.5, and was

---

among slaves in Prince George's County inventories to census returns in 1755 and 1776, concluding that inventories do provide a reliable demographic profile. Kulikoff discusses this issue in his dissertation on Prince George's County in the 18th century (Brandeis University, in progress).

[8] Craven, *White, Red, and Black*, 98-100.

[9] There is evidence of higher mortality for male slaves in the West Indies. See Richard S. Dunn, *Sugar and Slaves: The Rise of the Planter Class in the English West Indies, 1624-1713* (Chapel Hill, N. C., 1972), 315-317, and Orlando Patterson, *The Sociology of Slavery: An Analysis of the Origins, Development and Structure of Negro Slave Society in Jamaica* (London, 1967), 99, 107.

[10] Two hundred ninety-nine men and 181 women lived on plantations with 10 or more slaves. Dunn found evidence that large planters in the West Indies attempted to provide mates for each adult slave. *Sugar and Slaves*, 251, 315-316.

[11] Craven, *White, Red, and Black*, 100-101.

even higher before 1650. As late as 1704 the ratio among white adults in the four-county region was 1.807, higher than that of slaves listed in inventories between 1701 and 1710.[12] However, whites had a distinct advantage: they could move about in order to establish as normal a family life as the sexual imbalance in the population permitted. A young white man could also leave the region in search of a wife, thereby bringing the sex ratio among those who remained closer to one. The emigration of young men sharply lowered the sex ratio among whites in the four counties during the first decade of the eighteenth century, from 1.807 in 1704 to 1.348 in 1710.[13] Except for a few runaways, emigration was not an option open to blacks. Nor could a black move about freely within the region in order to establish a family. The restricted freedom of slaves aggravated the sexual imbalance revealed in the aggregate data.

Few planters owned large gangs of slaves in the seventeenth century. Only fifteen of the three hundred slaveowners who left inventories in the four counties between 1658 and 1710 held more than twenty slaves, and only thirty-eight owned more than ten. Nearly half owned only one or two. The slaves on many of the larger plantations, furthermore, were divided into small groups and set to work on outlying plantations or quarters. As a result, many slaves lived on plantations with only a few other blacks, a fact with long-term implications for race relations, the process of assimilation, and the survival of African cultural patterns in the New World. More than one-half of the slaves lived on plantations with ten or fewer blacks, nearly one-third on estates with five or fewer. The pattern of dispersed ownership described in Table II severely restricted the chances for social contact among blacks, making isolation and loneliness a prominent fact of life for Africans in the Chesapeake colonies.[14]

[12] *Md. Arch.*, XXV, 256. For sex ratios among white immigrants in the 17th century see Herbert Moller, "Sex Composition and Correlated Culture Patterns of Colonial America," *WMQ*, 3d Ser., II (1945), 113-153, and Craven, *White, Red, and Black*, 26-27.

[13] The emigration can be inferred from the census returns of 1704, 1710, and 1712 in *Md. Arch.*, XXV, 256, 258-259. See also John Seymour to the Board of Trade, June 23, 1708, C.O. 5/716/pt. III, and Edward Lloyd to the Board of Trade, Nov. 4, 1710, C.O. 717/pt. II, P.R.O. Transcripts, Lib. Cong.

[14] Because decedents are older and therefore probably wealthier than the living population, Table II may overstate the concentration of slave ownership. Any adjustment would only strengthen my argument. On the relationship of age and wealth see Alice Hanson Jones, "Wealth Estimates for the American Middle Colonies, 1774," *Economic Development and Cultural Change*, XVIII (1970), 86-97, and Russell R. Menard *et al.*, "Opportunity and Inequality: The Distribution of Wealth on the Lower Western Shore of Maryland, 1638-1705," *Maryland Historical Magazine*, LXIX (1974), 176-178.

TABLE II

DISTRIBUTION OF SLAVES ON MARYLAND'S LOWER WESTERN SHORE, 1658 TO 1710

No. of slaves per estate	No. estates	% estates	Cum. %	No. slaves	% slaves	Cum. %
1-2	145	48.3	48.3	198	12.2	12.2
3-5	70	23.3	71.6	273	16.9	29.1
6-10	47	15.7	87.3	356	22.0	51.1
11-20	23	7.7	95.0	340	21.0	72.1
21+	15	5.0	100.0	451	27.9	100.0
	300	100.0		1618	100.0	

A diversity of tribal origins and the "Babel of Languages" among slaves in Maryland perhaps increased the African's sense of isolation.[15]

The dispersed ownership pattern heightened the imbalance created by the sex ratio among adults. Only 16 percent of the men and 23 percent of the women lived on plantations with an equal sex ratio, while only 41 percent of the men and 53 percent of the women lived on estates where there were fewer than twice as many adults of one sex as the other. One hundred fourteen of the 525 men (22 percent) and 68 of the 363 women (19 percent) lived on plantations with no members of the opposite sex in their age category. The sex ratio in the aggregate population placed definite limits on the opportunities for family life among slaves; the dispersed ownership pattern prevented slaves from taking full advantage of such possibilities for contact with persons of the opposite sex as the sexual imbalance permitted. Together they placed formidable barriers in the way of affectionate relationships between men and women, denying many blacks a fundamental human opportunity.

Some slaves did form families, however, which whites sanctioned or

[15] See the comment of Olaudah Equiano, an African taken to Virginia as a slave in the 18th century, on his response to being unable to talk to other slaves, in John W. Blassingame, *The Slave Community: Plantation Life in the Antebellum South* (New York, 1972), 16. But see also Gov. Alexander Spotswood's warning that the "Babel of Languages" among slaves should not be allowed to lull Virginians into a false sense of security, for "freedom Wears a Cap which Can Without a Tongue, Call Togather all Those who Long to Shake of[f] The Fetters of Slavery," in H. R. McIlwaine and J. P. Kennedy, eds., *Journals of the House of Burgesses of Virginia* (Richmond, Va., 1905-1915), *1710-1712*, 240.

205

at least recognized. Appraisers occasionally grouped slaves into family units in inventories, giving explicit recognition to the bond between husband, wife, and children.[16] Some masters not only acknowledged the existence of slave families, but granted those families considerable independence. Henry Ridgely, for example, had three outlying quarters run by blacks. The quarters were amply supplied with livestock, bedding, household utensils, and tools, and there is no evidence of direct white supervision. Apparently Mingo, Dick, and Toby, whose names identify the quarters, ran relatively independent operations, often making their own decisions about the organization of work, with some responsibility for the success of the farm and for the maintenance and discipline of their dependents. Their lives perhaps resembled those of poor tenants or of men who farmed shares.[17]

Mingo, Dick, and Toby had acquired a measure of freedom and responsibility. Their positions required judgment and skill as well as strength and stamina, but their experience was hardly typical. The work of the majority of slaves was physically demanding, dull, and repetitive, offering blacks little challenge and only a slight possibility of better employment. Most slaves were kept to the routine tasks of raising tobacco and corn and tending livestock. For variety they could look only to the nearly endless round of menial odd jobs necessary to the operation of any farm. Opportunities for occupational mobility—to move from field hand to house servant or overseer of a quarter, or to learn a trade and work as a cooper, carpenter, or blacksmith—were virtually nonexistent in the seventeenth century. The inventories suggest that perhaps a dozen of the 525 adult males appraised in the four counties before 1710 held positions that paralleled those of Mingo, Dick, and Toby, while only four of the 525 were described as skilled craftsmen.[18] Few masters could afford the luxury of diverting slaves from tobacco to personal service, and few plantations were large enough to require full-time craftsmen or overseers.[19] What supervisory, skilled, and service occupations were avail-

[16] For examples see Testamentary Proceedings, III, 23-24; Inventories and Accounts, II, 128, 305, V, 143-145, 19½A, 28, VIII, 404-406, XA, 10, XIIIA, 122.

[17] Ridgely's inventory is in Inventories and Accounts, XXXIIB, 71. For other examples see Testamentary Proceedings, V, 178-179; Inventories and Accounts, VIIC, 105-107; Prince George's County Inventories, BB#1, 137-141.

[18] See above, n. 17; Prince George's County Inventories, BB#1, 117; Charles County Inventories, 1677-1717, 74, 290.

[19] But see Gov. Francis Nicholson's statement that "most people have some of them as their domestick servants: and the better sort may have 6 or 7 in those

able, furthermore, were awarded to English servants, who spoke their master's language, had often acquired a trade before migrating, and appeared on the plantations of nearly every slaveowner.[20] Seventeenth-century plantation life offered bound laborers few chances for occupational advancement. Given the height of linguistic and cultural barriers and the depth of racial prejudice, unassimilated African slaves could not compete with white indentured servants for the few good jobs that did exist. Plantation work routines did little to alleviate the dreary isolation that slavery forced upon most blacks in the early colonial period.

The isolation of blacks may have been mitigated by visiting in the evening, on Sundays and holidays, or by running away. The literature conveys the impression that slaves had more freedom of movement in the seventeenth century than later, but the evidence is not very firm.[21] There are complaints of blacks wandering about from plantation to plantation on visits, of "continual concourse of Negroes on Sabboth and holy days meeting in great numbers," and of slaves getting "Drunke on the Lords Day beating their Negro Drums by which they call considerable Numbers of Negroes together in some Certaine places." According to Gov. Francis Nicholson, visiting, even at distances of thirty or forty miles, was "common practice."[22] Yet it is impossible to determine, even crudely, how many blacks were able to make social contacts with slaves from other plantations or how frequently such contacts occurred. The wide dispersal of ownership, and in particular the unbalanced sex ratio on most plantations, must have driven blacks to exploit whatever chances

---

circumstances." Nicholson to the Board of Trade, Aug. 20, 1698, *Md. Arch.*, XXIII, 499. Nicholson is usually a reliable witness, but this assertion is clearly an exaggeration.

[20] For servants' skills see Mildred Campbell, "Social Origins of Some Early Americans," in James Morton Smith, ed., *Seventeenth-Century America: Essays in Colonial History* (Chapel Hill, N. C., 1959), 71. Their presence on the estates of most slaveowners is apparent in the inventories.

[21] At least this is the impression conveyed if it is assumed that legislation and case law provide a rough guide to the actual status and privileges of blacks. Despite their disagreements, the participants in the debate over the origins of slavery and race prejudice agree that the law of slavery tended toward increased severity during the late 17th and early 18th centuries. Winthrop D. Jordan, *White Over Black: American Attitudes Toward the Negro, 1550-1812* (Chapel Hill, N. C., 1968), 71-83; Carl N. Degler, "Slavery and the Genesis of American Race Prejudice," *Comparative Studies in Society and History*, II (1959-1960), 49-66; Oscar and Mary F. Handlin, "Origins of the Southern Labor System," *WMQ*, 3d Ser., VII (1950), 199-222.

[22] *Md. Arch.*, XXXVIII, 48; Somerset County Judicials, 1707-1711, 1, Hall of Records; Nicholson to the Board of Trade, Aug. 20, 1698, *Md. Arch.*, XXIII, 498.

presented themselves, whether surreptitious or open, whether sanctioned by their masters or forbidden, to relieve the isolation and loneliness that resulted from the demographic conditions of slavery on Maryland's lower Western Shore.

A surplus of males among adults of working age was not the only peculiarity of the slave population. Few children appear in the inventories: appraisers listed less than one slave under age 16 for every two adults between 16 and 50. In addition, the ratio of children to adults shows only the slightest upward tendency through the period under study. The small proportion of children reinforces the impression of a stunted family life for most blacks in early colonial Maryland.

While the difficulty of assessing the impact of immigration on the age structure makes certainty impossible, the small proportion of children does suggest that the slave population did not increase by natural means. Growth depended instead on immigration. Model life tables indicate that in populations with adult life expectancies that approximate those found among whites in Maryland of this period and that are growing by natural means, the ratio of persons under 16 to persons 16 to 50 should approach one.[23] In the West Indies, where it has been established beyond doubt that slaves suffered a net natural decline in the seventeenth and early eighteenth centuries, the black population contained a slightly higher proportion of children than in the four Maryland counties.[24]

The proportion of children in the inventories, furthermore, exaggerates the ability of the slave population to reproduce itself. Between 1658 and 1710 the sex ratio among slave children identifiable by sex was 1.405. Perhaps girls outnumbered boys among those who could not be so identified, or perhaps among children female mortality was much higher than male mortality. More likely, many of the children were not native

[23] For life expectancies among whites see Lorena S. Walsh and Russell R. Menard, "Death in the Chesapeake: Two Life Tables for Men in Early Colonial Maryland," *Md. Hist. Mag.*, LXIX (1974), 211-227. Model life tables are available in Ansley J. Coale and Paul Demeny, *Regional Model Life Tables and Stable Populations* (Princeton, N. J., 1966), and United Nations, Dept. of Social Affairs, Population Branch, *Age and Sex Patterns of Mortality: Model Life-Tables for Under-developed Countries* (New York, 1955). See the comments on their use in T. H. Hollingsworth, *Historical Demography* (Ithaca, N. Y., 1969), esp. 339-353.

[24] Dunn, *Sugar and Slaves,* 316. For a survey of census returns that helps place the proportion of children in the Maryland slave population in context see Robert V. Wells, "Household Size and Composition in the British Colonies in America, 1675-1775," *Journal of Interdisciplinary History*, IV (1973-1974), 543-570.

to the colony but had immigrated. The sexual imbalance probably reflects the predominance of boys among children in the immigrant population.

The apparent failure of the initial slave population to reproduce itself is significant. Much of the recent scholarly literature has been concerned with a comparison of slave systems in the Americas. In particular, historians have debated which of the several forms of slavery was most harsh and dehumanizing, an issue on which there has been more speculation than hard evidence. Most scholars have followed Frank Tannenbaum in arguing that slavery was milder in the Latin colonies than in the regions settled by the English.[25] Yet, as Philip Curtin has pointed out, slaves in British North America enjoyed a rapid rate of natural increase, if the entire colonial period is considered, while in most Latin colonies deaths outnumbered births among blacks. Since the ability to reproduce is a fundamental indicator of well-being, this fact is a powerful criticism of Tannenbaum's hypothesis.[26] While it is clear that by the late eighteenth century the slave population of the United States was growing by natural means, perhaps it had not always done so. The first slaves in Maryland, like blacks elsewhere in the Americas, apparently failed to reproduce themselves fully, a finding that provides support for historians who have been impressed by the similarities of the African experience in the New World.[27]

[25] Frank Tannenbaum, *Slave and Citizen: The Negro in the Americas* (New York, 1946); Stanley M. Elkins, *Slavery: A Problem in American Institutional and Intellectual Life* (Chicago, 1959); Herbert S. Klein, *Slavery in the Americas: A Comparative Study of Virginia and Cuba* (Chicago, 1967). For a dissenting view see Carl N. Degler, *Neither Black Nor White: Slavery and Race Relations in Brazil and the United States* (New York, 1971). On the debate see C. Vann Woodward, *American Counterpoints: Slavery and Racism in the North-South Dialogue* (Boston, 1971), 47-77, and Eugene D. Genovese, "The Treatment of Slaves in Different Countries: Problems in the Applications of the Comparative Method," in Laura Foner and Eugene D. Genovese, eds., *Slavery in the New World: A Reader in Comparative History* (Englewood Cliffs, N. J., 1969), 202-210.

[26] Curtin, *Atlantic Slave Trade*, 92-93.

[27] Maryland was not the only North American region in which slaves experienced an initial natural decline: at times during the 18th century the black populations in South Carolina, Philadelphia, and the province of New York registered an excess of deaths over births. On South Carolina see Peter H. Wood, *Black Majority: Negroes in Colonial South Carolina from 1670 through the Stono Rebellion* (New York, 1974), 153-154, 159-166. On Philadelphia see Gary B. Nash, "Slaves and Slaveowners in Colonial Philadelphia," *WMQ*, 3d Ser., XXX (1973), 232-241. On New York cf. the record of slave imports in U. S. Bureau of the Census, *Historical Statistics of the United States: Colonial Times to 1957* (Washington, D. C., 1960), series Z298-302, with the census returns of 1723 and 1731 in Evarts

Why so few children? The adult sex ratio would seem the most likely culprit, for the number of women of childbearing age in a population is one of the most important determinants of the birth rate. Among Maryland slaves, however, its influence seems relatively minor. If the excess men are excluded, the ratio of children to adults increases to .596, suggesting that even if the sex ratio were equal the population would still have registered a net natural decline, especially if many of the children were immigrants. On plantations with a sex ratio of one, the ratio of children to adults was .500, barely an improvement over that in the aggregate population. Sexual imbalance among adults seems an insufficient explanation of the small proportion of children in the slave population.[28]

Perhaps there were so few children because the slave women found in inventories were recent immigrants who had not been in the colony long enough to bear many children. No doubt this had some depressing effect on the number of children, but, like the sex ratio, it seems a relatively minor influence. In an attempt to obtain a rough estimate of the effect of the number of years slaves had been in Maryland on the proportion of children appearing in inventories, I have examined the biographies of decedents to identify those who had inherited slaves. Thirteen such men were identified. Presumably the 111 adult slaves found in their inventories had been in Maryland longer than most blacks. The ratio of children to adults among these slaves was .580, only slightly higher than that in the aggregate population. Moreover, the sex ratio among children in the inventories of men who had inherited slaves was 2.733, suggesting that the higher proportion of children on their estates resulted more from purchases than from births. This is not an entirely satisfactory test, but it does suggest that the number of years slave women had been in Maryland is of little importance in accounting for the small proportion of children. The profile of the population found in inventories between 1691 and 1700, a period characterized both by heavy black immigration and by a relatively high ratio of children to adults, lends additional weight to this conclusion.[29] The age structure of the slave population in the four-

---

B. Greene and Virginia Harrington, comps., *American Population before the Federal Census of 1790* (New York, 1932), 96-97. In compiling population estimates for *Historical Statistics,* Stella H. Sutherland apparently assumed that Virginia's slave population experienced a natural decline in the early 18th century. Cf. series Z14 with Z294-297.

[28] Roughly equal sex ratios among black adults did not result in natural increase in the West Indies. Dunn, *Sugar and Slaves,* 316.

[29] For slaves brought to Maryland in the 1690s see above, n. 5. If the inter-

county region before 1710 is probably not simply a reflection of the age distribution of immigrants. It reflects as well the failure of Africans to reproduce themselves fully in the New World.

The small number of children may have been a consequence of an extreme alienation among black women. Craven has recently noted that "many comments have been made upon the morbidity, at times expressed in suicide, of the African after reaching America, and the unwillingness of some women to bring a child into the condition of enslavement."[30] Unfortunately, the persuasiveness of this proposition depends almost entirely on the scholar's inclination, for the evidence that could subject it to a test—a survey of the attitudes of imigrant slave women—is unavailable.[31]

Attitudes other than morbidity may have depressed the birth rate. Most West African tribes—the principal home of immigrant slaves in the British colonies—practised polygynous marriage, usually an effective means of birth control. While it seems unlikely that polygyny could withstand the pressures generated by black sex ratios in the Chesapeake, some of the associated attitudes toward child rearing and sexual intercourse may have survived.[32] In particular, West African women usually nursed their children for two or three years and abstained from sexual intercourse until the infant was weaned. Such practice produces an interval between live births of three to four years, much longer than that usually found among European women in the colonies. If widely followed, this practice would severely depress the birth rate among African-born slave women.[33]

---

pretation advanced later in this essay is correct, the rise in the proportion of children in the 1690s reflects an increase in the child/woman ratio among native slaves born in the wake of the first wave of black immigration in the middle and late 1670s.

[30] Craven, *White, Red, and Black*, 101.

[31] See Blassingame, *Slave Community* (esp. Samuel Hall's comment on his mother's reaction to enslavement, quoted p. 22), and Patterson, *Sociology of Slavery*, 106ff.

[32] In the West Indies, where the sex ratio was approximately equal, blacks occasionally practiced polygynous marriage. Dunn, *Sugar and Slaves*, 251; Patterson, *Sociology of Slavery*, 106. According to Edward Kimber, slaves on the Eastern Shore of Maryland practiced polygyny in the mid-1740s. "Eighteenth Century Maryland as Portrayed in the 'Itinerant Observations' of Edward Kimber," *Md. Hist. Mag.*, LI (1956), 327.

[33] Melville J. Herskovits, *Dahomey: An Ancient West African Kingdom*, I (New York, 1938), 239-353; George P. Murdock, *Africa: Its Peoples and Their Cultural History* (New York, 1959); Paul Bohannan, *Africa and Africans* (Garden City, N. Y., 1964), 158-173; Patterson, *Sociology of Slavery*, 110. For birth intervals among European women in the colonies see Robert V. Wells, "Quaker Marriage Patterns in a Colonial Perspective," *WMQ*, 3d Ser., XXIX (1972), 440.

Chronic ill-health and high mortality doubtless limited the reproductive capacity of African-born slave women. Among white male immigrants in Maryland during the seventeenth century, expectation of life at age 20 was only about 23 years.[34] Whether black females died younger or older than white males, it seems safe to assume that their expectation of life was short and that many were afflicted with the chronic ailments that sapped the strength of the white population.[35] In addition, so short an expectation of life among adults indicates a high level of infant and childhood mortality that would lower the proportion of children in the slave population and limit the ability of blacks to reproduce themselves.[36]

Maryland's slave population did not experience a net natural decline throughout the colonial period. At the time of the first federal census, approximately 50 percent more blacks lived in Maryland and Virginia alone than had immigrated to all of British North America before 1790.[37] By 1755 there were more slave children than adults in the four-county region, indicating a substantial rise in the number of births and a rapid natural increase.[38] When did natural increase begin? Why did it occur? Again, data on the age and sex characteristics of the slave population from inventories provide a basis for speculation.

Table III presents a profile of the slave population in Charles and Prince George's counties drawn from inventories taken between 1711 and

[34] Walsh and Menard, "Death in the Chesapeake," *Md. Hist. Mag.,* LXIX (1974), 215.

[35] See Philip D. Curtin, "Epidemiology and the Slave Trade," *Political Science Quarterly,* LXXXIII (1968), 190-216, and Patterson's comments on the influence of gynecological problems on the fertility of slave women in Jamaica in *Sociology of Slavery,* 109-110.

[36] On inferring infant and childhood mortality from adult expectation of life see the model life tables cited in n. 23. A word of caution is required here. It is not clear that, given the expectation of life for males at age 20 in the Chesapeake colonies, one can then consult the appropriate model life table to determine the expectation of life at birth. It seems reasonable to assume that infant and childhood mortality in the Chesapeake was high, but whether a model life table based on the experience of late 19th- and 20th-century populations can tell us exactly how high seems an open question. See Hollingsworth, *Historical Demography,* 339-353; Walsh and Menard, "Death in the Chesapeake," *Md. Hist. Mag.,* LXIX (1974), 219-222; and Jack Ericson Eblen, "New Estimates of the Vital Rates of the United States Black Population During the Nineteenth Century," *Demography,* XI (1974), 302.

[37] Greene and Harrington, comps., *American Population,* 133, 155; Curtin, *Atlantic Slave Trade,* 72-75.

[38] *Gentleman's Mag.,* XXXIV (1764), 261. This census understates the number of slave women in Prince George's County by 1,000.

TABLE III

PROFILE OF SLAVES IN CHARLES AND PRINCE GEORGE'S COUNTIES,
MARYLAND, 1711 TO 1730

	1711-1720	1721-1730
Males 0-15	84	185
Females 0-15	78	164
Sex ratio	1.077	1.128
Sex unknown 0-15	20	34
Total 0-15	182	383
Males 16-50	209	287
Females 16-50	120	188
Sex ratio	1.742	1.526
Total 16-50	329	475
Old males	26	53
Old females	21	47
Sex ratio	1.238	1.128
Old sex unknown	3	2
Total old	50	102
Slaves, age, sex unknown	34	14
Total slaves	595	974
ratio 0-15/16-50	.553	.806
ratio 0-15/females 16-50	1.517	2.037
ratio females 0-15[a]/females 16-50	.733	.963

[a] Assuming that ½ of the children not identified by sex were females.

1730.[39] In constructing the table, I have followed the procedures used for Table I. Although it shares the earlier table's imprecision at the edges of each age category and should be used with the same caution, it is adequate for my purpose. Table III describes a slight increase in the proportion of children in the years between 1711 and 1720, and a more substantial gain during the decade beginning in 1721. The increase appears even more pronounced when the relatively equal sex ratio among children is considered. The 1720s, these data suggest, marked a watershed for the slave population on Maryland's lower Western Shore.[40]

[39] Charles County Inventories, 1673-1717; 1717-1735; Prince George's County Inventories, BB#1, 1696/7-1720; TB#1, 1720-1729; PD#1, 1729-1740. Lois Green Carr generously supplied the data for Prince George's from 1711 to 1720.
[40] In 1724 Hugh Jones noted that slaves "are very prolifick among themselves." Jones, *The Present State of Virginia . . .*, ed. Richard L. Morton (Chapel Hill,

Table III also provides some clues to the reasons for the growing number of children. This increase was clearly not the result of a decline in the sex ratio. There was, in fact, a slightly higher proportion of men in the 16 to 50 age category during the 1720s than in the period 1658 to 1710. This suggests that planters had not yet recognized the benefits of natural increase among slaves.[41] Had planter interest in black reproduction suddenly increased, one would expect to find evidence of an effort to eliminate the sexual imbalance. However, on plantations with ten or more slaves, whose owners were usually wealthy enough to adjust sex ratios through purchase, men outnumbered women by nearly two to one in the 1720s.[42]

The high sex ratio suggests that the increase in the number of children occurred despite a continuing high rate of black immigration. Had the rate of immigration declined, one result would have been a movement of the sex ratio toward equality, especially given the apparently higher mortality rate for men and the increasing number of native-born slaves among whom the numbers of men and women were roughly equal. The fact that a sex ratio as high as that of the seventeenth century was maintained despite a growing population of native-born adults and higher male mortality suggests an increase in the rate of black immigration in the 1720s. The number of slaves brought into Virginia in this decade provides support for this argument.[43]

While the sex ratio was fairly stable, the ratio of children to women was not. From 1658 to 1710 appraisers listed just over one child under 16 for each woman aged 16 to 50; by the 1720s this ratio had nearly doubled. Two processes could account for the rise in the child-woman ratio: a decline in the rate of infant and childhood mortality, or an increase in the number of births per woman. Both were probably at work. The expectation of life for white adult males lengthened in the eighteenth century, an improvement doubtless accompanied by an increase in the

---

N. C., 1956), 75. See also Gov. William Gooch to the Council of Trade and Plantations, July 23, 1730, in W. Noel Sainsbury *et al.*, eds., *Calendar of State Papers, Colonial Series: America and West Indies* (London, 1937), *1730*, no. 348.

[41] Dunn attributes the beginnings of natural increase among slaves in the West Indies in the late 18th century to such a recognition. *Sugar and Slaves,* 324-325.

[42] Two hundred one men and 111 women (sex ratio = 1.811) lived on plantations with 10 or more slaves.

[43] *Historical Statistics,* series Z294-297. The record of imports for the late 1720s is probably incomplete. See also the testimony of Mr. Hunt, active in the slave trade, before the Board of Trade, May 4, 1726, "that of late years there are annually imported into Maryland between 500 and 1,000 negroes." *Journal of the Commissioners for Trade and Plantations from January 1722-3 to December 1728* (London, 1928), 254.

chances of survival beyond infancy and childhood.[44] A similar decline in black mortality would help explain the increase in the proportion of children in the slave population.

There are several reasons to assume an increase in the number of births in the 1720s, all associated with a growing number of native-born women in Maryland's slave population. The slaves who arrived in the four counties during the seventeenth century did not fully reproduce themselves, but they did have some children. By the 1720s natives must have formed a demographically significant proportion of the black population. Perhaps in part because of differences in attitude (presumably, natives were more thoroughly assimilated and less alienated than immigrants[15]), but primarily because their reproductive life in the colony was longer, native women bore more children in Maryland than did their immigrant mothers.

African-born slaves in the New World, Curtin has noted, were "subject to the epidemiological factors that affect all people who move from one disease environment to another. Most important immunities to disease are acquired in childhood. To move into a new disease environment as an adult normally exacts some price in higher rates of morbidity and mortality among the immigrants." As a result, Curtin suggests, African-born slaves died younger and were more often sickly than creoles.[46] Studies of adult expectation of life demonstrate that native-born white men suffered less from chronic ill-health and lived longer than their immigrant parents. Improved health and longevity among native-born black women would result in an extension of the average reproductive life and a rise in the number of births per woman. However, among white males in the seventeenth century, the expectation of life at age 20 was only slightly longer for natives than for immigrants.[47] If the experience of black women was similar to that of white males, improvements in health and longevity are not, by themselves, a sufficient explanation of the increase in the child-woman ratio.

An analogy with Europeans in the Chesapeake suggests not only that the reproductive years were extended by longer expectation of life for

[44] Walsh and Menard, "Death in the Chesapeake," *Md. Hist. Mag.,* LXIX (1974), 218-219.

[15] Mullin, *Flight and Rebellion, passim.*

[46] Curtin, *Atlantic Slave Trade,* 19; Curtin, "Epidemiology and the Slave Trade," *PSQ,* LXXXIII (1968), 190-216.

[47] Walsh and Menard, "Death in the Chesapeake," *Md. Hist. Mag.,* LXIX (1974), 218-219.

natives, but that they also began earlier. Most white women who immigrated to the Chesapeake in the seventeenth century came as indentured servants. They were usually in their early twenties when they arrived and were bound for a four-year term. Some were purchased by planters as wives, and others had illegimate children while still servants, but most completed their terms and married before giving birth. Thus the mean age at marriage for immigrant women must have been about 25 years, perhaps higher. For native-born white women the mean age at first marriage in the seventeenth century may have been as low as 16 years, and it was certainly under 20.[48] Perhaps the experience of black women was similar. There seems no reason to assume that native-born slave women bore their first child at a later age than whites, while an average age at arrival of somewhat more than 20 years fits well with what little is known about the ages of slaves purchased by traders in Africa.[49] A recent study of age at marriage among whites in Charles County has found that native-born women, on the average, married seven or eight years younger than had their immigrant mothers.[50] If the age at which black women had their first child in the colony fell as sharply, native females probably had several more children in Maryland than did women born in Africa.

Given the prevailing sex ratio in the 1720s and before, there must have been strong pressure for native-born black women to begin sexual intercourse at an early age. The inventories yield evidence that they were in fact young when they conceived their first child. Twenty inventories filed in Maryland between 1711 and 1730 that associated a woman and her children and listed their ages were discovered. By subtracting the age of

[48] Craven, *White, Red, and Black*, 27-28. Mean age at first marriage for 58 women born in Somerset County, Md., before 1680 was 16.4 years. Calculated from a register of vital events in Somerset County Deeds, IKL, Hall of Records. Mean age at first marriage for women born in Charles County before 1680 was 17.8 years. Calculated by Lorena S. Walsh from a register of vital events in Charles County Court and Land Records, Q#1, P#1. Mean age at first marriage for women born in Prince George's County before 1700 was 17.9 years. Calculated by Allan Kulikoff from published genealogies. For evidence of contemporary recognition of the importance of youthful marriages for the rapid growth of both the black and the white populations in the Chesapeake see Gooch to Council of Trade and Plantations, July 23, 1730, in Sainsbury *et al.,* eds., *Cal. State Papers, 1730,* no. 348.

[49] Davies, *Royal African Company,* 300. Patterson suggests that slave women were usually between 15 and 25 when purchased in Africa, but introduces little supporting evidence. *Sociology of Slavery,* 109.

[50] Lorena S. Walsh, "Charles County, Maryland, 1658-1705: A Study of Chesapeake Social and Political Structure" (Ph.D. diss., Michigan State University, in progress).

the oldest child plus nine months from the age of the mother, a rough estimate of the age at first conception is possible: 18.7 years on the average for these twenty women. This figure should be considered an upper bound for the mean age at which native-born women initially conceived. The first child of several of the women may have died before the inventory was taken. Furthermore, some of the women may have been immigrants, although appraisers were more likely to record the ages of native than of immigrant slaves. Allan Kulikoff, working with a larger number of observations and in a period when the chances of inflating the result by including immigrants had fallen, has found a mean age at initial conception of just over 17 years for slave women appearing in Prince George's County inventories between 1730 and 1750.[51]

A summary of the argument may prove helpful at this point. The immigrant slave population possessed several characteristics that tended to depress the rate of natural increase. African-born slaves suffered from high rates of mortality and morbidity, an unbalanced sex ratio, and perhaps an extreme alienation expressed in part as an unwillingness to have children. Most important, immigrant women were well advanced in their child-bearing years when they arrived in the colony. As a result, the initial immigrant population failed to reproduce itself. They did have some children, however, and these children transformed the demographic character of slavery in Maryland. The native-born lived longer and were less sickly than their immigrant forebears, they were more thoroughly assimilated, and there was among them a relatively equal ratio of men to women. Most important, native women began their reproductive careers at a much younger age than their immigrant mothers. Creole women had enough children to improve the natural growth rate in the slave population despite a continuing heavy black immigration, a still unbalanced sex ratio, and the apparent failure of their masters to appreciate fully the benefits of a self-perpetuating labor force.[52] Although a good deal of

[51] Kulikoff discusses age at first conception along with other aspects of slave demography in his dissertation. For an example of the nature of the evidence used to estimate age at conception see Inventories and Accounts, XXXVIC, 223. For a similar method applied in different circumstances see Peter Laslett, "Age at Menarche in Europe since the Eighteenth Century," *Jour. Interdisciplinary Hist.,* II (1971-1972), 228-234.

[52] I should emphasize that I am not arguing that fertility necessarily increased, but merely that native-born slave women had opportunity for sexual intercourse in Maryland for a larger proportion of their reproductive lives than did immigrants. A finding of constant age-specific fertility rates for native and immigrant women would not be incompatible with the argument. However, it is likely that

additional evidence is needed before this argument can be more than an interesting hypothesis, it does seem to account for the changing age and sex profile of the slave population. Certainly it is a line of inquiry worth pursuing.

If this interpretation of the demography of slavery is correct, there are some striking parallels between the white and black populations in Maryland. Short life expectancies, high mortality, a surplus of males, and a late age at marriage for women also characterized white immigrants. As a result they suffered a net natural decline. The native-born, however, were healthier, lived longer, married at earlier ages, and had enough children to reverse the direction of reproductive population change.[53]

There are also parallels between the demographic history of slavery in Maryland and the experience of African colonial populations elsewhere in the Americas. Curtin has reported that Africans in the New World usually experienced an initial period of natural population decline. He found the growth of a native-born population the critical process in the transition from a negative to a positive natural growth rate. "As a general tendency," he argues, "the higher the proportion of African-born in any slave population, the lower its rate of natural increase—or, as was more often the case, the higher its rate of natural decrease."[54] In Curtin's view, the improved health and longevity of the creoles and the equal sex ratio

---

age-specific fertility did increase because of declining morbidity and because of attitudinal changes associated with assimilation.

[53] The demography of whites in the colonial Chesapeake is discussed in Craven, *White, Red, and Black*, 1-37; Irene W. D. Hecht, "The Virginia Muster of 1624/5 as a Source for Demographic History," *WMQ*, 3d Ser., XXX (1973), 65-92; and Russell R. Menard, "Immigration to the Chesapeake Colonies in the Seventeenth Century: A Review Essay," *Md. Hist. Mag.*, LXVIII (1973), 323-329. Preliminary investigation suggests that most initial immigrant populations in British colonial North America experienced a period of negative or at least very low natural increase after the first wave of immigration, followed by a rapid increase once native-born adults emerged as a significant proportion of the population. The initial growth rate and the interval between first settlement and the beginnings of rapid natural increase varied widely from region to region, apparently depending on mortality rates, the sex ratio among immigrants, and whether or not the initial settlers were followed by continuous waves of immigration, but the basic demographic mechanism—a fall in age at marriage from immigrant to native-born women—seems to have been nearly universal. I hope to pursue this topic soon. For some suggestive evidence see P. M. G. Harris, "The Social Origins of American Leaders: The Demographic Foundations," *Perspectives in American History*, III (1969), 314; Daniel Scott Smith, "The Demographic History of Colonial New England," *Journal of Economic History*, XXXII (1972), 176-177; and Robert V. Wells, "Quaker Marriage Patterns," *WMQ*, 3d Ser., XXIX (1972), 415-442.

[54] Curtin, *Atlantic Slave Trade*, 28.

among slaves born in the Americas were primarily responsible for the increased growth rate. The experience of slaves in the four counties suggests that Curtin may have overestimated the role of the sex ratio and of mortality and missed the significance of the decline in the age at which women had their first child in the New World. However, the Maryland data do support his belief that the growth of a native-born group of slaves was the key factor in the transition from a naturally declining to a naturally increasing population.

Whether or not these speculations on the changing process of growth in the slave population stand the test of further research, the sharp rise in the proportion of children among blacks in southern Maryland in the 1720s is symptomatic of a series of changes that combined to alleviate the dreary isolation of Africans in the Chesapeake as the eighteenth century progressed. The most important of these changes were rooted in the growth of the black population, an increased concentration of the ownership of slaves, improved sex ratios, and the gradual assimilation of Africans and their offspring into an American colonial culture.

The slave population of the four-county region grew rapidly during the first half of the eighteenth century, from about 3,500 in 1710 to more than 15,000 by 1755, a growth rate of 3.33 percent a year. At that rate, there were approximately 7,000 slaves in the area by 1730. Rapid growth led to a sharp rise in density. During the seventeenth century slaves were thinly spread across the four counties; as late as 1704 there were fewer than one and one-half slaves per square mile in the region. By 1730 this number had increased to about four, by 1755 to over nine.[55]

An increased concentration of ownership accompanied this growth. A comparison of Tables II and IV demonstrates that slaves were more heavily concentrated on large estates in the 1720s than they had been during the seventeenth century. In particular, the proportion of slaves who lived on plantations with only a few other blacks registered a marked decline. Rapid growth, greater density, and the increased concentration of the slave population enlarged the opportunities for social contact among blacks both within and without the plantation.

By the 1720s the proportion of slaves in the region who were natives

[55] Population data for 1710 and 1755 are from *Md. Arch.*, XXV, 258-259, and *Gentleman's Mag.*, XXXIV (1764), 261. The four counties contain 1,662 square miles. Morris L. Radoff and Frank F. White, Jr., comps., *Maryland Manual, 1971-1972* (Annapolis, Md., 1972), 817.

TABLE IV

DISTRIBUTION OF SLAVES IN CHARLES AND PRINCE GEORGE'S COUNTIES,
MARYLAND, 1721 TO 1730

No. of slaves per estate	No. estates	% estates	Cum. %	No. slaves	% slaves	Cum. %
1-2	40	34.2	34.2	57	5.9	5.9
3-5	26	22.2	56.4	105	10.8	16.7
6-10	26	22.2	78.6	188	19.3	36.0
11-20	14	12.0	90.6	198	20.3	56.3
21+	11	9.4	100.0	426	43.7	100.0
	117	100.0		974	100.0	

of Maryland was growing rapidly as blacks born in the wake of the great migration at the turn of the century came of age and had children of their own. Precision is impossible, but it seems likely that by 1730 most slaves were Maryland-born, although among adults Africans may still have predominated. Many of the Africans, furthermore, were by then long-term residents of the province. As a result, the slave population was more thoroughly acculturated than during the seventeenth century. The isolation that resulted from different tribal origins dissolved as English supplanted the variety of languages spoken by Africans upon arrival, as Christianity displaced African religions, and as slaves created a common culture from their diverse backgrounds in the Old World and their shared experience in the New.[56] These relatively acculturated blacks were more sophisticated about slavery than their seventeenth-century predecessors, better able to exploit its weaknesses and to establish and sustain a wider

[56] On the differences in language and religion between African and country-born slaves see the statement by the Virginia House of Burgesses in 1699 "that Negroes borne in this Country are generally baptized and brought up in the Christian Religion but for Negroes Imported hither," among other reasons, "the variety and Strangeness of their Languages . . . renders it in a manner impossible to attain to any Progress in their Conversion." McIlwaine and Kennedy, eds., *Journals of Burgesses, 1695-1696*, 174. See also Jordan, *White Over Black*, 184; Jones, *Present State of Virginia*, ed. Morton, 99; Mullin, *Flight and Rebellion*, 17-19; and Wood, *Black Majority*, 133-142, 167-191. Allan Kulikoff explores the cultural differences between African and native-born blacks in "From African to American: Slave Community Life in Eighteenth-Century Maryland" (paper presented at the Hall of Records Conference on Maryland History, June 1974).

variety of personal relationships despite their bondage and the limitations imposed by the demographic characteristics of the slave population.[57]

The rise of an assimilated native-born slave population combined with the growing concentration of labor on the estates of large planters to make a greater variety of jobs available to blacks within the plantation system. By the 1720s many planters could afford to divert slaves from field work to domestic service, and many plantations were large enough to require the services of supervisory personnel and full-time craftsmen. At the same time, fewer planters owned indentured servants who could compete with blacks for the better positions. Furthermore, the gradual diversification of the Chesapeake economy, particularly the beginnings of local industry and the growth of small urban centers, created more non-farm jobs. As a result, more and more slaves were able to escape the routine drudgery of tobacco and move from field work to more rewarding and challenging (and often more unsettling) jobs as domestics, artisans, industrial workers, and overseers.[58]

Counts based on occupational designations in inventories understate the proportion of artisans in the population because of the occasional failure of appraisers to record a skilled slave's achievement. Nevertheless, inventories provide a useful guide to changes in the jobs held by blacks. Before 1710 only 4 of the 525 adult male slaves who appear in inventories in the four counties were described as craftsmen; from 1711 to 1725 only 3 of 283 men in Charles and Prince George's estates were artisans. In the late 1720s—roughly a generation after the heavy migration at the turn of the century—the number of skilled slaves rose sharply: between 1726 and 1730, 13 of the 213 men (6 percent) in Charles and Prince George's inventories were skilled workmen. Seven were carpenters, two were coopers, one was a blacksmith, one a "tradesman," and two, perhaps representing an elite among black artisans, were skilled in both cooperage and carpentry.[59]

A tax list that survives for Prince George's County in 1733 provides some insight into the proportion of blacks who had attained supervisory positions. Seventy-nine quarters occupied by slaves appear; on thirty-seven no taxable-age white is listed. Ten of the thirty-seven quarters

[57] On the increased competence of acculturated slaves see Mullin, *Flight and Rebellion, passim.*

[58] For the often unsettling impact of job mobility see *ibid.*, 72-82, 98-103.

[59] Charles County Inventories, 1717-1735, 290, 291; Prince George's County Inventories, TB#1, 1720-1729, 6, 34, 68, 79, 81, 129, 317, 340. See also Jones, *Present State of Virginia,* ed. Morton, 76.

contained only two taxable slaves; another quarter had only one. On these, the lives of the slaves perhaps paralleled those of poor white tenants. Like Mingo, Dick, and Toby, these slaves apparently operated small family farms away from their master's home plantation. Eleven of the thirty-seven quarters contained three or four adult slaves, while between five and twenty taxable adults lived on the remaining fifteen. Some of the slaves on these larger operations must have enjoyed some measure of responsibility, status, and power.[60] If it is assumed that one black on each of the thirty-seven quarters held a position that approximated that of an overseer, 3 percent of the slave men in the county in 1733 were so employed. To these thirty-seven should be added another handful of slaves who lived either on the home plantations of widows with no resident white man or on estates where adult blacks greatly outnumbered adult whites. In such situations black men probably assumed some of the responsibility for operating the farm and for supervising the work of other slaves.[61]

A firm estimate of the number of slaves engaged in domestic service during the 1720s is impossible, but there can be little doubt that their ranks were swelled as the wealth and labor force of the great planters grew. Nor is it possible to measure the number who found work at the stores and taverns located in the several service centers (most still too small to deserve the name of towns) that were beginning to emerge in the region or in the minor industrial enterprises organized by wealthy planter-merchants.[62] However, when these possibilities are added to the chances to acquire a craft or a supervisory job, it becomes reasonable to suggest

[60] For the freedom and power of men in such positions see the example of Charles Calvert's black overseer who harbored a runaway slave for about a month in the winter of 1728-1729, *Maryland Gazette* (Annapolis), Dec. 24-31, 1728, Jan. 21-28, 1729. See also Mullin, *Flight and Rebellion*, 171-172.

[61] The tax list is in the Black Books, II, 109-124, Hall of Records. Because the list does not distinguish slaves by sex, it has been necessary to estimate the number of black men by applying a sex ratio of 1.500 to the total number of taxable-age slaves.

[62] For examples of blacks in non-farm jobs see the references to the slaves at a copper mine owned by John Digges and at mills owned by John Hoope and William Wilkinson, Prince George's County Tax List, 1733, Black Books, II, 121, and Charles County Inventories, 1717-1735, 208. See also Michael W. Robbins, "The Principio Company: Iron-making in Colonial Maryland, 1720-1781" (Ph.D. diss., George Washington University, 1972), 92-93, 99-101. Mullin, *Flight and Rebellion*, esp. 94-96, reports slaves working at a wide variety of jobs in 18th-century Virginia. On the small urban centers in the region in the 1720s see Allan Kulikoff, "Community Life in an Eighteenth-Century Tobacco County: Prince George's County, Maryland, 1730-1780" (paper presented at the annual meeting of the Eastern Historical Geography Association, October 1973).

that by 1730 as many as 10 to 15 percent of the slave men in the region were able to escape the monotonous work of the field hand. To be sure, the job opportunities for even the most talented, industrious, and competent black men were still severely restricted, but they had expanded since the seventeenth century.

Occupational opportunities for women were even more limited. For them, work as domestics, at the spinning wheel and loom, or caring for slave children, offered almost the only alternatives to agricultural labor. Even the women who did obtain such positions had often spent much of their working lives in the fields, moving to more sedentary tasks after they were, like Edward Lloyd's Bess, "past working in the Ground by Age."[63] Throughout the colonial period it is likely that the proportion of slave women who worked as common field hands was greater than that of men.[64] However, the increasing size of the labor force on the largest plantations and the growth of the proportion of children did permit more women to leave the fields as the eighteenth century advanced.

Sometime after 1730 a rough balance between the sexes was attained. Answers to such questions as when and how the balance was established, whether sudden and dramatic or gradual and little noticed, whether reflecting a decision by planters or simply the result of the growing number of native-born slaves, must await further research. The predominance of males in the black population approached insignificance by 1755, when the sex ratio among adult slaves in the four counties was only 1.105.[65] The near balance between the sexes ended the barracks-like existence forced upon many black men in the early colonial period and made it possible for a larger proportion of slaves to create a more settled and, by English standards if not by African, more nearly normal family life in the New World.[66]

Occupational mobility, cultural assimilation, and, most important, a growing opportunity for social contact, intimate personal relationships, and a stable family life made slavery a less isolating and dehumanizing

---

[63] Because of her age, Bess "set in the house and spin." Testamentary Papers, Box 25, folder 34, Hall of Records. For examples of younger women working as domestics see Prince George's County Inventories, TB#1, 1720-1729, 81, 129.

[64] Patterson reaches the same conclusion for Jamaica. *Sociology of Slavery*, 157.

[65] The census of 1755 in *Gentleman's Mag.*, XXXIV (1764), 261, understates the number of slave women in Prince George's County by 1,000.

[66] Allan Kulikoff discusses family life among slaves in 18th-century Prince George's County in "From African to American."

experience than it had been in the seventeenth century. It is ironic that, as the law of slavery hardened, as white racism deepened, and as the identification of blacks with bondage became firmly ingrained, demographic processes seldom studied by historians of Africans in the Chesapeake region made slavery more tolerable and slaves better able to cope with their oppression.

FROM SERVANTS TO SLAVES: THE TRANSFORMATION OF THE CHESAPEAKE LABOR SYSTEM

*Russell Menard**

University of Minnesota
Minneapolis

Why, in the decades surrounding 1700, did Chesapeake planters turn their labor force from one dominated by white servants bound for a term of years into one dominated by black slaves held for life? There would seem, on the surface at least, no compelling necessity, nothing inevitable about the transformation. Unlike sugar and rice, tobacco was not a crop that Englishmen believed themselves unsuited to cultivate. Indeed, until the end of the seventeenth century most Chesapeake tobacco was made by Englishmen; even after the rise of slavery Englishmen and their descendents continued to work in tobacco fields, sometimes as servants to substantial planters, more often as planters in their own right on small family farms. Why, then, the rise of slavery along the tobacco coast?

Briefly stated, this essay contends that the usual answer, which stresses the superior profitability of slaves, is not satisfactory. Chesapeake planters did not abandon indentured servitude because they preferred slaves; rather, a decline in the traditional labor supply forced planters to recruit workers from new sources, principally but not exclusively from Africa. The inquiry begins with a review of the literature, taking up first what economists and historians have had to say about the roots of coerced labor in general and then turning to specific assessments of the transformation in the Chesapeake. It next attempts a history of the growth of slavery along the tobacco coast using evidence on immigration, the relative size, composition, and distribution of the unfree work force, and the price of labor in the Chesapeake colonies as well as data on wages, prices, and the growth of population in England. The essay then explores regional variations in the growth of slavery within the Chesapeake before concluding with a discussion of the impact of the shift from servants to slaves on the ownership and distribution of labor.

---

*Menard is Assistant Professor of History, University of Minnesota. He would like to thank Lois Green Carr, Dorothy Clift, Paul G. E. Clemens, Stanley Engerman, George Green, P. M. G. Harris, Allan Kulikoff, Gloria Main, Richard B. Sheridan and Lorena S. Walsh for helpful criticism. Earlier versions of this paper were read at the annual meetings of the Southern Historical Association in 1972 and the American Historical Association in 1976. Support for research was provided by the National Science Foundation (GS# 32272) and the National Endowment for the Humanities (RS#-23687-76-431) through grants to the St. Mary's City Commission.

I

There is a long tradition among economists that—and there is more than a touch of irony here—associates slavery with the widespread availability of free or nearly free land.[1] The classic statement of the economic consequences of free land in the American colonies remains Adam Smith's:[2]

> Every colonist gets more land than he can possibly cultivate. He has no rent, and scarce any taxes to pay. No landlord shares with him in its produce, and the share of the sovereign is commonly but a trifle. He has every motive to render as great as possible a produce, which is thus to be almost entirely his own. But his land is commonly so extensive, that with all his own industry, and with all the industry of other people whom he can get to employ, he can seldom make it produce the tenth part of what it is capable of producing. He is eager, therefore, to collect labourers from all quarters, and to reward them with the most liberal wages. But those liberal wages, joined to the plenty and cheapness of land, soon make those labourers leave him, in order to become landlords themselves, and to reward, with equal liberality, other labourers, who soon leave them for the same reason they left their first master.

But Smith, and those historians associated with Frederick Jackson Turner who developed this insight into a long-dominant interpretation of American history, looked largely at the bright side of free land's consequences. Under some conditions free land promotes opportunity, relative equality of condition, family farms, and political democracy; under others it tends toward rigid social stratification, slavery, plantation agriculture, and oligarchy.[3]

The key to the paradox is apparent in Smith's recognition of the landowner's eagerness "to collect labourers from all quarters." If

---

1. For recent statements of the relation between free land and forced labor see Evsey D. Domar, "The Causes of Slavery or Serfdom: A Hypothesis," *Journal of Economic History*, XXX (1970), 18-32; Douglass C. North and Robert Paul Thomas, *The Rise of the Western World: A New Economic History* (New York, 1973); John Hicks, *A Theory of Economic History* (New York, 1969).

2. Adam Smith, *An Inquiry into the Nature and Causes of the Wealth of Nations* (New York, 1937), 532.

3. Smith, of course, was not oblivious to slavery in British America and perhaps sensed its relation to free land, as witness this passage which follows immediately that quoted above: "In other countries rent and profit eat up wages, and the two superior orders of people oppress the inferior one. But in new colonies the interest of the superior orders obliges them to treat the inferior one with more generosity and humanity; *at least where that inferior one is not in a state of slavery.*" *Ibid.* (Italics mine).

land of uniform quality and location is freely available its ownership has no economic value. Landowners, if they are to obtain income beyond what they can produce with their own hands, must impose restrictions on the labor force. They must discover ways of preventing workers from acquiring land and of preventing landowners from bidding wages up to the point where they consume the entire product of the laborer, leaving nothing for the landlord to appropriate.[4] A high land/man ratio creates a demand among landowners for unfree labor precisely because it drives wages up and offers widespread opportunities for workers to become landlords. In short, free land was an important pre-condition for both the slave-based, gentry dominated colonial South and the small farmer communities of early New England.

Recently, efforts to formalize the relationship between free land and slavery have come in for some criticism.[5] Evsey Domar, who has given the free land-slavery hypothesis its clearest statement, has also provided one of the sharpest critiques. "The presence of free land by itself," Domar notes, is "neither a necessary nor a sufficient condition for the existence" of slavery.[6] As to its necessity, the fundamental requirement is not abundant natural resources but the potential of labor to produce a surplus beyond "subsistence," which is possible when all land is under cultivation. As to its sufficiency, it is clear that workers can be either the beneficiaries or the victims of free land. All the model can assert is that in an agricultural economy in which land and labor are the only factors of production, free land, free workers, and a leisure class of non-working landowners cannot exist together. The actual position of workers—whether they are enslaved, capture the entire product of their labor, or occupy a position between the two extremes—is a political issue. As the model stands, politics is exogenous.

Furthermore, the model only states that landlords will restrict workers if they can. It does not specify the form those restrictions will take. From the landowner's perspective, slavery, serfdom, and indentured servitude represent potential solutions to the problem

---

4. This assumes a technology sufficient to generate a surplus above "subsistence," for without a surplus there is no economic incentive for enslavement.

5. See especially Stanley L. Engerman, "Some Considerations Relating to Property Rights in Man," *Journal of Economic History*, XXXIII (1973), 43-65; Robert Evans, Jr., "Some Notes on Coerced Labor," *ibid.*, XXX (1970), 861-866; Arcadius Kahan, "Notes on Serfdom in Western and Eastern Europe," *ibid.*, XXXIII (1973), 86-99; Robert Brenner, "Agrarian Class Structure and Economic Development in Pre-Industrial Europe," *Past and Present*, LXX (1976), 30-75.

6. Domar, "Causes of Slavery or Serfdom," 21.

posed by free land. All restrict the mobility of the worker by preventing his escape from the landlord's grip and forbidding his acquisition
of land, with the important differences that in the case of servitude
the restrictions are temporary and in the case of serfdom the worker
is bound to the land, not its owner. And, although they do not prevent
the price of labor from approximating its average product, the surplus
is captured by the landlord rather than the worker. Since it makes a
great difference to the worker whether he is enslaved, enserfed, or indentured, inability to predict the form of servitude is a severe weakness in the model. The last words, although doubtless not for long,
are those of John Meyer: "any kind of growing economy wherein
labor commands a good price combined with a political environment
within which one man can enslave other men, will be sufficient to
create the institution of slavery in some form or another."[7]

Despite its inadequacies, historians of the Chesapeake would be
unwise to dismiss the free land hypothesis. Some relaxation of assumptions is required to more closely approximate reality, but the
model is not an inaccurate description of the situation among English
tobacco growers in the seventeenth-century Chesapeake.[8] Moreover,
it isolates those elements critical to the issue at hand: a shortage of
labor which, because of the abundance of nearly free land, could not
be overcome simply by raising wages, created a desire among landowners to restrict the mobility of workers. However, while the model
highlights conditions which made unfree labor desireable, it offers little help in accounting for the switch to slaves late in the seventeenth
century. For more than fifty years, Chesapeake planters met their
demand for labor with indentured servants. And, although in the eyes
of aspiring rentiers it perhaps had disadvantages, servitude appears to
have been a largely satisfactory institution. For a time it at least permitted planters to expand the size of their labor force and therefore of
their plantations without resort to slavery, despite the brevity of servants' terms. The model, then, is incomplete when applied to the
Chesapeake: it simply does not tell us why slaves replaced servants
along the tobacco coast.

---

7. Meyer, "Comment on Papers by Engerman, Goldin, and Kahan," *Journal of
Economic History*, XXXIII (1973), 105.
8. On this point compare the modified version of the free land-slavery hypothesis in
Domar, "Causes of Slavery or Serfdom," 19-20, with the description of Chesapeake
society in the middle decades of the 17th century provided by Russell R. Menard,
"Economy and Society in Early Colonial Maryland" (Ph.D. diss., University of Iowa,
1975), 213-277, and Thomas J. Wertenbaker, *The Planters of Colonial Virginia* (Princeton, N.J., 1922), 38-83.

II

Historians have offered a simple answer to the question of why slaves replaced servants: profit. In most accounts, servants and slaves are treated as competing forms of labor, vying for the planter's allegiance. In that competition, servitude suffered disadvantages that made the outcome inevitable. Servants were unruly and difficult to discipline, served for only short terms, needed replacement within a few years, and were relatively expensive. Slaves were easier to control, served for life, reproduced themselves, and, in spite of a higher initial investment, were cheaper than servants in the long run. Given the relative cost advantages of slavery, historians have argued, the demand for servants, and consequently the numbers arriving annually, declined as the availability of slaves increased. The critical event in this process was the destruction of the Royal African Company's monopoly in 1698 which led to a sharp increase in the supply of slaves to the Chesapeake.[9]

This argument employs a series of untested assertions. There is, for example, no hard evidence that slaves were easier to discipline than servants, although the argument that blacks could be treated more severely than whites and were more readily identifiable if they attempted escape is persuasive. Nor is there evidence that planters were fully aware of the benefits of a self-perpetuating labor force in the seventeenth century. Quite the contrary, for what data exist, as limited and unsatisfactory as they may be, suggest that the first slave owners did little to encourage high fertility among their bondsmen and that blacks were unable to fully reproduce.[10] In addition, there has as yet been no successful effort to demonstrate that slaves were a more

---

9. The most persuasive presentation of this argument is Lewis C. Gray, *The History of Agriculture in the Southern United States to 1860*, 2 vols. (Washington, D.C., 1932), I, 349-350, 361-371. See also Wertenbaker, *Planters of Colonial Virginia*, 126-129, 137, and Richard Pares, *Merchants and Planters. Economic History Review*, Supplement, IV (1960), 14-25. For a more recent version placing new emphasis on a sub-theme in the traditional argument but still essentially compatible with it, see Edmund S. Morgan, "Slavery and Freedom: The American Paradox," *Journal of American History*, LIX (1972), 5-29, esp. 25-27. Morgan has elaborated and qualified the argument of this essay in *American Slavery, American Freedom: The Ordeal of Colonial Virginia* (New York, 1975), 295-315. For an interpretation that closely follows Morgan see T.H. Breen, "A Changing Labor Force and Race Relations in Virginia, 1660-1710," *Journal of Social History*, VII (1974), 3-25. For the view of an economist that differs in detail but is essentially compatible with my understanding of the transformation see Richard N. Bean, "The British Trans-Atlantic Slave Trade, 1650-1775" (Ph.D. diss., University of Washington, 1971).

10. Russell R. Menard, "The Maryland Slave Population, 1658 to 1730: A Demographic Profile of Blacks in Four Counties," *William and Mary Quarterly*, 3d Ser.,

profitable short-run investment than servants.[11] My suspicion is—if the returns from natural increase are excluded from the equation, and seventeenth and early eighteenth-century planters reveal little interest in slave rearing—that efficiency of management was a more important determinant of the rate of return than the type of labor employed. In fact, it would not be surprising to find that unassimilated Africans were less productive than English servants who came to the Chesapeake knowing their master's language and something of his work routines. Most important, no one has yet attempted to test the traditional argument's fundamental proposition: that planter demand for indentured labor declined as the supply of slaves increased.

Table 1

Ratios of Servants to Slaves from Maryland Probate Inventories, 1674-1699.

Date	Four Lower Western Shore Countries	All Maryland
1674-1679	2.64	3.88
1680-1684	1.54	1.36
1685-1689	1.86	1.58
1690-1694	.44	.28
1695-1699	.64	.34

Source: Data gathered by a project of the St. Mary's City Commission, "Social Stratification in Maryland," funded by the National Science Foundation (GS-32272); Philip M. Payne, "Slaveholding and Indentured Servitude in Seventeenth-Century Maryland, 1674-1699" (M.A. thesis, University of Maryland, 1968), 64, 85.

The first task is to date the transition: when did black slaves replace white servants as the principle source of unfree labor in the Chesapeake colonies? Probate inventories and tax lists indicate that blacks came to predominate about 1690. On Maryland's lower Western Shore, servants outnumbered slaves by more than two and one-

XXXII (1975), 29-54; Wesley Frank Craven, *White, Red, and Black: The Seventeenth-Century Virginian* (Charlottesville, Va., 1971), 100-101. On this point the apparently inconsistent attitude of Robert Bristow—his indifference to the ratio of men and women among his slaves and his disappointment to "find noe increase of them but all loss"—is worth noting. Bristow to John Grason, 15 Nov. 1707, and to Thomas Booth, 30 Oct. 1710, Bristow Letter Book, Virginia State Library, Richmond.

11. Gloria L. Main attempted to measure the relative returns on servants and slaves in the 17th century and concluded that slaves were more profitable. "Personal Wealth in Colonial America: Explorations in the Use of Probate Records from Maryland and Massachusetts, 1650-1720" (Ph.D. diss., Columbia University, 1972), 195-203. However, slight changes in Main's assumptions concerning maintenance costs, the length of terms, and slave longevity, changes that I believe the evidence supports, reverse her result.

half to one in probate inventories taken in the middle to late 1670s. By the early 1690s, the relative position of the two groups had changed: more than twice as many slaves as servants appeared in inventories taken between 1690 and 1694. In Maryland as a whole, the change was even more striking. Between 1674 and 1679, there were nearly four servants for every slave found in inventories; in the early 1690s, there were nearly four slaves for every servant. With the exception of a brief period from 1698 to 1702, when the two groups were roughly equal in size, slaves dominated the unfree labor force along Maryland's tobacco coast for the remainder of the colonial period.[12]

Table 2

Ratios of Servants to Slaves from York County, Virginia, Probate Inventories, 1637-1705.

Date	Servants/Slaves
1637-1644	____ a
1645-1653	1.50
1657-1662	1.81
1665-1669	9.66
1670-1674	1.90
1675-1679	1.91
1680-1684	1.90
1685-1689	.27
1690-1694	.07
1695-1699	.02
1700-1705	.12

[a] Four inventories containing one servant and no slaves appeared in the records.
Source: York County Deeds, Orders, Wills, etc., Nos. 1-12, 1633-1706, Virginia State Library, Richmond.

Scattered evidence from Virginia suggests that this timing was not peculiar to Maryland, although more data are required before the case can be considered closed. In the prime tobacco lands between the James and Rappahanock rivers the transition was especially rapid and

12.   Between 1698 and 1702, 316 slaves and 336 servants appeared in inventories taken in the four counties on Maryland's lower Western Shore—Calvert, Charles, Prince George's, and St. Mary's. Menard, "Economy and Society in Early Colonial Maryland," 386. For evidence on the changing proportion of servants and slaves in other regions of Maryland that describes a pattern similar to that reported here see Carville V. Earle, *The Evolution of a Tidewater Settlement System: All Hallow's Parish, Maryland, 1650-1783* (Chicago, 1975), 46, and Main, "Personal Wealth in Colonial America," 35.

dramatic. According to probate inventories, servants outnumbered slaves in York County by about two to one in the 1670s. This proportion was reversed during the late 1680s, and, by the next decade, servants had all but disappeared from the county. York inventories probated during the 1690s listed nearly twenty-five slaves for each indentured laborer. In Surry, a Southside county outside of the sweet-scented tobacco belt, the transition was less dramatic but the timing was the same. Tax lists reveal that slaves first achieved a numerical majority over servants in Surry in 1688.[13] Of course, York and Surry are not all of Virginia, but, in terms of wealth, soil quality, and intensity of commitment to slavery, they perhaps comprehend the extremes of the colonial economy.[14] That slaves first outnumbered servants in both at approximately the same time suggests that it is reasonable to project this pattern to Virginia as a whole.

These data are not incompatible with the traditional interpretation, although the shift in the composition of the labor force occurred roughly a decade earlier than is usually supposed. One could still contend that planter demand for servants declined as the supply of slaves increased. Were that the case the following sequence would be expected: an increase in the supply of slaves, a decline in the price of servants, and, finally, a decline in the supply of servants. The evidence describes a different pattern: a decline in the supply of servants followed by an increase in the price of indentured labor and in the supply of slaves.

Reliable direct measures of the number of servants and slaves brought to the Chesapeake during the seventeenth century are not available. One is tempted to use Virginia headright records for this purpose, but recent investigations indicate that they accurately describe neither the volume nor the pace of immigration.[15] However, Maryland headrights, while they do not provide a measure of volume and do not include blacks, can be made to yield a description of

13. Kevin P. Kelly, "The Structure of Household Labor in Late Seventeenth-Century Virginia: Surry County, A Case Study" (Unpubl. paper presented to the Southern Historical Association, Dallas, 1974). For the geographical distribution of sweetscented and oronoco tobaccos in Virginia see Colonial Office Group, Class 5, Piece 1319, folio 220, Public Record Office, London. Hereafter cited as C.O. 5/1319, f. 220.

14. Morgan, *American Slavery, American Freedom*, 227-230.

15. For an attempt to use Virginia headrights for this purpose see Craven, *White, Red, and Black*. On the inadequacy of headrights see the comments on Craven's effort in Edmund S. Morgan, "Headrights and Head Counts: A Review Article," *Virginia Magazine of History and Biography*, LXXX (1972), 361-371, and Russell R. Menard, "Immigration to the Chesapeake Colonies in the Seventeenth Century: A Review Essay," *Maryland Historical Magazine*, LXVIII (1973), 323-329.

trends in servant imports. Despite sharp short-term fluctuations, these describe a rapid increase in the number of servants brought to Maryland from the middle 1630s to the middle 1660s. Migration peaked in 1664, and then levelled out, revealing no tendency either to increase or decline to 1681, when the headright records stop. (See Figure 1). Further evidence is provided by the record of servants whose terms were regulated by the county courts. Beginning in 1660 in Virginia and 1661 in Maryland, masters were required to bring servants who arrived in the colonies without indentures to court to have their ages judged and their terms of service recorded. The resulting records measure the pattern of servant imports. Series for York and Lancaster counties, Virginia, appear in Table 3; series for several other Chesapeake counties are presented elsewhere. These data indicate that, within a context of short-term movements regulated largely by business cycles in the tobacco trade, the number of servants imported remained stable in the 1660s and 1670s and then fell off in the 1680s and 1690s.[16] Given the rapid growth of population in the Chesapeake colonies in the last half of the seventeenth century, this evidence suggests that the supply of servants declined relative to the number of plantation owners after the early 1660s, a decline that gained speed in the last two decades of the century.

If the decline in the supply of servants were a product of a fall in planter demand as the availability of slaves increased, evidence of substantial black immigration should appear before the mid 1660s. If such a migration occurred it has left few traces in the surviving records. Slaves did reach the Chesapeake colonies during the middle decades of the seventeenth century. By Governor Berkeley's estimate, 2000 blacks, about 5% of the population, lived in Virginia in 1671.[17] But it was not until at least a decade after the decline in the supply of servants that the number of blacks imported each year rose above a trickle and it was the end of the century before the supply of slaves proved dependable.

Edmund Jennings, based on coversations with "some ancient Inhabitants" and his own recollection, offered a history of Virginia slave imports to the Board of Trade in 1708. After reporting the arrival of over 6600 slaves in the preceeding nine years, he noted "that be-

---

16. Menard, "Economy and Society in Early Colonial Maryland," 159; William Hand Browne, et al., eds., Archives of Maryland . . . (Baltimore, 1883), 1, 409-419, hereafter cited as Md. Arch.; William W. Hening, ed., The Statutes at Large: Being a Collection of All the Laws of Virginia (Richmond, 1809-23).

17. Evarts B. Green and Virginia D. Harrington, American Population before the Federal Census of 1790 (New York, 1932), 136.

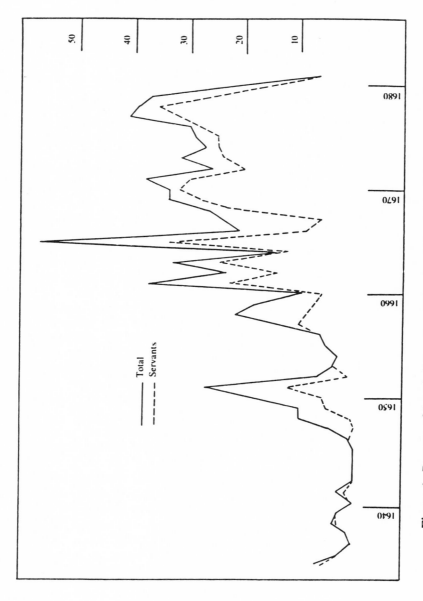

Figure 1. Pattern of Immigration from Maryland Headright Entries, 1634-1681.

Table 3
Number of Servants Registered in York and Lancaster Counties,
Virginia, 1660-1710.

Date	York	Lancaster	Date	York	Lancaster
1660	13	5	1690	0	2
1661	9	17	1691	4	1
1662	8*	21	1692	1	3
1663		21	1693	7	0
1664		10	1694	0	16
1665	1	10	1695	0	0
1666	3	2	1696	1	16
1667	25	24	1697	0	8
1668	10	50	1698	1	17
1669	30	26	1699	2	42
1670	21	20	1700	10	8
1671	18	11	1701	3	3
1672	10	7	1702	1	1
1673	26	3	1703	0	7
1674	24	32	1704	0	1
1675	20	25	1705	1	3
1676	23*	17*	1706	1	1
1677	3*	9*	1707		0
1678	12	12	1708		2
1679	37	10	1709		0
1680	21	8	1710		1
1681	17	9			
1682	13	7			
1683	5	1			
1684	4	3			
1685	2	8			
1686	2	13			
1687	1	6			
1688	3	5			
1689	3	4			

*Records incomplete.
Source: York and Lancaster County Orders, Virginia State Library, Richmond.

fore the year 1680 what negros were brought to Virginia were imported generally from Barbados for it was very rare to have a Negro ship come to this County directly from Africa." "Since that time," Jennings continued, "and before the year 1698, the Trade of Negros became more frequent, tho not in proportion to what it hath been of late, during which the Affrican Company sent several Ships and others by their Licence (as I have been informed) having bought their Slaves of the Company brought them in hither for Sale."[18] In a letter of the same year, Governor John Seymour offered a similar description of Maryland's trade: "before the year 1698, this province has been supplyd by some small Quantitys of Negro's from Barbados and other her Ma'tys Islands and Plantations, as Jamaica and New England Seaven, eight, nine or ten in a Sloope, and sometymes larger Quantitys, and sometymes, tho very seldom, whole ship Loads of Slaves have been brought here directly from Affrica by Interlopers, or such as have had Lycenses, or otherwise traded there." Since 1698, Seymour reported, nearly 3000 slaves, the large majority fresh from Africa, had arrived in Maryland.[19]

The history of the Chesapeake slave trade that emerges from the comments of Seymour and Jennings is reasonably accurate, although two minor changes are needed. First, Jennings should have dated the beginnings of a direct supply from Africa to the mid-1670s rather than 1680. The Royal African Company scheduled two ships to carry 650 slaves to the Chesapeake in 1674 and two ships in 1675. Although there is no record that the ships reached their destination, the £4608 in Virginia bills that appear on the Company's books in 1676 indicate that some slaves arrived. We also know that the Company delivered 120 Africans in 1678 and 177 in 1679. In addition, two Company ships with 404 slaves called at Barbados on their way to Virginia in the summer of 1679, although again there is no evidence that they actually reached the tobacco coast.[20] In sum, it is almost certain that the Company delivered at least 500 slaves to the Chesapeake between 1674 and 1679, and the number may have been well over 1000.

Second, both Jennings and Seymour emphasize the sharp increase in the quantity of slaves supplied to the Chesapeake with the end of

18. Jennings to Board of Trade, 27 Nov. 1708, in Elizabeth Donnan, ed., *Documents Illustrative of the History of the Slave Trade to North America* (Washington, D.C., 1930-35), IV, 88-90.

19. Seymour to Board of Trade, 18 Nov. 1708, *ibid.*, 21-23.

20. Craven, *White, Red, and Black*, 106; Morgan, *American Slavery, American Freedom*, 306; Donnan, *Documents Illustrative of the Slave Trade*, 1, 250, IV, 53-55; K. G. Davies, *The Royal African Company* (London, 1957), 359; C.O. 1/31, f. 32; C.O. 1/34, ff. 109, 110.

the Royal African Company's monopoly in 1698, an emphasis tending to underestimate the volume and obscure the pattern of slave imports in the last quarter of the seventeenth century. The supply of slaves to the Chesapeake grew steadily after 1674 when direct shipments from Africa began. Royal African Company records indicate that seven ships capable of carrying 1300 to 1400 slaves were dispatched for Virginia and Maryland during the 1680s.[21] In addition, it is in that decade that the first record of an interloper active in the Chesapeake appears.[22] Company interest in Virginia and Maryland fell off in the 1690s: only two ships destined for the tobacco coast are mentioned in its records. But independent traders, responding to a severe labor shortage and rising slave prices, took up the slack. Altogether, it is likely that some 1300 slaves from Africa arrived in the two colonies between 1690 and 1697. For the entire decade, the total may have reached 2500.[23] Furthermore, shipments of slaves from the West Indies to the Chesapeake probably increased over the last quarter of the seventeenth century. Trade between the islands and the tobacco coast expanded, and, given the depression and heavy slave deliveries of the period between the early 1680s and mid-1690s, sugar planters were doubtless more willing than previously to export blacks.[24] On the whole, Jennings and Seymour were correct: the arrival of more than 9000 slaves in the decade following 1700 was a substantial gain over the preceeding 25 years. But perhaps that gain represents as much an acceleration of existing trends as a sharp break with the past.

Despite these qualifications, the major point to emerge from the letters of Jennings and Seymour stands: before 1698 and the end of the

---

21. Morgan, *American Slavery, American Freedom*, 306; Treasury Group, Class 70, Piece 61, folios 3-4, 6, 30, 57, 170. Hereafter cited as T. 70/61, ff. 3-4.

22. C.O. 5/1308, ff. 18-45; Craven, *White, Red, and Black*, 87, 106; Morgan, *American Slavery, American Freedom*, 305.

23. On the company's lack of interest in Virginia in the 1690s see Royal African Company to William Sherwood, 14 Jan. 1695/6, where they assert that "at present we have no concerns in Yr Parts." T. 70/57, ff. 120-121, and Morgan, *American Slavery, American Freedom*, 306. On the response of independent traders to the labor shortage see T. 11/13, f. 8. For slaves brought to the Chesapeake see below, Table 6, and T. 11/13, ff. 1, 8; T. 70/61, ff. 83, 106, 165-166; Donnan, *Documents Illustrative of the Slave Trade*, IV, 65.

24. Between 1684 and 1696, 15,000 slaves were brought to Barbados by the Royal African Company, which may have accounted for as little as one half of the total deliveries. Over the same period the slave population declined by 4600. Admittedly, mortality was frightful on the island, but it is hard to avoid the conclusion that Barbados exported a substantial number of slaves from the mid-1680s to the mid-1690s. Richard S. Dunn, *Sugar and Slaves: The Rise of the Planter Class in the English West Indies, 1624-1713* (Chapel Hill, 1972), 87, 205, 230; Davies, *Royal African Company*, 337, 362, 365-366.

monopoly the supply of slaves to the Chesapeake was small, unreliable, and inadequate to the needs of tobacco planters for labor. An increase in the supply of slaves did not precede and thereby produce the decline in the importation of indentured servants. The sequence was the reverse: the decline in the supply of servants occurred at least a decade before blacks began to arrive in the Chesapeake from Africa in large numbers and over thirty years before the supply of slaves became dependable.

Probate inventories provide further evidence of the relative supplies of servants and slaves available to tobacco planters. Table 4 reports the numbers of servants and slaves per inventory in York County for the period 1637 to 1705. The supply of servants rose across the middle decades of the century, peaked about 1660, and then began a rapid decline. The supply of slaves, on the other hand, did not begin to increase steadily until the 1680s, 20 years after the supply of servants turned downward. Inventories from the lower Western Shore of Maryland yield similar results, although neither the decline in servants nor the increase in slaves was as dramatic as in York.

It would be an error to dismiss the decade after the ending of the Royal African Company's monopoly as unimportant to the rise of slavery in the Chesapeake. At least 10,348 slaves arrived in Maryland and Virginia from 1698 to 1709, a figure that probably excludes some

Table 4

Servants and Slaves per Probate Inventory, York County, Virginia, 1637-1705.

Date	Number Inventories	Servants per Inventory	Slaves per Inventory
1637-1644	4	.25	0.00
1645-1653	25	.60	.40
1657-1662	18	2.11	1.17
1665-1669	14	2.07	.21
1670-1674	23	1.65	.87
1675-1679	36	1.17	.61
1680-1684	24	.79	.42
1685-1689	30	.30	1.10
1690-1694	32	.16	2.25
1695-1699	37	.05	2.73
1700-1705	57	.30	2.60

Source: See Table 2.

Table 5
Servants and Slaves per Probate Inventory, Lower Western Shore of
Maryland, 1638-1705.

Date	Number Inventories	Servants per Inventory	Slaves per Inventory
1638-1642	21	.86	0.00
1658-1661	20	1.75	.15
1662-1664	48	.88	.15
1665-1667	58	1.69	.33
1668-1670	54	1.57	.43
1671-1674	92	1.21	.17
1675-1677	210	1.14	.34
1678-1680	91	.97	.57
1681-1684	108	1.21	.80
1685-1687	174	1.06	.45
1688-1690	97	.92	.76
1691-1693	48	.96	2.00
1694-1696	155	.36	.68
1697-1699	262	.48	.81
1700-1702	168	1.28	1.23
1703-1705	142	1.03	2.04

Source: St. Mary's City Commission Project, "Social Stratification in Maryland."

substantial shiploads direct from Africa and certainly does not count numerous small groups of slaves brought from the West Indies.[25] Yet even these did not at first satisfy the demand for labor, a demand long frustrated by declining supplies of white servants and the disruptions

---

25. Neither the slaves on the Fairfax, which arrived in York River from Africa on 30 May 1698, nor those on the African Galley, which arrived in the James on 25 Nov. 1699, appear in Table 6. C.0. 5/1441, ff. 25, 54. For numerous examples of slaves from the West Indies brought to Virginia between 1698 and 1705 see *ibid., passim.* A digression on a recent article by Herbert S. Klein is perhaps in order here. Klein has presented evidence that as late as 1710 to 1718, 53% of the slaves brought to Virginia were from the West Indies and only 42% were from Africa. However, British slavers often stopped in the West Indies to test the market and perhaps sell part of their cargo before moving on to the Chesapeake, thus seriously distorting Klein's figures. If it is assumed that all ships registered in Great Britain that appear in the records of slave imports as from the West Indies had in fact merely stopped at the Islands on their way to the Chesapeake from Africa, then only 16.5% of the slaves brought to Virginia between 1710 and 1718 were from the West Indies and 78% were from Africa. This is perhaps an extreme assumption, but it seems closer to the mark than Klein's. "Slaves and Shipping in Eighteenth-Century Virginia," *Journal of Interdisciplinary History,* III (1975), 383-412; Donnan, *Documents Illustrative of the Slave Trade,* IV, 175-182. Some evidence of ships from Africa stopping in the West Indies on the way to the Chesapeake

Table 6

Slaves Imported to Maryland and Virginia from Africa, 1695-1709.

Date	Virginia	Maryland	Total
1695		160	
1696		196	
1697		32	
1698		477	
1699		352	
1700	229	320	549
1701	796	64	860
1702	481	337	818
1703	156	55	211
1704	987	200	1187
1705	1639	442	2081
1706	1013	163	1176
1707	713	357	1070
1708	593	648	1241
1709	326		

Source: C.O. 5/749/pt. II; Md. Arch., XXV, 257; Margaret S. Morriss, *Colonial Trade of Maryland, 1689-1715* (Baltimore, 1914), 77-80; Donnan, *Documents Illustrative of the Slave Trade*, IV.

of war and then accelerated by the return of peace and prosperity.[26] "There were as many buyers as negros," Francis Nicholson noted in 1700 in a comment on the sale of 230 slaves in York River, "and I think that, if 2000 were imported, there would be substantial buyers for them."[27] Blacks brought better prices than ever before and, for a time, the Chesapeake surpassed Jamaica as the most profitable slave

appears in the lists out of which Klein constructed his measures. Compare the duplicate entries for the Peterborough, Parnel Galley, and Nightingale, three Bristol ships which brought 392 slaves to Virginia in 1718, which appear in one set of documents as from Barbados and in another as from Africa. Donnan, *Documents Illustrative of the Slave Trade*, IV, 177, 181, 183, 186. See also Royal African Company to Messrs. Horne, Thomas, and Willy, 23 Oct. 1701, T. 70/58, f. 17; William Griffith and Henry Palmer to Thomas Starke, 15 Jan. 1693/4, High Court of Admiralty Papers, Class 42, Piece 2; Capt. Edward Holden to the Owners of the Greyhound, 26 May 1723, Donnan, *Documents Illustrative of the Slave Trade*, IV, 100.

26. John M. Hemphill, II, "Virginia and the English Commercial System, 1689-1733: Studies in the Development and Fluctuations of a Colonial Economy under Imperial Control" (Ph.D. diss., Princeton University, 1964), 5-51.

27. Nicholson to Board of Trade, 1 Aug. 1700, Donnan, *Documents Illustrative of the Slave Trade*, IV, 173.

market in British America.[28] Nor did demand fall off with the return of war and depression in 1703. Frenzied buying continued, more blacks were imported, and prices advanced even higher, until, by the end of the decade, planters had "ruined the Credit of the Country."[29] Still, slaves did not drive servants from the tobacco coast; servitude was already in decline for other reasons. The rise of black slavery was more a consequence than a cause of the decline of white servitude; it perhaps hastened the process, but it did not begin it.

III

Although slaves did not drive indentured servants out of the Chesapeake colonies during the seventeenth century, one could still contend that the supply fell in response to a decline in planter demand. Were that the case, a decline in price should preceed the decline in supply. In order to test this possibility, I collected values for male indentured servants with at least four years to serve from Maryland and Virginia probate inventories. The resulting prices, which appear in Table 7, should be used with caution, especially those at the beginning and end of the series. For the years 1662 to 1709, the prices are reliable: they are based on numerous observations drawn from all of Maryland and have been exchanged into constant money values by a commodity price index. After 1710 the prices have been drawn only from the four counties on the lower Western Shore of Maryland and represent many fewer observations. In addition, the slight decline they describe may not accurately reflect the course of servant prices in the Chesapeake as a whole. The lower Western Shore had a relatively high concentration of blacks by the early eighteenth century and demand for white labor there may have fallen off sooner than in areas with a proportionately smaller slave work force. In Talbot County, for example, which had a much lower percentage of blacks, prices for servants remained high until the late 1720s.[30] The prices before 1662, drawn from inventories of York, Northampton, Norfolk,

---

28. Letters of Royal African Company to Capt. James Prowde, 23 Oct. 1701, to Charles Chaplin, *et al.*, 7 Dec. 1704, to Charles Thomas and Benjamin Bullard, 25 Jan. 1705, to Edward Chester, 25 Jan. 1705, to William Fry, 25 Jan, 1705, and to Phillip Broom, 25 Jan. 1705, T. 70/58, ff. 18, 154, 159-162.

29. Edmund Jennings to Board of Trade, 27 Nov. 1708, in Donnan, *Documents Illustrative of the Slave Trade*, IV, 89.

30. For regional differences in the proportion of slaves see below. For Talbot County servant prices see Paul G. E. Clemens, "From Tobacco to Grain: Economic Development on Maryland's Eastern Shore, 1660-1750" (Ph.D. diss., University of Wisconsin, 1974), 171.

Table 7
Prices of Servants and Slaves, 1641-1720.[a]

Date	Price of Servants in Pounds Tobacco	Price of Servants in £ Constant Value	Price of Slaves in £ Constant Value	Psl/Pser.
1641-43	1100			
1644-46	1375			
1647-49	1650			
1650-52	1900			
1653-55	1567			
1656-58	1275			
1659-61	1435	11.0		
1662-64	1600	10.0		
1665-67	2100	9.0		
1668-70	2050	10.0		
1671-73	2000	8.5		
1674-76	1900	8.0	23.0	2.88
1677-79	1900	9.0	23.5	2.61
1680-82	2950	11.0	25.5	2.32
1683-85	2900	10.5	23.0	2.19
1686-88	3200	11.5	23.0	2.00
1689-91	3800	12.0	22.0	1.83
1692-94	3150	10.0	24.5	2.45
1695-97	3050	10.5	25.5	2.43
1698-1700	2700	11.5	26.5	2.30
1701-03	3100	12.0	28.0	2.33
1704-06	3600	12.5	28.5	2.28
1707-09	2950	11.0	29.0	2.64
1710-12		10.5	28.5	2.71
1713-15		10.0	28.5	2.85
1716-18		10.5	30.5	2.90
1719-20		11.0	36.0	3.27

[a] Servant prices are for males with 4+ years to serve; slave prices of prime-male-field hands, aged 18 to 36.
Source: Maryland & Virginia Probate Inventories (see text).

Lancaster, and Northumberland counties, are also based on only a few observations and no commodity price index exists to permit their translation into constant values. In the table they are presented only in terms of pounds of tobacco; this serves as a proxy for a constant value series to the extent that tobacco prices changed with a pattern similar to the prices of all other commodities.[31] Moreover, changes in mortality may have had a profound impact on prices around mid-century. In the 1640s and early 1650s, the possibility of dying soon after arrival was sufficiently high to make seasoned hands with only two or three years to serve more valuable than new servants with twice the time remaining on their contracts.[32]

Despite all these difficulties, the price series is adequate to my purpose. In particular, it is most reliable in the fifty years following 1660 when the transformation of the Chesapeake labor force occurred. And, the price of servants did not behave as the traditional argument demands. Servant prices were steady from the mid-1640s to the early 1660s, increased slowly in the mid-1670s, rose sharply to the late 1680s, peaked about 1690, and then remained stable for the next twenty years, despite fairly violent short-term fluctuations. In short, the price of servants rose as the supply declined and blacks replaced whites as the majority among bound laborers in the Chesapeake. This is a strong criticism of the traditional argument: the supply of servants did not fall in response to a decline in planter demand.

The price ratios of servants to slaves during the period of transition provide further evidence of relative demand for the two types of labor. In the mid-1670s, when servants were still fairly plentiful and cheap, slaves were valued at nearly three times indentured laborers in inventories. Then, as the supply of servants fell and their price rose, the appraised values of the two forms of labor moved gradually together until, by 1690, slaves were worth less than twice as much as servants. The ratio jumped sharply in the early 1690s as the price of slaves surged upward but then immediately stabilized at about 2.3, substantially below the level of the 1670s, where it remained for over a decade. It was not until about 1708, by which time the unfree labor force was largely black and slavery well established, that the price of slaves pulled away from that of servants and the ratio reached and then surpassed its level during the 1670s. The ratio is not a pure measure of relative demand for servants and slaves: obviously, supply played a role, and the tobacco coast was only a small part of the total market for slaves. Nonetheless, it does not suggest that planters pre-

---

31. For tobacco prices before 1660 see Russell R. Menard, "A Note on Chesapeake Tobacco Prices, 1618-1660," *Virginia Magazine of History and Biography*, LXXXIV (1976), 401-410.

32. See, for examples, Norfolk Wills and Deeds, C, 1651-56, 19; Northampton Orders, Deeds, Wills, etc., #3, 1645-51, 180; York Deeds, Orders, Wills, etc., #1, 1633-1694, 143, Virginia State Library. On the decline of deaths during seasoning see Morgan, *American Slavery, American Freedom*, 180-185.

ferred slaves to servants when the labor force moved from white to black. In fact, they seem to have preferred servants, or, perhaps more accurately, they were reluctant to exchange laborers they were used to for workers who were unfamiliar and, doubtless to some, a bit frightening. If price ratios reflect relative demand, it was only after blacks had come to predominate among bound laborers that planters expressed a clear preference for slaves.

Why, then, if planters did not perfer slaves to servants, did they increase their holdings in slaves and decrease them in servants during the late seventeenth century? Further consideration of servant migration patterns provides some clues. Despite violent and distinctly cyclical fluctuations in the number of immigrants and a paucity of evidence, there is a discernible trend in the supply of servants to the Chesapeake colonies relative to the number of potential labor owners. If my reading of the limited data is correct, the supply of servants increased more rapidly than the number of households in the Chesapeake from 1640 until the early to middle 1660s. As a result, planters were able to expand their labor force, and therefore the size of their operations, without resort to slaves. The price of indentured labor seems to have remained stable across this period, although changes in mortality and limited evidence make it impossible to speak with assurance.

Opportunity soon undermined the ability of supply to keep ahead of demand. Many of the servants who came to Maryland and Virginia in the 1640s and 1650s completed their terms, accumulated capital, purchased land, and entered the market for indentured labor. The process described by Adam Smith operated in the early Chesapeake: cheap land and scarce labor forced planters to pay high wages to servants once they became free, permitting a quick transition from agricultural laborer to yeoman planter.[33] As a result of the rapid growth in the number of farms, the number of servants arriving in the Chesapeake had to increase each year in order to keep pace with de-

---

33. On the course of opportunity in the Chesapeake see Russell R. Menard, ``From Servant to Freeholder: Status Mobility and Property Accumulation in Seventeenth-Century Maryland,'' *William and Mary Quarterly*, 3d Ser., XXX (1973), 37-64; Menard, ``Economy and Society in Early Colonial Maryland,'' 213-277; Lois Green Carr and Russell R. Menard, ``Immigration and Opportunity: Servants and Freedmen in Early Colonial Maryland,'' in Thad W. Tate and David L. Ammerman, eds., *Essays in Chesapeake History: The Seventeenth Century* (Chapel Hill, forthcoming); Wertenbaker, *Planters of Colonial Virginia*, 60-83; Lorena S. Walsh, ``Servitude and Opportunity in Charles County, Maryland, 1658-1705,'' in Aubrey C. Land, Lois G. Carr, and Edward C. Papenfuse, eds., *Law, Society, and Politics in Maryland History* (Baltimore, 1977).

mand. If the number of new arrivals merely remained steady, or even if it increased but more slowly than the number of households, planters would face a labor shortage.

The turning point was reached in the mid-1660s. The number of servants brought to Maryland and Virginia, after growing steadily across the middle decades of the century, peaked in about 1665, and then levelled out, or at least grew at a slower rate, before registering an absolute decline in the 1680s. The rate of farm formation also declined, but much less steeply than the supply of servants: the number of plantations in the Chesapeake colonies expanded at roughly three percent per year during the last third of the seventeenth century.[34] As a result, the ratio of servants to plantations fell and the price of indentured labor rose.

Ratios of taxables per household provide a direct measure of the relative supply of labor and of the impact that the decline in servant immigration had on the size of the Chesapeake work force. The most complete series is for Lancaster County. It shows about four taxables per household in the early 1650s rising steadily to a peak of 5.5 in the mid-1660s. The ratio then began a gradual slide, falling to 4.5 by 1670, less than 3.5 by the mid-1670s, around 3 during the 1680s, finally reaching a low of 2.6 in the middle 1690s. The ratio jumped to 3.5 by 1700 and remained at about that level until the 1720s, when it again began to climb. Similar measures for other Chesapeake counties describe the same pattern, although in none was the ratio as high as in Lancaster.[35] During the last third of the seventeenth century, when the initial thrust toward heavy investment in slaves occurred, Chesapeake planters faced a severe labor shortage, a shortage produced by the failure of white immigration to keep pace with the growth in farms.[36]

---

34. The expansion of farms in the Chesapeake can be measured by counting households on the tax lists cited below in figure 2 and note 35. See also the number of estate inventories of heads of households probated in the counties on the lower Western Shore of Maryland reported in Russell R. Menard, P. M. G. Harris, and Lois Green Carr, "Opportunity and Inequality: The Distribution of Wealth on the Lower Western Shore of Maryland, 1638-1705," *Maryland Historical Magazine*, LXIX (1974), 177.

35. Ratios of tithables per household are available for Northampton County for 1664 to 1677 in Morgan, *American Slavery, American Freedom*, 425. Morgan's series can be extended back to 1661 from tax lists in Northampton County Orders, 1657-1664, 102-104, 138, 175-176, Virginia State Library. Figures for Surry County for 1688 to 1703 are available in Kevin P. Kelly, "Economic and Social Development of Seventeenth-Century Surry County, Virginia" (Ph.D. diss., University of Washington, 1972). A series for Accomack County, 1663 to 1695, is available from Stratton Nottingham, comp., *Accomack Tithables (Tax Lists), 1663-1695* (Onancock, Va., 1931).

36. Complaints of a labor shortage along the tobacco coast and in particular of inadequate supplies of indentured servants begin in 1670 and appear regularly until well

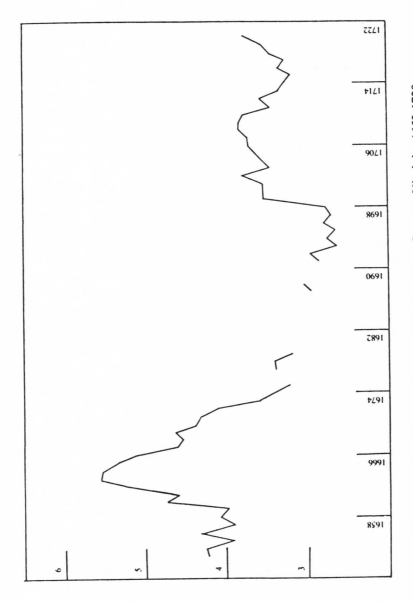

Figure 2. Taxables per Household in Lancaster County, Virginia, 1653-1720.
Source: Lancaster County Orders, Virginia State Library, Richmond.

Why did the supply of servants prove inadequate during the last third of the seventeenth century? This is a complex question for which no simple answer will do. However, we can make a beginning by offering a framework for understanding English trans-Atlantic migration patterns and then looking at indicators of the size of the potential immigrant group and of changes in the relative attractiveness of the various destinations available to Englishmen on the move. To begin with, it is important to place the process of migrating to the Chesapeake under indentures in context. A young Englishman of the seventeenth century who found life at home constricting, who sought greater opportunities or simply a change of scene had several options. He could try Maryland or Virginia of course, but there were other choices. He could go to the West Indies, New England, Pennsylvania. or the Carolinas. He could join the army or navy. If he lived in a village he could move to a town. And there was always London, the colonies' most serious competitor for immigrants. In sum, moving to the New World should be considered within a broad context of English migratory patterns in which colonies competed with each other and with places in England for new recruits.[37]

Within this framework, three factors regulated the size of the English-Chesapeake migratory stream: the intensity of the recruiting effort; the size of the potential migrant group; and the attractiveness of the Chesapeake region relative to other possible destinations. The

into the eighteenth century. See, for examples, William Wakeman to Joseph Williamson, 22 Apr. 1670, *Calendar of State Papers, Domestic, Charles II*, v. 10, *1670*, 178; Anthony Thorold to James Hickes, 11 June 1670, State Papers Group, Class 29, Peice 276, #115, PRO; Owen Wynne Collection, Ms. 211, ff. 75-76, Codrington Library, Oxford; Order of Treasury to Commissioners of Customs, 6 Dec., 1692, T. 11/13, 8; Maryland House of Delegates to Board of Trade, 8 June 1697, *Md. Arch.*, XIX, 540; Francis Nicholson to Board of Trade, 13 July 1697, *Calendar of State Papers, Colonial, America and West Indies, 1696-1697*, vol. 15, #1178, p. 550; Board of Trade of Nicholson, *ibid.*, 1697-1698, vol. 16, #49, p. 28; *Md. Arch.*, XXII, 381; *ibid.*, XXVI, 117-118; John Seymour to Board of Trade, 23 June 1708, C.O. 5/716, #54; Royal African Company to Gavin Corbin, 20 April 1708, T. 70/58, 332; Edmund Jennings to Board of Trade, 28 Nov. 1708, C.O. 5/1316, #16; Letters of Higginson and Bird to Thomas Walker, William Kenny, and Charles Fleming, 30 Sept. 1718, Higginson and Bird Letterbook, Galloway-Maxcy-Markoe Family Papers, vol. 75, #s 1600, 1601, and 1602, Library of Congress; Robert Bristow to John Baylor, 24 Nov. 1717, 12 Dec. 1719, Bristow Letterbook.

37. Migration patterns within pre-industrial England are the subject of a growing literature. John Patten, "Patterns of Migration and Movement of Labour to Three Pre-industrial East Anglian Towns," *Journal of Historical Geography*, II (1976), 111-129, is a useful starting point and serves as a guide to earlier work. English migration to the colonies remains a neglected subject in early American history. Recent investigations include Craven, *White, Red, and Black*, 1-37, and T.H. Breen and Stephen Foster, "Moving to the New World: The Character of Early Massachusetts Immigration," *William and Mary Quarterly*, 3d Ser., XXX (1973), 189-222.

first, intensity of recruitment, will not submit to measurement, although it is likely, particularly over the short-run as merchants responded to changes in the price of tobacco, that this was a powerful influence.[38] For the moment, we will hold recruitment constant in our model, an assumption soon to be relaxed. The remaining factors—size of the migrant group and relative attractiveness of the Chesapeake—can be measured, albeit indirectly and with less precision than one would like: both changed in ways that tended to reduce the number of servants willing to try their luck in tobacco.

The size of the migrant group in seventeenth-century England was a function of total population, an assertion that must be qualified by a recognition that migration was highly age, sex, and probably class specific (young men of the middling classes in their late teens and early twenties predominated) and that the propensity to migrate varied with time. Nevertheless, changes in the rate of population growth can provide a rough index to changes in the size of the migrant group. Despite disagreement over the absolute size of total population and the rates and sources of change, it is clear that England's population grew at a slower rate during the last half of the seventeenth century than during the first. The most reliable estimates describe an annual growth rate of .4 to .5% for roughly 200 years, beginning from a base of 2.5 million in the mid-fifteenth century and reaching 5.8 million in 1650, where total population stagnated for approximately 75 years before beginning another rapid swing upward toward the middle of the eighteenth century.[39] Recent work based on parish registers suggests that the timing of changes in the growth rate of the migrant group fits the pattern of Chesapeake migration with great precision. Aggregation of baptisims and burials indicate a shift from high to low in the growth rate of English population, in large part the result of a sharp fall in the birth rate, in the mid-1640s.[40] Other things being equal, a decline in the birth rate in the mid-1640s would lead to a reduction in the growth

---

38. Menard, "Immigration to the Chesapeake Colonies in the Seventeenth Century," 323-329.

39. E.A. Wrigley, *Population and History* (New York, 1969), 78; Ronald Lee, "Population in Preindustrial England: An Econometric Analysis," *Quarterly Journal of Economics*, LXXXVII (1973), 581-607; J.D. Chambers, *Population, Economy, and Society in Pre-Industrial England* (London, 1972), 9-32.

40. E.A. Wrigley, "Family Limitation in Pre-industrial England," *Economic History Review*, 2d Ser., XIX (1966), 82-109, esp. 106; M. Drake, "An Elementary Exercise in Parish Register Demography," *ibid.*, XIX (1962), 438-441; Peter Laslett and Karla Oosteveen, "Long Term Trends in Bastardy in England: A Study of the Illegitimacy Figures in the Parish Registers and in the Reports of the Registrar General, 1561-1960," *Population Studies*, XXVII (1973), 267.

of potential migrants and, therefore, of the number of servants bound for the Chesapeake roughly twenty years later, in the mid-1660s.

Of course, other things were not equal but rather tended to reduce the appeal of the tobacco coast relative to other destinations. In part this was a function of the pattern of population growth. During the sixteenth and early seventeenth centuries real wages in England fell as a growing number of workers competed for a relatively constant supply of natural resources. According to Thorold Rogers, "the lowest point was reached just about the outbreak of the great war between King and Parliament."[41] Relieved of the pressure of a rapidly growing work force, real wages rose across the last half of the seventeenth century. Rising real wages worked to reduce the size of the migrating population and, for those who still chose to move, to increase the attractiveness of destinations within England. In addition to the general course of real wages, several other factors limited the success of Chesapeake planters in the competition for workers. Within England, for example, the rebuilding of London in the aftermath of the great fire provided employment at good wages for thousands of potential servants.[42] Somewhat later, the wars at the turn of the century sharply reduced the stream of immigrants, although why—whether an unwillingness of merchants to invest in the Chesapeake during depression, alternative employment in the army or navy, or a reluctance of servants to risk an Atlantic crossing in time of war—is a puzzle.[43] Within the colonies, a decline in opportunities in Maryland and Virginia may have discouraged immigration, although it is not clear that even the most sophisticated and knowledgeable of Englishmen, let alone improverished young workers, knew that the tobacco coast was no longer a good poor man's country.[44] Perhaps more important, the Chesapeake was losing its position as

---

41. Rogers, *Six Centuries of Work and Wages: The History of English Labor* (New York, 1884), 522. On the course of real wages in England see E.H. Phelps Brown and Sheila V. Hopkins, "Seven Centuries of Building Wages," *Economica*, n.s., XXII (1955), 195-206; "Seven Centuries of the Prices of Consumables, compared with Builder's Wage-rates," *ibid.*, XXIII (1956), 296-314; "Wage-rates and Prices: Evidence for Population Pressure in the Sixteenth Century," *ibid.*, XXIV (1957), 289-306; Joan Thirsk, ed., *The Agrarian History of England and Wales, vol. IV, 1500-1640* (Cambridge, 1967), 865.

42. T.F. Reddaway, *The Rebuilding of London After the Great Fire* (London, 1940).

43. See above, note 36.

44. On the decline of opportunities in the Chesapeake region see the sources cited above, note 33. On the failure of knowledgeable Englishmen to perceive the decline see the report of the Board of Trade prepared in late 1697 on which of the several American colonies offered the best opportunities for ex-soldiers in C.O. 324/6, ff. 196-203.

the most attractive New World region. During the 1630s, poor Englishmen who decided to cross the Atlantic could choose among three destinations, but in the 1640s sugar and disease gave Barbados a bad reputation and the failure of New England to find a staple crop prevented the growth of a lively demand for servants.[45] These developments narrowed the options and focused the greatest part of the English trans-Atlantic migratory stream on the tobacco coast. After 1680, the opening up of Pennsylvania and the beginning of rapid development in the Carolinas ended this near monopoly and diverted migrants away from Maryland and Virginia.[46] In sum, changes in the size of the migrating population and in the relative attractiveness of the Chesapeake colonies combined to reduce the supply of indentured servants available to tobacco planters in the years after 1665.

Merchants and planters responded to the shortage by looking for alternative sources of labor. The last decades of the seventeenth century witnessed not only a shift from white to black workers, but a brief revival of interest in American Indians as a source of labor[47] and, more important, a substantial change in the character and origins of those who came as servants. During the middle decades of the century the majority of servants who came to the Chesapeake were English males in their late teens and early twenties, children of the middling ranks of England's families. After 1665, the proportion of young men of middling origins shrank as the number of women, Irishmen, laboring poor, and, especially after 1718, convicts in the servant population grew.[48]

This shift in the provenance of indentured servants combined with changes in the distribution of labor, in the wealth and status of masters, and in opportunities to produce a general deterioration in the status of servants. Around mid-century, the ownership of bound labor was widespread. Most small planters owned servants and most servants were owned by small planters. The servant bound to a small planter was probably not isolated from his master's family. Such men

---

45.   Craven, *White, Red, and Black*, 29.

46.   From 1681 to 1685, 8000 settlers, at least one-third of them indentured servants, immigrated to Pennsylvania from England. Gary B. Nash, *Quakers and Politics: Pennsylvania, 1681-1726* (Princeton, N.J., 1968), 50. On the rise of South Carolina as a competitor for servants see Peter H. Wood, *Black Majority: Negroes in Colonial South Carolina from 1670 through the Stono Rebellion* (New York, 1974).

47.   Morgan, *American Slavery, American Freedom*, 330; Wood, *Black Majority*, 39; Philip M. Payne, "Slaveholding and Indentured Servitude in Seventeenth-Century Maryland, 1674-1699" (M.A. thesis, University of Maryland, 1968), 42.

48.   For documentation of the change in origins of indentured servants see Menard, "Economy and Society in Early Colonial Maryland," 414-417.

could not afford separate servant's quarters detached from their homes. Often, servants must have been fully integrated into family life, sharing meals, sleeping under the same roof, treated like a poor relation or at times like a son or daughter. Nor could small planters afford to exempt themselves or their families from the hard work of farming. Masters and servants working side by side in the fields must have been a common sight in the Chesapeake in the 1650s and 1660s. Masters and servants, furthermore, often shared a common social origin in England and a common experience in moving to the New World. Most small planters, like the bound laborers they commanded, were drawn from the middling ranks of English society and had frequently arrived in the Chesapeake under indentures. In short, despite important differences in legal status, the social distance between master and servant was often narrow. Given the widespread opportunities available at mid-century, it was a gap a servant could expect to cross once out of his time.[49]

Both the gap and the difficulty of the crossing increased as the eighteenth century approached. As the labor shortage gained intensity, small planters were forced from the ranks of labor owners and servants became concentrated on the estates of the wealthy. These new masters, most of whom had either been born in the colonies or arrived from England as free men with capital, had little in common with their bondsmen, particularly as the middling Englishmen in the servant population were gradually replaced by the Irish, the laboring poor, and convicts. Nor did such masters work in the fields or integrate bound laborers into their families except in well-defined servile roles. In addition, the chances that an ex-servant would join the ranks of Chesapeake planters fell off sharply in the last quarter of the century. Servants who completed their terms in Maryland and Virginia after 1680 found little opportunity for advancement. Most left the tobacco coast in search of better prospects elsewhere. The last decades of the seventeenth century witnessed not only the growth of black slavery, but the sharp decline of the position and prospects of white servants in Chesapeake society.

By 1710, Chesapeake planters were irrevocably wedded to slave labor. Slaves accounted for nearly 20% of the region's population and in parts of the tidewater the proportion approached 40%. Thirty years earlier, slaves had been of only slight importance in the Chesapeake, making up less than 5% of the inhabitants of Maryland and Virginia.[50]

---

49. This and the next paragraph are based on the sources cited in note 33.
50. Green and Harrington, *American Population*, 137.

The growth of slavery, it has been said, was the product of an "unthinking decision," and so it was in the sense that planters did not perceive the social consequences of the act nor realize that they were transforming their labor system. That is, planters did not make a collective decision to increase their investment in slaves. But they did make a series of discrete, individual choices, and these, while unthinking in a larger sense, were hardly irrational. After 1665, when planters found the supply of servants inadequate to meet their needs, they purchased slaves in an effort to continue to expand their labor force, or at least maintain its size.

IV

Although slaves came to outnumber servants throughout the tobacco coast at about the same time, there were noticeable regional variations in the intensity of commitment to slavery. The magnitude of these variations can be measured with precision in Maryland from the census of 1710.[51] The central counties on the Western Shore—Calvert, Prince George's, and Anne Arundel—where blacks made up 30% of the population, reveal by far the heaviest investment in slaves. They are followed by a group of counties immediately north and south, Charles, St. Mary's, and Baltimore, where the percentage black ranged between 15 and 20. The Eastern Shore makes a third region where, with the exception of Kent County, blacks accounted for roughly 10 to 15% of the inhabitants. The central counties of the Eastern Shore show a larger proportion of blacks than those to the north and south.

It is impossible to offer so precise a description of the distribution of slaves in Virginia. My impression, based largely on naval office returns and the appearance of blacks in probate records, is that in the early eighteenth century the counties between the James and the Rappahanock had the highest concentration of slaves along the tobacco coast, a concentration that diminished gradually as one moved away from the York River and back from the bay. This region was followed by the counties between the Rappahanock and the Potomac, which perhaps held the same proportion of slaves as the central Western Shore of Maryland. Here the percentage black seems to have been highest near the bay and along the Rappahanock, gradually declining toward the north and west. A third group of counties, with roughly the same proportion of slaves as appear on the Maryland

51. The census returns are in *Md. Arch.*, XXV, 258-259. On their reliability see Menard, "Economy and Society in Early Colonial Maryland," 396-413.

Eastern Shore, included Accomack, Northampton, and the south side of the James River, although the plantations immediately along the south bank of the James may have had nearly the same proportion of blacks as those across the river.[52]

These regional variations in the distribution of slaves seem to have been shaped by the geography of tobacco cultivation, although a substantial amount of research is necessary before one can speak with assurance. In general, those counties most successful in the tobacco industry—which produced the best grades of sweetscented for the English market, whose economies show the least evidence of diversification and the most devotion to the staple, and whose commerce was dominated by London merchants—had the highest concentration of slaves. Those counties that were marginal producers of tobacco—which grew poor quality oronocco all marked for re-export to the continent, whose tobacco was carried by ships from the lesser outports, which were most heavily involved in the coastal and West Indian trade, and which had made the most progress with diversification—had the smallest proportion of blacks. The counties that fell between these extremes in investment in slavery produced the better grades of oronocco, were visited as often by Liverpool and Bristol ships as by those from London, and tended to show some evidence of diversification, particularly during periods of depression in the tobacco trade.[53]

If it stands, this relationship between the distribution of slaves and the geography of tobacco cultivation may help unravel what Gloria Main has called a quiet paradox of Chesapeake history.[54] As Main points out, the transformation of the Chesapeake labor force from white servants to black slaves occurred during a period of stagnation in the tobacco economy. Three phases marked the growth of the Chesapeake tobacco industry during the colonial period. The first, lasting from the introduction of commercial tobacco cultivation to the early 1680s, witnessed rapid expansion at a gradually decelerating rate of the amount of the staple grown in Maryland and Virginia. The third, stretching from the second decade of the eighteenth century to 1775, was also a period of expansion, less rapid than the first, as the

---

52. P.M.G. Harris, Lois G. Carr, and I are now engaged in a systematic study of Virginia probate records that should permit a more precise description of regional variations in the distribution of slaves.

53. I am now preparing an essay on the Chesapeake economy that will document these regional patterns.

54. "Maryland and the Chesapeake Economy, 1670 to 1720," in Land, Carr, and Papenfuse, eds., *Law, Society, and Politics in Maryland History*.

amount of tobacco produced grew steadily at roughly 2% a year. Sandwiched between these two long eras of expansion was a much shorter period of stagnation, lasting from the mid-1680s to about 1715, during which, and despite an extraordinary surge around the turn of the century, tobacco production levelled out, fluctuating around 28 million pounds for nearly thirty years.[55] However, the Chesapeake work force continued to grow during the period of stagnation; approximately 27,000 taxables in Maryland and Virginia in 1685 had become nearly 50,000 by 1715, an annual growth rate of about 2%.[56] The paradox is apparent: Chesapeake planters bought slaves in the late seventeenth and early eighteenth centuries, presumably to make more tobacco, at a time when the work force as a whole was devoting gradually less energy to the weed.

If I am correct about the relationship of tobacco to slaves, the paradox is more apparent than real. Aggregate data on British imports accurately describe a period of stagnation in the Chesapeake tobacco economy as a whole but may conceal a shifting regional pattern in which some areas expanded production while others contracted, moving away from the staple and toward a more diverse economy built upon the West Indian and coastal trades and a heightened degree of local self-sufficiency. The long depression that began about 1680 and, with two brief interruptions, lasted for more than thirty years, served as a sorting-out period for the Chesapeake economy.[57] Marginal producers who made a low grade of tobacco on poor quality land found that growing the staple was no longer profitable and turned to other tasks. Planters on the better tobacco lands, who made crops of higher quality and had access to the best markets, took up the slack and expanded their output of tobacco without raising the amount produced in the region as a whole. This process shaped the spread of slavery in the Chesapeake. Around the turn of the century, slavery grew most rapidly in regions where tobacco cultivation remained profitable. Where tobacco proved unprofitable, slavery grew more slowly. Planters in such areas had to wait until after 1710, when the

---

55.   On the growth of the Chesapeake tobacco industry see Menard, "Economy and Society in Early Colonial Maryland," 278-335; Menard, Harris, and Carr, "Opportunity and Inequality," 178-184; Jacob M. Price, "The Economic Growth of the Chesapeake and the European Market, 1697-1775," *Journal of Economic History*, XXIV (1964), 496-511; U.S. Bureau of the Census, *Historical Statistics of the United States, Colonial Times to 1970* (Washington, D.C., 1975), II, series Z 441-472.
56.   Menard, "Economy and Society in Early Colonial Maryland," 456; Greene and Harrington, *American Population*, 125, 139.
57.   The best account of the depression is Hemphill, "Virginia and the English Commercial System," 5-51.

Chesapeake tobacco industry began a period of renewed expansion, before they could command black laborers in large numbers.

V

What impact did the shift from servants to slaves have on the ownership and distribution of labor in the Chesapeake colonies? A consideration of the relationship between wealth and the ownership of servants and slaves among householders on the lower Western Shore of Maryland during the last half of the seventeenth century as described by probate inventories provides some clues. Small planters often owned servants. Few of the very poorest householders owned labor, but once a planter passed the £20 mark the likelihood that an indentured servant would appear in his inventory increased rapidly. More than half the planters worth £70 to £100 sterling owned servants, while servants appeared in nearly all estates worth more than £125. On the other hand, few small planters owned slaves, and only in inventories appraised at over £200 did more than half the estates regularly contain slaves.

Table 8
Percent of Householders who owned Labor by Total Estate Value, 1658-1720.

Total Estate Value	1658-1670	1671-1680	1681-1690	1691-1699	1700-1710	1711-1720
0-19.9 sterling	0.0	3.0	0.0	4.2	2.8	0.0
20-29.9	19.0	28.6	5.7	8.3	7.9	9.5
30-49.9	50.0	42.3	31.6	17.2	28.6	8.3
50-89.9	70.6	53.6	50.7	26.2	58.7	56.5
90-149.9	88.9	82.0	76.7	52.6	76.6	60.0
150+	89.2	93.8	96.9	90.8	95.3	100.0
Total	60.0	59.0	48.8	35.1	55.1	44.7
20-149.9	57.6	53.6	43.1	23.3	45.1	33.0

Source: For the years 1658 to 1705 the data are from Calvert, Charles, St. Mary's and Prince George's counties, St. Mary's City Commission, NSF project. For the years 1706 to 1720, the data are from Prince George's County only, and were supplied by Lois Green Carr.

Apparently, there were two distinct yet overlapping labor markets in the Chesapeake colonies. Small planters largely confined their labor purchases to servants; wealthier planters bought both servants and slaves. Doubtless this reflects the high initial cost of slaves: small planters could not afford £25 to £30 for a slave, but they could afford

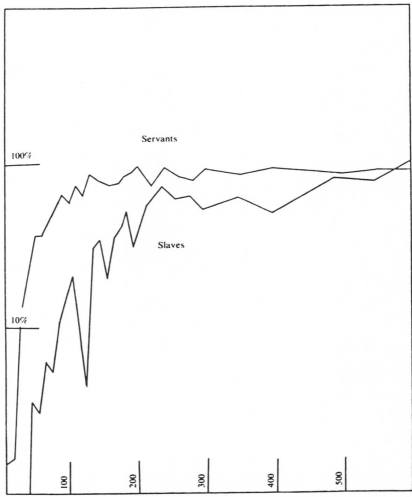

Figure 3. Proportion of Householders Owning Servants and
Slaves by Total Estate Value, 1658-1705.

£9 to £12 for a servant. As a result, small planters found it
increasingly difficult to acquire labor as the supply of servants
declined and the Chesapeake economy became increasingly
dependent upon slaves.

Their difficulty is illustrated by Maryland probate inventories. In
the 1660s, nearly 60% of the planters worth £20 to £150 owned labor;
by the 1710s only a third did so. Planters in the £30 to £50 range were

particularly hard hit. At the beginning of the period one-half of them owned labor when they died, a proportion that had fallen to less than 10% by the decade ending in 1720. On the other hand, the proportion of planters worth more than £150 who owned labor actually increased between 1658 and 1720. Initially at least, slavery solved the labor problem for only the wealthier Chesapeake planters.

Later in the eighteenth century demand for indentured servants did decline and small planters did solve their labor problem. By the 1750s, servants had all but disappeared from estate inventories along the tobacco coast, prices for indentured labor had fallen, and slaves regularly appeared in the estates of small planters. The evidence required for a full analysis of this process has yet to be gathered—in particular there are data to suggest major regional variations which, when finally pinned down, should prove illuminating—but some speculation is possible.[58]

The beginnings of rapid natural increase among slaves was perhaps the critical event. Evidence on age structure from estate inventories suggests that blacks experienced a net natural decline until about the 1720s, when the rise of a sizeable group of native-born slaves reversed the direction of natural population change.[59] This had a profound effect on the relative demand for servants and slaves. First, with the beginnings of rapid natural growth, slaves emerged as a clearly more profitable investment than servants in the eyes of planters. Second, natural increase permanently solved the problem of finding an adequate labor supply. Large planters expanded the size of their labor force and slaves became available to tobacco growers further down on the wealth scale. By the 1750s, planters worth as little as £60 sterling often owned slaves; in the seventeenth century slaves appeared regularly only in estates worth more than £200. Furthermore, by the 1750s slaves were often hired out. Planters who did not own slaves for life could still command their labor for a briefer period.[60]

Demographic change among whites may also have reduced demand for indentured servants. As a result of high mortality and a late age at marriage for men, immigrant planters seldom had sons to help with

---

58. Lois G. Carr and I explore this process in detail in an essay now in preparation, tentatively titled "Servants, Slaves, and Masters: The Ownership and Distribution of Labor in St. Mary's County, Maryland, 1638-1800."

59. Menard, "The Maryland Slave Population," 29-54.

60. On slave hiring in the eighteenth century see Allan L. Kulikoff, "Tobacco and Slaves: Population, Economy, and Society in Eighteenth-Century Prince George's County, Maryland" (Ph.D. diss., Brandeis University, 1976), 242-248.

running the family farm. The typical male indentured servant who survived his term and lived long enough to acquire a plantation married in his late 20s or early 30s and died in his early 40s, before his sons were old enough for field work. Native-born men married sooner lived longer, had larger families, and thus more often had sons of an age to join them in the fields.[61] The increasing supply of sons perhaps led to a fall in demand for indentured servants. At the very least it helped relieve the labor shortage that hit small planters when the supply of servants declined in the late seventeenth century.

But it was not merely that the distribution of labor had come full circle, that small planters were once able to command labor, lost that ability, and later regained it. Slavery did bring permanent change to the way labor was distributed in the Chesapeake because it permitted planters to accumulate more workers than ever before. During the seventeenth century, when indentured servants were the majority of bound laborers, plantations manned by large numbers of workers were rare. In the eighteenth century, when slaves predominated, large plantations were more common. In part, this was a function of the growth and distribution of wealth; the Chesapeake gentry of the mid-eighteenth century were richer than their forebears and used their greater wealth to control more labor. But it was also a function of slavery. Slaves bound for life were a more permanent and thus more easily accumulated form of labor than servants for a term of years. After 1720, furthermore, slavery grew through reproductive increase. With luck, a planter who simply let nature run its course could find himself transformed from owner of a few blacks to master of many. Slavery made the rise of large plantations possible and thus added a new feature to the landscape of the tobacco coast. By the mid-eighteenth century that feature had become, for the native gentry at least, a principal symbol of Chesapeake society.[62]

VI

The widespread availability of free land and consequent chronic labor shortage encouraged the use of unfree labor in the Chesapeake colonies. For a time, however, indentured servitude supplied tobacco

---

61. The evidence for this summary of white male life experience is presented in Lorena S. Walsh and Russell R. Menard, "Death in the Chesapeake: Two Life Tables for Men in Early Colonial Maryland," *Maryland Historical Magazine*, LXIX (1974), 211-227, and Russell R. Menard, "Immigrants and Their Increase: The Process of Population Growth in Early Colonial Maryland," in Land, Carr, and Papenfuse, eds., *Law, Society, and Politics in Maryland History*.

62. On the growth of large plantations, see Kulikoff, "Tobacco and Slaves."

planters with sufficient workers. Through the middle decades of the seventeenth century, the supply of servants to Maryland and Virginia grew more rapidly than the number of households. As a result, planters were able to meet their needs for labor with young men from farming and artisan families without heavy recruiting among groups they considered less desirable. Planters, however, depended on a steady increase in the number of young Englishmen willing to seek their fortunes in tobacco, a situation in turn dependent upon the high birth rate and secular decline in real wages that characterized English society before 1650. Just prior to mid-century, the birth rate fell and England's population stopped growing, or at least grew at a slower pace. Chesapeake planters felt the impact of the fall in the early 1660s when a decline in the number of young men entering the work force and a rise in real wages led to a growing reluctance on the part of middling Englishmen to try their luck in the colonies. Tobacco planters faced a labor shortage, a shortage aggravated by growing colonial demand as the Chesapeake continued to expand and rapid development began in the middle colonies and the Carolinas. A dwindling supply of middling Englishmen forced planters to draw more heavily on other groups— women, Irishmen, convicts, the poor, Indians, and, most important, Africans—to meet their needs for labor. Chesapeake planters did not abandon indentured servitude; it abandoned them.

The Chesapeake labor system was transformed in the decades surrounding 1700. As the supply of white workers declined, planters turned to slaves and to servants less like themselves for labor. A landscape dominated by family farms worked by a small planter, his family, and a servant or two witnessed the rise of large plantations supervised by a rich and powerful gentry and manned by black slaves. Indentured servitude did not disappear, but it did change. The composition of the immigrant group altered and the social distance between master and servant increased. Opportunities, once abundant, declined, and former servants often left the Chesapeake for more recently established colonies were material progress was still likely. In the course of a few decades, the tobacco coast moved from a labor system that promised poor men eventual integration into the society they served to one that kept a majority of its laborers in perpetual bondage and offered most of the others a choice between poverty and emigration.

Of course, the transformation went beyond the labor system. In the process of exchanging white workers for black the tobacco coast became a slave society. And, as Frank Tannenbaum has told us, slave society was "not merely for the blacks, but for the whites, not merely for the law, but for the family, not merely for the labor system, but for the culture—the total culture. . . . Nothing escaped, nothing, and no one."[63] It would be presumptuous, in a conclusion to so narrowly focused an essay, to attempt even an enumeration of all the ways in which slavery changed life along the Chesapeake. However, if this essay has illuminated the process that first brought blacks to Maryland and Virginia in large numbers, it should help in the task of building answers to the larger questions that slavery raises.

---

63. *Slaves and Citizen: The Negro in the Americas* (New York, 1946), 117.

Slavery and Freedom: The American Paradox

EDMUND S. MORGAN

AMERICAN historians interested in tracing the rise of liberty, democracy, and the common man have been challenged in the past two decades by other historians, interested in tracing the history of oppression, exploitation, and racism. The challenge has been salutary, because it has made us examine more directly than historians have hitherto been willing to do, the role of slavery in our early history. Colonial historians, in particular, when writing about the origin and development of American institutions have found it possible until recently to deal with slavery as an exception to everything they had to say. I am speaking about myself but also about most of my generation. We owe a debt of gratitude to those who have insisted that slavery was something more than an exception, that one fifth of the American population at the time of the Revolution is too many people to be treated as an exception.[1]

We shall not have met the challenge simply by studying the history of that one fifth, fruitful as such studies may be, urgent as they may be. Nor shall we have met the challenge if we merely execute the familiar maneuver of turning our old interpretations on their heads. The temptation is already apparent to argue that slavery and oppression were the dominant features of American history and that efforts to advance liberty and equality were the exception, indeed no more than a device to divert the masses while their chains were being fastened. To dismiss the rise of liberty and equality in American history as a mere sham is not only to ignore hard facts, it is also to evade the problem presented by those facts. The rise of liberty and equality in this country was accompanied by the rise of slavery. That two

This paper was delivered as the presidential address of the Organization of American Historians at Washington, D.C., April 6, 1972. Edmund S. Morgan is professor of history in Yale University.

[1] Particularly Staughton Lynd, *Class Conflict, Slavery, and the United States Constitution: Ten Essays* (Indianapolis, 1967).

·5·

such contradictory developments were taking place simultaneously over a long period of our history, from the seventeenth century to the nineteenth, is the central paradox of American history.

The challenge, for a colonial historian at least, is to explain how a people could have developed the dedication to human liberty and dignity exhibited by the leaders of the American Revolution and at the same time have developed and maintained a system of labor that denied human liberty and dignity every hour of the day.

The paradox is evident at many levels if we care to see it. Think, for a moment, of the traditional American insistence on freedom of the seas. "Free ships make free goods" was the cardinal doctrine of American foreign policy in the Revolutionary era. But the goods for which the United States demanded freedom were produced in very large measure by slave labor. The irony is more than semantic. American reliance on slave labor must be viewed in the context of the American struggle for a separate and equal station among the nations of the earth. At the time the colonists announced their claim to that station they had neither the arms nor the ships to make the claim good. They desperately needed the assistance of other countries, especially France, and their single most valuable product with which to purchase assistance was tobacco, produced mainly by slave labor. So largely did that crop figure in American foreign relations that one historian has referred to the activities of France in supporting the Americans as "King Tobacco Diplomacy," a reminder that the position of the United States in the world depended not only in 1776 but during the span of a long lifetime thereafter on slave labor.[2] To a very large degree it may be said that Americans bought their independence with slave labor.

The paradox is sharpened if we think of the state where most of the tobacco came from. Virginia at the time of the first United States census in 1790 had 40 percent of the slaves in the entire United States. And Virginia produced the most eloquent spokesmen for freedom and equality in the entire United States: George Washington, James Madison, and above all, Thomas Jefferson. They were all slaveholders and remained so throughout their lives. In recent years we have been shown in painful detail the contrast between Jefferson's pronouncements in favor of republican liberty and his complicity in denying the benefits of that liberty to blacks.[3] It has been

    [2] Curtis P. Nettels, *The Emergence of a National Economy 1775-1815* (New York, 1962), 19. See also Merrill Jensen, "The American Revolution and American Agriculture," *Agricultural History*, XLIII (Jan. 1969), 107-24.
    [3] William Cohen, "Thomas Jefferson and the Problem of Slavery," *Journal of American History*, LVI (Dec. 1969), 503-26; D. B. Davis, *Was Thomas Jefferson An Authentic Enemy of Slavery?* (Oxford, 1970); Winthrop D. Jordan, *White over Black: American Attitudes Toward the Negro, 1550-1812* (Chapel Hill, 1968), 429-81.

tempting to dismiss Jefferson and the whole Virginia dynasty as hypocrites. But to do so is to deprive the term "hypocrisy" of useful meaning. If hypocrisy means, as I think it does, deliberately to affirm a principle without believing it, then hypocrisy requires a rare clarity of mind combined with an unscrupulous intention to deceive. To attribute such an intention, even to attribute such clarity of mind in the matter, to Jefferson, Madison, or Washington is once again to evade the challenge. What we need to explain is how such men could have arrived at beliefs and actions so full of contradiction.

Put the challenge another way: how did England, a country priding itself on the liberty of its citizens, produce colonies where most of the inhabitants enjoyed still greater liberty, greater opportunities, greater control over their own lives than most men in the mother country, while the remainder, one fifth of the total, were deprived of virtually all liberty, all opportunities, all control over their own lives? We may admit that the Englishmen who colonized America and their revolutionary descendants were racists, that consciously or unconsciously they believed liberties and rights should be confined to persons of a light complexion. When we have said as much, even when we have probed the depths of racial prejudice, we will not have fully accounted for the paradox. Racism was surely an essential element in it, but I should like to suggest another element, that I believe to have influenced the development of both slavery and freedom as we have known them in the United States.

Let us begin with Jefferson, this slaveholding spokesman of freedom. Could there have been anything in the kind of freedom he cherished that would have made him acquiesce, however reluctantly, in the slavery of so many Americans? The answer, I think, is yes. The freedom that Jefferson spoke for was not a gift to be conferred by governments, which he mistrusted at best. It was a freedom that sprang from the independence of the individual. The man who depended on another for his living could never be truly free. We may seek a clue to Jefferson's enigmatic posture toward slavery in his attitude toward those who enjoyed a seeming freedom without the independence needed to sustain it. For such persons Jefferson harbored a profound distrust, which found expression in two phobias that crop up from time to time in his writings.

The first was a passionate aversion to debt. Although the entire colonial economy of Virginia depended on the willingness of planters to go into debt and of British merchants to extend credit, although Jefferson himself was a debtor all his adult life—or perhaps because he was a debtor—he hated debt and hated anything that made him a debtor. He hated it because it limited his freedom of action. He could not, for example, have freed his slaves so long as he was in debt. Or so at least he told himself. But it was the impediment not simply to their freedom but to his own that bothered him. "I am miserable," he wrote, "till I shall owe not a shilling. . . ."[4]

The fact that he had so much company in his misery only added to it. His Declaration of Independence for the United States was mocked by the hold that British merchants retained over American debtors, including himself.[5] His hostility to Alexander Hamilton was rooted in his recognition that Hamilton's pro-British foreign policy would tighten the hold of British creditors, while his domestic policy would place the government in the debt of a class of native American creditors, whose power might become equally pernicious.

Though Jefferson's concern with the perniciousness of debt was almost obsessive, it was nevertheless altogether in keeping with the ideas of republican liberty that he shared with his countrymen. The trouble with debt was that by undermining the independence of the debtor it threatened republican liberty. Whenever debt brought a man under another's power, he lost more than his own freedom of action. He also weakened the capacity of his country to survive as a republic. It was an axiom of current political thought that republican government required a body of free, independent, property-owning citizens.[6] A nation of men, each of whom owned enough property to support his family, could be a republic. It would follow that a nation of debtors, who had lost their property or mortgaged it to creditors, was ripe for tyranny. Jefferson accordingly favored every means of keeping men out of debt and keeping property widely distributed. He insisted on the abolition of primogeniture and entail; he declared that the earth belonged to the living and should not be kept from them by the debts or credits of the dead; he would have given fifty acres of land to every American who did not have it—all because he believed the citizens of a republic must be free from the control of other men and that they could be free only if they were economically free by virtue of owning land on which to support themselves.[7]

---

[4] Julian P. Boyd, ed., *The Papers of Thomas Jefferson* (18 vols., Princeton, 1950-   ). X, 615. For other expressions of Thomas Jefferson's aversion to debt and distrust of credit, both private and public, see *ibid.*, II, 275-76, VIII, 398-99, 632-33, IX, 217-18, 472-73, X, 304-05, XI, 472, 633, 636, 640, XII, 385-86.

[5] Jefferson's career as ambassador to France was occupied very largely by unsuccessful efforts to break the hold of British creditors on American commerce.

[6] See Caroline Robbins, *The Eighteenth-Century Commonwealthman: Studies in the Transmission, Development and Circumstance of English Liberal Thought from the Restoration of Charles II until the War with the Thirteen Colonies* (Cambridge, Mass., 1959); J. G. A. Pocock, "Machiavelli, Harrington, and English Political Ideologies in the Eighteenth Century," *William and Mary Quarterly*, XXII (Oct. 1965), 549-83.

[7] Boyd, ed., *Papers of Thomas Jefferson*, I, 344, 352, 362, 560, VIII, 681-82.

If Jefferson felt so passionately about the bondage of the debtor, it is not surprising that he should also have sensed a danger to the republic from another class of men who, like debtors, were nominally free but whose independence was illusory. Jefferson's second phobia was his distrust of the landless urban workman who labored in manufactures. In Jefferson's view, he was a free man in name only. Jefferson's hostility to artificers is well known and is generally attributed to his romantic preference for the rural life. But both his distrust for artificers and his idealization of small landholders as "the most precious part of a state" rested on his concern for individual independence as the basis of freedom. Farmers made the best citizens because they were "the most vigorous, the most independant, the most virtuous. . . ." Artificers, on the other hand, were dependent on "the casualties and caprice of customers." If work was scarce, they had no land to fall back on for a living. In their dependence lay the danger. "Dependance," Jefferson argued, "begets subservience and venality, suffocates the germ of virtue, and prepares fit tools for the designs of ambition." Because artificers could lay claim to freedom without the independence to go with it, they were "the instruments by which the liberties of a country are generally overturned."[8]

In Jefferson's distrust of artificers we begin to get a glimpse of the limits —and limits not dictated by racism—that defined the republican vision of the eighteenth century. For Jefferson was by no means unique among republicans in his distrust of the landless laborer. Such a distrust was a necessary corollary of the widespread eighteenth-century insistence on the independent, property-holding individual as the only bulwark of liberty, an insistence originating in James Harrington's republican political philosophy and a guiding principle of American colonial politics, whether in the aristocratic South Carolina assembly or in the democratic New England town.[9] Americans both before and after 1776 learned their republican lessons from the seventeenth- and eighteenth-century British commonwealthmen; and the commonwealthmen were uninhibited in their contempt for the masses who did not have the propertied independence required of proper republicans.

John Locke, the classic explicator of the right of revolution for the pro-

[8] *Ibid.*, VIII, 426, 682; Thomas Jefferson, *Notes on the State of Virginia*, William Peden, ed. (Chapel Hill, 1955), 165. Jefferson seems to have overlooked the dependence of Virginia's farmers on the casualties and caprice of the tobacco market.
[9] See Robbins, *The Eighteenth-Century Commonwealthmen*; Pocock, "Machiavelli, Harrington, and English Political Ideologies," 549-83; Michael Zuckerman, "The Social Context of Democracy in Massachusetts," *William and Mary Quarterly*, XXV (Oct. 1968), 523-44; Robert M. Weir, "'The Harmony We Were Famous For': An Interpretation of Pre-Revolutionary South Carolina Politics," *ibid.*, XXVI (Oct. 1969), 473-501.

tection of liberty, did not think about extending that right to the landless poor. Instead, he concocted a scheme of compulsory labor for them and their children. The children were to begin at the age of three in public institutions, called working schools because the only subject taught would be work (spinning and knitting). They would be paid in bread and water and grow up "inured to work." Meanwhile the mothers, thus relieved of the care of their offspring, could go to work beside their fathers and husbands. If they could not find regular employment, then they too could be sent to the working school.[10]

It requires some refinement of mind to discern precisely how this version of women's liberation from child care differed from outright slavery. And many of Locke's intellectual successors, while denouncing slavery in the abstract, openly preferred slavery to freedom for the lower ranks of laborers. Adam Ferguson, whose works were widely read in America, attributed the overthrow of the Roman republic, in part at least, to the emancipation of slaves, who "increased, by their numbers and their vices, the weight of that dreg, which, in great and prosperous cities, ever sinks, by the tendency of vice and misconduct to the lowest condition."[11]

That people in the lowest condition, the dregs of society, generally arrived at that position through their own vice and misconduct, whether in ancient Rome or modern Britain, was an unexamined article of faith among eighteenth-century republicans. And the vice that was thought to afflict the lower ranks most severely was idleness. The eighteenth-century's preferred cure for idleness lay in the religious and ethical doctrines which R. H. Tawney described as the New Medicine for Poverty, the doctrines in which Max Weber discerned the origins of the spirit of capitalism. But in every society a stubborn mass of men and women refused the medicine. For such persons the commonwealthmen did not hesitate to prescribe slavery. Thus Francis Hutcheson, who could argue eloquently against the enslavement of Africans, also argued that perpetual slavery should be "the ordinary punishment of such idle vagrants as, after proper admonitions and tryals of temporary servitude, cannot be engaged to support themselves and their families by any useful labours."[12] James Burgh, whose *Political Disquisi-*

---

[10] C. B. Macpherson, *The Political Theory of Possessive Individualism* (Oxford, 1962), 221-24; H. R. Fox Bourne, *The Life of John Locke* (2 vols., London, 1876), II, 377-90.

[11] Adam Ferguson, *The History of the Progress and Termination of the Roman Republic* (5 vols., Edinburgh, 1799), I, 384. See also Adam Ferguson, *An Essay on the History of Civil Society* (London, 1768), 309-11.

[12] Francis Hutcheson, *A System of Moral Philosophy* (2 vols., London, 1755), II, 202; David B. Davis, *The Problem of Slavery in Western Culture* (Ithaca, 1966), 374-78. I am indebted to David B. Davis for several valuable suggestions.

tions earned the praises of many American revolutionists, proposed a set of press gangs "to seize all idle and disorderly persons, who have been three times complained of before a magistrate, and to set them to work during a certain time, for the benefit of great trading, or manufacturing companies, &c."[13]

The most comprehensive proposal came from Andrew Fletcher of Saltoun. Jefferson hailed in Fletcher a patriot whose political principles were those "in vigour at the epoch of the American emigration [from England]. Our ancestors brought them here, and they needed little strengthening to make us what we are. . . ."[14] Fletcher, like other commonwealthmen, was a champion of liberty, but he was also a champion of slavery. He attacked the Christian church not only for having promoted the abolition of slavery in ancient times but also for having perpetuated the idleness of the freedmen thus turned loose on society. The church by setting up hospitals and almshouses had enabled men through the succeeding centuries to live without work. As a result, Fletcher argued, his native Scotland was burdened with 200,000 idle rogues, who roamed the country, drinking, cursing, fighting, robbing, and murdering. For a remedy he proposed that they all be made slaves to men of property. To the argument that their masters might abuse them, he answered in words which might have come a century and a half later from a George Fitzhugh: that this would be against the master's own interest, "That the most brutal man will not use his beast ill only out of a humour; and that if such Inconveniences do sometimes fall out, it proceeds, for the most part, from the perverseness of the Servant."[15]

In spite of Jefferson's tribute to Fletcher, there is no reason to suppose that he endorsed Fletcher's proposal. But he did share Fletcher's distrust of men who were free in name while their empty bellies made them thieves, threatening the property of honest men, or else made them slaves in fact to anyone who would feed them. Jefferson's own solution for the kind of situation described by Fletcher was given in a famous letter to Madison, prompted by the spectacle Jefferson encountered in France in the 1780s, where a handful of noblemen had engrossed huge tracts of land on which to hunt game, while hordes of the poor went without work and without

[13] James Burgh, *Political Disquisitions: Or, An ENQUIRY into public Errors, Defects, and Abuses* . . . (3 vols., London, 1774-1775), III, 220-21. See the proposal of Bishop George Berkeley that "sturdy beggars should . . . be seized and made slaves to the public for a certain term of years." Quoted in R. H. Tawney, *Religion and the Rise of Capitalism: A Historical Essay* (New York, 1926), 270.

[14] E. Millicent Sowerby, ed., *Catalogue of the Library of Thomas Jefferson* (5 vols., Washington, 1952-1959), I, 192.

[15] Andrew Fletcher, *Two Discourses Concerning the Affairs of Scotland; Written in the Year 1698* (Edinburgh, 1698). See second discourse (separately paged), 1-33, especially 16.

bread. Jefferson's proposal, characteristically phrased in terms of natural right, was for the poor to appropriate the uncultivated lands of the nobility. And he drew for the United States his usual lesson of the need to keep land widely distributed among the people.[16]

Madison's answer, which is less well known than Jefferson's letter, raised the question whether it was possible to eliminate the idle poor in any country as fully populated as France. Spread the land among them in good republican fashion and there would still be, Madison thought, "a great surplus of inhabitants, a greater by far than will be employed in cloathing both themselves and those who feed them. . . ." In spite of those occupied in trades and as mariners, soldiers, and so on, there would remain a mass of men without work. "A certain degree of misery," Madison concluded, "seems inseparable from a high degree of populousness."[17] He did not, however, go on to propose, as Fletcher had done, that the miserable and idle poor be reduced to slavery.

The situation contemplated by Madison and confronted by Fletcher was not irrelevant to those who were planning the future of the American republic. In a country where population grew by geometric progression, it was not too early to think about a time when there might be vast numbers of landless poor, when there might be those mobs in great cities that Jefferson feared as sores on the body politic. In the United States as Jefferson and Madison knew it, the urban labor force as yet posed no threat, because it was small; and the agricultural labor force was, for the most part, already enslaved. In Revolutionary America, among men who spent their lives working for other men rather than working for themselves, slaves probably constituted a majority.[18] In Virginia they constituted a large majority.[19] If Jefferson and Madison, not to mention Washington, were unhappy about that fact and yet did nothing to alter it, they may have been restrained, in part at least, by thoughts of the role that might be played in the United States by a large mass of free laborers.

When Jefferson contemplated the abolition of slavery, he found it inconceivable that the freed slaves should be allowed to remain in the country.[20]

[16] Boyd, ed., *Papers of Thomas Jefferson*, VIII, 681-83.

[17] *Ibid.*, IX, 659-60.

[18] Jackson Turner Main, *The Social Structure of Revolutionary America* (Princeton, 1965), 271.

[19] In 1755, Virginia had 43,329 white tithables and 60,078 black. Tithables included white men over sixteen years of age and black men and women over sixteen. In the census of 1790, Virginia had 292,717 slaves and 110,936 white males over sixteen, out of a total population of 747,680. Evarts B. Greene and Virginia D. Harrington, *American Population before the Federal Census of 1790* (New York, 1932), 150-55.

[20] Jefferson, *Notes on the State of Virginia*, 138.

In this attitude he was probably moved by his or his countrymen's racial prejudice. But he may also have had in mind the possibility that when slaves ceased to be slaves, they would become instead a half million idle poor, who would create the same problems for the United States that the idle poor of Europe did for their states. The slave, accustomed to compulsory labor, would not work to support himself when the compulsion was removed. This was a commonplace among Virginia planters before the creation of the republic and long after. "If you free the slaves," wrote Landon Carter, two days after the Declaration of Independence, "you must send them out of the country or they must steal for their support."[21]

Jefferson's plan for freeing his own slaves (never carried out) included an interim educational period in which they would have been half-taught, half-compelled to support themselves on rented land; for without guidance and preparation for self support, he believed, slaves could not be expected to become fit members of a republican society.[22] And St. George Tucker, who drafted detailed plans for freeing Virginia's slaves, worried about "the possibility of their becoming idle, dissipated, and finally a numerous banditti, instead of turning their attention to industry and labour." He therefore included in his plans a provision for compelling the labor of the freedmen on an annual basis. "For we must not lose sight of this important consideration," he said, "that these people must be *bound* to labour, if they do not *voluntarily* engage therein. . . . In absolving them from the yoke of slavery, we must not forget the interests of society. Those interests require the exertions of every individual in some mode or other; and those who have not wherewith to support themselves honestly without corporal labour, whatever be their complexion, ought to be compelled to labour."[23]

It is plain that Tucker, the would-be emancipator, distrusted the idle poor regardless of color. And it seems probable that the Revolutionary champions of liberty who acquiesced in the continued slavery of black labor did so not only because of racial prejudice but also because they shared with Tucker a distrust of the poor that was inherent in eighteenth-century conceptions of republican liberty. Their historical guidebooks had made them fear to enlarge the free labor force.

That fear, I believe, had a second point of origin in the experience of the American colonists, and especially of Virginians, during the preceding cen-

[21] Jack P. Greene, ed., *The Diary of Colonel Landon Carter of Sabine Hall, 1752-1778* (2 vols., Charlottesville, 1965), II, 1055.
[22] Boyd, ed., *Papers of Thomas Jefferson*, XIV, 492-93.
[23] St. George Tucker, *A Dissertation on Slavery with a Proposal for the Gradual Abolition of It, in the State of Virginia* (Philadelphia, 1796). See also Jordan, *White over Black*, 555-60.

tury and a half. If we turn now to the previous history of Virginia's labor force, we may find, I think, some further clues to the distrust of free labor among Revolutionary republicans and to the paradoxical rise of slavery and freedom together in colonial America.

The story properly begins in England with the burst of population growth there that sent the number of Englishmen from perhaps three million in 1500 to four-and-one-half million by 1650.[24] The increase did not occur in response to any corresponding growth in the capacity of the island's economy to support its people. And the result was precisely that misery which Madison pointed out to Jefferson as the consequence of "a high degree of populousness." Sixteenth-century England knew the same kind of unemployment and poverty that Jefferson witnessed in eighteenth-century France and Fletcher in seventeenth-century Scotland. Alarming numbers of idle and hungry men drifted about the country looking for work or plunder. The government did what it could to make men of means hire them, but it also adopted increasingly severe measures against their wandering, their thieving, their roistering, and indeed their very existence. Whom the workhouses and prisons could not swallow the gallows would have to, or perhaps the army. When England had military expeditions to conduct abroad, every parish packed off its most unwanted inhabitants to the almost certain death that awaited them from the diseases of the camp.[25]

As the mass of idle rogues and beggars grew and increasingly threatened the peace of England, the efforts to cope with them increasingly threatened the liberties of Englishmen. Englishmen prided themselves on a "gentle government,"[26] a government that had been releasing its subjects from old forms of bondage and endowing them with new liberties, making the "rights of Englishmen" a phrase to conjure with. But there was nothing gentle about the government's treatment of the poor; and as more Englishmen became poor, other Englishmen had less to be proud of. Thoughtful men could see an obvious solution: get the surplus Englishmen out of England. Send them to the New World, where there were limitless opportunities for work. There they would redeem themselves, enrich the mother country, and spread English liberty abroad.

The great publicist for this program was Richard Hakluyt. His *Principall*

---

[24] Joan Thrisk, ed., *The Agrarian History of England and Wales*, Vol. IV: *1500-1640* (Cambridge, England, 1967), 531.
[25] See Edmund S. Morgan, "The Labor Problem at Jamestown, 1607-18," *American Historical Review*, 76 (June 1971), 595-611, especially 600-06.
[26] This is Richard Hakluyt's phrase. See E. G. R. Taylor, ed., *The Original Writings & Correspondence of the Two Richard Hakluyts* (2 vols., London, 1935), I, 142.

Navigations, Voiages and Discoveries of the English nation[27] was not merely the narrative of voyages by Englishmen around the globe, but a powerful suggestion that the world ought to be English or at least ought to be ruled by Englishmen. Hakluyt's was a dream of empire, but of benevolent empire, in which England would confer the blessings of her own free government on the less fortunate peoples of the world. It is doubtless true that Englishmen, along with other Europeans, were already imbued with prejudice against men of darker complexions than their own. And it is also true that the principal beneficiaries of Hakluyt's empire would be Englishmen. But Hakluyt's dream cannot be dismissed as mere hypocrisy any more than Jefferson's affirmation of human equality can be so dismissed. Hakluyt's compassion for the poor and oppressed was not confined to the English poor, and in Francis Drake's exploits in the Caribbean Hakluyt saw, not a thinly disguised form of piracy, but a model for English liberation of men of all colors who labored under the tyranny of the Spaniard.

Drake had gone ashore at Panama in 1572 and made friends with an extraordinary band of runaway Negro slaves. "Cimarrons" they were called, and they lived a free and hardy life in the wilderness, periodically raiding the Spanish settlements to carry off more of their people. They discovered in Drake a man who hated the Spanish as much as they did and who had the arms and men to mount a stronger attack than they could manage by themselves. Drake wanted Spanish gold, and the Cimarrons wanted Spanish iron for tools. They both wanted Spanish deaths. The alliance was a natural one and apparently untroubled by racial prejudice. Together the English and the Cimarrons robbed the mule train carrying the annual supply of Peruvian treasure across the isthmus. And before Drake sailed for England with his loot, he arranged for future meetings.[28] When Hakluyt heard of this alliance, he concocted his first colonizing proposal, a scheme for seizing the Straits of Magellan and transporting Cimarrons there, along with surplus Englishmen. The straits would be a strategic strong point for England's world empire, since they controlled the route from Atlantic to Pacific. Despite the severe climate of the place, the Cimarrons and their English friends would all live warmly together, clad in English woolens, "well lodged and by our nation made free from the tyrannous Spanyard, and quietly and courteously governed by our nation."[29]

[27] Richard Hakluyt, *The Principall Navigations, Voiages and Discoveries of the English nation* . . . (London, 1589).

[28] The whole story of this extraordinary episode is to be found in I. A. Wright, ed., *Documents Concernings English Voyages to the Spanish Main 1569-1580* (London, 1932).

[29] Taylor, ed., *Original Writings & Correspondence*, I, 139-46.

The scheme for a colony in the Straits of Magellan never worked out, but Hakluyt's vision endured, of liberated natives and surplus Englishmen, courteously governed in English colonies around the world. Sir Walter Raleigh caught the vision. He dreamt of wresting the treasure of the Incas from the Spaniard by allying with the Indians of Guiana and sending Englishmen to live with them, lead them in rebellion against Spain, and govern them in the English manner.[30] Raleigh also dreamt of a similar colony in the country he named Virginia. Hakluyt helped him plan it.[31] And Drake stood ready to supply Negroes and Indians, liberated from Spanish tyranny in the Caribbean, to help the enterprise.[32]

Virginia from the beginning was conceived not only as a haven for England's suffering poor, but as a spearhead of English liberty in an oppressed world. That was the dream; but when it began to materialize at Roanoke Island in 1585, something went wrong. Drake did his part by liberating Spanish Caribbean slaves, and carrying to Roanoke those who wished to join him.[33] But the English settlers whom Raleigh sent there proved unworthy of the role assigned them. By the time Drake arrived they had shown themselves less than courteous to the Indians on whose assistance they depended. The first group of settlers murdered the chief who befriended them, and then gave up and ran for home aboard Drake's returning ships. The second group simply disappeared, presumably killed by the Indians.[34]

What was lost in this famous lost colony was more than the band of colonists who have never been traced. What was also lost and never quite recovered in subsequent ventures was the dream of Englishman and Indian living side by side in peace and liberty. When the English finally planted a permanent colony at Jamestown they came as conquerors, and their government was far from gentle. The Indians willing to endure it were too few in numbers and too broken in spirit to play a significant part in the settlement.

[30] Walter Raleigh, *The Discoverie of the large and bewtiful Empire of Guiana*, V. T. Harlow, ed. (London, 1928), 138-49; V. T. Harlow, ed., *Ralegh's Last Voyage: Being an account drawn out of contemporary letters and relations* . . . (London, 1932), 44-45.

[31] Taylor, ed., *Original Writings & Correspondence*, II, 211-377, especially 318.

[32] Irene A. Wright, trans. and ed., *Further English Voyages to Spanish America, 1583-1594: Documents from the Archives of the Indies at Seville* . . . (London, 1951), lviii, lxiii, lxiv, 37, 52, 54, 55, 159, 172, 173, 181, 188-89, 204-06.

[33] The Spanish reported that "Although their masters were willing to ransom them the English would not give them up except when the slaves themselves desired to go." *Ibid.*, 159. On Walter Raleigh's later expedition to Guiana, the Spanish noted that the English told the natives "that they did not desire to make them slaves, but only to be their friends; promising to bring them great quantities of hatchets and knives, and especially if they drove the Spaniards out of their territories." Harlow, ed., *Ralegh's Last Voyage*, 179.

[34] David Beers Quinn, ed., *The Roanoke Voyages 1584-1590* (2 vols., London, 1955).

Without their help, Virginia offered a bleak alternative to the workhouse or the gallows for the first English poor who were transported there. During the first two decades of the colony's existence, most of the arriving immigrants found precious little English liberty in Virginia.[35] But by the 1630s the colony seemed to be working out, at least in part, as its first planners had hoped. Impoverished Englishmen were arriving every year in large numbers, engaged to serve the existing planters for a term of years, with the prospect of setting up their own households a few years later. The settlers were spreading up Virginia's great rivers, carving out plantations, living comfortably from their corn fields and from the cattle they ranged in the forests, and at the same time earning perhaps ten or twelve pounds a year per man from the tobacco they planted. A representative legislative assembly secured the traditional liberties of Englishmen and enabled a larger proportion of the population to participate in their own government than had ever been the case in England. The colony even began to look a little like the cosmopolitan haven of liberty that Hakluyt had first envisaged. Men of all countries appeared there: French, Spanish, Dutch, Turkish, Portuguese, and African.[36] Virginia took them in and began to make Englishmen out of them.

It seems clear that most of the Africans, perhaps all of them, came as slaves, a status that had become obsolete in England, while it was becoming the expected condition of Africans outside Africa and of a good many inside.[37] It is equally clear that a substantial number of Virginia's Negroes were free or became free. And all of them, whether servant, slave, or free, enjoyed most of the same rights and duties as other Virginians. There is no evidence during the period before 1660 that they were subjected to a more severe discipline than other servants. They could sue and be sued in court. They did penance in the parish church for having illegitimate children. They earned money of their own, bought and sold and raised cattle of their own. Sometimes they bought their own freedom. In other cases, masters

[35] Morgan, "The Labor Problem at Jamestown, 1607-18," pp. 595-611; Edmund S. Morgan, "The First American Boom: Virginia 1618 to 1630," *William and Mary Quarterly*, XXVIII (April 1971), 169-98.

[36] There are no reliable records of immigration, but the presence of persons of these nationalities is evident from county court records, where all but the Dutch are commonly identified by name, such as "James the Scotchman," or "Cursory the Turk." The Dutch seem to have anglicized their names at once and are difficult to identify except where the records disclose their naturalization. The two counties for which the most complete records survive for the 1640s and 1650s are Accomack-Northampton and Lower Norfolk. Microfilms are in the Virginia State Library, Richmond.

[37] Because the surviving records are so fragmentary, there has been a great deal of controversy about the status of the first Negroes in Virginia. What the records do make clear is that not all were slaves and that not all were free. See Jordan, *White over Black*, 71-82.

bequeathed them not only freedom but land, cattle, and houses.[38] Northampton, the only county for which full records exist, had at least ten free Negro households by 1668.[39]

As Negroes took their place in the community, they learned English ways, including even the truculence toward authority that has always been associated with the rights of Englishmen. Tony Longo, a free Negro of Northampton, when served a warrant to appear as a witness in court, responded with a scatological opinion of warrants, called the man who served it an idle rascal, and told him to go about his business. The man offered to go with him at any time before a justice of the peace so that his evidence could be recorded. He would go with him at night, tomorrow, the next day, next week, any time. But Longo was busy getting in his corn. He dismissed all pleas with a "Well, well, Ile goe when my Corne is in," and refused to receive the warrant.[40]

The judges understandably found this to be contempt of court; but it was the kind of contempt that free Englishmen often showed to authority, and it was combined with a devotion to work that English moralists were doing their best to inculcate more widely in England. As England had absorbed people of every nationality over the centuries and turned them into Englishmen, Virginia's Englishmen were absorbing their own share of foreigners, including Negroes, and seemed to be successfully moulding a New World community on the English model.

But a closer look will show that the situation was not quite so promising as at first it seems. It is well known that Virginia in its first fifteen or twenty years killed off most of the men who went there. It is less well known that it continued to do so. If my estimate of the volume of immigration is anywhere near correct, Virginia must have been a death trap for at least another fifteen years and probably for twenty or twenty-five. In 1625

[38] For examples, see Northampton County Court Records, Deeds, Wills, etc., Book III, f. 83, Book V, ff. 38, 54, 60, 102, 117-19; York County Court Records, Deeds, Orders, Wills, etc., no. 1, ff. 232-34; Surry County Court Records, Deeds, Wills, etc., no. 1, f. 349; Henrico County Court Records, Deeds and Wills 1677-1692, f. 139.

[39] This fact has been arrived at by comparing the names of householders on the annual list of tithables with casual identifications of persons as Negroes in the court records. The names of householders so identified for 1668, the peak year during the period for which the lists survive (1662-1677) were: Bastian Cane, Bashaw Ferdinando, John Francisco, Susan Grace, William Harman, Philip Mongum, Francis Pane, Manuel Rodriggus, Thomas Rodriggus, and King Tony. The total number of households in the county in 1668 was 172; total number of tithables 435; total number of tithable free Negroes 17; total number of tithable unfree Negroes 42. Thus nearly 29 percent of tithable Negroes and probably of all Negroes were free; and about 13.5 percent of all tithables were Negroes.

[40] Northampton Deeds, Wills, etc., Book V, 54-60 (Nov. 1, 1654).

the population stood at 1,300 or 1,400; in 1640 it was about 8,000.[41] In the fifteen years between those dates at least 15,000 persons must have come to the colony.[42] If so, 15,000 immigrants increased the population by less than 7,000. There is no evidence of a large return migration. It seems probable that the death rate throughout this period was comparable only to that found in Europe during the peak years of a plague. Virginia, in other words, was absorbing England's surplus laborers mainly by killing them. The success of those who survived and rose from servant to planter must be attributed partly to the fact that so few did survive.

After 1640, when the diseases responsible for the high death rate began to decline and the population began a quick rise, it became increasingly difficult for an indigent immigrant to pull himself up in the world. The population probably passed 25,000 by 1662,[43] hardly what Madison would have called a high degree of populousness. Yet the rapid rise brought serious trouble for Virginia. It brought the engrossment of tidewater land in thousands and tens of thousands of acres by speculators, who recognized that

[41] The figure for 1625 derives from the census for that year, which gives 1,210 persons, but probably missed about 10 percent of the population. Morgan, "The First American Boom," 170n-71n. The figure for 1640 is derived from legislation limiting tobacco production per person in 1639-1640. The legislation is summarized in a manuscript belonging to Jefferson, printed in William Waller Hening, *The Statutes at Large; Being a Collection of All the Laws of Virginia, from the First Session of the Legislature, in the Year 1619* (13 vols., New York, 1823), I, 224-25, 228. The full text is in "Acts of the General Assembly, Jan. 6, 1639-40," *William and Mary Quarterly*, IV (Jan. 1924), 17-35, and "Acts of the General Assembly, Jan. 6, 1639-40," *ibid.* (July 1924), 159-62. The assembly calculated that a levy of four pounds of tobacco per tithable would yield 18,584 pounds, implying 4,646 tithables (men over sixteen). It also calculated that a limitation of planting to 170 pounds per poll would yield 1,300,000, implying 7,647 polls. Evidently the latter figure is for the whole population, as is evident also from Hening, *Statutes*, I, 228.

[42] In the year 1635, the only year for which such records exist, 2,010 persons embarked for Virginia from London alone. See John Camden Hotten, ed., *The Original Lists of Persons of Quality* . . . (London, 1874), 35-145. For other years casual estimates survive. In February 1627/8 Francis West said that 1,000 had been "lately receaved." Colonial Office Group, Class 1, Piece 4, folio 109 (Public Record Office, London). Hereafter cited CO 1/4, f. 109. In February 1633/4 Governor John Harvey said that "this yeares newcomers" had arrived "this yeare." Yong to Sir Tobie Matthew, July 13, 1634, "Aspinwall Papers," *Massachusetts Historical Society Collections*, IX (1871), 110. In May 1635, Samuel Mathews said that 2,000 had arrived "this yeare." Mathews to ? , May 25, 1635, "The Mutiny in Virginia, 1635," *Virginia Magazine of History and Biography*, I (April 1894), 417. And in March 1636, John West said that 1,606 persons had arrived "this yeare." West to Commissioners for Plantations, March 28, 1636, "Virginia in 1636," *ibid.*, IX (July 1901), 37.

[43] The official count of tithables for 1662 was 11,838. Clarendon Papers, 82 (Bodleian Library, Oxford). The ratio of tithables to total population by this time was probably about one to two. (In 1625 it was 1 to 1.5; in 1699 it was 1 to 2.7.) Since the official count was almost certainly below the actuality, a total population of roughly 25,000 seems probable. All population figures for seventeenth-century Virginia should be treated as rough estimates.

the demand would rise.[44] It brought a huge expansion of tobacco production, which helped to depress the price of tobacco and the earnings of the men who planted it.[45] It brought efforts by planters to prolong the terms of servants, since they were now living longer and therefore had a longer expectancy of usefulness.[46]

It would, in fact, be difficult to assess all the consequences of the increased longevity; but for our purposes one development was crucial, and that was the appearance in Virginia of a growing number of freemen who had served their terms but who were now unable to afford land of their own except on the frontiers or in the interior. In years when tobacco prices were especially low or crops especially poor, men who had been just scraping by were obliged to go back to work for their larger neighbors simply in order to stay alive. By 1676 it was estimated that one fourth of Virginia's freemen were without land of their own.[47] And in the same year Francis Moryson, a member of the governor's council, explained the term "freedmen" as used in Virginia to mean "persons without house and land," implying that this was now the normal condition of servants who had attained freedom.[48]

Some of them resigned themselves to working for wages; others preferred a meager living on dangerous frontier land or a hand-to-mouth existence, roaming from one county to another, renting a bit of land here, squatting on some there, dodging the tax collector, drinking, quarreling, stealing hogs, and enticing servants to run away with them.

The presence of this growing class of poverty-stricken Virginians was

[44] Evidence of the engrossment of lands after 1660 will be found in CO 1/39, f. 196; CO 1/40, f. 23; CO 1/48, f. 48; CO 5/1309, numbers 5, 9, and 23; Sloane Papers, 1008, ff. 334-35 (British Museum, London). A recent count of headrights in patents issued for land in Virginia shows 82,000 headrights claimed in the years from 1635 to 1700. Of these nearly 47,000 or 57 percent (equivalent to 2,350,000 acres) were claimed in the twenty-five years after 1650. W. F. Craven, *White, Red, and Black: The Seventeenth-Century Virginian* (Charlottesville, 1971), 14-16.

[45] No continuous set of figures for Virginia's tobacco exports in the seventeenth century can now be obtained. The available figures for English imports of American tobacco (which was mostly Virginian) are in United States Bureau of the Census, *Historical Statistics of the United States, Colonial Times to 1957* (Washington, D.C., 1960), series Z 238-240, p. 766. They show for 1672 a total of 17,559,000 pounds. In 1631 the figure had been 272,300 pounds. Tobacco crops varied heavily from year to year. Prices are almost as difficult to obtain now as volume. Those for 1667-1675 are estimated from London prices current in Warren Billings, "Virginia's Deploured Condition, 1660-1676: The Coming of Bacon's Rebellion" (doctoral dissertation, Northern Illinois University, 1969), 155-59.

[46] See below.

[47] Thomas Ludwell and Robert Smith to the king, June 18, 1676, vol. LXXVII, f. 128, Coventry Papers Longleat House, American Council of Learned Societies British Mss. project, reel 63 (Library of Congress).

[48] *Ibid.*, 204-05.

not a little frightening to the planters who had made it to the top or who had arrived in the colony already at the top, with ample supplies of servants and capital. They were caught in a dilemma. They wanted the immigrants who kept pouring in every year. Indeed they needed them and prized them the more as they lived longer. But as more and more turned free each year, Virginia seemed to have inherited the problem that she was helping England to solve. Virginia, complained Nicholas Spencer, secretary of the colony, was "a sinke to drayen England of her filth and scum."[49]

The men who worried the uppercrust looked even more dangerous in Virginia than they had in England. They were, to begin with, young, because it was young persons that the planters wanted for work in the fields; and the young have always seemed impatient of control by their elders and superiors, if not downright rebellious. They were also predominantly single men. Because the planters did not think women, or at least English women, fit for work in the fields, men outnumbered women among immigrants by three or four to one throughout the century.[50] Consequently most of the freedmen had no wife or family to tame their wilder impulses and serve as hostages to the respectable world.

Finally, what made these wild young men particularly dangerous was that they were armed and had to be armed. Life in Virginia required guns. The plantations were exposed to attack from Indians by land and from privateers and petty-thieving pirates by sea.[51] Whenever England was at war with the French or the Dutch, the settlers had to be ready to defend themselves. In 1667 the Dutch in a single raid captured twenty merchant ships in the James River, together with the English warship that was supposed to be defending them; and in 1673 they captured eleven more. On these occasions Governor William Berkeley gathered the planters in arms and at least prevented the enemy from making a landing. But while he stood off the Dutch he worried about the ragged crew at his back. Of the able-bodied men in the colony he estimated that "at least one third are Single freedmen (whose Labour will hardly maintaine them) or men much in debt, both which wee may reasonably expect upon any Small advantage the Enemy may gaine upon us, wold re-

[49] Nicholas Spencer to Lord Culpeper, Aug. 6, 1676, *ibid.*, 170. See also CO 1/49, f. 107.

[50] The figures are derived from a sampling of the names of persons for whom headrights were claimed in land patents. Patent Books I-IX (Virginia State Library, Richmond). Wyndham B. Blanton found 17,350 women and 75,884 men in "a prolonged search of the patent books and other records of the times . . . ," a ratio of 1 woman to 4.4 men. Wyndham B. Blanton, "Epidemics, Real and Imaginary, and other Factors Influencing Seventeenth Century Virginia's Population," *Bulletin of the History of Medicine*, XXXI (Sept.-Oct. 1957), 462. See also Craven, *White, Red, and Black*, 26-27.

[51] Pirates were particularly troublesome in the 1680s and 1690s. See CO 1/48, f. 71; CO 1/51, f. 340; CO 1/52, f. 54; CO 1/55, ff. 105-106; CO 1/57, f. 300; CO 5/1311, no. 10.

volt to them in hopes of bettering their Condicion by Shareing the Plunder of the Country with them."[52]

Berkeley's fears were justified. Three years later, sparked not by a Dutch invasion but by an Indian attack, rebellion swept Virginia. It began almost as Berkeley had predicted, when a group of volunteer Indian fighters turned from a fruitless expedition against the Indians to attack their rulers. Bacon's Rebellion was the largest popular rising in the colonies before the American Revolution. Sooner or later nearly everyone in Virginia got in on it, but it began in the frontier counties of Henrico and New Kent, among men whom the governor and his friends consistently characterized as rabble.[53] As it spread eastward, it turned out that there were rabble everywhere, and Berkeley understandably raised his estimate of their numbers. "How miserable that man is," he exclaimed, "that Governes a People wher six parts of seaven at least are Poore Endebted Discontented and Armed."[54]

Virginia's poor had reason to be envious and angry against the men who owned the land and imported the servants and ran the government. But the rebellion produced no real program of reform, no ideology, not even any revolutionary slogans. It was a search for plunder, not for principles. And when the rebels had redistributed whatever wealth they could lay their hands on, the rebellion subsided almost as quickly as it had begun.

It had been a shattering experience, however, for Virginia's first families. They had seen each other fall in with the rebels in order to save their skins or their possessions or even to share in the plunder. When it was over, they eyed one another distrustfully, on the lookout for any new Bacons in their midst, who might be tempted to lead the still restive rabble on more plundering expeditions. When William Byrd and Laurence Smith proposed to solve the problems of defense against the Indians by establishing semi-independent buffer settlements on the upper reaches of the rivers, in each of which they would engage to keep fifty men in arms, the assembly at first reacted favorably. But it quickly occurred to the governor and council that this would in fact mean gathering a crowd of Virginia's wild bachelors and furnishing them with an abundant supply of arms and ammunition. Byrd had himself led such a crowd in at least one plundering foray during the rebellion. To put him or anyone else in charge of a large and permanent gang of armed men was to invite them to descend again on the people whom they were supposed to be protecting.[55]

[52] CO 1/30, ff. 114-115.
[53] CO 1/37, ff. 35-40.
[54] Vol. LXXVII, 144-46, Coventry Papers.
[55] Hening, *Statutes*, II, 448-54; CO 1/42, f. 178; CO 1/43, f. 29; CO 1/44, f. 398;

The nervousness of those who had property worth plundering continued throughout the century, spurred in 1682 by the tobacco-cutting riots in which men roved about destroying crops in the fields, in the desperate hope of producing a shortage that would raise the price of the leaf.[56] And periodically in nearby Maryland and North Carolina, where the same conditions existed as in Virginia, there were tumults that threatened to spread to Virginia.[57]

As Virginia thus acquired a social problem analagous to England's own, the colony began to deal with it as England had done, by restricting the liberties of those who did not have the proper badge of freedom, namely the property that government was supposed to protect. One way was to extend the terms of service for servants entering the colony without indentures. Formerly they had served until twenty-one; now the age was advanced to twenty-four.[58] There had always been laws requiring them to serve extra time for running away; now the laws added corporal punishment and, in order to make habitual offenders more readily recognizable, specified that their hair be cropped.[59] New laws restricted the movement of servants on the highways and also increased the amount of extra time to be served for running away. In addition to serving two days for every day's absence, the captured runaway was now frequently required to compensate by labor for the loss to the crop that he had failed to tend and for the cost of his apprehension, including rewards paid for his capture.[60] A three week's holiday might result in a years extra service.[61] If a servant struck his master, he was to serve another year.[62] For killing a hog he had to serve the owner a year and the informer another year. Since the owner of the hog, and the owner of the servant, and the informer were frequently the same man, and since a hog was worth at best less than one tenth the hire of a servant for a year, the law was very profitable to masters. One Lancaster master was awarded six years extra service from a servant who killed three of his hogs, worth about thirty shillings.[63]

CO 1/47, ff. 258-260, 267; CO 1/48, f. 46; vol. LXXVIII, 378-81, 386-87, 398-99, Coventry Papers.

[56] CO 1/48 passim.

[57] CO 1/43, ff. 359-365; CO 1/44, ff. 10-62; CO 1/47, f. 261; CO 1/48, ff. 87-96, 100-102, 185; CO 5/1305, no. 43; CO 5/1309, no. 74.

[58] Hening, Statutes, II, 113-14, 240.

[59] Ibid., II, 266, 278.

[60] Ibid., II, 116-17, 273-74, 277-78.

[61] For example, James Gray, absent twenty-two days, was required to serve fifteen months extra. Order Book 1666-1680, p. 163, Lancaster County Court Records.

[62] Hening, Statutes, II, 118.

[63] Order Book 1666-1680, p. 142, Lancaster County Court Records.

The effect of these measures was to keep servants for as long as possible from gaining their freedom, especially the kind of servants who were most likely to cause trouble. At the same time the engrossment of land was driving many back to servitude after a brief taste of freedom. Freedmen who engaged to work for wages by so doing became servants again, subject to most of the same restrictions as other servants.

Nevertheless, in spite of all the legal and economic pressures to keep men in service, the ranks of the freedmen grew, and so did poverty and discontent. To prevent the wild bachelors from gaining an influence in the government, the assembly in 1670 limited voting to landholders and householders.[64] But to disfranchise the growing mass of single freemen was not to deprive them of the weapons they had wielded so effectively under Nathaniel Bacon. It is questionable how far Virginia could safely have continued along this course, meeting discontent with repression and manning her plantations with annual importations of servants who would later add to the unruly ranks of the free. To be sure, the men at the bottom might have had both land and liberty, as the settlers of some other colonies did, if Virginia's frontier had been safe from Indians, or if the men at the top had been willing to forego some of their profits and to give up some of the lands they had engrossed. The English government itself made efforts to break up the great holdings that had helped to create the problem.[65] But it is unlikely that the policy makers in Whitehall would have contended long against the successful.

In any case they did not have to. There was another solution, which allowed Virginia's magnates to keep their lands, yet arrested the discontent and the repression of other Englishmen, a solution which strengthened the rights of Englishmen and nourished that attachment to liberty which came to fruition in the Revolutionary generation of Virginia statesmen. But the solution put an end to the process of turning Africans into Englishmen. The rights of Englishmen were preserved by destroying the rights of Africans.

I do not mean to argue that Virginians deliberately turned to African Negro slavery as a means of preserving and extending the rights of Englishmen. Winthrop Jordan has suggested that slavery came to Virginia as an unthinking decision.[66] We might go further and say that it came without

---

[64] Hening, *Statutes*, II, 280. It had been found, the preamble to the law said, that such persons "haveing little interest in the country doe oftner make tumults at the election to the disturbance of his majesties peace, then by their discretions in their votes provide for the conservasion thereof, by makeing choyce of persons fitly qualifyed for the discharge of soe greate a trust...."

[65] CO 1/39, f. 196; CO 1/48, f. 48; CO 5/1309, nos. 5, 9, 23; CO 5/1310, no. 83.

[66] Jordan, *White over Black*, 44-98.

a decision. It came automatically as Virginians bought the cheapest labor they could get. Once Virginia's heavy mortality ceased, an investment in slave labor was much more profitable than an investment in free labor; and the planters bought slaves as rapidly as traders made them available. In the last years of the seventeenth century they bought them in such numbers that slaves probably already constituted a majority or nearly a majority of the labor force by 1700.⁶⁷ The demand was so great that traders for a time found a better market in Virginia than in Jamaica or Barbados.⁶⁸ But the social benefits of an enslaved labor force, even if not consciously sought or ·recognized at the time by the men who bought the slaves, were larger than the economic benefits. The increase in the importation of slaves was matched by a decrease in the importation of indentured servants and consequently a decrease in the dangerous number of new freedmen who annually emerged seeking a place in society that they would be unable to achieve.⁶⁹

If Africans had been unavailable, it would probably have proved impossible to devise a way to keep a continuing supply of English immigrants in their place. There was a limit beyond which the abridgment of English liberties would have resulted not merely in rebellion but in protests from England and in the cutting off of the supply of further servants. At the time of Bacon's Rebellion the English commission of investigation had shown more sympathy with the rebels than with the well-to-do planters who had engrossed Virginia's lands. To have attempted the enslavement of English-born laborers would have caused more disorder than it cured. But to keep as slaves black men who arrived in that condition *was* possible and apparently regarded as plain common sense.

The attitude of English officials was well expressed by the attorney who reviewed for the Privy Council the slave codes established in Barbados in 1679. He found the laws of Barbados to be well designed for the good of his majesty's subjects there, for, he said, "although Negros in that Island are punishable in a different and more severe manner than other Subjects are for Offences of the like nature; yet I humbly conceive that the Laws

---

⁶⁷ In 1700 they constituted half of the labor force (persons working for other men) in Surry County, the only county in which it is possible to ascertain the numbers. Robert Wheeler, "Social Transition in the Virginia Tidewater, 1650-1720: The Laboring Household as an Index," paper delivered at the Organization of American Historians' meeting, New Orleans, April 15, 1971. Surry County was on the south side of the James, one of the least wealthy regions of Virginia.

⁶⁸ See the letters of the Royal African Company to its ship captains, Oct. 23, 1701; Dec. 2, 1701; Dec. 7, 1704; Dec. 21, 1704; Jan. 25, 1704//5, T70 58 (Public Record Office, London).

⁶⁹ Abbot Emerson Smith, *Colonists in Bondage: White Servitude and Convict Labor in America 1607-1776* (Chapel Hill, 1947), 335. See also Thomas J. Wertenbaker, *The Planters of Colonial Virginia* (Princeton, 1922), 130-31, 134-35; Craven, *White, Red, and Black*, 17.

there concerning Negros are reasonable Laws, for by reason of their numbers they become dangerous, and being a brutish sort of People and reckoned as goods and chattels in that Island, it is of necessity or at least convenient to have Laws for the Government of them different from the Laws of
England, to prevent the great mischief that otherwise may happen to the
Planters and Inhabitants in that Island."⁷⁰ In Virginia too it seemed convenient and reasonable to have different laws for black and white. As the
number of slaves increased, the assembly passed laws that carried forward
with much greater severity the trend already under way in the colony's labor laws. But the new severity was reserved for people without white skin.
The laws specifically exonerated the master who accidentally beat his slave
to death, but they placed new limitations on his punishment of "Christian
white servants."⁷¹

Virginians worried about the risk of having in their midst a body of men
who had every reason to hate them.⁷² The fear of a slave insurrection hung
over them for nearly two centuries. But the danger from slaves actually
proved to be less than that which the colony had faced from its restive and
armed freedmen. Slaves had none of the rising expectations that so often
produce human discontent. No one had told them that they had rights.
They had been nurtured in heathen societies where they had lost their freedom; their children would be nurtured in a Christian society and never
know freedom.

Moreover, slaves were less troubled by the sexual imbalance that helped
to make Virginia's free laborers so restless. In an enslaved labor force
women could be required to make tobacco just as the men did; and they
also made children, who in a few years would be an asset to their master.
From the beginning, therefore, traders imported women in a much higher
ratio to men than was the case among English servants,⁷³ and the level of

⁷⁰ CO 1/45, f. 138.
⁷¹ Hening. *Statutes*, II, 481-82, 492-93; III, 86-88, 102-03, 179-80, 333-35, 447-62.
⁷² For example, see William Byrd II to the Earl of Egmont, July 12, 1736, in Elizabeth
Donnan, ed., *Documents Illustrative of the History of the Slave Trade to America* (4 vols.,
Washington, 1930-1935), IV, 131-32. But compare Byrd's letter to Peter Beckford, Dec. 6,
1735, "Letters of the Byrd Family," *Virginia Magazine of History and Biography*, XXXVI
(April 1928), 121-23, in which he specifically denies any danger. The Virginia assembly
at various times laid duties on the importation of slaves. See Donnan, ed., *Documents
Illustrative of the History of the Slave Trade*, IV, 66-67, 86-88, 91-94, 102-17, 121-31, 132-
42. The purpose of some of the acts was to discourage imports, but apparently the motive
was to redress the colony's balance of trade after a period during which the planters had
purchased far more than they could pay for. See also Wertenbaker, *The Planters of Colonial
Virginia*, 129.
⁷³ The Swiss traveler Francis Ludwig Michel noted in 1702 that "Both sexes are usually
bought, which increase afterwards." William J. Hinke, trans. and ed., "Report of the
Journey of Francis Louis Michel from Berne Switzerland to Virginia, October 2, (1) 1701-
December 1, 1702: Part II," *Virginia Magazine of History and Biography*, XXIV (April

discontent was correspondingly reduced. Virginians did not doubt that discontent would remain, but it could be repressed by methods that would not have been considered reasonable, convenient, or even safe, if applied to Englishmen. Slaves could be deprived of opportunities for association and rebellion. They could be kept unarmed and unorganized. They could be subjected to savage punishments by their owners without fear of legal reprisals. And since their color disclosed their probable status, the rest of society could keep close watch on them. It is scarcely surprising that no slave insurrection in American history approached Bacon's Rebellion in its extent or in its success.

Nor is it surprising that Virginia's freedmen never again posed a threat to society. Though in later years slavery was condemned because it was thought to compete with free labor, in the beginning it reduced by so much the number of freedmen who would otherwise have competed with each other. When the annual increment of freedmen fell off, the number that remained could more easily find an independent place in society, especially as the danger of Indian attack diminished and made settlement safer at the heads of the rivers or on the Carolina frontier. There might still remain a number of irredeemable, idle, and unruly freedmen, particularly among the convicts whom England exported to the colonies. But the numbers were small enough, so that they could be dealt with by the old expedient of drafting them for military expeditions.[74] The way was thus made easier for

---

1916), 116. A sampling of the names identifiable by sex, for whom headrights were claimed in land patents in the 1680s and 1690s shows a much higher ratio of women to men among blacks than among whites. For example, in the years 1695-1699 (Patent Book 9) I count 818 white men and 276 white women, 376 black men and 220 black women (but compare Craven, *White, Red, and Black,* 99-100). In Northampton County in 1677, among seventy-five black tithables there were thirty-six men, thirty-eight women, and one person whose sex cannot be determined. In Surry County in 1703, among 211 black tithables there were 132 men, seventy-four women, and five persons whose sex cannot be determined. These are the only counties where the records yield such information. Northampton County Court Records, Order Book 10, 189-91; Surry County Court Records, Deeds, Wills, etc., No. 5, part 2, 287-90.

[74] Virginia disposed of so many this way in the campaign against Cartagena in 1741 that a few years later the colony was unable to scrape up any more for another expedition. Fairfax Harrison, "When the Convicts Came," *Virginia Magazine of History and Biography,* XXX (July 1922), 250-60, especially 256-57; John W. Shy, "A New Look at Colonial Militia," *William and Mary Quarterly,* XX (April 1963), 175-85. In 1736, Virginia had shipped another batch of unwanted freedmen to Georgia because of a rumored attack by the Spanish. Byrd II to Lord Egmont, July 1736, "Letters of the Byrd Family," *Virginia Magazine of History and Biography,* XXXVI (July 1928), 216-17. Observations by an English traveler who embarked on the same ship suggest that they did not go willingly: "our Lading consisted of all the Scum of Virginia, who had been recruited for the Service of Georgia, and who were ready at every Turn to mutiny, whilst they belch'd out the most shocking Oaths, wishing Destruction to the Vessel and every Thing in her." "Observations in Several Voyages and Travels in America in the Year 1736," *William and Mary Quarterly,* XV (April 1907), 224.

the remaining freedmen to acquire property, maybe acquire a slave or two of their own, and join with their superiors in the enjoyment of those English liberties that differentiated them from their black laborers.

A free society divided between large landholders and small was much less riven by antagonisms than one divided between landholders and land-less, masterless men. With the freedman's expectations, sobriety, and status restored, he was no longer a man to be feared. That fact, together with the presence of a growing mass of alien slaves, tended to draw the white set-tlers closer together and to reduce the importance of the class difference between yeoman farmer and large plantation owner.[75]

The seventeenth century has sometimes been thought of as the day of the yeoman farmer in Virginia; but in many ways a stronger case can be made for the eighteenth century as the time when the yeoman farmer came into his own, because slavery relieved the small man of the pressures that had been reducing him to continued servitude. Such an interpretation conforms to the political development of the colony. During the seventeenth century the royally appointed governor's council, composed of the largest property-owners in the colony, had been the most powerful governing body. But as the tide of slavery rose between 1680 and 1720 Virginia moved toward a government in which the yeoman farmer had a larger share. In spite of the rise of Virginia's great families on the black tide, the power of the council declined; and the elective House of Burgesses became the dominant organ of government. Its members nurtured a closer relationship with their yeo-man constituency than had earlier been the case.[76] And in its chambers Vir-ginians developed the ideas they so fervently asserted in the Revolution: ideas about taxation, representation, and the rights of Englishmen, and ideas about the prerogatives and powers and sacred calling of the indepen-dent, property-holding yeoman farmer—commonwealth ideas.

In the eighteenth century, because they were no longer threatened by a dangerous free laboring class, Virginians could afford these ideas, whereas in Berkeley's time they could not. Berkeley himself was obsessed with the experience of the English civil wars and the danger of rebellion. He de-spised and feared the New Englanders for their association with the Puri-tans who had made England, however briefly, a commonwealth.[77] He was

[75] Compare Lyon G. Tyler, "Virginians Voting in the Colonial Period," *William and Mary Quarterly*, VI (July 1897), 7-13.

[76] John C. Rainbolt, "The Alteration in the Relationship between Leadership and Con-stituents in Virginia, 1660 to 1720," *William and Mary Quarterly*, XXVII (July 1970), 411-34.

[77] William Berkeley to Richard Nicolls, May 20, 1666, May 4, 1667, Additional Mss. 28,218, ff. 14-17 (British Museum, London).

proud that Virginia, unlike New England, had no free schools and no printing press, because books and schools bred heresy and sedition.[78] He must have taken satisfaction in the fact that when his people did rebel against him under Bacon, they generated no republican ideas, no philosophy of rebellion or of human rights. Yet a century later, without benefit of rebellions, Virginians had learned republican lessons, had introduced schools and printing presses, and were as ready as New Englanders to recite the aphorisms of the commonwealthmen.

It was slavery, I suggest, more than any other single factor, that had made the difference, slavery that enabled Virginia to nourish representative government in a plantation society, slavery that transformed the Virginia of Governor Berkeley to the Virginia of Jefferson, slavery that made the Virginians dare to speak a political language that magnified the rights of freemen, and slavery, therefore, that brought Virginians into the same commonwealth political tradition with New Englanders. The very institution that was to divide North and South after the Revolution may have made possible their union in a republican government.

Thus began the American paradox of slavery and freedom, intertwined and interdependent, the rights of Englishmen supported on the wrongs of Africans. The American Revolution only made the contradictions more glaring, as the slaveholding colonists proclaimed to a candid world the rights not simply of Englishmen but of all men. To explain the origin of the contradictions, if the explanation I have suggested is valid, does not eliminate them or make them less ugly. But it may enable us to understand a little better the strength of the ties that bound freedom to slavery, even in so noble a mind as Jeffersons. And it may perhaps make us wonder about the ties that bind more devious tyrannies to our own freedoms and give us still today our own American paradox.

[78]Hening, *Statutes*, II, 517.

The Labor Problem at Jamestown, 1607–18

EDMUND S. MORGAN

THE STORY OF JAMESTOWN, the first permanent English settlement in America, has a familiar place in the history of the United States. We all know of the tribulations that kept the colony on the point of expiring: the shortage of supplies, the hostility of the Indians, the quarrels among the leaders, the reckless search for gold, the pathetic search for a passage to the Pacific, and the neglect of the crucial business of growing food to stay alive. Through the scene moves the figure of Captain John Smith, a little larger than life, trading for corn among the Indians and driving the feckless crew to work. His departure in October 1609 results in near disaster. The settlers fritter away their time and energy, squander their provisions, and starve. Sir Thomas Gates, arriving after the settlement's third winter, finds only sixty men out of six hundred still alive and those sixty scarcely able to walk.

In the summer of 1610 Gates and Lord La Warr get things moving again with a new supply of men and provisions, a new absolute form of government, and a new set of laws designed to keep everybody at work. But when Gates and La Warr leave for a time, the settlers fall to their old ways. Sir Thomas Dale, upon his arrival in May 1611, finds them at "their daily and usuall workes, bowling in the streetes."[1] But Dale brings order out of chaos. By enlarging and enforcing the colony's new law code (the famous *Lawes Divine, Morall and Martiall*) he starts the settlers working again and rescues them from starvation by making them plant corn. By 1618 the colony is getting on its feet and ready to carry on without the stern regimen of a Smith or a Dale. There are still evil days ahead, as the Virginia Company sends over men more rapidly than the infant colony can absorb them. But the settlers, having found in tobacco a valuable crop for export, have at last gone to work with a will, and Virginia's future is assured.

The story probably fits the facts insofar as they can be known. But it does

An earlier version of this paper was read at the annual meeting of the American Historical Association on December 29, 1968. I wish to express my thanks to those who offered criticisms at that time and also to Helen M. Morgan and to Professors J. H. Hexter, Lawrence Stone, William N. Parker, and William B. Foltz who read the paper subsequently and made valuable suggestions.

[1] Ralph Hamor, *A True Discourse of the Present State of Virginia* (London, 1615; Richmond, 1957), 26.

not quite explain them. The colony's long period of starvation and failure may well be attributed to the idleness of the first settlers, but idleness is more an accusation than an explanation. Why did men spend their time bowling in the streets when their lives depended on work? Were they lunatics, preferring to play games rather than clear and plow and plant the crops that could have kept them alive?

The mystery only deepens if we look more closely at the efforts of Smith, Gates, La Warr, and Dale to set things right. In 1612 John Smith described his work program of 1608: "the company [being] divided into tennes, fifteenes, or as the businesse required, 4 hours each day was spent in worke, the rest in pastimes and merry exercise." Twelve years later Smith rewrote this passage and changed the figure of four hours to six hours.[2] But even so, what are we to make of a six-hour day in a colony teetering on the verge of extinction?

The program of Gates and La Warr in the summer of 1610 was no more strenuous. William Strachey described it:

it is to be understood that such as labor are not yet so taxed but that easily they perform the same and ever by ten of the clock have done their morning's work: at what time they have their allowances [of food] set out ready for them, and until it be three of the clock again they take their own pleasure, and afterward, with the sunset, their day's labor is finished.[3]

The Virginia Company offered much the same account of this period. According to a tract issued late in 1610, "the setled times of working (to effect all themselves, or the Adventurers neede desire) [requires] no more pains than from sixe of clocke in the morning untill ten, and from two of the clocke in the afternoone till foure."[4] The long lunch period described for 1610 was also a feature of the *Lawes Divine, Morall and Martiall* as enforced by Dale. The total working hours prescribed in the *Lawes* amounted to roughly five to eight hours a day in summer and three to six hours in winter.[5]

It is difficult, then, to escape the conclusion that there was a great deal of unemployment or underemployment at Jamestown, whether it was the idleness of the undisciplined in the absence of strong government or the idleness of the disciplined in the presence of strong government. How are

[2] John Smith, *Travels and Works*, ed. Edward Arber and A. G. Bradley (Edinburgh, 1910), 1: 149; 2: 466.
[3] L. B. Wright, ed., *A Voyage to Virginia in 1609* (Charlottesville, 1964), 69–70.
[4] *A True Declaration of the Estate of the Colonie in Virginia* (London, 1610), reprinted in Peter Force, ed., *Tracts and Other Papers* (Washington, 1844), 3. no. 1: 20; Smith, *Travels and Works*, 2: 502. Captain Daniel Tucker maintained a similar program in Bermuda in 1616: "according to the Virginia order, hee set every one [that] was with him at Saint Georges, to his taske, to cleere grounds, fell trees, set corne, square timber, plant vines and other fruits brought out of England. These by their taske—Masters by breake a day repaired to the wharfe, from thence to be imployed to the place of their imployment, till nine of the clocke, and then in the after-noone from three till Sunneset." *Ibid.*, 653.
[5] For the Colony in Virginia Brittannia: *Lawes Divine, Morall and Martiall* (London, 1612), 61–62.

we to account for this fact? By our standards the situation at Jamestown demanded hard and continuous work. Why was the response so feeble?

One answer, given by the leaders of the colony, is that the settlers included too many ne'er-do-wells and too many gentlemen who "never did know what a dayes work was."[6] Hard work had to wait until harder men were sent. Another answer may be that the Jamestown settlers were debilitated by hunger and disease. The victims of scurvy, malaria, typhoid, and diphtheria may have been left without the will or the energy to work. Still another answer, which has echoed through the pages of our history books, attributed the difficulty to the fact that the settlement was conducted on a communal basis: everybody worked for the Virginia Company and everybody was fed (while supplies lasted) by the company, regardless of how much he worked or failed to work. Once land was distributed to individuals and men were allowed to work for themselves, they gained the familiar incentives of private enterprise and bent their shoulders to the wheel.[7] These explanations are surely all valid—they are all supported by the testimony of contemporaries—and they go far toward explaining the lazy pioneers of Jamestown. But they do not reach to a dimension of the problem that contemporaries would have overlooked because they would have taken it for granted. They do not tell us what ideas and attitudes about work, carried from England, would have led the first English settlers to expect so little of themselves in a situation that demanded so much. The Jamestown settlers did not leave us the kind of private papers that would enable us to examine directly their ideas and attitudes, as we can those of the Puritans who settled New England a few years later. But in the absence of direct evidence we may discover among the ideas current in late sixteenth- and early seventeenth-century England some clues to the probable state of mind of the first Virginians, clues to the way they felt about work, whether in the Old World or the New, clues to habits of thinking that may have conditioned their perceptions of what confronted them at Jamestown, clues even to the tangled web of motives that made later Virginians masters of slaves.

ENGLISHMEN'S IDEAS about the New World at the opening of the seventeenth century were based on a century of European exploration and settlement. The Spanish, whose exploits surpassed all others, had not attempted to keep their success a secret, and by the middle of the sixteenth century Englishmen interested in America had begun translating Spanish histories

---

[6] Smith, *Travels and Works*, 2: 487.
[7] A much more sophisticated version of this explanation is suggested by Professor Sigmund Diamond in his discussion of the development of social relationships in Virginia, "From Organization to Society: Virginia in the Seventeenth Century," *American Journal of Sociology*, 63 (1958): 457–75; see also his "Values as an Obstacle to Economic Growth: The American Colonies," *Journal of Economic History*, 27 (1967): 561–75.

and memoirs in an effort to rouse their countrymen to emulation.[8] The land
that emerged from these writings was, except in the Arctic regions, an
Eden, teeming with gentle and generous people who, before the Spanish
conquest, had lived without labor, or with very little, from the fruits of a
bountiful nature.[9] There were admittedly some unfriendly exceptions who
made a habit of eating their more attractive neighbors; but they were a
minority, confined to a few localities, and in spite of their ferocity were
scarcely a match for Europeans armed with guns.[10] Englishmen who visited
the New World confirmed the reports of natural abundance. Arthur Bar-
lowe, for example, reconnoitering the North Carolina coast for Walter
Raleigh, observed that "the earth bringeth foorth all things in aboundance,
as in the first creation, without toile or labour," while the people were
"most gentle, loving, and faithfull, void of all guile, and treason, and such
as lived after the manner of the golden age. . . ."[11]

English and European readers may have discounted the more extravagant
reports of American abundance, for the same authors who praised the land
often gave contradictory accounts of the hardships they had suffered in it.
But anyone who doubted that riches were waiting to be plucked from
Virginia's trees had reason to expect that a good deal might be plucked
from the people of the land. Spanish experience had shown that Europeans
could thrive in the New World without undue effort by exploiting the
natives. With a mere handful of men the Spanish had conquered an
enormous population of Indians in the Caribbean, Mexico, and Peru and
had put them to work. In the chronicles of Peter Martyr Englishmen
learned how it was done. Apart from the fact that the Indians were
naturally gentle, their division into a multitude of kingdoms, frequently
at odds with one another, made it easy to play off one against another.
By aiding one group against its enemies the Spaniards had made themselves masters of both.[12]

The story of English plans to imitate and improve on the Spanish strategy
is a long one.[13] It begins at least as early as Francis Drake's foray in Panama
in 1572–73, when he allied with a band of runaway slaves to rob a Spanish
mule train carrying treasure from Peru across the isthmus to Nombre de

[8] See especially the translation of Peter Martyr, in Richard Eden, *The Decades of the new
worlde or west India* (London, 1555); a useful bibliographical history is John Parker, *Books to
Build an Empire* (Amsterdam, 1966).

[9] Gustav H. Blanke, *Amerika im Englishen Schrifttum Des 16. und 17. Jahrhunderts*
Beitrage Zur Englischen Philologie, 46 (Bochum-Langendreer, 1962), 98–104.

[10] Since Peter Martyr, the principal Spanish chronicler, identified most Indians who resisted
the Spaniards as cannibals, this became the familiar sixteenth-century epithet for unfriendly
Indians. It is doubtful that many tribes actually practiced cannibalism, though some certainly did.

[11] D. B. Quinn, ed., *The Roanoke Voyages 1584–1590*, Works issued by the Hakluyt Society,
2d ser., 104, 105 (London, 1955), 1: 108.

[12] Eden, *Decades, passim.* For English awareness of the Spanish example, see Smith, *Travels
and Works*, 2: 578–81, 600–03, 955–56, and Susan M. Kingsbury, ed., *The Records of the
Virginia Company of London* (Washington, 1906–35), 3: 558, 560–62.

[13] I have dealt with this subject in a work still in progress.

Dios on the.Caribbean.[14] The idea of joining with dissident natives or slaves either against their Spanish masters or against their wicked cannibalistic neighbors became an important ingredient in English plans for colonizing the New World. Martin Frobisher's experiences with the Eskimos in Baffin Land and Ralph Lane's with the Indians at Roanoke[15] should perhaps have disabused the English of their expectations; but they found it difficult to believe that any group of natives, and especially the noble savages of North America, would fail to welcome what they called with honest pride (and some myopia) the "gentle government" of the English.[16] If the savages first encountered by a colonizing expedition proved unfriendly, the thing to do was to make contact with their milder neighbors and rescue them from the tyranny of the unfriendly tribe, who must be their enemies and were probably cannibals to boot.[17]

The settlers at Jamestown tried to follow the strategy, locating their settlement as the plan called for, near the mouth of a navigable river, so that they would have access to the interior tribes if the coastal ones were hostile. But as luck would have it, they picked an area with a more power-ful, more extensive, and more effective Indian government than existed anywhere else on the Atlantic Coast. King Powhatan had his enemies, the Monacans of the interior, but he felt no great need of English assistance against them, and he rightly suspected that the English constituted a larger threat to his hegemony than the Monacans did. He submitted with ill grace and no evident comprehension to the coronation ceremony that the Virginia Company arranged for him, and he kept his distance from James-town. Those of his warriors who visited the settlement showed no disposition to work for the English. The Monacans, on the other hand, lived too far inland (beyond the falls) to serve as substitute allies, and the English were thus deprived of their anticipated native labor.[18]

They did not, however, give up their expectations of getting it eventually. In 1615 Ralph Hamor still thought the Indians would come around "as they are easily taught and may by lenitie and faire usage . . . be brought,

[14] Irene A. Wright, ed., *Documents concerning English Voyages to the Spanish Main 1569-1580*, Works issued by the Hakluyt Society, 2d ser., 71 (London, 1932), gives the original sources, both English and Spanish.

[15] Richard Collinson, ed., *The Three Voyages of Martin Frobisher*, Works issued by the Hakluyt Society, 1st ser., 38 (London, 1867), 131, 141-42, 145-50, 269, 271, 280-89; Quinn, *Roanoke Voyages*, 1: 275-88.

[16] The phrase "gentle government" is the younger Hakluyt's, in a proposal to make use of Drake's Negro allies from Panama for a colony at the Straits of Magellan. E. G. R. Taylor, ed., *The Original Writings and Correspondence of the two Richard Hakluyts*, Works issued by the Hakluyt Society, 2d ser., 76, 77 (London, 1935), 1: 142.

[17] *Ibid.*, 121, 2: 241-42, 246-49, 257-65, 275, 318, 342.

[18] The secondary literature on the Indians of Virginia is voluminous, but see especially Nancy O. Lurie, "Indian Cultural Adjustment to European Civilization," in J. M. Smith, ed., *Seventeenth-Century America* (Chapel Hill, 1959), 33-60. The most helpful original sources, on which most of our information is necessarily based, are Smith, *Travels and Works*, and William Strachey, *The Historie of Travell into Virginia Britania* (composed 1612), ed. L. B. Wright and V. Freund, Works issued by the Hakluyt Society, 2d ser., 103 (London, 1953), 53-116.

being naturally though ingenious, yet idley given, to be no lesse industrious, nay to exceede our English.''[19] Even after the massacre of 1622 Virginians continued to dream of an Indian labor supply, though there was no longer to be any gentleness in obtaining it. Captain John Martin thought it better to exploit than exterminate the Indians, if only because they could be made to work in the heat of the day, when Englishmen would not. And William Claiborne in 1626 invented a device (whether mechanical or political is not clear) that he claimed would make it possible to keep Indians safely in the settlements and put them to work. The governor and council gave him what looks like the first American patent or copyright, namely a three-year monopoly, to "have holde and enjoy all the benefitt use and profitt of this his project or inventione," and they also assigned him a recently captured Indian, "for his better experience and tryall of his inventione."[20]

English expectations of the New World and its inhabitants died hard. America was supposed to be a land of abundance, peopled by natives who would not only share that abundance with the English but increase it under English direction. Englishmen simply did not envisage a need to work for the mere purpose of staying alive. The problem of survival as they saw it was at best political and at worst military.

ALTHOUGH ENGLISHMEN long remained under the illusion that the Indians would eventually become useful English subjects, it became apparent fairly early that Indian labor was not going to sustain the founders of Jamestown. The company in England was convinced by 1609 that the settlers would have to grow at least part of their own food.[21] Yet the settlers themselves had to be driven to that life-saving task. To understand their ineffectiveness in coping with a situation that their pioneering descendants would take in stride, it may be helpful next to inquire into some of the attitudes toward work that these first English pioneers took for granted. How much work and what kind of work did Englishmen at the opening of the seventeenth century consider normal?

The laboring population of England, by law at least, was required to work much harder than the regimen at Jamestown might lead us to expect. The famous Statute of Artificers of 1563 (re-enacting similar provisions from the Statute of Laborers of 1495) required all laborers to work from five in the morning to seven or eight at night from mid-March to mid-September, and during the remaining months of the year from day-break to night. Time out for eating, drinking, and rest was not to exceed

---

[19] *True Discourse*, 2. See also Strachey, *Historie of Travell*, 91–94; Alexander Whitaker, *Good Newes from Virginia* (London, 1613), 40.

[20] Susan M. Kingsbury, ed., *The Records of the Virginia Company of London* (Washington, 1906–35), 3: 705–06; H. R. McIlwaine, ed., *Minutes of the Council and General Court of Colonial Virginia* (Richmond, 1924), 111.

[21] *Records of the Virginia Company*, 3: 17, 27.

Hard at work in old England. Woodcut from *Robert, the Devil*. Printed by W. de Worde [1502?] (STC 21070, 21071). Photograph: Edward Hodnett, *English Woodcuts, 1480–1535* (London, 1935).

two and a half hours a day.[22] But these were injunctions not descriptions. The Statute of Laborers of 1495 is preceded by the complaint that laborers "waste much part of the day . . . in late coming unto their work, early departing therefrom, long sitting at their breakfast, at their dinner and noon-meat, and long time of sleeping after noon."[23] Whether this statute or that of 1563 (still in effect when Jamestown was founded) corrected the situation is doubtful.[24] The records of local courts show varying efforts to enforce other provisions of the statute of 1563, but they are almost wholly silent about this provision,[25] in spite of the often-expressed despair of masters over their lazy and negligent laborers.[26]

[22] R. H. Tawney and Eileen Power, eds., *Tudor Economic Documents* (London, 1924), 1: 342. For some seventeenth-century prescriptions of long working hours, see Gervase Markham, *A Way to get Wealth* (13th ed.; London, 1676), 115–17; Henry Best, *Rural Economy in Yorkshire in 1641*, Surtees Society, *Publications*, 33 (Durham, 1857), 44. See also L. F. Salzman, *Building in England down to 1540* (Oxford, 1952), 61–65.

[23] 11 Henry 7, cap. 22, sec. 4; Douglas Knoop and G. P. Jones, *The Medieval Mason* (Manchester, 1933), 117.

[24] Tawney and Power, *Tudor Economic Documents*, 1: 352–63.

[25] A minor exception is in J. H. E. Bennett and J. C. Dewhurst, eds., *Quarter Sessions Records . . . for the County Palatine of Chester, 1559–1760*, Publications of the Record Society for the Publication of Original Documents relating to Lancashire and Cheshire, 94 (Chester, 1940), 95–96, where a master alleged that his apprentice, John Dodd, "hath negligently behaved him selfe in his service in idleinge and sleepinge in severalle places where he hath been comanded to work." But sleeping (from eight in the morning till two in the afternoon and beyond) was only one of Dodd's offenses. On the enforcement of other provisions in the statute, see Margaret G. Davies, *The Enforcement of English Apprenticeship . . . 1563–1642* (Cambridge, Mass., 1956); R. K. Kelsall, *Wage Regulation under the Statute of Artificers* (London, 1938); and R. H. Tawney, "The Assessment of Wages in England by Justices of the Peace," *Vierteljahrschrift für Sozial- und Wirtschaftsgeschichte*, 11 (1913): 307–37, 533–64.

[26] E. S. Furniss, *The Position of the Laborer in a System of Nationalism* (Boston, 1920), 117–

It may be said that complaints of the laziness and irresponsibility of workmen can be met with in any century. Were such complaints in fact justified in sixteenth- and early seventeenth-century England? There is some reason to believe that they were, that life during those years was characterized by a large amount of idleness or underemployment.[27] The outstanding economic fact of the sixteenth and early seventeenth century in England was a rapid and more or less steady rise in prices, followed at some distance by a much smaller rise in wages, both in industry and in agriculture. The price of provisions used by a laborer's family rose faster than wages during the whole period from 1500 to 1640.[28] The government made an effort to narrow the gap by requiring the justices in each county to readjust maximum wages at regular intervals. But the wages established by the justices reflected their own nostalgic notions of what a day's work ought to be worth in money, rather than a realistic estimate of what a man could buy with his wages. In those counties, at least, where records survive, the level of wages set by the justices crept upward very slowly before 1630.[29]

Wages were so inadequate that productivity was probably impaired by malnutrition. From a quarter to a half of the population lived below the level recognized at the time to constitute poverty. Few of the poor could count on regular meals at home, and in years when the wheat crop failed, they were close to starvation.[30] It is not surprising that men living under these conditions showed no great energy for work and that much of the population was, by modern standards, idle much of the time. The health manuals of the day recognized that people normally slept after eating, and the laws even prescribed a siesta for laborers in the summer time.[31] If they slept longer and more often than the laws allowed or the physicians recommended, if they loafed on the job and took unauthorized holidays, if they worked slowly and ineffectively when they did work, it may have

34; E. P. Thompson, "Time, Work-Discipline, and Industrial Capitalism," *Past and Present*, no. 38 (1967): 56–97.

[27] D. C. Coleman, "Labour in the English Economy of the Sixteenth Century," *Economic History Review*, 2d ser., 8 (1956), reprinted in E. M. Carus Wilson, ed., *Essays in Economic History* (London, 1954–62), 2: 291–308.

[28] E. H. Phelps Brown and Sheila V. Hopkins, "Seven Centuries of Building Wages," *Economica*, 2d ser., 22 (1955): 95–206; "Seven Centuries of the Prices of Consumables, compared with Builders' Wage-Rates," *ibid.*, 2d ser., 23 (1956): 296–314; "Wage Rates and Prices: Evidence for Population Pressure in the Sixteenth Century," *ibid.*, 2d ser., 24 (1957): 289–306; H. P. R. Finberg, ed., *The Agrarian History of England and Wales*, 4, *1500–1640*, ed. Joan Thirsk (Cambridge, 1967), 435–57, 531, 583–695.

[29] Tawney, "Assessment of Wages," 555–64; Kelsall, *Wage Regulation*, 67–86. Tawney and Kelsall both argue that the enforcement of maximum wages according to the statute of 1563 demonstrates a shortage of labor; but except in a few isolated instances (there may well have been local temporary shortages) the evidence comes from the period after the middle of the seventeenth century.

[30] Coleman, "Labour in the English Economy," 295; Peter Laslett adduces figures to show that actual starvation was probably rare among English peasants (*The World We Have Lost* [London, 1965], 107–27), but there can be little doubt that they were frequently close to it and chronically undernourished. See Carl Bridenbaugh, *Vexed and Troubled Englishmen* (New York, 1968), 91–98.

[31] Thomas Elyot, *The Castel of Helthe* (London, 1541), fols. 45–46; Thomas Cogan, *The*

been due at least in part to undernourishment and to the variety of chronic diseases that undernourishment brings in its train.[32]

Thus low wages may have begot low productivity that in turn justified low wages.[33] The reaction of employers was to blame the trouble on deficiencies, not of diet or wages, but of character. A prosperous yeoman like Robert Loder, who kept close track of his expenses and profits, was always bemoaning the indolence of his servants. Men who had large amounts of land that they could either rent out or work with hired labor generally preferred to rent because labor was so inefficient and irresponsible.[34]

Even the division of labor, which economists have customarily regarded as a means of increased productivity, could be a source of idleness. Plowing, for example, seems to have been a special skill—a plowman was paid at a higher rate than ordinary farm workers. But the ordinary laborer's work might have to be synchronized with the plowman's, and a whole crew of men might be kept idle by a plowman's failure to get his job done at the appropriate time. It is difficult to say whether this type of idleness, resulting from failure to synchronize the performance of related tasks, was rising or declining; but cheap, inefficient, irresponsible labor would be unlikely to generate pressures for the careful planning of time.

The government, while seeking to discourage idleness through laws requiring long hours of work, also passed laws that inadvertently discouraged industry. A policy that might be characterized as the conservation of employment frustrated those who wanted to do more work than others. English economic policy seems to have rested on the assumption that the total amount of work for which society could pay was strictly limited and must be rationed so that everyone could have a little,[35] and those with family responsibilities could have a little more. It was against the law for a man to practice more than one trade or one craft.[36] And although large numbers of farmers took up some handicraft on the side, this was to be discouraged, because "for one man to be both an husbandman and an Artificer is a gatheringe of divers mens livinges into one mans hand."[37] So as not to take

Haven of Health (London, 1589), 231–39; *The Englishmens Doctor, or The School of Salerne* (orig. pub. London, 1608) (New York, 1920), 77.

[32] E. P. Thompson, "Time, Work Discipline, and Industrial Capitalism."

[33] On the prevalence of such a vicious circle in pre-industrial countries, see W. F. Moore, *Industrialization and Labor* (Ithaca, 1951), 106–13, 308. But see also E. J. Berg, "Backward-Sloping Labor Supply Functions in Dual Economies—The Africa Case," *Quarterly Journal of Economics*, 75 (1961): 468–92. For a comparison of Tudor and Stuart England with modern underdeveloped countries, see F. J. Fisher, "The Sixteenth and Seventeenth Centuries: The Dark Ages in English Economic History," *Economica*, 2d ser., 24 (1957): 2–18.

[34] G. E. Fussell, ed., *Robert Loder's Farm Accounts 1610–1620*, Camden Society, 3d ser., 53 (London, 1936); Lawrence Stone, *The Crisis of the Aristocracy, 1558–1641* (New York, 1965), 295–97; Thirsk, *Agrarian History*, 198.

[35] Compare Bert F. Hoselitz, *Sociological Aspects of Economic Growth* (Glencoe, 1960), 33–34.

[36] 37 Edward 3, c.6. *A Collection in English of the Statutes now in Force* (London, 1594), fols. 22–23; Calendar of Essex Quarter Session Rolls (microfilm in the University of Wisconsin Library), 4: 228; 17: 124.

[37] Tawney and Power, *Tudor Economic Documents*, 1: 353.

work away from his elders, a man could not independently practice most trades until he had become a master through seven years of apprenticeship. Even then, until he was thirty years old or married, he was supposed to serve some other master of the trade. A typical example is the case of John Pikeman of Barking, Essex, a tailor who was presented by the grand jury because he "being a singleman and not above 25 years of age, does take in work of tailoring and works by himself to the hindrance of other poor occupiers, contrary to the law."[38]

These measures doubtless helped to maintain social stability in the face of a rapid population increase, from under three million in 1500 to a probable four and a half million in 1640 (an increase reflected in the gap between wages and prices).[39] But in its efforts to spread employment so that every able-bodied person would have a means of support, the government in effect discouraged energetic labor and nurtured the workingman's low expectations of himself. By requiring masters to engage apprentices for seven-year terms and servants (in agriculture and in most trades) for the whole year rather than the day, it prevented employers from hiring labor only when there was work to be done and prevented the diligent and effective worker from replacing the ineffective. The intention to spread work is apparent in the observation of the Essex justices that labor by the day caused "the great depauperization of other labourers."[40] But labor by the year meant that work could be strung out to occupy an unnecessary amount of time, because whether or not a master had enough work to occupy his servants they had to stay and he had to keep them. The records show many instances of masters attempting to turn away a servant or apprentice before the stipulated term was up, only to have him sent back by the courts with orders that the master "entertain" him for the full period.[41] We even have the extraordinary spectacle of the runaway master, the man who illegally fled from his servants and thus evaded his responsibility to employ and support them.[42]

In pursuit of its policy of full employment in the face of an expanding population, the government often had to create jobs in cases where society offered none. Sometimes men were obliged to take on a poor boy as a servant whether they needed him or not. The parish might lighten the burden by

[38] April 1594. Calendar of Essex Quarter Sessions Rolls, 16: 165. See also the indictment (1589) of four bachelors for taking up the trade of poulterer, which "hindreth other powre men." *Ibid.*, 15: 54. While the statute seems to allow single men and women under thirty to set up in trade unless their services are demanded by a master, the courts, in Essex County at least (where the earliest and most extensive records are preserved), required such persons to find themselves a master. Moreover, the court was already issuing such orders before the statute of 1563. See *ibid.*, 1: 85, 116.
[39] See note 28.
[40] Calendar of Essex Quarter Sessions Rolls, 4: 128.
[41] For examples: William LeHardy, ed., *Hertfordshire County Records*, 5 (Hertford, 1928): 191–92, 451; E. H. Bates, ed., *Quarter Sessions Records for the County of Somerset*, 1, Somerset Record Society, 23 (London, 1907), 11–12, 21; B. C. Redwood, ed., *Quarter Sessions Order Book 1642–1649*, Sussex Record Society, 54 (1954). 34, 44, 46, 128, 145–46, 188, 190.
[42] For examples: *Hertfordshire County Records*, 5: 376; *Quarter Sessions Records for Somerset*, 1: 97, 193, 258, 325.

paying a fee, but it might also fine a man who refused to take a boy assigned to him.[43] To provide for men and women who could not be foisted off on unwilling employers, the government established houses of correction in every county, where the inmates toiled at turning wool, flax, and hemp into thread or yarn, receiving nothing but their food and lodging for their efforts. By all these means the government probably did succeed in spreading employment. But in the long run its policy, insofar as it was effective, tended to depress wages and to diminish the amount of work expected from any one man.

Above and beyond the idleness and underemployment that we may blame on the lethargy and irresponsibility of underpaid labor, on the failure to synchronize the performance of related tasks, and on the policy of spreading work as thinly as possible, the very nature of the jobs to be done prevented the systematic use of time that characterizes modern industrialized economies. Men could seldom work steadily, because they could work only at the tasks that could be done at the moment; and in sixteenth- and seventeenth-century England the tasks to be done often depended on forces beyond human control: on the weather and the seasons, on the winds, on the tides, on the maturing of crops. In the countryside work from dawn to dusk with scarcely an intermission might be normal at harvest time, but there were bound to be times when there was very little to do. When it rained or snowed, most farming operations had to be stopped altogether (and so did some of the stages of cloth manufacture). As late as 1705 John Law, imagining a typical economy established on a newly discovered island, assumed that the persons engaged in agriculture would necessarily be idle, for one reason or another, half the time.[44]

To be sure, side by side with idleness and inefficiency, England exhibited the first signs of a rationalized economy. Professor J. U. Nef has described the many large-scale industrial enterprises that were inaugurated in England in the late sixteenth and early seventeenth centuries.[45] And if the development of systematic agricultural production was advancing less rapidly than historians once supposed, the very existence of men like Robert Loder, the very complaints of the idleness and irresponsibility of laborers, the very laws prescribing hours of work all testify to the beginnings of a rationalized economy. But these were beginnings only and not widely felt. The laborer who seemed idle or irresponsible to a Robert Loder probably did not seem so to himself or to his peers. His England was not a machine for producing wool or corn. His England included activities and pleasures

[43] Bates, *Quarter Sessions . . . Somerset*, 114, 300; Redwood, *Order Book* (Sussex), 96, 146, 194; W. L. Sachse, ed., *Minutes of the Norwich Court of Mayoralty*, Norfolk Record Society, 15 (Norwich, 1942), 78, 216.
[44] Coleman, "Labour in the English Economy"; E. P. Thompson, "Time, Work Discipline, and Industrial Capitalism"; Keith Thomas, "Work and Leisure in Pre-Industrial Society," *Past and Present*, no. 29 (1964): 50–66.
[45] J. U. Nef, *The Conquest of the Material World* (Chicago, 1964), 121–328.

and relationships that systematic-minded employers would resent and that modern economists would classify as uneconomic. At the opening of the seventeenth century, England was giving him fewer economic benefits than she had given his grandfathers so that he was often ready to pull up stakes and look for a better life in another county or another country.[46] But a life devoted to more and harder work than he had known at home might not have been his idea of a better life.

PERHAPS WE MAY now view Jamestown with somewhat less surprise at the idle and hungry people occupying the place: idleness and hunger were the rule in much of England much of the time; they were facts of life to be taken for granted. And if we next ask what the settlers thought they had come to America to do, what they thought they were up to in Virginia, we can find several English enterprises comparable to their own that may have served as models and that would not have led them to think of hard, continuous disciplined work as a necessary ingredient in their undertaking.

If they thought of themselves as settling a wilderness, they could look for guidance to what was going on in the northern and western parts of England and in the high parts of the south and east.[47] Here were the regions, mostly wooded, where wastelands still abounded, the goal of many in the large migrant population of England. Those who had settled down were scattered widely over the countryside in isolated hovels and hamlets and lived by pasture farming, that is, they cultivated only small plots of ground and ran a few sheep or cattle on the common land. Since the gardens required little attention and the cattle hardly any, they had most of their time to themselves. Some spent their spare hours on handicrafts. In fact, they supplied the labor for most of England's minor industries, which tended to locate in pasture-farming regions, where agriculture made fewer demands on the inhabitants, than in regions devoted to market crops. But the pasture farmers seem to have offered their labor sporadically and reluctantly.[48] They had the reputation of being both idle and independent. They might travel to the richer arable farming regions to pick up a few shillings in field work at harvest time, but their own harvests were small. They did not even grow the wheat or rye for their own bread and made shift to live in hard times from the nuts and berries and herbs that they gathered in the woods.

[46] On the geographical mobility of the English population, see E. E. Rich, "The Population of Elizabethan England," *Economic History Review*, 2d ser., 2 (1949–50): 249–65; and Peter Laslett and John Harrison, "Clayworth and Cogenhoe," in H. E. Bell and R. L. Ollard, eds., *Historical Essays 1600–1750 Presented to David Ogg* (New York, 1963), 157–84.

[47] This paragraph and the one that follows are based on the excellent chapters by Joan Thirsk and by Alan Everitt, in Thirsk, *Agrarian History*.

[48] Thirsk, *Agrarian History*, 417–29; Joan Thirsk, "Industries in the Countryside," in F. J. Fisher, ed., *in the Economic and Social History of Tudor and Stuart England* (London, 1961), 70–88. See also E. L. Jones, "Agricultural Origins of Industry," *Past and Present*, no. 40 (1968): 58–71. Lawrence Stone, "An Elizabethan Coalmine," *Economic History Review*, 2d ser., 3 (1950): 97–106, especially 101–02; Thirsk, *Agrarian History*, xxxv, 111.

Jamestown was mostly wooded, like the pasture-farming areas of England and Wales; and since Englishmen used the greater part of their own country for pasture farming, that was the obvious way to use the wasteland of the New World. If this was the Virginians' idea of what they were about, we should expect them to be idle much of the time and to get grain for bread by trading rather than planting (in this case not wheat or rye but maize from the Indians); we should even expect them to get a good deal of their food, as they did, by scouring the woods for nuts and berries.

As the colony developed, a pasture-farming population would have been quite in keeping with the company's expectation of profit from a variety of products. The Spaniards' phenomenal success with raising cattle in the West Indies was well known. And the proposed employment of the settlers of Virginia in a variety of industrial pursuits (iron works, silk works, glass works, shipbuilding) was entirely fitting for a pasture-farming community. The small gardens assigned for cultivation by Governor Dale in 1614 will also make sense: three acres would have been far too small a plot of land to occupy a farmer in the arable regions of England, where a single man could handle thirty acres without assistance.[49] But it would be not at all inappropriate as the garden of a pasture farmer. In Virginia three acres would produce more than enough corn to sustain a man for a year and still leave him with time to make a profit for the company or himself at some other job—if he could be persuaded to work.

Apart from the movement of migrant workers into wastelands, the most obvious English analogy to the Jamestown settlement was that of a military expedition. The settlers may have had in mind not only the expeditions that subdued the Irish[50] but also those dispatched to the European continent in England's wars. The Virginia Company itself seems at first to have envisaged the enterprise as partly military, and the *Lawes Divine, Morall and Martiall* were mostly martial. But the conception carried unfortunate implications for the company's expectations of profit. Military expeditions were staffed from top to bottom with men unlikely to work. The nucleus of sixteenth-century English armies was the nobility and the gangs of genteel ruffians they kept in their service, in wartime to accompany them into the field (or to go in their stead), in peacetime to follow them about

---

[49] Hamor, *True Discourse*, 16–17; Peter Bowden, in Thirsk, *Agrarian History*, 652. It is impossible to determine whether the settlers had had direct experience in pasture farming, but the likelihood that they were following familiar pasture-farming procedures and may have been expected to do so by the company is indicated by the kind of cattle they brought with them: swine, goats, neat cattle, and relatively few horses. When they proposed to set plows going, they were to be drawn by oxen as was the custom in pasture-farming areas. In arable farming areas it was more common to use horses. The company's concern to establish substantial herds is evident in the *Lawes Divine, Morall and Martiall* in the provisions forbidding slaughter without government permission.

[50] See Howard M. Jones, *O Strange New World* (New York, 1964), 167–79; David B. Quinn, "Ireland and Sixteenth Century European Expansion," in *Historical Studies, Papers Read at the Second Conference of Irish Historians* (London, 1958); *The Elizabethans and the Irish* (Ithaca, 1966), 106–22. Professor Quinn and Professor Jones have both demonstrated how the subjugation of Ireland served as a model for the colonization of America. Ireland must have been in the minds of many of the settlers at Jamestown.

as living insignia of their rank.[51] Work was not for the nobility nor for those who wore their livery. According to the keenest student of the aristocracy in this period, "the rich and well-born were idle almost by definition." Moreover they kept "a huge labor force . . . absorbed in slothful and parasitic personal service." Aside from the gentlemen retainers of the nobility and their slothful servants the military expeditions that England sent abroad were filled out by misfits and thieves whom the local constables wished to be rid of. It was, in fact, government policy to keep the able-bodied and upright at home and to send the lame, the halt, the blind, and the criminal abroad.[52]

The combination of gentlemen and ne'er-do-wells of which the leaders at Jamestown complained may well have been the result of the company's using a military model for guidance. The Virginia Company was loaded with noblemen (32 present or future earls, 4 countesses, 3 viscounts, and 19 barons).[53] Is it possible that the large number of Jamestown settlers listed as gentlemen and captains came from among the retainers of these lordly stockholders and that the rest of the settlers included some of the gentlemen's personal servants as well as a group of hapless vagabonds or migratory farm laborers who had been either impressed or lured into the enterprise by tales of the New World's abundance? We are told, at least, that persons designated in the colony's roster as "laborers" were "for most part footmen, and such as they that were Adventurers brought to attend them, or such as they could perswade to goe with them, that never did know what a dayes work was."[54]

If these men thought they were engaged in a military expedition, military precedent pointed to idleness, hunger, and death, not to the effective organization of labor. Soldiers on campaign were not expected to grow their own food. On the other hand they *were* expected to go hungry often and to die like flies even if they never saw an enemy. The casualty rates on European expeditions resembled those at Jamestown and probably from the same causes: disease and undernourishment.[55]

But the highest conception of the enterprise, often expressed by the leaders, was that of a new commonwealth on the model of England itself.

[51] W. H. Dunham, *Lord Hastings' Indentured Retainers 1461–1483*, Connecticut Academy of Arts and Sciences, *Transactions*, 39 (New Haven, 1955); Gladys S. Thompson, *Lords Lieutenants in the Sixteenth Century* (London, 1923); Stone, *Crisis of the Aristocracy*, 199–270.

[52] Stone, *Crisis of the Aristocracy*, 331; Lindsay Boynton, *The Elizabethan Militia 1558–1638* (Toronto, 1967); Thompson, *Lords Lieutenants*, 115.

[53] Stone, *Crisis of the Aristocracy*, 372. About fifty per cent of the other members were gentry. See Theodore K. Rabb, *Enterprise and Empire: Merchant and Gentry Investment in the Expansion of England 1575–1630* (Cambridge, Mass., 1967).

[54] Smith, *Travels and Works*, 2: 486–87.

[55] The expedition of the Earl of Essex in 1591 to assist Henry IV of France met with only a few skirmishes, but only 800 men out of 3,400 returned. Thompson, *Lords Lieutenants*, 111. Even the naval forces mustered to meet the Armada in 1588 suffered appalling losses from disease. In ten of the largest ships, in spite of heavy replacements, only 2,195 out of the original complement of 3,325 men were on the payroll by September. The total loss was probably equal to the entire original number. Lawrence Stone, "The Armada Campaign of 1588," *History*, 29 (1944): 120–43, especially 137–41.

Yet this, too, while it touched the heart, was not likely to turn men toward hard, effective, and continuous work.[54] The England that Englishmen were saddled with as a model for new commonwealths abroad was a highly complex society in which the governing consideration in accomplishing a particular piece of work was not how to do it efficiently but who had the right or the duty to do it, by custom, law, or privilege. We know that the labor shortage in the New World quickly diminished considerations of custom, privilege, and specialization in the organization of labor. But the English model the settlers carried with them made them think initially of a society like the one at home, in which each of them would perform his own special task and not encroach on the rights of other men to do other tasks. We may grasp some of the assumptions about labor that went into the most intelligent planning of a new commonwealth by considering Richard Hakluyt's recommendation that settlers include both carpenters and joiners, tallow chandlers and wax chandlers, bowyers and fletchers, men to rough-hew pike staffs and other men to finish them.[57]

If Jamestown was not actually troubled by this great an excess of specialization, it was not the Virginia Company's fault. The company wanted to establish at once an economy more complex than England's, an economy that would include not only all the trades that catered to ordinary domestic needs of Englishmen but also industries that were unknown or uncommon in England: a list of artisans the company wanted for the colony in 1611 included such specialists as hemp planters and hemp dressers, gun makers and gunstock makers, spinners of pack thread and upholsterers of feathers.[58] Whatever idleness arose from the specialization of labor in English society was multiplied in the New World by the presence of unneeded skills and the absence or shortage of essential skills. Jamestown had an oversupply of glassmakers and not enough carpenters or blacksmiths, an oversupply of gentlemen and not enough plowmen. These were Englishmen temporarily baffled by missing links in the economic structure of their primitive community. The later jack-of-all-trades American frontiersman was as yet unthought of. As late as 1618 Governor Argall complained that they lacked the men "to set their Ploughs on worke." Although they had the oxen to pull them, "they wanted men to bring them to labour, and Irons for the Ploughs, and harnesse for the Cattell." And the next year John Rolfe noted that they still needed "Carpenters to build and make Carts and Ploughs, and skilfull men that know how to use them, and traine up our cattell to draw them; which though we indeavour to effect, yet our want of experience brings but little to perfection but planting Tobacco."[59]

---

[54] For typical statements implying that Virginia is a new commonwealth on the English model, see the *Lawes Divine, Morall and Martiall*, 47–48; Robert Johnson, *The New Life of Virginia*, in Force, *Tracts*, 1, no. 7: 17–18.
[57] Taylor, *Writings of the two Richard Hakluyts*, 2: 323, 327–38.
[58] Alexander Brown, *The Genesis of the United States* (Boston, 1890), 1: 469–70.
[59] Smith, *Travels and Works*, 2: 538, 541.

TOBACCO, AS WE KNOW, was what they kept on planting. The first shipload of it, sent to England in 1617, brought such high prices that the Virginians stopped bowling in the streets and planted tobacco in them. They did it without benefit of plows, and somehow at the same time they managed to grow corn, probably also without plows. Seventeenth-century Englishmen, it turned out, could adapt themselves to hard and varied work if there was sufficient incentive.

But we may well ask whether the habits and attitudes we have been examining had suddenly expired altogether. Did tobacco really solve the labor problem in Virginia? Did the economy that developed after 1618 represent a totally new set of social and economic attitudes? Did greater opportunities for profit completely erase the old attitudes and furnish the incentives to labor that were needed to make Virginia a success? The study of labor in modern underdeveloped countries should make us pause before we say yes. The mere opportunity to earn high wages has not always proved adequate to recruit labor in underdeveloped countries. Something more in the way of expanded needs or political authority or national consciousness or ethical imperatives has been required.[60] Surely Virginia, in some sense, became a success. But how did it succeed? What kind of success did it have? Without attempting to answer, I should like very diffidently to offer a suggestion, a way of looking ahead at what happened in the years after the settlement of Jamestown.

The founders of Virginia, having discovered in tobacco a substitute for the sugar of the West Indies and the silver of Peru, still felt the lack of a native labor force with which to exploit the new crop. At first they turned to their own overpopulated country for labor, but English indentured servants brought with them the same haphazard habits of work as their masters. Also like their masters, they were apt to be unruly if pressed. And when their terms of servitude expired—if they themselves had not expired in the "seasoning" that carried away most immigrants to Virginia—they could be persuaded to continue working for their betters only at exorbitant rates. Instead they struck out for themselves and joined the ranks of those demanding rather than supplying labor. But there was a way out. The Spanish and Portuguese had already demonstrated what could be done in the New World when a local labor force became inadequate: they brought in the natives of Africa.

For most of the seventeenth century Virginians were unable to compete for the limited supply of slaves hauled across the ocean to man the sugar plantations of the Americas. Sugar was a more profitable way to use slaves than tobacco. Moreover, the heavy mortality of newcomers to Virginia

---

[60] Moore, *Industrialization and Labor*, 14–47; Melville J. Herskovits, "The Problem of Adapting Societies to New Tasks," in Bert F. Hoselitz, *The Progress of Underdeveloped Areas* (Chicago, 1952), especially 91–92. See also William O. Jones, "Labor and Leisure in Traditional African Societies," Social Science Research Council, *Items*, 23 (1968): 1–6.

made an investment in Africans bound for a lifetime more risky than the same amount invested in a larger number of Englishmen, bound for a term that was likely to prove longer than a Virginia lifetime.

But Virginians continued to be Englishmen: the more enterprising continued to yearn for a cheaper, more docile, more stable supply of labor, while their servants loafed on the job, ran away, and claimed the traditional long lunch hour. As the century wore on, punctuated in Virginia by depression, discontent, and rebellion, Virginia's position in the market for men gradually improved: the price of sugar fell, making it less competitive with tobacco; the heavy mortality in the colony declined, making the initial outlay of capital on slaves less risky; and American and European traders expanded their infamous activities in Africa. The world supply of slaves, which had fallen off in the second quarter of the seventeenth century, rose sharply in the third quarter and continued to rise.[61]

With these developments the Virginians at last were able to acquire substitute natives for their colony and begin, in their own English way, to Hispanize Virginia. By the middle of the eighteenth century Africans constituted the great majority of the colony's entire labor force.[62] This is not to say that plantation slavery in Virginia or elsewhere can be understood simply as a result of inherited attitudes toward work confronting the economic opportunities of the New World. The forces that determined the character of plantation slavery were complex. But perhaps an institution so archaic and at the same time so modern as the plantation cannot be fully understood without taking into consideration the attitudes that helped to starve the first settlers of the colony where the southern plantation began.

[61] On the last point, see Philip D. Curtin, *The Atlantic Slave Trade: A Census* (Madison, 1969), 119. I hope to deal elsewhere with the other developments that brought slavery to Virginia.
[62] In 1755 the total number of white tithables in the colony was 43,329, of black tithables 59,999. Evarts B. Greene and Virginia D. Harrington, *American Population before the Federal Census of 1790* (New York, 1932), 150–51. Tithables were white men and black men and women over sixteen. Black women were tithable because they were made to work like men.

Perspectives in American History, New Series, I, 1984.

BLACK LIFE IN
EIGHTEENTH-CENTURY CHARLESTON

Philip D. Morgan

IN 1777 a Frenchman arrived in Charleston to begin a five-month tour of the American colonies. He was immediately struck by the demeanor of the city's slaves, which contrasted sharply with that of French West Indian bondmen with whom he was familiar. "The Anglo-American slaves," he observed, "have a peculiar kind of pride and bearing; without degenerating into insolence, it at least gives the impression that they regard a man who is not their master simply as a man, not a tyrant." In contrast to St. Domingue, where slaves were prompt to salute any white man and received blows "without murmur," these Anglo-American slaves impressed the traveler by their "proud bearing or serenity in the presence of a white man."[1]

Apparently, Charleston's slaves did not act like slaves. They were not servile; they were proud, haughty, self-confident. Perhaps urban life served to undermine the traditional disciplines of slavery. Perhaps urbanization loosened the restraints of bondage to the point where the sense of racial order was imperiled. Perhaps slavery was in jeopardy in Charleston around 1777. Hindsight, on the other hand, invests these speculations — and the traveler's remarks — with considerable irony, for the supposedly cowed slaves on St. Domingue would soon rise up in the most successful slave revolt in the New World, while Charleston's haughty slaves were not able, even during the turmoil of the Revolutionary War, to mount any real opposition to the established order. There appears to be a paradox here worthy of investigation.

The author wishes to thank the American Association for State and Local History for its support.
    1. *On the Threshold of Liberty: Journal of a Frenchman's Tour of the American Colonies in 1777,* ed. and trans. Edward D. Seeber (Bloomington, Ind., 1959), pp. 14–15. Although the author seems to be referring to all Anglo-American slaves and although his journal is less a travel account than a travel reminiscence, this description of slaves in the context of a discussion of Charleston is not, in my view, accidental.

187

TABLE 1

The Population of Charleston at Selected Points in the Eighteenth Century

Social groups	1720[a]	1760[b]	1770[b]	1790[c]	1800[c]
Black slaves	1,390	4,451	5,833	7,684	9,819
Free blacks	—	23	24	586	1,024
Whites	1,415	4,124	5,030	8,089	9,626
Totals	2,805	8,598	10,887	16,359	20,469
Percentage black	49	52	54	51	53
Percentage of lowcountry black population in town	12	8	9	10	10

[a] Peter H. Wood, *Black Majority: Negroes in Colonial South Carolina from 1670 through the Stono Rebellion* (New York, 1974), pp. 146–147.
[b] Office of Public Treasury, General Tax Receipts and Payments, 1760–1770 (South Carolina Department of Archives and History, Columbia).
[c] U.S. Bureau of the Census, First and Second Censuses.

I

The demography of eighteenth-century Charleston was disquieting to many of its white residents. For most of the century, blacks congregated in larger numbers and in a more confined space in this one city than anywhere else on the North American mainland. By about 1720 when Charleston crossed the urban "threshold" of 2,500 inhabitants, the town boasted a sizable concentration of about 1,400 blacks.[2] Subsequently, eighteenth-century Charleston always contained a black majority (see Table 1). In 1775 Charleston's black population stood at over 6,000 — more than one and a half times the size of the combined black populations of Boston, New York, and Philadelphia.[3] In another generation, despite the severe losses of the Revolutionary War, the city's black population almost doubled. In 1800 it stood at 11,000.

Since the city served as a mecca and entrepot for a wide variety of transient bondmen, the black presence was even more imposing to the casual eye than the resident totals would indicate. On the eve of the American Revolution the city's 6,000 or more resident blacks were probably aug-

2. Penelope J. Corfield, *The Impact of English Towns 1700–1800* (Oxford, 1982), p. 6.
3. For the black population of northern cities see Gary B. Nash, "Forging Freedom: The Emancipation Experience in the Northern Seaport Cities 1775–1820," in *Slavery and Freedom in the Age of the American Revolution*, ed. Ira Berlin and Ronald Hoffman (Charlottesville, Va., 1983), p. 5.

mented, at any one time, by an additional 1,000 to 1,500 transient slaves.[4] Since some whites left the city in the summer months, it is perhaps not so surprising that visitors calculated that blacks outnumbered whites by as many as three or four to one.[5]

Had any of Charleston's residents been able to assess the city's population structure in more measured fashion, their unease might have been somewhat allayed. First, the black population in Charleston was not growing faster than in the hinterland. In 1720 about one in ten lowcountry blacks lived in town; this proportion remained relatively constant throughout the rest of the century (see Table 1). Second, most lowcountry parishes were overwhelmingly black; from a regional perspective, Charleston was distinctive for having only a slight black majority. No lowcountry parish could claim as high a proportion of nonslaveholding whites as could be found in the city. In the late eighteenth century their share of the city's white population stood at over one quarter.[6] Third, the vast majority of urban slaves, unlike those in the neighboring countryside, were owned in small groups (see Table 2). Blacks were widely distributed throughout households and lived side by side with whites. Masters were therefore in a strong position to monitor and control their slaves' activities. Finally, urban whites were not confronted with a disproportionate share of single, restless, male slaves: in fact, by the middle of the century, black women outnumbered men—and this in a society where there was a shortage of black women (see Table 3).[7]

II

If the demography of Charleston could simultaneously produce unease and offer reassurance, the same might be said of the town's economy. The

4. This estimate is based on the number of Africans and resident slaves put up for sale in the city in an average month (about 600), the number of runaways in town (estimated by one observer in 1772 at 200), and the errand boys, messengers, boatmen, fishermen, market vendors, invalids in the city hospitals, and apprentices who were temporarily to be found in the town, which I estimate at anywhere from 200 to 400.

5. T. P. Harrison, "Journal of a Voyage to Charleston in So. Carolina by Pelatiah Webster in 1765," *Publications of the Southern History Association* (Washington, D.C., 1898), II, 134; "Charleston, S.C., in 1774 as Described by an English Traveller," *South Carolina Historical Magazine*, 9 (1865): 34. The Frenchman thought the ratio was seven or eight blacks to one white: *On the Threshold of Liberty*, p. 13. Just before the Revolution, some Charlestonians began to summer on the adjoining islands and in the northern colonies. See Carl Bridenbaugh, *Myths and Realities: Societies of the Colonial South* (Baton Rouge, La., 1952), pp. 95–96.

6. For demographic data on the lowcountry countryside, see my "Black Society in the Lowcountry 1760–1810," in Berlin and Hoffman, *Slavery and Freedom*, pp. 85–96.

7. Women outnumbered men in eighteenth-century English towns. See Corfield, *Impact of English Towns*, p. 99.

TABLE 2

Pattern of Slaveowning in Charleston, 1730–1800

| | Size of Estate | | | | | Number |
Years	1–9	10–19	20–29	30–49	50 +	of Slaves
1730s	73	18	10	—	—	197
1740s	60	40	—	—	—	471
1750s	35	48	18	—	—	699
1760s	55	33	9	3	—	1222
1770s	43	46	8	3	—	1324
1780s	48	31	16	5	—	1329
1790	46	41	10	3	—	7684
1790s	46	43	9	2	—	1475
1800	46	36	12	5	1	9819

SOURCE: Records of the Secretary of the Province, 1730–1736; South Carolina Inventory Books II to CC; and Charleston District Inventory Books vols A, B, and C (South Carolina Department of Archives and History, Columbia); together with U.S. Bureau of the Census, First and Second Censuses.

TABLE 3

The Structure of the Slave Population in Charleston, 1730–1799

Sex and Age Ratios	1730s	1740s	1750s	1760s	1770s	1780s	1790s
Men/women	1.02	1.11	0.87	0.94	1.12	0.97	0.89
Children/women	1.11	1.08	1.06	1.17	0.96	1.12	1.24
Boys/girls	1.38	1.24	1.02	1.30	1.39	1.05	1.15
Old men/old women	0.40	0.83	0.83	1.07	0.53	0.49	0.87
Number of slaves	197	471	699	1,222	1,324	1,329	1,475

SOURCE: Same as Table 2.

near-monopoly of certain activities by blacks, their persistent attempts to enlarge upon their economic independence, their alleged abuse of their earning and spending powers brought them into considerable conflict with urban whites. And yet, at the same time, these hard-won occupational opportunities, the advantages and privileges they brought in their wake, the measure of freedom involved in hiring and living out were highly valued by slaves. The latitude extended to, and assumed by, urban blacks offered them a stake, however tenuous, in the established order. This double-edged quality to the black role in Charleston's economic life can be illustrated in many ways.

Perhaps the greatest economic opportunity for urban blacks lay in the system of "self-hire" or "hiring out," as it was known. There were two ways to rent out the services of slaves in the eighteenth century. In one, masters were responsible for the hire arrangement; in the other, the slave was given permission to market his or her services. Neither system was common in rural areas but the second was almost exclusively urban. Of the first type, perhaps the most common form in town was the renting out of porters and laborers. Indeed, by the latter half of the eighteenth century, the rates of porterage and the locations of porters' stands were public knowledge. But even then, moonlighting was always possible. A slave named Ishmael, belonging to James Laurens, seems to have taken advantage of this opportunity, for he "brought in 30/- said he had earned as a Porter." Henry Laurens, who was responsible for renting out Ishmael's services, gave him "the Money together with a Reprimand which [Ishmael] thought a good Couplet."[8] "Self-hire" made sense where the slave offered a specialized service and was in constant demand. Such was the case with a painter who "very often undertakes jobs of his own head" or a pilot who "hired himself out, particularly in carrying vessels up the river." On the eve of the Revolution, ten percent of Savannah's adult black population were said to "live by themselves & allow their master a certain sum p. week"; the proportion was probably much higher in the more economically developed city of Charleston.[9]

Slaves who "hired their own time" had a considerable measure of independence. Required by their masters to pay a certain sum of money either weekly or monthly, they could save or freely spend whatever they earned above the stipulated amount. In addition, masters were not too particular about how their slaves acquired their wages. Female market vendors, for example, were said to "buy and sell on their own accounts, what they please, in order to pay their wages, and get as much more for themselves as they can; for their owners care little, how their slaves get the money, so they

8. Commissioners for regulating and taking care of the streets of Charlestown, *South Carolina Gazette* (hereafter, *SCG*), August 25 and October 8, 1764; Henry Laurens to James Laurens, July 2, 1775, Henry Laurens Papers (South Carolina Historical Society, Charleston).

9. Rawlins Lowndes, *South Carolina Gazette and Country Journal* (hereafter, *SCG & CJ*), January 30, 1770; Elizabeth Tucker, *South Carolina and American General Gazette* (hereafter, *SC & AGG*), August 5, 1768; Rev. Samuel Frink to Society for the Propagation of the Gospel, July 8, 1771, C/Am/8/51 (SPG Archives, London).

are paid." Such slaves inhabited a veritable "twilight zone" between bondage and freedom. Consider, for example, the quandary of a Savannah resident who, in 1784, assumed responsibility for a female slave who had been hired out in Charleston. In a letter to a Charlestonian, he declared that he had "no objection to send for her here [because] I know she is capable, but I presume [she] has been so long her own Mistress, and so attached to Caro'a that she woud with great reluctance come here."[10]

From the masters' perspective, slaves who "hired their own time" had opportunities not only to exploit, but also to abuse, their economic situation. Two examples will suffice to suggest this potential. In 1759 the friends of Thomas Sacheverelle had made a practice of crediting his slave Thom for articles the bondman had purchased out of his own earnings. "To free himself from such debts," Thom began defrauding his master of "a good deal of money." In order to put a halt to this practice, Sacheverelle declared that all sales must stop and that he be informed of all work agreements entered into by his slave. Apparently, Thom was still to be allowed to handle money. Some forty years later, another master faced another kind of common difficulty. His gifted twenty-three-year-old slave was "a very excellent and expeditious Taylor, can cut out and take measure; is also a very smart and capable Waiting Man, can shave and dress, has occasionally worked as a Jobbing Carpenter, and at building Clay Houses . . . and will do as much of any thing he knows in a given time, as any black man in the country." He was only offered for sale because his master was "obliged to hire him out, and the fellow having the handling of so much money, has of late been several times in liquor."[11] What is interesting here is that the master saw no alternative but sale for the wayward slave who "hired his own time."

Many slaves who marketed their own services also lived beyond the purview of whites. Although the 1740 slave act specifically prohibited the

10. The "Stranger," *SCG*, September 24, 1772; J. Clay to R. Deane, April 24, 1784, *Collections of the Georgia Historical Society*, 8 (1913): 212. As early as 1698 an act for the better ordering of slaves referred to the practice of "self-hire" and the problems it created; MSS Acts no. 168 (South Carolina Department of Archives and History, Columbia).

11. Thomas Sacheverelle, *SCG*, October 6, 1759; Bartholomew Carroll. *City Gazette*, June 24, 1800. Advertisements for slaves who were "abusing" their "self-hire" arrangements were frequent. In July 1798, for example, a slaveowner in Prince William Parish offered a $100 reward for information concerning his runaway slave woman, Pleasant. She had been "permitted last summer and winter to hire herself in Charleston, [but] her conduct was so remiss in neglecting to pay her wages, that in February last she was ordered home." Pleasant, however, failed to comply with the order and managed to conceal herself in the city for at least six months. William Smith, *South Carolina State Gazette* (hereafter, *SC State Gazette*), July 21, 1798.

renting of rooms, houses, or stores to slaves, the practice persisted. According to the "Stranger," "many rooms, kitchens, &c. are hired to or for the use of slaves in this town; and, by such slaves, let to others, in subdivisions, which serve as places of concealment for run-aways, stolen goods, &c." A fire which broke out in Meeting Street in 1772 consumed "some wooden buildings . . . inhabited by Negroes," which were more than likely the homes of slaves who paid a double rent—not just for their dwellings but also for the use of their own time and effort. The same was probably true of the fire that occurred in Anson Street in 1805 which razed a small grocery shop and "a number of small huts adjoining, occupied by negroes." And even where "self-hired" slaves did not live in rented houses of their own, they possessed a measure of flexibility in their living arrangements unavailable to most other slaves. Thus, a slave carpenter, who was "in possession of a ticket by which he was authorized to work at his trade in Charleston," lived for the most part "at the house in Broad St. of Mr. Blakeley, to whom his wife belongs."12

Urban artisans, particularly those who effected their own hiring arrangements, had access to money and goods well beyond the expectation of any rural slave. The earning power of an urban slave can occasionally be measured precisely. For example, before leaving South Carolina (which he did on May 23, 1759), Benjamin Stead, a Charleston merchant, directed that his slave Bevis be freed as soon as he could produce £500 (South Carolina currency) "from the profits arising from his labour." This, Bevis was able to do by January 15, 1762. By her will dated February 23, 1763, Elizabeth Akin ordered that her mulatto slave John Gough should have his freedom as soon as he paid £250 to her executors. He accomplished this within nine months. He, in turn, received the sum of £50 "to enable him to purchase Tools, that he might get his livelihood by his Trade."13 The skilled slave who could clear a profit of £250 in 1760 would have produced enough money to buy a prime African slave.

Although manumissions were never numerous in the eighteenth-century

12. Thomas Cooper and David J. McCord, eds., *The Statutes at Large of South Carolina* (Columbia, S.C., 1836–1841), VII, 412–413; The "Stranger," *SCG*, September 24, 1772; *SC & AGG*, January 14, 1771; *Charleston Courier*, June 17, 1805 (these references are probably not to outbuildings or kitchens, where most slaves lived. For such references, see *SCG*, August 20, 1763; Jonathan Scott, *SC & AGG*, January 19, 1776); Jacob Drayton, *City Gazette*, July 25, 1797.

13. Benjamin Stead's deed of manumission to Bevis, January 15, 1762, Miscellaneous Records, LL, 495–496 (South Carolina Archives); (Stead's departure is mentioned in *SCG*, May 26, 1759); Elizabeth Akin's deed of manumission to John Gough, November 21, 1763, *ibid.*, MM, 7–8. All sums of money will be given in terms of South Carolina currency, unless otherwise stated. The rate of exchange averaged around £700 per £100 sterling for the half-century before the Revolution.

lowcountry, a significant proportion involved urban slaves who purchased themselves for considerable sums of money. Thus, in 1773 George Flagg, a painter, freed his slave Friday on receipt of £1,000. Four years later a slave woman bought herself for the same sum "being the earnings and gains arising from her labours and Industry from time to time . . . allowed to carry on and transact."[14] Slaves might employ white intermediaries as well as contract directly with their masters. David Brown, a shipwright, declared that he had bought a slave woman, "but the Principal part of the Purchase Money . . . was her own Property and by her Delivered to me to Purchase her Freedom." In 1778 John Speid bought a slave woman Betty from Francis Britton for £2,000 "which was her own Money and my name was only made use of for her Benefit."[15]

Slave hawkers, who as early as the 1730s were a prominent feature of town life, also had access to money. In 1733 Negro "Hucksters of corn, pease, fowls, &ca" were to be found both "Night and Day on the several Wharfes, . . . buy[ing] up many Articles necessary for the support of the Inhabitants."[16] Slave peddlers were not only encountered on the wharves but on almost any street corner, hawking everything from cakes, tarts, confectionary, and bread to cooked rice, milk, fruit, oysters, fish, vegetables, chestnuts, even sand.[17] Most of these slaves ostensibly peddled just their masters' goods, but buying produce on their own account, trading with other slaves, and selling their own wares (such as provisions, for slaves were "suffered to cook [and] bake") also encroached upon their primary duties. Moreover, by the late eighteenth century, slaves held their own unofficial

14. George Flagg's deed of manumission to Friday, July 21, 1773, Miscellaneous Records, PP, 568–569; Alexander Hewat's deed of manumission to Diana, April 16, 1777, *ibid.*, SS, 49–50. For an analysis of lowcountry manumissions on the question of self-purchase, see my "Black Society," p. 116 and Larry D. Watson, "The Quest for Order: Enforcing Slave Codes in Revolutionary South Carolina, 1760–1800" (PhD diss., University of South Carolina, 1980), p. 170.

15. David Brown's deed of manumission to Doll, May 18, 1765, Miscellaneous Records, MM, 276–277; John Speid's deed of manumission to Betty, September 29, 1778, *ibid.*, RR, 572.

16. Presentments of the Grand Jury for Charlestown, *SCG*, March 30, 1734. See also Mr. Watson, *ibid.*, July 16, 1737; George Austin, *ibid.*, December 29, 1737; James Taylor, *ibid.*, March 29, 1746; Elizabeth Bullock, *ibid.*, December 6, 1751.

17. For one reference to each item, see Eliza Johnson, *SCG & CJ*, September 30, 1766; Ichabod Attwell, *State Gazette of South Carolina* (hereafter, *State Gazette of SC*), February 13, 1786; Frederick Smith, *Royal Gazette*, December 26, 1781; Claudius Gaillard, *City Gazette*, August 16, 1790; Presentments of the Grand Jury of Charlestown, *SCG*, May 24, 1773; Leonard Graves, *SCG & CJ*, January 27, 1767; Richard Powers, *SCG*, February 26, 1753; Margaret Remington, *SC & AGG*, January 19, 1776; Caspar C. Schutt, *SC State Gazette*, February 10, 1796; John-Crew Robinson, *et al.*, *SCG*, October 8, 1772; Timothy and Mason, *SC State Gazette*, October 15, 1796; John Gensel, *Charleston Courier*, February 10, 1803.

Sunday market on South Bay.[18] These opportunities for blacks posed problems for whites: forestalling, selling at "exorbitant prices," trafficking with "Country Negroes," harboring runaways—all were complaints leveled at black hucksters.[19]

Once public markets were established, blacks soon came to dominate them. The lower market (on the Bay), which was founded in 1739 primarily as a meat market, was a particular haunt of slave vendors. By the middle of the century advertisements for slave runaways occasionally refer to a sighting in the lower market or to a slave with specialized butchering skills.[20] In 1772 two Charleston residents observed that "the Butchering Business in the Lower Market of Charles-Town has for many years past been carried on by Negroes." In the same year the "Stranger" attributed the "exorbitant prices" at the lower market to the virtual monopoly exerted by "black butchers."[21] Butchering was obviously a lucrative business. In 1755 Susannah Jones freed her slave, "commonly called & known by the name of Abraham Jones," because of his "long and faithful service" to her and because he paid her £300. A year later, Abraham Jones, now described as a free black butcher, purchased his son Jacob for £200 and set him free. In 1757 Mathew Daniels, another free black butcher, freed his wife Betty and their three children after purchasing them for £700.[22]

18. Presentments of the Grand Jury of Charles Town, *SCG*, January 25, 1770; *ibid.*, *SCG & CJ*, June 20, 1775; Presentments of the Grand Jury for the District of Charlestown, *State Gazette of SC*, June 20, 1791.

19. Carl Bridenbaugh, *Cities in Revolt: Urban Life in America 1743–1776* (New York, 1955), p. 82; Presentments of the Grand Jury for the Province, *SCG*, November 5, 1737; Presentments of the Grand Jury, *ibid.*, November 5, 1744. See also the section on female market vendors below.

20. On Charleston's markets, see Carl Bridenbaugh, *Cities in the Wilderness: The First Century of Urban Life in America 1625–1742* (New York, 1938); pp. 193, 351, 352; and Bridenbaugh, *Cities in Revolt*, p. 80; and George C. Rogers, Jr., *Charleston in the Age of the Pinckneys* (Norman, Okla., 1969), pp. 86–87. For the pertinent runaway advertisements, see, for example, Samuel Smith, *SCG*, May 1, 1744; Samuel Smith, *ibid.*, February 1, 1746; John Wilson, *ibid.*, January 19, 1760; Stephen Miller and Isaac Legare, *ibid.*, August 17, 1765; George Saxby, *SCG & CJ*, April 18, 1769.

21. Francis Rivers and Robert Farquhar, *SCG & CJ*, February 4, 1772; The "Stranger," *SCG*, September 24, 1772. A runaway was taken up at the lower market (Workhouse, *ibid.*, October 13, 1767); and a Negro man was stabbed by a Negro butcher there (*City Gazette*, August 14, 1790).

22. Susannah Jones's deed of manumission to Abraham Jones, 1755, Miscellaneous Records, KK, 209–211; Providence Hutchinson's deed of sale to Abraham Jones, April 24, 1756 and Abraham Jones's deed of manumission to Jacob, October 16, 1756, *ibid.*, KK, 405–407; John Edwards' deed of sale to Mathew Daniels, July 7, 1757 and Mathew Daniels' deed of manumission to Betty, Matt, Quash, and Betty, July 12, 1757, *ibid.*, LL, 254–255. For another striking case involving a butcher, see Elizabeth Fidling's deed of manumission to Carolina, February 9, 1768, and Carolina Lamboll's deed of manumission to Jane, January 19, 1779, *ibid.*, RR, 585–586; Carolina Lamboll's deed of manumission to Quash, September 9, 1785, *ibid.*, UU, 427–428; and Carolina Lamboll's deed of manumission to Pompey, October 9, 1784, *ibid.*, VV, 105–106.

Perhaps the most striking figure among Charleston's butchers was a "mustee" slave named Leander. In 1770 he purchased himself for the considerable sum of £900. His white intermediary, Jacob Willeman, observed how this amount "was delivered to [him] by . . . Leander from time to time as Monies which he had by his great care dilligence and industry in his business Trade or Occupation of a Butcher for several years last past got together and Earned."[23] Leander continued to show a keen eye for the main chance. Seven years later, the Commissioners of the Markets were convinced that the "good People of this State are greatly imposed on by Free Negroes who usually attend the Market to sell veal, Mutton, &ca on commission." Consequently, they ordered that no free black or slave could sell any item in the markets without a ticket specifying the sale price. This did not stop Leander who, at about the same time, was tried and convicted of extortion in the lower market for selling veal at 40/- a leg or loin while possessed of a ticket specifying a sale price of 30/-.[24] Apparently, this setback did little to halt Leander's material progress. In 1786, now with the surname Fairchild, Leander had become a slaveowner for, in that year, he freed his slave Robin in return for £45. Four years later, he purchased his daughter and grandson (also named Leander) by making a downpayment of £50 and agreeing to secure the balance by a "mortgage of negros." He subsequently freed these members of his family.[25]

Blacks also dominated the fish market. In 1770 a separate building specializing in the sale of fish was built at the foot of Queen Street. The act regulating this new establishment explicitly acknowledged the preeminent role of blacks: "the business of Fishing," it declared, "is principally carried on by Negroes, Mulattoes, and Mestizoes." Indeed, this had long been the case.[26] An identifiable group of "fishing Negroes" had emerged in the town during the first half of the century. In 1737 a runaway slave was "lately seen with the fishing Negroes, at the Markett place"; three years later, a Charleston resident warned "all Negroes" against carrying her slave, Lancaster, "a Fishing"; and, in 1750, a slave who had been a runaway upward of two years was said to be "harboured by his father Robin,

23. Jacob Willeman's deed of manumission to Leander, October 11, 1770, Miscellaneous Records, OO, 385–386.

24. Commissioners of the Markets, *Gazette of the State of South Carolina* (hereafter, *Gazette of State of SC*), May 5, 1777; *ibid.*, May 12, 1777.

25. Leander Fairchild's deed of manumission to Robin, December 16, 1786, Miscellaneous Records, WW, 346–347; Leander Fairchild's deed of manumission to Nancy and Leander, November 9, 1790, *ibid.*, ZZ, 255.

26. Commissioners of Workhouse and Market, *SCG*, October 25, 1770.

a noted fisherman in this town."[27] Also around midcentury Dr. Alexander Garden's botanical investigations led him to seek the assistance of the city fishermen. This proved frustrating, he reported, because "most or indeed all of them are negroes, whom I find it impossible to make understand me rightly what I want."[28]

This virtual monopoly exercised by slave fishermen proved more than an incidental vexation. According to a white observer in 1772, slave fishermen were able "at their pleasure, to supply the town, with fish or not." He claimed that they could "exact whatever price they think proper, for that easily-procured food"; consequently, the price of drumfish had risen almost tenfold the past decade. The demeanor of a runaway slave who was "carrying on the fishing business between town and James-Island" would only have confirmed the "Stranger"'s worst suspicions. According to his owner, this slave's "insolent behaviour to several, since absent, is known."[29] The independent character of slave fishermen may have rested, in part, on their *de facto* ownership of canoes. According to the "Stranger," many slaves were "permitted to keep boats, canows, &c." One Charleston household boasted three slave fishermen but no boats or canoes, perhaps indicating that they belonged to the slaves. One runaway slave who was "possessed of a canoe" was thought to be fishing in and around the city. In 1778 during the fire of Charleston Elkanah Watson observed how "every vessel, shallop, and negro-boat was crowded with the distressed inhabitants."[30]

Slaves also dominated the local maritime and riverine traffic centered on Charleston. Schooner services either linking inland plantations and towns to Charleston or connecting it to contiguous coastal towns were operated very largely by slaves. A Camden merchant in the late eighteenth

27. Kennedy O'Brien, *SCG*, November 5, 1737; Elizabeth Smith, *ibid.*, December 25, 1740; John McQueen, *ibid.*, January 15, 1750. See also David Arnett, *ibid.*, November 5, 1737 and Christopher Holson, *ibid.*, September 15, 1758.

28. Garden to Mr. Ellis, March 25, 1755 in *A Selection of the Correspondence of Linnaeus and other Naturalists, from the original manuscripts*, comp. James Edward Smith (London, 1821), I, 349.

29. The "Stranger," *SCG*, September 24, 1772; Paul Hamilton, *SC & AGG*, November 18, 1780. See also Nathaniel Blundell, *SCG*, February 26, 1763; James Steven, *ibid.*, June 15, 1765; *SCG & CJ*, February 18, 1766; Thomas Patterson, *SC & AGG*, December 30, 1774; George Sommers, *SCG & CJ*, January 3, 1775; Benjamin Simons, *SC & AGG*, May 1, 1776; John M'Ilraith, *ibid.*, July 30, 1779; Benjamin Mazyck, *ibid.*, July 30, 1779; Thomas Corbett, Jr., *SCG*, March 7, 1799; John Roberts, *City Gazette*, March 14, 1799; Mr. Belzon, *ibid.*, July 11, 1799.

30. The "Stranger," *SCG*, September 24, 1772; inventory of Daniel Chopard, August 3, 1770, Inventory Book Y, 306–307 (South Carolina Archives); and his estate, *SCG*, August 30, 1770; Henry Osborne, *City Gazette*, April 7, 1794; Elkanah Watson, *Men and Times of the Revolution* (New York, 1856), p., 45.

century referred to a boat coming up from Charleston that had "only negros on board"; the Duc de La Rochefoucauld-Liancourt mentioned that the crews on the Savannah-Charleston packets in the early national era were comprised mostly of slaves.[31] About a fifth of the skilled posts occupied by urban slaves involved work on water, either as sailors, boatmen, pilots, or fishermen (see Table 4).

Not surprisingly, these were the occupational groups that produced the most runaways. A slave like Scipio, aged about fifty years, and said to be "plausible and sensible," probably did not agonize long over his decision to abscond from his boat while it was in the city and "engage with some [other] boat or fisherman." He was, after all, as his master put it, "very knowing by water and an exceeding good Boatman, having been many years a patroone [helmsman]." Similarly, absenteeism probably held few terrors for an accomplished slave like Jamaica-born Charles, aged about twenty-eight, a "compleat waiting man and as compleat a seaman as any Negro can be," a man who had been on two voyages to England and was "most of the last war a french-horn man."[32] The resourcefulness of Abraham, a member of a lowcountry schooner's crew, was most impressive. "After skulking about town some time, and actually hiring himself as a free seaman with a Capt. Allen," Abraham learned, according to his master, that he was "advertised [as a runaway] by beat of drum." Consequently, he shipped himself aboard Mr. Thomas Waring's sloop, which was destined for Port Royal, in the hope that he might reach St. Augustine. However, at Port Royal Creek he was "discovered" (presumably as a runaway) by the "black patroon," who handed him over to the master of a packet sloop bound for Charleston. However, Abraham was not so easily thwarted. He stole a boat from the sloop and "escaped to Mr. Goven's on St. Helena Island, where giving out that he was going to Major Butler's he left the boat, and has not been heard of since."[33]

All-slave crews with black coxswains at the helm became regular targets of complaint in the countryside. In 1762 residents of one Cooper River parish pointed out that "divers boats [were] plying there having only slaves go in them by which all manner of pilfering was facilitated." Three years

31. John Chesnut to Robert Henry, April 15, 1794, John Chesnut Letterbook (Library of Congress); François Alexandre Frédéric, duc de la Rochefoucauld Liancourt, *Travels through the United States of North America . . .* , (London, 1799), I, 618. A number of boating accidents involved blacks: *State Gazette of SC*, December 29, 1785; *ibid.*, March 6, 1786; *Charleston Courier*, May 19, 1807; *ibid.*, August 11, 1807.
32. James Donnom, *SCG & CJ*, November 11, 1766; Hugh Hughes, *ibid.*, January 21, 1772.
33. James Parsons, *SC & AGG*, August 21, 1777.

TABLE 4

Occupation among Male Slaves belonging to Charleston Residents, 1730–99

	Iᵃ	Rᵇ		I	R
Tradesmen	201 (54%)	102 (32%)	Specialist Tradesmen	37 (10%)	62 (19%)
carpenter	73	17	barber	9	10
cooper	33	12	painter	8	6
shoemaker	24	17	caulker	4	2
bricklayer	22	13	ship carpenter	4	8
taylor	12	8	ropemaker	2	–
blacksmith	7	5	baker	3	4
tanner	7	6	silversmith	2	–
butcher	7	4	gunsmith	1	–
sawyer	6	8	chimney sweep	1	–
sadler	5	6	brazier	1	–
wheelwright	4	3	potter	1	–
currier	1	3	brickmaker	1	–
Watermen	75 (20%)	114 (36%)	cabinetmaker	–	7
boatman	64	43	doctor	–	4
fisherman	8	6	sailmaker	–	3
pilot	3	3	distiller	–	2
sailor	–	62	house carpenter	–	2
Household slaves	44 (12%)	23 (7%)	chairmaker	–	1
waiting man	22	11	goldsmith	–	1
cook	8	3	jeweller	–	1
house slave	5	2	self-hired	–	11
gardner	4	2	Semiskilled slaves	15 (4%)	19 (6%)
waiter	3	–	laborer	11	–
coachman	2	4	porter	3	5
drummer	–	1	marketman	1	6
			shop assistant	–	2
			carter	–	6
			Total	372	320

ᵃ I (Inventoried sample) is same as in Table 2.
ᵇ R (Runaway sample) is from Charleston Library Society, South Carolina Newspapers, 1732–82 (microfilm) (The Johns Hopkins University, Baltimore). For the years after 1782: extant issues of the *South Carolina Weekly Gazette* (1783–86), *South Carolina Gazette and General Advertiser* (1783–85), *Gazette of the State of South Carolina* (1783–85), *Columbian Herald* (1784–89), *State Gazette of South Carolina* (1785–89), *Charleston Morning Post* (1786–87), and *City Gazette* (1787–89), Charleston Library Society, Charleston, S.C.; and microfilm copies of *State Gazette of South Carolina* (1790–1802), *City Gazette* (1790–1801), *Columbian Herald* (1790–96), *Columbia Gazette* (1794), *Charleston Courier* (1803–6), and *Times* (1803), University of South Carolina, Columbia.

later a Savannah River planter reported a theft from his plantation and attributed it to the "common practice for trading boats and others to land their people, and remain whole nights and days on the plantation." In 1767 inhabitants from many parts of South Carolina objected to the practice of the Comptroller of H.M. Customs in issuing permits, "several of which are to common Negro slaves," thereby affording "a Shelter for illicit traffick."[34] Nobody had a kind word for "Boat Negroes."

Even the specialized economic activities of the city were infiltrated by blacks. Skilled artisan workshops like that of gunsmiths, silversmiths, goldsmiths, cabinetmakers, and chairmakers employed slaves.[35] Shipbuilding and ship repairing were heavily reliant on slave labor: so much so that some shipwrights petitioned for relief from this black competition.[36] The city's Grand Jurors thought it "a very great GRIEVANCE" that "the manufacturing of Candles and Soap in Charles Town" was "generally left to Negroes by Night as well as by Day."[37] The carrier of the *South Carolina Gazette,* the bell-ringer at the parish church, and the fiddler at the young ladies' and gentlemen's dancing school were all slaves.[38] Even medical expertise could be claimed by urban slaves. Perhaps in some cases this came from working for white specialists—a slave who had been "brought up by [a] Doctor from a Boy to tend in his Shop" was said to be "capable of performing many Cures"—but others probably drew more on their native traditions.[39] An Ibo slave named Simon was said to be "well known in town and country and pretends to be a doctor"; another was said to "give himself out for a DOCTOR"; a third passed "for a Doctor among people of his color, and it is supposed practices in that capacity about town."[40]

Slave women enjoyed much wider occupational opportunities in town than in the countryside. Certainly most female slaves, even in town, held menial, unrewarding positions; but, by the middle of the century, per-

34. Several of the inhabitants of the parish of St. Thomas and St. Dennis, *SCG,* April 3, 1762; John Stevens, *Georgia Gazette,* June 27, 1765; remonstrance of divers inhabitants of the Province of South Carolina to Mark Robinson; November 1767, Garth Papers (South Carolina Historical Society).

35. For one example of each, see John Dodd, *SCG,* October 11, 1770; inventory of Andrew Dupey, September 10, 1743, Inventory Book WPA 115, 317–318; Jacob Valk, *SC & AGG,* February 5, 1778; John Pacerow, *Gazette of State of SC,* August 12, 1778; John Fisher, *SC & AGG,* February 21, 1781.

36. Carl Bridenbaugh, *The Colonial Craftsman* (New York, 1950), p. 140; Richard B. Morris, *Government and Labor in Early America* (New York, 1946), p. 184; Joseph A. Goldenberg, *Shipbuilding in Colonial America* (Charlottesville, Va., 1976), pp. 63–65.

37. Presentments of the Grand Jury for Charlestown, *SCG,* October 31, 1774.

38. The Printer, *SCG,* June 14, 1740 (see also The Printer, *City Gazette,* July 1, 1797); Gilbert Chalmers, *SCG,* September 8, 1785; Elias Bate, *ibid.,* November 8, 1751.

39. Mary-Magdalen Schwartzkopff, *SCG,* September 17, 1772. Perhaps this was the same slave who ran away from Jacob-Nicholas Schwartzkopff in 1771 and was said to be "well known, especially among the negroes, being employed by them as a Doctor," *SCG,* January 3, 1771.

40. Jacob Martin, *SCG,* October 9, 1749; Jacob Valk, *Gazette of State of SC,* May 12, 1777; James George, *City Gazette,* June 19, 1797.

haps as many as a quarter of them served in specialized roles as house servants, seamstresses, cooks, or washerwomen (see Tables 5 and 6). The role of a washerwoman was hardly glamorous, but it afforded a measure of independence from white owners and provided some companionship with fellow blacks. In 1743 one slave woman was described as having "been

TABLE 5

Occupations among Female Slaves belonging to Charleston Residents, 1730–99

	I	R
House slave	35	4
Washerwoman	30	7
Cook	30	2
Seamstress	21	4
Marketwoman	—	9
Self-hired	—	4
TOTAL	116	30

SOURCE: Same as Table 4.

TABLE 6

Skilled Slaves among Adult Slaves belonging to Charleston Residents, 1730–99

	I			R		
	skilled	adults	%	skilled	adults	%
men						
1730s–50s	61	117	52%	56	156	36%
1760s–70s	146	217	67%	145	320	45%
1780s–90s	165	245	67%	119	279	43%
women						
1730s–50s	13	93	14%	6	84	7%
1760s–70s	40	165	24%	18	93	19%
1780s–90s	63	170	37%	8	107	7%

SOURCE: Same as in Table 4.

used to wash and iron in houses in this Town." Presumably, she went from house to house carrying out her task. In 1775 a slave named Chloe belonging to James Laurens was required to "work at a stated Washerwoman's & to bring in her Wages weekly 30/ per Week & maintain Stepny [her son]."[41] The presence of separate "negro washing-houses" also created covert opportunities for runaway slave women. One slave mother, seven months pregnant, and with a thirteen-year-old boy and five-year-old girl in tow, was thought to be working among the "negro washing-houses or kitchens" because she had formerly done so for "23 months together." Similarly, an African-born woman managed to stay at large for at least two years, even though her master knew "she had been in Charleston the greatest part of her time since her absence, passes for a free wench, and it is said washes and irons for a livelihood."[42]

A large proportion of the market vendors were women. Typical were John Stanyarne's Bella, "well known in Charles Town, being almost every day at Market selling divers Things"; or Margaret Remington's Phillis and Elsey, "well known in town, having been used to sell oysters for these 13 years past"; or Eliza Hill's Peg, who "walked the streets with a tray on her head with peaches."[43] So ubiquitous did such women become that the Charleston Grand Jury was provoked in 1768 to complain of the "many idle Negro wenches, selling dry goods, cakes, rice, &ca in the markets," while in 1779 it was "the excessive number of Negro Wenches, suffered to buy and sell about the streets, corners and markets of Charlestown" that proved particularly offensive. So powerful was their influence that even a runaway boy was thought to have "been decoyed and harboured by some of the huckster wenches."[44] But the best description of their activities comes from the "Stranger," who commented at length on the slave women to be found around the town's lower market. They were

seated there from morn 'til night, and . . . [had] such a connection with, and influence on, the country negroes who come to that market, that they generally find means to ob-

41. Mrs. Flavell, *SCG*, October 24, 1743; Henry Laurens to James Laurens, July 2, 1775, Laurens Papers.

42. Stephen Hartley, *SCG.*, October 13, 1757; Henry Bell, *State Gazette of SC*, August 14, 1786. See also Mary Ellis, *SCG*, February 3, 1757; Thomas Ladson, *SC & AGG*, May 1, 1776; William Hort, *Gazette of State of SC*, June 16, 1777. "Hiring out" as a seamstress was also quite common. See, for example, Richard Park Stobo, *SCG*, March 21, 1761; Peter Timothy, *SCG & CJ*, May 20, 1766.

43. John Stanyarne, *SCG*, November 10, 1746; Margaret Remington, *ibid.*, November 25, 1777; Eliza Hill, *City Gazette*, September 2, 1793.

44. Presentments of the Grand Jury of the Province, *SC & AGG*, January 29, 1768; Presentments of the Grand Jury of Charlestown District, *ibid.*, December 3, 1779; William McKimmy, *ibid.*, August 27, 1778.

tain whatever they may chuse, in preference to any white person; and thus they forestall and engross many articles, which some few hours afterwards you must buy from them at 100 or 150 per cent advance. I have known those black women to be so insolent, as even to wrest things out of the hands of white people, pretending they had been bought before, for their masters or mistresses, yet expose the same for sale again within an hour after, for their own benefit. I have seen the country negroes take great pains, after having been first spoke to by those women, to reserve whatever they chose to sell to them only, either by keeping the particular articles in their canows, or by sending them away, and pretending they were not for sale; and when they could not be easily retained by themselves, then I have seen the wenches so briskly hustle them about from one to another, that in two minutes they could no longer be traced. I have seen these very negro women surround fruit-carts, in every street, and purchase amongst them, the whole contents, to the exclusion of every white person.[45]

Urban slaves, but especially women, were singled out for their "excessive and costly apparel" and for the "extravagance of their dress," further testimony to their earning power. A Charleston domestic was said to "dress . . . gay at times"; a seamstress was "very fond of dressing well, wears her hair very long, and has appeared lately in mourning clothes for the death of her mother"; while the owner of a runaway sail-maker simply pointed out that his slave's dress "excels that of his Master."[46] Urban slave women were particularly noted for "dress[ing] in Apparel quite gay and beyond their condition." If the wardrobe of one runaway who escaped from her Charleston home in October 1784 was typical one begins to see why. She carried "all her cloaths among which were a jacket shift, and apron of new white linen, a black callimanco petticoat, a blue Negro cloth coat, and do. jacket with red neck binding, a new check apron, two coats of red furniture check much faded; her other aprons, jackets and shifts, making in the whole six suits, were osnabrugs and dowlas; also two new blankets, and two old, with four handkerchiefs."[47] A collection of clothes like this helps explain a mysterious report "in general circulation" in September 1793, which stated that "authorized persons are going about this city for the purpose of depriving negroes of their clothes."[48]

45. The "Stranger," *SCG*, September 24, 1772. A more positive comment on a female market vendor, but one that confirms her independence, comes from an advertisement of sale for a "market woman who has never failed in the regular payment of her weekly wages." James O'Hear, *City Gazette*, April 27, 1795.

46. Presentments of the Grant Jury of Charlestown, *SCG*, June 3, 1774; *ibid.*, May 24, 1773; Joseph Wigfall, *Royal Gazette*, October 24, 1781; Thomas Farr, *SC & AGG*, November 4, 1780; Patrick Byrne, *City Gazette*, July 19, 1797.

47. Presentments of the Grand Jury, *SCG*, November 5, 1744; James Thompson, *Gazette of State of SC*, November 18, 1784. A runaway man was actually seen in woman's clothes: James Smith, *SC & AGG*, February 11, 1779.

48. *City Gazette*, September 2, 1793.

III

Precisely because the city generated opportunities, urban blacks attracted a more intense opposition and hostility from whites than their rural counterparts ever faced. This was as true of their social activities as of their economic experiences. The vaunted flexibility of urban slavery provoked, at best, a continuous stream of complaints and, at worst, persistent efforts to curb the social opportunities pursued by blacks. And yet, the flexibility of urban slavery was real. Blacks continued to find ways to circumvent the restrictions imposed on them. Ironically, their hard-won gains served to bind many bondmen to the existing social order.

The relationship between black and white manual workers reflects this ambivalence particularly well. Unlike blacks in the surrounding countryside, Charleston's slaves were thrown into close proximity with large numbers of white mechanics and laborers. It requires no feat of imagination to conceive how this enforced commingling led to hostility. White workers were openly resentful of the competition they faced from their black counterparts. One after another during the course of the century, shipwrights, helmsmen, chimney sweeps, house carpenters, bricklayers, cordwainers, master coopers, painters, glaziers, paperhangers, and master tailors banded together to complain that blacks were taking their jobs.[49] Their inability to halt this process was hardly designed to make them look kindly upon neighboring blacks.

No doubt lower-class whites were primarily responsible for much of the random violence to which urban blacks were subject. Presumably the lower orders comprised the majority of the town watchmen who, on more than one occasion, drew the fire of town authorities for their "disorderly behaviour." One time, the charge was specific: the watchmen were accused of "beating and abusing Negroes sent on Errands by their Masters with Tickets."[50] Boston King, born a lowcountry slave in about 1760, was a personal witness to such abuse. His most vivid memories of his early life in South Carolina concern his four-year apprenticeship in Charleston. During

49. The story of these groups' resentments is told, in fragmented fashion, in the secondary literature. See Bridenbaugh, *Cities in the Wilderness*, p. 359 and *Cities in Revolt*, p. 88; Morris, *Government and Labor*, pp. 184–185; Bridenbaugh, *Colonial Craftsmen*, pp. 140–141; Winthrop D. Jordan, *White Over Black: American Attitudes Toward the Negro, 1550–1812* (Chapel Hill, N.C., 1968), p. 406; and Marina Wikramanayake, *A World in Shadow: The Free Black in Antebellum South Carolina* (Columbia, S.C., 1973), p. 101.

50. Presentments of the Grand Jury, *SCG*, January 25, 1772.

that time, he suffered a series of beatings at the hands of his tradesman master. On one occasion, King incurred the wrath of a white journeyman who accused him of theft. For the offense, King recollected, "I was beat and tortured most cruelly, and was laid up three weeks before I was able to do any work."[51]

The natural hostility that arose between lower-class whites and blacks was not, however, implacable. Divisions within the ranks of white mechanics, for instance, presented opportunities to blacks. The more successful craftsmen who employed slaves felt much less threatened by black competition. The response of a group of master shipwrights to others of their trade who had complained about the black economic threat was probably typical. They declared that "his Majesty's ships have been repaired and refitted only by the assistance of Our slaves, And . . . without these slaves the worst consequences might ensue." Even a house painter who hoped to recommend himself to potential customers with the news that he would not "trust to Negroes (which is too common) to perform the finishing part of the Business," was at the same time advertising for "two smart Negro Boys . . . as Apprentices." Another Charleston painter was much more positive about his slaves' abilities, for they had, he noted proudly, "transacted the Whole of his Business, without any hired Assistance." Timothy Ford claimed that barbers were "supported in idleness & ease by their negroes who do the business; and in fact many of the mechaniks bear nothing more of their trade than the name."[52]

Some white artisans, by freeing their slaves, were directly responsible for producing the very competitors at which their fellow tradesmen railed. Richard Lampert, a white wheelwright, seems to have been instrumental in creating a family of free black wheelwrights, also with the surname Lampert.[53] Hugh Cartwright, a successful bricklayer, was responsible for enabling Thomas Cole, his former slave, to establish himself as a free black

51. "Memoirs of the Life of Boston King, a Black Preacher," *Methodist Magazine*, 21 (1798): 106. See also the behavior of a printer toward his slaves: Christopher Gould, "Robert Wells, Colonial Charlestown Printer," *South Carolina Historical Magazine*, 79 (1978): 27.

52. J. H. Easterby, ed., *Journal of South Carolina Commons House of Assembly September 14, 1742–January 27, 1744* (Columbia, S.C., 1954), pp. 547–550; Mr. Booth, *SCG*, March 22, 1773; John Allwood, *ibid.*, March 8, 1773; Joseph W. Barnwell, ed., "Diary of Timothy Ford, 1785–1786," *South Carolina Historical Magazine*, 13 (1912): 142

53. Richard Lampert's deed of manumission to Kingston Lampert, October 30, 1750 and subsequent oath, January 23, 1751, Miscellaneous Records, HH, 381–383; Robert Wells's deed of sale to John Lampert, November 4, 1760, *ibid.*, LL, 577. See also John Lampert's deed of manumission to George, April 10, 1782, *ibid.*, TT, 128–129.

bricklayer. After his master's death, Cole engaged Cartwright's former attorney to help him purchase his wife and two children.[54]

Other lower-class whites actively undermined the traditional disciplines of slavery. Some employed blacks illegally. Joseph Tobias harbored three slaves belonging to George Marshall for two months in 1766. Marshall not only claimed the loss of their labor but also argued that "by keeping the evil and vicious company of him the said Joseph," his slaves had "contracted a habit of Laziness Idleness & wickedness which will forever hereafter render" them unprofitable. A generation later, the master of a runaway slave made public his suspicions "that there are certain despicable characters in this city who harbour and encourage the desertion of negroes from their owners; and by furnishing them with tickèts in their master's name render their recovery extremely difficult."[55] Some whites participated in crimes with blacks. Poor dram-shop keepers were prepared to break the law by selling liquor to slaves — and thereby make a tidy profit. The lower orders might even share the same interests. In 1774 Charleston's public authorities declared a Mr. Gordon "a Mountebank" and a "public Nuisance and Deluder of the lower and Ignorant Part of the Community" because his "Exhibitions not only lead White People but great Numbers of slaves to Idleness and Dissipation."[56]

An urban milieu obviously facilitated more fraternization among blacks than was possible in the countryside. While blacks made the most of these opportunities, white hostility mounted. In 1712 legislation was directed against the numerous slaves who entered Charleston on Sundays and holidays in order to "drink, quarrel, fight, curse and swear and profane the Sabbath . . . resorting in great companies together." By the 1730s and 1740s it was the "disorderly" assembling, "caballing," and "rioting" of urban blacks themselves that provoked alarm. A gathering of blacks one Sunday evening in 1732 when "nigh 200 Negroes met together on the Greene" was particularly newsworthy because it led to the stabbing of a valuable

54. John Rattray's deed of manumission to Thomas Cole, August 20, 1755, Miscellaneous Records, KK, 205; Benjamin Smith's deed of manumission to Ruth, Tom, and Barbary, May 5, 1763, *ibid.*, LL, 603–604.

55. Charles Fraser Commonplace Book, p. 59 (and see also p. 49) (College of Charleston); Henry Gibbes, *State Gazette of SC*, March 4, 1790.

56. Presentments of the Grand Jury of Charlestown, *SCG*, February 28, 1774. On crimes and dram-shop keepers, see below. The fears of the town authorities concerning the fraternization of poor whites and blacks in late colonial Charleston is discussed in Walter J. Fraser, Jr., "The City Elite, 'Disorder' and the Poor Children of Pre-Revolutionary Charleston," *South Carolina Historical Magazine*, 84 (1983): 167–179.

black slave.⁵⁷ By 1744 such assemblies had seemingly become more wide-spread, for a city Grand Jury complained of slaves "caballing in great Numbers through most parts of the Town, especially on the Sabbath Day." Twenty years later, the problem had escalated even further, for slaves were said to go "at all times in the night . . . about [the] streets, rioting, [and] . . . often gather in great numbers on the Sabbath Day, & make riots, where it is not in the power of the small number of watchmen to suppress them."⁵⁸ At the root of these complaints lay fears for personal safety, but white sensibilities were also offended. The alleged rowdiness of slaves, their "prophane swearing," their "playing at Dice and other games," and their "talking obscenely in the most public manner" were regular targets of city jurors.⁵⁹ In 1774 the jurors summed up their general grievances by observing that "Negroes in Charles-town are become so obscene in their language, so irregular and disorderly in their conduct, and so superfluous in their Numbers" as to make imperative an act regulating their behavior.⁶⁰

Liquor was more readily available in town than in the countryside. As early as 1693 the governor of South Carolina was complaining of the presence of "very disorderly houses" where "strong liquors" were sold to the lower orders of white society and to "Great numbers of Negroes" who were drawn to town "knowing they can have drinck . . . for mony or what else they bring."⁶¹ By the middle years of the century a variety of incidental references indicates that the problem had magnified. An advertisement for a runaway slave mentioned a sighting at a tavern; a mistress who objected to her hired slave's failure to turn over his wages explained that the money was lost "either by Gaming or spend[ing] among the lettle Punch-Houses"; in 1744 the city Grand Jury named twelve establishments that had been caught "retailing liquors to Negroes"; a few years later a master threatened to prosecute any person who sold liquor to his slave butcher; in 1763 a writer to the *South Carolina Gazette* claimed that the dram-shop owners who sold liquor to slaves had "raised by it in a few years considerable fortunes from the most indigent circumstances."⁶²

57. Cooper and McCord, *Statutes at Large*, VII, 354; presentments of the Grand Jury of Charles-town, *SCG*, March 30, 1734; *ibid.*, March 26, 1737; *ibid.*, November 5, 1737; *ibid.*, November 8, 1742.

58. Presentments of the Grand Jury, *ibid.*, November 5, 1744; *ibid.*, June 2, 1766. For other such complaints, see *ibid.*, April 15, 1745 and May 1, 1756.

59. Presentments of the Grand Jury, *SCG & CJ*, November 17, 1767; *ibid.*, January 25, 1770; *ibid.*, June 20, 1775.

60. *Ibid.*, October 31, 1774.

61. Governor's message, April 10, 1693, Miscellaneous Records of the Secretary of the Province, 1692–1700, 46–47 (South Carolina Archives).

62. James Mathewes, *SCG*, June 5, 1742; Elizabeth Smith, *ibid.*, October 17, 1741; Presentments

On the eve of the Revolution about one in thirteen of all the dwellings in Charleston was a licensed tippling house; and presumably there were others that operated illegally. Well might an owner offer his house servant for sale for "too frequently getting to the Dram-Shops (these too numerous Pests that are a Scandal to this Town, and bid fair to ruin every Black Servant in it)." And well might the "Stranger" report that "at all times, nay, even at noon-day, many dram-shops are crowded with negroes, some of the keepers of which are indeed cautious enough to have private passages for them to enter by.—Shameful inattention!"[63] By the late eighteenth century masters seemed to strike a more matter-of-fact note, as if aware of the intractability of the problem. The following descriptions of runaway slaves suggest as much: "is very fond of rum," "an artful, drunken rascal," "can sing psalms and is a lover of brandy," "is very fond of liquor, went off in a small canoe, and was very drunk at the time," "drinks all the rum he can get," "Boat Fellow, commonly called *Drunken Sandy*."[64]

Opportunities to participate in Anglo-American religious activities were much greater in town than in the countryside. As always, an opportunity for blacks posed a dilemma for whites. The two-edged quality of black religious life in an urban setting is well illustrated in an incident that occurred in the mid-1770s. At this time, at least two blacks associated with the Methodist faith were preaching in Charleston: Thomas, a slave of John Edwards, a Methodist preacher in town, and David, trained in England and sent to the lowcountry by the Countess of Huntingdon. In late 1774 or early 1775 David came close to being lynched. At the house of Patrick Hinds, a noted bootmaker in town, David delivered an inflammatory speech to a group of assembled blacks in which he proclaimed that

the Jews of old treated the Gentiles as Dogs & I am informed the people of this Country use those of my Complection as such[.] I dont mean myself Thank God. I am come from a better Country than this, I mean old England but let them remember that the Children

---

of the Grand Jury, *ibid.*, April 5, 1745; Presentments of the Grand Jury, *ibid*, March 19, 1763. See also Samuel Smith, *ibid.*, January 1, 1752; Presentments of the Grand Jury, *ibid.*, May 1, 1756; *ibid.*, June 2, 1766; *ibid.*, November 17, 1767; *ibid.*, January 29, 1768; *ibid.*, May 17, 1768. Complaints from the 1760s onward were almost annual.

63. Sampson Neyle, *SCG*, April 11, 1771; The "Stranger," *SCG*, September 24, 1772. See Bridenbaugh, *Cities in Revolt*, pp. 227 and 358 for the number of tippling houses and dwellings in late colonial Charleston. See also Robert M. Weir, *Colonial South Carolina: A History* (Millwood, N.Y., 1983), pp. 123 and 170.

64. John Wells, Jr., *SC & AGG*, September 24, 1778; John Walters Gibbs, *ibid.*, November 5, 1778; warden of workhouse, *ibid.*, September 10, 1779; Paul Pritchard, *State Gazette of SC*, June 23, 1785; James Kennedy, *City Gazette*, July 3, 1798; Robert Giles, *ibid.*, September 14, 1799.

of Israel were delivered out of the hands of Pharo and he and all his Host were drowned in the Red Sea and God will deliver his own People from Slavery.[65]

David was quickly hustled out of Charleston to the Bethesda orphanage in Georgia. He still persisted in his "shocking delusion," as one minister termed it, thinking himself "a second moses . . . called to deliver his people from slavery"; whereas his mission, as the local residents conceived it, "was to preach a Spiritual Deliverance to these People, not a temporal one." David's "problem," so one of his colleagues surmised, was that "he can't bear to think of any of his own colour being slaves." Only after David was discreetly shipped back to England did the furor subside.[66]

Later in the eighteenth century the Methodists began to make further headway among the city's blacks. In the mid-to-late 1780s "truly Amazing" reports of black participation in Methodist meetings began to emanate from the city. "Hundreds" of blacks were said to attend their services; one minister reported that "to hear them tell what God has done for their Souls . . . would almost create a Heaven in your soul." In the mid-1790s the Methodist "Society of Blacks" approximated five hundred.[67] At the same time, Methodist successes created problems. In 1793 William Hammett, a Methodist preacher in the city, came face to face with the harsher realities of urban slaveholding. A slaveowner wrote him about her "servant Peggy [who] has done everything bad except beating me"; in retribution, she asked Hammett to deny Peggy the sacrament. Hammett replied that he was "sorry to be informed that any person who partakes of my holy ordinances under my care should act improperly, as it is what I never admit of . . . But as I do not judge prematurely in these cases, I beg the accused and her accuser may be brought before me, and shall act accordingly." As no specific charges were leveled, Hammett reasoned that he had to investigate, but "however well intended my lenity was,"

65. John Edwards to the Countess of Huntingdon, January 16, 1775, A3/6/10, Countess of Huntingdon's American Papers (Westminster College, Cambridge [England]). See also *ibid.*, January 11, 1775, A3/6/9; William Piercey to the Countess of Huntingdon, November 28, 1774, A4/1/9; presentments of the Grand Jury, *SCG*, March 27, 1775.

66. William Piercey to the Countess of Huntingdon, March 25, 1775, A4/2/6; James Habersham to the Countess of Huntingdon, April 19, 1775 and to Robert Keen, May 11, 1775, "Letters of James Habersham," *Collections of the Georgia Historical Society*, VI (1904): 238–244.

67. John Cossom to the Countess of Huntingdon, March 25, 1785, A3/12/19; Thomas Hill to the Countess of Huntingdon, April 12, 1788; A3/12/20; Oliver Hart to J. Hart, April 18, 1785, Oliver Hart Papers (University of South Carolina, Columbia); *Extracts of the Journals of the late Rev. Thomas Coke . . .* (Dublin, 1816), p. 248. See also Journal of George Wells, September 11, December 3, 1791 (Lovely Lane Museum, Baltimore); *The Journal and Letters of Francis Asbury*, ed. Elmer T. Clark (London, 1958), I, 739; II, 6, 78; III, 160.

he continued, "my name was cast out as evil and my note handed about thro' the highest circles of the community, and the worst construction put upon it, . . . even that I put the Maid and Mistress on a footing, and of course intended to introduce equality which would overset slavery." Hammett learned his lesson well. He soon sided with "the highest circles of the community," established a plantation, and stocked it with slaves. As one of his former colleagues acidly put it, "no one was more strenuous against slavery than he, while destitute of the power of enslaving."[68]

If an urban setting facilitated the search for religious passion, it also promoted the gratification of sexual passions. Indeed, the lowcountry capital became renowned for the most openly-displayed interracial liaisons in British North America. As was to be expected of a port, prostitutes (most of whom were probably black) were widely available. A runaway slave man, for example, was said to be "intimate with abundance of black prostitutes" in town, while a slave woman was thought to be harbored in "those houses where sailors frequent."[69] Visitors to Charleston were generally appalled at the level of miscegenation. Johann Bolzius longed "to get out this sinful city [where] . . . [t]he Europeans commit dreadful excesses with the Negro girls"; Henry Muhlenburg found "many blacks who are only half black, the offspring of those white Sodomites who commit fornication with their black slave women."[70] What was most distinctive about Charlestonian attitudes, as Winthrop Jordan has emphasized, was the relatively relaxed view taken of interracial unions. According to Josiah Quincy, "the enjoyment of a negro or mulatto woman is spoken of as quite a common thing: no reluctance, delicacy or shame is made about the matter." An Englishman, who had recently arrived in Charleston, revealed how readily he had adapted to the city's mores when he declared to a friend that there were some blacks who "deserve every attention that can be paid them." A Charleston lady could refer in her diary to "Gentlemen" visiting

---

68. Journal of William Hammett, May 10, 1793 (University of South Carolina); *Journals of Thomas Coke*, p. 217. When Hammett broke away from the orthodox Methodists in the early 1790s, he persuaded twenty-four whites and thirty-five blacks to join him: Thomas Morrell to Ezekiel Cooper, February 20, 1792, Ezekiel Cooper Collection, XV, no. 36 (Garrett Theological Seminary, Evanston, Ill.). Another interesting insight into the opposition faced by Methodists is the treatment meted out to the Rev. George Dougherty in 1800. See James Harper to Ezekiel Cooper, 1800, Ezekiel Cooper Collection, XV, no. 22, and *Journal of Francis Asbury*, II, 266.

69. James Reid, *SCG*, November 14, 1761; Margaret Peronneau, *SC & AGG*, October 15, 1779.

70. George Fenwick Jones, "John Martin Boltzius' Trip to Charleston, October 1742," *South Carolina Historical Magazine*, 82 (1981): 101; *The Journals of Henry Melchior Muhlenberg . . . .*, trans. Theodore G. Tappert and John W. Doberstein (Philadelphia, 1942–1958), I, 58.

"Mulatto Girls." John Davis met some gentlemen on his travels who were "laughing over their nocturnal adventures in *Mulatto Alley* at Charleston."[71]

Since Charlestonians seem to have adopted a benign view of miscegenation, wherein lies the problem? First, we may suspect that the sense of shock registered by so many visitors to Charleston must have been communicated to at least some residents. Indeed, there is evidence that some Charlestonians were themselves dismayed at local behavior. In 1743 the members of one Grand Jury emphatically denounced the "TOO COMMON PRACTICE OF CRIMINAL CONVERSATIONS WITH NEGRO AND OTHER SLAVE WENCHES."[72] Most important, perhaps, while the sexual exploitation of black women was unlikely to produce unease among whites, a world turned upside down, one where black women aspired to a measure of equality with their white counterparts, could never be viewed with equanimity. In 1772 the "Stranger" caustically observed that there was "scarce a new mode [of dress] which favourite black and mulatto women slaves are not immediately enabled to adopt." Ebenezer Hazard seemed most disturbed at the egalitarian implications of the "black dances" that occurred in Charleston, which "many of the first gentlemen (so called) attend" and at which many of the black women "dress elegantly, and have no small acquaintance with polite behaviour." During the Revolutionary War, a Charlestonian found no better illustration of the "shame and perfidy [to which] the Officers of that once great nation (Britain) has arriv'd" then their attendance at "an Ethiopian Ball" where female slaves "dress'd up in taste, with the richest silks, and false rolls on their heads, powder'd up in the most pompous manner." A public investigation followed a "Negro dance" that the Charleston Guard discovered in 1795. Most disturbing was the presence of a white magistrate; indeed, as one of the black women was taken into custody, she handed him "her Head Dress and Bonnet and desired him to take Care of it for her."[73]

71. Jordan, *White Over Black*, pp. 145–147, who quotes Quincy; L. Dalton to Mr. Gibbs, 1796, Miscellaneous Manuscripts (Library of Congress); diary of Catherine De Rosset, July 8, 1798, De Rosset Family Papers (Southern Historical Collection, University of North Carolina, Chapel Hill); John Davis, *Travels of four years and a half in the United States of America* (Bristol, 1803), p. 355. For a reference to a slave woman in Mulatto Alley, see the Charles Fraser Commonplace Book, p. 123.
72. Presentments of the Grand Jury of the Province, *SCG*, March 28, 1743.
73. The "Stranger," *SCG*, September 24, 1772; H. Roy Merrens, "A View of Coastal South Carolina in 1778: The Journal of Ebenezer Hazard," *South Carolina Historical Magazine*, 73 (1972): 190; Daniel Stevens to John Wendell, February 20, 1782, in *Massachusetts Historical Society Proceedings*, 48 (1915): 342; depositions of Peter S. Ryan, William Johnson, James Allison, James McBride, and Henry Moses, November 7, 1795, General Assembly, Governor's Messages, no. 650, November 24, 1795, 9–30 (South Carolina Archives).

Since many sexual encounters between whites and blacks were undoubtedly exploitative in character, wherein were the opportunities for blacks?
They resided in the tangible benefits that at least some black women were
able to extract for their intimacies with whites. George Dick, a mariner,
left all his property to Jenny Dick, a free black, who lived with him as
his servant and to Alexander Dick, his natural son. And if a slave mother
gained nothing for herself, she might still entertain hopes for her children. Take the case of the mulatto slave woman who gave birth to a
Charleston butcher's child. She belonged to Mrs. Frost who refused to
sell the daughter to her white father. The father died in 1740. His plans
for his child did not expire with him; but they had to wait another twenty-six
years, until Mrs. Frost died, before his executors could purchase his daughter,
set her free, and bestow £350 on her, the balance of her father's estate.[74]
A fifth of the more than one thousand slaves who received freedom in
South Carolina between 1760 and 1800 were mulattoes, usually children;
and most of these were freed at the behest of white men.[75]

  · Interracial sexual activity helped, then, to produce a sizable free black
population which, although not exclusively an urban phenomenon, was
predominantly so. In 1790 a third of the province's free blacks resided
in Charleston; and perhaps a half lived in the city and nearby environs.[76]
Free blacks were the most feared and the most privileged segment of the
black population. At one time or another, most of the "problems" associated with urban slaves were attributed to their fraternization with free
blacks. The doubling of the free black population in Charleston during
the 1790s, particularly the introduction of many light-skinned *gens de
couleur* from St. Domingue, alarmed the town authorities.[77] At the same
time, opportunities were quite obviously more available to free blacks than
to slaves: opportunities to organize their own churches, mutual aid societies, and schools, to become slaveholders, to find niches within the economy

---

74. Will of George Dick, October 24, 1773, Charleston County Wills, XV (1771–1774), 609–610
(South Carolina Archives); Robert Raper to Thomas Boone, March 5, 1770, Robert Raper Letterbook
(West Sussex Record Office, England) (on microfilm at the South Carolina Historical Society). See
also will of Abraham Newton, April 8, 1790, Charleston County Wills, XXIII (1786–1793), 635;
Elias Ball's deed of sale to William Ellis, July 9, 1746 and William Ellis' deed of manumission to
William, October 28, 1746, Miscellaneous Records, GG, 75–76.

75. Watson, "Quest for Order," pp. 171–172.

76. Wikramanayake, *A World in Shadow*, pp. 21–22.

77. *Ibid.*, pp. 18, 142, 160, *passim*. See also Ira Berlin, *Slaves Without Masters: The Free Negro
in the Antebellum South* (New York, 1974), part 1.

as hairdressers, pastry cooks, butchers, and the like, and even to serve their country during wartime.[78]

The ambivalent position of free blacks can best be illustrated through two individuals. The first is Thomas Jeremiah or "Jerry," as he was known. Perhaps no eighteenth-century free black took fuller advantage of the opportunities available in an urban setting. He first distinguished himself as a fire fighter, then utilized this public reputation to set himself up as a fisherman, all the while acting as a harbor pilot. By the time of his death, he was a slaveholder and reputed to be worth more than £1,000 sterling. The governor of South Carolina described him as a man "of considerable property, one of the most valuable and useful men in his way in this province." According to a more jaundiced observer, he was "a forward fellow, puffed up by prosperity, ruined by Luxury and debauchery and grown to an amazing pitch of vanity and ambition." His dizzying ascent was brought to an abrupt halt in the summer of 1775 when he was sentenced to death for plotting an insurrection. A harbinger of doom occurred four years earlier when Jerry was convicted of assaulting a white ship captain. Sentenced to one hour in the stocks and ten lashes, Jerry only escaped punishment through the governor's pardon. In 1775 his crime was such that not even the governor's pardon (which was extended) could save him. Whether Jerry actually plotted an insurrection against the state is unclear; he protested his innocence to the last; many prominent whites, including the governor himself, believed him; but there was damning black testimony and apparent perjury from Jerry himself. In a very real sense, however, Jerry's fall can be attributed to his unusually elevated and precarious position within Charleston society. Either this induced him to envisage a role for blacks, one in which he would have "the Chief Command," in the imminent war between Britain and America; or it made him the best available scapegoat for patriot forces who wanted both to intimidate other black harbor pilots and promote military preparedness. Either way, Jerry was a victim of his own success.[79]

78. Wikramanayake, A World in Shadow, pp. 61, 73, 103, 110, and passim; see also Berlin, Slaves Without Masters, part 1.

79. This portrait of Jerry is built from a wide range of primary sources, the most interesting of which is the set of letters exchanged between Henry Laurens, Lord William Campbell, and Alexander Innes, August 1775, in the Laurens Papers. There are two recent secondary accounts of the Jerry "affair." See Peter H. Wood, " 'Taking Care of Business,' " in The Southern Experience in the American Revolution, ed. Jeffrey J. Crow and Larry E. Tise (Chapel Hill, N.C., 1978), pp. 283–287. For a fuller version, and one close to my own interpretation, see Weir, Colonial South Carolina, pp. 200–203.

Of much less public moment, but just as instructive for understanding the daily reality of life for Charleston's free blacks, was an incident involving a free black woman named Mary Edy. On August 30, 1782, around 5 p.m., a squabble developed between Mary Edy and Ann Fowler, a white resident of Queen Street. The dispute became so intense that the two of them spilled out into the street, each striking the other, until passersby finally separated them. Conflicting testimony makes it unclear who was primarily responsible for the affray. At the root of the fracas lay a debt that Mary owed Ann. The latter had apparently detained Mary's eldest girl in order to have it met. If a free black woman's child could be kept from her in this way, this is but one further confirmation of the precarious status of free blacks in the city. At the same time, however, four white witnesses came to Mary's defense. At one trial Ann Fowler's action against Mary Edy for assault was dismissed; the outcome of a second trial, brought in the face of the white woman's charge of judicial favoritism toward a free black, is unknown. At the very least, free blacks were not necessarily without white allies—even on the bench.[80]

Since, among other things, the presence of a relatively large free black population made it easier for slaves to pass as free within the town, Charleston acted as a magnet for runaway slaves. About a quarter of all colonial South Carolina runaway slaves whose destinations were reported in newspaper advertisements were said to be lurking in or making for the city. Certainly, the colonial capital attracted more fugitives than it lost.[81] An opportunity for blacks posed a problem of discipline for whites, since runaways could stay at large for surprisingly long periods within the town. Perhaps the record goes to a slave woman who was absent for at least seven years around the middle of the century. In 1765 her master reported that she now called "herself free Mary and sometimes free Hannah, has [had] three children since her absenting herself, lives in or near Charlestown, takes in washing, was lately seen in the lower market."[82] An advertisement for an urban runaway often included a recent sighting: Chloe had "been

80. Record of Court of Justices and Freeholders in Charlestown, September 19, 1782, and accompanying testimony, Rugeley Papers (Bedford County Record Office, England).

81. Between five and six hundred colonial advertisements reported Charleston as a probable destination (the imprecision reflects those cases where both a possible rural and urban destination were reported). For more quantitative information of this and subsequent points concerning this runaway population, see my "En Caroline du Sud: Marronnage et Culture Servile," *Annales, Economies, Sociétés, Civilisations*, numéro 3 (mai-juin 1982): 574–590.

82. Stephen Miller and Isaac Legare, *SCG*, August 17, 1765. See also, for example, William Bruce, *ibid.*, November 26, 1744; John McQueen, *ibid.*, January 15, 1750; James Irving, *ibid.*, May 4, 1752.

several times seen on board his majesty's ship Mercury"; Nanny was "every night in town"; and Jupiter "was frequently seen in Charleston at Mr Barkers in Friend Street where he has a mother."[83] The failure to apprehend such conspicuous runaways says much about the town's policing powers and the black community's harboring capacities.

Runaway slaves could realistically seek sanctuary within Charleston because of its opportunities for casual employment. Charleston's wharves, its shipping, markets, wash-houses, and kitchens represented varied sources of support for the fugitive slave.[84] In addition, particular social groups were noted for harboring runaways: free blacks were always a target of suspicion; groups of "Jamaica negroes," "Bermuda negroes," and, later in the century, "French negroes" were singled out for taking in their own.[85] But most runaways who headed for Charleston were seeking the support of friends and relatives. The runaway who had "a large acquaintance in town" or "many companions" or "a numerous Acquaintance" was not unusual.[86] Most common of all, however, was the fugitive who was thought to be harbored by an immediate member of his family or a more distant relative — aunts and cousins were suspected on more than one occasion.[87]

One of the problems that contemporaries associated with runaways — and, more generally, with urban places — was a high incidence of crime. One can imagine the embarrassment felt by provincial authorities when they heard of the indignity suffered by a Catawba chief. As a loyal friend to South Carolina, he had brought a number of Tuscarora scalps to Charleston; on his way home, he lay down to sleep just outside the town walls and was promptly robbed by a band of runaway slaves "who lurk

83. Jonathan Scott, *SCG*, September 10, 1763; Leonard Bodell, *ibid.*, March 10, 1764; James Carson, *City Gazette*, June 26, 1797. For similarly precise street or house sightings, see James St. John, *SCG*, September 12, 1741; James Reid, *ibid.*, November 14, 1761; John Mitchell, *SC & AGG*, July 9, 1778; *ibid.*, December 6, 1780; Joseph Wigfall, *Royal Gazette*, September 10, 1782.

84. For an example of each see Catherine Cattell, *SCG*, November 10, 1746; Alex Inglis, *SC & AGG*, June 4, 1778; James Donnom, *SCG*, May 2, 1769; Stephen Hartley, *ibid.*, May 28, 1750; Wellin Calcott, *SC & AGG*, October 5, 1772.

85. For an example of each see Peter Timothy, *SCG & CJ*, May 20, 1766; John Champneys, *ibid.*, March 3, 1772; White Outerbridge, *SCG*, November 27, 1752; David Haig, *City Gazette*, April 13, 1797.

86. Peter Sanders, Jr., *SCG*, November 14, 1761; Smith and Nutt, *ibid.*, November 27, 1762; William Hort, *SCG & CJ*, July 25, 1775. One master "constantly offered among negroes of his [runaway's] acquaintance to forgive him if he returned of his accord": Charles Atkins, *Royal Gazette*, June 20, 1780.

87. For slaves said to have "many relations," see Francis Roche, *SCG*, January 16, 1762; John Chapman, *SCG & CJ*, March 10, 1767; Thomas Patterson, *SC & AGG*, December 30, 1774; William Roberts, *SCG*, March 27, 1775. For slaves said to have aunts, cousins, or both, see Andrew Letch, *SCG*, June 12, 1753; Francis Roche, *SCG & CJ*, October 20, 1767; William M'Donnald, *City Gazette*, March 2, 1797; John Glen, *ibid.*, August 4, 1797.

about the Town, having no fear of being disturb'd by the Patrol."[88] Though there are no available statistics, it seems likely that crime was both more frequent and more organized in town than in the countryside. Two examples—one early and the other late in the century—will make the point. The robbery of £2,000 worth of goods, which occurred in 1735, and the suspected involvement of "a great many Negroes," not to mention whites, was virtually unthinkable outside an urban environment. Similarly, at the end of the century, Charleston authorities were to be found cautioning against "a gang of black house-breakers who now infest the city"; at about the same time, a rash of "daring assaults" and "street robberies" were conducted during daylight hours, perhaps marking Charlestonians' first experiences of street muggings.[89] The capacity of the black underworld to unload stolen goods should not be underestimated, for slaves were caught stealing objects as utilitarian as bricks and firewood, as cumbersome as sails, rigging, and house furniture, and as valuable as watches. One slave even attempted to buy a thousand cigars with a stolen banknote.[90]

The crime that white Charlestonians feared above all else was arson; and lurking behind this spectre was the nightmare of an accompanying rebellion. Alarm bells were set ringing with particular urgency in the early 1740s. The severe fire of November 1740 raised suspicions of slave involvement; rumors reached northern ports of an accompanying insurrection; one Charleston merchant was fearful enough to write his brother in London telling him "of the great Risque we Run from an Insurrection of our Negroes." However, no such insurrection occurred, nor were any slaves implicated in the fire. But nine months later, a slave who was said to look "upon every White Man he should meet as his declared Enemy" was burned alive for allegedly attempting to torch the town.[91] Other scares occurred at regular intervals thereafter. A visitor to Charleston in 1774, for example, was present at a fire which was soon extinguished but observed that "on such occasions the citizenry must also turn out under arms on account

88. *SCG*, July 10, 1736.

89. *SCG*, June 21, 1735; *City Gazette*, September 23, 1800; *Charleston Times*, April 13, December 13 and 17, 1803; *Charleston Courier*, July 13, 1805.

90. Court of Justices and Freeholders, November 19, 1773, Miscellaneous Records, PP, 624; John Marley, *SCG*, November 28, 1761; Parish Transcripts, September 18, 1752 (New York Historical Society); Court of Justices and Freeholders, February 7, 1774, Miscellaneous Records, PP, 652–653; Moses Naur, *City Gazette*, November 21, 1800. But see Bridenbaugh, *Cities in Revolt*, p. 303.

91. *The Letterbook of Robert Pringle*, ed. Walter B. Edgar (Columbia, S.C., 1972), I, 273; *SCG*, August 15, 1741. See also Peter H. Wood, *Black Majority: Negroes in Colonial South Carolina from 1670 through the Stono Rebellion* (New York, 1974), pp. 294–297; Bridenbaugh, *Cities in the Wilderness*, pp. 212, 371–372; Rogers, *Charleston*, pp. 27–28.

of the many Negro slaves who are prone to seize upon such opportunities to rebel." Five years later, a Jamaican-born slave was executed for trying to set fire to the town.[92]

A second major cluster of suspicions arose during the 1790s. The most spectacular incident, one that neatly points up the ambivalence of urban slaveholding, occurred in the summer of 1796. The burning down of three hundred houses produced the usual fears of slave involvement; news even reached a visitor in Philadelphia that the fire was "part of a plan formed by the negro slaves in that state who are said to be ripe for insurrection."[93] At the same time, however, a Charlestonian, while acknowledging that "we are now rather in a critical situation, several attempts to set the Town on fire have been since detected and frustrated, every trifle sets the whole city in an uproar," calmly pointed out that "whites are more suspected as the perpetrators of such dreadful acts than Negroes who are in general very active and clever at an alarm of fire." Indeed, a slave named Will belonging to Major Charles Lining gained his freedom for his part in saving St. Philip's church from the fire of 1796. In fact, blacks had long been used as part of the city's fire-fighting force.[94] The black role in Charleston's fires could therefore range all the way from feared incendiaries to valued fire fighters.

Did the distinctive problems posed by an urban black majority necessitate a strong police force? The evidence is somewhat mixed and contradictory. Certainly, urban masters relied more heavily on public agencies for disciplining their slaves than was possible in the countryside. And these police powers were not negligible. Throughout the eighteenth century Charleston relied primarily on an armed watch to maintain order during the night, when a curfew was imposed on slaves. Initially, the watch consisted of a constabulary and an unpaid, rotating citizen force; but, from 1703 onward (with occasional reversions to the previous system), it was put on more of a military footing, with the appointment of commanders

92. *Journals of Muhlenberg*, II, 593; *Gazette of State of SC*, March 24, 1779.

93. Sir Robert Liston to Lord Grenville, July 6, 1796, MS 5583, f. 35, Sir Robert Liston Papers (National Library of Scotland, Edinburgh). For other 1790s scares, see *City Gazette*, November 22, 1797; J. Alison to Jacob Read, December 5, 1797, Jacob Read Papers (University of South Carolina); Mary Pinckney to Mrs. Manigault, February 5, 1798, Manigault Family Papers (University of South Carolina); *SC State Gazette*, July 6, 1798; *City Gazette*, July 10, 1798.

94. Nathaniel Bowen to Henry Hill, June 17, 1796, Bowen-Cocke Papers (South Carolina Historical Society); record of manumission for Will Philip Lining, Miscellaneous Record Book III (1796–1799), 334–336. For black fire-fighters, see Bridenbaugh, *Cities in Revolt*, p. 105. For a study of Charleston fires in the nineteenth century, see Jane H. Pease and William H. Pease, "The Blood-Thirsty Tiger: Charleston and the Psychology of Fire," *South Carolina Historical Magazine*, 79 (1978): 281–295.

and other ranks and the call for the enlistment of a specified number of civilian watchmen, some of whom had to turn out each night. An annual salary scale was listed for all ranks within the watch. The size and turnout of the watch fluctuated almost yearly, depending in part on the observable foreign threat. For most of the century no more than eighteen men had to turn out on any one night. In fact, this nightly turnout, specified in the act of 1708, was not exceeded until 1769, when it was doubled to thirty-six men. The alarm of 1776 saw this number augmented to fifty-one.[95] In addition, in 1734 two mounted patrols comprising a captain and eight men apiece were hired and paid to ride alternately at weekends and holidays. Six years later these companies were reduced to a captain and five men; and monthly patrol duties were instituted.[96] A third force was occasionally available. As the 1761 act on the town watch noted, "it frequently happens that some Detachment of his Majesty's Regular Troops are Posted in or near Charles town at the Public Barracks." When this happened, the legislators permitted the watch to suspend its duties. A visitor to the city in 1753 observed the presence of a company of regular soldiers, which served to "intimidate the black slaves."[97]

This varied police force was far more imposing in theory than in fact. For one thing, it seems that by the late colonial period the militia rarely patrolled in the city. The armed watch became responsible for discipline on weekends and holidays as well as week nights.[98] This produced much public disquiet, for the watch was not noted for effectiveness or efficiency.

95. The size and turnout of the armed watch can only be gauged by exploring both printed and manuscript acts. The published acts of 1685, 1698, 1701, 1703, 1704, 1708, 1709, 1741, and 1767 are printed in full in Cooper and McCord, *Statutes at Large*, VII, 1, 7, 17, 22, 38, 49, 54; III, 587; IV, 257. See also the 1806 ordinance regulating the city guard in *A Digest of the Ordinances of the City Council of Charleston, From the Year 1783 to October 1844 . . .* (Charleston, 1844), pp. 88-95. The unpublished acts of 1696, 1707, 1713, 1723, 1726, 1733, 1737, 1761, 1769, and 1776 are available at the South Carolina Archives. Also helpful are Bridenbaugh, *Cities in the Wilderness*, pp. 64-67, 215-220, 374-378, and his *Cities in Revolt*, pp. 107-110, 297-299.

96. Cooper and McCord, *Statutes at Large*, III, 398 and 568. See also III, 456, 681; IV, 541; VII, 441; IX, 631-691.

97. An act for establishing, keeping and maintaining the Watch, no. 905, 1761, MSS Acts; Walter L. Robbins, ed. and trans., "John Tobler's Description of South Carolina (1753)," *South Carolina Historical Magazine*, 71 (1970): 146. Reliance on British troops did not necessarily endear them to South Carolinians. In 1757 a British soldier complained of the delays in the construction of a new barracks in Charleston. He pointed out that the residents were "very saving," and added, "they're extremely pleased to have soldiers protect their Plantations, but will feel no inconvenience from them, making no great difference between a soldier and a Negro." Henry Boquet to the Earl of Loudoun, August 25, 1757, Henry Boquet Papers, Add MSS 21631, ff. 71-72 (British Library).

98. Complaints about the watch, which were particularly vociferous in the early 1770s, indicate that it was now the body primarily responsible for keeping order on weekends and holidays.

In 1745 an officer of the watch was reprimanded for "entertaining seamen and Negroes at unseasonable Hours." A generation later, the practice had apparently magnified, for complaints were heard against "the number of Licenses which are annually granted to Watchmen, or their Wives, to keep Dram-Shops, whereby it becomes their Interest to encourage Negroes, and others to frequent their Houses."[99] Most disturbing was the laxness of the watch, recruited largely, it seems, from tradesmen, artificers, and laborers. In 1745 a tavernkeeper in Elliott Street was asked to calculate the time at which the watch passed by his door. He replied that "ever since he lived there, he never remembered to have seen the Guard pass thro' that street." In 1773 the city Grand Jury observed that "it is well known that not one Half of the Number of Men required by Law do attend their Duty on Sunday, and at Night; that in the Afternoon on Sundays the Watch House is frequently shut up and not a Man on Duty." The previous year the watch was accused of failing to confine some slaves who were without tickets, whereby "the Negroes in general disregard them, and if they can but raise the sum of Ten (shillings) to pay for their Release, are not afraid of being out all night."[100] Even when slaves were locked up, their incarceration does not appear to have been very confining. A runaway woman, charged to the Provost Marshall's care in 1731, was said to have "great Liberty in the prison, [she] lived in great plenty and done much work with Needle & has also kept up a constant communication with some country Negroes." Escapes from the public jail and workhouse were not uncommon.[101]

---

99. Presentments of the Grand Jury for the Province, *SCG*, April 15, 1745; *ibid.*, October 29, 1772.
100. *Ibid.*, May 24, 1773; *ibid.*, January 25, 1772. See also *SCG & CJ*, June 20, 1775. Even when the watch did its job, individual masters could still find grounds for complaint. See Thomas Wright, *SCG*, October 30, 1762 and John Remington, *ibid.*, November 6, 1762.
101. South Carolina Assembly Journal, April 2, 1731, CO5 432 (Public Record Office, London). For escapes, see Christopher Holson, *SCG*, September 18, 1762; Roger Pinckney, *ibid.*, December 30, 1766. There is mixed opinion about the effectiveness of Charleston's nineteenth-century police force. Michael Hindus in his comparison of the South Carolina and Massachusetts criminal justice systems stresses Boston's early commitment to a professional police force. Only when whites came into Charleston in sizable numbers in the 1850s did the city establish a comparable force. Until then, all whites had "police powers" over blacks and a professional force was deemed unnecessary. Hindus, *Prison and Plantation: Crime, Justice, and Authority in Massachusetts and South Carolina, 1767–1878* (Chapel Hill, N.C., 1980), pp. xix, 37–39. Jane Pease and William Pease, on the other hand, in their comparison of Charleston and Boston in the 1830s, argue that the civilian watch was much more formidable in Charleston than in Boston precisely because of the presence of black slaves. Jane H. Pease and William H. Pease, "Social Structure and the Potential for Urban Change: Boston and Charleston in the 1830s," *Journal of Urban History*, 8 (1982): 175.

IV

The poor performance of eighteenth-century Charleston's guardians of the peace raises in acute form the paradox with which this essay began. Were the instruments of social control in a parlous state in Charleston in the late eighteenth century? Had the "free air" of city life effectively undermined the traditional disciplines of slavery? If so, it is no wonder that Charleston's slaves appeared self-possessed, almost arrogant. On the other hand, perhaps we should reverse the logic. If Charleston's police powers were so weak, might this not indicate the presence of significant stabilizing forces within the town's social fabric? Perhaps the latitude, diversity, and fluidity of urban slavery were as much a strength as a weakness. How can this situation be explained?

First, there is the matter of Charleston's police powers. The inefficiency of the public watch was a testament to the strength of the unofficial "police" powers all whites held over blacks. Certainly, significant divisions existed among whites, but whenever blacks were thought to pose a threat to the community (defined exclusively in white terms), free men generally banded together. In December 1765, for instance, when some "Negroes . . . mimick'd their betters in crying out *'Liberty,'* " Henry Laurens described how "here in Town *all* were Soldiers in Arms for more than a Week" (my emphasis). The scale of this general mobilization is indicated by the public accounts: for twelve days a white man and two Negroes fixed bayonets to six hundred guns and installed flints in about one thousand muskets.[102] In an emergency, Charleston did not rely on its watch, but on its adult white male population.

White supremacy was a more effective policeman than any watchman could ever be. Charleston's slaves were, of course, surrounded by more whites than any of their rural cousins. Far more vital to the slave in the street than the activities of the public watch was the disposition of individual whites. Consider what happened to the "poor negro, a member of the [Methodist] society" who was employed "to snuff the candles . . . in chapel." He had the temerity to ask a stranger from North Carolina to refrain from talking during a sermon; whereupon the visitor "beat him unmercifully with a stick." Even though the "rioter" was later imprisoned, the ease with which a black could be assaulted even during a religious

---

102. *The Papers of Henry Laurens*, ed. George C. Rogers, Jr., *et al.* (Columbia, S.C., 1976 on), V, 53; South Carolina Commons House Journal, 1765–1768, June 3, 1766, p. 131 (South Carolina Archives).

service, and apparently with no attempt made at intervention, speaks loudly
of the level of personal violence to which blacks were always liable.[103] Appropriately, when in 1773 Charleston's Grand Jury moved to check the
"intolerable Insolence of the Negroes," they recommended, not a more
active watch, but the erection of public stocks in every cross-street in order
that "every white Person" (who, by virtue of skin color, had the power
to "whip Negroes found without Tickets") could more easily confine the
offenders.[104]

Such widely invested powers and the confidence bred of military superiority help explain why masters failed to carry arms to church as the
law stipulated. More than that, when they complied with the law, it might
be in letter only for, in 1767, they were seen "delivering the arms to negroes
to keep during divine service." Or it might explain why, in 1772, city grand
jurors could complain of "Negroes being allowed to keep Horses and carry
Fire-Arms." Or it might explain why, on one muster day in 1754, some
gentlemen "delivered their Fire Arms to Negroes to carry home (and which
they charged and discharged several times as they went along the streets
to the great Terror of many Ladies)."[105] By implication, such incidents did
not frighten white men — or so at least it would appear.

Second, although many of the distinctive problems ascribed to urban
blacks aroused much public disquiet, they were not always as threatening
as the jeremiads claimed. The presence of runaways probably added to
the incidence of urban crime, but the ability of slaves to enjoy a change
of scene, visit a relative, or go underground probably siphoned off as much
potential disorder as it created. Slaves could assemble in greater numbers
and more readily in town than in the countryside. Threatening as these
gatherings often appeared, they were more important for allowing slaves
their own communal outlet, for absorbing and deflecting potential black
resentment. The same argument applies to the numerous tippling houses
found in Charleston. In some respects, they threatened the general order
and conventions of established society: in them, blacks fraternized with
lower-class whites, engaged in their "corrupting" games, exchanged stolen
goods, and got drunk. Surely here was a breeding ground of crime, promiscuity, and disorder? And yet these institutions served as an important focus
for communal activity, channeling it in more "harmless" directions, such

103. *Journals of Thomas Coke*, p. 169. Olaudah Equiano tells of being threatened by violence
in Charleston's markets. See Olaudah Equiano, *The Interesting Narrative of*... (New York, 1791), I, 270.
104. Presentments of the Grand Jury of Charlestown, *SCG*, February 22, 1773.
105. *Ibid.*, *SCG & CJ*, November 17, 1767; *ibid.*, *SCG*, January 25, 1772; *SCG*, October 17, 1754.

as gambling and drinking, than might otherwise have been the case.[106]

Third, the flexibility of urban master-slave relations, which expanded as the century progressed, also served to frustrate and defuse black hostility. The chances of being freed, while never widespread, were much greater in town than in the countryside.[107] Some urban masters were carried along by a rising tide of humanitarianism. In his will of 1803 John Huger requested his heirs "to regard my Negroes as humble friends, and their own fellow Creatures, and to treat them with all the humanity and compassion, and to give them all the indulgence which existing circumstances can admit of."[108] By the late eighteenth century masters were displaying a heightened concern for the integrity of the slave family,[109] and they were also willing to consider slaves' wishes in other areas. Some slaves simply wished to change masters, either temporarily or permanently. One master noted how he gave his slave "a ticket to look for a mastr in Town where he was brought up & wished to live"; two urban masters entered into an agreement to transfer a slave woman among themselves because she "desire[d] to live with" one rather than the other; the owners of a sawyer offered him for sale "on account of his wish to decline living with them any longer."[110]

But perhaps the most striking development occurred in the economic realm. By the late eighteenth century, a slave's desire to change employment was more readily honored. This is, in turn, a reflection on the level

106. For a similar argument, in a different context, see Peter Clark, "The Alehouse and the Alternative Society," in *Puritans and Revolutionaries: Essays in Seventeenth-Century History presented to Christopher Hill,* ed. D. Pennington and K. Thomas (Oxford, 1978), pp. 49–61.

107. Morgan, "Black Society," p. 116; Watson, "Quest for Order," pp. 189–190.

108. Will of John Huger, October 12, 1803, Charleston County Will Book, 1800–1807, pp. 431–436.

109. Morgan, "Black Society," pp. 124–129; see also pp. 113–118. As this essay notes, there was evidence of heightened racism in the late eighteenth century; at the same time, there was also heightened respect. Take, for example, the runaway advertisement of 1795 for groom Ned, "well known in and about Charleston and thro'out every part of this state, and the states of Georgia and North Carolina as a keeper of race horses." His master described him as "handsome, well made, with a long and bushy head of hair, frequently platted at the sides and cued"; he had a "full and manly look." Ned's appearance obviously made quite an impression on his owner: John McPherson, *City Gazette,* August 24, 1795.

110. Jonathan Sarrazin, *City Gazette,* January 1, 1796; William Woodrop's deed of sale to James Lennox, April 1756, Miscellaneous Records, KK, 368; *City Gazette,* September 22, 1800. An owner of a runaway slave was moved to make the following concession: "Whereas a negro fellow (well known in this town), named TOM a carpenter by trade, was purchased for me, at the sale of Mrs. Wright, and who has absented himself ever since, without any reason whatever, except that he does not chuse to live in the country; in order therefore that the said Fellow may be satisfied, I do hereby promise that the said TOM may, by applying to Mr. Williamson, have a ticket to look for another master, and no notice taken of his past conduct, provided he returns within a month." Isaac McPherson, *SC & AGG,* July 30, 1778.

of artisanal specialization achieved by urban slaves. Thus, "a complete waiting man," "born and bred" in town, was put up for sale because he was currently employed "to attend in a store which does not seem to suit his inclination"; a "young negro man who has been bred a tallow chandler, but dislikes greasy work" was offered for sale to anybody who would let him take care of horses; a sailor was sold "for no other reason than that he declines going to sea [but] would wish in preference to work about the city"; a house servant who "discover[ed] an inclination to the carpenter's trade" was permitted to pursue his chosen path.[111]

Slaves were not simply the inert recipients of their masters' heightened solicitude. Some returned the favor. The set piece intended to convey the depths of the slaves' attachment to their master was that scene, the stuff of which legends are made, when the long-absent patriarch returned home to be warmly greeted by joyful dependents. The myth had at least some basis in fact. Even if such occasions are interpreted as ritualized events, with a certain amount of role-playing on all sides, some receptions seem too effusive to be explained away as a set of cynical maneuvers. Henry Laurens, for instance, was obviously moved by the welcome he received when he returned to his Charleston home in 1774 after an absence of three years:

I found no body here but three of our old Domestics Stepney, Exeter, & big Hagar. These drew tears from me by their humble & affectionate Salutes & Congratulations, my knees were clasped, my hands kissed, my very feet embraced & nothing less than a very, I can't say fair, but full Buss of my Lips would satisfy the old Man weeping & Sobing in my Face. The kindest enquiries over & over again were made concerning Master Jackey, Master Harry, Master Jemmy [Laurens' children, still in Europe]. They encircled me, held my hand, hung upon me, I could scarcely get from them. Ah said the old man, I never thought to see you again. I broke my way through these humble sincere friends, thanking them a thousand times for such marks of their affection & proceeded to Broad Street.[112]

---

111. Printer, *SCG*, February 1, 1770; Gibbs and Graham, *Columbian Herald*, April 17, 1786; Jacob Cohen, *SC State Gazette*, April 18, 1798; John Webb, *City Gazette*, July 8, 1799.

112. Henry Laurens to John Laurens, December 12, 1774, Laurens Papers. As early as 1680 a Charleston resident referred to the "many trusty negroes" in town: Maurice Mathews, "A Contemporary View of Carolina in 1680," *South Carolina Historical Magazine*, 55 (1954): 158. Another person who explicitly touted the trustworthiness of urban slaves was Governor James Glen. In counting up the province's assets in the event of a foreign invasion, he estimated upward of one thousand well armed men in Charleston and, "in an emergency, the town negroes, whose fidelity may be depended on [and who] might be armed." Glen to the Duke of Newcastle, July 2, 1744, *Collections of the South Carolina Historical Society* (Charleston, S.C., 1858), II, 288. Finally, for a more personal statement of the "faithfulness" of urban slaves, see George Seaman to Lady Pitcalny, March 1, 1756, Ross of Pitcalnie Muniments, GD 199/227 (Scottish Record Office).

Some urban slaves could show a face that would have been unrecognizable to the Frenchman from St. Domingue.

This, in turn, suggests a fourth consideration favoring the stability of the urban order. The opportunities enjoyed by urban blacks served to create a larger range of differences between them than was the case among rural blacks. The black community in Charleston was deeply fragmented. Most obviously, there was a much more extensive occupational hierarchy in town, with several identifiably specialized groups. Many urban blacks were propelled into the marketplace as competitors for jobs and wages. There were various ethnic loyalties that divided urban blacks—not just African nationalities but also a number of different West Indian identities.[113] Not surprisingly, when blacks came together to fraternize in town, conflicts arose.[114] There was also the division between the free and enslaved sectors of the black community, which was more pronounced in town than in the countryside. And while there were certainly intimate ties between the two, friction could easily arise as free blacks tried to make their way in white society and thereby distance themselves from slaves. In 1800 the governor of South Carolina recognized that free blacks "associate with slaves, in terms of great familiarity, yet, on the least offence, they institute actions of slander, assault, and battery, and other actions of oppressive nature against them." There was even a significant division within the free black community between the light- and the dark-skinned.[115]

But the most significant division, again evident in other parts of the lowcountry but not as salient as in town, was that between the more and less assimilated slaves. The cosmopolitan nature of city life sped up the process of acculturation and accentuated the gap between slaves who were highly knowledgeable of white ways and those who were literally just off the ships. For an early example of sophistication one can do no better than to listen to a visitor's complaint about the number of would-be lawyers

113. Apart from the Bermudian, Jamaican, and French Negroes mentioned earlier, virtually the whole range of African ethnic groups were to be found among urban runaways or captives, together with Indian slaves, slaves from Barbados, St. Kitts, St. Thomas, St. Domingue, the East Indies, and every mainland colony. In addition, a few were described as Portuguese-, Spanish-, or Italian-born. For particularly cosmopolitan slaves, see John Brown, *SCG & CJ*, May 23, 1769; John Brown, *ibid.*, November 13, 1770 (different slaves).

114. Examples of conflict among blacks include *SCG*, October 28, 1732; Court of Justices and Freeholders, Janaury 30, 1770, Miscellaneous Records, OO, 205; *City Gazette*, August 14, 1790.

115. Governor's message no. 5, November 26, 1800, General Assembly (South Carolina Archives). See also Wikramanayake, *A World in Shadow*, pp. 73–75; Berlin, *Slaves Without Masters*, pp. 58, 73–74. But see Robert L. Harris, Jr., "Charleston's Free Afro-American Elite: The Brown Fellowship Society and the Humane Brotherhood," *South Carolina Historical Magazine*, 82 (1981): 289–310.

in Charleston. In 1734 he had overheard "a Blackamore openly in the street say 'That an Officer may break open a House by night or day, and as long as he has a good warrant, may lawfully kill any body in his own defence.'" After citing other more "ignorant" legal opinions, the stranger added the following postscript: "I shew'd this to a Friend, who inform'd me there is a Black man in this town, who is called *Lawyer* (from his constant attendance on the Courts) perhaps he was the person above mentioned, if so, I beg his pardon, because he (in all probability) may have a better guess at the matter in Dispute than any of the rest." Just two years before this conversation took place, a slave named Sambo, with the nickname "the Lawyer," was advertised as a runaway in the pages of the *South Carolina Gazette*.[116]

If there were never very many slaves who acquired a smattering of legal knowledge, the general level of sophistication waxed rather than waned. Some slaves in the late eighteenth century played European musical instruments; others played Anglo-American games such as huzzle-cap, pitch penny, trap-ball, and fives; one slave understood "French cookery"; another wore "goggles" to compensate for weak eyes; another sported a watch on a chain; others wore wigs; and some could read and write.[117] Indeed, in 1800 the Charleston City Council authorized the watch to "break doors, gates, or windows" in order to disperse any gatherings "for the purpose of mental instruction" of the blacks.[118]

Yet, though some urban slaves became sophisticated, eighteenth-century Charleston's enslaved population always included recent African immigrants. They must often have offered a poignant contrast to their more self-confident and assured creole brethren. There was the "new Negro" man who was "supposed to have lost himself in or about Charles Town . . . , answers readily to the name of ACHILLES, but understands no other English." Or, in 1737, there were the four Angolans who returned to the wharf from which they had been sold two months previously: they spoke no English and did not know their master's name. Perhaps they hoped

116. *SCG*, November 9, 1734; Ribson Hutchinson, *ibid.*, September 16, 1732. For slaves fully living up to eighteenth-century society's conception of the penitent criminal and giving their religiously-inspired speeches at the foot of the gallows, see *SCG*, April 6, 1734 and April 12, 1739.

117. Morgan, "Black Society," p. 133; Mark A. DeWolfe Howe, ed., "Journal of Josiah Quincy, Junior, 1773," *Massachusetts Historical Society Proceedings*, 49 (1915–1916): 455; Rogers, Barker, and Lord, *City Gazette*, March 29, 1797; Samuel Warner, *SC & AGG*, April 18, 1764.

118. City of Charleston, Ordinances, December 20, 1800, as cited in Richard C. Wade, *Slavery in the Cities: The South 1820–1860* (New York, 1964), p. 175. There was a school for blacks in operation in Charleston from the 1740s through the 1760s.

to find a way home to Africa.[119] A half-century later, Angolan groups were still in evidence: six of them ran off from a merchant and were thought to be harbored in town. Three Senegambians, two of whom were brothers, made off, still with their identification cards hanging around their necks.[120] There was much else to remind the visitor of Africa: a glimpse of filed teeth, a slave with ethnic markings, a snatch of a conversation in an African language, the sight of a woman carrying a pail of water on her head, the central role of black women in the markets, the playing of an African dice game such as papaw, or the passing of funeral processions which, according to an act of 1750, were "frequent" occurrences, often attended by a "great concourse of slaves."[121] While all this added to the cosmopolitan flavor of eighteenth-century Charleston, it did not make for a cohesive black community.

Finally, we must consider the seeming anomaly of those "proud" slaves described by the visiting Frenchman in 1777. There is no doubt that many of Charleston's slaves behaved precisely as depicted. Another visitor to Charleston was just as impressed by the demeanor of urban bondmen:

Few of the [town blacks], when questioned by a white man, will return any answer; and most of those who vouchsafe to do so, will, in a surly and insolent tone, tell him, 'they belong to their Masters—are going (either) home, or, to their wives—or, to a DANCE': Not many will Condescend to pay the compliment of taking off their hats to a white man, who by his appearance, appears below affluence.

This visitor has also given us a striking portrait of a "Country Dance" in which a party of urban slaves participated, testimony to their independence and autonomy. On any given Sunday, he estimated, one in ten of Charleston's blacks left town to gather with their rural counterparts. Meetings of two hundred or more were not uncommon.[122]

119. Caleb Lloyd, *SCG*, May 11, 1765; *ibid.*, January 22, 1737.
120. George Savage, *SCG*, July 30, 1785; *ibid.*, August 30, 1785. A slave woman of the "Gulla country," who had "been two years in the country, and speaks a few words of English badly," ran away from her Broad Street home: Stueart and Barre, *Columbian Herald*, August 29, 1785.
121. In turn, see Workhouse, *SCG & CJ*, June 19, 1770; Workhouse, *SCG*, July 3, 1762; the workhouse jailer had African slaves interpret for him; Thomas White, *SCG*, January 16, 1762; for a cautious assessment of the role of black women in New World markets, see Sidney W. Mintz and Douglas Hall, "The Origins of the Jamaican Internal Marketing System," *Yale University Publications in Anthropology*, No. 57 (New Haven, 1960), 23–24; *Laurens Papers*, VIII, 128; an act for keeping the Streets in Charlestown clean, no. 775, 1750, MSS Acts.
122. The "Stranger," *SCG*, September 17, 1772. Another perceptive account of the urban black population comes from the early nineteenth century: Sidney Walter Martin, "Ebenezer Kellogg's Visit to Charlestown, 1817," *South Carolina Historical Magazine*, 49 (1948): 9–11.

But we do not need to rely on visitors in order to catch glimpses of self-confident, assured slaves. One Charleston slaveowner reported that his runaway slave, a mere stripling of seventeen years, "has told me to my face, 'he can go when he pleases, and I can do nothing to him, nor shall I ever get a copper for him.'" The braggadocio of another urban slave was equally irritating to his master: "though he is my property," the owner reminded himself, "he has the audacity to tell me he will be free, that he will serve no Man, and that he will be conquered or governed by no man." Witnesses in a legal dispute concerning a female cook reported variously that she was "rather impudent," was often seen "drink[ing] at home & sometimes in a dram-shop," had run away four times from one owner, and had once struck a former mistress. The judge in the case decided that no misrepresentation had occurred in her sale because no witness denied she was an industrious worker, "only that she has got drunk sometimes, and is very high spirited & impudent."[123] Apparently, such characteristics were not unusual in an urban domestic.

Even the town's black children were disrespectful. A lady who exercised daily on the road leading from Charleston informed the residents that "repeatedly Boys and *even very small ones*, accompanied by *Negro Boys* are imprudently intrusted by their parents with Guns, and often shoot across the road, by which means danger will often happen by accident, either by their shot or frightening the horses." Taken to task by the harassed lady, one of the black boys responded that "he *belonged to himself* and *did not care.*"[124]

The insouciance of the urban slave runaway is captured in one master's claim that his fugitive could be "very easily caught, as he is very lazy [and] sleeps pretty late." Insolence more aptly characterizes another urban slave who was sold "for no other fault than being too much her own mistress. If locked out at ten o'clock, she jumps the fence and forces a window open to get into the house." But the ultimate in self-possession must be reserved for the "negro man [who] stole into the house No 2 St. Michael's Alley,

123. John Fisher, *SC & AGG,* February 21, 1781; Joshua Eden, *SCG,* November 7, 1775; *Rousel v. McCartey,* June 1795, no. 55, Thomas Waties Papers (University of South Carolina). A Charleston mistress offered her valuable seamstress for sale "on account of her having too great a spirit for a mistress to manage," Printer, *SCG & CJ,* November 8, 1768. See also two letters dated November 2 and 8, 1782, in the Peter Horry Papers, Peter Force Collection (Library of Congress). In 1808 a Savannah resident talked of his slave "taking such advantage of me thinking I was in his power — He endeavored to impress on my mind that [I] need not calculate on his doing me any good unless he had his own way." Hugh Ross to William Page, June 17, 1808, William Page Papers (University of North Carolina).

124. *Charleston Courier,* November 7, 1806.

and, while the family were at supper in the adjoining room began to pack up every thing that was portable; but perceiving himself seen by a young girl, he told her he was come for his master's great coat, and gave her a hat to carry into the next room, while he leisurely walked down stairs and escaped."[125]

But whether such behavior was ultimately destabilizing is another matter. If, as Henry Laurens once declared (in reference to his brother's town slaves), "Your Negroes in some measure govern themselves," why should they relinquish this *de facto* self-government for a suicidal assault on white society?[126] To ask this rhetorical question is not to portray urban slaves as cringing or fawning individuals, fearful of losing whatever toehold they had managed to establish within the urban social system — for, as we have seen, just the opposite was true. However, although their assurance — translated as "sauciness" or "impudence" in the vocabulary of eighteenth-century masters — posed problems for whites, it also served to bind the slave to the existing order. Assurance does not, after all, imply restiveness. Nor, to use the Frenchman's description, does "serenity."

Thus it seems reasonable to argue that slavery in Charleston was more, not less, secure than it was in the surrounding countryside. Rather than being the weak link in the lowcountry social system, Charleston might more accurately be termed the linchpin. Here was one place where the numbers of whites were roughly equal to blacks, where black women even outnumbered black men, where blacks were widely distributed throughout households, and where blacks lived side by side with whites. If the urban social structure stacked high odds against black opposition, their subordination was further maintained in a number of more or less subtle ways — from the habitual arrogance of whites to the naked power of an armed watch, from the masters' fine clothes to the arbitrary power of individual slaveowners, from the etiquette of the street to the powers invested in all whites to assault blacks almost with impunity.

Reassured though they may have been by this wide range of coercive powers, white residents were constantly expressing unease at the activities of their slaves. They were engaged in a persistent struggle to minimize

125. Laval, *State Gazette of SC*, August 2, 1793; M. Russell, *City Gazette*, July 24, 1800; *ibid.*, April 3, 1788. A visitor to Charleston in the early nineteenth century whirled around in "astonishment" at the sight of a "six feet three tall" black man who "came coursing down the side walk with a flourishing gait & swaggering knee." John Hammond Moore, ed., "The Abiel Abbot Journals: A Yankee Preacher in Charleston Society, 1818–1827," *South Carolina Historical Magazine*, 68 (1967): 250–251.

126. Henry Laurens to James Laurens, January 1776, Laurens Papers.

black fraternization, deny blacks alcohol, avoid radical religious messages, suppress any leveling tendencies arising from interracial sexual unions, restrain the slaves' taste for finery, stamp out crime, and thwart any potential rebellions. And there is no denying that urban whites had justifiable cause for their disquiet. An inflammatory preacher like David or a truculent free black like Jerry could exert a powerful influence on their fellow blacks in an urban setting. Were a conspiracy to develop, men like these would undoubtedly be in the forefront.

However, while privileged slaves were most likely to form the vanguard of a rebellion, they were also the most likely to betray it. After all, they had the most to lose should it fail. In the privacy of a rented dwelling, in the musty backroom of a dram-shop, in the communal fellowship of a religious meeting, or simply in the companionship of fellow black workers, urban slaves enjoyed a latitude denied their rural cousins. And this latitude proved precious to them and served to deflect discontent and defuse any serious insurrectionary impulses they may have had. If rebellion was easier to organize in a city, it was also easier to betray.[127] And, of course, it was also much easier to repel.

V

The larger significance of this story of black life in eighteenth-century Charleston lies in two areas. First, it speaks to the vexed question of slave resistance. More than one historian has been puzzled by the relative absence of slave revolts in the lowcountry region of South Carolina and Georgia.[128] To such bemusement there is one simple and straightforward response. As Eugene Genovese so spiritedly put it, what right have we to "tell others, and retrospectively at that, when, how, and why to risk

127. This is, in my view, the lesson to be drawn from the Vesey conspiracy. There is, of course, considerable dispute about whether a conspiracy actually existed. Richard C. Wade has argued this position in his "The Vesey Plot: A Reconsideration," *Journal of Southern History*, 30 (1964): 143–161. Many others have disputed his contentions. Perhaps the most sensible interpretation is that adopted by Professor Freehling, who hints at his position in a luminous footnote, from which I have borrowed. Although he explores the conspiracy as South Carolinians viewed it rather than as objective truth, he sides with the governor of that period, Thomas Bennett, who believed that a serious conspiracy was afoot, but doubted that it involved more than eighty blacks or that it ever came close to fruition. William W. Freehling, *Prelude to Civil War: The Nullification Controversy in South Carolina, 1816–1836* (New York, 1968), pp. 53–65 (footnote on p. 54).

128. Michael Mullin, "British Caribbean and North American Slaves in an Era of War and Revolution, 1775–1807," in *The Southern Experience*, pp. 235–238; Winthrop D. Jordan, "Why Didn't Slaves Rebel?" *New York Review of Books*, 27 (1980), 18.

their lives and those of their loved ones"?[129] And yet, on Genovese's own checklist of factors favoring slave revolt, the most eligible locale on the North American mainland was certainly the lowcountry region. Blacks heavily outnumbered whites; African numbers and influence were significant; plantations were large; absenteeism during the summer months was common; divisions within the ruling class occurred; and autonomous black leadership emerged; and the terrain favored the formation of runaway bands.[130] However, for nearly two hundred years only one major revolt took place. Perhaps, as Peter Wood has suggested, the explanation lies in the white counter-offensive that followed this one insurrection — that of Stono in 1739. From that point, lowcountry slave society was, in his words, characterized by "a heightened degree of white repression and a reduced amount of black autonomy."[131]

If, as it now appears, this twin process of increased repression and reduced autonomy is somewhat at variance with other developments in the post-Stono countryside, it is wholly inadequate as a description of the history of slavery in Charleston.[132] White repression certainly cannot be discounted, but the instruments of urban social control grew no more markedly draconian after Stono. Black autonomy was certainly not reduced; the reverse was true. And, if the argument of this essay is sound, the absence of these two developments did not render Charleston's social fabric any more unstable. The prospects of a successful slave revolt were less favorable in Charleston than in the surrounding countryside. Since all avenues in the lowcountry led directly to Charleston, we may have located one of the key reasons behind the region's relative quiescence. The common saying — as Charleston goes, so goes the country — has broader implications than might at first be imagined.[133]

This is not to say that the conditions of urban slavery always or necessarily militated against insurrection. In some regions, at certain times, this was palpably not true. In a place like New York City in the early eighteenth century, slaves obviously stood more chance organizing for a revolt than in the surrounding countryside.[134] In British Caribbean islands like

129. Eugene D. Genovese, *From Rebellion to Revolution: Afro-American Slave Revolts in the Making of the Modern World* (Baton Rouge, La., 1979), p. 1.

130. *Ibid.*, pp. 11–12.

131. Wood, *Black Majority*, p. 326.

132. See my "Black Society," pp. 83–141.

133. Weir, *Colonial South Carolina*, p. 123. See also Bridenbaugh, *Myths and Realities*, p. 54 and *passim*.

134. Kenneth Scott, "The Slave Insurrection in New York in 1712," *New York Historical Society Quarterly*, 45 (1961): 43–74.

Barbados and Jamaica the opposite was true. The major port cities of Bridge-town and Kingston played much the same linchpin role as did Charleston in the lowcountry.[135] One should, it seems, avoid the contemporary ur-banists' desire to subsume all urban experiences under one general pat-tern and instead explore comparable regional urban systems.[136]

Second, the story of black life in eighteenth-century Charleston throws light on the major debate concerning urban slavery in North America. That debate was sparked some twenty years ago by the opening line of Richard Wade's seminal study, *Slavery in the Cities*: "By 1860 slavery was disintegrating in Southern cities." Although Wade contended that the process of disintegration accelerated in the 1850s, his broader point was that slavery and cities were profoundly incompatible. As he succinctly ex-plained, "the cause of slavery's difficulty in the city was the nature of urban society itself."[137] Put simply, slaves could not be controlled in cities. The restraints of bondage were loosened to the point where urban slavery col-lapsed from within. This argument has been criticized, but mainly with quantitative information to prove that there was growth in demand for urban slave services in the immediate antebellum decades, and hence that the vigor of urban slavery was unimpaired in 1860.[138]

Perhaps a more telling criticism is available if a longer time perspective is taken. The history of the one eighteenth-century city on the mainland that was dominated by slavery provides a good vantage point from which to assess the nature of urban slavery. All of the corrosive acids generated by city life, and which Wade identified as eroding the "peculiar institu-tion," were as much at work in eighteenth-century Charleston as in any antebellum southern city. A process of disintegration that takes place over a few decades may seem plausible enough. But our credibility becomes strained when the point of collapse is antedated to about 1800, for one historian of urban slavery has claimed that "towns were rapidly getting

135. This is my reading of Michael Craton, *Testing the Chains: Resistance to Slavery in the British West Indies* (Ithaca, N.Y., 1982). To my knowledge, there are no detailed studies of black life in the major British Caribbean port cities. But, for suggestive material, see Colin G. Clarke, *Kingston, Jamaica: Urban-Development and Social Change, 1692–1962* (Berkeley, 1975), p. 27.

136. Bridenbaugh in his two volumes on the urban experience is guilty of this charge. The "new" urban history also adopts this premise. See, for example, Sam Bass Warner, Jr., "If All the World were Philadelphia: A Scaffolding for Urban History, 1774–1930," *American Historical Review*, 74 (1968): 26–43, and the essay volumes edited by Stephan Thernstrom and Richard Sennett, and Leo F. Schnore, respectively.

137. Wade, *Slavery in the Cities*, p. 246.

138. Claudia Dale Goldin, *Urban Slavery in the American South 1820–1860: A Quantitative History* (Chicago, 1976).

out of control" in the late eighteenth century.[139] And the argument begins to lose all force when the alleged "deficiencies" of urban slavery can be traced over one hundred and fifty years. An institution that was unraveling for a century and a half deserves credit for surviving. One final assessment, then, of the larger significance of eighteenth-century Charleston's black life is that the city did indeed create its own kind of slavery—and a viable form it proved to be.

139. Mullin, "British Caribbean and North American Slaves," p. 242.

RETHINKING AMERICAN NEGRO SLAVERY
FROM THE VANTAGE POINT OF THE COLONIAL ERA

Gerald W. Mullin

History Department
California State University
Sacramento

A surge of interest in Afro-American history has pushed to the fore a familiar and important controversy—the relationship between ante-bellum society and its most distinctive institution, the plantation.[1] Generally historians have construed the plantation either as a kind of seigniorial manor and the planter's way of life, or as a factory in the field and simply the planter's business. Constructions of this weight require a solid foundation, but scholars who have used the plantation as little more than a literary device, a metaphor for Southern values and ways, have not built well.

The plantation would be a more reliable guide to Southern society if we saw it from microcosmic, long-range, and comparative perspectives, which clarified the perameters—regional variations in settlement patterns and crops—as well as the center, the relationships among the institution's major components—organization, work routines, and the roles of planter, overseer, and slave. Most important, an effective model of the plantation would show the connections between institution and society, and indicate how historical change for one component influenced the development of the others.

This arduous but rewarding task cannot be done here in an exploratory essay about plantation organization, and the planter's role (an invaluable way of linking the institution to society and to major historical developments), as they changed through time.[2] To do this requires that a sharper distinction be made between colonial and ante-bellum plantations, and that attention be shifted both from the drama of sectional conflict to the humdrum reality of plantation routines, and from the master class to those blacks and whites whose everyday, ordinary existences were massively and profoundly influenced by the structures and rhythms of staple production.

---

1. Ernie Isaacs, Eugene Genovese, Stanley Elkins and Eric McKitrick made helpful suggestions (some of which I followed). But I'm responsible for the finished product, which is intended to be suggestive about several problems that can only be resolved by rigorous quantitative and comparative analysis.

2. Two brilliant and useful investigations of the applicability of role theory to slavery are Stanley M. Elkins, *Slavery, A Problem in American Institutional and Intellectual Life* (Chicago, 1959), Part III, esp. 123ff; and Kenneth M Stampp, "Rebels and Sambos: The Search for the Negro's Personality in Slavery," *The Journal of Southern History* 37 (August 1971): 367-392.

I

Latin Americanists have been more sensitive to the historical, folk, and routine dimensions of plantations than U. S. scholars; and they have been in more general agreement about the plantation's essential characteristics. Caribbean area specialists, particularly, who are often anthropologists and sociologists (or historians inclined to approach societies ethnographically), take a long and comparative view of features common to all plantation regions from the Chesapeake Bay to British Guyana, from the sixteenth through the nineteenth centuries. In the context of post-Roman European history, writes Sidney Mintz, the plantation was an absolutely unprecedented social, economic and political institution, which stemmed from the growing European demand for a wider range of foodstuffs and raw materials.[3] The large-scale production of these staples was only feasible in humid, tropical and semitropical regions of open resources. Richard Sheridan, an economic historian who has spent a lifetime studying sugar and slavery in the Caribbean, has recently drawn together the indispensable elements of plantation America:

> The New World plantation represented a combination of African labour, European technology and management, Asiatic and American plants, European animal husbandry, and American soil and climate . . . . Animate sources of energy, such as plants, domesticated animals, and Negro slaves, were combined with inanimate energy captured by windmills, water wheels, and sailing vessels. The plantation was truly an innovation in the Schumpeterian sense. It established new trade routes and shipping lanes, shifted millions of hoe cultivators from one side of the Atlantic to the other, determined the movement and direction of capital, induced the growth of temperate zone colonies to supply intermediate products, produced a class of *nouveau riche* planters and merchants, and became a prize in the contest for power and plenty among the mercantile nations of Europe.[4]

A hemispheric and colonial perspective dramatizes the institution's relentless development, while advancing the useful notion that plantations were a basic force for urbanization. After the

3. Sidney W. Mintz, Foreword to Ramiro Guerra y Sánchez, *Sugar and Society in the Caribbean* (New Haven, 1964), p. 14.
4. Richard B. Sheridan, "The Plantation Revolution and the Industrial Revolution, 1625-1775," *Caribbean Studies* 9 (October 1969): 7. Cf Sidney M. Greenfield, "Slavery and the Plantation in the New World: The Development and Diffusion of a Social Form," *Journal of Inter-American Studies* 11 (January 1969): 44-57; Charles Wagley, "Plantation America: A Culture Sphere," in Vera Rubin, ed., *Caribbean Studies: A Symposium* (Seattle, 1960), pp. 3-13; and Edgar T. Thompson, "The Plantation," in Thompson and Everett C. Hughes, eds., *Race: Individual and Collective Behavior* (New York, 1958), pp. 225-33.

Amerindian and later the white yeomanry were destroyed by the mid-seventeenth century they were replaced by large plantations run by Negro slaves for a small and powerful planter elite (Barbados is the best and most familiar example of this process). Eventually, throughout the Americas in the eighteenth and nineteenth centuries, many big sugar (and some rice, cotton, coffee and cocoa) plantations became factories in the field, which included processing operations and equipment ranging from crude tobacco curing sheds to large sugar mills and distilleries. The large-scale, highly rationalized plantation, a remorseless engine of profit and change, transformed economies by creating backward linkages, that is, inducements to investments in such plantation inputs and transportation facilities as ships, farm implements, and slave provisions (clothing and food); and forward linkages, or inducements to investments in industries in the Mother Country that produced consumer goods for the factors who set up shop in plantation towns, ports, processing and warehouse sectors.[5] In appropriating large areas in which the rural population (slaves or their descendants freed by revolution or emancipation) had to concentrate, in bringing improvements in transportation and communication, and routinizing work practices and establishing company stores, the great Latin American plantation did "its powerful best to create a factory situation albeit a rural one."[6]

Unfortunately these arguments have not been fully exploited by historians of the ante-bellum South, whose investigations of the nature of slavery and the sectional conflict may be divided for convenience into two interpretations. One view presents the War as an inevitable conflict between two social systems, North and South, each with its own territorial base; and, as a War for Southern Independence generated by a small, entrenched and highly self-conscious ruling class, dedicated to the reactionary ideology that slavery was a positive good even though it was economically backward and unprofitable. The world these slaveholders made was essentially patriarchal and premodern ("semi-feudal" or "seigniorial"), and based on plantations that reflected this ethos: they were not economically rational (that is, based on the most advanced methods for maximizing profit), because their most important function was non-economic—enhancing the slaveholders' "aspirations to luxury, ease and accomplishment." Master-slave relationships were cast in the same mold: the typical master, a benevolent patriarch who shunned cruelty and system, dealt with his slaves paternalistically. The most persuasive spokes-

5. *Ibid*, pp 7-8, 21ff.
6. Mintz citing Professor Henry Wallich (1950) in Guerra y Sánchez, *Sugar and Society*, p. 37.

man for this argument is Eugene Genovese:

> Slavery gave the South a social system and a civilization.
> . . . [that] increasingly grew away from the rest of the
> nation and from the rapidly developing sections of the
> world. . . .
>
> The plantation Society that had begun as an appendage
> of British capitalism ended as a powerful, largely autono-
> mous civilization. . . . [The] essential element in this
> distinct civilization was the slaveholder's domination. . . .
>
> The premodern quality of the Southern world was im-
> parted to it by its dominating slaveholding class. . . . The
> planters commanded Southern politics and set the tone of
> social life. Theirs was an aristocratic, anti-bourgeois spirit. .
> . . The planter typically recoiled at the notions that profit
> should be the goal of life; that the approach to production
> and exchange should be internally rational and uncompli-
> cated by social values; that thrift and hard work should be
> the great virtues.[7]

In brief the plantation regime was economically retrogressive,
antagonistic to the dynamic commercial and industrial economy
of the North, and both reinforced and drew upon the elite's easy-
going, leisured and anti-bourgeois way of life.

The other major interpretation may be illustrated by Barrington
Moore Jr., who in *Social Origins of Dictatorship and Democracy:
Lord and Peasant in the Making of the Modern World*, argued that
the South was an integral—not an antagonistic—part of the North
American economy, and an indispensable contributor to its rapid
growth and transformation in the early nineteenth century. In his
words:

> Up until about 1830 it [cotton] was the most important
> cause of the growth of manufacturing in this country. . . .
> From 1840 to the time of the Civil War, Great Britain drew
> from the Southern states four-fifths of all her cotton im-
> ports. Hence it is clear that the plantation operated by
> slavery was no anachronistic excrescence on industrial
> capitalism. It was an integral part of this system and one of
> its prime motors in the world at large.[8]

The Civil War stemmed from a competitive relationship among
regional economies: the West, as well as the North and South; but,
it was a war between varieties of capitalism—agricultural versus
commercial enterprise. In this framework the planter was basically

7. Eugene Genovese, *The Political Economy of Slavery* (New York, 1961), pp. 3,
15-16, 28.

8. Barrington Moore Jr., *Social Origins of Dictatorship and Democracy: Lord and
Peasant in the Making of the Modern World* (Boston, 1966), p. 116.

an entrepreneur, his plantation a business that systematically organized labor and capital to generate profits and political power; and, the normal relationship between slaves and their masters was that of labor and management. While a preponderant majority of slaveholders (who were never more than half of the white population) owned fewer than three or four slaves, the great majority of bondsmen belonged to the rich. Planters who owned more than thirty slaves, Kenneth Stampp notes, "were the ones who achieved maximum efficiency, the most complex economic organization, and the highest degree of specialization within their labor forces."[9] Robert Fogel, among other econometricians, has reinforced the work of Moore and Stampp. Arguing that the rate of growth of the per capita income in the South exceeded the national average, that slavery was the growth stock of the 1850s, he concludes:

> Thus when slaveowners invested in slaves, it was not because they were doddering idiots wedded to an economically moribund institution. Nor was it because they were noblemen who were sacrificing their personal economic interests to save the country from the threat of barbarism. Perhaps slaveowners were nobly motivated. If so, they were well rewarded for their nobility—with average rates of return in the neighborhood of 10 or 12 per cent per annum. . . . Perhaps the most startling of the new findings is the discovery that Southern agriculture was nearly 40 per cent more efficient in the utilization of its productive resources than was Northern agriculture.[10]

These conflicting views are based on two kinds of sources, each with its own code words and concepts, that point to different realities of slavery. The first view of the plantation regime as premodern and economically backward draws heavily on the writings of a very special segment of the slaveowning elite, the pro-slavery propagandists, the house intellectuals and politicians, who arrived late on the scene, and if they were not usually completely separated from plantations and slaves, certainly viewed the system from the studies and verandas of the Great House. If truth is what emerges from a dialogue with our opposites, the apologists' opposites, audience and message are especially informative. While defending slavery against the abolitionists for European and Non-slaveholding readers in both the North and South, the proslavery writers were more intimately connected to national culture than

---

9. Stampp, *The Peculiar Institution, Slavery in the Ante-Bellum South* (New York, 1956), pp. 38; also 41-2, 325; see too Lewis C. Gray, *History of Agriculture in the Southern United States to 1860*, 2 vols. (New York, 1941), I: 302.

10. Robert W. Fogel, "Historiography and Retrospective Econometrics," *History and Theory* 9 (1970): 248.

they realized. "As industrial capitalism took more and more hold in the North," Moore writes, "articulate Southerners emphasized whatever aristocratic and preindustrial traits they could find in their own society: courtesy, grace, cultivation, the broad outlook versus the alleged money-grubbing outlook of the North." This message, part of a familiar intellectual tradition, was not uniquely Southern: "Such [anti-bourgeois] notions crop up everywhere as industrialization takes hold, even to some extent without industrialization. The spread of commercial agriculture in a precommerical society," Moore reminds us, "generates various forms of romantic nostalgia."[11]

But there is little "romantic nostalgia" in such ante-bellum plantation records as ledgers, account-, day-, and farmbooks. Documents of this kind,[12] which clearly support the second interpretation—ante-bellum slavery as agricultural capitalism—were created by men, working among slaves, for their own information and profit; and they provide a richer, more intimate and reliable, picture of the ordinary reality of slavery and plantations than a view based on the pro-slavery writers. The scene inferred from the ledgers is corroborated by another major source—essays (in agricultural journals) for an audience of planters and farmers about ideal plantation conditions. Together these documents are not ideological, but essentially about something much more tangible and immediate to the lives and livelihoods of whites and blacks, who were living slavery and not simply talking about it; namely, the most advanced methods possible for growing staples with slave labor.

But documents from an earlier period indicate that plantation organization was not always so businesslike; nor were relations between planter and slave so comparable to those between modern management and labor. Instead, the web of plantation relations before 1800 was shaped by entirely different circumstances—the planters' reactions to colonial status and 'uncivilized' Africans.

Narrowing the focus initially to eighteenth-century sources, restores a sense of slavery's development in time, and helps resolve the conflicting views of North American plantations: before Inde-

---

11. Moore, *Social Origins of Dictatorship and Democracy*, pp. 122-23.
12. Plantation Record Book, 1853-65 Evans (Nathaniel, and Family) Papers: Plantation Record Book, 1859-66, Le Blanc Family Papers: Vital Register, 1832-62, McCutcheon (Samuel) Papers: Pre Aux Cleres Plantation Book, 1852-54: McCollam (Andrew and Ellen E.), 1847 Record: William J. Palfrey Plantation Diaries, 1852-59; and the "Comite" Plantation Record Book, 1857, J. G. Kilbourne Papers, Louisiana State University Archives. Kollock Plantation Records, 1837-60; Manigault Plantation Records for Gowrie and Silk Hope, vols. 2-4: John Edwin Fripp Plantation Account Books; Arnold-Screven Papers, vol. 4 Plantation Journal, Southern Historical Collection, University of North Carolina Archives. See also Memorandum of Directions. . . 1846, Charles Crommelin Papers; and the James A. Tait Memorandum Book, 1831-40, Alabama State Archives.

pendence the plantation, as a cog in an imperial apparatus controlled thousands of miles away in Great Britain, was the center of the rich planter's life, and his way of achieving autonomy while coping with the psychological as well as the political and economic abuses of colonial status,[13] but following revolution, the creation of national sovereignty and an American economic system, large plantations were no longer all-consuming experiences for whites compensating for a sense of powerlessness inherent in colonial status; but rather, business enterprises for owners who much of the time lived or traveled elsewhere.

This significant change in the plantation's function, critically important for an understanding of how it shaped the lives of blacks and whites, is conveyed in the following contemporary descriptions. Landon Carter, a rich Virginian of the Revolutionary generation, said his mansion, Sabine Hall, was "an excellent Little fortress. . . , built on a Rock of Independency." Nearly a century later an anonymous contributor to a southern agricultural magazine wrote, "a plantation might be considered as a piece of machinery."[14]

These conflicting images—a fortress, conveying impressions of a rural, self-sufficient landed aristocracy, and a machine, evoking pictures of factories, standardized processes and interchangeable parts—reflect faithfully the prevailing values and aspirations of their eras, and point to significant developments in plantation organization from the early 1700s to Emancipation and the end of the Civil War in the 1860s.

II

Slavery in the colonial era was not simply a prelude to antebellum slavery. In the eighteenth century, particularly, its uniqueness stemmed from a process that had passed from the scene by 1800: the first stirrings of an American nationalism, —eventually of revolutionary dimensions that was shaped by the coming of age of the only landed aristocracy in America; and Africans, who slowly became Negroes as they changed their Old World customs and adjusted to the cruel realities of plantation slavery. A view of these distinctive attributes, from one eighteenth-century slave society in which planters saw Africans as peasants and themselves as manor lords with a civilizing mission, is provided by a boastful

---

13. These themes are developed more fully in my book *Flight and Rebellion: Slave Resistance in Eighteenth-Century Virginia* (New York, 1972), esp. chs. I and II.
14. Landon Carter to the editors of the *Virginia Gazette* (Purdie and Dixon, editors), fall 1769 cited in Jack P. Greene, *Landon Carter: An Inquiry into the Personal Values and Social Imperatives of the Eighteenth-Century Gentry* (Charlottesville, 1965), p. 26; "Management of Slaves," *The Southern Cultivator* 4 (March 1846): 44.

letter from a wealthy tobacco planter to an English earl:

> Besides the advantage of a pure Air, we abound in all kinds of Provisions without expense (I mean we who have Plantations). I have a large Family of my own. . . . Like one of the Patriarchs, I have my Flocks and my Herds, my Bond-men and Bond-women, and every Soart of Trade amongst my own Servants, so that I live in a kind of Independence on every one but Providence. However this Soart of Life is without expense, yet it is attended with a great deal of trouble. I must take care to keep all my people to their Duty, to set all the Springs in motion. . . . But then 'tis an amusement in this silent Country and a continual exercise of our Patience and Economy.
> Another thing My Lord that recommends this Country very much—we sit securely under our vines and our fig trees without any danger to our property. . . . [Although] we have often needy Governors, and pilfering convicts sent among us.[15]

William Byrd's paternalistic attitudes and feudal images are deceptive. For in his or any colonial setting 'sitting securely under vines and fig trees' was largely wishful thinking. Forced to deal with circumstances unknown to their nineteenth-century counterparts, Byrd and his countrymen talked about patriarchal independence, when in reality they were destined to be colonial planters and slaveowners in a mercantilist Empire: as colonists they were obliged to recognize that authority for the most important decisions for their country originated outside its boundaries in England. As planters they had to submit to the Mother Country's control of manufactured goods, credit arrangements and prices, and as slaveowners, they exploited Africa as a cheap and consistent source of labor, only to gradually realize how thoroughly dependent they were on slaves.

Byrd's idyll was defined by space as well as time. In the midst of British officials and Africans at various stages of socialization, slaveowners expressed a need to be free in ways best suited to their local topographic, demographic and urban conditions. In the tobacco colonies an extensive network of navigable rivers, a chronic absence of town life, and the gentry's ambition to be "independent on Every one but Providence," scattered settlers far into the interior of the country where they built the large and comparatively self-sufficient plantations that were the focus of their lives. Determined to be autonomous tobacco planters encouraged cultural change among slaves, because their tanneries, blacksmith and carpentry shops required literate, skilled artisans.

15. William Byrd II, Westover, Virginia, to the Earl of Orrery, July 5, 1726, *Virginia Magazine of History and Biography* 32 (December 1924): 27.

In Virginia, the oldest area of permanent settlement in British America, "living bravely," on autarkic, self-contained, plantations maintained by black craftsmen, was an old, resilient tradition stemming from the settlers' Elizabethan origins. In 1649 Captain Samuel Matthews' plantation was described in this way:

> He hath a fine house, and all things answerable to it; he sowes yeerly store of Hempe and Flax, and causes it to be spun; he keeps Weavers, and hath a Tan-house, causes Leather to be dressed, hath eight Shoemakers employed in their trade, hath forty Negroes servants, brings them up to Trades in this house; He yeerly sowes abundance of Wheat, Barley, etc. The Wheat he selleth at four shillings the bushell, Kills store of Beeves and sells them to victuall the ships when they come thither; hath abundance of Kine, a brave Dairy, Swine great store, and Pottery, . . . keeps a good house, lives bravely.[16]

Samuel Matthews was the product of what one historian has appropriately called "the World We Have Lost."[17] Colonial Virginia, whose values were set in Matthews' days of the early seventeenth century, was part of that world; a premodern society —small-scale, corporate, God-fearing and deferential, in which slave-owners were paternalistic and plantations were manors, "little Fortress[es] of Independency"—that is, once they came to be economically self-sufficient and diversified, as Africans (or usually their American-born children) were assimilated and trained as artisans. In these circumstances then the tobacco gentry's patriarchal model for plantation organization was clearly a reaction to a particular time and place.

In the rice-growing region of South Carolina, however, settled more than fifty years later by Barbadians and Englishmen of the Restoration Era, a different kind of river system, a much higher percentage of unacculturated and untrained Africans among all slaves, and one of the largest cities in colonial America produced different relationships between the land and its settlers.[18] The low country planters, concentrated on a plain of sea islands and marsh

---

16. Cited in Gray, *History of Agriculture in the Southern United States*, 1: 453.

17. Peter Laslett, *The World We Have Lost* (London, 1965), *passim*

18. This view of South Carolina is based on my own interpretations of the following sources in the State Archives, Columbia: Records in the British Public Record Office Relating to South Carolina, 1663-1782 ("Sainsbury Transcripts"), 36 volumes (particularly correspondence between officials in the colony and England relating to staples, slave trade, religion and insurrections); Manuscripts of the Society for the Propagation of the Gospel in Foreign Parts in South Carolina (microfilm of Library of Congress Transcripts); a quantitative study of all 664 estate inventories in the Charleston District, Charleston County Wills (C. W. A. Project typescripts), vol. VII, 1752-56; vol. XI, 1758-61; and a sample of 600-odd fugitive slave notices; advertisements for slaves taken up and jailed in the Charleston workhouse, and plantation and land sale notices in the *South Carolina Gazette*, 1732-1775, (U. C. Berkeley microfilm collection). On the rice planters' wealth, M. Eugene Sirmans, *Colonial South Carolina, A Political History, 1663-1763* (Chapel Hill, 1966), p. 226.

that was extremely productive agriculturally but most unhealthy, grew only rice on specialized—not diversified—plantations, employed few black artisans, and spent much of their time in Charleston, the source of the urban goods and services that the tidewater tobacco planters had to produce on their own plantations. Rice in fact made so much more money than tobacco (the weed's market declined severely after 1750, producing a string of bankruptcies and forcing planters into wheat and general farming) that by mid-century the low country had the highest per capita income in America, and probably the fastest growth rate in the world. By the 1750s a monoculture society had developed and, in important ways, South Carolina was similar to British West Indian society: that is, a colony characterized by a well defined urban export area (and a city rather than the plantation as the focus for white society and culture), great fortunes and extensive planter absenteeism.

III

Further comparisons between rice and tobacco regions, as an indication of what ante-bellum plantations changed from, should be made from the slave's vantage point. A view from the bottom up accomplishes (as it should) much more than simply a reconstruction of the lives and settings of a neglected and historically silent people. Examining the reactions of Africans illuminates a process (if shorthand is admissible) in which plantation society once small-scale, corporate and colonial came to be populous, individualistic and sovereign; and planters inclined to be paternalistic fathers became impersonal businessmen.

In the colonial era slave behavior was largely accountable to the extent of planter absenteeism, the slave's origin (birthplace), job and degree of cultural change (as seen in the most plentiful and reliable sources on slaves, those describing resistance).[19] For our purposes, the relationships between acculturation levels and styles of resistance, on the one hand, and the planter's role, on the other, are most informative about comparisons between colonial and ante-bellum plantations.

Acculturation was the process in which native Africans, while learning English and other ways whites would have them behave, changed their customs and became Negroes. This process was marked by three stages, and often lasted more than a generation (especially in South Carolina). Native Africans (referred to as "outlandish"), at the first level of socialization, seldom learned

---

19.   This section is based on my *Flight and Rebellion*, ch 2.

English well, nor lost the essentials of an African orientation. When forced into field labor, they were called "new Negroes," a second stage of acculturation; and, as they began the slow, and sometimes demoralizing process of cultural change, their reactions were dramatically transformed into individualistic rather than collective patterns.

Philosophically as well as socially Africans were aliens, whose acts of rebellion often exposed novel preconceptions and expectations about relations with others and the way the world worked. As a communal and tribal folk, they saw slavery as a temporary misfortune, to be confronted cooperatively, and rejected totally. In the colonial period Africans were the only slaves reported as runaways in large groups who often traveled into the wilds, where they attempted to reestablish village life as they knew it before they were enslaved. But assimilated blacks (especially artisans), the third level of acculturation, typically resisted slavery alone, and in ways that were not nearly as threatening to the slave system. They ran off and often hired themselves out in cities, where in a labor starved economy talented runaways (white servants as well as slaves) often achieved a modicum of freedom, which was impossible within the confines of the plantation.

The concept of cultural change dramatizes the historical dimension of slavery, while providing a more precise way of talking about slave behavior. But "acculturation" is a rather stilted, dormant word, which does not begin to convey a sense of the tragic confrontation among races in colonial America. The epic European conquest, settlement, and importation of Africans (which brought nearly 200,000 slaves to the eighteenth-century mainland) set in motion massive but often intimate, encounters between blacks and whites, that profoundly shaped our basic cultural modalities (sex, diet, domesticity, language, politics and religion) in ways that are still only little understood.

Documents about Africans in South Carolina are most informative about the unique mood and feeling of colonial slavery. In the Carolina low county slaves in organized, war-like groups, often fled to the frontier, the Spanish presidio at St. Augustine, Florida; or, rebelled and fought back.

In September 1739 Angolans, who were part of a large and poorly supervised road crew on the Stono River, led one of the largest slave uprisings ever in North America. Although Africans were usually as competent as Indians in surviving in the wilderness, they were occasionally confused by their isolation on the rice plantations, as well as their rapid movement from a west to an east coast, which distorted ways of making the world intelligible (by calculating direction and time). The Stono insurrectionists were no exception. After burning several plantations and killing a score of whites, Sunday night, September 9, their force grew rapidly from twenty to sixty, "some say a Hundred," by additions of "new Negroes." Monday morning they "burnt all before them without Opposition," swept south and west through the hamlet of Jacksonboro; and, later in the day, "thinking they were now victorious over the whole Province," they halted in a field, and set to Dancing, Singing and beating Drums, to draw more Negroes to them." But the Africans had marched only ten miles to the Pon Pon River, where they were eventually surrounded, scattered or shot. The rebellion ended after the murder of twenty-one whites and more than forty blacks, but two years later Settlement Indians were still presenting claims to the legislature for rebels whom they had tracked down and killed. [20]

These violent rituals of a society groping toward basic arrangements between races rarely occurred after 1750. Acculturation, which diffused black anger by making slaves less cooperative, proceeded rapidly. And by the end of the slave trade in 1807, "White Over Black," already an intrinsic part of what it meant to be an American in the New Nation, was also largely an uncontested reality.

The extent and quality of planter absenteeism—how slaveowners executed the role of master—was another major variable determining slave behavior. Absenteeism was not so much a question of whether or not an owner lived at home; but rather, the degree to which the plantation was his base of operations, the way he oriented himself to the world; how much he came and went, and so, the extent to which he was personally involved in its daily supervision. Slave owners whose only home was the plantation, whose families lived amongst the artisans and household servants of the home quarter (all of whom in turn served as models of cultural change for "new Negroes"), were the real patriarchs in Southern history. Their knowledge of each slave, and willingness to intervene in the blacks' domestic lives, ensured both a faster rate of assimilation and degree of compliance than those whose slaves, supervised by overseers and black drivers, lived among their own.

Africans were in part the creatures of ecological perameters and the overriding objectives of plantation production, but acculturation was a two-way street. Slaves exerted significant influence of their own, and, at a crucial moment, when planters for the first

20. *Gentleman's Magazine*, New Series, 10 (1740), 127-29; Newton D. Mereness, ed., *Travels in the American Colonies* (New York, 1916), pp. 222-23; Governor William Bull to the Board of Trade, Charleston, October 5, 1739, South Carolina Records in the British Public Record Office ("Sainsbury Transcripts") 20: 179-80.

time were working out the best techniques for growing staples with slaves. In order to curb resistance (which in the colonial period was so often African—that is, persistent, organized and dangerous), planters soon realized that they must either live at home, or provide a rationalized system of rules, routine and command, a clearly perceived hierarchy of authority, as a substitute for their own constant surveillance, worrisome attention to detail, encouragement of cultural change by example, and paternalistic treatment of slaves. Eighteenth-century tobacco plantations and the larger ante-bellum enterprises best illustrate these two ways of organizing staple production for profit, status and power. The situation in South Carolina is more confusing, but suggestive, because the sources, which are so sparse and thin, offer glimpses of the more progressive managerial styles that characterized large ante-bellum plantations.

The patriarchal role—which did not survive the change from the Colonial to the Early National period—was most highly refined in the Chesapeake Bay region. Tobacco patriarchs lived on their plantations and took their fatherly roles seriously, while habitally referring to their slaves as "my people," "my Bondsmen," "the black members of my family." They saw slave rebelliousness as a transgression of the Fifth Commandment, "Honour thy Father and thy Mother," and assumed that both master and slave had certain rights and obligations: "I must again desire that you will keep Tommy strictly to his Duty & obedience"; "cruelty to the poor slaves is a thing I always Abhored. I would think myself happy could I keep them to there [sic] duty without being Obliged to correct them." Or "began this morning to enforce my resolution of correcting the drunkenes[s] in my family by an example of Nassau." Patriarchs also controlled the most important decision made for slaves—task allotment, placing them in the house, fields or workshops. They doctored blacks who were ill and as a matter of course participated in their slaves' family lives, while moving new mates to the same quarter, placing a promising child in a workshop at a parent's request and generally enforcing their moral codes on the Africans. [21]

But the planter's execution of these considerable responsibilities was seriously impaired by a failure to achieve real self-determination in the Empire, which in a declining tobacco market sharpened his need to be a competent father, one who saw plantation authority as absolute and indivisible. Masters used trusted slaves to

21. George Pitt to Mr. Robert Prentis, Stratford-on-Avon, England, February 1, 1775, Prentis Family Papers, Alderman Library, University of Virginia; Charles Dabney to John Blair Jr., and Mary Ambler, April 1, 1769, Dabney Papers, Southern Historical Collection; Jack P. Greene, ed., *The Diary of Colonel Landon Carter of Sabine Hall, 1752-1778,* 2 vols. (Charlottesville, 1966), I: 363.

report directly about activities on the satellite quarters; and insisted that overseers treat slaves as they would (that is "benevolently"), while refusing to give them the means to make crops without "Driving and Storming."[22] Consequently relations among tobacco planters, overseers and slaves were typically chaotic; and overseers were especially vulnerable to the field slaves' petty rebelliousness.

Nonetheless the tobacco planter's presence was formidable. His direct supervision of slaves and routine channeled rebelliousness into reactions that were sporadic and non-cooperative, or at worst, into such low-keyed campaigns of sabotage as stealing, tool breaking and truancy. As the Virginia slave population became comparatively assimilated by mid-century, there were virtually no African uprisings which to the end of the colonial period haunted the rice planter's imagination. In fact in Virginia slaves at the other end of the acculturation scale, the relatively advantaged artisans, were the most troublesome, first as runaways (not simply "outlying" truants) and then as insurrectionists (who organized Gabriel Prosser's conspiracy in 1800). But, in South Carolina planters concentrated their fear of black on Africans, singling out some tribesmen aboard slavers as more dangerous than others; while Virginians in the slave market were unconcerned about the 'national character' of particular tribes, since Africans were expected to become Negroes as soon as possible.[23]

The few surviving documents about colonial rice plantations, where absenteeism was extensive and blacks remained African longer, present a different picture of the relationship between cultural change, rebelliousness and performance of the role of planter. While examining ways of teaching Africans English so they could be more readily proselytized, a Charleston minister for the Society for the Propagation of the Gospel in Foreign Parts, momentarily looked into the heart of [a] distinctive plantation culture. What he saw was:

> a Nation within a Nation. In all Country Settlements, they [the slaves] live in contiguous Houses and often 2, 3 or 4 Famillys of them in One House. . . . They labour together and converse almost wholly among themselves.[24]

The nature of absenteeism that made this cultural autonomy possible is illuminated in the Josiah Smith Junior Letterbook

22. Cornelius Hall to John H. Norton, October 1791, Norton Papers, Colonial Williamsburg Research Center.
23. Elizabeth Donnan, "The Slave Trade into South Carolina Before the Revolution," *American Historical Review* 33 (July 1928): 816-17.
24. Revd. Alexander Garden to the Secretary, May 6, 1740, cited in Frank J. Klingberg, *An Appraisal of the Negro in Colonial South Carolina* (Washington, 1941), p. 106.

(1770 - 1775), one of the few records of a colonial rice plantation surviving as more than a fragment.[25] Commuting between Charleston and Georgetown (the epicenter of rice cultivation until the 1870s), Smith pursued his own business interests while managing two plantations for George Austin (once a partner with Henry Laurens in the largest slave trading company in North America), who lived in England. The tone of Smith's letters, and the patterns of authority and decision-making they reveal, were characteristically ante-bellum: the owner was non-resident, impersonal toward his slaves, and delegated authority rationally; his steward or manager visited the plantation to report on the nature of the market, and on major decisions concerning personnel, equipment and buildings. Most important, overseers and black drivers (prevalent in ante-bellum records for large plantations, but in the colonial period mentioned only in South Carolina sources) were clearly in charge of daily activities. So the Josiah Smith Letterbook contrasts sharply with the documentation concerning the old fashioned paternalism of Chesapeake Bay society.

But tobacco planters were businesslike in their own way. Their intimate knowledge of slaves and planting was essentially the "command experience" so often cited as the basis for their ascendancy at the national level during the Revolutionary and Early National periods. Living as fathers among their black and white families, they were hard-working manor lords, who spent hours a day in the saddle, riding about the only domain in which they enjoyed real power and independence, and scrutinizing overseers, slaves, livestock and crops:

> Rode out this day. Corn except where the land is very stiff is coming up and with a broad blade.
> Mill dam in tolerable good order but a little wanting to make things there very strong, and troughs to let the ponds from the runs into the canals run off into the meadow which is to be.
> Making tobacco hills. Potatoes came up, want weeding.
> Fork Corn not quite done in the Peach orchard. Therefore Cotton can't be planted there before next Monday, the old May day.
> Wheat looks tolerable, only a trespass from the Cowpen last Monday night.[26]

Landon Carter, one of the more scrupulous planters, even took to

---

25. Southern Historical Collection photographic copy of the original ms in the South Carolina Historical Society, Charleston. See also David R. Chesnutt, "South Carolina's Penetration of Georgia in the 1760s: Henry Laurens as a Case Study," *South Carolina Historical Magazine* 73 (October 1972): 204 for Laurens' attempts to use a new style of agent-overseer system of management.

26. Greene, ed., *Landon Carter's Diary*, II: 1038.

calculating the labor required, per plant per row, in an early time-and-motion study:

> I find it wondered at how any hand can tend 28,000 corn hills planted at any distance. But surely it cannot be reasonable to do so, when it is considered that at 2 feet and 7 an acre holds 3,111 corn hills and at 6 and 5 it holds only 1,452; for it is in such a case evident that at 7 and 2 the care contains more than double to what it does when planted at 6 and 5 by 202 hills. Allow then that at 6 and 5 ten thou[s]and hills only are tended; it will amount to near 7 acres that are worked each hand. Now at 7 and 2, 7 acres will contain 21,777 so that there only wants 6,223 to make up 28,000. Now that is Exactly 4 hill[s] short of 2 acres, So that the hand that tends 28,000 is only to tend 9 acres. And cannot a hand tend 9 acres of ground?[27]

Carter's entrepreneurial instincts were shared by his fellow planters throughout British America, but kept in check while they had to be colonial patriarchs and businessmen. His methods foreshadowed a more rationalized approach to plantation organization that changed the character of master-slave relationship on large ante-bellum plantations. As agriculture became increasingly commercialized, as part of the profound changes accelerated or set in motion in the South by the Revolution, the management of slaves and plantations became less personal and more uniform and routine.

IV

This development took place against the backdrop of a familiar story—the winning of Independence, the political and economic crises of the 1780s and, under the aegis of the Federalist Party, the establishment of national government, and an American economic system of centrally controlled commerce, banks and currency.

Less well known is the "economic revolution in the South" (Lewis C. Gray), where a switch to wheat, general farming and slave raising were only the most obvious indications of fundamental change.[28] Economic reorientation had been in motion since the non-importation agreements. Following Independence, wartime salt-, rope-, and ship-works, textile, forge and munitions manufactures (of which many had recruited and trained women, juveniles and slaves in the 1770s) continued to generate urbanization, population growth and expectations.[29] As usual slaves were conspicuous participants in these developments, and provide a useful way of evaluating the social impact of basic economic

27. *Ibid.*, II: 679.
28. Gray, *History of Agriculture in the Southern United States*, II: 613ff.
29. Mullin, *Flight and Rebellion*, ch. 4.

changes. In analyzing Gabriel Prosser's conspiracy, St. George Tucker in 1801 told the Virginia State legislature that:

> There is a progress in human affairs which may indeed be retarded, but which nothing can arrest. . . . Of such sort is the advancement of knowledge among the negroes of this country. . . . Every year adds to the number of those who can read and write. . . .
>
> In our infant country, where population and wealth increase with unexampled rapidity. . . . the growth and multiplication of our towns tend a thousand ways to enlighten and inform them. The very nature of our government, which lends us to recur perpetually to the discussion of natural rights, favors speculation and inquiry.[30]

Ante-bellum planters were also buffeted by the fierce currents Tucker knew so well. They enjoyed the mixed blessings of national sovereignty and a market economy of specialized, interdependent sections bound together by the instruments of a "Transportation Revolution"—canals, paddleboats, and eventually railroads. They lived in a society, which in outlawing the slave trade and enfranchising non-landholders, was less aristocratic and more democratic and egalitarian in tone than their forefathers'. They also enjoyed greater space.[31]

In breaking out of colonial boundaries — including geographical ones from Delaware to Georgia, and plunging greedily into the deep South, from the Floridas to the arid lands of western Texas— ante-bellum pioneers and adventurers contributed to a new social order characterized by one foreign observer after another in essentially the same manner: fortunes and families were made and lost in the twinkling of an eye; the business cycle was like a cannon ball loose in the hold of a rolling ship, because in America rather suddenly enterprise had become a religion. And in the South as well as the North, it was worshipped passionately. America, Francis J. Grund, an English immigrant observed, was a vast workshop with a sign at its entrance: "No admission here, except on business."[32]

---

30. [St. George Tucker], *Letter to a Member of the General Assembly of Virginia on the Subject of the Late Conspiracy of the Slaves, with a Proposal for their Colonization* (Richmond, 1801), Virginia State Library microfilm

31. This section is based on: documents in Edwin C. Rozwenc, ed., *Ideology and Power in the Age of Jackson* (New York, 1964), esp. 7-21, Pts. I and II; Edward Pessen, *Jacksonian America: Society, Personality and Politics* (Homewood, Ill., 1969), esp. chs. 2, 4-6; Douglass C. North, *The Economic Growth of the United States, 1790-1860* (New York, 1961); Marvin Fisher, *Workshops in the Wilderness* (New York, 1967); Douglas T. Miller, *The Birth of Modern America, 1820-1850* (New York, 1970), and Sigmund Diamond, "Values as an Obstacle to Economic Growth: The American Colonies," *Journal of Economic History* 27 (December 1967): 561-75.

32. Cited in Richard Hofstadter, *The American Political Tradition* (New York, 1948), p 57.

The boom-or-bust economy of the Jacksonian Era, like a freshly tapped keg of beer—bubbly, effervescent, and on top, largely foam—checked the development of another relatively stable and coherent ruling class of slaveowners; while accelerating mobility in a new, an American, society which favored expectant capitalists whose careers contrasted sharply with the lives of the lordly barons of Westover and Sabine Hall, who had moved in a more stately, three-quarter-time, in smaller, more elegant spaces filled with European art and music. The new leaders, like their hero Andrew Jackson, were "one-generation aristocrats," of "half-shod elegance"—suitable creatures of a comparatively raw and untried society possessing few of the traditions and refinements of the old colonial order.[33]

"It is imperative, indeed, to conceive it [the ante-bellum South] as having remained more or less fully in the frontier stage of a great part—maybe the greater part—of its history," wrote Wilbur J. Cash, who understood nineteenth-century planters as well as anyone. In his famous portrait of the rude origins from which they never completely recovered, Cash directed attention to a shrewd and useful criteria for evaluating a new elite's real nature and influence—longevity and stability (both geographical and structural). The colonial "gentleman," accustomed to a comparatively aged and mellow world," was abruptly rejected by Cash as a candidate for ante-bellum leadership. "Like every aristocrat, he required above all things a fixed background, the sense of absolute security and repose which proceeds from an environment which moves in well-worn grooves." Instead the new rich came from among "the strong, the pushing, the ambitious [of] the old coon-hunting population of the backcountry."[34]

Alexis de Tocqueville also understood the mysterious and potent connections between terrain, settlement patterns and class structure. Moving his analysis of Jacksonian America from the more settled East to the new states of the West and South where democracy had reached its "utmost limits," he argued that "society ha[d] no existence." "Founded offhand and as it were by chance, the inhabitants are but of yesterday" and the elite was "so completely disabled that we can scarcely assign to it any degree of influence."[35]

The transformation in the early nineteenth-century of the social and political setting for American Negro slavery changed the

33. See Hofstadter's memorable characterizations of the ante-bellum nouveau riche in *ibid.*, pp. 54-67.
34. Wilbur J. Cash, *The Mind of the South* (New York, 1941), pp. 10-20.
35. Alexis de Tocqueville, *Democracy in America*, "Social Conditions of the Anglo-Americans" Henry Reeve text rev. by Francis Bowen, Phillips Bradley, ed., 2 vols. (New York, 1946), I: 53ff.

planter's role and the mood of the documents he left about slavery. Planters were no longer colonists burdened by a need to make plantations self-sufficient and themselves patriarchs "independent on every one but Providence." Instead masters could be masterful in a more rational and profitable manner, by allowing the plantation to realize its potential, as an enterprise that concentrated most efficiently manpower, expertise and capital in the production of staples. But as the large plantation changed from a way of life to a business, new and ominous techniques were developed for regulating and routinizing the lives of slaves.

Sensitive to the currents of the day, arbiters of the new agriculture, and publishers of the popular farm journals, demanded accountability and a systemization of production: "The plantation is a piece of machinery . . . . To operate successfully, all of its parts should be uniform and exact, and the impelling force regular and steady." "No more beautiful picture of human society can be drawn than a well organized plantation. . . . A regular and systematic plan of operation of the plantation is greatly promotive of easy government. Have, therefore, all matters as far as possible reduced to a system." [36]

With the routinization of plantation operations came an even more important change: for ante-bellum slaves, most of whom lived on large plantations, slavery was no longer familial and domestic, but an impersonal and bureaucratic institution. The "Management of Negroes" articles in southern agricultural journals, written by editors, travelers, planters and overseers, encouraged slaveholders to devise more effective, manipulative techniques: "Make him [the slave] as comfortable at home as possible"; "treat your negro *well* and he will respond to it with fidelity and honesty; kind words, humane consideration, justness in discipline, unhesitating authority when required, forbearance towards venal offenses, arous[e] pride of character." [37]

Masters no longer aspired to be patriarchs but personnel managers, experts in motivational psychology: "I have found very little trouble in bringing them all under my system . . . by exciting his pride I elevate the man." If slaves on Sundays insisted on dressing "in the ridiculous finery which they sometimes display, and which often provides a smile," they should not be mocked, because such dress as this "aids very materially in giving them self-respect." [38]

---

36 "Management of Slaves," *De Bow's Review* 18 (June 1855): 718. *Southern Cultivator* 4 (March 1846): 44.
37. "Management of Slaves." *Southern Cultivator* 4 (March 1846): 44; "Treatment of Slaves—Mr. Guerry," *ibid.* 18 (August 1860): 258.
38. "Management of Negroes – Duties of Masters, &c.," *ibid.* 18 (June 1860): 177; "Overseers at the South," *De Bow's Review* 21 (September 1856): 279.

The new outlook encouraged a restructuring of the plantation community.[39] On many large units economic diversification by slave artisans (an important means of advancement for talented slaves) was all but abandoned. Aside from a household vegetable garden, a few pigs and corn fields, big plantations produced staples and little else. Most slaves were "hands" reduced to field regimens under a clearly defined chain of command—overseers, sub-overseers, drivers and foremen; and each moment of the day was as accountable and organized as the actual weighing and recording of cotton sacks at dusk.

> Then begins another push, which continues until the whole crop is gathered and housed. During 'picking time'. . . the hands are regularly roused, by a large bell or horn, about the first dawn of day, or earlier so that they are ready to enter the field as soon as there is sufficient light to distinguish the bolls. . . . The hands remain in the field until it is too dark to distinguish the cotton, having brought their meals with them. For the purpose of collecting the cotton, each hand is furnished with a large basket, and two coarse bags about the size of a pillow case, with a strong strap to suspend them from the neck or shoulders. The basket is left at the end of the row, and both bags taken along; when one bag is full as it can well be crammed, it is laid down in the row, and the hand begins to fill the second in the same way. As soon as the second is full, he returns to the basket, taking the other bag as he passes it, and empties both into the basket, treading it down well, to make it contain the whole day's work. The same process is repeated until night; when the basket is taken upon his head and carried to the scaffold-yard, to be weighed. There the overseer meets all hands at the scales, with the lamp, slate, and whip.[40]

As large plantations became factories-in-the-field planters did all they could to make field workers contented charges. The ante-bellum counterparts—of piped-in Muzak in automobile assembly plants and lunch-hour group therapy sessions to iron-out feelings of rebelliousness in large-scale Japanese industries—were all present: slave chapels with licensed ministers; nurseries for small children whose mothers worked in the fields, and games, contests

---

39. On the structure of the Southern export and import markets, and degree of plantation self-sufficiency (importations of pork and corn, particularly) a good place to begin is Harold D. Woodman, ed., *Slavery and the Southern Economy, Sources and Readings* (New York, 1966); and an issue of *Agricultural History* 44 (January 1970) devoted to "The Structure of the Cotton Economy of the Antebellum South," esp. Robert E. Gallman, "Self-Sufficiency in the Cotton Economy of the Ante-bellum South." See also James C. Bonnor, "Advancing Trends in Southern Agriculture, 1840-60," *Agricultural History* 22 (October 1948); and Edwin A. Davis, *Plantation Life in the Florida Parishes of Louisiana, 1836-1846, As Reflected in the Diary of Bennet H. Barrow* (New York, 1943), esp. pp. 25-26, 28-29, 37-38.

40. J. H. Ingrahm cited in Charles S. Sydnor, *Slavery in Mississippi* (Baton Rouge, 1933, 1966), p. 13. Cf Gray, *History of Agriculture in the Southern United States*, I: 553-54.

and rewards to encourage productivity and to make slavery fun. Planters large and small were quite frank about their motives for keeping slaves happy and presumably docile. But even "happiness" should be standardized. "Tattler" in the *Southern Cultivator* (November 1850) wrote: "When at work, I have no objection to their whistling or singing some lively tune, but no *drawling* tunes are allowed in the field, for their motions are almost certain to keep time with the music."[41]

The process of making the plantation "a perfect society," and the worker "comfortable at home," may have cost some slaves their individuality. If "Sambo" existed, that docile passive creature of the plantation's infantilizing tendencies, he was a product of the largest, late ante-bellum plantations.[42] In the last years of slavery, rebelliousness changed, and may have decreased as a result of this tendency toward closure of the institution from all external and internal disruption: in the colonial period virtually every plantation record is filled with instances of boondoggling, feigned illnesses, truancy, and theft, but similar nineteenth-century records contain only rare accounts of rebellious slaves of any kind. When resistance did occur (usually on smaller, more loosely organized plantations) it was typically self-defeating, violent and often deadly.

In transforming the familial and domestic character of colonial slavery, the wealthy ante-bellum planter created an alienating world for his slaves. Herbert Marcuse tells us that "free choice among a wide variety of goods and services does not signify freedom if these goods and services sustain social controls over a life of toil and fear—that is, if they sustain alienation."[43] Many slaves, reduced to mere numbers in account- and day-books were undoubtedly alienated; too enmeshed in a system with all of its small rewards to see ways out.

The new reality of plantation slavery revealed in the "Management of Negroes" articles was faithfully replicated in the records of many large plantations. In comparison with colonial crop-and day-books, entries for ante-bellum slaves were more abstract, uniform—and predictable:

---

41. "Tattler," "Management of Negroes," *Southern Cultivator* 8 (November 1850), p. 163.

42. On Sambo see Elkins, *Slavery*, p. 82; and Stampp, "Rebels and Samboes," *Journal of Southern History* 37 (August 1971): 367-92.

43. Herbert Marcuse, *One-Dimensional Man: Studies in the Ideology of Advanced Industrial Society* (Boston, 1964), pp. 7-8.

NAMES	Mon	Tues	Wed	Thur	Fri	Sat	Sun	Total/Sick
Richard	Roll logs	Ploughed	Hauled	Hauled	Ploughed	Chopped		
Emma	Cleaning up trash	Clear new ground	Clean up ground	Clean up ground	Scraped ditches	Shrubing		
Big Henry	Pile and Burn	Shrubing over Bayou	Burned	Burn	Cleaned new ground	Cleaned new ground [44]		

and,

> 1840. When a negro gets to be 50 years old his task must be reduced from 50 rows to 40. When a woman has a child her task must be 40 rows instead of 50. All the negroes under 20 years must have less than a full task, say from 17 to 20 years of age about 45 rows. All of the age of 11, 12, and 13 years to work two to a task. They all go out at 10 years old and the first year must work with their mothers and both together make one task.[45]

The most astute and informative contemporary observer of antebellum plantation life, Frederick Law Olmsted, left this unforgettable picture of the field hands' stultifying world-of-work:

> They are constantly and steadily driven up to their work, and the stupid, plodding, machine-like manner in which they labor is painful to witness. This was especially the case with the hoe-gangs. One of them numbered nearly two hundred hands (for the force of two plantations was working together), moving across the field in parallel lines, with a considerable degree of precision. I repeatedly rode through the lines at a canter, with other horsemen, often coming upon them suddenly, without producing the smallest change or interruption in the dogged action of the laborers, or causing one of them to lift an eye from the ground.[46]

Planters' attitudes had changed about slaves and their duties and responsibilities toward them. Their new industrial consciousness made it possible to see themselves as estate managers rather than patriarchs, and to delegate to the slaves' supervisors the necessary authority to assure a smooth operation. As an effective substitute for their own constant presence on the plantation, planters established strict and comprehensive rules and regulations for overseers that dealt with all major components of the plantation operation —from the slaves' bedding, diet and housing, to the most intimate details of their religious, fraternal and family lives. Managers and

44. Record Book, 1859-66 (entries for February 25-March 2), Le Blanc Family Papers, Louisiana State University Archives.
45. James A. Tait, Memorandum Book, 1831-40, Alabama State Archives.
46. Frederick Law Olmsted, *A Journey in the Back Country* (New York, 1863), pp. 81-2.

overseers kept careful records of marriages, births and deaths and physician's visits, the quantities of clothing, supplies and implements received from the planter; and quarterly inventories of stock, tools and crops, and daily accounts of cotton picked by each hand.

A quiet but significant advance in the technology of record-keeping accompanied the rationalization of plantation organization. In place of cramped and hurried notes taken in the margins or blank sheets of hand-sized almanacs, reformers like Thomas Affleck of Mississippi published detailed printed ledger pages, that brought together in one place several of the miscellaneous records usually kept by staple producers. The colonial almanacs were "comic absurdities" when compared to the new comprehensive ledgers, which Robert Williams argues were "essentially consistent with the intent and purpose of modern cost-accounting, and followed the best and most advanced principles of efficient administrative management."[47] The account books, for example, considered the often neglected factors of capital depreciation, labor costs, and social welfare. One of these new ledgers, which allowed the planter to lay out a coherent plan for his operations while providing him with a quick summary of his property and its workings, was advertised in *De Bow's Review* in 1850:

PLANTATION ACCOUNTS

Thomas Affleck, of Mississippi, published, several years ago, a Plantation Record and Account Book, of which Weld & Co., of New Orleans, are now the agents and part proprietors. . . . There are heads for inventories of stock, implements and tools; for daily records of events on the plantation; for quarterly abstracts; of cotton picked each day, names of negroes picking, averages, &c.; of articles furnished to the negroes during the year; of overseers' supplies; of birth and deaths on place; of physicians' visits and names etc. of patients; of bales [of] cotton made; average weight and sales; with full and ample directions to the planter in enabling him to keep the accounts with greatest ease.

Price. — No. 1, for a plantation of forty hands, or under, $2.50. No. 2, for a plantation of eighty hands, or under, $3.00. . . .

---

47. Robert Williams, "Thomas Affleck: Missionary to the Planter, the Farmer, and the Gardener," *Agricultural History* 31 (July 1957): 46.

The planting community and the press have fully recognized the simplicity and completeness of this work, and its
perfect adaptation to the end in view — that of affording to
planters and their overseers a plain and uniform book of
blanks, embracing every record and account necessary to be
kept upon a plantation.[48]

Paradoxically, we associate capitalistic enterprise with "Yankee
ingenuity"; but trends toward strict routine and accountability
were evident on southern plantations much earlier than in
northern mills. This is not surprising. Planters realized that they
had long controlled an indispensable factor for rationalizing such
enterprises as plantations: a disciplined labor force. Slaves not
only guaranteed built-in growth through their natural increase; but
in slavery there were not strikes, lock-outs or even endemic turn-
overs of personnel. That planters enjoyed a slave's labor for a
lifetime in itself probably offset the profits lost by the slaves'
noncooperativeness.

Southern agricultural entrepreneurs knew what they were doing
economically. Drawing upon a much longer and more consistent
tradition of large-scale enterprise, with a much more disciplined
and predictable labor force, than their northern counterparts, they
were able sooner to get down to fundamentals: producing staples
efficiently. Ironically, the organizers of the partial and regional
pre-war industrial revolution in the Northeast first had to contend
with potentially the most disruptive issue in the country: the
impact of a new, untried system of enterprise on small-scale
agrarian society.[49] There is a separate reality to different kinds of
historical records: the assumptions and values behind the ante-
bellum plantation accounts and articles in agricultural magazines
stand in sharp contrast to the homilies on chastity produced by
northern textile mill owners and managers for their farm-girl
operatives. Obviously, the culture of Industrial Man, which has a
long history in our work oriented society, had a distinctly
southern bias in ante-bellum America. And it may now be profitable to follow the example of Caribbean area scholars by also
construing the large nineteenth-century plantation as an urbaniz-
ing force creating—not conservative, suspicious, frugal and tradi-
tionalistic peasants—but landless, wage-earning, store-buying
countrymen, who had nothing to sell but their labor.[50]

Exceptions to this frame of reference were the small planters,
who were the real patriarchs and inheritors of the paternalism that

---

48. *De Bow's Review*, 8 (January 1850): 98.
49. Charles L. Sanford, ed., *In Quest of America, 1810-1824* (New York, 1964),
pp. 21, 351; Foster Rhea Dulles, *Labor in America* (rev. ed., New York, 1960), pp. 74-5;
and Herbert G. Gutman, "Work Culture, and Society in Industrializing America,
1815-1919," *American Historical Review* 78 (June 1973): 531-88, esp. 540-41, 550-54.
50. Cf Mintz in Guerra y Sánchez, *Sugar and Society*, p. 37.

pervaded colonial slave society. Clement Eaton (in *The Growth of Southern Civilization*) introduces a typical small slaveholder, James T. Burroughs, well known as the owner of Booker T. Washington. In this family, Burroughs and his sons worked all day in the fields beside their few prime hands, and everyone ate, slept, procreated and died beneath the same roof.[51] The letters of Rachel O'Connor, who grew cotton with sixteen slaves on Bayou Sarah, West Feliciana Parish, Louisiana, and some of Olmsted's marvelous travel reports, indicate clearly that old ways of slavery were very much alive in the ante-bellum era.[52] But these pockets of paternalism were usually located far from the routes to market, the navigable rivers, canals and railroads. One senses that, had the Civil War not intervened, they would have been victims of an evolutionary process—reptiles in an age of mammals.

The ante-bellum South was not a semi-feudal society dominated by a class of men defending an anti-bourgeois and unprofitable way of life. From the earliest times, however, the South had been locked into the most backward sector of Old World capitalistic imperialism, the New World plantation areas.[53] As tragic actors in this special niche, all Southerners, from the mightiest planter to the lowest slave, acquired a colonized mentality, fortified and refined by the interpersonal dynamics of the master-slave relationship. Even the application of the most advanced methods for maximizing profits from agriculture could not change that destiny. For this unhappy society civil war would be a painful but cathartic renewal.

---

51. Clement Eaton, *A History of the Old South*, 2nd ed. (New York, 1966), p. 235; also, "A Small Planter," "Management of Negroes," *De Bow's Review* 11 (October 1851): 371.

52. Weeks (David, and Family) Papers, Louisiana State University Archives; esp. Rachel's letters to Mary Weeks, January 11, 1830, June 4, 1832 and September 4, 1840; and to her brother, November 20, 1833, April 25, 1834, and July 30, 1836.

53. Stanley J. and Barbara H. Stein, eds., *The Colonial Heritage of Latin America: Essays on Economic Dependence in Perspective* (New York, 1970); and Caio Prado, *The Colonial Background of Modern Brazil* (Berkeley, 1967).

The Colonial Militia and Negro Manpower

By Benjamin Quarles

In the mainland colonies of British America there existed no homogeneous militia system, operating under a central command. Instead, each colony maintained and controlled its own independent militia force. Yet on one point, the use of the Negro for military service, policy became uniform throughout the colonies. Slave or free, Negroes were excluded from the militia, save as noncombatants or in unusual emergencies. This policy of semi-exclusion became so prevalent as to constitute a basic tenet of American military tradition.[1]

Since most of the Negroes were slaves, one of the major reasons for their exemption from military service was the concept that the servant's duty to his master superseded any obligation owed as a citizen to the colony or local community. Provincial legislatures, sensitive to the property rights of the master, were impressed by claims that tampering with his labor supply struck at the roots of colonial prosperity.[2] Hence legislation to enlist non-freemen for

[1] The preparation of this article was made possible by a Social Science Research Council grant for research in the history of military policy.

[2] This feeling was also demonstrated in the difficulties encountered by crown officials in trying to recruit indentured servants for the royal army. Governor Horatio Sharpe, for example, informed William Shirley in February, 1756, that unless recruiting officers stopped signing up apprentices and servants in Maryland, "an insurrection of the people is likely to ensue." William H. Browne et al. (eds.), *Archives of Maryland* (66 vols., Baltimore, 1883-   ), VI, 342. A similar letter came from the governor of Pennsylvania. Robert Hunter Morris to William Shirley, February 16, 1756, Charles H. Lincoln (ed.), *Correspondence of William Shirley* (2 vols., New York, 1912), II, 391-92. "I did give private orders," wrote a New Jersey governor, "to be very cautious of inlisting servants." Lewis Morris to William Gooch, July 14, 1740, *The Papers of Lewis Morris* (Newark, 1852), 96. This "cautious" attitude toward the enlistment of servants in the provincial armies is dealt with in Cheesman A. Herrick, *White Servitude in Pennsylvania* (Philadelphia, 1926), 233-53; Abbot E. Smith, *Colonists in Bondage* (Chapel Hill, 1947), 278-84; and Richard B. Morris, *Government and Labor in Early America* (New York, 1946), 282-90.

the militia usually stipulated that the consent of the master must first be obtained.

A second important reason for this limited use of the Negro was an understandable reluctance to put a gun in his hands. Furnishing military "accoutrements" to a slave and training him as a potential soldier was thought to be asking for trouble. Going through military evolutions on training day, a musket in his hands, might arouse notions of revolt in the slave. Furthermore, in time of actual warfare a bondman might disappear,[3] or even show up in the ranks of the enemy — French, Spanish, or Indian. In the military use of Negroes, "there must be great caution used," wrote a group of Carolina patentees, "lest our slaves when armed might become our masters."[4]

To prevent Negro enlistments, statute law lent its weight to custom. As might be expected, Virginia's enactments were earlier and more numerous than those of her sister colonies. In January, 1639, came the first prohibitory law: "All persons except negroes" were to be provided with arms and ammunition.[5] In the 1690's a Council order enjoined militia officers from enlisting "Physicians, Chirurgeons, Readers, Clerks, Ferrymen, Negroes."[6] Other enactments at the turn of the century forbade Negroes from holding any military office and slaves from serving "in horse or foot."[7]

Fear of slave uprisings subsided with time in the colony and the legislature eased somewhat the limitations on non-whites. Under a law of 1723 free Negroes, mulattoes,[8] and Indians might be enlisted as drummers or trumpeters. Moreover, in case of invasion, insurrection, or rebellion, these groups would be required to march with the militia and do "the duty of pioneers, or such other servile

[3] "If any servant upon pretence of going to the wars against the enemy do run away from his master's service," warned the New York legislature in 1684, "he shall if taken be greviously punished at the direction of the Governor and Council." *The Colonial Laws of New York* (5 vols., Albany, 1894-1896), I, 161-62.

[4] "Agent for Carolina and Merchants Trading Thither" to Board of Trade, July 18, 1715, William L. Saunders (ed.), *Colonial Records of North Carolina* (10 vols., Raleigh, 1886-1890), II, 197.

[5] William W. Hening (ed.), *The Statutes at Large: Being a Collection of All the Laws of Virginia* (13 vols., Philadelphia and New York, 1810-1823), I, 226.

[6] Henry R. McIlwaine (ed.), *Executive Journals of the Council of Colonial Virginia, 1680-1739* (4 vols., Richmond, 1925-1930), I, 526; also "The Randolph Manuscript," *Virginia Magazine of History and Biography* (Richmond), XX (April, 1912), 117.

[7] Hening (ed.), *Statutes at Large of Virginia*, III, 251, 336.

[8] Virginia defined a mulatto as the "child of an Indian and the child, grand child, or great grand child, of a negro." *Ibid.*, III, 252.

labour as they shall be directed to perform." [9] But Virginia went no further. By subsequent militia acts these Negroes and Indians, although eligible to summons, were prohibited from carrying arms.[10] Furthermore, any exempted Negro who presumed to show up at a muster was to be fined one hundred pounds of tobacco, "and shall immediately give security to the . . . commanding officer, for paiment of the same." [11]

Similar policies evolved above the Potomac. As early as 1643, Plymouth, having joined the New England Confederation and deeming it necessary to establish a militia, stipulated that no one should be permitted to enlist "but such as are of honest and good report, & freemen." [12] But it was Massachusetts, New England's oldest and strongest permanent colony, that set the pattern of military policy in that region. Shortage of manpower in early Massachusetts fostered widespread encouragement of militia training, and even the parents of children from ages ten to sixteen were urged to permit them to take instruction in the handling of small arms.[13] An enactment followed in 1652 specifying that militia enlistments were to include "all Scotsmen, Negers and Indians inhabiting with or servants to the English." [14] This measure was of short duration. Four years later the legislature prohibited the mustering in of Negroes or Indians, explaining the step as necessary in the interests of "the better ordering and settling of severall cases in the military companyes." [15]

Henceforth, despite the perennial difficulties of procuring militiamen,[16] Massachusetts officially held to this policy of exclusion. Governor Simon Bradstreet, writing to his superiors in England in 1680, indicated that enlistment in the militia was non-selective, "except Negroes and slaves whom wee arme not." [17] In 1693 a re-

[9] *Ibid.*, IV, 119.

[10] Act of 1738, *ibid.*, V, 17; Act of 1755, *ibid.*, VI, 533; Act of 1757, *ibid.*, VII, 95.

[11] *Ibid.*, IV, 119.

[12] Nathaniel B. Shurtleff *et al.* (eds.), *Records of the Colony of New Plymouth in New England* (12 vols., Boston, 1855-1861), II, 61.

[13] Nathaniel B. Shurtleff (ed.), *Records of the Governor and Company of the Massachusetts Bay in New England* (5 vols., Boston, 1853-1854), II, 99.

[14] *Ibid.*, III, 268.

[15] *Ibid.*, 397.

[16] For these difficulties see Jack S. Radabaugh, "The Militia of Colonial Massachusetts," *Military Affairs* (Washington), XVIII (Spring, 1954), 10-11.

[17] Simon Bradstreet to Privy Council, May 18, 1680, James Savage (ed.), "Gleanings from New England History," *Collections of the Massachusetts Historical Society*, 3rd series, VIII (Boston, 1843), 336.

affirmation came from the General Court: Negroes were included among those "exempted from all trainings." [18]

Exclusionary legislation of the Virginia and Massachusetts type soon became standard practice. Connecticut in 1660 forbade Negroes from serving in the watch or train bands. [19] Twenty years later the Maryland assembly ordered that "all negroes and slaves whatsoever shall be exempted the duty of trayning or any other millitary service," a prohibition that was re-enacted in 1715. [20] New Hampshire in 1718 exempted Negroes from training, [21] and New Jersey in 1760 ruled against the enlistment of slaves without the written permission of the masters. [22] In Philadelphia as late as the opening of the Revolutionary War, the Committee of Safety ordered to the workhouse one David Owen, "a person suspected of enlisting Negroes." [23]

The exemption of Negroes from militia duty seemed to put them in a privileged class with clergymen, public officials, and other notables. Hence Massachusetts devised the practice of labor service. A law of 1707, after pointing out that Negroes shared the benefit of military protection without bearing a commensurate responsibility, stipulated that they should "do service equivalent to trainings." This was spelled out as "so many day's work yearly" in street cleaning, highway maintenance, and other service for the common benefit. Moreover, in times of peril, Negroes were required "to make their appearance at parade" and, once there, to do as directed. Failure to report was finable at five shillings for each day's neglect of duty; the penalty for not showing up in time of danger was twenty shillings or eight days' labor. [24]

[18] *Acts and Laws of the General Court of Massachusetts, 1692 to 1719* (London, 1724), 51.

[19] James H. Trumbull and Charles J. Hoadly (eds.), *Public Records of the Colony of Connecticut* (15 vols., Hartford, 1850-1890), I, 349. For the relationship between military defense and slave legislation in the Puritan colonies see Lorenzo J. Greene, *The Negro in Colonial New England, 1620-1776* (New York, 1942), 126-27.

[20] *Archives of Maryland*, VII, 56; *Laws of Maryland* (Annapolis, 1744), 143.

[21] *Acts and Laws of His Majesty's Province of New-Hampshire in New-England* (Portsmouth, 1771), 95.

[22] Samuel Nevill (ed.), *The Acts of the General Assembly of the Province of New Jersey* (2 vols., Woodbridge, 1752-1761), II, 267.

[23] *Colonial Records of Pennsylvania, 1683-1790* (16 vols., Philadelphia, 1852-1853), X, 427.

[24] *Acts and Laws of Massachusetts, 1692 to 1719*, p. 242. During the first year after the law was passed 33 Negroes in Boston spent a total of 218 days of labor in public works. George H. Moore, *Notes on the History of Slavery in Massachusetts* (New York, 1866), 60-61. From the time of the enactment of the measure much of Boston's

Watch service, rather than labor, was preferred in Rhode Island. Here in 1676 the legislature decreed that "a negro man capable of watch . . . shall be lyable to that service." [25] This step was in line with the colony's avowed determination to make all citizens "observant," either actively or passively, of military affairs; but watch service did not necessitate carrying firearms.

An armed slave was an anomaly seldom tolerated in normal times by the provincial legislatures. Hence the barring of Negroes from the militia was commonly supplemented by laws to keep weapons out of their hands. Again Virginia took the lead. In 1680 the Jamestown assembly prohibited Negroes from carrying clubs, swords, guns, or other weapons of defense or offense. The preamble of this measure explained that it was necessary because "the frequent meeting of considerable numbers of negroe slaves under pretence of feasts and burialls is judged of dangerous consequence." [26] Restated in 1705, the law substituted "slave" for "negroe or other slave," [27] but an enactment of 1723 removed any doubt: arms were to be carried by "no negro, mulatto, or indian whatsoever," under penalty of a whipping not to exceed twenty-nine lashes. [28]

Similar precautions were taken by other provincial bodies. Negro arms-bearing was prohibited in Pennsylvania in 1700; a colored person convicted of carrying a gun, pistol, fowling piece, club, "or other weapons whatsoever" would receive twenty-one lashes on the bare back. [29] South Carolina's comprehensive slave code of 1712 required every master to have all "negro houses" searched fortnightly for guns, swords, clubs, or other "mischievous" weapons. [30] The Delaware counties prohibited blacks from bearing arms or serving in the militia "upon any pretense whatsoever." This action, taken

road maintenance was done by impressed Negroes. Carl Bridenbaugh, *Cities in the Wilderness* (New York, 1955), 163.

[25] John R. Bartlett (ed.), *Records of the Colony of Rhode Island and Providence Plantations in New England* (10 vols., Providence, 1856-1865), II, 536. New Hampshire's comprehensive militia act of 1718, although barring Negroes from the trainings, did not list them among the groups exempt from "military watchings and wardings."

[26] Hening (ed.), *Statutes at Large of Virginia*, II, 481.

[27] *Ibid.*, III, 459.

[28] *Ibid.*, IV, 131.

[29] James T. Mitchell and Henry Flanders (eds.), *Statutes at Large of Pennsylvania from 1682 to 1801* (16 vols., Harrisburg, 1896-1908), II, 79. Reaffirmed five years later (*ibid.*, 235-36), this law was not repealed until after the colonial period (1780).

[30] Thomas Cooper and David J. McCord (eds.), *Statutes at Large of South Carolina* (10 vols., Columbia, 1836-1841), VII, 353.

in 1741 after the news of a Negro plot to burn New York, was considered necessary, the authorities explained, because the counties were now exposed not only to foreign enemies "but to the insults also or insurrections of our own slaves." [31]

In cases where frontier defense or game hunting might dictate arming the slave, appropriate safeguards were required. In Virginia, slaves on frontier plantations might use guns, but only if properly licensed. As a further safeguard, only the master could procure such a permit for his servant.[32] A New Jersey ruling of 1694 allowed slaves to carry firearms if accompanied by the master or his representative.[33] Similarly, North Carolina in 1729 forbade slaves to hunt with dog or gun unless accompanied by a white man.[34] Maryland permitted its bondmen to carry offensive weapons only when on the master's premises.[35]

The general policy, therefore, in colonial America was to exclude the Negro from military participation and arms-bearing. But times of peril made for hard choices; in such a season it might be necessary to take a calculated risk. The arming of slaves was considered particularly risky in time of war; indeed, much of the legislation of Negro exclusion came when enemy danger threatened most. "The villany of the Negroes on an emergency of gov't is w't I always feared," wrote Governor Robert Dinwiddie, of Virginia, when informed of trouble with the Negroes near Fort Cumberland during the early months of the French and Indian War.[36]

Yet equally serious in wartime was the paucity of manpower. It was this shortage that often overcame customary caution. South Carolina, exposed to enemy attack and heavily populated with Negroes, perhaps best illustrates the provincial problem of using slaves as soldiers. Faced with an Indian threat following the outbreak of Queen Anne's War, the colony in 1703 authorized masters to arm their slaves if enemy invasion materialized.[37] Taking the big step a year later, the assembly ordered masters to furnish slaves,

---

[31] *Laws of the Government of New-Castle, Kent, and Sussex upon Delaware* (Philadelphia, 1741-1742), 178.

[32] Hening (ed.), *Statutes at Large of Virginia*, IV, 131.

[33] Aaron Leaming and Jacob Spicer (eds.), *The Grants, Concessions, and Original Constitutions of the Province of New-Jersey* (Philadelphia, 1758), 341.

[34] *Laws of the State of North Carolina* (2 vols., Raleigh, 1821), I, 125.

[35] *Laws of Maryland*, 144.

[36] Dinwiddie to Charles Carter, July 18, 1755, in Robert A. Brock (ed.), *Official Records of Robert Dinwiddie* (2 vols., Richmond, 1883-1884), II, 101.

[37] Cooper and McCord (eds.), *South Carolina Statutes*, VII, 33.

upon summons, for the provincial militia. Payment for their service would be made from public funds.[38] Typical of legislation authorizing Negro enlistments (and military legislation generally), this measure had a time limit; in this instance the law was to continue in force for only two years.

In 1708 the assembly passed a more comprehensive bill. Its preamble reaffirmed the necessity, in time of actual invasion, of enlisting trusted slaves, "accoutred and armed with a lance or hatchet or gun" supplied from the provincial stores. A slave who killed or captured an enemy would be freed; a slave disabled while fighting would be liberated and thereafter maintained "at the charge of the public." [39]

When Indian troubles persisted after Queen Anne's War, the assembly again authorized the use of Negroes in the militia. In May, 1715, a month after the outbreak of the Yamassee War, Governor Charles Craven informed London that he had "caused about two hundred stout negro men to be enlisted." This step was necessary, he explained, because there were so few white men ("not above fifteen hundred") in the colony.[40] Within five years the assembly again ordered that in time of danger masters were to make available to militia officers the services of trusted slaves from ages sixteen to sixty. It provided also that a slave who killed or captured an enemy was to receive ten pounds from "the Public Receiver for every killing or taking." [41]

During the following two decades South Carolina felt no need for slave recruits. But in 1739, faced by the menace of the Spanish garrison at St. Augustine, the colony again took the venturesome step. Asserting that "Negroes and slaves have behaved themselves with faithfulness and courage and demonstrated that in some instances faith and trust may be put in them," the assembly authorized the governor to empower militia captains to enlist "recommended" slaves. Only at a time of general alarm and invasion would they be armed; then each enlisted slave would be furnished with a gun, a hatchet, a powder horn, a shot pouch with ammunition and bullets for twenty rounds, and six spare flints. For killing an enemy, taking him alive, or capturing his colors, liberation was to be the reward. A

[38] *Ibid.*, 347-49.
[39] *Ibid.*, 349-51.
[40] Charles Craven to Secretary of State Charles Townshend, May 23, 1715, Saunders (ed.), *Colonial Records of North Carolina*, II, 178.
[41] Cooper and McCord (eds.), *South Carolina Statutes*, III, 108-10.

slave who fought well enough "to deserve public notice" would receive yearly "a livery coat and pair of breeches made of good red
Negro Cloth turned up with blue, and a black hat, and pair of black
shoes, and shall that day in every year during their lives on which
such action was performed be freed and exempted from all personal
service or labor." [42]

A year later, when an expedition to reduce the St. Augustine garrison was proposed, General James E. Oglethorpe suggested that
one thousand Negroes be drafted, of whom eight hundred would be
military laborers and two hundred would be armed for combat.[43]
The assembly voted that the pay for such slaves "shall be £10 Currency per Month, the Owners running all Hazzards" that might attend the expedition. A later provision specified, however, that the
masters of any slaves between twenty and fifty years of age who were
killed in action would be paid a sum "not exceeding £250 per
Head." [44]

Before the South Carolina experiment of using blacks in the
militia could be tested, a slave uprising took place in September,
1739, at Stono, less than twenty miles from the capital. Another
full-scale slave conspiracy followed nine months later in Charles
Town itself.[45] To the alarmed South Carolinians two things seemed
clear: the rebellious Negroes had been in possession of firearms; and
they had undoubtedly been urged on, albeit not openly, by the
Spaniards. The reaction was prompt. Faced with Negro revolts and
plots, the lawmakers reversed their position. On December 11,
1740, the assembly ordered "that the law for encouraging armed
Negroes, and for making them useful for the defense of the province
be speedily revised." [46] A permanent damper fell on Negro enlistment in the militia. Twenty years later, with the colony beset
by trouble with the Cherokees, a motion to arm five hundred Negroes
was defeated by the deciding vote of the presiding officer.[47]

[42] South Carolina Acts, 1733-1739 (Law Library, Library of Congress). The acts
down to 1736 were printed; those for the period after 1736 are handwritten and un-
paged.

[43] For Oglethorpe's military labor proposal see J. Harold Easterby (ed.), *The
Colonial Records of South Carolina* (7 vols., Columbia, 1951-   ), II, 175-78. For the
suggestion on Negro troops see John Tate Lanning (ed.), *The St. Augustine Expedition of 1740* (Columbia, 1954), 97.

[44] Easterby (ed.), *Colonial Records of South Carolina*, II, 195, 309.

[45] Herbert Aptheker, *American Negro Slave Revolts* (New York, 1943), 187-89.

[46] Easterby (ed.), *Colonial Records of South Carolina*, II, 420.

[47] John R. Alden, *John Stuart and the Southern Colonial Frontier* (Ann Arbor,
1944), 113-14.

The South Carolina experience was duplicated in Georgia. Three years before the Revolutionary War the Georgia assembly voted to arm slaves if such a step became necessary, and masters were required to furnish militia officers with lists of all their capable and trustworthy slaves between ages sixteen and sixty. Remarkably similar to the South Carolina law of 1739, this act promised freedom to slaves who killed or captured an enemy. A slave who fought bravely would receive annually a supply of bright-colored clothes, and be excused from labor on the anniversaries of his heroism.[48] But the provisions of this act were not carried out. Subsequent incidents, such as that of the ten slaves who ran amuck in St. Andrew's Parish after killing their overseer,[49] seemed to bring sober second thoughts concerning the arming of the Negro.

Georgia was not unique in holding misgivings and in taking precautionary steps. But in colonial America official attitudes toward arming the Negro did not always mirror actual practice. A case in point is the French and Indian War period during which colored men were enlisted in both southern and northern colonies. A few illustrative instances may be noted. In Granville County, North Carolina, under date of October 8, 1754, a muster roll of Colonel William Eaton's company lists five Negroes and two mulattoes, a roll of Captain John Glover's company lists three Negroes, and that of Captain Osborn Jeffreys lists five Negroes.[50] And in Virginia, General Edward Braddock wrote from Williamsburg in 1755: "There are here numbers of mulattoes and free Negroes of whom I shall make bat men, whom the province are to furnish with pay and frocks." [51]

In the French and Indian War the colony of New York made extensive use of the Negro.[52] So did Connecticut; in her wartime

[48] Allen D. Candler (ed.), *Colonial Records of the State of Georgia* (26 vols., Atlanta, 1904-1916), XIX, Part I, 324-29.

[49] Ulrich B. Phillips (ed.), *Plantation and Frontier Documents, 1649-1863* (2 vols., Cleveland, 1909), II, 118-19.

[50] Walter Clark (ed.), *The State Records of North Carolina* (26 vols., Winston and Goldsboro, 1886-1907), XXII, 370-72. After the war customary precautions were resumed; by an act of 1768 overseers of six slaves or more were to be fined if they appeared at musters. Luther L. Gobbel, "The Militia in North Carolina in Colonial and Revolutionary Times," *Historical Papers of the Trinity College Historical Society* (Durham), XII (1916), 42.

[51] Edward Braddock to Robert Napier, March 17, 1755, Stanley Pargellis (ed.), *Military Affairs in North America, 1748-1765* (New York, 1936), 78.

[52] For the names of Negroes serving in New York companies, with such descriptive data as date of enlistment, age, birthplace, occupation, stature, militia company, and

militia colored men served in twenty-five different companies.[53] In Rhode Island, James Richardson of Stonington, advertising in May, 1763, for his Negro servant, reported him as having served as a soldier earlier that year.[54] The town of Hingham, Massachusetts, recruiting men in 1758 for the prosecution of the war, included two Negroes, Primus Cobb and Flanders, among the thirty-six privates in Captain Edward Ward's company.[55] Jeremy Belknap expressed the belief that in Massachusetts as a whole the number of slaves declined by 1763 "because in the two preceding wars, many of them were enlisted either into the army or on board vessels of war, with a view to procure their freedom." [56]

In fine, despite the laws, Negroes were enlisted. This difference between policy and practice is but another illustration of the colonial dilemma with respect to the use of slaves as soldiers. "They are . . . necessary, but very dangerous domestics," commented a prominent South Carolina physician in 1763.[57] To arm the Negroes was hazardous, but the latent military strength they represented was undeniable — a manpower potential often too badly needed and too readily available to be ignored.

officer who did the enlisting, see "Muster Rolls of New York Provincial Troops, 1755-1764," *Collections of the New-York Historical Society for 1891* (New York, 1892), 60, 182, 284, 364, 385, 398, 402, 406, 418, 420, 426, 427, 440, 442, 498. One Negro, Salomon Jolly, is designated as free ; the others, presumably, were slaves.

[53] "Rolls of Connecticut Men in the French and Indian War" (2 vols.), I, 322, II, 437, *Collections of the Connecticut Historical Society*, Vols. IX, X (Hartford, 1903-1905). The number of companies is derived from a page check of the regimental and militia affiliations of the Negroes listed (barring duplications) in the indexes of these two volumes.

[54] "Eighteenth Century Slaves as Advertised by Their Masters," *Journal of Negro History* (Washington), I (April, 1916), 200.

[55] *History of the Town of Hingham, Massachusetts* (3 vols., Hingham, 1893), I, 265.

[56] "Queries Respecting the Slavery and Emancipation of Negroes in Massachusetts, Proposed by the Honorable Judge Tucker of Virginia, and Answered by the Reverend Dr. Belknap," *Collections of the Massachusetts Historical Society*, 1st series, IV (Boston, 1795), 199.

[57] George Milligen-Johnston, *A Short Description of the Province of South-Carolina* (London, 1770), reprinted in Chapman J. Milling (ed.), *Colonial South Carolina: Two Contemporary Descriptions* (Columbia, 1951), 136.

The Legal Status of the Slave in South Carolina, 1670-1740

By M. EUGENE SIRMANS

THE LEGAL STATUS OF THE NEGRO SLAVE WAS EVENTUALLY THE same in all the British colonies on the North American mainland, for by the middle of the eighteenth century the law in each of those colonies adjudged the slave to be his master's personal chattel. Despite their final unanimity the colonies arrived at chattel slavery on different roads. Following the trail pioneered by Virginia and Maryland, most provinces treated Negroes as perpetual servants for several decades prior to the legal adoption of chattel slavery. South Carolina took a somewhat different route. Before it made the Negro slave a chattel, it first experimented with other approaches to the legal problems involved.

In tracing the evolution of chattel slavery in South Carolina the colony's relationship with Barbados demands particular attention. Historians used to assume that immigrants to South Carolina from the West Indies "brought with them the slave code of those islands, especially that of Barbados,"[1] and that South Carolina copied its slave laws from those of Barbados. Some years ago this generalization was challenged by Oscar and Mary Handlin, who contended that South Carolina could not have borrowed its slavery customs from Barbados or any other island colony, because the "labor system of those places was not yet fully evolved" when South Carolina adopted its first slave laws and because statutory chattel slavery never existed in the islands.[2]

Throughout the history of Negro servitude in Barbados, the colonists there disliked specific legal definitions of slavery and preferred the institution to be defined by custom rather than by law. Consequently, their slave laws dealt with the control of slaves instead of their legal status. This enabled Barbados to impose upon the Negro the conditions of servitude desired by his master

---

[1] Edward McCrady, "Slavery in the Province of South Carolina, 1670-1770," in American Historical Association, *Report* (1895), 644.

[2] Oscar and Mary F. Handlin, "Origins of the Southern Labor System," *William and Mary Quarterly*, s. 3, VII (April 1950), 206.

without English interference.[3] Nevertheless, Barbadians did develop a system of slavery—extralegal though it was—possibly as early as the 1630's, but certainly by the 1650's when one commentator observed, "They [Negroes] and the generation are Slaves to their owners to perpetuity." Barbadians of the time referred to Negroes as slaves, and slavery was the normal condition of Negroes. They served their masters for life, and Negro children inherited the status of their parents.[4] Custom, not law, defined the Negro's status. The system continued to be informal until 1668, when the assembly enacted a law defining slaves as real estate, or freehold property. Four years later the assembly amended the law by making the slave a personal chattel in payment of his master's debts. The laws of 1668 and 1672 were the colony's final words on the status of slaves. Thereafter, Barbados avoided further questions of legal status and passed only laws relating to police control, of which the most important was the comprehensive slave code of 1688.[5]

Barbados exerted its influence on South Carolina from the beginnings of the younger colony. A Barbadian, Sir John Colleton, was the prime mover in securing the proprietary charter for Carolina. Many of the first settlers were Barbadians, and the first Negroes in South Carolina came from Barbados. It would be reasonable to assume that the Barbadians brought their slavery practices with them, and the surviving evidence supports such an assumption. There may have been a Barbadian source even for the provision in John Locke's Fundamental Constitutions of Carolina that said, "Every freeman of Carolina, shall have absolute power and authority over his negro slaves . . . ."[6] Locke corresponded with Sir Peter Colleton, a proprietor and resident of Barbados,[7] and he

[3] *Ibid.*, 219-20; James Stephen, *The Slavery of the British West-India Colonies* . . . (2 vols., London, 1824-1830), I, 14-15.

[4] Winthrop D. Jordan, "The Influence of the West Indies on the Origins of New England Slavery," *William and Mary Quarterly*, s. 3, XVIII (April 1961), 248-50; the quotation is from "A Briefe Discription of the Ilande of Barbados" in Vincent T. Harlow (ed.), *Colonising Expeditions to the West Indies and Guiana, 1623-1667* (Hakluyt Society, *Works*, s. 2, No. 55 [London, 1925]), 44-45, quoted in Jordan, "The Influence of the West Indies on the Origins of New England Slavery," 249.

[5] Richard Hall (comp.), *Acts Passed in the Island of Barbados, from 1643, to 1762, Inclusive* (London, 1764), 64-65, 93-94, 112-21; Richard Hall, *An Abridgement of the Acts in Force, in the Island of Barbados, from 1643, to 1762, Inclusive* (London, 1764), 60; John Poyer, *The History of Barbados, from . . . 1605, till . . . 1801* (London, 1808), 132-33, 136-40.

[6] William L. Saunders (ed.), *The Colonial Records of North Carolina, 1662-1776* (10 vols., Raleigh, 1886-1890), I, 204.

[7] Maurice Cranston, *John Locke: A Biography* (New York, 1957), 120, 156.

may well have acquired his knowledge of slavery from this source.

South Carolina differentiated between white servants and Negroes from the first and treated the Negroes as slaves. For example, the Grand Council in 1672 and 1673 sentenced white servants to extra service as a punishment, but never Negroes, thus tacitly recognizing that Negroes already served for life.[8] In its first years South Carolina had but few persons who were subject to involuntary servitude. There was only a small number of Negroes and perhaps a slightly larger number of Indian captives, a group that always shared the Negro's status in South Carolina.[9] More important and more numerous than either were the white servants. The first laws relating to servitude therefore applied primarily to white servants, with provisions applying to Negroes and Indians added almost as an afterthought. Such laws were concerned only with the policing of the unfree population and made no explicit reference to legal status. Implicit in the laws, however, was a distinction between white servants and nonwhite slaves; the statutes followed the example of the Grand Council by providing extra service as punishment for white servants but never for Negroes or Indians.[10]

The first South Carolina law relating solely to slavery was passed by the assembly in 1690, a time when the government of the colony was under the control of a political faction headed by former Barbadians. The law of 1690 drew upon the Barbadian acts of 1668 and 1672 for its definition of slavery, retaining the meaning though not the wording of the Barbadian definition. The South Carolina statute provided that slaves "as to payment of debts, shall be deemed and taken as all other goods and chattels ... and all negroes shall be accounted as freehold in all other cases whatsoever, and descend accordingly." In other words, except in payment of the master's debt, slaves were to be freehold property.

[8] Grand Council Journals, January 10, October 8, 18, 1672, August 30, 1673, in South Carolina Historical Society, Collections (5 vols., Charleston, 1857-1897), V, 373-74, 413-14, 427. For other examples of differentiation between white servants and Negroes, see Alexander S. Salley (ed.), Warrants for Land in South Carolina, 1672-1711 (3 vols., Columbia, 1910-1915), I, 55, 70, 94.

[9] Although South Carolina enslaved a large number of Indians, more than any other colony, their presence there did not exert a discernible influence on the legal development of slavery. The absence of such an influence may be explained by the fact that most of the captured Indians were immediately shipped out of the colony and sold in the West Indies. On this subject, see Almon Wheeler Lauber, Indian Slavery in Colonial Times Within the Present Limits of the United States (New York, 1913), 105-106, 240.

[10] Thomas Cooper and David J. McCord (eds.), Statutes at Large of South Carolina (14 vols., Columbia, 1836-1875), II, 22-23. This law is apparently a re-enactment of an earlier law of the same nature, see ibid., II, v.

Clauses relating to the policing of slaves came from earlier servant laws but with the addition of special controls for slaves. Slaves needed written permission to leave their masters' residences; slave-owners were required to make regular searches of slave quarters for weapons; and slaves who ran away or struck their masters faced severe penalties, among which were whipping, branding, slitting the nose, and emasculation.[11]

The unusual feature of the South Carolina act of 1690 was its definition of the slave as freehold property. Freehold slavery was common in the Caribbean, whether the colony was English, French, Spanish, or Portuguese, but rare on the mainland. As freehold property the Negro enjoyed a higher legal status than he did as chattel, because freehold was a higher form of property than chattel. Freehold property was attached to a landed estate and could not be moved; its holder legally had a right only to its use and not absolute ownership. Freehold slavery thus implied that a master had a right to the slave's services rather than to the slave himself. On the other hand, chattels were defined as the owner's personal belongings which he could dispose of as he pleased. In short, freehold slavery attached the slave to land, like a serf, while chattel slavery attached him to a master, a condition unknown in English law and a uniquely North American development.[12]

The slave act of 1690, passed during the administration of the rebel governor, Seth Sothell, was disallowed by the proprietors along with all other laws passed during Sothell's governorship. South Carolina did not yet really need a slave law as slaveholding was not to become widespread until about five years later, when the colony began to produce a marketable staple that required a large labor force. After planters began to cultivate rice successfully and to demand cheap labor, the South Carolina assembly passed a new slave bill in 1696, a bill so comprehensive in its control of the slave's life as to deserve the designation of South Carolina's first slave code.

The assembly again borrowed from Barbados. The South Caro-

---

[11] *Ibid.*, VII, 343-47. On the political control of the colony by a Barbadian faction, see M. Eugene Sirmans, *Masters of Ashley Hall: A Biographical Study of the Bull Family of Colonial South Carolina, 1670-1737* (unpublished Ph.D. thesis, Princeton University, 1959), 68-69, 75-77.

[12] William Blackstone, *Commentaries on the Laws of England* (4 vols., London, 1765-1769), Bk. II, chs. 7, 24; "Chattels Personal" and "Freehold" in Giles Jacob, *The Law Dictionary*, T. E. Tomlins, ed. (2 vols., London, 1797); Stephen, *Slavery of British West-India Colonies*, I, 63-69.

lina law of 1696 was copied from the Barbados slave code of 1688. The assembly of South Carolina enacted verbatim the Barbadian statute's preamble and three fourths of its provisions for policing the slave population. As in the Barbadian law, the preamble to the South Carolina bill stated that special legislation was necessary to govern slaves, because Negroes had "barbarous, wild, savage Natures" and were "naturally prone and inclined" to "Disorders, Rapines, and Inhumanity." The South Carolina code re-enacted the provisions of the act of 1690 relating to the control of slaves, and it added others from the Barbadian code on the prevention of slave crimes and the trial of miscreant slaves. A new clause, enacted by the South Carolina assembly in 1696, tried to eliminate potentially dangerous gatherings of slaves by directing the constables of Charles Town to break up slave assemblies on the Sabbath.[13]

Once again the most unusual part of the law was its definition of a slave. The law stated, "All Negroes, Mollatoes, and Indians which at any time heretofore have been bought and Sold or now are and taken to be or hereafter Shall be Bought and Sold are hereby made and declared they and their Children Slaves to all Intents and purposes." [14] This definition, which was solely the product of the South Carolina assembly, was unique in colonial America. Vague to the point of being cryptic, the definition followed the general policy of Barbados and other island colonies but went further. The purpose of the islanders in resting slavery upon custom instead of law had apparently been to obviate interference from authorities in England; perhaps the South Carolina legislators were seeking to achieve the same end. If so, they succeeded, for neither the proprietors nor the Crown intervened in the slave practices of South Carolina as long as the code of 1696 remained in force.

The simple but broad definition of slaves as "Slaves to all Intents and purposes" made custom the arbiter of slavery in South Carolina. The question remains, however, of just what that custom was. The surviving evidence that bears on this question is fragmentary and inconclusive, but it is all on one side. It indicates that it was the custom of South Carolina in the early eighteenth century to

---

[13] Governor Archdale's Laws [1696] (South Carolina Archives, Columbia), fol. 60-66. David J. McCord omitted this law from his and Cooper's edition of the South Carolina statutes but included the re-enactment of it in 1712; see Cooper and McCord (eds.), *Statutes at Large of South Carolina*, VII, 352-65. This has led several historians to date the first passage of the law incorrectly as 1712; see, for example, McCrady, "Slavery in South Carolina," 645.

[14] Archdale's Laws, fol. 60.

treat slaves as chattels. In a promotional tract of 1712, John Norris wrote, "When these people [Negroes] are thus bought, their Masters, or Owners, have then as good a Right to and title to them, during their lives, as a Man has here to a Horse or Ox, after he has bought them." [15] This sounds like chattel slavery. But Norris was only a pamphleteer and not a jurist or even an official of the colony. A more explicit statement by an official was offered in 1725 by Arthur Middleton, who was then acting governor of the colony. He said flatly that slaves "have been and are always deemed as goods and Chattels of their Masters."[16]

The court records of a colony often provide the best indication of the slave's status, but some of the more important sets of South Carolina's judicial records offer few clues to the problem of status. The only provincial court of common pleas sat in Charles Town, and none of its records are extant for the period before 1733. No case that came before the court after that date involved the status of a Negro or Indian. The post-1733 records are only judgment books, so there is no way to tell whether slaves were attached by writs of ejectment or replevin, the first of which would indicate freehold slavery and the second, chattel slavery.[17] The records of the court of vice-admiralty contain the one surviving record of a court case involving in any way the status of Negroes, but it is an inconclusive one. In 1736 a sea captain found three Negroes adrift in a canoe off the coast of South Carolina. The court of vice-admiralty treated the Negroes as salvage and sold them at auction. The case does not prove that the court defined slaves as chattel property, because it might have treated freehold property the same way in the unlikely event that a house or a barn had been found adrift at open sea.[18]

[15] John Norris, *Profitable Advice for Rich and Poor . . .* (London, 1712), 17-18.
[16] Journal of the Council of South Carolina, September 10, 1725, Colonial Office Papers (Public Record Office, London; microfilm in Library of Congress), s. 5, CCCCXXVIII, fol. 108. The first historian of South Carolina, Alexander Hewatt, misquoted Middleton and gave the statement an entirely different meaning; he quoted Middleton as saying, "Negroes were real property, such as houses and land, in Carolina." See Hewatt's *An Historical Account of the Rise and Progress of the Colonies of South Carolina and Georgia* (2 vols., London, 1779), in B. R. Carroll (ed.), *Historical Collections of South Carolina* (2 vols., New York, 1836), I, 270-71. Hewatt's misquotation has been widely accepted as accurate; see, for example, David D. Wallace, *The History of South Carolina* (4 vols., New York, 1934), I, 375.
[17] Records of the Court of Common Pleas: Judgment Books, 1733-1791 (South Carolina Archives).
[18] South Carolina Admiralty Records, 1716-1763 (Federal Records Center, East Point, Ga.), C (1736-38), 146-62; D (1738-47), 19.

Better evidence as to the slave's legal status is to be found in the colony's probate proceedings, the records of the Court of Chancery, and the records of slave sales. The probate proceedings are the only surviving judicial records in which the court system dealt regularly with slaves. When a will was probated, the governor—acting in his capacity of provincial ordinary—ordered an inventory of the decedent's personal estate. The inventories listed and evaluated all his personal chattels: his clothes, cattle, horses, hogs, furniture, china, even his chamber pots. The inventories included servants only very rarely and never listed real estate of any kind; they made no mention of lands, houses, warehouses, barns, or other buildings. In other words, probate inventories included personal chattels but- not freehold property or, except rarely, servants. The inventories always included the decedent's slaves, which strongly suggests that in probate proceedings slaves were considered chattels rather than real estate or servants of some kind. The practice of listing slaves with personal chattels began as early as 1693 and continued as long as slavery existed in South Carolina.[19] That it was the custom to treat slaves as chattels is confirmed by records of the Chancery Court. In three different cases involving the divisions of estates, the only ones of their kind to come before the Chancery Court before 1740, the court classified slaves with the decedent's personal goods, not with his real estate.[20] The legal form used by South Carolinians to sell Negroes provides additional confirmation that slaves were treated as chattels by custom long before they were defined as such by law. Slaves were transferred from one owner to another by indenture; land was always sold by lease and release.[21] The available evidence, then, indicates that under the vague definition of slavery in the code of 1696 South Carolinians began treating their slaves as personal chattels nearly half a century before the code of 1740 formally inaugurated chattel slavery.

The assembly made no basic changes in the slave code until 1740, although it re-enacted the original law three times and

[19] Wills, Inventories of Estates, and Miscellaneous Records [title varies], 1671-1868 (office of judge of probate court, Charleston, S. C.). I have found only two inventories out of more than 200 for the period 1693-1740 that listed freehold property of any kind. A total of 25 white servants appear in the inventories prior to 1740; see Warren B. Smith, *White Servitude in Colonial South Carolina* (Columbia, 1961), 135-36.

[20] Anne King Gregorie (ed.), *Records of the Court of Chancery of South Carolina, 1671-1779* (Washington, 1950), 278-80, 383-85.

[21] Mesne Conveyances, 1719-1800 (office of register of mesne conveyances, Charleston).

amended it twice after 1696.[22] Believing that "if negroes are well used, they never run" away, South Carolinians did not enforce the harsher police provisions of this code of 1696.[23] Most slave owners chose to deal gently with their bondsmen, but they did not trust them. They feared a slave insurrection, and with good reason. Small groups of Negroes initiated slave revolts in 1714 and 1720, but their masters managed to put down both outbursts before they became general.[24] Meanwhile, as the production of rice and other crops expanded, the number of slaves in the colony increased, and after 1708 the population of South Carolina included more Negroes than whites. In 1730 the colony entered into a period of unprecedented prosperity, and planters began to import slaves at the rate of 2,500 a year. After a decade of this high rate of importation, Negroes outnumbered whites by 39,000 to 20,-000.[25] The flow of slaves into South Carolina was so great that in 1738 a Georgian commented, "Our Neighbours at Charles Town, I hear have their Belly-full of 'em . . . ."[26]

The rapid influx of Negroes into South Carolina after 1730 helped to produce a crisis in the institution of slavery. The ever-growing number of slaves made it impossible for slave owners to

[22] Cooper and McCord (eds.), *Statutes at Large of South Carolina*, VII, 352-96.

[23] *Manuscripts of the Earl of Egmont: Diary of Viscount Percival, Afterwards First Earl of Egmont, 1730-1747* (Historical Manuscripts Commission, *Sixteenth Report* [3 vols., London, 1920-1923]), III, 201. See also Francis LeJau to Secretary, Society for the Propagation of the Gospel, June 30, 1707, in Frank J. Klingberg (ed.), *The Carolina Chronicle of Dr. Francis LeJau, 1706-1717* (Berkeley, 1956), 26-27; William Bull, Jr., to the Earl of Hillsborough, November 30, 1770, Records in the British Public Record Office Relating to South Carolina, 1711-1782 (South Carolina Archives), XXXII, 382; Hewatt, *Historical Account*, in Carroll (ed.), *Collections*, I, 349-50; and Howell M. Henry, *The Police Control of the Slave in South Carolina* (Emory, Va., 1914).

[24] LeJau to Secretary, S.P.G., January 22, 1714, in Klingberg (ed.) *LeJau Chronicle*, 136-37; Francis Varnod to same, January 10, 1722, Manuscripts of the Society for the Propagation of the Gospel (office of the Society for the Propagation of the Gospel, London; transcripts and microfilm, Library of Congress), s. A, XVII, 171; Richard Ludlam to Secretary, July 2, 1722, *ibid.*, XVIII, 83.

[25] Governor and Council to Proprietors, September 17, 1708, in *Records in the British Public Record Office Relating to South Carolina, 1663-1710* (5 vols., Atlanta and Columbia, 1928-1947), V, 203; J. H. Easterby (ed.), *The Colonial Records of South Carolina: The Journal of the Commons House of Assembly, 1736-1750* (9 vols., Columbia, 1951-1962), 1741-1742, 460 (March 3, 1742); E. B. Greene and V. D. Harrington, *American Population Before the Federal Census of 1790* (New York, 1932), 174; Elizabeth Donnan, "The Slave Trade into South Carolina Before the Revolution," *American Historical Review*, XXXIII (July 1928), 807.

[26] William Stephens to the Trustees of Georgia, January 19, 1738, in Allen D. Candler (ed.), *The Colonial Records of the State of Georgia, 1732-1782* (26 vols., Atlanta, 1904-1916), XXII, pt. 1, 76.

continue the traditionally indulgent treatment of their slaves and at the same time maintain discipline among them. Enforcement of the slave code, never efficient, became almost nonexistent, and owners lost control of their slaves. As many as two hundred Negroes sometimes engaged in drinking parties in Charles Town, while many slaves openly defied the law by buying and selling goods in the Charles Town market.[27] Then in 1738 the Spanish governor of Florida stirred up South Carolina's Negroes by publishing a royal edict that promised freedom to all English slaves who made good their escape to St. Augustine. Spain and England were approaching war, and the edict attempted to forestall English aggression on the southern frontier by encouraging slave unrest and exploiting South Carolina's fears of its slave population. Publication of the edict was followed by several successful escapes by parties of runaways from South Carolina and an unknown number of abortive attempts. News of the escapes, combined with lax enforcement of slave laws, made many whites believe that a general slave insurrection could begin at any moment.[28]

The assembly of South Carolina ignored all the signs of warning and acted as if it were blind to the dangers of unrest among the slaves. It clung to the old laws and passed no corrective legislation, other than an ineffective patrol law, and it failed to meet the challenge of the Spanish edict.[29] The assembly was more concerned with conventional politics. The council and Commons House were entangled in a prolonged struggle for control of the purse, and every attempt to relieve the crisis growing out of the slavery situation fell a victim to that struggle.[30]

The insurrection that had been brewing finally broke out on Sunday, September 9, 1739, although in fact it was less an insurrection than an attempt by slaves to fight their way to St. Augustine. The trouble started on Saturday night when about twenty slaves, led by a Negro named Jemmy, broke into a warehouse near

---

[27] Charles Town *South-Carolina Gazette*, October 28, 1732; Presentments of the Grand Jury, March 20, 1735, Records in the British P.R.O. Relating to S. C., XVII, 304.

[28] Journal of the Upper House, 1721-1773 (South Carolina Archives), VII, 142-43 (January 19, 1739); William Bull, Sr., to the Duke of Newcastle, May 9, 1739, Records in the British P.R.O. Relating to S. C., XX, 40-41.

[29] Cooper and McCord (eds.), *Statutes at Large of South Carolina*, III, 395-99, 456-61; Easterby (ed.), *Commons Journal*, 1736-1739, 604, 673 (January 24, March 16, 1739).

[30] See for example Easterby (ed.), *Commons Journal*, 1736-1739, 362, 547, 681, 707 (December 13, 1737, March 22, 1738, April 2, May 30, 1739).

the Stono river and armed themselves with guns, ammunition, and other military supplies. The armed slaves killed ten whites and burned several houses on Sunday morning. Then, with flags flying, drums beating, and shouts of "liberty," about sixty slaves set out to march to St. Augustine. Lieutenant Governor William Bull, who had escaped the initial outburst only by fast riding, called out the militia, which caught the fleeing slaves at four o'clock that afternoon. The Negroes fought bravely, but the militia outnumbered them, and many of the Negroes had drunk too much rum. By sunset the insurrection had ended, with forty Negroes and twenty whites dead.[31]

Two other abortive uprisings followed the Stono insurrection, but the assembly remained preoccupied with its internal struggles.[32] It was not until May 1740 that the Commons and council agreed on a new slave code, one which represented a new departure in South Carolina's slave laws. The law defined slaves as personal chattels. This was the first precise definition of slavery since the disallowed act of 1690; slavery no longer rested upon custom but upon law. Thus, in 1740, South Carolina definitely and finally abandoned its Barbadian traditions of slavery and set the institution upon the legal foundations developed in other English mainland colonies.

In other respects, the slave code of 1740 was more consistent with the practices of the institution in South Carolina. The assembly sought to maintain the tradition of kind treatment of slaves by enacting provisions designed to keep "the owners and other persons having the care and government of slaves" from "exercising too great rigour and cruelty over them." The law forbade masters to work their slaves on Sunday or more than fourteen or fifteen hours a day during the week. Owners were required to provide sufficient food and clothing. If a white were accused of killing or maiming a slave he was to face a jury trial, and, if found guilty, he could be fined up to £100 sterling. A second and equally traditional goal of the slave code was to make sure that the slave "be kept in due subjection and obedience." The assembly re-enacted all the old provisions regulating the slave's conduct and added new ones. The law outlawed all assemblies of slaves, forbade the

---

[31] "An Account of the Negroe Insurrection in South Carolina," in Candler (ed.), *Colonial Records of Georgia*, XXII, pt. 2, 232-36. See also William Bull, Sr., to the Board of Trade, October 5, 1739, Records in the British P.R.O. Relating to S. C., XX, 179-80.

[32] Petition of Assembly, July 26, 1740, *ibid.*, 300-301; Easterby (ed.), *Commons Journal*, 1739-1741, 324, 327 (May 2, 1740).

sale of alcohol to them, and prohibited them from learning to write.[33] At the same time it passed the new slave code, the assembly strengthened the patrol system by vesting responsibility for it in the militia. It also tried to reduce the number of Negroes being shipped to the colony by raising the import duty.[34]

The new slave code was permitted to go into effect despite some opposition in England, where the Crown's legal advisers seemed suddenly aware of chattel slavery. In 1748 the Board of Trade's legal counsel, Mathew Lamb, recommended disallowance of the South Carolina code on the grounds that the colonial law conflicted with an act of Parliament of 1732 designed to help English merchants recover debts in the colonies. One of the provisions of this act directed that slaves be treated as real estate in the recovery of colonial debts. Lamb considered that the act sanctioned freehold slavery but not chattel slavery. The Board of Trade, however, took no action on the South Carolina slave code, and the code remained in force, although three years later the Board secured the disallowance of a Virginia law because it defined slaves as chattels.[35] The Crown's permissive treatment of the code of 1740 may well have been due to the intercession of Charles Town merchants, who often owned slaves and who enjoyed considerable influence with the Board of Trade.

In South Carolina the slave code of 1740 worked well. It seemed to have found the balance between kindness and discipline required to keep slaves in good order, for there were no further slave rebellions in the colonial period. A few changes in the law were found necessary, but they were minor. For example, the assembly had to amend the patrol law, but by 1750 the patrols functioned efficiently.[36] In some other instances, the assembly found provisions of the 1740 law too severe on the slaves and either amended the law accordingly or else permitted it to be ignored.

---

[33] The slave code of 1740 is in Cooper and McCord (eds.), *Statutes at Large of South Carolina*, VII, 397-417.

[34] *Ibid.*, III, 556-73.

[35] Mathew Lamb to Board of Trade, November 2, 1748, Records in the British P.R.O. Relating to S. C., XXIII, 261; Leo F. Stock (ed.), *Proceedings and Debates of the British Parliaments Respecting North America, 1542-1754* (5 vols., Washington, 1924-1941), IV, 150; James Curtis Ballagh, *A History of Slavery in Virginia* (Baltimore, 1902), 63-68; Gerald Montgomery West, *The Status of the Negro in Virginia During the Colonial Period* (New York, [1889?]), 11, 27-32.

[36] Cooper and McCord (eds.), *Statutes at Large of South Carolina*, III, 681-85; Klaus G. Loewald and others (trans. and eds.), "Johann Martin Bolzius Answers a Questionnaire on Carolina and Georgia," *William and Mary Quarterly*, s. 3, XIV (April 1957), 234.

Most notably, it allowed the Society for the Propagation of the Gospel to operate a grammar school for fifty to sixty Negro boys in Charles Town.[37]

Thus did South Carolina evolve chattel slavery in a manner unique among American colonies. In the seventeenth century it imported the slave pattern of Barbados in piecemeal fashion, adopting first the Barbadian definition of a slave as freehold property and then the comprehensive Barbadian slave code. It was under South Carolina's own deliberately vague definition of a slave, however, that South Carolinians developed chattel slavery without benefit of legislative action and without interference from England. Not until after the slave insurrections of 1739 did the colonists completely abandon the Barbadian approach to slavery and write chattel slavery into law.

[37] Cooper and McCord (eds.), *Statutes at Large of South Carolina*, VII, 420-25; James Glen to Board of Trade, January 29, 1752, Records in the British P.R.O. Relating to S. C., XXV, 7-8; Robert Smith to Secretary, S.P.G., July 25, 1759, Manuscripts of the S.P.G., s. B, V, No. 252.

From African Captivity to American Slavery: The Introduction of Black Laborers to Colonial Louisiana

By DANIEL H. USNER, JR.

Durham, North Carolina

The importation of Africans to Louisiana in 1719 immediately affected the French colony and inexorably altered its destiny. Since 1700 explorers and colonists qualified their predictions of prosperity on the lower Mississippi Valley with exhortations for African slaves. For twenty years the strategically located garrison on the Gulf of Mexico remained only a nominal buffer against British and Spanish encroachments on the Mississippi. Canadian soldiers, sailors, and *voyageurs* were both unwilling and ill-prepared to deforest the land and cultivate the soil. A diminishing store of merchandise aggravated their precarious dependence on surrounding Indian nations for food supplies. After France conceded its languishing settlement to John Law's company in 1717, over one thousand European criminals and contract laborers arrived. Most of them died of disease or starvation; the remaining population in 1721 consisted of 178 *engagés* working for 853 French settlers.[1]

Amidst this wasteful transportation of European vagabonds, prostitutes, and salt smugglers, five hundred Africans arrived from Guinea during the summer of 1719. In contrast to white paupers and prisoners, these black captives were eagerly anticipated and carefully selected. The company instructed the two slaver captains destined for Louisiana "not to trade for any negro or negress who is more than thirty years of age, as far as possible, or less than eight."

---

[1] Dunbar Rowland and Albert Sanders, eds., *Mississippi Provincial Archives, 1701–1740*, 3 vols. (Jackson, 1929), III, 25, 35–36, cited hereafter as *MPA*; *The Census Tables for the French Colony of Louisiana From 1699 Through 1732*, compiled and translated by Charles R. Maduell, Jr. (Baltimore, 1972), p. 16; James D. Hardy, Jr., "The Transportation of Convicts to Colonial Louisiana," *Louisiana History*, VII, No. 3 (1966), 220.

25

The colony, however, needed much more than "well-made and healthy Africans." Captains Du Coulombier and Herpin were ordered to purchase "a few who know how to cultivate rice," as well as some "hogsheads of rice suitable for planting." In their search for an agricultural staple and labor force, Louisiana colonists were conscious of examples and limitations imposed by a firmly established South Atlantic economy. Since wealthy French and English planters dominated sugar production in the West Indies, they turned to rice, indigo, tobacco, and silk as potential sources of commerce and wealth. Ambitious colonists pleaded agricultural ignorance and requested permission to purchase Negroes who understood the cultivation of these crops from Santo Domingo and Carolina. An avaricious glance at production in the Caribbean and Carolina motivated French efforts to procure knowledgeable agriculturists from West Africia.[2]

Before any slavers reached Louisiana, colonists attempted several times to obtain Negroes "to clear" the land. Relying heavily on English precedent in Carolina, Governor Bienville repeatedly sought authority to trade Indian slaves for Negroes in the islands. He recommended an exchange rate of three Indians for each Negro. In 1710 the minister of marine and colonies officially prohibited such trade, considering it "not practicable," and stating "it may be possible" to "induce French vessels" to import Negroes from Africa once war ended in Europe. Meanwhile a few well-to-do settlers bargained with Santo Domingo merchants for black servants. Bienville sent a brigantine to Havana in 1707 to meet Pierre Le Moyne d'Iberville, his brother and founder of French Louisiana, who intended to sell some Negroes captured from English Caribbean plantations. Iberville's death in the Nevis campaign, however, made it a "fruitless" voyage. With only about twenty Negro slaves in 1712, colonists expressed willingness to receive pirates who could procure Negroes. The black slaves who reached Louisiana before 1719 were profitably employed at necessary jobs. In 1720 Bienville traded Laurent, one of these early Louisiana Negroes, to the company for

[2] *MPA*, II, 82, 101–102, 111, 178; Elizabeth Donnan ed., *Documents Illustrative of the History of the Slave Trade to America* (Washington, D.C., 1935), IV, 635–638. For African contribution to rice cultivation in South Carolina, see: Peter H. Wood, *Black Majority: Negroes in Colonial South Carolina from 1670 through the Stono Rebellion* (New York, 1974), pp. 58–62.

three recently imported Africans. The company desperately needed a good, but cheap, blacksmith at Mobile.[3]

Without sufficient finances and without voluntary laborers, the colony needed to employ slaves at various tasks. In 1717 Commissary-General Hubert urged that Negroes be used to "drive carts loaded with the King's goods" and be taught "the different trades of the workmen maintained by the King." Diverse and specialized slave labor would save wages and reduce costly food consumption. French permanence on the Gulf of Mexico depended largely on the colony's ability to replace expensive and inefficient white workers with unsalaried and coercible black workers. Blacks, forced to toil on a strange continent, applied this white need to their own survival and self-defense. Whites simultaneously applied black labor to their own wealth and esteem. Within a decade these economic, social, and psychological links between labor exploitation and racial subjugation forged an inseparable chain around colonial Louisiana.[4]

As the first cargo of Africans disembarked on the sandy, uncleared Gulf islets, the weak French garrison was engaged in a struggle against the nearby Spanish outpost at Pensacola. After several months of cruel imprisonment and confinement, these captives were thrust amidst a European colonial war. A group of Negroes immediately began to work on fortifications at Pensacola. The rest went to Dauphin Island to assist with its evacuation. Sixty Negroes remained with 250 soldiers to defend the island. Early in August Joseph Le Moyne Sérigny, commander of the campaign, learned "through fugitive slaves" that French soldiers deserted Pensacola, which was subsequently recaptured by the Spanish. On returning to Dauphin Island, he discovered the soldiers' barracks "burned to the ground as a result of sabotage." Once the Spanish assault ended, the Council of Commerce reported losses incurred by several runaway slaves. Deserting soldiers and Negroes were ubiquitous problems for frontier authorities in colonial America. The situation was aggravated in Louisiana by the proximity of Spanish refuge at Pensacola.[5]

---

[3] *MPA*, II, 20–29, 73, III, 40, 141, 282; Nancy Miller Surrey, *The Commerce of Louisiana During the French Regime, 1699–1763* (New York, 1916), pp. 228–229.

[4] *MPA*, II, 230.

[5] Glenn R. Conrad, trans., ed., annot., *Immigration and War Louisiana, 1718–1721*, U.S.L. History Series (Lafayette, 1970), pp. 21–27; Joan Cain and Virginia Koenig, trans.,

While colonial officials formulated means of compensating losses caused by runaway slaves, over a thousand Africans "were dying of hunger and wretchedness on the sands of Fort St. Louis." Freighters left for Vera Cruz and the West Indies in search of wheat needed to feed starving survivors of the Atlantic crossing. The *Affriquain* left Juida with 280 slaves; only 180 of these persons were alive when the ship reached Dauphin Island on March 17, 1721. The *Duc de Maine* and the *Néreide* each lost 56 slaves. The entire human cargo on the *Charles* perished when it burned more than fifty leagues from the coast. The few surviving crew members "suffered greatly from thirst and hunger, having been reduced to loading their launch with a few negroes for their subsistence." Under such hapless circumstances, Africans' dread of European cannibalism was realized. Meanwhile colonists failed to manage the subsistence of 2,000 slaves arriving at Louisiana between June 1719 and October 1721. The census of November 1721 records only 680 African survivors.[6]

With the arrival of African slaves, colonists were prepared to move their settlement from the barren gulf coast to the fertile valley of the Mississippi River. The new Company of the Indies distributed land concessions from the mouth of the river to the Indian village of Natchez. Prospective planters, however, faced prolonged inundations of the river, pestilent swamps, and dense forests. Bienville selected the site of New Orleans as the capital for its strategic location, certainly not for its terrain and environment. While some slaves were transported to company mines at Illinois or sold to local concessionaires, most Africans who escaped death on Dauphin Island were employed at making New Orleans a habitable city. Some built levees and drainage ditches along the river. Others cleared the forests and prepared timber for vessels and houses. Swarms of alligators and mosquitoes, creatures familiar to Africans, kept the French away from the city during this preliminary labor. Within a year of African migration to New Orleans, black slaves were planting and preparing corn, beans, and rice for the subsistence of themselves and their masters.[7]

Historical Journal of the Settlement of the French in Louisiana, attributed to Jean-Baptiste Bénard de La Harpe, U.S.L. History Series (Lafayette, 1971), p. 115; *MPA*, II, 216, III, 255.

[6] La Harpe, *Journal*, 167–169, 190; Maduell, *Census Tables*, p. 21.

[7] *MPA*, II, 310; Baron Marc de Villiers, "A History of the Foundation of New Orleans,

Two concessions at Natchez, situated about 200 miles above New Orleans, began to successfully plant tobacco. Father Pierre de Charlevoix, a Jesuit priest descending the Mississippi in 1721, described Natchez as the "finest, most fertile, and most populous canton of all Louisiana." Free from the river's inundations and abundant in open land and clear streams, this enclave of the Natchez Indians was long considered the best site for plantation agriculture. Charlevoix reported the concessions there wanting "nothing to make an improvement of the land but negroes, or hired servants." He advised against the former because they "are always strangers: and who can be assured that by continually increasing in our colonies, they will not one day become formidable enemies?" Despite the indifferent traveler's foreboding, settlers hurried thirty black slaves to the St. Catherine concession. White tobacco workers were returning to France.[8]

On July 18, 1721, the director of St. Catherine, Jean-Baptiste Faucon-Dumanoir, wrote from Natchez: "You may be assured, gentlemen, that tobacco, rice, and silk will thrive in this colony as well as in any spot on earth, but remember that without a great many negroes you cannot expect any profit, since the white laborers can barely feed themselves." Faucon-Dumanoir assured company officials that "indigo will grow well here provided a man of experience should be engaged for this culture." He also needed skilled workers, especially locksmiths, edge-tool makers, and sawyers, "to teach their trade to the negroes, for if we succeed in training and perfecting them, they will, in the course of time, bring you large profits; if necessary, they will be sold at four times their cost and in case of need, their labor would bring more than what we gain on our culture."[9]

Throughout the colony European contract farmers and workers were leaving because of inhospitable surroundings and insufficient salaries. Returns on the company's large investment increasingly depended on its ability to import large numbers of African slaves.

1717–1722," *Louisiana Historical Quarterly*, III (1920), 195, hereafter cited as *LHQ*, with volume and page number.

[8] B. F. French, ed., "Historical Journal of Father Pierre Francois Xavier de Charlevois," *Historical Collections of Louisiana*, 7 vols. (New York, 1846–51), III, 140–141, 154–156, 159.

[9] "Excerpt from a letter written by Mr. Faucond du Manoir, Director General of the Colony of Ste Catherine, July 18, 1721," *LHQ*, II (1919), 164–169.

Negroes' subsistence could easily be provided for with Indian corn and beans. The abundance of rice already cultivated by blacks would sufficiently pay for newly imported slaves. By 1726, most slaves were arriving from the Senegal region. These West Africans were quite familiar with geographical conditions similar to those along the Mississippi. On his voyages up the Senegal River between 1697 and 1715, André Brüe observed that its inundations contributed greatly to the "rich and fruitful" soil which "abounds in maiz of both kinds; rice, pulse, tobacco, and indigo." The agricultural experience of Senegalese slaves provided an early source of wealth for French settlers. Small planters reportedly purchased a few slaves and grew rice on uncleared patches of land within the bounds of large concessions. Disgruntled concessionaires, having to employ their slaves at larger tasks of constructing levees and ditches, were then forced to buy rice from these small slaveholding trespassers.[10]

Louisiana colonists were long denied the quantity of slaves necessary for producing rice, indigo, or tobacco as staples. Throughout the 1720s they demanded more and more Africans. Some well-financed concessions, however, managed to accumulate enough slaves for intensive agricultural production. The St. Catherine and White Earth plantations at Natchez produced exportable tobacco through Negro labor until the Indians destroyed them in 1729. The Natchez War, in fact, upset the company's plans to establish a tobacco factory there with thirty black workers. Five concessions at Chapitoulas, just three leagues above New Orleans, maintained 315 Negro adults and 126 Negro children by 1731. Through the labor of these people, a white population of 53 established profitable indigo factories.[11]

The settlement with the densest black population stood across the river from Chapitoulas. Here 940 Negro adults and 280 Negro children were distributed among 54 landholdings and 2 mills along the river. Three free Negroes also lived in the area, alongside 206

[10] *MPA*, II, 321, 351, 629–630, III, 423, 447, 519; Thomas Astley, *A New General Collection of Voyages and Travels* (London, 1745–47), II, 49; Philip Curtin, *Economic Change in Precolonial Africa: Senegambia in the Era of the Slave Trade* (Madison, 1975), p. 17; Surrey, *Commerce*, p. 232.

[11] *MPA*, I, 80, II, 396–399, 629–630; "Letter from Father du Poisson, Oct. 3, 1727," Reuben Gold Thwaites (ed.), *The Jesuit Relations and Allied Documents, Travels and Explorations of the Jesuit Missionaries in New France, 1610–1791*, 73 vols. (Cleveland, 1900), LXVII, 281, 311; *Census Tables*, 116.

white masters, 31 *engages*, and 7 Indian slaves. In the middle of these concessions stood the colony's largest plantation; its 201 Negro adults and 29 Negro children were owned by the Compagnie des Indes and directed by Le Page du Pratz. Under Le Page's scrutiny these slaves cultivated the colony's best tobacco and cotton.[12]

During the 1720s most Negroes performed agricultural labor between New Orleans and Natchez, and a growing black population began to concentrate within this 200-mile stretch of alluvial soil along the Mississippi. Slaves left on the gulf coast were generally employed at manufacturing timber products, one of the most lucrative staples during the colony's early development. When not producing food products in the winter months, Negroes made "all sorts of timber," stave-wood, shingles, planks, beams, and planking, for commerce with Santo Domingo. At Mobile company Negroes went into the cypress swamps to cut wood, with which Dubreuil's Negroes made shingles. The dangers encountered by slaves in swamps infested with alligators and mosquitoes perhaps proved too expensive for private slaveholders.[13]

The abundance of decayed and fallen pine trees along the Gulf of Mexico made pitch and tar manufacture a profitable industry in colonial Louisiana. In 1723 Widow Belsaguy, a manufacturer at Mobile, requested four Negroes to "teach them the trade and in three years she will make them perfect." Governor De La Chaise supported her request "because she would be responsible for the negroes in case of [their] death before the end of the three years." By 1726, black apprentices were replacing white coopers, "whose food and wages carry off all the profits." The elaborate process of tar manufacture operated by Louisiana Negroes during the 1720s merits the description provided by Le Page:

> When they have a sufficient number of these trees, that are fit for the purpose, they saw them in cuts with a cross-cut saw, about two feet in length; and while the slaves are employed in

[12] *Census Tables*, pp. 121–122; Le Page du Pratz, *The History of Louisiana* (1763), facsimile reproduction of 1774 English edition, Joseph Tregle, Jr., ed., Louisiana American Revolution Bicentennial Commission Publication (Baton Rouge, 1975), pp. 193–195.

[13] *MPA*, II, 393, 494, III, 521; Thomas Hutchins, *An Historical Narrative and Topographical Description of Louisiana and West Florida* (Philadelphia, 1784), pp. 38–39; John G. Clark, *New Orleans 1718–1812, An Economic History* (New Orleans, 1969), p. 29.

sawing them, others split these cuts lengthwise into small pieces, the smaller the better. They sometimes spend three or four months in cutting and preparing the trees in this manner. In the mean time they make a square hollow in the ground, four or five feet broad, and five or six inches deep: from one side of which goes off a canal or gutter, which discharges itself into a large and pretty deep pit, at the distance of a few paces. From this pit proceeds another canal, which communicates with a second pit; and even from the first square you make three or four such trenches, which discharge themselves into as many pits, according to the quantity of wood you have, or the quantity of tar you imagine you may draw from it. Then you lay over the square hole four or five pretty strong bars of iron, and upon these bars you arrange cross-wise the split pieces of pine, of which you should have a quantity ready; laying them so, that there may be a little air between them. In this manner you raise a large and high pyramid of the wood, and when it is finished, you set fire to it at the top. As the wood burns, the fire melts the resin in the pine, and this liquid tar distills into the square hole, and from thence runs into the pits made to receive it.[14]

The Superior Council, Louisiana's judicial and military oligarchy, relied on two sources of black labor for construction of New Orleans. Since the company owned all imported Africans, it was entitled to their labor until auction time. Of the 88 slaves who survived the 1723 voyage from Gorée Castle on the Senegal coast, 50 worked on the levee, 35 built huts on the company's plantation, and 3 became sailors. Negroes intended for sale to Spanish merchants also temporarily worked in New Orleans. In November, 1727, the council decided to maintain Africans already granted to inhabitants until the levee was finished. A statute labor law provided the other means of completing the capital. Inhabitants were required to supply Negro labor squads for thirty days of public works. While grantees and officials argued over who should feed them, these blacks "cut down the trees at the two ends of the town as far as Bayou St. John in order to clear this ground and to give air to the city and to the mill." They also dug canals and entrenchments for both cultivation and defense.[15]

---

[14] *MPA*, II, 384, III, 521; "Instructions for M. Duvergier, Director Ordonnateur of the Colony of Louisiana, Sept. 15, 1720,"*LHQ*, XV (1932), 426; Le Page, *History*, pp. 217–218.
[15] *MPA*, II, 372–373, 427–428, 547–549, 591–593; "Records," *LHQ*, I (1918), 234–236.

While Frenchmen demanded more slaves for their own prosperity and colony's development, the mortality of human deprivation and emigration took its toll on enslaved Africans. Senegalese captives who eventually reached Louisiana in the late 1720s were kept for months in slave prisons at Gorée, where they "had only one meal per day and drank brackish water." Between June, 1728, and June, 1729, three slavers embarked from Gorée with 1,287 slaves. Most of the 1,051 survivors who reached the Mississippi River were attacked by scurvy immediately after disembarkation. Unable to hospitalize the hundreds of sick, colonial officials sold them at auction. Their dire need for slaves led settlers to "outbid each other for the scurvied, consumptive and ulcerated" Negroes, raising the price for them as high as 1,000 *livres*.[16]

The fate of the *Venus*'s cargo tragically reveals the vicious cycle of human desolation and economic desperation involved in the Atlantic slave trade. Eighty-seven Africans died in passage; 43 died on arrival. Two-thirds of the remaining disease-ridden people died almost immediately after auction. Approximately 7,000 Africans reached Louisiana between 1718 and 1735. The black population in 1735 was only 3,400.[17]

As loss of African lives and colonial property continued, a few French surgeons profited from periodic visits and inadequate remedies. The company's plantation was fortunate enough to have an African physician, who taught Le Page his secret cures for yaws and scurvy. For yaws he prescribed an ointment consisting of powdered iron rust and citron juice and warned against the mercurial medicine used by surgeons, which proved fatal to their patients. He applied an ointment made from scurvy grass, ground-ivy, and water-cresses to the infected gums of scurvied victims. "The negro who taught me these remedies, observing the great care I took of both the negro men and negro women, taught me likewise the cure of all the distempers to which the women are subject; for the negro women are as liable to diseases as the white women."[18]

[16] *MPA*, II, 575–576, 620–621, 638; "Historical Memoirs of M. Dumont," *Historical Collections*, V, 119.

[17] *MPA*, II, 659–660, 668; Philip Curtin, *The Atlantic Slave Trade: A Census* (Madison, 1969), pp. 82–83.

[18] "Bill for Services Rendered to Mr. Pailhoux's Negroes furnished on 10, March, 1726 by Pouyadon De Latour, surgeon major of New Orleans," *LHQ*, I (1918), 153; Le Page, *History*, pp. 378–380.

The importation of African slaves was extremely fatal, but much more frequent than European immigration. Decreasing availability of white workers combined with increasing profitability of black labor to escalate the apprenticeship of slaves to reliable skilled artisans. Consequently many newly arrived Africans immediately entered a separate and diverse class of black artisanship. For Senegalese farmers this must have been an especially dramatic experience; in Senegambia occupational people such as blacksmiths and leather workers belonged to an endogamous social caste, or nĕno, distinct from free men and bondsmen. Throughout the first decade of Louisiana slavery, Africans with strong agricultural and communal traditions suddenly found themselves performing highly individualized tasks.[19]

Company and privately owned slaves were apprenticed to brickmakers, joiners, blacksmiths, locksmiths, sculptors, wheelwrights, saddlers, masons, and carpenters. Contracts provided that "after three years they would have them fully trained," usually within three years, artisans would receive between 200 and 400 *francs* per slave. Governor Périer suggested that the company train Negroes at different trades in Paris. Although this policy was not enacted, the directors encouraged the apprenticeship of "some already in the colony." "Those people once trained" would cost the company nothing. By the end of 1728, Périer confidently reported: "We are placing negroes as apprentices with all the workmen who we think are good and honest men, and if the same practice had been followed when they were first sent to the colony, we could at present do without several white men, although the workmen do not seek to perfect the negroes in their trades because they feel distinctly that that will harm them in the future." Immediate needs did not preclude anxiety over the potential economic and social dangers posed by black artisans.[20]

Skilled black workers became a significant factor in the growth of colonial cities. The census of 1732 indicates that 15 out of 59 New Orleans tradesmen and merchants owned Negroes, whom they

---

[19] Curtin, *Economic Change*, pp. 29–30; for analysis of Negro artisanship in colonial Virginia see: Gerald W. Mullin, *Flight and Rebellion: Slave Resistance in Eighteenth-Century Virginia* (New York, 1972).

[20] *MPA*, I, 127, II, 494, 553–554, 599, 602, 626–627, 639; "Records," *LHQ*, IV (1921), 230, 355–356.

housed and trained in their shops. Thirty-seven of the 252 Negroes then residing in the city belonged to skilled white craftsmen. Carpenters, joiners, and blacksmiths owned more Negro slaves than other artisans, but blacks worked at a variety of specialties ranging from hospital service to ironworking. Occupational and personal proximity of these Negroes with white inhabitants invited interracial mixture and emancipation. Well into the nineteenth century, a growing class of free blacks and mulattoes and an expanding group of black artisans contributed profoundly to the economic welfare, as well as the cultural wealth, of New Orleans.[21]

Since Iberville landed on the Gulf Coast in 1699, deserting soldiers and sailors plagued the French colony. The reliability of these people not having improved by 1723, Governor De La Chaise urged that the company employ black sailors. "It would be better for you to have negroes to serve as sailors than your convicts and your white men who must have French provisions. The two negroes of Suratte whom we brought here in the *Galatée* are now good sailors, so when some come, give orders, Gentlemen, that those who you think suitable be retained in order to make sailors of them." In May 1724, Antoine Beauvais, a free mulatto cooper whose sight was impaired, requested to "serve the company as a sailor." The Superior Council granted Antoine the job for fifteen *livres* per month with rations. The Council's March 25, 1729, report of the navy included: "We are putting as many blacks as we can in the place of the white men."[22]

Shifting sand bars, shallow channels, and the buildup of trees carried by the river created peculiar problems for navigators at the Mississippi mouth. The black rowers manning the boats that guided vessels through the ticklish delta were as important as a good pilot. In 1727, fifty-five company Negroes resided at Fort Balise. When not meeting ships they removed the large quantities of timber that continuously blocked passage. The company daily

---

[21] Census Tables, pp. 123–141; MPA, II, 558–559; for the economic and cultural role of Negroes in antebellum New Orleans see: Joseph Tregle, "Early New Orleans Society; A Reappraisal," *Journal of Southern History*, 18 (1952), 20–36; Robert Reinders, "The Free Negro in the New Orleans Economy, 1850–1860," *Louisiana History*, VI (1965), 273–285; and Marcus Christian, *Negro Ironworkers of Louisiana, 1718–1900* (New Orleans, 1972).

[22] "Journal of Diron d' Artaguette, Sept. 1, 1722–Sept. 10, 1723," Newton D. Mereness, ed., *Travels in the American Colonies* (New York, 1916), p. 20; MPA, II, 346, 372–373, 634.

diminished naval expenses by "making only blacks, and few white men, sailors."[23]

After 1723 most Louisiana slaves came from the Senegal region, where Africans already experienced naval and military employment by a white ruling minority. Colonial development on the Mississippi coincided with commercial development on the Senegal. Blacks played vital roles in both processes, from positions of strength in Africa and weakness in America. The use of African sailors in Louisiana reveals how the situation of French colonists on the Mississippi resembled that of French merchants on the Senegal. Both groups were comprised of people scattered along troublesome rivers and dependent upon the same central authority in Paris. The Compagnie des Indes employed European criminals and forced workers as soldiers in both West Africa and America. But geographical factors necessitated multifunctional and intensive labor, for which Europeans turned to Africans.[24]

Frenchmen on the Senegal employed four major occupational groups of Africans: interpreters, domestic servants, sailors, and bambaras—people enslaved from the interior region and stationed as soldiers at forts and factories. During the 1720s the term bambara had several meanings. The Bambaras were an ethnic group comprising the dominant people of the emerging Segu and Kaarta kingdoms. Victims of Bambara wars, enslaved and transported westward, were also classified as Bambara slaves. The French used the term bambara for any Senegalese slave soldier. Most Senegalese slaves who reached Louisiana between 1723 and 1730 were evidently captured Bambaras. André Brüe described the French slave trade in 1722: "It is allowed, that this trade with the Mandigos can supply the Company with no slaves, but Bambaras Negroes. But then these Negoes are the best in all Africa for work, being strong, gentle, tractable, and faithful; not subject to sullenness, or to run away as the Guinea Negroes frequently are." Owners of Bambara slaves in Louisiana would have questioned Brüe's assessment of their character.[25]

---

[23] Le Page, *History*, pp. 130–131; *MPA*, II, 565, III, 388–392, 439–443.

[24] Curtin, *Economic Change*, pp. 112–115.

[25] André Delcourt, *La France et les establissements francais au Senegal entre 1713 et 1763* (Paris, 1952), pp. 128–131; Curtin, *Economic Change*, pp. 178–179; Astley, *Collection of Voyages*, p. 158.

At the time of Brüe's report, a Bambara named Samba led a revolt against the French at Fort Arguin. The Dutch subsequently captured the fort and held it for two years. On recovering Fort Arguin for France in 1724, Périer de Salvert condemned Samba to slavery in America. During passage to Louisiana, he plotted mutiny, but was discovered and enchained. Starting life anew as a company slave in the colony, Samba served as interpreter for slave cases before the Superior Council. He also became commander of the company's Negroes and confidant of director Le Page du Pratz. Samba's constructive involvement in colonial affairs ended in 1730 when he conspired to revolt. His experience in service and insurrection was emblematic of slavery's dilemma for both white and black Louisianians.[26]

Demographic, economic, and geographical conditions in Louisiana made slaveholders' needs, demands, and power as uncertain and flexible as the Mississippi delta. Slaves were involved more actively in the evolution of its economy and social structure than is assumed. The *Code Noir*, which is often overemphasized, provided a weak framework for people unfamiliar with Africans and inexperienced with slavery. This code, which originated in France and reached Louisiana through the Caribbean islands in 1724, imposed restrictions on slaves and free negroes and responsibilities on slaveholders. Frontier conditions and economic interests, however, militated against the social order that it was supposed to shape from slavery. It was almost impossible to promote religious instruction, sexual separation, and kind treatment along the damp, mosquito-infested banks of the Mississippi.[27]

Father Raphael, a Capuchin priest, reported that "even in the most populated places the instruction of the negro and Indian slaves is entirely neglected since the masters think only of deriving profit from the work of these poor wretches. . . . The majority die without baptism, . . . although the negroes ask for nothing better than to be instructed and baptized. . . ." Raphael was encouraged by the peculiar "religious pliability" of Africans and infuriated by the

---

[26] Astley, *Collection of Voyages*, pp. 6–14; Le Page, *History*, p. 80.

[27] For traditional treatment of Louisiana's Black Code see: Alice Dunbar-Nelson, "People of Color in Louisiana," *Journal of Negro History*, I (1916), 359–374; William Riddell, "Le Code Noir," *Journal of Negro History*, X (1925), 321–329; and Donald Everett, "Free People of Color in Colonial Louisiana," *Louisiana History*, VII (1966), 5–20.

"lack of religion on the part of their masters." He urged "that the ordinances of the black code against masters who abuse their slaves and make them work on Sundays and feast days will be put in force, for although the number of those who maintain young Indian women or negresses to satisfy their intemperance is considerably diminished, there still remain enough to scandalize the church and to require an effective remedy."[28]

The Superior Council heard several cases of slave overwork and mutilation. Captain de Merveilleux petitioned against his overseer in September, 1727, for ruining one of his most valuable slaves. Choucoura, an arrested runaway, was apparently bound tightly by his hands and given 600 rawhide lashes by Jean Gaulaz. Through this "inhuman punishment" he lost two fingers from his right hand and two finger tips from his left hand. Another "brutish overseer" was charged with raping and beating slave women in the open field, stinting slaves of their necessary provisions, and "causing frequent abortion among the slave women by corporal punishment in pregnancy."[29]

While the black code provided a legal channel for emancipation, the scarcity of white women amidst a growing black population created the real conditions for a rising free Negro class. French colonists immediately recognized the need to both limit and utilize the middling position of these people. The first free Negro mentioned in colonial records was Louis Congo, who became the colony's executioner "as the price of his freedom." When a company slave named Johnny had been assigned this job, he ran to his cabin and cut off his hand with an axe. For this show of courage, he was made commander of the company's Negroes. Louis Congo's first victim was a Negro, "burned alive for killing a Frenchman." In August, 1726, "three runaway savages" murderously attacked the black executioner. The employment of free Negroes to capture runaway slaves also promoted control over slavery. But as demonstrated in one case before the Superior Council, intraracial hostility was not ensured. André, a free Negro, was imprisoned for shooting into the water and allowing a fugitive Negro to disappear.[30]

[28] *MPA*, II, 482, 521; The term religious pliability is taken from Melville J. Herskovits, *The Myth of the Negro Past* (Boston, 1941), pp. 141, 220.

[29] "Records," *LHQ*, I (1918), 228, IV (1921), 224–229, 521, V (1922), 91–94.

[30] "Memoirs of Dumont," 121; La Harpe, *Journal*, p. 213; "Records," *LHQ*, III (1920), 414,

Despite the black code, John Mingo, a free English-speaking Negro from Carolina, married a slave named Thérèse. His contract with her owner provided that he "pay as much as possible each year" to redeem her value of 1500 *francs*. Thérèse was allowed a ration of rice, corn, beans, and sweet potatoes from the plantation, and her "children, if any be born meanwhile, shall also be free." Two years later on October 21, 1729, the couple hired themselves to De Chavannes, Thérèse as a domestic servant and John as overseer of his slaves. Free Negroes could petition and testify in court. But they could be reduced to slavery for immoral conduct or inability to pay fines and debts.[31]

The black code especially broke down in New Orleans, where slaves freely roamed the streets and traversed legal barriers. To save on food costs, masters allowed blacks to work for non-slaveholders on Saturdays and Sundays. Negroes living around the capital "generally turned their two hours at noon to account by making faggots to sell in the city." Many black residents sold ashes or fruits. With money so earned some Negroes purchased their freedom or enjoyed French luxuries. Prohibition against sexual promiscuity was as ineffective as that against economic independence. The census of New Orleans for 1732 lists 229 white "men capable of bearing arms" and 169 white "women and marriageable girls," a disproportionate sex ratio worsened by an incessant transient male population. The city's black population consisted of 102 "negroes" and 74 "negresses," whose distribution was determined by their owners. Blark marketing and miscegenation made New Orleans a seedbed for free men and women of color.[32]

IV, 520; Laura Foner, "The Free People of Color in Louisiana and St. Domingue: A Comparative Portrait of Two Three-Caste Slave Societies," *Journal of Social History*, III (1970), 406–430; *Census Tables*, p. 113:

Census of 1731 for the banks of the Mississippi River

Women and marriageable girls	209
Children of the family	390
European engagees	119
Men capable of bearing arms	377
Negro slaves	2529
Negro children	819
Indian slaves	47

[31] "Records," *LHQ*, I (1918), 238, IV (1921), 236, 355, 520; H. E. Sterkx, *The Free Negro in Antebellum Louisiana* (Rutherford, 1972), p. 24.

[32] "Memoirs of Dumont," 120; *Census Tables*, p. 123.

Although the black code forebade slaves of different masters from assembling by day or night, blacks managed to gather regularly in large numbers. The labor statute for public works brought slaves from all along the river into New Orleans for periods of thirty days. Common work projects and close physical contact created opportunity for developing communication and communal identity. New Orleans, with its black artisan population, free negro class, and statute slave laborers greatly enhanced the emergence of a creole culture and language. On Sundays Negroes came "together to the number of three or four hundred" and made their own kind of Sabbath. According to Le Page they sold stolen goods to each other and committed many crimes at these "tumultuous meetings" of song and dance. Outside the town's rear gate African slaves— agricultural laborers, construction workers, skilled artisans, sailors, and even maroons—could meet for ceremony and conspiracy.[33]

Many slaves, driven by despair over permanent captivity or periodic cruelty, often fled alone into the wilderness. Others resolutely sought their African homeland or Spanish refuge. Amidst the confusion and turmoil of the Pensacola war, several of the first Africans to reach the colony swam from Dauphin Island. Some, perhaps, reached the mainland and found refuge among the Spanish. European explorers long before realized the significant role that African slaves might play in their struggle for supremacy in America. In his 1678 *Memoir on the Necessity of Fitting out an Expedition to take Possession of Louisiana*, Robert Cavelier de la Salle proposed that "Mulattoes, Indians, and Negroes," once promised their liberty, would assist the French in driving their Spanish masters from Mexico. He also suggested their role in defending a colony. "Indians, Mulattoes, and Negroes, armed and freed by this first success from the terror which they have of the Spaniards, would be able to dispute the advance of the largest army which could be raised in Mexico. Besides which, they would stake all, in order not to be again reduced to a state of slavery." Now with a Spanish fort so near at Pensacola, the envisioned colony of La Salle had to secure its own slaves from enemy interference.[34]

[33] Le Page, *History*, p. 387; George W. Cable, "The Dance in Place Congo," *Century Magazine*, XXXI (Feb. 1886), 517–532; Cable, "Creole Slave Songs," *Century Magazine*, XXXI (April, 1886), 807–828.
[34] *Historical Collections*, I, 27, 33.

The colonial frontier posed a peculiar dilemma for Negro slaves. Runaway Africans, in a foreign and hostile country, often had to choose among different nations of slaveholders, including Indians. Confined on an increasingly slaveholding continent, the black maroon found freedom only in the uninhabited or uninhabitable wilderness. In 1720 "a young negro about twenty," belonging to Le Page, ran away with his wife into the woods, "where his youth and want of experience made him believe he might live without the toils of slavery." This marooned African couple were members of the first human cargo that reached Louisiana. Le Page had purchased both for 1,320 *livres*, or 55 £ sterling, and taken them to Natchez. On being found by the Tonica Indians, they were carried to a village and given to a Frenchman, for whom they subsequently worked. The young man "died of a defluxion on the breast" after being returned to his rightful owner.[35]

Some cases of runaway slaves were obviously explicable. A Negro woman bought by a government official in New Orleans "went mad, and subsequently ran off to the bush, never to come again." David, of the Bambara nation, ran away "because his master broke a finger for him." He killed a heifer in complicity with some other Bambaras, who fled from Adrien Gilbert "because underfed." Another Bambara named Pierot, aged 27 or 28, ran away from Jean Dalby "because [he was] too sick and afraid of punishment." African maroons travelling eastward along the Gulf Coast, either seeking Spanish Pensacola or Africa, were frequently recovered at Mobile. Le Page explained that some Negroes "have killed or drowned themselves" and several "have deserted," all "from an apprehension that the white men were going to drink their blood."[36]

The anxiety of both races concerning slave maroonage is clearly illustrated in the case of Biron, a Bambara who arrived on the *Aurore* in 1726. Biron ran away several times within two years. On July 7, 1728 he "absented himself" once again and was pursued by

---

[35] Le Page, *History*, pp. 24, 29; for a discussion of the precarious position of Negro slaves in frontier societies see: A. Irving Hallowell, "American Indians, White and Black: The Phenomenon of Transculturation," *Current Anthropology*, IV (1963), 519–531; William S. Willis, "Anthropology and Negroes on the Southern Colonial Frontier," James Curtis and Lewis Gould, eds., *The Black Experience in America* (Austin, 1970).

[36] "Records," *LHQ*, II (1919), 194, IV, 348, 357; Le Page, *History*, p. 377.

his master, Jean Soubagne. When Soubagne found him "sitting amidst the cane" outside New Orleans, Biron "fled into the depth of the woods." While being enchained after capture, he jumped on Soubagne's gun "and made himself master of it." Soubagne managed to seize Biron "whilst awaiting help from the other negroes, and took the gun away from him for fear that he might fire on him. . . ."[37]

The attorney general of the Superior Council charged Biron with "rebellion against his master, all the more punishable from the fact that the number of negroes is increasing in this colony, and that one would not be in safety on the distant plantations, that this negro is now a prisoner." Not speaking French, Biron was interrogated through Samba, the Bambara rebel and mutineer who was now a Christian and sworn to translate faithfully. According to Samba, Biron "said that his master might fire at him, that it was not in the intention of using it against his master and that when he seized the gun it was broken." The Council convicted Biron for running away and ordered that he "be whipped by the public executioner at the foot of the gallows, warning him moreover, not to run away in future under penalty of much greater penalties."[38]

The punishment of runaway slaves reflected both the frequency of black maroonage and the intensity of white fear. M. Dumont described the formula:

> When a negro maroons, that is, runs away, he is flogged when taken. . . . He is laid flat on his face on the ground, his two legs kept together, and his arms extended and tied to two stakes so that he forms a letter Y. In this state he receives a hundred or sometimes two hundred blows of a carter's whip. While this is going on, a lighted brand must be kept ready to apply to his face when he does not cry; for it often happens that in their rage at the punishment, negroes have choked themselves by thrusting their tongue over their palate and actually sucking it in. When their skin is thus in shreds, it is rubbed with a sponge dipped in pepper and vinegar. . . . After this punishment they are put in irons and kept fasting until they promise to behave better.[39]

[37] "Records," *LHQ*, IV (1921), 491. "Trial and Sentence of Biron, Runaway Negro Slave, Before the Superior Council of Louisiana, 1728," *LHQ*, VIII (1925), 23–25.

[38] "Trial and Sentence," *LHQ*, VIII (1925), 23–25.

[39] "Memoirs of Dumont," 120–121; Sidney Mintz, "Toward an Afro-American History,"

Maroon communities constituted slavery's greatest threat to Louisiana during the 1720s. These elusive villages provided runaway slaves with their most effective means of physical survival and political resistance. They significantly resembled Bambara banditry along the Senegal River, in both practice and population. During the Bambara wars, when political authority weakened, men from a single village or group of nearby villages secretly formed an association called tō. These bandits, or *tegereya*, would disappear into the bush, make quick raids on unsuspecting neighbors, and sell their plunder away from home. In Louisiana the unsuspecting neighbors were French planters, and the plunder was generally livestock. On August 17, 1726, Attorney General Fleuriau, owner of eight Negroes, exhorted "prompt and sweeping action against runaway slaves, lest soon the community be raided by whole gangs thereof. Let the neighborhood *Indians* watch out for such runaways and arrest them. Find the ringleaders and deal with them stringently."[40]

Coalescence of Negro and Indian runaway slaves seriously endangered a colony surrounded by various Indian nations. Sansoucy, an Indian slave, "took refuge in a village called *des Natanapallé* where there were fifteen other fugitive slaves." Possessing eleven guns and some ammunition, these maroons "meant to defend themselves if molested for capture." Godin of the Oquelonex tribe, a young man belonging to company cashier Duval, "ran away by mad impulse with slaves of Sieur Tisserant." Beyond Lake Pontchartrain he joined a party of other fugitives, whose chief also belonged to Tisserant, and lived there for two years. Governor Périer argued against continuing the traffic of Indian slaves in May, 1728. ". . . these Indian slaves being mixed with our negroes may induce them to desert with them, as has already happened, as they may maintain relations with them which might be disastrous to the colony when there are more blacks."[41]

Maroon communities served as economic markets, as well as

Journal of World History, 13 (1971), 321: "The sharpest evidence of slave resistance, then, is not the historical record of armed revolts, important though these were, so much as the codes that legalized branding, flogging, burning, the amputation of limbs, hamstringing and murder to keep the slaves 'nonviolent.' "

[40] "Records," *LHQ*, III (1920), 414; Curtin, *Economic Change*, p. 181.

[41] "Records," *LHQ*, III (1920), 443–444; *MPA*, II, 573.

places of refuge. Slave pilferage continuously troubled colonists, who had to keep constant vigilance over their livestock. While working on the levee in 1727, five Negroes killed two cows and ran away from New Orleans. Between Chapitoulas and New Orleans about five Bambara fugitives, all aged in their twenties and belonging to different concessions, stole a heifer, bacon, corn, and some hens. Changereau was captured and admitted to eating some of the meat, but denied stealing it. He attributed the heifer's theft to Doctor Manadé's runaway Negro. François, belonging to St. Julien across the river, took no part in killing any cattle, but "stole some bacon and sold it to another negro for tobacco." Sabany, a Bambara slave of Villainville's New Orleans concession, denied having run away. But some marooned comrades gave him fresh meat in a cabin at Bienville's concession, which stood on the opposite bank of the Mississippi.[42]

The French relied heavily on local Indian nations for restitution of marooned Africans. The majority of runaways convicted by the Superior Council were captured by Indians, who received weapons, ammunition, and alcohol as bounty. The employment of Indian slave catchers served a dual purpose for white masters: it created an effective deterrent against costly maroonage and promoted hostility between the two most populous races. The presence of a single Negro among a neighboring village caused alarm among the small French population. Bienville made peace with the Natchez in 1723 on condition "that they bring in dead or alive a negro who has taken refuge among them for a long time and makes them seditious speeches against the French nation and who has followed them on occasions against our Indian allies." Dumont described this Negro as a free black who went over to the Indians, and "even made himself head of a party. It was justly feared that he would teach them our way of attack and defense." The Natchez chief, Tatooed Serpent, turned over his head and the heads of some hostile warriors for ten bottles of brandy.[43]

[42] *MPA*, II, 393, 563; "Records," *LHQ*, I (1918), 226, IV (1921), 348, V (1922), 246–247.

[43] *MPA*, II, 563, III, 385–387, 421; "Records," *LHQ*, V (1922), 97; "Cabildo Archives," *LHQ*, III (1920), 79; "Memoirs of Dumont," 56. The best general discussions of Negro-Indian relations during this period are Willis, "Anthropology and Negroes," 33; and Gary B. Nash, *Red, White, and Black: The Peoples of Early America* (Englewood Cliffs, 1974), pp. 290–297, 310–319.

Colonists' dread of Indian-Negro cooperation and their dependence on each race for vital needs placed them in a difficult bind; one that could only be escaped by eliminating the least needed people. This dilemma for French colonists in Louisiana became a great danger during the Natchez War of 1729–1730. Before making their deadly assault on the colony's most advanced settlement, the Natchez Indians convinced several Negroes, including two foremen of the White Earth plantation, that they would be free with them. Despite warnings, which even caused settlers to arm their slaves, the Natchez settlement was taken by surprise when a friendly visit became a bloody massacre. The Indians killed the men and captured their women and children as slaves. The 280 black slaves now found themselves in a state of quasi-freedom, caught in a struggle among Natchez warriors, French soldiers, and Choctaw mercenaries.[44]

News of the Natchez massacre set off a wave of fear at New Orleans. Governor Périer struggled to mobilize a military expedition among people who were even frightened of the Chaouchas, a nation of thirty warriors below New Orleans. To both ease white anxiety and secure Negro-Indian antagonism, Périer sent Negro volunteers to destroy the Chaouchas. The example of this mission, "which they executed with as much promptness as secrecy," kept the other small nations along the river "in a respectful attitude." "If I had been willing to use our negro volunteers I should have destroyed all these little nations which are of no use to us, and which might on the contrary cause our negroes to revolt. . . ." But the use of a much needed, but much-to-be feared, black soldiers demanded careful consideration. Like all colonial officers in America, Périer dared not use all Negro volunteers to destroy Indian nations "for fear of rendering [them] . . . too bold and of inclining them perhaps to revolt after the example of those who joined the Natchez."[45]

On January 27, 1730, a force of colonial soldiers, including fifteen black volunteers and nearly 500 Choctaw allies, caught the Natchez by surprise. They reportedly killed about a hundred Indians and recovered 54 women and children and 100 Negroes. But

[44] *MPA*, I, 58, 63, 80.
[45] *MPA*, I, 64–65, 71.

as Périer learned on January 31, "this defeat would have been complete if it had not been for the negroes who prevented the Choctaws from carrying off the powder and who by their resistance had given the Natchez time to enter the two forts." Once inside the forts Negroes assisted the Natchez in their use of French cannons. After two weeks the assault at Natchez ended when the Indians escaped their forts and fled westward. Many recovered Negroes were now in the hands of the Choctaws, who refused to release them without sufficient reward. The scattering of these black captives among Choctaw villages added fuel to the mounting fires of racial anxiety and national hostility. Afraid that these slaves would either settle with the Choctaws or be sold to the English, Louisiana officials immediately negotiated for their restitution. Meanwhile they abandoned to the Choctaws "three Negroes who had been most unruly, and who had taken the most active part in behalf of the *Natchez*." These black rebels were then "burned alive with a degree of cruelty which has inspired all the Negroes with a new horror of the Savages, but which will have a beneficial effect in securing the safety of the Colony."[46]

To those Negroes who "proved loyally useful" to the French at Natchez and the Illinois post, officials had promised their freedom. On May 13, 1730, Attorney General Fleuriau ordered that the promise be fulfilled. He also suggested that a "military company organized among the like elect negroes" be organized for "instant call against the Indians on occasion." A free black militia was subsequently formed and actively participated in war against the Chickasaws during the 1730s. A despondent Governor Périer offered a revealing assessment of the Natchez conflict: "The negroes to the number of fifteen who were permitted to take arms did deeds of surprising valor. If these soldiers had not been so expensive and so necessary to the colony it would have been safer to use them than ours who seem expressly made for Louisiana, they are so bad."[47]

Louisiana's first great racial crisis culminated in New Orleans. While waiting for reinforcements from France, colonists spent a dreadful summer in 1730. Repeated rumors of Indian invasion

---

[46] *MPA*, I, 68–70, 105, 110–113; "Letter from Father le Petit, July 12, 1730," *Jesuit Relations*, LXVIII, 197–199.

[47] "Records," *LHQ*, IV (1921), 524; *MPA*, I, 70.

maintained a state of white alarm and created opportune conditions for black conspiracy. On "receiving a violent blow from a French soldier for refusing to obey him," a Negro woman passionately proclaimed "that the French should not long insult negroes." That evening a suspicious Le Page du Pratz skulked about the company's slave quarters. From one of the huts, he heard some Negroes scheming "a design to rid themselves of all the French at once, and to settle in their room, by making themselves masters of the capitol, and all the property of the French." Samba, the trusted overseer and interpreter for the Compagnie des Indes, was among the eight Negroes who headed the conspiracy.[48]

Subjected to the torture of burning matches, the conspirators refused to confess. On discovering Samba's insurrectionary experience in West Africa and on the Atlantic Ocean, Le Page drew up a memorial describing his seditious past. This evidence before the council and further threats of torture compelled Samba to "directly own all the circumstances of the conspiracy." After the others confessed "the eight negroes were condemned to be broke alive on the wheel, and the woman to be hanged before their eyes; which was accordingly done, and prevented the conspiracy from taking effect." The conspirators' heads were posted at both ends of New Orleans and at Chapitoulas, where the black population was most dense and white anxiety most intense.[49]

The 1730 slave conspiracy awakened white colonists to the delicate balance that had to be maintained between the services and threats offered by the black population. Forebodings of disaster demanded restrictions on already developing social realities such as arming blacks and allowing them to assemble. The conspiracy warned Negroes, on the other hand, of their distressing position in a society based on racial slavery. Resistance against slavery weakened economic self-defense and advancement as effective means of transcending slavery. The effectiveness of these means and the consequent diversity within the black population, both in function and color, militated against the success of overt resistance. Incongruous response patterns enhanced incompatible black interests.

[48] "Memoirs of Dumont," 99–100; Le Page, *History*, p. 77.
[49] Le Page, *History*, 77–79; George W. Cable, *The Creoles of Louisiana* (London, 1885), pp. 32–33.

By January, 1731, when the Compagnie des Indes resigned its Louisiana monopoly, the population of the Lower Mississippi consisted of 1,721 European settlers and 3,600 African slaves. The difficult task of providing a slowly developing colony with a desired and dreaded black labor force now fell upon the French government. As the importation of Africans diminished during the following decade, colonists needed to both consolidate and control black slaves. Certain demographic and economic conditions, especially a lack of white women, artisans, and soldiers, contributed to the peculiar emergence of a free Negro population and a regular militia of Negro troops. But the overwhelming scarcity of black laborers in Louisiana created a pattern of race relations largely resembling slavery in other North American colonies.[50]

The French forcibly removed Negroes from their African homeland onto an American frontier, but not without paying a great price. With agricultural and skilled labor needed for colonial development came an oppressed and discontented people who threatened colonial order. By 1731 French colonists' increasing dependence on enslaved Africans prescribed strict limitations on the role and status of that allegedly inferior race. Within this tightening polarity of value and danger, displaced and diverse Africans created an autonomous and antagonistic community.

[50] *Census Tables*, pp. 113, 123.

Blacks in Virginia: A Note on the First Decade

Alden T. Vaughan*

AMID the historiographical wrangling that has in recent years focused on the origins of American slavery and race prejudice, at least one item of agreement has held firm: almost nothing is known about the status of blacks in America until 1630 or later.[1] Unhappily for our attempts to understand the emergence of Negro servitude, information on the early years remains frustratingly sparse. However, the evidence for the 1620s is not so lacking or as unrevealing as has long been supposed.

Two principal sources and a smattering of lesser items tell much about how white Virginians viewed blacks during the first decade of African importation. What the sources reveal is not a solution to the slavery v. servitude puzzle; they do not make clear how many of the Africans in Virginia were being held in permanent bondage nor what effect conversion to Christianity may have had on the Negro's status. The sources do, however, shed some light on these matters. They also show with disturbing clarity that the black men and women brought to Virginia from 1619 to 1629 held from the outset a singularly debased status in the eyes of white Virginians. If not subjected to permanent and

* Mr. Vaughan is a member of the Department of History, Columbia University.
[1] The principal disputants have been Oscar and Mary F. Handlin, "Origins of the Southern Labor System," *William and Mary Quarterly*, 3d Ser., VII (1950), 199-222; Carl N. Degler, "Slavery and the Genesis of American Race Prejudice," *Comparative Studies in History and Society*, II (1959), 49-66; Winthrop D. Jordan, "Modern Tensions and the Origins of American Slavery," *Journal of Southern History*, XXVIII (1962), 18-30; and Jordan, *White Over Black: American Attitudes Toward the Negro, 1550-1812* (Chapel Hill, 1968). Other contributions to the debate include Paul C. Palmer, "Servant into Slave: The Evolution of the Legal Status of the Negro Laborer in Colonial Virginia," *South Atlantic Quarterly*, LXV (1966), 355-370; Louis Ruchames, "The Sources of Racial Thought in Colonial America," *Journal of Negro History*, LII (1967), 251-272; and George M. Fredrickson, "Toward a Social Interpretation of the Development of American Racism," in Nathan I. Huggins *et al.*, eds., *Key Issues in the Afro-American Experience*, I (New York, 1971), 240-254. For a discussion of earlier treatments of the subject, see Stanley Elkins, *Slavery: A Problem in American Institutional and Intellectual Life* (Chicago, 1959), 38-40.

inheritable bondage during that decade—a matter that needs further evidence—black Virginians were at least well on their way to such a condition. For the Elizabethan Englishmen's deep-rooted antipathy to Africans, so well documented by Winthrop D. Jordan in *White Over Black*, reveals itself in a variety of subtle ways in the records of early Virginia.

The very earliest references to black men in British America leave uncertain their status but suggest that most, but not all, were held as servile laborers. John Rolfe's two letters concerning the events of August 1619 are our only surviving accounts of the arrival of the first Negroes. In a letter of January 1620 to Sir Edwin Sandys, Treasurer of the Virginia Company, Rolfe described the arrival the previous year of a Dutch man-of-war which "brought not any thing but 20. and odd Negroes, which the Governor and Cape Marchant bought for victualles. . . ."[2] Rolfe's other mention of the event is even less fulsome; in a letter reprinted in John Smith's *Generall Historie of Virginia* . . . Rolfe reported that "about the last of August came in a dutch man of warre that sold us twenty Negars. . . ."[3] Clearly the arrival of the first Africans meant little to Rolfe; clearly also they were considered items of merchandise. But so were white indentured servants whose labor could also be bought and sold, and they too were occasionally mentioned with a callousness that matches Rolfe's.

There is no further reference to blacks until 1624. On the last day of November of that year, *"John Phillip* A negro Christened in *England* 12 yeers since"* testified in a suit against a white man. Phillips, it appears, was no slave and perhaps not even a servant; his conversion to Christianity had taken place before he reached the colony and from his testimony before the General Court it seems likely that he was a member of a ship's crew.[4] About a year later the Court ordered that the "negro caled by the name of *brase* shall belonge to *Sir Francis Wyatt,* Governor etc., As his servant"; this was probably the same black man that a month earlier had been assigned by the Court to Lady Yeardley, wife of the former governor, who was ordered to allow the Negro "monthly for

[2] Susan Myra Kingsbury, ed., *The Records of the Virginia Company of London,* III (Washington, D. C., 1933), 243.

[3] Edward Arber and A. G. Bradley, eds., *Travels and Works of Captain John Smith* (Edinburgh, 1910), II, 541.

[4] H. R. McIlwaine, ed., *Minutes of the Council and General Court of Colonial Virginia, 1622-1632, 1670-1676* (Richmond, 1924), 33.

his labor forty pownd waight of good marchantable tobacco for his labor
and service so longe as he remayneth with her."[5] These court entries
and the evidence that survives concerning Anthony Johnson, a Negro
who eventually claimed headrights for Africans *he* imported into Virginia, make clear that not all of the blacks who entered Virginia in the
decade after 1619 were thrust into permanent bondage. A few may have
arrived as free men, while others undoubtedly served a period of service
from which they were released into freedom much as were white indentured servants. From the legal standpoint the black and white servants
differed only in the absence, so far as we know, of any written terms of
indenture by which the servant had engaged in service. The distinction
may have been important, though. Most English servants came voluntarily with contract in hand. The blacks came under duress and were
sold, most likely, for as long a period of service as the purchaser desired
or the law decreed. But since Virginia had no relevant laws, and since
those of England were sufficiently vague as to permit almost any interpretation, the probability is that many purchasers of blacks held them for
life or at least far longer than white servants.[6]

That such a construction of the evidence is likely receives strong support from two colony-wide censuses taken in the middle of the decade.
On orders of the Virginia Company of London, the colonial authorities
in February 1624, compiled a "List of the Livinge and Dead in Virginia"
in each of the twenty-three clusters of settlement that then comprised
the colony. The original of this document survives in the Public Record
Office in London, and it was printed as early as 1874 in the *Colonial
Records of Virginia*.[7] The list gives evidence of twenty-two blacks among

[5] *Ibid.*, 72-73.
[6] Jordan, *White Over Black*, Chap. 2.
[7] The original document, filed in the West Room of the Public Record Office,
London, is more legible than the microfilm copies in the Virginia Colonial Records
Project and more accurate than the printed versions contained in the *Colonial
Records of Virginia* (Richmond, 1874). However, because discrepancies between the
original and printed versions are slight and for the most part irrelevant to the purposes of this paper, citations will be to the *Colonial Records of Virginia* except
where otherwise noted. The manuscript is in C.O. 1/3, Public Record Office (Virginia Colonial Records Project Microfilm). The census also appears in John Camden Hotten, ed., *The Original Lists of Persons . . . Who Went from Great Britain
to the American Plantations, 1600-1700* (London, 1874). Biographical sketches of
some of the residents listed in the census can be found in Edward D. Neill, "A
Study of the Virginia Census of 1624," *New-England Historical and Genealogical
Register*, XXXI (1877), 147-153, 265-272, 393-401.

the living and one as having died since the previous April. What is most striking about the appearance of these blacks in the census is that although most of them had been in America for five years, none is accorded a last name and almost half are recorded with no name at all. Typical entries read "one negar," "A Negors Woman," or in the case of Flowerdew Hundred, as:

$$
\begin{array}{l}
\underline{\hspace{4cm}} \\
\underline{\hspace{4cm}} \\
\underline{\hspace{4cm}} \quad\quad \text{vj} \quad \left\{ \begin{array}{l} \text{negors} \\ \text{negors} \\ \text{negors} \\ \text{negors} \\ \text{negors} \\ \text{negors}^8 \end{array} \right. \\
\underline{\hspace{4cm}} \\
\underline{\hspace{4cm}} \\
\underline{\hspace{4cm}}
\end{array}
$$

By contrast, very few entries for non-Negroes have incomplete names. Occasionally a first name is absent and the omission indicated by a dash, and a few listings of presumably white servants appear as "A servant of Mr. Moorewood's," or "Mary, a maid." Two Italian glassmakers are designated by their surnames only.[9] There are also a few entries for whites in the 1624 census on a level of impersonality that approaches the listings of the Negroes: "two Frenchmen," "Symon, an Italien," and "Thomas, an Indian."[10] One can only speculate on what such listings reveal about the attitudes of ethnocentric Englishmen toward persons of other nationalities, but the point to be made here is that Negroes as a group received by far the scantiest and most impersonal entries in the census. Ten of the twenty-three are without first or last names, the rest have first names only. By contrast, the same page that records two Frenchmen anonymously also lists two others with full names and a third with a surname only. Similarly, an Italian, Bernardo of the glass works, is followed on the list by "Mrs. Bernardo" in marked contrast to the entries for black women, none of whom is designated as married, although it seems implausible that some were not. In short, the census of 1624 suggests the early appearance of an attitude deeply prejudicial toward blacks in Virginia.

More telling is the census taken a year later.[11] The "Muster of Inhab-

---

[8] *Colonial Records of Virginia*, 40. I have used here the arrangement and spacing of the original manuscript.

[9] *Ibid.*, 47, 49.

[10] *Ibid.*, 50, 58, 53.

[11] C.O. 1/3, P.R.O. (Va. Col. Rec. Proj.). The document has been printed, with

itants in Virginia," of January and February 1625, like its predecessor, is arranged by plantations, beginning in this case with the "Colledge-land," and running through more than a score of localities. Again a name, or at least an identifying label, is given to each inhabitant. But in addition, for most men and women the census shows age, date of arrival in Virginia, and ship of passage, plus for each free family its possessions in houses, armaments, munitions, food staples, and livestock. The result-ing gold mine of military, economic, and demographic data has barely been tapped by historians and thus far has received its most extensive attention from genealogists.[12] But like the census of 1624, that of 1625 tells much about the status of black men and women in British America.

Again, twenty-three Negroes appear. Nine of them lived in James City, seven at Percy's Hundred, three at Elizabeth City, two at War-rasquoke, one in the "Neck of land near James City," and one at "Eliza-beth Citty beyond Hampton River"—a fairly wide geographical distribu-tion of black laborers. Of particular interest is the nearly even balance in sex: twelve men and eleven women, an indication that the sexual disparity of the West Indies, where a severe shortage of females had grave im-plications for population increases and for social adjustment, found from the outset no parallel on the mainland.[13]

Compared to the 1624 census, the 1625 report is more complete as

---

omission of the data on armaments and other possessions, in Hotten, ed., *Original Lists*, 201-265; and in its entirety in Annie Lash Jester and Martha Woodruff Hiden, eds., *Adventurers of Purse and Person: Virginia 1607-1625* (Princeton, 1956), 5-69. A convenient tabular summation of the data can be found in A. C. Quisenberry, "The Virginia Census, 1624-25," *Virginia Magazine of History and Biography*, VII (1899-1900), 264-267.

[12] Two early historians who made extensive use of the census are Alexander Brown, *The First Republic in America* . . . (Boston, 1898), 610-628; and Philip Alexander Bruce, *Economic History of Virginia in the Seventeenth Century*, II (New York, 1896), 70-72. Recently Edmund S. Morgan has drawn perceptively on the census in "The First American Boom: Virginia, 1618 to 1630," *WMQ*, 3d Ser., XXVIII (1971), 169-198. But significantly the only published versions of the muster appear in essentially genealogical works: Hotten, ed., *Original Lists;* Jester and Hiden, eds., *Adventurers of Purse and Person.*

[13] Philip D. Curtin, "Epidemiology and the Slave Trade," *Political Science Quarterly*, LXXXIII (1968), 211-215; and Curtin, *The Atlantic Slave Trade: A Census* (Madison, 1969), esp. 28. Much work remains to be done on the impact of sex ratio on the adjustment of blacks to new environments, its impact on the frequency and severity of slave revolts, and the correlation between sex ratio—with its important bearing on population growth—and white attitudes toward the slave trade.

well as more ambitious. Very few names are incomplete; age is indicated for the vast majority of inhabitants, and the remaining information—date and ship of arrival, provisions, cattle, etc.—shows few gaps. But again most of the Negroes are relegated to anonymity or partial identification. For example, the muster of Abraham Peirsey's "servants" lists thirty-six individuals, including seven blacks. Four of them are Negro men and are so designated, with no names, first or family, no date or ship of arrival, no age; the others are entered as "Negro woman," and "Negro woman and a young Child of hers." All of Peirsey's twenty-nine white servants, however, are recorded with full names and ship and date of arrival; ages are given for twenty-seven of the twenty-nine.[14] Similarly, of the twenty-four servants at James City, full information is given on all except the wife of one (who presumably arrived in the same ship as her husband and is therefore deficient only in age), and the eight blacks who are shown as: "Negro Men 3 Negro Woemen 5."[15]

Continuing the practice of the 1624 census, given names do appear for some blacks, and in a few instances additional information is recorded. Hence the muster of Capt. William Peirce includes "Angelo a Negro Woman in the *Treasuror*."[16] That entry may be significant: other entries show that *Treasurer* brought colonists to Virginia in 1613, 1614, 1615, 1617, and 1618, and from other sources it is known that the ship returned to Virginia in the fall of 1619 with a load of Negroes but was not permitted to land her human cargo for fear of arousing Spanish animosity. Perhaps the ship identification on Angelo is in error, or perhaps she alone came ashore from *Treasurer* in 1619, but barring such possibilities, Angelo's arrival in Virginia would precede by from one to six years the date usually assigned for the advent of blacks in Virginia.[17] Neither John Rolfe, it will be remembered, nor any other

[14] Jester and Hiden, eds., *Adventurers of Purse and Person*, 21-22.
[15] *Ibid.*, 27.
[16] *Ibid.*, 29.
[17] *Treasurer* was a controversial vessel in the 17th century and has remained one ever since. After making several trips to America for the Company, beginning in 1613 or earlier, in 1618 she arrived in Virginia under Capt. Daniel Elfrith with a commission from the Duke of Savoy to prey on Spanish shipping. Lt. Gov. Samuel Argall, a part owner of the vessel, dispatched her to the West Indies where she fell in with a Dutch man-of-war (more likely a privateer also under license from the Duke of Savoy), which soon captured a cargo of Negroes which she sold

contemporary claimed that the Dutch ship brought the *first* Negroes to Virginia.

On five of the Negroes recorded in the 1625 census we have fuller entries, although only one received a complete listing: "John Pedro, a Neger aged 30 in the *Swan* 1623." This was probably the "John, a negro" of the 1624 report, who along with several other servants of Capt. Francis West appears "At the Plantation over against James Cittie" in 1624, and in 1625 at "Elizabeth Cittie Beyond Hampton River, Beinge the Companyes land."[18] In the case of John Pedro we have not only a full listing but a full name, the only black other than the aforementioned John Phillips of the 1624 General Court records to so appear in the decade from 1619 to 1629. We do, however, know the surname of three Negroes at Elizabeth City, listed in 1624 only as Anthony and Isabella, Negroes. In the 1625 report their entry reads "Antoney Negro: Isabell Negro: and William Theire Child Baptised." This undoubtedly was the Anthony Johnson who subsequently became free and later owned black servants himself.[19]

---

in Virginia. *Treasurer* acquired some Negroes too, but finding a hostile reception at Jamestown, where the new governor George Yeardley feared repercussions from the Spanish if he allowed the landing of goods seized by an English ship during peacetime, she sailed to Bermuda and there unloaded her human cargo on the Earl of Warwick's estate. "Stark rotten" when she reached Bermuda late in 1619, *Treasurer* apparently did not sail again. Bruce, *Economic History of Virginia,* II, 66-70; Kingsbury, ed., *Virginia Company Records,* III, 219-222; and Edward D. Neill, *Virginia Vetusta . . .* (Albany, N. Y., 1885), 112-116, 201-202. Cf. Brown, *First Republic,* 324-327; and Brown, *The Genesis of the United States . . . ,* II (Boston, 1890), 885-886, 987, where he argues that *Treasurer,* not the Dutch ship, brought the first group of 20 or more Negroes to Virginia. The surviving evidence does not seem to support Brown's contention. See also James Curtis Ballagh, *A History of Slavery in Virginia* (Baltimore, 1902), 7-9, who contends that *Treasurer* landed one Negro, Angelo. Ballagh bases his conclusion on Brown, whose findings are dubious, and on the 1625 census, which as noted above lists Angelo as having arrived on *Treasurer* but does not specify the year. Her date of arrival may have been 1618 or earlier. The most thorough account of the *Treasurer* episode is Wesley Frank Craven, *The Dissolution of the Virginia Company* (New York, 1932), 127-133. Two recent works by Craven, both stressing the possibility of blacks arriving before 1619 and in a number exceeding 20, appeared too late to be considered in this article. See "Twenty Negroes to Jamestown in 1619?" *Virginia Quarterly Review,* XLVII (1971), 416-421; and *White, Red, and Black: The Seventeenth-Century Virginian* (Charlottesville, Va., 1971), 77-82.

[18] Jester and Hiden, eds., *Adventurers of Purse and Person,* 62; *Colonial Records of Virginia,* 46.

[19] *Colonial Records of Virginia,* 51; Jester and Hiden, eds., *Adventurers of Purse*

The remaining two blacks whose entries show more than a given name are "Antonio a Negro in the *James* 1621" and "Mary a Negro Woman in the *Margarett and John* 1622," both at Warrasquoke.[20] Significant in these listings is evidence that blacks continued to enter Virginia, perhaps at the rate of two or three per year, and on English ships that also carried free and indentured whites, thus presumably coming from England and either bringing a black or two from there, or stopping in the West Indies where a few blacks may have been purchased for importation to Virginia.

Once in Virginia the black servants may or may not have fared much like their white servant counterparts. However, there are strong hints from the census of 1625 that they were a different category of labor: witness the absence for most of the blacks of age and date of arrival—crucial data for white servants since terms of indenture usually stipulated service for a specified number of years or until a specified age. Furthermore, although most of the blacks of the 1625 census had been in Virginia for six years, none of them is shown as free; all are either specifically listed under the heading of "servants" or are included in the holdings of free white men who held white as well as black "servants." In most cases the blacks are at the end of such lists of "servants," sometimes accompanied by an Indian, and, as already noted, usually accorded no name or other data. The overall impression conveyed by the census of 1625, then, is of a significantly inferior position for the Negro in the social structure of white Virginia.

The impression gains further credence from the will of George

---

and Person, 49; Court Records of Northampton County, Land Patents of Virginia, 1643-1651, Bk. II, 326, 1651-1654, 161-162, Virginia State Library, Richmond. Because of his relative prosperity and his ownership of black servants, Johnson has received considerable attention from historians. See Susie M. Ames, *Studies of the Virginia Eastern Shore in the Seventeenth Century* (Richmond, 1940), 102-104; John H. Russell, *The Free Negro in Virginia, 1619-1865* (Baltimore, 1913), 24-25; Russell, "Colored Freemen as Slave Owners in Virginia," *Jour. Negro Hist.,* I (1916), 234-237; and James H. Brewer, "Negro Property Owners in Seventeenth-Century Virginia," *WMQ,* 3d Ser., XII (1955), 576-578. While there is no doubt that Anthony Johnson and his family were free by 1652, the evidence does not support a claim that he had escaped bondage "within three years of the landing of the first Negroes at Jamestown." See "Anthony Johnson, Free Negro, 1622," *Jour. Negro Hist.,* LVI (1971), 71-76. In 1625 he and his family belonged to Capt. William Tucker.

[20] Jester and Hiden, eds., *Adventurers of Purse and Person,* 46.

Yeardley, governor from 1619 to 1621 and again from 1626 to 1627, who wrote his will in 1627, eight years after the date generally accepted for the arrival of the first Africans. To his heirs Sir George left "goode debts, chattels, servants, negars, cattle or any other thing."[21] The "negars" may of course have been "servants" too, but a separate category for them as distinct from his other servants suggests at the very least that Governor Yeardley considered blacks apart, and presumably inferior, and certainly a species of property. At the most, the sequence of Yeardley's listing in which Negroes come between servants and cattle implies a status lower than servants, perhaps relegated to servitude for life, a crucial step on the path toward a system of permanent and inheritable slavery based primarily on color.

For the remainder of the decade, evidence of Africans in Virginia is again shrouded in obscurity. From papers preserved in the Public Record Office we know that at least a few more blacks entered the colony, but the number and circumstances are not clear. In 1628 a Captain Guy or Gay in *Fortune* seized a ship near Angola with some Negroes on board; he sent them to Virginia to be sold for tobacco.[22] That same year an unspecified number of blacks were sent to the colony on board *Straker*.[23] Unfortunately the records in these cases tell us too little. But presumably the black population of Virginia had grown by 1629 to a figure somewhat greater than the "20 and odd" of ten years before. Some natural increase had taken place, some fresh imports had arrived, and because of the probability that most of the blacks were young and healthy on arrival and had in many cases undoubtedly been "seasoned" to English diseases in Britain or the Indies, the mortality rate would likely have been low.

What the evidence of the decade after 1619 tells us is inconclusive but not insignificant. It shows with alarming clarity that blacks from the outset suffered from a prejudice that relegated them to the lowest rank in the colony's society, and there are strong hints that bondage for blacks did not follow the same terms as for whites. There is a suggestion,

[21] MS 2y327a, Virginia Historical Society, Richmond.
[22] H.C.A. 13/47, P.R.O. (Va. Col. Rec. Proj.); John Ellzey to Edward Nicholas, May 13, 1628, in John Bruce *et al.,* eds., *Calendar of State Papers, Domestic Series, Charles I, 1628-1629* (London, 1859), 110, Ellzey to Nicholas, May 27, 1628, *ibid.,* 131; Bruce, *Economic History of Virginia,* II, 73-74.
[23] H.C.A. 13/47, P.R.O. (Va. Col. Rec. Proj.).

too, that a small but growing traffic in slaves had begun in which Virginia served as the final destination. Finally, there is evidence that a few blacks, principally if not exclusively those who had been converted to Christianity before their arrival in Virginia, may have held a higher status than other blacks and eventually obtained their freedom. But on balance, the scattered evidence of the first decade strongly supports the contentions of Winthrop Jordan and Carl Degler that a deep and pervading racial prejudice served as an early and inevitable precursor to American Negro slavery.

NEGRO IMPORT DUTIES IN COLONIAL VIRGINIA
A Study of British Commercial Policy and Local Public Policy

by DAROLD D. WAX [*]

ON November 25, 1775, Lord Dunmore's Proclamation of Emancipation, issued on November 7, was printed in Dixon and Hunter's *Virginia Gazette*. Declaring martial law in Virginia, it also granted freedom to those Negroes who, able to bear arms, joined His Majesty's forces.[1] A long editorial accompanied the Proclamation and commented on this attempt by Virginia's last royal governor to incite the slave population to rebel. It said in part:

> Long have the Americans, moved by compassion, and actuated by sound policy, endeavoured to stop the progress of slavery. Our Assemblies have repeatedly passed acts laying heavy duties upon imported Negroes, by which they meant altogether to prevent the horrid traffick; but their humane intentions have been as often frustrated by the cruelty and covetousness of a set of English merchants, who prevailed upon the King to repeal our kind and merciful acts, little indeed to the credit of his humanity.

Bound up in this statement is an interpretation of the Negro slave trade and slavery that gained wide acceptance during the American Revolution. Local residents had made determined efforts, and for all the right reasons, to limit the institution and to prohibit the trade, while England, responding to the pressures of merchants engaged in the profitable slave traffic, had developed policies which frustrated these colonial aims and instead encouraged the Negro trade. This view, for example, came close to being written into the final draft of the Declaration of Independence.[2] In modified form, it is an interpretation that has found its way into standard histories of the Negro in America and into general histories of the English colonies.[3] One historian, discussing Virginia, gave classic expression to this

---

* Dr. Wax is associate professor of history at Oregon State University, Corvallis, Oregon.

[1] For a facsimile of broadside, see Francis L. Berkeley, Jr., *Dunmore's Proclamation of Emancipation* (Charlottesville, Va., 1941), frontispiece.

[2] See Carl Becker, *The Declaration of Independence, a Study in the History of Political Ideas* (New York, 1958), pp. 212-213; also Cornel Lengyel, *Four Days in July: The Story Behind the Declaration of Independence* (Garden City, N. Y., 1958), pp. 174-177, 245-248.

[3] For representative statements see the following: James C. Ballagh, *A History of Slavery in Virginia* (Baltimore, 1902), p. 11; W. E. B. DuBois, *The Suppression of the African Slave-Trade to the United States of America, 1638-1870* (New York, 1965), p. 4; Clarence L. Ver Steeg, *The Formative Years, 1607-1763* (New York, 1963), p. 192; Daniel P. Mannix and Malcolm Cowley, *Black Cargoes: A History of the Atlantic Slave Trade, 1518-1865* (New York, 1962), p. 173; John Hope Franklin, *From Slavery to Freedom: A History of Negro Americans* (New York, 1967), pp. 73-74; Arthur Zilversmit, *The First Emancipation: The Abolition of Slavery in the North* (Chicago and London, 1967), pp. 47-48. Lorenzo Johnston Greene, *The Negro in*

point of view: "In this legislation [i.e., Negro duty legislation]," wrote James C. Ballagh,

as well as in the candid statements of representative Virginians, we find most conclusive proofs of the early hostile attitude of the colonists toward a negro population, as well as of their powerlessness to shape their economic and social development where it conflicted with the general plan of English commercial policy. No colony made a more strenuous and prolonged effort to prevent the imposition of negro slavery upon it, and no State a more earnest attempt to alleviate or rid itself of that burden than Virginia.[4]

Plainly, if this interpretation is accepted, the British must be charged with forcing both the slave trade and the institution of slavery on an incensed but helpless people who opposed the wholesale introduction of Negroes and who made repeated attempts through the passage of duty legislation to restrict the numbers brought to the colonies.

Before this interpretation is allowed to stand any longer, however, it should be challenged, at least to the extent that some crucial questions be explored. There was no critical examination of these questions when they were first framed a generation ago and there has been none since. What, it needs to be asked, were the circumstances under which these duty acts were passed? What purpose or purposes lay behind the acts? What conflict of interests was involved in the passage of this legislation? And, finally, what were the motives of the British government as it passed judgment on these acts?[5] It is the aim of this paper to examine these questions in the light of the historical experience of the colony of Virginia.

Virginia was not the only mainland colony to place duties on imported Negroes, though four of those colonies—New Hampshire, Connecticut, Delaware, and North Carolina—enacted no duty legislation during the colonial era.[6] Of the remainder, South Carolina alone was more persistent than Virginia in pursuing a policy of levying duties on imported

---

Colonial New England (New York, 1968), offers these typical remarks: "The British government, furthermore, encouraged and protected the [slave] traffic and vetoed every attempt of the colonists to hinder or to abolish it" (p. 24); "Finally, the mother country refused to permit any encumbrance upon the slave trade, whether for regulatory or revenue purposes. Whenever it was discovered that the colonies were taxing slave imports, the British Parliament, throughout the colonial period, immediately ordered such duties repealed" (p. 56). A more balanced and certainly more rare view is in Lewis Cecil Gray, *History of Agriculture in the Southern United States to 1860* (Washington, 1933), I, 356-358.

[4] Ballagh, *History of Slavery in Virginia*, p. 14.

[5] Elizabeth Donnan, ed., *Documents Illustrative of the History of the Slave Trade to America* (Washington, 1930-1935), IV, 7.

[6] A twenty-shilling duty passed by the Pennsylvania Assembly in 1700 was enforced briefly in Delaware (J. T. Mitchell and Henry Flanders, eds., *The Statutes at Large of Pennsylvania From 1682 to 1801* [Harrisburg, 1896-1915], II, 108-109).

slaves. Only Maryland, which enacted a Negro duty law in 1695, taxing new Negroes at the rate of 10s per head, preceded Virginia in passing this type of legislation.[7]

The first Negro duty statute in Virginia became law in June 1699; effective immediately and to be enforced for three years, it taxed indentured servants at the rate of 15s per head and "every negro or other slave" at the rate of 20s per head. Laws passed in 1701, 1704, and 1706 continued this same levy on slaves.[8] Then in 1710 a new law increased the duty to £5, where it remained by virtue of acts passed in 1712 and 1714 until late in the year 1718, when it was allowed to expire.[9] Although there were two attempts to reestablish the duty in the 1720's, both bills were nullified by the home government. These disallowances meant that for more than a decade Negroes entered duty free, for not until 1732 was a plan devised for taxing imported slaves which was acceptable to English officials.[10]

This new plan shifted payment of the duty from the importer to the buyer and substituted an *ad valorem* assessment in place of the specific levy. Set at five percent, this duty was extended by four later statutes to July 1751, when it expired.[11] The Assembly revived the five percent duty in April 1752 and, after one renewal in 1753, then began to increase the levy. Beginning in 1754 the *ad valorem* levy was raised to ten percent, with enforcement provided for until February 1770 through passage of three subsequent laws (in 1755, 1759, and 1763). Further, due to the exigencies of war, the duty was increased to twenty percent in 1755, where it remained until reduced by law to ten percent in 1760.[12]

In 1767, however, the General Assembly returned to a higher duty policy,

---

[7] Jeffrey R. Brackett, *The Negro in Maryland: A Study of the Institution of Slavery* (Baltimore, 1890), pp. 41-44.

[8] William Waller Hening, ed., *The Statutes at Large: Being a Collection of all the Laws of Virginia From the First Session of the Legislature in the Year 1619* (Richmond and Philadelphia, 1809-1823), III, 193-195, 212-213, 225, 229-235. The Act of 1704 is listed by title only in Hening; for the full text see Waverly Keith Winfree, "Acts Not in Hening's Statutes, 1702- 1732, with a Biographical Sketch of William Waller Hening" (unpublished M.A. thesis, College of William and Mary, 1959), pp. 73-75.

[9] Hening, *Statutes*, III, 482, IV, 30. Full texts of the acts of 1710 and 1712 are in Winfree, "Acts Not in Hening's Statutes," pp. 105-116, 132-137. The Act of 1714 is not listed in either Hening or Winfree, but see H. R. McIlwaine, ed., *Journals of the House of Burgesses of Virginia* (Richmond, 1905-1915), 1712-1714, 1715, 1718, 1720-1722, 1723-1726, pp. 116-117; hereafter cited as J.H.B.

[10] Hening, *Statutes*, IV, 118, 182, for titles only; for full texts see Winfree, "Acts Not in Hening's Statutes," pp. 269-281, 338-347.

[11] Hening, *Statutes*, IV, 317-332, 394, 469-474; V, 28-31, 160-161, 318-319. For four years, beginning in 1740, a supplementary law increased the duty to ten percent *ad valorem* (*ibid.*, V, 92-94).

[12] *Ibid.*, VI, 217-221, 353-354, 417-420, 461-470, VII, 69-87, 282-283, 338-339, 357-363, 381-383, 639-642, VIII, 190-192.

restoring the twenty percent *ad valorem* rate. After this law was nullified by the home government, new laws passed in 1769 once more raised the total duty to twenty percent. Negro duty legislation came to an end in 1772 with a statute placing a ten percent duty on slaves entered from Africa and substituting a flat £5 in place of the former twenty percent *ad valorem* duty on slaves imported from other colonies. This law as well as one of those passed in 1769 was disallowed in England.[13]

The mere chronology of the Negro duty legislation enacted by the Virginia General Assembly is extremely complex. The frequency with which such statutes were passed together with their overlapping nature and varying levies makes it exceedingly difficult to maintain a clear picture of the rates enforced at any given time. It is also difficult to assess with confidence the motivations which were at work and which lay behind the passage of the duty laws, for it is not always clear just what Virginians were trying to accomplish when they legislated in this fashion. Were there economic and social forces helping to determine the course of action? Were these attempts to restrict and control the number of Negroes brought to Virginia? Or were they, as some have argued, definite efforts to prohibit the slave trade? How important, in the final analysis, was the revenue motive; could it be that Virginians, in certain instances at least, were motivated by nothing more than the need to discover additional sources of revenue for the support of local government?

The revenue motivation seems to have been crucial in the early years, beginning with the act of 1699. Colonel Francis Nicholson had returned to Virginia as governor in 1698, after an absence of nearly seven years, and his instructions and commission were read to the General Assembly which met at Jamestown on April 27, 1699. A portion of his instructions focused on the revenue problem and stated that "A Duty to be raised upon liquors imported unto the said Colony would be the most Easie meanes that can be found out for the better Support of that Government." But other means, it was said, would have to be searched for in order to raise the necessary funds "to defray the Contingent Charges of that Government."[14] Besides revenue matters, other major items of business at this Assembly session were the selection of a new site for the capital city and provision for construction of a new capitol at this site.[15] The Council, in a resolution adopted on May 16, 1699, recommended to the Burgesses "to take Care to raise money

---

[13] Hening, *Statutes*, VIII, 237-238, 336-337, 342-348, 530-532.
[14] J.H.B., *1695-1696, 1696-1697, 1698, 1699, 1700-1702*, p. 136.
[15] Richard L. Morton, *Colonial Virginia* (Chapel Hill, N. C., 1960), I, 357.

enough, to pay the publick Debts, already Contracted and build the State House, and also to make such other Sufficient provisions for the Security, Defence, and all other Contingencies which may happen to the Government." [16] The result was the Negro duty bill which became law in June 1699, "For laying an imposition upon servants and slaves . . . towards building the Capitoll," taxing imported slaves at the rate of 20s per head. [17]

Further work on the capitol and the concomitant need for additional revenue were responsible for the duty acts passed in 1701, 1704, and 1706, all of which maintained the 20s levy. On August 26, 1701, for example, Governor Nicholson laid before the Burgesses for their consideration some twenty-one propositions, one of which asked that they "renew the Imposition Acts." [18] They answered by preparing a new Negro duty bill which, when it was read a third time and passed on September 19, was sent to the Council along with a bill "giving further directions in building the Capitol and for building a publick prison." [19]

Meanwhile, the duty legislation was yielding a revenue and this was being spent on public projects, including construction of the capitol. In November 1706 and again in April 1707 Council President Edmund Jennings ordered Benjamin Harrison, treasurer of the impositions on liquors and slaves, to pay sums of £400 and £700 respectively to Henry Cary, who was responsible for the capitol construction. [20] In a letter to the home government dated June 24, 1708, Jennings discussed the valuable revenue features of the most recent duty act, which had by then expired:

> The Act of Assembly wch imposed that usefull and necessary duty on Liquors & Slaves imported into this Colony expired on the 24th of last month, it hath raised about four thousand pounds whereof three thousand was appropriated to the building a house for the Governor. The outside work of this House is expected to be finished this Summer, wch will exhaust the whole fund appointed for that building, and the Overplus of those impositions cannot be applyed towards finishing it without ye Direction of the Assembly, but I shall take all necessary Care for haveing that work Carryed on and finished as Soon as may be. [21]

By December 1710, when the first £5 duty law was passed, there were new forces operating to influence the decision to tax Negroes at a higher rate.

---

[16] H. H. McIlwaine, Wilmer L. Hall, *et al.*, eds., *Executive Journals of the Council of Colonial Virginia* (Richmond, 1925-1966), I, 435, hereafter cited as *E.J.C.*
[17] Hening, *Statutes*, III, 193-195.
[18] *J.H.B.*, 1695-1696, 1696-1697, 1698, 1699, 1700-1702, pp. 268-270.
[19] *Ibid.*, p. 302.
[20] Edmund Jennings to Benjamin Harrison, November 20, 1706, Colonial Papers, 1692-1706, and same to same, April 1707, Colonial Papers, 1707-1714, Virginia State Library.
[21] President of the Council to Lord Sunderland, June 24, 1708, *ibid.*

An expanding slave population was increasing the possibility of insurrection, and reports were circulated of Negro plots and conspiracies.[22] Fear of a rebellion was aggravated and new suspicions were broadcast when a slave plot was uncovered in the spring of 1710. As the evidence accumulated and slaves from at least three counties—Surry, Isle of Wight, and James City— were implicated in the planned uprising, the government acted swiftly to counter the threat. There were large-scale arrests and an executive proclamation called for assistance in apprehending the presumed ringleader, Negro Peter, either dead or alive. Still, there was no hysteria and most of the Negroes were released without punishment.[23]

But the implications of the Negro plot were being felt in Virginia months later. In his inaugural message, read to the Burgesses on October 26, 1710, Governor Alexander Spotswood thought it worthwhile to underscore the need for precautionary measures, for an expanding slave population posed special problems.[24] Edmund Jennings had touched on the same point—the alarming increase of Negroes—two years before in a report to the Board of Trade. He added that Virginians had overextended themselves in purchasing slaves and were now "sensibly convinced of their Error which has in a manner ruined the Credit of the Country."[25]

It is not surprising that the Assembly which convened at Williamsburg in October 1710 should have reimposed a duty on Negroes, and a £5 duty at that. The higher duty was clearly intended as something more than a revenue measure, though revenue was not irrelevant. Spotswood, for example, in his inaugural address, asked the Burgesses to appropriate a "farther Sume of Mony for The Speedy perfecting the Governors house."[26] But while he wished to encourage the passage of revenue bills, he believed the £5 levy on new Negroes to be nearly prohibitive.[27] A few months after passage of the bill, in a letter to home officials, Spotswood said that in his judgment "so high a Duty on Negroes was intended to discourage the importation." He added that he had tried to reduce the amount of the duty

but they urged what is really true, that the Country is already ruined by the great number of negros imported of late years, that it will be impossible for them in many Years to discharge the Debts already contracted for the purchase of those Negroes, if fresh supplys be still poured in upon them while their tobacco continues so little

---

[22] There were rumors of Negro discontent in Virginia in 1687, 1694, and 1703 (*E.J.C.*, I, 86-87, 317; II, 311-312).

[23] *Ibid.*, III, 234-235, 236, 243, 575.

[24] *J.H.B.*, 1702/3-1705, 1705-1706, 1710-1712, p. 240.

[25] Donnan, *Documents*, IV, 88-90.

[26] *J.H.B.*, 1702/3-1705, 1705-1706, 1710-1712, p. 240.

[27] *Ibid.*, p. 281.

valuable, but that the People will run more and more in Debt, and must be forced to imploy their hands upon other Manufacturers.

The Burgesses, he said, were unanimous in their decision to lose the bill rather than "to go contrary to the general inclination of the Country in this particular."[28]

When the Assembly continued the £5 duty for three years in November 1712, it stated that there was "no better Expedient found to Lessen the Levy by the Poll or to defray any publick Charge than Impositions of that Nature." Revenue raised by this act was to go toward relieving their distressed neighbors in North Carolina, to purchase for them 900 yards of duffels and to raise £1000 for their use.[29] The further extension of the £5 duty for two years, till December 1718, meant that for eight years Virginia enforced a duty policy that was intended both to raise revenue and to restrict, but not prohibit, the slave trade. Records show that the £5 duty did not end the traffic in slaves, for during this eight-year period 4,415 Negroes entered Virginia through the five naval districts.[30]

Slaves were also imported in substantial numbers in the years after 1718, when no duty was being collected.[31] A committee of the Council appointed in 1723 to examine the state of the tobacco trade spoke of "the daily encrease of the number of People Employed in making of Tobacco by the Importation of Negros, as well as by the encrease of the Inhabts." The growing black population had not lessened fear of an insurrection, and in the autumn of 1722 there was once again evidence of a Negro conspiracy.[32]

Thus, in passing the "Act for laying a Duty on Liquor and Slaves" in 1723, the Assembly referred to "the vast numbers of Negro slaves which are daily imported and increased among us" as well as to the "late discovered Conspiracies among these Slaves wholly to destroy Your Majesties good Subjects Inhabiting here." But revenue considerations were not slighted, for it was said that years of experience supported the view that "the only method easy to be born here in raising funds is by laying Duties on Liquors and Slaves imported." The act recited the list of public projects which had been aided in the past by the duty legislation, among them the governor's

---

[28] R. A. Brock, ed., *The Official Letters of Alexander Spotswood, Lieutenant-Governor of the Colony of Virginia, 1710-1722* . . . (Richmond, 1882), I, 52-53.

[29] Winfree, "Acts Not in Hening's Statutes," p. 132.

[30] Donnan, *Documents*, IV, 175-181.

[31] *Ibid.*, IV, 183-189.

[32] *E.J.C.*, IV, 20, 31, 49.

house, a general court building, and a public magazine and jail.[33]

Although the duty levied by the act of 1723 was only 40s, much less than the £5 rate assessed between 1710 and 1718, Governor Hugh Drysdale was sufficiently concerned to caution the Burgesses against interfering with this branch of English commerce. After learning that a new Negro duty bill was being considered in the House, he sent over an instruction from the home government dated September 27, 1717, "relating to the passing of Acts wch may affect the Trade & Shipping of Great Brittain."[34] Although concerned about the bill, Drysdale did sign it, thereby winning the approval of the "Generality of ye Country." Robert Carter, himself a slave factor who sold Negroes in Virginia, told a correspondent that the governor "hath passed two Laws, that some very much Condemn as a breach of his Instruct[ions], but in ye doing It hath Very much Enhanct his Value with Ye Generalty of the People." Carter wrote that one of these laws placed an impost on liquors and slaves, which "is but ye Constant Law yet ye Country has made their refuge to raise money by when they were out of Cash."[35]

Just as Drysdale gave his support to a Negro duty law in 1723, so his eventual successor, William Gooch, was recruited and lent his assistance in trying to convince royal authorities that they should allow the duty act of 1728 to stand. Passed in March and to be effective for three years after receiving the King's approval, this act reiterated the need for revenue. In the past, the preamble stated, revenue from duty laws had gone for many useful public projects.[36] Gooch's letter to the Board of Trade, however, hinted that Virginians might want to restrict Negro imports. Having presented his case for additional revenue, Gooch added, "But besides, tis the common topick among the People that while the like or a greater Duty on Negroes subsists & has continued for a long time in Maryland a Proprietary Government, it is hard that they who are under his Majesty's immediate Government should be restrained from the same means of securing & improving their Country."[37]

The possibility of establishing a duty program that would be accepted by home officials presented itself in April 1732. An instruction received at that time prohibited "the laying any Duty to be paid by the Importer on any Negro's brought into this Country for Sale," and seemed to imply that

---

[33] Winfree, "Acts Not in Hening's Statutes," p. 269.
[34] E.J.C., IV, 40.
[35] Robert Carter to ? (torn), July 2, 1723, Letter Books of Robert Carter, 1723-32, University of Virginia Library.
[36] Winfree, "Acts Not in Hening's Statutes," p. 338.
[37] William Gooch to My Lords, n.d. (1728), William Gooch Papers (typescript), I (1727-1731), 43-44, Virginia Historical Society.

levies not imposed directly on the importers would be permitted.[38] Thus, Governor Gooch defended the duty act of 1732, which placed a five percent *ad valorem* duty on the buyer, by arguing that it conformed with the instruction.[39]

Gooch returned to this argument—that the duty had been shifted from the importer to the buyer—on later occasions. And he was always quick to point out that the duty laws enforced after 1732 did raise revenue. He said in 1734 that the duties on Negroes and liquors were "designed for defraying the public Charge of the Colony, and for lessening the common Poll-tax." In 1746 he lamented the fact that "This Branch of the Revenue is greatly lessen'd since the Commencement of the War with the French King."[40] Revenue demands undoubtedly were of importance in the Negro duty program that was pursued after 1732. Lewis Burwell, who was acting governor in 1750, wrote to home officials in November of that year and told them it would be necessary to convene the Assembly during the following summer, since the impost on slaves would expire in July 1751 and his government would have to continue the law "to pay the public Debts."[41] Revenue was collected under the *ad valorem* system because Negroes continued to enter the colony; the slave trade was not severely restricted.[42] After the duty had been increased from five to ten percent in 1740, for example, a prospective slave trader expressed no fear that it might inhibit the traffic:

Mr. Barclay tells me you were commining [sic] with him in the Negro trade. Am of opinion its a very profitable one; the merchants from Bristol carry it on with good success. Negroes have sold high this year. £20 for men £18 women; Our last Assembly has laid an additional duty on Slaves 5 pc more so that the duty on negroes now is 10 pc paid by the purchaser; if you Should ever think proper to try a trade of that kynd here I hope youl let Mr. Barclay & I have the Consignment make no doubt but shall be able to render you as agreeable a Sale as any other could.[43]

Pressures generated after 1754 by renewed conflict with the French led the Assembly to increase the duty on Negroes, first advancing the levy to ten percent and then the next year, 1755, raising it to twenty percent. Although financial considerations were prominent—the Assembly required

---

[38] *E.J.C.*, IV, 265.
[39] William Gooch to My Lords, July 18, 1732, Gooch Papers, II (1732-1740), 287-288.
[40] William Gooch to My Lords, November 20, 1734, November 26, 1735, *ibid.*, II, 362, 419-420; III (1741-1751), 851.
[41] Lewis Burwell to My Lords, November 24, 1750, *ibid.*, III, 1057-1058.
[42] See Donnan, *Documents*, IV, 189 ff.
[43] Francis Jerdone to Neill Buchanan, July 8, 1740, Jerdone Account & Letter Book, 1736-1737, 1738-44, Jerdone Papers, Earl Gregg Swem Library, College of William and Mary.

funds with which to maintain the colony's defenses and to protect its citizens —the effect of these increases was to restrict the slave traffic. One Virginian, active in the slave trade in the late 1750's, described the situation this way:

> The Slaves that have already been imported lately into this Colony, have afterwards been marched or carry'd by water either to Maryland or North Carolina, in order to evade a duty which we have here of 20 pct on the Sales, when when [sic] laid on was rather intended as a prohibition, notwithg that very heavy duty on all Slaves imported and sold here, all persons the inhabitants have a Liberty to import what Number they please duty free, provided they are for the importers own use, which is the occasion of the Sales being made in Maryland & Carolina, they being the two most convenient provinces & boundaries of this Colony, where the people goes and Buys & imports them for their own Use.

This observer went on to predict that the Assembly at its next session "will make some new Law with respect to the importation of Slaves into the Colony, as they find this present Law can very easyly be evaded, when I imigine they will either reduce the present duty, or enact an entire prohibition."[44]

At its next session, which began on November 1, 1759, the Assembly did indeed reexamine the existing duty legislation and consider proposals for rendering the system more workable. The one duty law passed required payment of a twenty percent *ad valorem* charge on slaves brought in from adjoining colonies. The Assembly also considered "lessening the Duties laid upon Slaves imported" from Africa, though reductions were not provided for until the next year.[45]

That some were opposed to a duty scale which acted as a partial prohibition of the Negro trade became more clear at the legislative session of May 1760. Ever since 1755 a twenty percent levy had been enforced in Virginia, but now a rider attached to an act "for raising the Sum of £32,000 for the Relief of the Garrison of Fort Loudoun, in the Cherokee Country," reduced the duty to ten percent. The act declared that the "said additional duty of ten percentum hath been found very burthensome to the fair purchaser, a great disadvantage to the settlement and improvement of the lands in this colony, introductive of many frauds, and not to answer the end thereby intended, inasmuch as the same prevents the importation of slaves, and thereby lessens the fund arising from the duties upon slaves."[46]

The high rates on slaves entering Virginia after 1754 were designed partly

---

[44] William Allason to Robert Allason, July 30, 1759, William Allason Letter Book, 1757-1770, Allason Papers, Virginia State Library.

[45] Hening, *Statutes*, VII, 338-340; J.H.B., *1758-1761*, pp. 148-149.

[46] *Ibid.*, pp. 171-179; Hening, *Statutes*, VII, 363.

to raise revenue at a time of severe military crisis. But it must be noted, too, that some Virginians had special reasons for wanting to raise a revenue in precisely this manner. There was, for example, apparently the same conflict in Virginia as in other colonies between the trading and the agrarian interests.[47] With respect to the levying of taxes, the question was what groups in society should bear the burden, that is, how should taxes be distributed? A Virginia slave trader said in 1751 that local merchants were unfairly saddled with taxes. Writing to a correspondent he said, "There was a Duty of 5 p Ct. upon Sales of Slaves, payable by the Buyers, which expired the 31st July last, but will probably be renewed next Session of Assembly." In this context he remarked on the heavy taxes borne by the trading interests:

Our misfortune is that the Legislature is cheifly composed of Country gentlemen who in their great Wisdoms think fit to lay the Burthen for the support of government upon Trade, not considering that they are nearly concerned in Increase or decay of it.[48]

More to the point is the recurring suggestion that the struggle over the passage of Negro duty legislation pivoted around a clash between large planters and small planters.[49] Large planters apparently were anxious or at least willing to restrict the importation of Negroes because this would add to the value of those already in the colony and in their possession. Less well-to-do planters—those who aspired to greater wealth and higher rank—were opposed to a duty policy that prevented them from acquiring property in slaves at reasonable prices. William Allason summarized the division in 1760:

The duty on Slaves seems now to be fixed for some time at 10 p ct. on the Sales and imagine our Assembly will let it remain so. for sometime past there has been great party amongst them. the Rich ones was for preventing Slaves being imported All together by the Exhorbitant duty of 20 p ct. the Poorer on the other hand was very Strenuous for reducing the duty as much as possible.[50]

Governor Francis Fauquier explained the rider attached to the Act for the relief of Fort Loudon, which in 1760 had reduced the duty to ten percent, in these terms also:

---

[47] See Jonathan Dickinson to Friend and Kinsman (Joshua Crosby), April 21, 1715, Jonathan Dickinson Letter Book, 1715-1721, Library Company of Philadelphia.

[48] Charles Steuart to Anthony Fakie, August 21, 1751, Charles Steuart Letter Book. 1751-53, 1754-63, microfilm copy, Colonial Williamsburg.

[49] J.H.B., 1758-1761, p. xvi.

[50] William Allason to Halliday and Dunbar, August 19, 1760, Allason Letter Book, 1757-1770, Allason Papers.

This Act was passed this Session in the lower House, but by a single voice, on account of this Clause; and it is apprehended will occasion a Battle in the next Session whenever the assembly meets again; for the contest on this occasion is between the old Settlers who have bred great quantity of Slaves, and would make a monopoly of them by a duty which they hoped would amount to a prohibition; and the rising Generation who want Slaves, and don't care to pay the Monopolists for them at the price they have lately bore, which was exceedingly high. These reasons your Lordpps may guess are not urged in the arguments on either side; but, I believe are the true foundation of the Squabble. [51]

Fauquier, like other crown officials before him, was careful to keep the home government fully informed of all Virginia legislation affecting the slave trade, for English authorities, since the early days of the Royal African Company, had done what they could to promote the traffic into the colonies. Periodic instructions reminded colonial governors of their responsibilities in this regard: the slave trade in general and the Company in particular were to be given every encouragement. [52] But despite the belief that the African trade was a vital artery in the network of British overseas commerce, the imperial government proved remarkably tolerant in its attitude toward the Negro duty legislation enacted in Virginia. Not until the late 1760's, as it became increasingly evident that residents were bent upon curtailing slave imports, did the home government begin consistently to disallow these laws.

The first Negro duty laws, for example, were not objected to by English officials; this was true even of the laws levying a £5 duty on slaves brought in between 1711 and 1719, for none of these was disallowed. It was not until passage of the law of 1723, and then only after strong pressure was exerted by English merchants involved in the trade, that the home government nullified a Virginia Negro duty statute. [53] Virginia's next attempt at passing a Negro duty law, the act of 1728, met a similar fate, although the organized opposition in England was less formidable than before. [54]

Thereafter, however, for the next thirty-five years following passage of the duty act of 1732, there was no English interference with the Virginia policy of taxing slave imports. The home government was apparently satisfied by the arrangement which charged the purchasers rather than the importers with payment of the duty. No doubt, too, it was responsive to

---

[51] J.H.B., 1758-1761, pp. 284-285.
[52] See, for example, Donnan, *Documents*, IV, 94-95.
[53] *Ibid.*, 103-117.
[54] *Ibid.*, 123-124.

colonial pleas that linked revenue plans with financial demands associated with the French wars. The Virginia Council noted the approving English policy in a comment to the governor in 1759: "And as all these Acts have been regularly transmitted to the Right Honble the Lords for Trade and Plantations, and no Objections have been made to them by their Lordships, or any of his Majesty's Ministers, the Council therefore reasonably conclude, that the said Acts are look'd upon to be no way inconsistent with the royal Instruction, inasmuch as that forbids the passing any Act for laying a Duty on Slaves to be paid by the Importer; whereas these several Acts direct the Duty to be paid by the Buyer."[55]

A more rigid English policy began to emerge in the late 1760's, and was manifested in the disallowance of three duty statutes enacted in the years just before the outbreak of the Revolution. Thus, the Assembly's attempt in 1767 to increase the duty by ten percent, raising the total levy to twenty percent, was nullified on August 12, 1768, without having ever been enforced.[56] Evidently a twenty percent *ad valorem* duty was now considered too high. English officials took the same position when the duty statutes enacted in 1769 came up for review, although the treatment accorded these laws may have been caused by a misunderstanding of the total levy which they imposed. Three statutes placing duties on slaves had been passed in 1769. One was "for continuing certain Acts of Assembly, imposing Duties on Slaves;" this continued the five percent rate for three additional years. Home officials, apparently confused by the frequent duty laws passed in Virginia, incorrectly believed that this law continued a ten percent levy. Given this misconception, they looked with disapproval on the other two duty acts passed at this session. The first levied an additional ten percent duty on slaves, increasing the total imposition to fifteen, not twenty percent as the home government would believe. The second, an "Act for the better support of the contingent charges of government," added another five percent, raising the total to twenty, not twenty-five percent.[57]

With the mistaken impression that the three mentioned acts would levy an *ad valorem* duty of twenty-five percent on Negro imports, home officials upon their receipt began a careful review. Their inclinations were reinforced by the protests of merchants engaged in transporting slaves to Virginia. Fifty-six Liverpool traders signed a petition objecting to the five percent increase provided by the act for the better support of the contingent charges

---

[55] *E.J.C.*, VI, 149-150.
[56] James Munro, ed., *Acts of the Privy Council of England, Colonial Series*, (Nendeln, Liechtenstein, 1966), V (1766-1783), 164-165.
[57] Hening, *Statutes*, VIII, 336-337, 342-348.

of government.[58] After study by the Board of Trade, a committee of the Privy Council ordered the Board to draft an additional instruction to the governor of Virginia "that he do not for the future give his assent without Your Majesty's permission first obtained to any Law, by which the Duties of ten perCent. upon Slaves imported into that Colony imposed by former Laws shall be increased."[59]

Council President William Nelson, who was acting governor at the time this instruction arrived, replied in a lengthy document which traced the history of Negro duty legislation in Virginia since 1732. In it he emphasized the revenue features of the acts and said that the increases of the duty in the 1750's had been related to the war with France and the defense of Virginia's frontiers. He also tried to make clear that had all of the acts passed in 1769 been allowed to stand the total duty on Negroes would have been twenty rather than twenty-five percent, as English officials believed.[60]

Virginia's last attempt while still an English colony to levy an import duty on Negroes came in 1772. The Burgesses who enacted this statute also drew up an address to the King urging that Virginia be permitted to legislate against the slave traffic, now termed "a Trade of great Inhumanity."[61] The governor who chose to sign and then to defend the duty statute of 1772 was Lord Dunmore. In giving his assent he approved an act which levied a ten percent *ad valorem* duty on slaves from Africa and replaced the former twenty percent duty on slaves from the colonies with a £5 levy. His defense of the act, dated May 1, 1772, was sincere and spirited though nonetheless unsuccessful. "The people of this Colony," he wrote to Lord Hillsborough,

are very anxious for an Act to lay an additional duty upon the importation of Slaves, in order to restrain the introduction of people, the Number of whom, already in the Colony, gives them Just cause to apprehend the most dangerous Consequence there from, and therefore makes it necessary that they should fall upon means, not only of preventing their increase, but, also of lessening their number, and the interest of the Country would Manifestly require the total expulsion of them.

Marshaling all the evidence that he could in support of the act, and trying to make the action of the Assembly seem as reasonable as possible, he stressed the large black population and its rapid increase both by natural causes and by importations of new Negroes. Such numbers added to the likelihood of

[58] Donnan, *Documents*, IV, 151-152.
[59] Munro, *Acts of the Privy Council of England, Colonial Series*, V (1766-1783), 286-288.
[60] William Nelson to My Lord, March 27, 1771, Records of the Public Record Office and British Museum, photocopies of transcripts in the Library of Congress, Box 3 (C. O. 5/1349), Virginia State Library.
[61] J.H.B., 1770-1772, pp. 257, 282-284.

an insurrection. And even if the people should enforce the slave codes and keep a watchful eye over their slaves, they realized that in time of war an enemy could with great ease make allies of them, who were "attached by no tye to their Masters or to the Country."[62]

In his reply Hillsborough anticipated disallowance of the act; he told Dunmore that "I must not flatter Your Lordship with a hope of Success in that business." When news arrived that the act had, as Hillsborough predicted, been disallowed, Dunmore replied, and quite correctly, that it was not contrary to the instruction of 1770, for it did not impose a duty higher than ten percent except for the £5 impost on slaves brought from other colonies, who had since 1759 been handled by special legislation.[63]

Thwarted by England and anxious to place restrictions on slave importations, Virginians had to await the time when they were free of imperial control and able to act without regard to imperial interests. A statute adopted in October 1778 ending the external slave trade coincided with local independence from England.[64]

Yet the more impressive evidence seems unmistakably clear; England had not pursued a consistent policy of invalidating Virginia Negro duty legislation. Of the nearly three dozen duty statutes passed by the Assembly, only five were unfavorably reviewed by the home government—those passed in 1723, 1728, 1767, 1769, and 1772. For most of the colonial period, Virginians were left relatively free to tax imported slaves as they pleased. And in passing these laws, they were seldom motivated by a desire to prohibit the slave trade. Need for revenue, fear of slave insurrection, over-extension of their credit, and the desire of some to limit slave importations so as to enhance the value of Negroes already in the colony, these considerations far outweighed any humanitarian impulse to end the traffic. Furthermore, the duties that were levied never completely checked the trade. Thus, in 1761, at a time when the prevailing duty stood at ten percent, one resident nevertheless spoke of the handsome profits to be derived from selling slaves: "at present it seems to be by farr the most profitable trade that we have in this part of the world."[65]

Throughout the colonial period, whenever economic conditions permitted, Virginia planters willingly purchased freshly imported Negro slaves. Among

[62] Donnan, *Documents*, IV, 153-154.

[63] Lord Hillsborough to Dunmore, July 1, 1772, and Dunmore to the Earl of Dartmouth, July 9, 1773, Records of the Public Record Office and British Museum, Box 4 (C.O. 5/1349-51).

[64] Donnan, *Documents*, IV, 164-165; Hening, *Statutes*, IX, 471-472.

[65] William Allason to Crosbies and Traffords, August 4, 1761, Allason Letter Book, 1757-1770, Allason Papers.

some, moreover, the competition was apparently keen for the privilege of acting as agents for English firms engaged in the slave trade.[66] Whatever might be true of other colonies, in Virginia it cannot be claimed that local humanitarian interests were overridden by imperial policy, for Virginians did little to discourage the slave trade and a great deal to insure that black laborers would always be available when needed.

[66] See Richard Corbin to Charles Gose, August 22, 1762, Richard Corbin Letter Book, 1761-1768 (copy), Virginia Historical Society; Charles Steuart to Messrs. Minivielles, William Moore, Jr., Isaac Depisa and Benj. Massiah, July 5, 1751, Steuart Letter Book, 1751-53, 1754-1763; and William Allason to Halliday and Dunbar, August 19, 1760, Allason Letter Book, 1757-1770, Allason Papers.

The Statutory Law of Slavery and Race in the Thirteen Mainland Colonies of British America

William M. Wiecek

W hen Rhode Island legislators began the gradual statutory abolition of slavery in their state in 1784, they declared in a preamble
that slavery "has gradually obtained [in Rhode Island] by unre-
strained custom and the permission of the laws."[1] This pithily restated the
accepted explanation of the legal origins of slavery in the American states. To
create slavery by law it was not necessary, as United States Supreme Court
Justice John McLean later observed, to pass legislation providing "that
slavery shall exist"; and no such statute was ever adopted in any American
jurisdiction.[2] Rather, as an anonymous Garrisonian abolitionist maintained
in a retrospective survey of the statutory law of slavery in the British
American mainland colonies, the legal origins of slavery are found in "the
provincial legislative acts, which establish and sanction the custom [of
slaveholding] and stamp it with the character of law."[3]

"Provincial legislative acts" did in fact validate and regulate many
customary elements of the legal relationship between white and black people
in the colonial period. Historians, judges, lawyers, and others have recurred
to them for nearly two centuries, sometimes to prove the legitimacy of
slavery, sometimes to mine materials for proslavery or antislavery propa-
ganda, sometimes to illustrate details of colonial life, but seldom for the
purpose of examining the ways in which law affected colonial society as a

Mr. Wiecek is a member of the Department of History, University of Mis-
souri–Columbia. Research for this article was indirectly supported by the National
Endowment for the Humanities, the Faculty Research Council of the University of
Missouri, and the John Carter Brown Library, Brown University, Providence,
Rhode Island. The article represents work in progress toward a book, tentatively
titled "The Sources of Antislavery Constitutionalism in America, 1760-1848."

[1] Act of 1784, John Russell Bartlett, ed., *Records of the Colony of Rhode Island
and Providence Plantations, in New England* (Providence, 1856-1865), X, 7-8,
hereafter cited as *R.I. Recs.*

[2] Miller v. McQuerry, 17 F. Cas. 336 (No. 9583) (C.C.D. Ohio 1853).

[3] "Constitutionality of Slavery," *Massachusetts Quarterly Review,* IV (1848),
463-509, esp. 472.

prelude to understanding the role of law in American experience.[4] Conceptually, the slave codes[5] and session laws of the colonies break down into seven analytical categories, comprising statutes that (1) either prohibited slavery or, contrariwise, sanctioned its elementary characteristics; (2) protected such rights as slaves were accorded; (3) provided for the noncriminal policing of slaves; (4) created a criminal law of slavery, classifying the crimes that slaves might commit and specifying the procedures by which they were to be tried and punished; (5) restricted the behavior of whites in dealing with slaves and free blacks; (6) regulated manumissions; and (7) restricted the behavior of free blacks.

Such a topical analysis has one unfortunate consequence: it suggests a static picture of colonial law, as if somehow at some point in the eighteenth century all the session laws of a colony were suddenly marshaled into a coherent and comprehensive order. In reality, statutory law at any time is in a process of development, with legislatures usually acting in response to particular problems perceived as urgent. When the colonial session laws had accumulated over the years to the point where they were difficult to collect in one place and actually in conflict among themselves, legislators appointed a committee of codification or revision to impose some order on the mess. This was the impetus behind the slave codes of the colonies, which were not true

---

[4] For surveys of these laws see Winthrop D. Jordan, *White over Black: American Attitudes Toward the Negro, 1550-1812* (Chapel Hill, N.C., 1968), chaps. 2-3; Edgar J. McManus, *Black Bondage in the North* (Syracuse, N.Y., 1973), chaps. 4-5; John Codman Hurd, *The Law of Freedom and Bondage in the United States,* I (Boston, 1858), 228-310; George M. Stroud, *A Sketch of the Laws relating to Slavery in the several States of the United States of America* (Philadelphia, 1827); and Philip S. Foner, *History of Black Americans: From Africa to the Emergence of the Cotton Kingdom* (Westport, Conn., 1975), 192-250, *passim.* For particular colonies see M. Eugene Sirmans, "The Legal Status of the Slave in South Carolina, 1670-1740," *Journal of Southern History,* XXVIII (1962), 462-473; Edgar J. McManus, *A History of Negro Slavery in New York* (Syracuse, N.Y., 1966), chap. 5; Paul C. Palmer, "Servant into Slave: The Evolution of the Negro Laborer in Colonial Virginia," *South Atlantic Quarterly,* LXV (1966), 355-370; Adele Hast, "The Legal Status of the Negro in Virginia, 1705-1765," *Journal of Negro History,* LIV (1969), 217-239; John T. Noonan, Jr., *Persons and Masks of the Law: Cardozo, Holmes, Jefferson, and Wythe as Makers of the Masks* (New York, 1976), 35-43; Edwin Olsen, "The Slave Code in Colonial New York," *Jour. Negro Hist.,* XXIX (1944), 147-165; and Marion Thompson Wright, "New Jersey Laws and the Negro," *ibid.,* XXVIII (1943), 156-199, esp. 161-171. See also Elsa V. Goveia, "The West Indian Slave Laws of the Eighteenth Century," *Revista de Ciencias Sociales,* IV (1960), 75-105. I omit, as not relevant to the present inquiry, statutes regulating the importation of slaves, indentured or other forms of servitude, and the tithable status of blacks.

[5] The word "code" is used loosely throughout this article to denote a codified collection of statues, usually having its origins in session laws enacted piecemeal over a period of time.

codes but rather attempts at tidying up or, in the case of South Carolina's 1690 code and Georgia's 1755 code, at incorporating wholesale and belatedly a ready-made body of law from a neighboring jurisdiction that had some legislative experience with the problem.

One of the oddities of the law of slavery in America is that, although all the thirteen colonies sanctioned slaveholding on the eve of the Revolution, some of the earliest statutory provisions concerning slavery had been adopted in order to abolish it entirely or in part. Rhode Island and Georgia banned slavery absolutely, New Jersey did so less categorically, and Massachusetts and New York prohibited all but certain types of slavery from being introduced.

Rhode Island's antislavery law of 1652 was the most stringent:

> Whereas, there is a common course practised amongst English men to buy negers, to that end they may have them for service or slaves forever; for the preventinge of such practices among us, let it be ordered, that no blacke mankind or white being forced by covenant bond, or otherwise, to serve any man or his assighnes longer than ten yeares, or untill they come to bee twentie four yeares of age, if they bee taken in under fourteen, from the time of their cominge within the liberties of this collonie. And at the end or terme of ten yeares to sett them free, as the manner is with the English servants. And that man that will not let them goe free, or shall sell them away elsewhere, to that end that they may bee enslaved to others for a long time, hee or they shall forfeit to the Collonie forty pounds.[6]

Whether this statute was applicable throughout Rhode Island is doubtful; it did not, in any event, prevent the development of slavery in the colony.[7] Newport was the northern mainland center of the slave trade, and retained that odious distinction throughout the period of the legitimate slave trade through 1807.[8] Thus the antislavery impact of the 1652 statute was modest.

The trustees of Georgia tried to exclude slavery for a decade after the founding of the colony in 1732.[9] The exclusion of slavery or, more correctly,

---

[6] *R.I. Recs.*, I, 243.

[7] Edward Channing, *The Narragansett Planters*, Johns Hopkins University Studies in Historical and Political Science, IV (Baltimore, 1886); Lorenzo Johnston Greene, *The Negro in Colonial New England* (New York, 1969 [orig. publ. New York, 1942]), 86-88.

[8] For the debate on the significance of the slave trade and the triangular trade to northern ports see Virginia Bever Platt, " 'And Don't Forget the Guinea Voyage': The Slave Trade of Aaron Lopez of Newport," *William and Mary Quarterly*, 3d Ser., XXXII (1975), 601-618.

[9] Act of 1734, Allen D. Candler, comp., *The Colonial Records of the State of Georgia* (Atlanta, 1904-1916), I, 49-52, hereafter cited as *Col. Recs. Ga.* See Darold

of Negroes was predicated mainly on the need to people the area with reliable free laborers who would not constitute a fifth column abetting the menacing Spanish presence to the south. Opposed from the outset by the settlers, this exclusionary policy was abandoned at the time the trustees surrendered their charter and Georgia became a royal colony; shortly thereafter the assembly adopted South Carolina's 1740 slave code as its basic law of slavery. The attempted prohibition of slavery in West Jersey was no more successful. Though the proprietors ordained that "all and every Person and Persons inhabiting the said Province, shall, as far as in us lies, be free from oppression and slavery," this ambiguous provision did not long forestall the introduction of slaves.[10]

The best-known exclusion of slavery in the colonial period, Article 91 of the Massachusetts *Body of Liberties* (1641), in reality acknowledged the legitimacy of certain kinds of slavery by a juxtaposition of Mosaic and international law: "There shall never be any bond slaverie, villinage or captivitie amongst us unless it be lawfull captives taken in just warres, and such strangers as willingly selle themselves or are sold to us. And these shall have all the liberties and Christian usages which the law of God established in Israell concerning such persons doeth morally require. This exempts none from servitude who shall be Judged thereto by Authoritie."[11] The reference to "strangers" derived from the distinction in the detailed regulations of Lev. 25:39-55 between "your brethren the children of Israel" and "the strangers that do sojourn among you." The former could not be sold as "bondmen" or ruled over "with rigor." But "strangers," who could be thus sold and ruled, came to be defined for the Puritans, and for other English settlers, as Indians and Negroes. The "Duke's Laws" of New York (1665) similarly recognized the legitimacy of enslaving those "judged thereunto by authority or such as willingly have sould or shall sell themselves."[12] Thus the Massachusetts law, and the New York statute derived from it, in reality recognized four legitimating bases of slavery, though at first glance they seem meant to exclude slavery.

From a late eighteenth-century perspective, the antislavery provisions of Rhode Island, Georgia, West Jersey, New York, and Massachusetts were anomalous and defunct. By the time of the Revolution, each of the mainland

---

D. Wax, "Georgia and the Negro Before the American Revolution," *Georgia Historical Quarterly*, LI (1967), 63-77.

[10] "The Concessions and Agreements of the Proprietors . . ." (1676), chap. 23, Aaron Leaming and Jacob Spicer, eds., *The Grants and Concessions, and Original Constitutions of the Province of New Jersey . . .*, 2d ed. (Somerville, 1881), 398; John E. Pomfret, *Colonial New Jersey: A History* (New York, 1973), 208-214.

[11] Max Farrand, ed., *The Laws and Liberties of Massachusetts* (Cambridge, Mass., 1929), 4.

[12] "Bond Slavery," in "The Duke of York's Laws, 1665-1675," *The Colonial Laws of New York . . .* (Albany, 1894-   ), I, 18.

colonies had at least the rudiments of a statutory law of slavery or race, and nine of them had fairly elaborate slave codes that specified one or more of four basic legal characteristics of American slavery.[13]

First, the statutes defined slavery as a lifetime condition, distinguishing it from servitude and other forms of unfree status, which lasted only for a term of years.[14] Second, with one early and short-lived exception, slave status was made hereditable through the mother.[15] In so providing, the American colonies reversed the common-law rule that personal status followed the condition of the father. Instead, they adopted the exotic continental formula summed up in the phrase *partus sequitur ventrem*—the condition of the offspring follows that of the mother. This would not be the last time that

[13] The codifying colonies, with the dates of enactment of their codes, were Delaware, 1721; Georgia, 1755, 1770; Maryland, 1715; New Jersey, 1713; New York, 1712; North Carolina, 1715, 1741; Pennsylvania, 1725; South Carolina, 1690 (disallowed), 1696, 1740; and Virginia, 1705, 1723, 1748. For brevity's sake the codes will be hereafter cited by colony and date—for example, New Jersey: 1713 code. Codes are printed in the Act of 1721, in *Laws of the Government of New-Castle, Kent and Sussex upon Delaware* (Philadelphia, 1741), 132-138, hereafter cited as *Laws of Del.* (1741); Acts of 1755 and 1770, *Col. Recs. Ga.*, XVIII, 102-144, XIX, Pt. 1, 209-249; Act of 1715, chap. 44, William Kilty, comp., *The Laws of Maryland . . .* , I (Annapolis, 1799), n.p., hereafter cited as *Laws of Md.;* Act of 1713, chap. 10, Samuel Neville, comp., *The Acts of the General Assembly of the Province of New-Jersey . . .* (n.p., 1752), 18; Act of 1712, chap. 250, *Col. Laws N.Y.*, I, 761-767; Act of 1715, chap. 46, and Act of 1741, chap. 24, William L. Saunders, Walter S. Clark, and Stephen B. Weeks, eds., *Colonial and State Records of North Carolina* (Raleigh, Winston, Goldsboro, and Charlotte, 1886-1914), XXIII, 62-66, 191-204, hereafter cited as *N.C. Recs.;* Act of 1725, chap. 4, *The Acts of Assembly of the Province of Pennsylvania* (Philadelphia, 1775), 143; Acts of 1690 (disallowed), 1696, and 1740, Thomas Cooper and David J. McCord, eds., *The Statutes at Large of South Carolina* (Columbia, 1836-1841), VII, 343-347, 352-365 (misdated 1712), 397-417, hereafter cited as *Statutes of S.C.;* Act of 1705, chap. 49, Act of 1723, chap. 4, and Act of 1748, chap. 38, William Waller Hening, ed., *The Statutes at Large; Being a Collection of all the Laws of Virginia . . .* (Richmond, 1809-1823), III, 447-462, IV, 126-134, VI, 104-112.

[14] Act of 1664, William Hand Browne, ed., *Archives of Maryland,* I (Baltimore, 1883), 533-534; Maryland: 1715 code. On the appearance of Maryland's *durante vita* provision see Jonathan L. Alpert, "The Origin of Slavery in the United States—The Maryland Precedent," *American Journal of Legal History,* XIV (1970), 189-221. See also Winthrop D. Jordan, "The Influence of the West Indies on the Origins of New England Slavery," *WMQ,* 3d Ser., XVIII (1961), 243-250. Act 12 (1670) and Act 1 (1682), Hening, ed., *Statutes at Large,* II, 283, 490-492. South Carolina: 1740 code. On the legal distinction between servitude and slavery generally see Richard B. Morris, *Government and Labor in Early America* (New York, 1946), 390-512.

[15] Act of 1706, chap. 160, *Col. Laws N.Y.*, I, 597-598. Act 12 (1662) and Act 1 (1696), Hening, ed., *Statutes at Large,* II, 170, III, 140. South Carolina: 1740 code. Georgia: 1755 code. The exception, immediately abandoned, was the 1664 Maryland statute cited in n. 14 above.

English legal tradition was bent to serve the needs of New World slave societies.

This innovation was made necessary by the fact that many children of slave mothers had white fathers. To permit these mulatto offspring to take the status of their father would not only be an anomaly—a slave woman raising her children to freedom presented obvious difficulties—but it would also lead to an unthinkable blurring of racial and social lines in a society that viewed miscegenation as a "stain and contamination" to white racial purity. Finally, the mulatto child represented an increase in the master's property if it grew up enslaved.

The third fundamental statutory characteristic of American slavery was racial identification. This appeared in the mainland colonies' first comprehensive slave code, South Carolina's of 1696, which in turn was modeled on the 1688 Barbados code.[16] The South Carolina law defined as slaves "all Negroes, Mullatoes, and Indians" who had been, or were to be, "bought and sold." The colony's 1740 codification added a fourth racial category, "mustizoes."[17] This code and Georgia's of 1755 also provided that in freedom suits the burden was always on the black (for example, Negro, Indian, mulatto, or mestizo) to prove that he was born of a free woman; a black was presumed a slave unless he could prove his free status.[18] This statutory presumption passed into the common law of southern jurisdictions after Independence, but was limited to persons visibly and exclusively of African descent.[19]

As an incident to the racial identification of slaves, the colonial codes provided that baptism or conversion to Christianity did not liberate slaves. Virginia's first codification, "An act concerning Servants and Slaves" (1705), accepted Christianity as conferring free status: slaves were all persons brought in by sea or land "who were not christians in their native country, (except Turks and Moors in amity with her majesty, and others that can make due proof of their being free in England, or any other christian country, before they were shipped, in order to transportation hither) . . .

[16] On the influence of the Barbadian code see Sirmans, "Legal Status of the Slave," *Jour. So. Hist.*, XXVIII (1962), 462-473; Jordan, *White over Black*, 84-85; and Richard S. Dunn, *Sugar and Slaves: The Rise of the Planter Class in the English West Indies, 1624-1713* (Chapel Hill, N.C., 1972), 110-116, 238-246.

[17] Virginia explicitly defined a mulatto as "the child, grandchild, or great-grandchild of a negro." Act of 1705, chap. 5, Hening, ed., *Statutes at Large*, III, 250-252. South Carolina: 1740 code. See Winthrop D. Jordan, "American Chiaroscuro: The Status and Definition of Mulattoes in the British Colonies," *WMQ*, 3d Ser., XIX (1962), 183-200.

[18] South Carolina: 1740 code. Georgia: 1755 code. To avoid awkwardness the word "black" herein will refer indiscriminately to these statutory categories of Negro, Indian, mulatto, and mestizo.

[19] Hudgins v. Wrights, 11 Va. (1 Hen. and M.) 134 (1806); Gobu v. Gobu, 1 N.C. (1 Tayl.) 164 (1802).

notwithstanding a conversion to christianity afterwards."[20] But as the New York assembly noted a year later, masters who wanted to baptize their slaves were "deterr'd and hindered thereof by a groundless opinion that hath spread itself in this Colony" that baptism would work an automatic liberation, and so specifically stated that it would not do so, a provision adopted elsewhere.[21] Virginia had earlier enacted such a provision in order that "diverse masters, freed from this doubt, may more carefully endeavour the propagation of christianity by permitting children, though slaves, or those of greater growth if capable to be admitted to that sacrament."[22]

The fourth and most troublesome of the elements of slavery for colonial legislators was the precise legal status of a slave as property. It took South Carolina and other southern colonies fifty years from the time of their first experiments with the subject to reach a final solution. The problem was whether a slave was to be considered realty (that is, property like land and buildings) or personalty (that is, chattels or movable property like horses and wagons) or some combination or modification of the two (for example, as "freehold," which in the context of South Carolina's 1696 code meant property annexed or attached to specific realty, analogous to the medieval status of villeinage regardant, where the villein was attached to the manor rather than to the lord), or as *sui generis*. By the mid-eighteenth century, southern jurisdictions had settled on the legal definition of a slave as a "chattel personal."[23] But before they did, a few of the southern colonies went through some peculiar contortions in efforts to make a human being into a vendible thing. Virginia in 1727 made it possible to "annex" a slave to lands, apparently in a humanitarian effort to prevent forced sales of slaves in decedents' estates.[24] Earlier the Old Dominion stated that slaves were realty, except that they were to be considered personalty for such matters as attachment for debt, recording of transfer, enfranchisement of owner, and suit for a slave in actions of detainer, trover, and conversion.[25]

When the statutes, by the mid-eighteenth century, had defined these four basic elements of slavery—lifetime status, *partus sequitur ventrem*, racial identification, and slave-as-chattel—slavery as a legal institution was fully fledged. Yet the laws dealing with these basic elements represented only

[20] Virginia: 1705 code, derived from Act 12 (1670) and Act 1 (1682), Hening, ed., *Statutes at Large*, II, 283, 490-492.

[21] Act of 1706, chap. 160, *Col. Laws N.Y.*, I, 597-598. See also Maryland: 1715 code, and South Carolina: 1696 code.

[22] Act 2 (1667), Hening, ed., *Statutes at Large*, II, 260.

[23] Act of 1748, chap. 2, *ibid.*, V, 432-439 (disallowed 1751). South Carolina: 1740 code. Georgia: 1755 code.

[24] Act of 1727, chap. 11, Hening, ed., *Statutes at Large*, IV, 222-228.

[25] Act of 1705, chap. 23, *ibid.*, III, 333-334.

a minute portion of colonial statutory output related to slavery. The bulk of colonial legislative efforts regulated the rights of blacks, their noncriminal police, and the law of slave crimes. It was these laws that constituted the heart of the black codes. They codified a system of racial etiquette, with a detailed catalogue of penalties for both blacks and whites who transgressed it, and with an occasional reward held out to slaves who acquitted themselves unusually in service to white society. Though the laws were made primarily with reference to slaves, they applied generally to all black persons, who posed a perceived threat to the purity and safety of whites. Not surprisingly, given the relative size of their slave and black populations, Virginia and South Carolina led the colonies in statutory output, while the output of New Hampshire and Connecticut was by far the least.

Statutory provisions directly or indirectly securing the rights of slaves were scanty. The only positively accorded right appears in South Carolina's code of 1740 and Georgia's derivative code of 1755, where blacks could bring suit to test the legality of their enslavement. They were permitted to secure appointment of a guardian *ad litem* (a necessary procedural step, since slaves, like lunatics and minors, were legally incompetent in the eyes of the law); this guardian could institute an "action of trespass in the nature of ravishment of ward," an old common law action.[26] Both substantive rights and procedures under the Georgia statute were extraordinarily liberal: defects in form were declared immaterial, and if the black prevailed, he could be awarded damages against the person holding him in slavery. But if he lost, the court of common pleas was empowered to administer suitable corporal punishment. Delaware also permitted similar freedom suits, and North Carolina's records note one instance of a freedom suit brought in that colony.[27]

Provisions negatively or indirectly securing the rights of slaves were more common. The South Carolina and Georgia codes stated that one of the purposes of their enactment was that "the owners and other persons having the care and government of slaves may be restrained from exercising too great rigour and cruelty over them." To that end both statutes required that the master or overseer provide "sufficient clothing, covering or food" and empowered justices of the peace to order relief for abused slaves and punish the responsible white by fine (though the white could exculpate himself by oath).[28] North Carolina went at the same objective indirectly by prohibiting

[26] South Carolina: 1740 code. Georgia: 1755 code. A guardian *ad litem* is a person appointed to conduct or defend a suit on behalf of an incompetent.

[27] Act of 1760, chap. 26, *Laws of the Government of New-Castle, Kent and Sussex, Upon Delaware*, II (Wilmington, Del., 1763), 51-54; *N.C. Recs.*, II, 550-551.

[28] South Carolina: 1740 code. See also Act of 1722, *Statutes of S.C.*, VII, 371-384, and Georgia: 1755 code.

payment to masters for slaves executed under sentence or under outlawry unless the master certified that the slave was "sufficiently cloathed" and had received "an Allowance not less than a Quart of Corn per Diem." The South Carolina and Georgia codes also prohibited the working of slaves on Sunday (with an exception for works of necessity and family service), and restricted the work day to between fourteen and sixteen hours.[29]

Denominating a slave a chattel was merely a way of giving legal recognition to an underlying economic fact: the slave was a capital investment. As such, he represented an expectation to his master and had to be protected like all other forms of capital. Prodded by the Board of Trade, the colonial assemblies prohibited cruel treatment of slaves and defended them from gratuitous injury, even by their masters.[30] South Carolina made the willful murder of a slave punishable by fine and incompetence to hold public office, while Georgia made the first offense subject to benefit of clergy but the second punishable by the laws of England. For what would be manslaughter today—a killing "on a sudden heat or passion, or by undue correction"— both South Carolina and Georgia imposed a lower fine. Still lower was the fine for anyone who should "wilfully cut out the tongue, put out the eye, castrate, or cruelly scald, burn, or deprive any slave of any limb or member, or . . . inflict any other cruel punishment, other than by whipping or beating with a horse-whip, cow-skin, switch or small stick, or by putting irons on, or confining or imprisoning." The smallest fine of all, plus damages to the master for loss of a slave's time, was for beating, maiming, or disabling a slave without "sufficient cause or lawful authority."[31] New Hampshire also made the killing of black "servants" punishable by death.[32] Virginia and North Carolina, in statutes similar to Georgia's, enacted the notorious "moderate correction" proviso, which exonerated the killing of "any Slave outlawed . . . or . . . any Slave in the Act of Resistance to his lawful Owner or Master, or . . . any Slave dying under moderate Correction."[33]

How effective these statutes were in deterring brutality is an open question. Responding to a petition for pardon of an overseer who had a captured runaway whipped to death, the Virginia Council in 1729 stated that to execute the overseer would "in all probability stir up the Negro's to a contempt of their Masters and Overseers, which may be attended with

[29] Act of 1753, chap. 6, *N.C. Recs.*, XXIII, 390; South Carolina: 1740 code. Georgia: 1755 code.

[30] Leonard Woods Labaree, ed., *Royal Instructions to British Colonial Governors, 1670-1776*, II (New York, 1935), 506-508.

[31] South Carolina: 1740 code. Georgia: 1755 code.

[32] Act of 1718, chap. 25, Albert S. Batchellor, comp., *Laws of New Hampshire*, II (Concord, 1913), 292, hereafter cited as *Laws of N.H.*

[33] Act 1 (1669), Hening, ed., *Statutes at Large*, II, 270. Act of 1774, chap. 31, *N.C. Recs.*, XXIII, 975-976.

dangerous consequences to this colony."[34] The effect of these laws was further diluted by statute (in Virginia) or by judge-made presumptions that in cases of slaves dying under punishment "it cannot be presumed that prepensed malice (which alone makes murther felony) should induce any man to destroy his owne estate."[35] In the same vein, the true intent of statutes prohibiting the killing of slaves was suggested by South Carolina's disallowed 1690 code, which punished the killing of a slave out of "wilfulness, wantoness, or bloody mindedness" by three months in prison and £50 damages to the owner.[36]

Of greater consequence in the day-to-day life of most slaves were restrictions on their less vital rights. The "trucking" statutes made it illegal for a slave to "give, Sell or Truck any Comodity Whatsover,"[37] a provision that in the island colonies was enacted to restrict competition for the benefit of white vendors.[38] Pennsylvania and the Carolinas barred slaves from hiring-out for wages on their own time.[39] Southern colonies variously prohibited slaves from owning cattle, horses, sheep, hogs, boats, or canoes, and, in South Carolina, from planting corn, peas, or rice for sale.[40] By contrast, the island colonies encouraged slaves to garden for themselves or raise livestock during their day-and-a-half weekend break, to market the produce, to act as higglers, and to keep the proceeds of these efforts.[41]

Georgia and South Carolina forbade teaching slaves to read or write,[42] while the Carolinas and Virginia forbade Negroes to vote or hold office, a

[34] Quoted in Arthur P. Scott, *Criminal Law in Colonial Virginia* (Chicago, 1930), 202.

[35] Act 1 (1669), Hening, ed., *Statutes at Large*, II, 270.

[36] South Carolina: 1690 code, 346.

[37] Act of 1708(?), *Acts and Laws of His Majesty's English Colony of Connecticut, in New-England, in America* (New Haven, 1769), 229-231. Act of 1684, chap. 18, *Col. Laws N.Y.*, I, 157-159. Act of 1715, chap. 290, *ibid.*, I, 845 (prohibited slaves from selling oysters in New York City). South Carolina: 1740 code (limited to Charleston). Georgia: 1755 code (with exception for licensed vendors). Acts of 1682, chap. 4, and 1694, chap. 2, Leaming and Spicer, eds., *Grants and Concessions*, 254, 340 (East Jersey).

[38] Goveia, "West Indian Slave Laws," *Revista de Ciencias Sociales*, IV (1960), 86.

[39] Pennsylvania: 1725 code. Act of 1758, chap. 7, *N.C. Recs.*, XXIII, 488-489. South Carolina: 1696 and 1740 codes (all pay must be given to the master).

[40] Act of 1723, chap. 15, *Laws of Md.*, I; Act 3 (1692), in Hening, ed., *Statutes at Large*, III, 102-103; Virginia: 1705 code. North Carolina: 1741 code. Act of 1714, revision of 1696 code, *Statutes of S.C.*, VII, 365-368; South Carolina: 1740 code. Georgia: 1755 code.

[41] Richard B. Sheridan, "Africa and the Caribbean in the Atlantic Slave Trade," *American Historical Review*, LXXVII (1972), 15-35, esp. 34.

[42] South Carolina: 1740 code. Georgia: 1755 code.

provision that might seem supererogatory were it not for occasional accounts of blacks voting.[43] South Carolina enacted a unique sumptuary law for slaves: because "many of the slaves in the Province wear clothes much above the condition of slaves," owners had to restrict them (excluding those in livery) from wearing "any sort of apparel whatso[e]ver, finer, other, or of greater value than negro cloth, duffils, kerseys, osnabrigs, blue linen, check linen or coarse garlix, or callicoes, checked cottons, or Scotch plaids."[44]

The armed black was a bugbear to whites, yet in times of invasion slaves might perform useful military or paramilitary service. Statutes governing militia and military service of slaves and free blacks oscillated between the horns of this dilemma. Connecticut and New Hampshire excluded "negar servts." from militia duty.[45] Massachusetts obliged free blacks to repair highways, clean the streets, or do other menial service in lieu of drilling with the trainbands, except during alarms, when they had to parade and perform such duties as might be assigned them by the commanding officer.[46] Virginia, South Carolina, and Georgia, particularly the latter two because of their exposed circumstances, could not afford the luxury of declining to draw on the black military manpower pool. Virginia excluded slaves from its militia but permitted free blacks, mulattoes, and Indians to be enlisted as "drummers or trumpeters." In times of invasion, insurrection, or rebellion such persons could "march with the militia, and . . . do the duty of pioneers [that is, military laborers], or such other servile labour."[47] This practice again contrasted with that of the island colonies, especially Jamaica, which enrolled free coloureds in its militia and reluctantly acquiesced in their embodiment in a regular army regiment, the Second West Indian.[48] South Carolina in 1704, when it had a long exposed frontier with the Spanish settlements southward, permitted enlistment of slaves during actual invasion and provided that if a slave were killed, his master was to be compensated. Four years later, the statute was amended to limit the number of slaves enrolled to the number of

[43] Act of 1705, chap. 5, Hening, ed., *Statutes at Large*, III, 250-252; Virginia: 1723 code. Act of 1715, *N.C. Recs.*, II, 214-215. Act of 1716, *Statutes of S.C.*, II, 683-691. Gov. William Gooch explained in 1736 that the Virginia antivoting act was the product of a recent insurrection scare that impelled the Burgesses to reemphasize the degraded status of free blacks. William Gooch to Alured Popple, May 18, 1736, reprinted in Emory G. Evans, "A Question of Complexion: Documents Concerning the Negro and the Franchise in Eighteenth-Century Virginia," *Virginia Magazine of History and Biography*, LXXI (1963), 411-415.

[44] South Carolina: 1740 code, 412.

[45] Act of 1718, chap. 21, *Laws of N.H.*, II, 287; J. Hammond Trumbull, ed., *The Public Records of the Colony of Connecticut . . .* (Hartford, 1850-1890), I, 349.

[46] Act of 1707, *Acts and Laws of Massachusetts-Bay* ([Boston, 1707]), 309.

[47] Act of 1723, chap. 2, Hening, ed., *Statutes at Large*, IV, 118.

[48] Edward Brathwaite, *The Development of Creole Society in Jamaica, 1700-1820* (Oxford, 1971), 107, 293-294.

whites (though it ironically referred to them as "our trusty slaves"), and to provide for the emancipation of wounded slaves.[49]

Georgia incorporated a bizarre provision in its militia act of 1755. In times of invasion it permitted the enrollment of slaves recommended by their owners or overseers, not to exceed one-third the total of whites in the regiment. Masters were paid per diem for their services, and full value for slaves killed or maimed. Those slaves would be liberated "who shall actually engage the Enemy, in times of Invasion of this Province, and Shall Couragiously behave themselves in Battle so as to kill any one of the Enemy, or take a prisoner alive or Shall take any of their Colours." For deeds of less valor, where a slave behaved "remarkably . . . in the Engagement, so as to deserve public Notice," he "shall be entitled to and receive from the public Treasury Yearly, and every Yr. a Livery Coat, and pair of Breeches, made of good red Negro Cloth turn'd up with Blue, and a Black Hat and pair of Black Shoes, and shall that Day in every Year (during their Lives) on which such Action Shall be perform'd be free'd and exempted from all personal Labour and Service to their owner or Manager."[50]

Comparable difficulties surrounded the problem of slaves' and other blacks' testimony in court. "Forasmuch as [blacks] are people of such base and corrupt natures, that the credit of their testimony cannot be certainly depended upon,"[51] they were generally prohibited from testifying against whites (Maryland was an exception), and, with variations in practice among the colonies, were permitted to testify only against other blacks, slave or free. Sometimes their testimony was admissible only in prosecutions for certain serious offenses; in other statutes it required the corroboration of "pregnant circumstances"; and sometimes its evidentiary weight was simply left to the discretion of the court.[52]

The law of slave police was based on two related but seemingly inconsistent premises: (1) for one of the basic purposes of slavery, forced labor, the master was left almost entirely to his own resources; the state did not intervene to force a slave to work; but (2) all of the slaveholding society, including nonslaveholding whites and even blacks, had to be mobilized to preserve discipline and to police slaves whose behavior did not conform. The result of these needs was an intricate regulation of slave behavior that, for

[49] Acts of 1704 and 1708, *Statutes of S.C.*, VII, 347-351.
[50] Acts of 1755 and 1773, *Col. Recs. Ga.*, XVIII, 7-47, esp. 43-44, XIX, Pt. I, 291-332.
[51] Act of 1732, chap. 7, Hening, ed., *Statutes at Large*, IV, 327.
[52] Act of 1702, chap. 123, and Act of 1706, chap. 160, *Col. Laws of N.Y.*, I, 519-521, 597-598. Act of 1717, chap. 13, and Act of 1751, chap. 14, *Laws of Md.*, I. Act of 1744, chap. 13, Hening, ed., *Statutes at Large*, V, 244-245; Act of 1748, chap. 38, *ibid.*, VI, 104-112. Act of 1746, chap. 2, *N.C. Recs.*, XXIII, 262. South Carolina: 1696 and 1740 codes. Georgia: 1770 code.

white persons, was not punishable under the law. This supplemented the
unwritten norm of black deference to whites and was a bridge to the harsher
criminal code applicable to slaves.

The need for slave policing was set forth in South Carolina's 1696 slave
code: slaves "are of barbarous, wild, savage natures, and such as renders
them wholly unqualified to be governed by the laws, customs, and practices
of this Province," making it necessary to "restrain the disorders, rapines and
inhumanity, to which they are naturally prone and inclined."[53] Virginia
found its laws as of 1723 "insufficient to restrain their tumultuous and
unlawful meetings, or to punish the secret plots and conspiracies carried on
amongst them."[54]

The statutes took care to prohibit a slave's self-liberation by running
away. Where escapes posed a special danger—as to an enemy in time of war,
or out of the colony to frontier areas surrounded by hostile European
colonists—[55] or where the runaways formed maroon colonies, the statutes
went farther, providing for outlawry and barbaric punishments. South Carolina's 1696 code required that if a slave ran away with intent to leave the
colony, he was to be put to death; otherwise he was to be given forty lashes
for the first offense and branded R on the right cheek for the second; for the
third, forty lashes and an ear cut off; for the fourth, if a male he "shall be
gelt," and if a female, branded R on the left cheek and her left ear cut off;
for a fifth offense, either death or "the cord of one of the slave's legs to be cut
off above the heel." This statute was not much mitigated by the passage of
time; a decade after the Stono Rebellion (1739), the runaway law was
amended to permit patrols to kill runaway groups of three or more if they did
not immediately surrender and to kill a "notorious runaway" (defined as one
absent twelve months or more) if he could not be taken.[56] Masters occasionally offered a greater reward for a runaway killed than for one taken alive
because the later statutes provided that the master would be reimbursed for
an outlawed slave who was killed, whereas a returned runaway would be a
continuing nuisance.[57]

[53] South Carolina: 1696 code, 352.

[54] Virginia: 1723 code, 126.

[55] Act of 1705, chap. 1149, *Col. Laws of N.Y.*, I, 582-584 (prohibiting running
away north of Albany so that "no Intelligence can be carried to the French at
Canada"), reenacted in 1745 (chap. 790, *ibid.*, III, 448), during a later phase of the
Great War for Empire.

[56] Act of 1751, *Statutes of S.C.*, VII, 420-425. See also South Carolina: 1740 code
(special bounties for runaways recaptured south of the Savannah River), and
Georgia: 1755 code, to the same effect (including a bounty of £1 for the "Scalp with
Two Ears of a Grown Man Slave") for runaways caught south of the Altamaha.
South Carolina: 1696 code, 360.

[57] See an advertisement of Robert Burton offering 20s. for Frank alive, and £10
for his head, in *Virginia Gazette* (Purdie and Dixon), Sept. 3, 1772.

Colonial legislatures enacted auxiliary statutes to make running away difficult. Slaves could not go off their plantation without a written pass signed by the master; a strange slave on a plantation could be ordered home and whipped for disobedience; a suspected runaway could be apprehended by any white person and sometimes by other blacks, taken to the nearest sheriff or constable, and sent back to his master with a whipping. Heavy penalties were imposed on whites and free blacks for harboring runaways.

The statutes commonly provided a reward, sometimes with compensation for travel costs, for persons who captured runaways and returned them either to the owner or to a sheriff or justice of the peace; the runaway himself received thirty-nine lashes. Virginia and North Carolina statutes permitted the hiring out or sale of slaves who could not give the name of their master (an effort to deal with the problem of unseasoned native Africans who did not speak English) or who would not do so—a particularly onerous provision for free blacks, who by definition could not give the name of any master if they were mistakenly seized as runaways.[58] Finally, Virginia and Rhode Island found it necessary to prohibit the carrying of slaves on ferries and vessels without the master's permission—an effort to stop waterborne escapes.[59]

A variant of the runaway problem was posed by "outlying" slaves and maroon colonies. The statutes routinely permitted the summary killing of outlying slaves when they offered resistance to recapture, or failed to return after a specified time, or had been outlawed, or committed depredations like hog- and chicken-stealing.[60] Masters were sometimes recompensed for slaves thus killed, indicating that the extermination of maroons transcended control of individual slaves and became an issue affecting the entire society. Virginia experimented for a time with dismemberment rather than death for outlying slaves; until 1769 this included castration.[61] The purpose of such punishment,

[58] Pennsylvania: 1725 code. New Jersey: 1713 code. Delaware: 1721 code. Act 1 (1670), Hening, ed., *Statutes at Large*, II, 277-279; Act of 1722, Waverly K. Winfree, comp., *The Laws of Virginia, Being a Supplement to Hening's* . . . (Richmond, 1971), 212-222; Act of 1753, chap. 7, Hening, ed., *Statutes at Large*, VI, 356-369. North Carolina: 1741 code (when hired out, slaves were to wear a collar with "P.G." [Public Gaol] stamped on it). South Carolina: 1740 code. Georgia: 1755 code.

[59] Act of 1757, *Acts and Laws of the English Colony of Rhode-Island and Providence-Plantations* . . . (Newport, 1767), 177-178; Acts of 1714 and 1718, *R.I. Recs.*, IV, 179, 234. Act of 1705, chap. 12, Hening, ed., *Statutes at Large*, III, 270-275.

[60] Act of 1729, chap. 4, *Laws of Md.*, I. Act 10 (1680), Hening, ed., *Statutes at Large*, II, 481-482; Act 16 (1691), *ibid.*, III, 86-88; Act of 1789, chap. 38, *ibid.*, VI, 104-112. North Carolina: 1741 code. Act of 1755, *Col. Recs. Ga.*, XVIII, 7-47.

[61] Virginia: 1705 and 1723 codes; Act of 1769, chap. 19, Hening, ed., *Statutes at Large*, VIII, 358-361.

as the Burgesses stated in 1705, was "terrifying others from the like practices."[62]

But terrifying did not always work. A fear of black Jacqueries maturing
into slave insurrections always lay near the surface of white consciousness. To
forestall this, as well as to help in the policing of potential runaways and
boisterous blacks, the statutes prohibited a wide array of slave behavior that
did not amount to criminal offenses: congregating on plantations or in town;
wandering off plantations without a pass; hunting or strolling with dogs;
riding horses ("whereby they convey intelligences from one part of the
country to another, and carry on their secret plots and contrivances for
insurrections and rebellions"); owning wooden swords, drums, and horns;
"rambling, riding, or going abroad in the night"; building churches; and
traveling in groups without a white man.[63] The southern colonies found it
necessary to make special provisions exempting overseers from militia duty,
requiring all white men subject to militia duty to go about armed, even to
church, and obliging commanding officers to leave behind a quarter of a
militia regiment marched out of its county.[64] In 1759, when half the
Charleston militia was sent out of the city to suppress a Cherokee uprising,
the other half had to remain behind as a constabulary force for the slaves.[65]

The northern colonies, by contrast, resorted chiefly to curfew laws for
blacks,[66] and to tippling statutes forbidding all persons to sell liquor to blacks
or otherwise entertain them.[67] Virginia and Georgia also forbade such black
conviviality, the former citing the nuisance of "setting up booths, arbours,
and stalls, at court-houses, race-fields, general-musters, and other public

[62] Virginia: 1705 code, 461.

[63] Act of 1702, chap. 123, *Col. Laws N.Y.*, I, 519-521. Act of 1705, chap. 29, *Acts
of Pennsylvania* (Philadelphia, 1775), 45-46. New Jersey: 1713 code. Act of 1723,
chap. 15, and Act of 1751, chap. 15, *Laws of Md.*, I. Virginia: 1705, 1723, and 1748
codes; Act of 1752, chap. 42, Hening, ed., *Statutes at Large*, VI, 295. North
Carolina: 1715 and 1741 codes; Act of 1745, chap. 10, and Act of 1753, chap. 6, *N.C.
Recs.*, XXIII, 234-239, 388-390. Act of 1686, *Statutes of S.C.*, II, 22-23; Act of 1722,
ibid., VII, 371-384; Act of 1737, *ibid.*, III, 456-461. South Carolina: 1740 code.
Georgia: 1755 code.

[64] Act 3 (1692), Hening, ed., *Statutes at Large*, III, 102-103. Act of 1766, chap. 3,
N.C. Recs., XXIII, 760-765. Act of 1743, *Statutes of S.C.*, VII, 417-419. Georgia:
1755 code; Act of 1755, *Col. Recs. Ga.*, XVIII, 7-47; Georgia: 1770 code.

[65] Carl Bridenbaugh, *Myths and Realities: Societies of the Colonial South*
(Baton Rouge, La., 1952), 69.

[66] Act of 1703, chap. 11, *The Acts and Resolves, Public and Private, of the
Province of the Massachusetts Bay . . .*, I (Boston, 1869), 535-536. Act of 1703, *R.I.
Recs.*, III, 492. Act of 1708(?), *Acts and Laws of Conn.*, 229-231; Pennsylvania: 1725
code. See also Act of 1757, *Col. Recs. Ga.*, XVIII, 214.

[67] Act of 1718, chap. 2, *Laws of N.H.*, II, 196. Act of 1698, chap. 10, *Acts and
Resolves of Mass. Bay*, I, 327. Acts of 1750 and 1770, *The Public Laws of the State of
Rhode-Island and Providence Plantations . . .* (Providence, 1798), 612, 611. New
York: 1712 code; Act of 1730, *Col. Laws of N.Y.*, II, 679-688.

places, where, not only the looser sort of people resort, get drunk, and commit many irregularities, but servants and negros are entertained, and encouraged to purloin their master's goods, for supporting their extravagancies."[68] Finally, Virginia and South Carolina prohibited blacks from owning weapons of any sort, except by license and in frontier areas.[69]

Though slaves were property in the eyes of the law, they were also human beings, and as such capable of offenses against the public peace. Hence special criminal codes were elaborated to deal with actions too severe to be handled by ordinary slave police regulations. A variety of motives prompted the enactment of substantive and procedural slave criminal codes. South Carolina and Georgia noted that "natural justice forbids that any person, of what condition soever, should be condemned unheard, and the order of civil government requires that for the due and equal administration of justice, some convenient method and form of trial should be established."[70] Moreover, "a speedy prosecution of negroes and other slaves for capital offences is absolutely necessarie, that others being detered by the condign punishment inflicted on such offenders, may vigorously proceed in their labours and be affrighted to commit the like crimes."[71] In addition, slave trials were an expense to the state (in capital cases in Virginia, for example, the slave had to be brought to Williamsburg for trial), and time spent in jail awaiting trial was down-time to the master.[72] Thus the procedural aspects of the law of slave crimes emphasized a crude form of justice, as well as speed and effect in trial and punishment.

The substantive law of slave crimes was divided into minor and major offenses, roughly paralleling the modern distinction between misdemeanors and felonies. The two petty offenses that appeared most frequently in the statutes were minor theft and striking whites. For a first offense for striking a white or attempting to do so, the usual punishment was a whipping; a second or third such offense was capital.[73] Pilfering, petty larceny, and perjury were similarly punishable, though South Carolina provided for cutting off an ear,

[68] Act of 1710, chap. 14, Hening, ed., *Statutes at Large*, III, 335-336. Georgia: 1755 code.

[69] Act 10 (1639), Hening, ed., *Statutes at Large*, I, 226; Virginia: 1723 code. South Carolina: 1690 and 1740 codes. See also New York: 1712 code, enacted in response to the 1712 insurrection.

[70] South Carolina: 1740 code, 400. Georgia: 1755 code.

[71] Act 3 (1692), Hening, ed., *Statues at Large*, III, 102-103.

[72] Act of 1702, chap. 123, *Col. Laws of N.Y.*, I, 519-521. See also Julius Goebel and T. Raymond Naughton, *Law Enforcement in Colonial New York: A Study in Criminal Procedure (1664-1776)* (New York, 1944), 418, and Scott, *Criminal Law in Colonial Virginia*, 45.

[73] Act of 1708(?), *Acts and Laws of Conn.*, 185. Act of 1702, chap. 123, *Col. Laws of N.Y.*, I, 519-521. Virginia: 1705 and 1748 codes. South Carolina: 1740 code. Georgia: 1755 and 1770 codes.

branding, or nose-slitting for second and third offenses.[74] Other minor offenses included selling stolen goods, possessing weapons, and, in Rhode Island and Delaware, attempted rape of a white woman.[75] Petty offenses were normally triable before a justice of the peace or a county court.

The related crimes of murder and insurrection led the list of capital slave offenses. Mass uprisings were extremely rare before the Gabriel insurrection in Virginia (1801) and almost as rare after that, although the whites' fears of such uprisings were not in any degree diminished by the fact that they were largely unrealistic. More commonplace, and just as unwelcome for the individual victim, were acts of what the law considered "petty treason" on the part of the blacks. Petty treason was a concept well known to the common law: the killing of persons in authority by those subject to them, such as parricide or the murder of a master by his apprentice. The colonies adapted it smoothly to control the behavior of blacks, with one major innovation: common law petty treason applied only to two individuals in a particular relationship; black petty treason, though primarily designed to prevent slaves from murdering overseers and masters, was broadened to range all blacks on one side and all whites on the other. Colonial statutes severely punished blacks who committed murder and manslaughter (usually, but not always, of whites); conspiracy to commit insurrection or rebellion; arson and burning of agricultural or manufactured produce; poisoning and attempted poisoning; and even such lesser offenses as inveigling runaways, robbery, killing or stealing cattle, burglary, and buggery.[76]

Courts that tried slaves for "heinous offenses" were sometimes given discretion to prescribe the mode of execution, as in New York, where punishments were to be inflicted "in such manner and with such Circumstances as the aggravation and Enormity of their crime . . . shall merit." The purpose of this latitude was "to deter others from offending in the like manner," "to the terror of other slaves."[77] Virginia and North Carolina

---

[74] Act of 1717, chap. 13, *Laws of Md.*, I. Act 6 (1699), Hening, ed., *Statutes at Large*, III, 179; Virginia: 1723 and 1748 codes. North Carolina: 1741 code. South Carolina: 1696 code.

[75] Act of 1743, *Acts and Laws of R.-I.*, 195. Act of 1708(?), *Acts and Laws of Conn.*, 229-231. New Jersey: 1713 code. *Laws of Del.* (1741), 65-68. Virginia: 1705 code.

[76] Act of 1708, chap. 181, *Col. Laws N.Y.*, I, 631; New York: 1712 code. Act of 1705, chap. 29, *Acts of Pa.*, 45. New Jersey: 1713 code; Act of 1768, chap. 475, Samuel Allinson, comp., *Acts of the General Assembly of the Province of New-Jersey . . .* (Burlington, 1776), 307. *Laws of Del.* (1741), 65-68. Act of 1751, chap. 14, *Laws of Md.*, I. Virginia: 1723 and 1748 codes; Act of 1732, chap. 7, Hening, ed., *Statutes at Large*, IV, 325-327. North Carolina: 1741 code. South Carolina: 1690 and 1740 codes; Act of 1751, *Statutes of S.C.*, VII, 420-425. Georgia: 1755 code.

[77] Act of 1708, chap. 181, *Col. Laws of N.Y.*, I, 631.

specifically permitted an offending slave to be castrated.[78] Maryland, in cases of petty treason or arson, provided that the slave's right hand first be cut off, then the slave hanged, the head chopped off, the corpse quartered, and the head and quarters "set up in the most public places of the county where such act was committed," as a terror to slaves who "have no sense of shame, or apprehension of future rewards or punishments."[79] Courts, particularly in New York, exercised this discretion with ferocity in times of insurrection scares. Blacks there were put to death by burning (in one recorded case, the sentence specified a slow fire to protract agony for eight to ten hours), being broken on a wheel, hanging in chains to die of starvation, and impaling.[80]

Despite whatever emotional satisfaction may have been derived from putting a slave felon to death, the loss of a slave represented a capital expense to the master which could not be disregarded. Hence the statutes provided that the master be reimbursed for the value of executed slaves.[81] A Georgia statute forthrightly admitted that this was done "in order to discourage any owners of slaves from concealing any crime committed by such slaves to the prejudice of the public welfare."[82] In 1778 a North Carolina court first valued the slave, then tried him, found him guilty, and sentenced him to be burnt.[83] Acknowledging the burden of paying for executed slaves, even when a ceiling was put on their value, South Carolina provided that when more than one slave was tried for the same offense, only one was to be put to death "as exemplary," the rest being either returned to their owner or deported.[84]

---

[78] Act of 1769, chap. 19, Hening, ed., *Statutes at Large*, VIII, 358-361. Act of 1758, chap. 7, *N.C. Recs.*, XXIII, 488-489 (repealed by Act of 1764, chap. 8, *ibid.*, 656).

[79] Act of 1729, chap. 4, *Laws of Md.*, I.

[80] Goebel and Naughton, *Law Enforcement in Colonial New York*, 118; McManus, *Negro Slavery in New York*, 95; Lord Cornbury to Board of Trade, Feb. 10, 1707/8, and Gov. Robert Hunter to Lords of Trade, June 23, 1712, in E. B. O'Callaghan and Berthold Fernow, eds., *Documents Relative to the Colonial History of the State of New York* (Albany, 1856-1887), V, 39, 341-342. For the orgy of executions, including 13 by burning, following the New York "Negro Plot" of 1741 see Daniel Horsmanden, *The New York Conspiracy*, ed. Thomas J. David (Boston, 1971 [orig. publ. New York, 1744]), 468-473.

[81] *Laws of Del.* (1741), 65-68. Act of 1751, chap. 14, *Laws of Md.*, I. Virginia: 1748 code. North Carolina: 1741 code (reimbursement to be paid out of a "pole-tax on all Slaves" in the colony). Georgia: 1755 code (£50 limitation on amount of reimbursement).

[82] Georgia: 1770 code, 223. See to the same effect South Carolina: 1740 code (which additionally provided for a £250 fine for masters who concealed slaves' crimes), and New Jersey: 1713 code.

[83] *N.C. Recs.*, XIII, 375.

[84] South Carolina: 1690 code (return to owner); Act of 1714, *Statutes of S.C.*, VII, 365 (deportation); South Carolina: 1740 code (one of several to be executed even where mercy was extended to all by the court for *in terrorem* effect).

The colonies determined that the usual criminal procedures in felony cases, including the empaneling of a jury, were unsuitable for slave trials, either because a slave could not be tried by peers or because the expense of a full-dress trial was too great.[85] The procedural law of slave crimes was designed to expedite the punishment of slaves (or their exoneration if they were found innocent) so as to diminish costs to the whole community and to assure masters of a fair hearing for their property. After experimenting unsatisfactorily with special quarter-sessions or justice-of-the-peace judiciaries like courts of Oyer and Terminer,[86] the colonies hit upon the successful expedient of creating special slave-trial courts composed of two to three justices of the peace and three to seven "substantial freeholders of the vicinity." Though the freeholders seem originally to have served in lieu of a jury, in time they took on mixed jury and judicial functions.[87]

The procedures before these courts were to be "summary and expeditious" and informal, but the master was permitted to defend the slave, charges sometimes had to be in writing, and the defense could call witnesses. Either unanimity or some specified majority was required for a death sentence. Students of the operation of these courts in Virginia and New York have concluded that despite the informality of the proceedings, the slaves enjoyed a higher level of justice in them than they would have received in the summary hearings provided for petty offenses. Criminal justice under these provisions "was often harsh, but it was uniform and not arbitrary. And it was rapid."[88]

The slave codes bound whites, too. The antebellum proslavery legalist,

[85] Act of 1705, chap. 11, Hening, ed., *Statutes at Large,* III, 269-270.

[86] In American jurisdictions a quarter-sessions court was a special court having criminal jurisdiction, usually limited to misdemeanors, that sat four times a year. Oyer and Terminer were courts of criminal jurisdiction, usually of felonies, sometimes following the English model in that they were called into existence on special occasions such as insurrections, and sometimes sitting by regular commission.

[87] The evolution of special slave courts can be traced in Act of 1702, chap. 123, and Act of 1708, chap. 181, *Col. Laws N.Y.,* I, 519-521, 631, and New York: 1712 code. Act of 1705, chap. 29, *Acts of Pa.,* 45. Act of 1695, chap. 3, Leaming and Spicer, eds., *Grants, Concessions,* 357 (East Jersey); New Jersey: 1713 code; Act of 1768, chap. 475, Allinson, comp., *Acts of N.J.,* 307 (reversion to trials in regular courts). *Laws of Del.* (1741), 65-68. Act of 1751, chap. 14, *Laws of Md.,* I. Act 3 (1692), Hening, ed., *Statutes at Large,* III, 102-103; Virginia: 1748 code; Act of 1765, chap. 26, Hening, ed., *Statutes at Large,* VIII, 137 (reversion to Oyer and Terminer); Act of 1772, chap. 9, *ibid.,* VIII, 522-523. North Carolina: 1741 code. South Carolina: 1740 code. Georgia: 1755 code; Act of 1765, *Col. Recs. Ga.,* XVIII, 649-688; Act of 1766, *ibid.,* 760-762; Georgia: 1770 code.

[88] Thad W. Tate, *The Negro in Eighteenth-Century Williamsburg* (Williamsburg, Va., 1965), 99; Goebel and Naughton, *Law Enforcement in Colonial New York,* 382.

John Codman Hurd, observed that South Carolina's colonial slave laws illustrate "how, even in the superiority which is conferred upon him by law, the action of the free inhabitant, though not himself a slave-owner, may, in many respects, be restricted through the existence of a slave-class."[89] His abolitionist contemporary, Ephraim Peabody, put it more bluntly: "the master is as much fettered to one end of the chain, as the slave is to the other."[90]

Probably the most irksome liability imposed on whites was the system of patrols necessary to the rural policing of slaves. South Carolina's patrol acts of 1737 and 1740 demonstrate the price whites paid to keep blacks orderly. White males were subject to enlistment for terms of twelve months without pay, and when enlistments fell short they could be drafted by the commissioners of patrols. Fines were imposed for drinking on duty because "many irregularitys have been committed by former patrols, arising chiefly from their drinking too much liquor before or during the time of their riding on duty." The patrolers had to contribute not only their time (and at night, at that) but also weapons and mounts, a burden that was resented by non-slaveholders who were drafted to police the human chattels of their more opulent neighbors.[91]

A perennial problem in slave societies was the connivance of whites at the running away of blacks. Early in the eighteenth century the Virginian grandee and diarist, William Byrd II, observed in his *History of the Dividing Line* that poor white North Carolinians refused to turn in runaways. "On the contrary, they find their account in settling such fugitives on some out-of-the-way corner of their land, to raise stocks for a mean and inconsiderable share, well knowing their condition makes it necessary for them to submit to any terms."[92] North Carolina may have been the most forward of the colonies in this respect, but it was not unique. Whites often assisted fugitive blacks in Virginia and elsewhere, sometimes perhaps out of sympathy, most often for cheap labor.[93]

Hence colonial statutes forbade enticing, inveigling, entertaining, or

[89] Hurd, *Law of Freedom and Bondage*, I, 309.

[90] [Ephraim Peabody], *Slavery in the United States: its Evils, Alleviations, and Remedies* (Boston, 1851), 4.

[91] Acts of 1737 and 1740, *Statutes of S.C.*, III, 456-461, 473. We need a thorough study of slave patrols. For South Carolina patrols see Peter H. Wood, *Black Majority: Negroes in Colonial South Carolina from 1670 through the Stono Rebellion* (New York, 1974), 274-275.

[92] William Byrd II, *History of the Dividing Line*, reprinted in Byrd, *A Journey to the Land of Eden and Other Papers* (New York, 1928), esp. 50.

[93] Gerald W. Mullin, *Flight and Rebellion: Slave Resistance in Eighteenth-Century Virginia* (New York, 1972), 110-120. White connivance is another topic that calls for investigation. For examples in South Carolina see Wood, *Black Majority*, 208-209.

harboring runaways or other slaves.[94] Virginia, Delaware, and South Carolina made slave-stealing a capital and nonclergyable offense.[95] But connivance and rustling were not the end of the problem; whites were also profitably careless in buying things from slaves. "Divers leud and evil-minded persons, for the sake of filthy lucre," the Massachusetts General Court complained, "do frequently receive from Indians, molato's, negro's, and other suspected persons"; hence that colony, like others, passed statutes that complemented those forbidding blacks to truck by authorizing twenty lashes for both seller and buyer if the goods happened to be stolen. New York provided for forfeiture of the value of such items, plus £5 to the master.[96]

Commercial intercourse was not the only kind that made problems. The other sort, sexual, received full attention in the antimiscegenation statutes of the colonies. Most colonies forbade interracial marriage and penalized white women for having a child by a black, usually by imposing a term of servitude for the mother and binding out the "abominable mixture and spurious issue" until the age of twenty-five to thirty.[97] In the case of children of slave mothers this provision sometimes enabled the mother's master to recoup the capitalized value of the child.

Manumission posed a particular problem for colonial legislators. New York declared that "it is found by Experience, that the free Negroes of this colony are an Idle slothful people and prove very often a charge on the place where they be"; Pennsylvania, Delaware, and Virginia agreed, adding that freedmen were a bad example to slaves, enticing them and acting as "fences."[98] To deal with this problem the legislatures either forbade freeing

[94] Act of 1702, chap. 123, *Col. Laws of N.Y.*, I, 519-521. Pennsylvania: 1725 code. Act of 1694, chap. 2, Leaming and Spicer, eds., *Grants, Concessions*, 340 (East Jersey). Delaware: 1721 code. Maryland: 1715 code; Act of 1751, chap. 14, *Laws of Md.*, I. North Carolina: 1715 code.

[95] "An Act for the more effectual preventing and punishing of . . . Horse-Stealing . . . ," *Laws of the Government of New-Castle, Kent and Sussex, upon Delaware* (Philadelphia, 1752), 208-211. Act of 1748, chap. 14, Hening, ed., *Statutes at Large*, V, 547-548 (disallowed). Act of 1754, *Statutes of S.C.*, VII, 426.

[96] Act of 1698, chap. 8, *Acts and Resolves of Mass. Bay*, I, 325. Act of 1702, chap. 123, and Act of 1730, chap. 560, *Col. Laws N.Y.*, I, 519-521, II, 679-688. Act of 1682, chap. 4, Leaming and Spicer, eds., *Grants, Concessions*, 254-255 (East Jersey); New Jersey: 1713 code. Delaware: 1721 code. Maryland: 1715 code. Virginia: 1705 code; Act of 1753, chap. 7, Hening, ed., *Statutes at Large*, VI, 356-369. Act of 1686, *Statutes of S.C.*, II, 22-23; Act of 1738, *ibid.*, III, 487.

[97] Act of 1705, chap. 10, *Acts and Resolves of Mass. Bay*, I, 578-579. Maryland: 1715 code; Act of 1717, chap. 13, *Laws of Md.*, I. Act 12 (1662), Hening, ed., *Statutes at Large*, II, 170; Act 16 (1691), *ibid.*, III, 86-88; Act of 1753, chap. 7, *ibid.*, VI, 356-369; Virginia: 1705 code. North Carolina: 1715 code. Act of 1717, *Statutes of S.C.*, III, 20.

[98] New York: 1712 code. Pennsylvania: 1725 code. Delaware: 1721 code. Act 16 (1691), Hening, ed., *Statutes at Large*, III, 86-88.

old or ill slaves, or required a manumitting master to post a bond or recognizance, so that the charge for a "decrepid" slave would not fall on the town or county. Alternatively, they provided that a manumitted slave, if unable to care for himself, would continue to be a charge on the master.[99] Virginia and South Carolina required any freed black to be sent out of the colony; Virginia later provided that manumission could be done only by act of the governor and council for "some meritorious services." An improperly manumitted slave could be sold back into slavery, a provision copied in North Carolina.[100]

Most of the colonial slave codes governed free blacks as well, simply because the statutes applied not to "slaves" but, in typical statutory language, to "any negro, mullato, or indian." Nonetheless, the special circumstances of free blacks made it necessary to enact a few provisions applying specifically to them. In New Jersey and New York they could not own real estate; in Virginia they could not own "christian" slaves, which, in context, meant that they could hold in slavery only persons racially similar to themselves.[101] In South Carolina free blacks could be sold into slavery for harboring fugitives, and in Rhode Island they could be bound out as servants for keeping disorderly taverns.[102] Pennsylvania and Delaware permitted the overseers of the poor to bind out as apprentices the children of indigent free blacks and, in Pennsylvania, any free black adult who shall "loiter and mispend his or her Time."[103]

Statutes are not evidence of actual social conditions. When a statute prohibits a certain type of behavior (for example, blacks striking whites), it is no more reasonable to infer from the enactment of the statute that such behavior was common than to infer that it was rare. Nor can we assume that the statutes were rigorously enforced by vigilant authorities. Again, it is as reasonable to infer that a statute's function was merely admonitory as to infer

[99] Act of 1703, chap. 1, *Acts and Resolves of Mass. Bay*, I, 519. Act of 1729, *R.I. Recs.*, IV, 415. Act of 1708(?), *Acts and Laws of Conn.*, 229-231. New York: 1712 code; Act of 1717, chap. 341, *Col. Laws N.Y.*, I, 922-923; Act of 1773, chap. 1608, *ibid.*, V, 533-534 (prohibited collusive sales to avoid manumission bond). Pennsylvania: 1725 code. New Jersey: 1713 code (prohibitive £200 surety requirement). Act of 1752, chap. 1, *Acts of the Assembly of the Province of Maryland . . . 1752* (Annapolis, 1752), 3-5.
[100] Act of 1691, chap. 16, Hening, ed., *Statutes at Large*, III, 86-88; Virginia: 1723 and 1748 codes. Act of 1723, chap. 5, *N.C. Recs.*, XXIII, 106-107. Act of 1735, *Statutes of S.C.*, VII, 396.
[101] New York: 1712 code. New Jersey: 1713 code. Act 5 (1670), Hening, ed., *Statutes at Large*, II, 280-281; Act of 1753, *ibid.*, VI, 356-369.
[102] "An Act for the breaking up of disorderly Houses kept by free Negroes and Mulattoes" (n.d.), *At the General Assembly . . . of Rhode-Island . . . in February . . . 1770* (Newport [1770]), 87-88. South Carolina: 1740 code.
[103] Pennsylvania: 1725 code, 144. Delaware: 1721 code.

that it was regularly executed. That slave courts *could* prescribe castration does not prove that they *did*. We must look to other sources for information on whether they did, how often, why, what deterred them when they did not, and so on. So if statutes in themselves do not furnish plain evidence of actual behavior, what do they tell us?

Statutory law is a distillation of some of the society's most cherished values, or at least of the values of the class that wields the hegemonic power that produces laws. Statutes are one way, and a solemn and formal one, for the elite that imposes its values on a society to state what those values are and how behavior should conform to them. No other social act performs this function so conspicuously and directly. Statutory law is thus a valuable window on the hopes and fears of a society, of its image of itself, and of the ways it hoped to shape the time to come.

Acknowledgments

Warren M. Billings, "The Cases of Fernando and Elizabeth Key: A Note on the Status of Blacks in Seventeenth-Century Virginia," *William and Mary Quarterly, 3rd Ser.*, 30 (1970): 467–74. Reprinted by permission of the *William and Mary Quarterly*.

James H. Brewer, "Negro Property Owners in Seventeenth-Century Virginia," *William and Mary Quarterly 3rd Ser.*, 12 (1955): 575–80. Reprinted by permission of the *William and Mary Quarterly*.

T.H. Breen, "A Changing Labor Force and Race Relations in Virginia, 1660–1710," *Journal of Social History* 7 (1973): 3–25. Reprinted by permission of the *Journal of Social History*.

Carl N. Degler, "Slavery and the Genesis of American Race Prejudice," *Comparative Studies in Society and History* 2 (1959): 49–66. Reprinted with the permission of Cambridge University Press.

Oscar Handlin and Mary F. Handlin, "Origins of the Southern Labor System," *William and Mary Quarterly, 3rd Ser.*, 7 (1950): 199–222. Reprinted by permission of the *William and Mary Quarterly*.

Whittington B. Johnson, "The Origin and Nature of African Slavery in Seventeenth Century Maryland," *Maryland Historical Magazine* 73, No. 3 (September, 1978): 236–45. Reprinted by permission of the *Maryland Historical Magazine*.

Winthrop D. Jordan, "American Chiaroscuro: The Status and Definition of Mulattoes in the British Colonies," *William and Mary Quarterly, 3rd Ser.*, 19 (1962): 183–200. Reprinted by permission of the *William and Mary Quarterly*.

Winthrop Jordan, "Modern Tensions and the Origins of American Slavery," *Journal of Southern History* 28 (1962): 18–30. Reprinted by permission of the *Journal of Southern History*.

Allan Kulikoff, "A 'Prolifick' People: Black Population Growth in the Chesapeake Colonies, 1700–1790," *Southern Studies* 16, No. 4 (Winter, 1977): 391–428. Reprinted by permission of *Southern Studies*.

Allan Kulikoff, "A 'Prolific' People: Black Population Growth in the Chesapeake Colonies, 1700–1790," William and Mary Quarterly, *3rd Ser.*, 35 (1978): 226–59. Reprinted by permission of the *William and Mary Quarterly*.

Russell R. Menard, "The Maryland Slave Population, 1658 to 1730: A Demographic Profile of Blacks in Four Counties," *William and Mary Quarterly, 3rd Ser.*, 32 (1975): 29–54. Reprinted by permission of the *William and Mary Quarterly.*

Russell R. Menard, "From Servants to Slaves: The Transformation of the Chesapeake Labor System," *Southern Studies* 16, No. 4 (Winter, 1977): 355–90. Reprinted by permission of *Southern Studies.*

Edmund S. Morgan, "Slavery and Freedom: The American Paradox," *Journal of American History* 59 (1972): 5–29. Reprinted by permission of the *Journal of American History.*

Edmund S. Morgan, "The Labor Problem at Jamestown, 1607–18," *American Historical Review* 76, No. 3 (1971): 595–611. Reprinted by permission of the *American Historical Review.*

Philip D. Morgan, "Black Life in Eighteenth-Century Charleston," *Perspectives in American History, New Series,* I (1984): 187–232. Reprinted with the permission of Cambridge University Press.

Gerald W. Mullin, "Rethinking American Negro Slavery from the Vantage Point of the Colonial Era," *Louisiana Studies* (now called *Southern Studies*) 12 (Summer, 1973): 398–422. Reprinted by permission of *Louisiana Studies.*

Benjamin Quarles, "The Colonial Militia and Negro Manpower," *Mississippi Valley Historical Review* (now called *Journal of American History*) 14 (March, 1959): 643–52. Reprinted by permission of the *Mississippi Valley Historical Review.*

M. Eugene Sirmans, "The Legal Status of the Slave in South Carolina, 1670–1740," *Journal of Southern History* 28 (November, 1962): 462–73. Reprinted by permission of the *Journal of Southern History.*

Daniel H. Usner, Jr, "From African Captivity to American Slavery: The Introduction of Black Laborers to Colonial Louisiana," *Louisiana History* 20 (Winter, 1979): 25–48. Reprinted by permission of *Louisiana History.*

Alden T. Vaughan, "Blacks in Virginia: A Note on the First Decade," *William and Mary Quarterly, 3rd Ser.*, 29 (July, 1972): 469–78. Reprinted by permission of the *William and Mary Quarterly.*

Darold D. Wax, "Negro Import Duties in Colonial Virginia," *Virginia Magazine of History and Biography* 79 (1971): 29–44. Reprinted by permission of the *Virginia Magazine of History and Biography.*

William M. Wiecek, "The Statutory Law of Slavery and Race in the Thirteen Mainland Colonies of British America," *William and Mary Quarterly, 3rd Ser.*, 34 (1977): 258–80. Reprinted by permission of the *William and Mary Quarterly.*